Evidentiality

Evidentiality

ALEXANDRA Y. AIKHENVALD

Research Centre for Linguistic Typology
La Trobe University

OXFORD
UNIVERSITY PRESS

This book has been printed digitally and produced in a standard specification
in order to ensure its continuing availability

OXFORD
UNIVERSITY PRESS

Great Clarendon Street, Oxford OX2 6DP

Oxford University Press is a department of the University of Oxford.
It furthers the University's objective of excellence in research, scholarship,
and education by publishing worldwide in

Oxford New York

Auckland Cape Town Dar es Salaam Hong Kong Karachi
Kuala Lumpur Madrid Melbourne Mexico City Nairobi
New Delhi Shanghai Taipei Toronto
With offices in
Argentina Austria Brazil Chile Czech Republic France Greece
Guatemala Hungary Italy Japan South Korea Poland Portugal
Singapore Switzerland Thailand Turkey Ukraine Vietnam

Oxford is a registered trade mark of Oxford University Press
in the UK and in certain other countries

Published in the United States
by Oxford University Press Inc., New York

© Alexandra Y. Aikhenvald, 2004

The moral rights of the author have been asserted

Database right Oxford University Press (maker)

Reprinted 2009

ISBN 978-0-19-920433-5

For Bob with visual and non-visual love

Plea

This book is far from being the last word on evidentiality systems. I welcome reactions, counterexamples, new ideas, and data, to further develop, refine, and improve the generalizations and hypotheses put forward here. Please send them to me at Research Centre for Linguistic Typology, La Trobe University, Bundoora, Victoria 3086, Australia (e-mail: a.aikhenvald@latrobe.edu.au, fax: 61-3-94673053).

Contents

Preface   xi
Acknowledgments   xiv
Abbreviations   xvi
Conventions   xxiv
List of Tables   xxv
List of Diagrams   xxvi
List of Schemes   xxvii

1 Preliminaries and key concepts   1

  1.1 Evidentiality: an illustration   1
  1.2 What is, and what is not, an evidential   3
    1.2.1 The nature of linguistic evidentials   3
    1.2.2 Expressing information source by means other
      than grammatical evidentials   10
  1.3 'Evidentials' as a linguistic term   11
  1.4 Challenges   17
  1.5 How this book is organized   19

2 Evidentials worldwide   23

  2.1 Evidentiality systems with two choices   25
    2.1.1 Evidentiality systems with two choices: an overview   26
    2.1.2 Evidentiality systems with two choices: analytic difficulties   38
  2.2 Evidentiality systems with three choices   42
  2.3 Evidentiality systems with four choices   51
  2.4 Evidentiality systems with five or more choices   60
  2.5 Information sources throughout the world : a summary   63

3 How to mark information source   67

  3.1 Grammatical means for evidential marking   67
  3.2 Markedness in evidentiality systems   70
    3.2.1 Functional markedness in evidentiality systems   71
    3.2.2 Formal markedness in evidentiality systems   72
    3.2.3 Evidentiality-neutral forms   75
    3.2.4 Omission of evidentials   78
  3.3 Scattered coding of evidentiality   80
  3.4 Several evidentiality subsystems in one language   82

3.5   Double marking of information source   87
3.6   How one evidential can occur more than once   95
3.7   Scope of evidentiality   96
3.8   Time reference of evidentials   99
3.9   Expression of evidentials: a summary   103

4 Evidential extensions of non-evidential categories   105

4.1   Non-indicative moods, modalities, and future   106
4.2   Perfect, resultative, and past tenses   112
4.3   Passives   116
4.4   Nominalizations   117
4.5   Complementation   120
4.6   Person-marking   123
4.7   Perceptual meanings in demonstratives   130
4.8   Reported speech as evidentiality strategy   132
      4.8.1 Marking reported speech   132
      4.8.2 Reported speech and reported evidentials:
             semantic affinities   135
      4.8.3 Reported evidential and reported speech:
             division of labour   137
      4.8.4 Grammaticalization of reported speech
             markers and incipient evidentials   140
4.9   Several evidentiality strategies in one language   142
4.10 Evidentiality strategies: what can we conclude?   144
4.11 Modal expressions and evidentiality strategies:
      where to draw the line?   147

5 Evidentials and their meanings   153

5.1   Semantic complexity in systems with two
      evidentiality choices   154
5.2   Semantic complexity in systems with three evidentiality choices 159
      5.2.1 Visual, or direct, evidential in systems with three choices 159
      5.2.2 Non-visual sensory evidential in systems with
             three choices   162
      5.2.3 Inferred evidential in systems with three choices 163
5.3   Semantic complexity within larger systems   166
      5.3.1 Semantic complexity of sensory evidentials   167
      5.3.2 Semantic complexity of inferred evidentials 174
5.4   Semantic complexity of reported evidentials   176
      5.4.1 Reported versus quotative   177
      5.4.2 Distinguishing secondhand and thirdhand information 178

5.4.3 Epistemic extensions of reported evidentials   179
5.4.4 Two reported evidentials in one language   185
5.5   Evidentials and their meanings: a summary   186
6 Evidentiality and mirativity   195
6.1 Mirative extensions in systems with two evidentiality choices   195
6.2 Mirative extensions in other evidentiality systems   200
6.3 Mirative extensions of evidentiality strategies   204
6.4 Evidentials as mirative strategies: a summary   207
Appendix. Mirativity: grammaticalized 'unprepared mind'?   209

7 Whose evidence is that? Evidentials and person   217
7.1 Evidentiality and nature of observer   217
7.2 Evidentiality and first person   219
7.2.1 'First person' effects in evidentials   219
7.2.2 Restrictions on evidential use in first person contexts   231
7.3 Evidentials and 'others'   233
7.3.1 When 'I' involves 'you'   233
7.3.2 Second and third persons with evidentials   234
7.4 Evidentials as implicit person markers   235
7.5 Information source and the observer: a summary   237

8 Evidentials and other grammatical categories   241
8.1 Evidentials and clause types   242
8.1.1 Evidentials in questions   242
8.1.2 Evidentials in commands   250
8.1.3 Evidentials in dependent clauses and other
       clause types   253
8.2 Evidentials and negation   256
8.3 Evidentials and non-indicative modalities   257
8.4 Evidentials, tense, and aspect   261
8.5 Evidentials and other categories   268
8.6 Evidentials and other grammatical categories: a summary   270

9 Evidentials: where do they come from?   271
9.1 Origins of evidentials   271
9.1.1 Grammaticalized verbs as source for evidentials   271
9.1.2 Deictic and locative markers as sources for evidentials   275
9.1.3 Evidentiality strategies as source for evidentials   276
9.1.4 Speech complements as source for evidentials   281
9.1.5 Copula constructions as source for evidentials   283

9.1.6 Other sources for evidentials   284
9.1.7 Etymologically heterogenous evidentials   285
9.1.8 Sources for evidentials: a summary   287
9.2 Evidentials and language contact   288
9.2.1 Evidentiality as an areal feature   288
9.2.2 Gain and loss of evidentials in language contact   294
9.2.3 Evidentials in contact languages   296
9.3 Evidentials and language obsolescence   299
9.4 Where do evidentials come from: a summary   302
Map. Evidentials worldwide: areal distribution   303

10 How to choose the correct evidential: evidentiality
in discourse and in lexicon   305

10.1 Preferred evidentials   305
10.2 Evidentiality and discourse   310
10.2.1 Evidentials and narrative conventions   310
10.2.2 Manipulating evidentials in discourse   315
10.3 Evidentials and the lexicon   324
10.4 How to choose the correct evidential: a summary   331

11 What are evidentials good for? Evidentiality, cognition, and
cultural knowledge   333

11.1 Evidentials, communication, and cognition   334
11.2 Metalinguistic perception of evidentials   339
11.3 Evidential conventions and knowledge   343
11.4 Cultural and cognitive correlates of evidentials:
some speculations   355
11.5 Evidentials in culture and cognition: a summary   360
Appendix. How children acquire evidentials   362

12 What can we conclude? Summary and prospects   365
12.1 Cross-linguistic properties of evidentials: a summary   366
12.2 Evidentials: prospects and avenues for further investigation   382

Fieldworker's guide. How to gather materials on evidentiality systems   385

Glossary of terms   391
References   397
Index of languages   429
Index of authors   439
Subject index   445

Preface

This book is about the grammatical means of expressing information source, known as evidentials. The linguistic categorization of information source has a direct bearing on human cognition, communication, types of knowledge, and cultural conventions. This is what makes a cross-linguistic study of evidentials important for all scholars dealing with human cognition and communication, including linguists, psychologists, anthropologists, and philosophers.

Languages with large systems of evidentials present a true challenge for the typologist. My first encounter with these unusual systems was through field-work on Tariana, a North Arawak language spoken in northwest Amazonia, and Tucano, its neighbour from the East Tucanoan family. The more I worked on the topic, the more exotic and unusual systems I encountered, especially among little-known South American languages. This book came into being as an attempt to integrate these systems into a broad, cross-linguistically based, typological framework.

This study can be used both as a sourcebook for further typological studies, and as a textbook. Its discussion is couched in terms of basic linguistic theory, the typological and functional framework of linguistic analysis in terms of which most grammars are cast, and in terms of which significant typological generalizations are postulated. All the generalizations in this book are inductively based.

The readers and myself share a common set of purposes—to gain an understanding of what evidentials in the languages of the world do, and how they work. For this purpose, I have tried to analyse the facts and to formulate hypotheses and conclusions in the clearest possible way. The complexity of the actual linguistic systems speaks for itself.

Chapter 1 provides an illustration of evidentials, and general background. The final chapter provides a summary of findings throughout the book. In order to get an idea of evidential systems attested in the languages of the world, all readers are advised to study Chapter 2. Those who are interested in how information source can be marked through means other than a dedicated evidentiality system should read Chapter 4. Readers interested in historical and comparative issues and in language contact can hone in on Chapter 9. Scholars whose primary interests lie in the area of discourse should focus on Chapter 10. Those with a particular interest in the area of cognition and communication can refer to Chapter 11. The core of the volume is in Chapters 3 to 8 which detail the grammatical status and ramifications of evidential systems.

For ease of reference, evidential systems have been assigned designations such as A1, B2, or C3. These are fully explained in Chapter 2. The reader may find it helpful to photocopy the summary list of these, from the section on conventions, and keep it by their side while reading the volume.

A note on the materials and sources used is in order. This study is based on the examination of the grammars of over 500 languages representing each major language family and each linguistic area across the globe. Special attention has been paid to data that has recently become available on the languages of South America and New Guinea. All information on Tariana and Baniwa, from the Arawak family, and some data on Tucano, come from my own fieldwork.

Only about a quarter of the languages of the world have grammatical evidentials. At our present stage of knowledge it would have been unwise to restrict the analysis to just a sample of the available set of languages. Instead, I have looked at every language with evidentials on which I could find data. This all-embracing approach allows me to make the typology proposed here as comprehensive as it can be at this time, without imposing artificial limitations dictated by this or that 'sampling strategy'. Due to limitations of space, I could not cite examples of all occurrences of every phenomenon (the book is not intended to be an exhaustive encyclopaedia of evidentiality across the world). I usually provide a particularly illustrative example, and mention others. (Suggestive but somewhat tangential examples are added in footnotes.) If a phenomenon is found in more than half of the languages under consideration I call it 'relatively frequent'. If it is found in a restricted number of languages (one to five), I cite all of them and indicate its rarity. Note, however, that what appears rare to us at the present stage of knowledge may turn out to be more frequent when we start learning more about hitherto little-known languages and areas. This is the reason why I choose not to give any statistical counts at this stage. Five hundred is no more than about one-tenth of all human languages (estimates concerning the overall number of languages vary: 5,000 appears to be a conservative consensus; see Dixon 1997: 116, and the lengthy discussion in Crystal 2000). It thus seems most judicious to follow a qualitative approach at the present time, postponing quantitative analysis until more reliable data is available and can be assessed.

The choice of languages and the sheer number of examples discussed for each language reflect the state of study of each of these, rather than my own preferences. Jarawara, Nganasan, and Desano—for each of which a detailed analysis is available—are quoted much more frequently than, for instance, Kulina, Nenets, or Piratapuya—for each of which there is as yet no good comprehensive grammar. In each case, I refer to the most reliable, firsthand data based on fieldwork and/or native speaker proficiency of the researchers. Assertions and conclusions that would be cast in visual evidentiality—had they been written in a language with obligatory evidentiality—form the basis for this book. 'Do not say that for which you lack adequate evidence' is one of Grice's Maxims of Quality which I have followed throughout the study.

Lists of languages (with genetic affiliation), of language families, and of linguistic areas considered are given in the index. Examples which come from my own work are not followed by the indication of a source. I preserve the language names and the orthography of the source (or use an accepted practical orthography, transcription, or transliteration) unless otherwise indicated. I have also followed the morphemic analysis as given by the source (e.g. Johanson's for Turkish or Floyd's for Wanka Quechua).

A note on the use of gender-differentiated pronouns: I use 'they' for generic reference, without specifying the speaker's gender. The masculine pronoun 'he' always implies that a speaker is a man. In many cultures shamans are typically male—the use of 'he' to refer to a shaman reflects this cultural convention.

A study like this could only be definitive when good and thorough analytic descriptions have been provided for most of the world's languages. At present, we are a long way from this ideal. Nevertheless, I hope that this study will provide a framework within which fieldworkers and typologists will be able to work, and which can be amended and adjusted as new data and new insights emerge.

It is my hope that this book will encourage people to study evidentials, especially in little-known or undescribed languages, going out into the field and documenting languages threatened by extinction (before it is too late to do so).

Acknowledgments

I am indebted to many people, of different continents and backgrounds.

My gratitude goes to all those native speakers who taught me their languages and how to be precise in marking information source: Cândido, José, Jovino, Graciliano, and Olívia Brito (Tariana of Santa Rosa), and Marino, Domingo, Ismael, Jorge, and Batista Muniz (Tariana of Periquitos); Humberto Baltazar and Pedro Ângelo Tomas (Warekena); Afonso, Albino, and João Fontes, Celestino da Silva, Cecília and Laureano da Silva and the late Marcília Rodrigues (Baniwa); the late Tiago Cardoso (Desano, Piratapuya) and Alfredo Fontes (Tucano). I am forever indebted to Pauline Luma Laki, James Laki, David Takendu, Yuamali, Gemaj, and so many others who revealed the beauty of their native Manambu (New Guinea) which provides an efficient communicative means without evidentials.

My deepest gratitude goes to my teachers of Estonian (the late Elsa and Maimu Endemann, Lembit Oiari, and Juuli Selvet), to the members of Eesti Noorte Grupp of Canberra—Reet Bergman, Krista Gardiner, and Reet Vallak—and to Aet and Boris Lees, who have provided an ongoing source of inspiration through simply speaking their mother tongue.

Indefatigable support came from those who patiently answered my questions on evidentials, provided me with references and additional sources and commented on earlier versions of this book—Anvita Abbi, Willem Adelaar, Janet Barnes, Edith Bavin, Gavan Breen, Eithne Carlin, Slava Chirikba, Alec Coupe, Éva Csató, Tim Curnow, Josephine Daguman, Rui Dias, Anthony Diller, Gerrit Dimmendaal, Pattie Epps, Marília Ferreira, Michael Fortescue, Nilson Gabas Júnior, Carol Genetti, Albina Girfanova, Antoine Guillaume, Valentin Gusev, Claude Hagège, Bernd Heine, Ken Hill, Jane Hill, Hans Henrich Hock, Lars Johanson, Brian Joseph, Ferenc Kiefer, Christa König, John Koontz, Nicole Kruspe, Ago Künnap, Yolanda Lastra, Mary Laughren, Terry Malone, Sérgio Meira, Cynthia Miller, Marianne Mithun, Knut Olawsky, Hella Olbertz, Tom Payne, Bill Poser, François Queixalos, Bob Rankin, Willem de Reuse, Lucy Seki, Janet Sharp, Alexei Shmelev, Elena Shmeleva, Chida Shuntaro, Elena Skribnik, Tonya Stebbins, Kristine Stenzel, Anne Storch, Clay Strom, Catherine Travis, Nikolai Vakhtin, Defen Yu, and Fernando Zúñiga.

This book arose as a revision of a lengthy position paper for the International Workshop on Evidentiality (La Trobe University, Melbourne 2001). A shorter version was published as Introduction to the volume *Studies in Evidentiality* (2003), which features papers presented at the Workshop. Participants of the Workshop deserve special thanks. This book would not have been possible but for the linguistic insights and analysis by Pilar Valenzuela, Slava Chirikba, R. M. W. Dixon, Michael Fortescue, Lars Johanson, Willem de Reuse, Sally McLendon, Lena Maslova, Brian Joseph, Ruth Monserrat, Victor Friedman, and Randy LaPolla.

I am most grateful to those who read through the whole draft of the book, or parts of it, and provided comments, corrections, and ideas—Willem Adelaar, Gavan Breen, Eithne Carlin, Bernard Comrie, Östen Dahl, Scott DeLancey, Michael Fortescue, Zygmunt Frajzyngier, Lars Johanson, Randy LaPolla, Marianne Mithun, Anne Storch, Catherine Travis, and Pilar Valenzuela. Invaluable comments on just about every page came from R. M. W. Dixon, without whose constant encouragement and support this book would not have appeared.

I gratefully acknowledge the Wenner Gren Foundation for a grant which made my fieldwork financially feasible. My warmest thanks go to Silvana and Valteir Martins and Lenita and Elias Coelho, without whose friendship and assistance a great deal of my fieldwork would have been impossible.

Adam Bowles carefully read through several drafts of this book and corrected it with his usual skill, perspicacity, dedication, and good humour. Thanks are equally due to him, and to Perihan Avdi for nobly assisting with the proofs. Siew Peng Condon provided a wonderful working atmosphere at the Research Centre for Linguistic Typology. This book would have been scarcely possible without her cheerful support.

The stimulating intellectual atmosphere of the Research Centre for Linguistic Typology within the Institute of Advanced Study at La Trobe University was instrumental in bringing this research to fruition. Last—but certainly not the least—I am deeply grateful to Professor Michael Osborne, the Vice-Chancellor and President of La Trobe University, who made this all happen.

Abbreviations

=	clitic boundary
1	first person
2	second person
3	third person
3sp	'space' impersonal third person subject
4	fourth person
A	transitive subject function
ABL	ablative
ABS	absolutive
ABSTR	abstract
ACC	accusative
ACT	active
ACT.PART.NOM	active participle nominative
ADM	admirative
ADV	adverb
ADVM	adverbial marker
AFAR	translocative (at a distance)
AFF	affix
AFFIRM	affirmative
AG	agentive
ALL	allative
ANAPH	anaphoric
ANIM	animate
ANT	anterior
ANTIC	anticipatory
AO	synthetic aorist
AOR	aorist
APPL	applicative
APPR	apprehensive
ART	article
ASP	aspect
ASSERT	assertive
ASSOC	associative
ASSOC.MOT	associated motion
ASSP	asserted past particle

ASSUM	assumed
ATTR	attributive
AUD	auditory
AUG	augmentative
AUX, aux	auxiliary
BEN	benefactive
C.INT	content interrogative mood
CATEG	category
CAUS	causative
CDN	conjunct dubitative neutral
CDP	conjunct dubitative preterite
CIRC	circumstantial
CL	classifier
CM	conjugation marker
CMPL	completive aspect
CNTR	contrast
CO.REF	co-reference
COM	comitative
COMP	comparative
COMPL	completive
COMPL.CL	complement clause marking
COND	conditional
CONF	confirmation
CONFIRM	confirmative particle
CONJ	conjunct person-marking
CONJUN	conjunction
CONT	continuous aspect
CONV	converb
COP	copula
CSM	change of state marker
CUST	customary
DAT	dative
DEB	debitive
DECL	declarative
DEF	definite
DEL	delimiting
DEM	demonstrative

DEP	dependent clause marking
DES	desiderative
DETR	detrimental
DIM	diminutive
DIR	directive
DIR.EV	direct evidential
DIR/INFR	direct/inferred
DISJ	disjunct person-marking
DIST	distal
DIST.IMPV	distal imperative
DISTR	distributive
DN	deverbal noun
DP	discourse particle
DPAST	direct past
DS	different subject
DSTR	distributive
DTRNZ	detransitivizer
du, Du	dual
DUB	dubitative
DUR	durative
DYN	dynamic
EMPH	emphasis
EP	epenthetic
ERG	ergative
EV	evidential
EXC	excessive
excl	exclusive
EXCLAM	exclamatory
EXIST	existential
EXPER	experiential
EXPER.PAST	experienced past
EXT	extent
F	future tense inflection
f, FEM	feminine
FIN	finite
FINAL.PART	final particle
FIRSTH	firsthand
FOC	focus

FP	far past
FR	frustrative
FUT	future
FUT.NOM	nominal future
FUT.PART	future tense particle
GEN	genitive
GER	gerund
HAB	habitual
HS	hearsay
HUM	human
IC	indirective copula
ILL	illative
IM	synthetic imperfect
IMM.PAST, IMM.P	immediate past
IMPARF	imparfait
IMPV	imperative
IMPERS	impersonal
IMPF	imperfective
IMPV.SEC	secondhand imperative
INAN	inanimate
INC	incompletive aspect
INCH	inchoative
incl	inclusive
IND	indicative
INDEF	indefinite
INDIR.COP	indirective copula
INESS	inessive
INF	infinitive
INF.NON.MIR	non-mirative inferential particle
INFR	inferred
INST	instrumental
INT	interjection (filler, pause particle)
INTER	interrogative
INTR	intransitive
INTRATERM.ASP	intraterminal aspect
INTRST	complement of interest
INV	inverse prefix class

IPAST	indirective past
IRR	irrealis
ITER	iterative
L	l-past (aorist and imperfect)
LAT	lative
LIG	ligature
LIM	limitative
LNK	linker
LOC	locative
LOGOPHOR	logophoric
m, MASC, M	masculine
MAN	purpose-manner converb
MIR	mirative
MOD	modal particle
MSD	masdar
N	neuter
NARR	narrative
NCL	noun class
NCM	non-compact matter classificatory verb stem
NEC	necessitative
NEG	negative
NEUT	neutral gender
nf	non-feminine
NF	non-final marker
NFIN	non-finite
NMLZ	nominalizer
NOM	nominative
NOM.PAST	nominal past
NOM.PERF	perfective nominalization
NOMN	nominalization
NON.EXPER	non-experienced
NON.IMM	non-immediate
NONFIRSTH	non-firsthand
NONVIS	non-visual
NP	noun particle
NPOSS	non-possessed
nsg	non-singular
NUM.CL	numeral classifier

NVEXP	non-visual experiential particle
NVOL	non-volitional
O	transitive object function
OBJ, obj	object
OBL	oblique
OBV	obviative
Oc	marker of O-construction type
ONOM	onomatopoeia
OPT	optative
OR	orientation (direction) marker
OV	objective version
p	person
P	past
P.INT	polar interrogative mood
PABS	past absolutive
PART	participle
PART.PRES	present participle
PARTVE	partitive
PASS	passive
PASS.PRES.NOM	present participle nominative
PASS.PRS.NOM.NT	passive participle present nominative neuter
PAST.COMPL	completed past
PAST.REL	past relative
PB	probabilitive
PC	particle of concord
PDR	past deferred realization particle
PDS	previous event, different subject
PEJ	pejorative
PERF	perfect
PERF.CONT	perfect continuous
PINDEF	past indefinite
PINF	physical inferential particle
pl, PL	plural
PLUPERF	pluperfect
POSS	possessive
POST	post-terminal aspect
POT	potential
PP1	incompletive participle
PP2	completive participle

PPAST	post-terminal past
PREF	prefix
PRES	present
PRES.PARTIC.PART.SG	present participle partitive singular
PREV	preverb
PREV.DIR.EV	previous direct evidence
PREV.EVID.EV	previous evidence evidential
PREVEN	preventive
PRIV	privative
PROCOMP	procomplement
PROD	product verbalizer
PROG	progressive
PROHIB	prohibitive
PROL	prolative
PRON	pronominal
PROP	proprietive
PROSP	prospective aspect
PROX	proximate
PROX.IMPV	proximate imperative
PS	passé simple
PSSI	previous event, same subject, intransitive matrix clause
PSST	previous event, same subject, transitive matrix clause
PURP	purposive
Q	question
QUOT	quotative
RA	repeated action
REC	reciprocal
REC.P	recent past
REFL	reflexive
REL	relative
REM.P	remote past
REP	reported
RNR	result nominalizer
S	(intransitive) subject function
SD	sudden discovery tense
SDS	simultaneous event, different subject
SENS.EV	sensory evidential
SEQ	sequence
SF	subject-focus

SFP	sentence final particle
sg, SG	singular
SIM	similarity
sIn	singular action, intransitive
SJ	subject case
SMU	submorphemic unit
SPEC	specific nominalizer and relativizer enclitic
SPEC	specifier
SPECL	speculative
SS	same subject
SSSI	simultaneous event, same subject, intransitive matrix clause
SSST	simultaneous event, same subject, transitive matrix clause
STA	stative prefix type
STAT	stative
SU	subjunctive marker
SUB	subordinating
SUBJ	subjunctive
SUBR	subordinator
SUPP	suppositive, presumptive
SWITCH.REF	switch reference
T	temporal
TAG	tag question particle
TERM	marker of non-subject
TOP	topic
TOP.NON.A/S	topical non-subject case
TR	transitive
TRANSFORM	transformative
TS	tense
VA	verbal adjective
VCL	verb class marker
VCLASS	verb class
VERT	vertical classifier
VIS	visual
VN	verbal noun
VOC	vocative
VOL	volitional
VP	verbal particle
YNQ	yes-no question particle

Conventions

The following conventions have been adopted for the ease of reference to evidentiality systems:

Systems with two choices are referred to with the letter A and a number, as follows:

A1. Firsthand and Non-firsthand

A2. Non-firsthand versus 'everything else'

A3. Reported (or 'hearsay') versus 'everything else'

A4. Sensory evidence and Reported (or 'hearsay')

A5. Auditory (acquired through hearing) versus 'everything else'

Systems with three choices are referred to with the letter B and a number, as follows:

B1. Direct (or Visual), Inferred, Reported

B2. Visual, Non-visual sensory, Inferred

B3. Visual, Non-visual sensory, Reported

B4. Non-visual sensory, Inferred, Reported

B5. Reported, quotative, and 'everything else'

Systems with four choices are referred to with the letter C and a number, as follows:

C1. Visual, Non-visual sensory, Inferred, Reported

C2. Direct (or Visual), Inferred, Assumed, Reported

C3. Direct, Inferred, Reported, Quotative

The only kind of system with five choices found in more than one language is referred to as D1:

D1. Visual, Non-visual sensory, Inferred, Assumed, and Reported

The discussion of each type is found in Chapter 2.

List of Tables

2.1 Semantic parameters in evidentiality systems   65

3.1 Subsystems of evidentials in Tucano depending on clause types   85

3.2 Double marking of information source: a summary   93

3.3 How to tell a lie in a language with obligatory
evidentiality: Tariana   98

4.1 Conjunct and disjunct copulas in Lhasa Tibetan   127

4.2 Reported evidential and reported discourse:
division of labour   140

4.3 Evidentiality strategies: a summary   147

5.1 Sensory evidentials in large systems   173

5.2 Semantic extensions in evidentiality systems with
two choices   188

5.3 Semantic complexity of evidentials in systems with
three choices   190

5.4 Semantic complexity of evidentials in systems with
four and five choices   191

6.1 Mirative extensions of evidentials: a summary   207

6.2 Restrictions on mirative extensions of evidentials
depending on other categories   208

7.1 First person effects in evidentials   238

8.1 Semantics of evidentials in interrogative clauses in
Tariana and in Tucano   247

8.2 Subsystems of evidentials in Tariana depending
on clause types   255

8.3 Co-occurrence of evidentials with modalities in Tariana   260

8.4 Evidentials, aspect, and tense in Yukaghir   263

8.5 Tense and evidentiality in Tariana and Tucano   265

8.6 Correlations between tense and evidentiality   267

9.1 Strategies employed in the development of the
tense-evidentiality system in Tariana   286

List of Diagrams

3.1   Correlations in question–response: Tariana and Tuyuca   86
10.1 Hierarchy of Preferred Evidentials in Tuyuca and Tariana   307
10.2 Hierarchy of Preferred Evidentials in Kashaya   308
10.3 How to choose the correct evidential: restrictions and
      preferences   331

List of Schemes

3.1 Formal markedness in evidentiality systems   73
3.2 Evidentiality subsystems in Jarawara   85
4.1 Evidential extensions for non-indicative moods
    in main clauses   110
4.2 Evidential extensions for non-indicative moods in
    non-main clauses   111
4.3 Evidential extensions for perfects and resultatives   116
4.4 The semantic range of evidentiality strategies   145
5.1 Meaning extensions for non-firsthand evidentials   158
6.1 Mirative extension of an evidential (I)   208
6.2 Mirative extension of an evidential (II)   209
6.3 Mirative extension of an evidential: deferred
    realization (III)   209
9.1 The development of non-firsthand evidentials out
    of perfects and resultatives   279

1

Preliminaries and key concepts

No two languages are entirely the same, nor are they entirely different. It is as if there were a universal inventory of possible grammatical and lexical categories and each language makes a different set of choices from this inventory. As Franz Boas (a founding father of modern linguistics) put it, languages differ not in what one can say but in what kind of information must be stated: 'grammar [...] determines those aspects of each experience that *must* be expressed' (Boas 1938: 132). One language may have a two-term gender system, while another has five genders and a third makes no gender distinctions at all in its grammar. Along similar lines, some languages have grammatical tense, and others do not.

In about a quarter of the world's languages, every statement must specify the type of source on which it is based—for example, whether the speaker saw it, or heard it, or inferred it from indirect evidence, or learnt it from someone else. This grammatical category, whose primary meaning is information source, is called 'evidentiality'. In Boas's words (1938: 133), 'while for us definiteness, number, and time are obligatory aspects, we find in another language location near the speaker or somewhere else, [and] source of information—whether seen, heard, or inferred—as obligatory aspects'.

1.1 Evidentiality: an illustration

Marking one's information source indicates how one learnt something. Languages vary in how many types of information sources they have to express. Many just mark information reported by someone else. Others distinguish firsthand and non-firsthand sources. In rarer instances, visually obtained data are contrasted with data obtained through hearing or smelling, or through various kinds of inference. These larger systems also tend to have a separate marker for reported information. Tariana, an Arawak language spoken in the multilingual area of the Vaupés in northwest Amazonia, has an even more complex system. In this language, one cannot simply say 'José played football'. Just like in all other indigenous languages from the same area, speakers have to specify whether they saw the event happen, or heard it, or know about it because somebody else told them, etc. This is achieved through a set of evidential markers fused with tense. Omitting an evidential results in an ungrammatical and highly unnatural sentence.

If one saw José play football, 1.1 would be appropriate (here and elsewhere evidential morphemes are in bold type), with -*ka* marking both visual evidential and recent past tense.

Tariana
1.1   Juse   irida   di-manika-**ka**
       José   football   3sgnf-play-REC.P.VIS
       'José has played football (we saw it)'

If one just heard the noise of a football game but could not see what is happening, 1.2 is the thing to say. Here, -*mahka* marks non-visual evidential and recent past.

Tariana
1.2   Juse   irida   di-manika-**mahka**
       José   football   3sgnf-play-REC.P.NONVIS
       'José has played football (we heard it)'

If one sees that the football is not in its normal place in the house, and José and his football boots are gone (and his sandals are left behind), with crowds of people coming back from the football ground, this is enough for us to infer that José is playing football. We then say 1.3, where -*nihka* marks inferred evidentiality and recent past tense.

Tariana
1.3   Juse   irida   di-manika-**nihka**
       José   football   3sgnf-play-REC.P.INFR
       'José has played football (we infer it from visual evidence)'

Suppose José is not at home on a Sunday afternoon. We know that he usually plays football on Sunday afternoon. Then, 1.4 is an option. Our assumption here is based on general knowledge about José's habits, with -*sika* marking assumed evidentiality and recent past tense.

Tariana
1.4   Juse   irida   di-manika-**sika**
       José   football   3sgnf-play-REC.P.ASSUM
       'José has played football (we assume this on the basis of what we already know)'

The difference between the 'assumed' evidential, as in 1.4, and the 'inferred', as in 1.3, lies in access to visual evidence of something happening and to the degree of 'reasoning' involved. The less obvious the evidence and the more the speaker has to rely on reasoning based on knowledge or on common sense, the more chance there is that the assumed evidential will be used. An inferred evidential refers to something based on obvious evidence which can be easily observed (even if the event itself was not seen). This illustrates two types of inference—the one based on visible result, and the other based on reasoning, general knowledge and, ultimately, conjecture.

And finally, if one learnt the information from someone else, then 1.5 is the only correct option, with *-pidaka* marking reported evidentiality and recent past tense.

Tariana

1.5   Juse   irida   di-manika-**pidaka**
      José   football   3sgnf-play-REC.P.REP
      'José has played football (we were told)'

Despite the recent surge of interest in evidentiality, it remains one of the least known grammatical categories. Evidentiality systems differ in how complex they are: some distinguish just two terms, for instance, firsthand and non-firsthand. Others have six, or even more, terms. Some languages differentiate between one evidential (often with the meaning of 'reported' or 'non-firsthand') and no evidentiality at all. The term 'verificational' or 'validational' is sometimes used in place of 'evidential'. There is an excellent summary of work on recognizing this category, and naming it, in Jacobsen (1986). A brief discussion of terminological problems is under §1.3.

1.2 What is, and what is not, an evidential

1.2.1 *The nature of linguistic evidentials*

Evidentiality is a linguistic category whose primary meaning is source of information. In the chapters that follow, we will see that this covers the way in which the information was acquired, without necessarily relating to the degree of speaker's certainty concerning the statement or whether it is true or not. One evidential morpheme often covers several related sources. For instance, one evidential typically refers to things one hears, smells and feels by touch. To be considered as an evidential, a morpheme has to have 'source of information' as its core meaning; that is, the unmarked, or default interpretation. Evidence for such interpretation comes from various quarters, not least native speakers' intuitions, and the possibility of lexical 'reinforcement'. That is, an evidential can be, optionally, rephrased with a lexical item, or one can add a lexical explanation to an evidential. A visual evidential would then be rephrased as 'I saw it', and a reported evidential with 'they told me'. We return to these 'semantic clues' to what evidentials mean and how native speakers explain them, in Chapter 5 and then in §11.2.

'Evidential' and 'evidence' as a linguistic category differs from 'evidence' in common parlance. According to the definition in the *Oxford English Dictionary*, 'evidence' covers 'the available facts, circumstances, etc. supporting or otherwise a belief, proposition, etc., or indicating whether or not a thing is true or valid'. In legal talk, evidence is 'information given personally or drawn from a document etc. and tending to prove a fact or proposition' and also 'statements or proofs admissible as testimony in a lawcourt'. Whatever has to do with providing this kind of 'evidence' is 'evidential'.

Now, the linguistic notion of evidentiality—as discussed by Boas (1938) and exemplified in 1.1–5 above—differs drastically from the conventional usage by a non-linguist. Linguistic evidentiality has nothing to do with providing proof in court or in argument, or indicating what is true and what is not, or indicating one's belief. All evidentiality does is supply the information source. The ways in which information is acquired—by seeing, hearing, or in any other way—is its core meaning. In Hardman's words (1986: 121), marking data source and concomitant categories is 'not a function of truth or falsity'. The truth value of an utterance is not affected by an evidential (cf. Donabédian 2001: 432). And, in fact, an evidential can have a truth value of its own. It can be negated and questioned, without negating or questioning the predicate itself (see §3.7). An evidential can even acquire its own time reference, distinct from that of the clause (see §3.8). Unlike most other grammatical categories, information source can be marked more than once in a clause, reflecting the same observer, or different observers, perceiving the information through different albeit compatible avenues (see §3.5).

This disparity between the common, or legal, notion of 'evidence' and 'evidential' is akin to that between linguistic borrowing and borrowing from a bank. Lay people—even first-year students of linguistics—are often puzzled: why is it so that one always has to repay a monetary loan, while loan words are never given back? Or take the term 'gender'. In politically correct varieties of Modern English this label has almost displaced the term 'sex'. As a result, 'gender' now has two distinct senses. The *Oxford Dictionary* states: 'gender' is 'the state of being male or female'. It also states that 'gender' as a linguistic term refers to the 'grammatical classification of nouns and related words, roughly corresponding to the two sexes and sexlessness'. In the same way the terms 'evidence' and 'evidential' each have two meanings: that of the courtroom and that of the linguist. This distinction, however, has not yet had time to percolate into dictionaries.

The unrecognized polysemy of the term 'evidence' and its derivative, 'evidential', has resulted in conceptual and terminological confusion. Most of all, this has influenced the ways in which linguists with a firm grounding in European languages came to understand evidentiality. For many scholars of Romance and Germanic languages, having a way of saying 'apparently' or 'I do not believe' is a good enough pretext to put 'evidentiality' in the title of their paper (e.g. Hassler 2002). Yet marking information source as a grammatical category does not imply any reference to validity or reliability of knowledge or information (pace Hassler 2002: 157, or Hoff 1986). Neither does linguistic evidentiality bear any straightforward relationship to 'truth', or responsibility, let alone relevance. This is quite unlike the non-linguistic use of the term— there evidence means 'proof', and 'evidential' means 'to do with proof'.

Linguistic evidentials can in fact be manipulated in rather intricate ways in telling lies. Either the information source may be correct, and the information false; or the other way round. Speakers' proficiency in evidentials is often a token of their status within a community and indicates how well they know the existing conventions. However, expressing an appropriate information source, and choosing the correct marking for it, has nothing to do with one's 'epistemic stance', point of view, or personal reliability.[1]

---

[1] An example of how the laymen's use of the term 'evidence' has affected some linguistic usage is a definition of evidentiality as ' "natural epistemology", the ways in which the ordinary people unhampered by philosophical traditions naturally regard the source and reliability of their knowledge' (Chafe and Nichols 1986: vii). This reflects a limited perspective: it presupposes that marking information source is the same as marking 'reliability'. Evidentials are indeed part of what is covered by the philosophical term 'epistemology' inasmuch as it relates to information source. Epistemology is defined as 'the philosophical theory of knowledge, which seeks to define it, distinguish its principal varieties, identify its sources, and establish its limits' (Bullock and Stallybrass 1988: 279). Note that this definition of epistemology does not include attitude to truth or reliability of information or of knowledge. Chung and Timberlake (1985: 244–6) correctly categorize evidentiality as an 'epistemological mode' to do with information source, using the term 'epistemology' in its conventional, philosophical meaning.

Unfortunately, the connection between evidentiality and 'reliability' of information has become quite entrenched: even Matthews (1997: 120), in what is by far the best dictionary of linguistics to date, defines evidential as 'particle, inflection which is one of a set that make clear the source or reliability of the evidence on which a statement is based'. In Chafe's terminology (1986), evidentiality in a 'narrow sense' refers to marking the **source** of knowledge. Evidentiality in a 'broad sense' is marking speaker's **attitude** towards his or her knowledge of reality. Such a view of evidentiality subsumes specification of probability, degree of precision or truth, and various other extensions typically expressed with modalities. This approach dilutes the sharp boundaries between evidentiality and various modalities, including hypotheticals, irrealis, and probabilitative moods. Ultimately this produces a conceptual and a terminological confusion, and fails to account for the numerous languages where evidentiality is fully independent from each of such categories (see, for instance, §8.3). The occasionally existing link between some evidential choices and the expression of certainty or uncertainty (see, for instance, §5.3.1 and §5.4.4) is then mistaken for a universal.

Along similar lines, Dendale and Tasmowski (2001: 343) claim that 'in the evidential systems of many languages, the forms marking the source of information also mark the speaker's attitude towards the reliability of that information'. (A similar stance underlies the discussion by Nuyts 2001.) Throughout

Linguistic evidentiality is a grammatical system (and often one morphological paradigm). In languages with grammatical evidentiality, marking how one knows something is a must. Leaving this out results in a grammatically awkward 'incomplete' sentence (cf. Valenzuela 2003: 34 on Shipibo-Konibo, a Panoan language from Peru). Those who cannot get their evidential right are in trouble: they are considered linguistically incompetent and generally not worth talking to. Only in some systems can an evidential be omitted if recoverable from the context. This is very much unlike languages where saying explicitly how you know things is a matter of choice for the speaker.

Not infrequently, languages employ means other than grammatical evidentiality to describe different types of knowledge, and of information source. As shown by Frajzyngier (1985: 252), the inherent meaning of unmarked indicative sentences in a number of languages is to 'express what the speaker wants to convey as truth'. In languages with evidentials, some evidentials—usually the ones to do with visually acquired knowledge—may be formally unmarked. Once again, this is different from an 'unmarked indicative sentence' in languages where evidentiality is not obligatory, and statements are typically left vague as to the source of information.

Evidentials may acquire secondary meanings—of reliability, probability, and possibility (known as epistemic extensions[2]), but they do not have to. A hypothetical modality may overlap with a non-firsthand evidential: both could be used for something one has not observed and thus has reservations about.

this book, I will show that this is far from universal, and definitely not an 'empirical fact' (pace Dendale and Tasmowski 2001: 342–3). Whether or not an evidential has an 'epistemic' extension (that is, an extension to do with probability or possibility) depends (a) on the structure of the evidential system; (b) on the terms within this system: for instance, epistemic extensions could be associated with reported evidentials in some and with inferred evidentials in other languages; and (c) on the overall structure of the language: if a language has a vast array of modalities with epistemic meanings, one can hardly expect highly specialized evidentials to have any such extensions. The view of evidentiality as type of 'epistemology' or 'epistemic modality' is ultimately based on an attempt to reconcile the 'exotic' facts of languages with large evidentiality systems, and modality-oriented familiar languages of Europe.

Along similar lines, I disregard attempts to apply poorly elaborated notions of 'weak' and 'strong' evidentiality which firstly do not draw a necessary line between modalities and source of information, and secondly are based on a highly restricted set of data, such as Mushin (2001a). In the same way, establishing correlations between inference and information source can only be achieved after a complete investigation of evidentiality as a grammatical category; this makes studies of lexical strategies referring to information source, such as Ifantidou (2001), premature and tangential for the analysis of grammatical expression of information source, despite the fact that evidential markers occasionally come from lexical sources (see §9.1.6).

[2] The term 'epistemic' has different meanings in different disciplines. It is defined, in the *Oxford English Dictionary* (1999), as 'of or relating to knowledge or degree of acceptance'. The philosophical term 'epistemics' signifies 'the scientific study of knowledge' (Bullock and Stallybrass 1988: 279). In common linguistic usage (e.g. Matthews 1997: 115) the word 'epistemic' is used very differently: it means 'indicating factual necessity, probability, possibility, etc.', rather than 'relating to knowledge'.

This does not make a modal into an evidential. Cross-linguistically, evidentiality, modality (relating to the degree of certainty 'with which something is said': Matthews 1997: 228), and mood (relating to a speech act) are fully distinct categories. In each case, it is important to determine primary meaning for each of these on language-internal grounds. The ways in which semantic extensions of evidentials overlap with modalities and such meanings as probability or possibility depend on the individual system, and on the semantics of each individual evidential term. For instance, using the reported evidential in Estonian may imply that the speaker simply acquired the information from someone else. Or the speaker could choose to use the reported evidential if he or she does not vouch for the veracity of the reported information. Reported evidential in larger systems—such as Quechua or Shipibo-Konibo—does not have such connotations. In many languages (e.g. Quechua or Tariana), markers of hypothetical modality and irrealis can occur in conjunction with evidentials on one verb or clause (see §8.3). This further corroborates their status as distinct categories.

Evidentiality is a category in its own right, and not a subcategory of any modality (see highly convincing arguments in de Haan 1999; Lazard 1999; 2001; and DeLancey 2001, and in studies of individual languages, e.g. Skribnik 1998: 205–6), or of tense-aspect.[3] Scholars tend to assume that evidentials are modals largely because of their absence in most major European languages, thus trying to explain an unusual category in terms of some other, more conventional, notion. There is simply no other place in a Standard Average European grammar where they could be assigned. For want of a better option, evidentials are then translated into European languages with epistemic markers. For instance, 1.4, 'José has played football (assumed)', can be translated into English using 'apparently' or 'probably' as a short cut. Those researchers who base their analysis of language data on the ways in which these data are glossed or translated into English are thus misled.[4]

That evidentials may have semantic extensions related to probability and speaker's evaluation of the trustworthiness of information does not make

[3] Pace Bybee (1985), Palmer (1987), van der Auwera and Plungian (1998), and Willett (1988). The proponents of such views hardly ever provide any justification for their treatment of evidentials, simply assuming that evidentials are modals (also see Dahl 1985: 148, 190). Palmer (1986: 51) considered evidentiality as 'indication by the speaker of his (lack of) commitment to the truth of the proposition being expressed', adding that 'it would be a futile exercise to try to decide whether a particular system (or even a term in a system in some cases) is evidential rather than a judgement' (70). Similarly, for Frajzyngier (1985: 250), it 'appears rather obvious that the different manners of acquiring knowledge correspond to different degrees of certainty about the truth of the proposition'. According to Trask (1999: 189), 'modality shades off imperceptibly into several other categories', one of which is said to be evidentiality. Throughout the book it will be demonstrated the ways in which such suggestions are inadequate.

[4] A prime example of this is Wierzbicka's 'reinterpretation' of examples in Chafe and Nichols (1986) on the basis of how they are translated into English (Wierzbicka 1994, 1996: 427–58).

evidentiality a kind of modality. This can be compared to the semantics of gender systems: in many languages feminine gender is associated with diminution, or endearment (see numerous examples in Aikhenvald 2000), and masculine gender with augmentative; this, however, does not mean that gender is a type of diminutive or augmentative category. The kinds of extensions one can get for a particular evidential meaning in a language largely depend on the structure of the evidentiality system and its place among other verbal categories.[5]

Evidentiality and mirativity—a category whose primary meaning is related to unprepared mind, new information, and speaker's surprise—are conceptually related, albeit distinct. Any evidential other than visual or firsthand may, but does not have to, extend to refer to 'unusual' and 'surprising' information (called 'mirative' by DeLancey 1997; see Lazard 1999 and DeLancey 2001 on difficulties associated with teasing apart the categories of evidentiality and mirativity).

Evidentiality can be expressed in a variety of ways. Some languages have dedicated affixes or clitics, while others have their evidentiality marking fused with another category (as with tense in Tariana). Evidentiality is not restricted to any type of language. Languages with evidentiality can be fusional, agglutinating or isolating; alternatively, they can be synthetic or polysynthetic.[6] Only occasionally do Creoles and Pidgins have evidentials; see Nichols (1986: 245) on Chinese Pidgin Russian, where evidentiality is the only obligatory category. Neither does the presence or absence of evidentiality depend on whether a language is head- or dependent-marking. No evidentials have been described for Sign Languages.

Evidentiality specifications may be made independently of clause type, modality, or tense-aspect choice. Alternatively, a choice in the evidentiality system may depend on tense, aspect, or clause type. As we will see below, a significant number of languages distinguish evidentiality only in the past, and just a few do so in the future. Dependencies between evidentiality and other categories are discussed in Chapter 8 below (in the spirit of Aikhenvald and Dixon 1998a).

The choice of evidentiality often correlates with person. Some evidentials may not occur in a first person context.[7] This is understandable: the idea of

---

[5] Attempts have been made to place all putatively evidential markers on a scale, from those that have 'context-free' semantic interpretations of source of information (that is, evidentials proper as discussed throughout this book) to those which may or may not have a conceptualized interpretation of source of information (such as one possible interpretation of English *must:* Mushin 2001a: 30–3). This approach suffers from lack of distinction between grammatical evidentiality and lexical and other means which may acquire evidential-like meaning extensions. Semantic extensions of evidentials can scarcely be arranged on any such a scale; see Chapter 5 for a discussion of evidentials and their meanings.

[6] Dahl (1985), on the basis of a small sample of languages, arrived at a conclusion that evidentials are only found in agglutinating languages. An investigation of a larger selection of languages does not confirm this.

[7] In some previous studies, attempts were made to reduce evidentiality to a kind of 'knowledge' of the first person speaker (Anderson 1986: 276). Evidentiality covers more than just person and relates only marginally to the 'speaker–hearer contract' (pace Givón 1982: 43).

using reported or inferred evidential when talking about oneself sounds counterintuitive. If these seemingly unusual choices are available in first person, they may produce additional semantic effects. An inferential or a reported evidential may describe something the speaker cannot remember, or does not want to take responsibility for, or did inadvertently. Evidentials may be mutually exclusive with certain moods and with modality markers. Typically, fewer evidentiality choices are available in questions and in commands than in statements. Quite a few languages simply do not employ evidentials in commands.

Evidentiality may form one obligatory inflectional system, with information source as its core semantics. Such systems are our main focus of study. Evidential meanings may be expressed in a variety of other ways, by using different grammatical mechanisms but not forming one coherent category. In some such cases, one can distinguish several evidentiality subsystems. In others, evidentiality specifications are 'scattered' all over the grammar. In other words, evidential meanings are there, but they do not form a single grammatical category. Languages with 'scattered' evidentiality may employ semantic parameters which diverge somewhat from those recurrent in languages with evidentiality as a single tightly knit and coherent category. The composition and status of evidentiality in each individual case is important to bear in mind if one wishes to achieve cross-linguistically valid generalizations (see §3.3).

Languages with evidentiality tend to develop conventions concerning preferred choices in different discourse genres. An evidential in itself may be considered a token of a genre. Speakers of languages with evidentials may say that a story is not a story without a reported evidential. An unexpected evidentiality choice may acquire additional stylistic overtones—of sarcasm, irony, or indignation. Evidentiality choices correlate with backgrounding, or foregrounding, a part of the narrative. All this contributes to the importance of evidentials for human communication and the ways in which speakers view the world.

Obligatory evidentials presuppose the requirement of explicitly stating the exact source of information, and may go together with certain cultural attitudes and practices. The spread of shared cultural practices from one people to another may affect the use of evidentials. The introduction of new cultural practices such as radio, television, or reading may provide additional semantic extensions for evidentials (see Chapter 11).

A strong argument in favour of the importance of evidentials for human cognition lies in their metalinguistic valuation and speakers' awareness of their necessity. An evidentially unmarked statement (if at all possible in a language) may be treated with suspicion and ultimately contempt. Those who cannot get their evidentials right may be branded as crazy, unreliable, and generally not worth talking to. Languages without evidentiality are often viewed as somehow deficient by those whose languages have evidentiality. Evidentials often make their way into contact languages (such as Spanish, Portuguese, and even English spoken by second language learners of American Indian extraction). And they readily spread through language contact.

1.2.2 *Expressing information source by means other than grammatical evidentials*

Every language has some way of referring to the source of information, but not every language has grammatical evidentiality. Having lexical means for optional specification of the source of knowledge is probably universal—cf. English *I guess, they say, I hear that*, etc., as well as lexical verbs such as *allege* (e.g. *the alleged killer of* X). A valuable discussion of 'parenthetic' expressions in English, which are widely used to optionally indicate the source of information, can be found in Urmston (1952) and Dixon (1991a: 209–15). These lexical means can be of different statuses. They may include adverbial expressions such as *reportedly*, or introductory clauses with complementation markers, such as *it seems to me that*, or particles, such as Russian *jakoby, mol*, and *deskatj* all indicating 'hearsay' (Rakhilina 1996). Adverbial phrases dealing with speaker's attitude in Japanese (Aoki 1986: 234–5) can also be considered a lexical way of referring to how information has been obtained and to its validation. Modal verbs are often used to express meanings connected with information source (cf., for example, Tasmowski and Dendale 1994, on 'evidential-like' interpretation of *pouvoir* 'be able to' in French; or King and Nadasdi 1999, on how French-English bilinguals employ verbs of opinion or belief which they—misleadingly—call 'evidentiality'). The semantic scope of such expressions ranges from information source to the degree of speaker's commitment to the veracity of the statement, e.g. English *reportedly* or its Estonian equivalent *kuuldavasti* (with the same meaning). However, Estonian also has a dedicated paradigm for reported evidential, while English has nothing of this sort. An exemplary discussion of how Hebrew and Arabic lack grammatical evidentiality is in Isaksson (2000).

Saying that English parentheticals are 'evidentials' is akin to saying that time words like 'yesterday' or 'today' are tense markers. These expressions are not obligatory and do not constitute a grammatical category; consequently, they are only tangential to the present discussion. Saying that English has 'evidentiality' (cf. Fox 2001) is misleading: this implies a confusion between what is grammaticalized and what is lexical in a language. Lexical expressions may, of course, provide historical sources for evidential systems (see Chapter 9). Lexical ways of indicating source of information may reinforce grammatical evidentials. Or one can add a lexical explanation to an evidentially marked clause, to disambiguate an evidential which has several meanings.

Throughout this book I will be concerned with just the grammatical coding of evidentiality. Grammar is taken to deal with closed systems, which can be realized through bound morphemes, clitics, and words which belong to full grammatical word classes, such as prepositions, preverbs, or particles. As I mentioned above, in almost all languages, source of information can be expressed lexically, for example, by adverbs such as 'reportedly' or 'apparently'. In itself, a semantic study of such expressions is a separate task. I won't attempt it here.

It is, however, worth mentioning that grammar and lexicon can and do interact. And evidentiality may well interact with the lexicon of a language in a variety of ways. Lexical classes of verbs can require certain evidentiality choices: for instance, internal states and processes, 'felt' rather than seen, are often cast in non-visual or non-firsthand evidential. Such preferences may get lexicalized as restricted evidentiality choices for predicate types and construction types. We return to this in Chapter 10.

Meanings to do with how people know things may be expressed in yet another indirect way, without developing a dedicated form with primarily evidential meaning. Non-evidential categories frequently acquire evidential extensions. A verbal form—e.g. conditional mood, or a perfect, or a passive—can develop an evidential-like meaning as a 'side effect' without having 'source of information' as its primary meaning (see the discussion in Lazard 1999). One of the best-known examples is the conditional in French (known as 'conditionnel d'information incertaine') used to relate information obtained from another source for which the speaker does not take any responsibility. In a few Iranian and Turkic languages, and also in Georgian, perfect has similar connotations, while in Kinyarwanda (Bantu: Givón and Kimenyi 1974) the choice of a complementation strategy correlates with the expressions of ways in which information was obtained. The term 'evidentiality system' in the sense proposed here is not appropriate for these systems. The extensions of grammatical categories and forms to cover evidential-like meanings will be referred to as an 'evidentiality strategy' (see Chapter 4). Historically, evidentiality strategies often develop into evidentials (see Chapter 9).

1.3 'Evidentials' as a linguistic term

Up until the late nineteenth century only those linguistic categories which were found in classical Indo-European languages were accorded due status and investigated in some depth. Since these languages have no grammaticalized information source, the concept of evidentiality had not made its way into linguistics until 'exotic' languages started being described in terms of categories relevant for them, rather than from a limited Indo-European perspective.

Pre-twentieth-century grammatical descriptions of Quechua and Aymara, languages with obligatory evidentials, are particularly instructive. In one of the earliest grammars of Quechua, *Grammatica o arte de la lengua general de los indios de los reynos del Peru* in 1560, Santo Tomás treats evidential particles, together with other morphemes which 'do not fit into the model of Romance languages' (Dedenbach-Salazar Sáenz 1997a: 297) as simply ornate particles with no meaning of their own ('de suyo nada significan: pero adornan, o ayudan a la significacion de los nombres, o verbos a que se añaden', '(they) do not mean anything of their own: but they adorn, or help the meaning of the nouns, or verbs to which they attach'). Along similar lines, the anonymous grammar of Quechua published in 1586 (Anónimo 1586: Dedenbach-Salazar Sáenz 1997a: 301) treats evidential markers as 'particulas diversas (...) que [...] siruen de ornatiuas' ('various particles (...) which [...] serve to adorn') (see further examples and discussion in Dedenbach-Salazar Sáenz 1997a).[8] Bertonio (1603), in his grammar of Aymara (see Calvo Pérez 1997; Hardman 1986: 113), considered the Aymara information source markers as 'ornate particles', since 'without them the sentence is perfectly fine'. Torres Rubio (1616: 244) also treated evidentials as particles 'which serve no other function than to adorn the sentence'. In Quechua and Aymara studies, the same attitude persisted until much later. Ráez (1917), in his description of Wanka Quechua, described the direct evidential suffix 'as a substitute for the copula in the present indicative tense' (Floyd 1999: 3). Ellen Ross (1963) called Aymara evidential markers 'emphatic suffixes', while Juan Enrique Ebbing (1965) called them 'suffixes of adornment and emphasis' (Hardman 1986: 113). Indo-European-oriented grammarians consistently overlooked the meaning of evidentials as markers of information source.[9]

Perhaps the first scholar who explicitly formulated the notion of obligatory information source was Boas. In his introduction to *The Handbook of American Indian Languages*, Boas (1911a: 43) states that 'each language has a peculiar tendency to select this or that aspect of the mental image which is conveyed by the expression of the thought'. Using the example *The man is sick*, he comments that 'this example might be further expanded by adding modalities of the verb', explaining how in Kwakiutl 'in case the speaker had not seen the sick person himself, he would have to express whether he knows by hearsay or by evidence that the person is sick, or whether he has dreamed it'. He goes on to say, in his

---

[8] Along similar lines, in his extensive grammar of Cuzco Quechua, Middendorf (1890: 80–1) considered the direct evidential as just an affirmative particle. Similar examples are too numerous to list.

[9] Not all language families have been so unlucky. According to Friedman (2003: 189) and Dankoff (1982: 412), the earliest description of an evidential 'unwitnessed/witnessed opposition' goes back to al-Kāšḡarī's eleventh-century compendium of Turkic grammar *Dīwān luḡat at-Turk*.

sketch of Kwakiutl (1911*b*: 443), that 'to suffixes expressing subjective relations belong those expressing the source of subjective knowledge—as by hearsay, or by a dream'. The four evidential suffixes in Kwakiutl are then listed under the heading 'suffixes denoting the source of information' (§32, p. 496). In his article 'Language' (1938), he mentions information source as an obligatory category in some languages (see §1.1 above). And in his essay 'Language and culture' (1942: 182), Boas goes on to comment on the potential usefulness of Kwakiutl-type evidentials for newspaper reporters.

Since Boas's work, evidentials have made their way into many grammars of North American Indian languages. The exact place of evidentials as a category in its own right took time to be fully defined. Quite a few scholars considered evidentials a kind of mood, mainly because of the verbal slot they go in. In his grammar of Tsimshian, Boas (1911*c*: 348–9) grouped evidentials together with 'modal suffixes' on these structural grounds. Sapir (1922) treated the 'inferential' evidential in Takelma as one of six tense-mode categories. And Swadesh (1939) analysed the quotative and the inferential evidential in Nootka as 'modes of evidence', within a larger chart of inflection of 'modes'.

The importance of marking information source as a separate category gradually became an integral part of various grammars of North American Indian languages. In a series of articles on Wintu, Dorothy Lee (1938, 1944, 1950, and 1959) recognized evidentials as a special category and discussed them under the label of 'suffixes giving the source of information' (1938: 102). See Jacobsen (1986: 4–5) on further mentions of grammaticalized information source.

Up until Jakobson (1957), the term 'evidential' was accorded a somewhat different meaning from the one employed since. Boas used it in the meaning of 'something for which there is evidence', that is, similar to 'inferred on the basis of visible traces'. This usage is obviously closer to the lay person's 'evidential' as something to do with evidence than 'evidential' as a generic term for information source; the usage we owe to Jakobson (1957). The gloss 'evidently: as is shown by evidence' appears as the translation for the suffix -*xEnt* in Kwakiutl (Boas 1911*b*: 496), and Boas (1947: 237; 245) listed this same suffix among 'a small group of suffixes expressing source and certainty of knowledge'. That is, the linguistic 'evidential' started its life as a term for a subtype of grammaticalized information source rather than a generic label (cf. Jacobsen 1986: 4).

The term 'evidential' as a label for a grammatical category broader than simple inference was first introduced by Jakobson in 1957 (reprinted in 1971: 135). The definition he gave is as follows: '$E^n E^{ns}/E^s$ evidential is a tentative label for the verbal category which takes into account three events—a narrated event (E^n), a speech event (E^s), and a narrated speech event (E^{ns}). The speaker reports an event on the basis of someone else's report (quotative, i.e. hearsay evidence), of a dream (revelative evidence), of a guess (presumptive evidence) or of his own previous experience (memory evidence).' He then illustrates evidentiality, using Bulgarian: 'Bulgarian conjugation distinguishes two semantically opposite sets of forms: "direct narration" ($E^{ns} = E^s$) *vs.* "indirect narration" ($E^{ns} \neq E^s$). To our question, what happened to the steamer Evdokija, a Bulgarian first answered: *zaminala* "it is claimed to have sailed", and then added: *zamina* "I bear witness; it sailed". '

Importantly, Jakobson was the first to draw a sharp distinction between mood and evidentiality as independent categories.[10]

The term 'evidential' to refer to grammaticalized information source appears to have become established by the mid-1960s (Jacobsen 1986: 6). Sherzer (1976) includes 'evidential or source of information markers' among areal features relevant for North American Indian languages.

Interest in evidentiality has grown during the past thirty years. The groundbreaking article by Barnes (1984), on Tuyuca, followed by Malone (1988), alerted linguists to the existence of complex multiterm evidentials in South America. Evidentiality became a recognized and widely acknowledged category in Quechua and Aymara studies (e.g. Levinsohn 1975, Jake and Chuquin 1979, Weber 1986, and especially Hardman (ed.) 1981 and Hardman 1986). Evidentials came to be recognized throughout the world—in Philippine languages (Ballard 1974), in Warlpiri (Laughren 1982), in Tibetan (DeLancey 1986), Japanese (Aoki 1986), and many more. Further work on various languages, language families, and language areas will be referred to throughout the rest of the book as required. A breakthrough in the studies of evidentiality was marked by a seminal collection of papers in Chafe and Nichols (1986), which drew together systems from all over the world. A first preliminary survey of evidentials was done by Willett (1988). As we will see throughout this book, this survey, however valuable, contains a number of inaccuracies and simplifications (see note 18 to Chapter 2).

A somewhat different view and different terminology for small evidential systems has been developed independently by European scholars. In contrast

---

[10] Unlike evidentials, which refer to information source, 'mood characterises the relation between the narrated event and its participants with reference to the participants of the speech event: in Vinogradov's formulation, this category "reflects the speaker's view of the character of the connection between the action and the actor or the goal"' (Jakobson 1971; also see Vinogradov 1947: 581). Vinogradov further expands this definition by saying that the category of mood 'expresses the evaluation of reality of the link between the action and its subject from the speaker's viewpoint, or the desire of the speaker to either accomplish or deny this connection. That is, the category of mood is a grammatical category in the verbal system, which defines the modality of the action, i.e. implies the relationship of the action to actuality as established by the speaker' (translation mine). This definition of modality/mood is basically similar to the one provided in the Glossary of terms, and that provided by Matthews (1997).

to North American Indian languages, many languages of Eurasia hardly ever have more than one or two evidential terms. The most frequent type of system is the one where, in Lazard's words (2001), 'evidentially marked discourse is opposed to neutral discourse'. One of the earliest attempts to label this evidentially marked form whose meaning is typically non-firsthand or indirect experience, and sometimes also secondhand information, comes from Décsy (1965: 184). In his analysis of languages from the Permic subgroup of Finno-Ugric, he used the term 'form of indirect experience' (*indirekte Erlebnisform*). The first analysis of this category, its expression and meaning is by Haarmann (1970). While recognizing the fact that 'indirect experience' can be expressed either lexically or grammatically in any language, Haarmann analyses it as an independent grammatical category well represented throughout Eurasia.[11]

Focus on languages which have one, typically non-firsthand, evidential contrasted with evidentially neutral forms gave rise to terminological conventions different from what became standard in North American Indian linguistics. The term used for such small systems in Guentchéva (1996) is *médiatif*, or 'mediative' (also see Lazard 1996, 1999, 2001). (This term is occasionally extended to larger systems. An alternative, proposed by Hagège 1995, is *médiaphorique*.) The corresponding term in the Turkic tradition, suggested by Johanson (1996, 1998, 2000a, b), is 'indirective'. This is, perhaps, a continuation of the tradition—originated by Haarmann (1970)—whereby 'indirect experience' is treated as a separate category, and not a subtype of a more general notion of information source, or evidentiality.

Another terminological tradition has been established for the languages of the Balkans. The confusion in the ways the term 'witnessed' was used to cover the evidentials in these languages led Aronson (1967) to propose a new term. He introduced the label 'confirmative', to 'describe Bulgarian evidentials in which the speaker is markedly vouching for the truth of the statement' (Friedman 2003: 190). In his own work Friedman (1978, 1979, 1981, 1982, 1986, 1994, 2000, and 2003) introduced the term 'nonconfirmative' as its opposite, 'to refer to evidentials that attenuate personal vouching by means of reportedness, inference, sarcasm, or surprise'. The opposition of confirmative and non-confirmative is that of firsthand versus non-firsthand (type A1 in §2.1 below). In the literature on Quechua, evidentials are often called 'validationals' or 'verificationals'. Grammarians of Aymara (e.g. Hardman 1986) call them 'data source markers'.

Guentchéva (1996) is a major collection of papers predominantly investigating small evidential systems, and covers only a few of the larger systems.

---

[11] This is in contrast to Weinreich's approach (1963: 120–1) to evidential categories (such as Hopi quotative and Bulgarian and Turkish non-firsthand) as kinds of mood, or 'pragmatic operators', akin to German subjunctive.

Johanson and Utas (2000) present an informed study of two-term evidentiality systems in Turkic, Iranian, and a few neighbouring languages. A typological overview accompanied by studies of several individual systems is in Aikhenvald (2003a). This typology is the precursor of the present book.

At present, evidentials seem to be 'the flavour of the month'.[12] Linguists of all trends and persuasions talk about evidentials and evidence, for all sorts of languages. Not surprisingly, the same term is applied and overapplied to different things. And yet there is no exhaustive cross-linguistic study of how languages deal with the marking of information source in their grammars. This book aims to fill this gap, based on the languages hitherto described. A further aim is to establish a common conceptual ground for the analysis of evidentials as a grammatical category, its semantics and expression, as well as development, loss, and correlations with other grammatical categories.

[12] During the past two decades, a surge of interest in 'evidentiality' has resulted in a large number of publications and definitions. Quite a few of these are misleading. For instance, Anderson (1986: 274–5) lists the following properties which he considers as 'definitional' for evidentials: '(a) evidentials show the kind of justification for a factual claim which is available to the person making that claim, whether direct evidence plus observation (no inference needed), evidence plus inference, inference (evidence unspecified), reasoned expectation from logic and other facts [...]; (b) evidentials are not themselves the main predication of the clause, but are rather a specification added to a factual claim about something else; (c) evidentials have the indication of evidence as in (a) as their primary meaning, not only as a pragmatic inference; (d) morphologically, evidentials are inflections, clitics or other free syntactic elements (not compounds or derivational forms)'. While points (a)–(c) are basically sound, point (d), which concerns the surface realization of the category, should not be among its definitional properties. For one thing, this criterion would not work for systems in which the distinction between inflectional and derivational categories is not clear-cut. Further criteria include (p. 277): '(i) evidentials are normally used in assertions (realis clauses), not in irrealis clauses, nor in presuppositions; (ii) when the claimed fact is directly observable by both speaker and hearer, evidentials are rarely used (or have a special emphatic or surprisal sense); and (iii) when the speaker (first person) was a knowing participant in some event (voluntary agent; conscious experiencer), the knowledge of that event is normally direct and evidentials are then often omitted'. All these points are highly arguable. Evidentials in some systems may be used in 'irrealis' clauses (depending on how the interactions between mood and modality, and evidentials, work in a particular language: see §8.3 below on the use of evidentials with conditional and irrealis in various languages); and the obligatoriness of evidentials depends on the particular system rather than on randomly chosen parameters such as (ii) and (iii). In Tuyuca (Barnes 1984) the evidentials are never omitted, whether the speaker is the 'knowing participant' or not. Finally, the last criterion 'second person in questions is treated as first person in statements', that is, a conjunct/disjunct (or locutor versus non-locutor) distinction in person-marking, is not at all necessarily linked to evidentiality (see §7.1–2).

De Haan (1997, MS, 1999) also offers criticism of Anderson's approach. However, the criteria which de Haan himself considers definitional hardly score any better (for instance, he states that 'evidentials do not show agreement with the speaker' and that they 'cannot be in the scope of negation').

Wierzbicka's treatment of evidentiality (1994, 1996: 427–58) (based on a reinterpretation of the limited data published in Chafe and Nichols 1986) is both misguided and simplistic. She defines evidentials through semantic 'primitives', such as 'know', whose universality is dubious. Thus, she is defining a grammatical category through lexical means (which are lacking from languages both with and without evidentiality). In contrast to Boas (1938: 133 quoted at the beginning of this section), she also does not make a distinction between evidentiality as a closed grammatical system and a lexical means of expressing meanings somehow related to 'source of knowledge'.

A cross-linguistically based typological analysis of grammatical evidentiality will provide us with insights as to how to investigate this phenomenon in new, previously undescribed languages. Limiting the notion of evidentiality to grammar will help us to avoid its 'extensions which start to stretch the sense beyond coherent definition', to use Matthews's expression (1997: 90).

Examples will be drawn from over 500 languages from all parts of the world. Grammatical evidentiality is not a terribly frequent phenomenon; it is only found in about 25 per cent of the world's languages. Most familiar languages—such as English, or French—lack it. This is why most of my examples come from relatively unknown languages, frequently overlooked by typologists and by linguists in general. My additional aim is to introduce these languages into linguistic circulation.

In this book I have been able to mention only a fraction of the available references on evidentials. Many works which discuss evidentiality or 'evidence' are not mentioned here, either because they are tangential to the general theme of this book or because the claims and the analyses are not fully substantiated or convincing,[13] or because a particular source merely provides additional examples of a point already amply exemplified. I hope to provide a useful overview of types of grammatical evidentials, and their functions and semantics across the world. But note that this volume is not intended to be an encyclopedia of evidentials.

1.4 Challenges

Evidential systems of varied size are scattered all over the world. They are particularly frequent in South American and North American Indian languages, in the languages of the Caucasus, and in the languages of the Tibeto-Burman family (see §9.2.1, and the Map at the end of Chapter 9). However, until recently, there was no comprehensive typological framework which would account for the analysis of varied evidential systems, their semantics, function, the ways in which they interact with other grammatical categories (such as person, negation, clause types), and so on. This has made writing grammars of previously undescribed or poorly documented languages with evidentiality a particularly daunting task.

The relative lack of comprehensive typologically informed grammars is a major challenge for a comprehensive typological analysis of any category. Evidentiality is no exception. European-oriented researchers often face difficulties in determining the exact meanings of this 'exotic' category. Hardman (1986: 113–14) provides a fascinating account of the 'blindness' of numerous

---

[13] As, for instance, is the case with 'evidentiality' in Dutch argued for by de Haan (1997).

researchers to evidentiality, or 'data-source marking', in Aymara, within the period from 1603 up until the late 1960s—evidentials were simply disregarded as 'ornate' optional particles (see further examples in §1.3). And yet, for Aymara speakers, using the right evidential is crucial: those who do not mark their information source are branded as arrogant 'liars' (see §11.1–2).

Sticking to a highly restrictive formalist framework often proves to be particularly detrimental in analysing unusual categories. Migliazza (1972), in his cross-dialectal grammar of Yanomami,—analysed within the framework of the transformational grammar of the time—missed evidentiality altogether. In fact, some Yanomami dialects have as many as four evidentials; for example, Xamatauteri (Ramirez 1994: 169–70; 316–17) with firsthand, non-firsthand, inferred, and reported. Sanuma, the Yanomami dialect described by Borgman (1990: 165–73), has three terms: firsthand, 'verification' (by seeing evidence or by hearing from someone who has firsthand knowledge of the state or event), and inferential. And Yanam (described by Gomez 1990: 97) shows just two evidentials, firsthand and non-firsthand.

The problem of detecting evidentials in a language may be aggravated by an inadequate fieldwork methodology. Basing one's grammar exclusively on asking questions and grammatical elicitation—translating from a lingua franca into the native language—and on sentences taken out of their context, leads to getting only a small part of the grammatical structure right. Speakers of Kamaiurá, a Tupí-Guaraní language with a very complex system of evidentials, often omit the markers of source of information in elicited sentences. Such sentences come out as unnatural, 'something artificial, sterile, deprived of colour' (Seki 2000: 347). Typologists must rely on careful grammatical descriptions—based on analysis of spontaneous texts in the language under study—unconstrained by any formalism which has a restricted vogue, in order to bring together language facts and their typological assessments.

One of the major challenges for a comprehensive study of evidentiality is the lack of good quality descriptions and in-depth analyses. Evidentiality—unlike case, gender, aspect, mood, or tense—is not found in familiar Indo-European languages and cannot be easily accounted for by the grammatical categories which well-known languages are expected to have. Those who follow formulaic guidelines for grammar writing may thus find it hard to accommodate evidentials. Hence the variability of the places in grammars where evidentiality is discussed. Evidentiality is sometimes looked upon as 'modality', or 'cognitive modality'. Or it is considered as a sort of 'mood'. Linguists are often at a loss to decide where exactly evidentiality belongs.

It is the purpose of this book to put evidentiality on the map as a category in its own right. Besides providing a cross-linguistically valid conceptual framework for investigating evidentiality worldwide, I aim to supply fieldworkers and grammar writers with appropriate analytic tools for disentangling varied facets of grammaticalized marking of information source in the world's languages. At the end of this book the reader will find a brief questionnaire for investigating evidentiality and evidentiality strategies. Its objective is to provide a checklist of main points without which evidentiality can scarcely be understood.

1.5 How this book is organized

My aim here is to present a functional-typological, empirically based account of grammatical evidentiality across the world's languages.[14] The categories and their properties are explained inductively—based on facts, not assumptions. As Bloomfield (1933: 20) put it: 'The only useful generalisations about language are inductive generalisations. Features which we think ought to be universal may be absent from the very next language that becomes accessible. . . . The fact that some features are, at any rate, widespread, is worthy of notice and calls for an explanation; when we have adequate data about many languages, we shall have to return to the problem of general grammar and to explain these similarities and divergences, but this study, when it comes, will not be speculative but inductive.'

In Chapter 2, I start with a survey of evidentiality systems attested in the world's languages. Evidential systems vary in their size and in the kinds of information sources expressed. Some languages mark just reported information; others distinguish firsthand and non-firsthand. Visually obtained data may be contrasted with data obtained through hearing or smelling, or through inference of various kinds. Many of these larger systems also have a separate marker for reported or secondhand information. Few have a special marker for 'thirdhand'. At the end of the chapter, I summarize the semantic parameters and the evidential systems so far attested.

No particular language type is associated with marking evidentiality. Just about any kind of morpheme can have an evidential meaning. Evidentials which refer to visually obtained or 'firsthand' information tend to be less formally marked than other evidentials. Circumstances in which evidentials may be omitted also vary from system to system. A language may have several subsystems of evidentiality. Some languages can indicate two information sources at once. An evidential can be negated or questioned. Evidentials can have their

---

[14] The analysis is cast in terms of basic linguistic theory, the fundamental typological theoretical apparatus 'that underlies all work in describing languages and formulating universals about the nature of human language', where 'justification must be given for every piece of analysis, with a full train of argumentation' (Dixon 1997: 132; see also Dixon 1994: xvi).

own 'truth value': using a wrong evidential is one way of telling a lie. These issues are discussed in Chapter 3.

Non-indicative moods and modalities, past tenses and perfects, passives, nominalizations, and complementation strategies can acquire a secondary usage to do with reference to an information source. So can person-marking. Perceptual meanings—visual or non-visual—can be encoded in demonstratives. Evidential extensions of these categories, which I call 'evidentiality strategies', are discussed in Chapter 4. Every language has some way of reporting what some-one else said to the speaker and of quoting another person's speech. Reported speech can be viewed as a universal evidential strategy. How reported speech is marked and how it compares to reported evidentials cross-linguistically are also discussed in this chapter.

Meanings expressed in evidentiality systems vary across the world's languages, and so do the extensions of varied evidentials. For instance, the core meaning of a reported evidential is always verbal report. Such an evidential may also acquire an overtone of 'doubt' ('This is what I have been told, but I don't vouch for it'). The core meaning of a visual evidential is something the speaker has seen (rather than heard, or inferred, or has been told). This evidential can be extended to relate generally known facts, and sometimes even to facts the speaker is sure of. The semantic complexity of evidentials of different sorts and systems is the topic of Chapter 5.

'Mirativity' is a category manifesting 'unexpected information' with over-tones of surprise and admiration. Its independence as a category in its own right rather than a semantic extension of evidentiality is now beyond doubt (since the seminal article by DeLancey 1997). A 'mirative' extension is typical for many evidentials which do not involve any visual or firsthand information. These are analysed in Chapter 6, in the context of the semantics and structure of a given evidential system. The appendix at the end of the chapter contains a few illustrative examples demonstrating the existence of a separate grammat-ical category of 'mirativity' in a number of languages.

When the source of information is stated, who is the observer? In other words, whose information source does the evidential reflect? The question of the identity of the observer is tightly linked to the interaction between eviden-tiality and the value of person. Chapter 7 shows how this works.

Different evidentiality choices may be available in a statement, a question, or a command; evidentiality choices may depend on choices made in a mood or modality, or under negation. The existing tendencies are considered in Chapter 8.

Every evidential has its own history, and a pathway of development. An evid-ential may go back to a verb of speech, or a verb of perception. Or it can develop out of another open or closed class via grammaticalization and reanalysis.

A small evidentiality system may develop out of one of the evidentiality strategies analysed in Chapter 4. Evidentiality is prone to borrowing and linguistic diffusion: evidentiality systems often arise, or can be lost, under the impact of language contact and are found in a variety of linguistic areas. Language obsolescence may result in their loss or drastic restructuring. As a result of language contact, languages—among them familiar European varieties, such as Andean Spanish—may develop evidentials. These issues are discussed in Chapter 9, alongside an overview of the distribution of evidentials across the world.

How to choose the correct evidential when confronted with more than one avenue for information acquisition? Rules for making a choice in these cases relate to 'preferred evidentials'. Evidentials often become conventionalized in different genres and styles of discourse. An unexpected evidential choice produces additional rhetorical effects. The choice of evidentials may partly depend on the lexical class of a verb, and there may be correlations between evidentials and the organization of the lexicon. This is the topic of Chapter 10.

And finally, what are evidentials good for? What makes them so important for human cognition and communication? Speaking a language with evidentials presupposes the requirement of explicitly stating the exact source of information; this may go together with certain cultural attitudes and practices, both traditional and modern. Speakers of languages with evidentials are usually aware of having to always say 'how you know it'. These issues are addressed in Chapter 11. What little we know about evidentials in child language acquisition is summarized in the appendix to this chapter.

Chapter 12 is a précis of the book. It contains a summary and a brief recapitulation of the overall conclusions. Here I also suggest further problems and further routes of investigation of evidentiality across the languages of the world.

A major objective of this book is to encourage scholars to undertake fieldwork-based in-depth investigations of evidentials all over the world. How should one go about it? A short fieldworker's guide provides suggestions to fieldworkers on how to gather materials on evidentiality systems, in terms of semantic, formal, and other parameters which have proved to be cross-linguistically relevant.

The book is accompanied by a glossary of linguistic terms used throughout, within the context of problems linked to evidentiality. This is provided in order to avoid terminological confusion, and to make sure the readers understand what the author means.

2

Evidentials worldwide

Evidentiality systems across the world vary in how complex they are, and in what meanings they encode. I start with some general observations about how evidential systems are organized and what labels will be used, and then discuss the kinds of systems attested, exemplifying their typical representatives. We first consider relatively simple systems with just two evidential options (§2.1). In §§2.2–3, we look at systems with three and four evidentials, and in §2.4 at larger systems. The recurrent semantic parameters in evidentiality systems are summarized in §2.5. Evidentials tend to spread across linguistic areas. A detailed discussion and a map illustrating their geographical distribution are in §9.2.1.

Evidentiality systems vary in terms of the number of information sources encoded and in terms of how these are marked. In a system with two choices, one term can be 'firsthand', and the other 'non-firsthand' (A1 below). Not infrequently, there is just one, overtly marked, evidential contrasted to an evidentiality-neutral 'everything else' form. The most frequent system of this latter kind is reported or hearsay versus 'the rest' (A3), or 'non-firsthand' versus 'the rest' (A2). Strictly speaking, systems of this kind have only one evidential 'term'. They have been included on a par with two-term systems because of the semantic similarities and tendencies towards historical development (see §5.1 and §9.1). Markedness in evidentiality systems is addressed in §3.2, with a typological perspective on systems with and without a 'default' or 'neutral' member.

The simplest evidentiality systems have just two choices. More complex ones involve more than six. The semantic domain covered by each evidential interrelates with that covered by others: in some systems a 'non-visual' evidential may extend to cover things heard and felt by touch, and in others it may be restricted just to what was heard. The labels we use for evidentials may sometimes be misleading if taken literally. For instance, in a small two-term system 'firsthand' may in fact cover information obtained through any physical sense: vision, hearing, smell, taste, and touch. In 2.1, from Jarawara (Arawá: Dixon 2003, 2004), a 'firsthand' evidential marks what the speaker could see, and the 'non-firsthand' refers to what he could not see. This may cover inference.

Jarawara

2.1   Wero   kisa-me-**no**,
       name   get.down-BACK-IMM.P.NONFIRSTH.m
       ka-me-**hiri**-ka
       be.in.motion-BACK-REC.P.FIRSTH.m-DECL.m
       'Wero got down from his hammock (which I didn't see), and went out
       (which I did see)'

The speaker saw Wero go out of the house and inferred he must have got down
from his hammock. But he did not see Wero get down from his hammock. This
explains the use of the non-firsthand evidential on the first verb.

In 2.2, also from Jarawara, the firsthand evidential describes the noise of the
boat that the speaker hears (before he could see the boat itself).

2.2   [moto   ati]   ka-tima-**re**-ka
       motorboat(m)   noise   be.in.motion-UPSTREAM-IMM.P.FIRSTH.m-DECL.m
       'The noise of the motorboat was coming upstream (the noise could be
       heard)'[1]

Similarly, in Yukaghir the 'firsthand' evidential can refer to any appropriate
sense, be it seeing, hearing or smelling. Alternatively, a visual term may cover
a combination of visual information and something personally witnessed, but
can never refer to strictly auditory data. This is the case in Kalasha and Khowar,
both Dardic (Bashir 1988: 48–54).

The non-firsthand in a two-term system may have a fairly wide range of
meanings: it may imply that the speaker heard about the action from some
secondary source, or made inferences about it, or participated in it directly
but was not in control. It is unlikely to refer to secondhand information if there
is a separate 'reported' evidential forming a special subsystem, as is the case in
Mỹky (isolate from Brazil: Monserrat and Dixon 2003).

In a multiterm system 'visual' most often refers to information obtained
through seeing, and not through other senses. Or there can be a catch-all
'direct' evidential, referring to any appropriate sense, as in Shipibo-Konibo
(Valenzuela 2003). These systems have no 'catch-all' non-firsthand, or non-
sensory, term. Non-firsthand information is marked depending on whether it
was reported (acquired through other people by 'hearsay'), or inferred on the
basis of physical evidence or reasoning and common sense. In Chapter 5, we
provide a detailed discussion of meanings and meaning extensions of each
evidential depending on the system it is in. Many linguistic traditions have
attempted to provide their own terminological flavours to essentially the same

---

[1] These two evidentials are called 'eyewitness' and 'non-eyewitness' by Dixon (2003, 2004).

concepts. In order to streamline the existing diversity, I have chosen the following cover-terms for each set of choices.

- 'Firsthand' and 'non-firsthand' has been reserved for systems with two choices in opposition to each other. (Alternatives found in the literature include 'experienced' and 'non-experienced', 'eyewitness' and 'non-eyewitness', and 'confirmative' and 'non-confirmative'.)
- If a language has a 'non-firsthand' form without its opposite value, we call it 'non-firsthand'. (Alternative terms in the literature include 'non-eyewitness', 'inferential', 'non-confirmative', 'indirective', and 'mediative'.)[2] (See §1.3.)
- The evidential whose meaning is 'verbal report' is termed 'reported'; alternative terms are hearsay and quotative. Here, 'quotative' is reserved for a reported evidential which involves exact indication of who provided the information.

If in doubt, the reader can check the terminological conventions and their equivalents in the literature in the Glossary. Throughout this book, I will mention terms used by individual authors in brackets (if different from the consensus).

A further note on presentation is in order. Individual systems have been assigned letter-nicknames, for ease of reference. Two-term systems are under A; three-term systems are under B; four-term systems under C, and five-term systems under D. Since there are rather few examples of well-analysed systems with more than five choices, these have not been assigned any letters. Problematic cases where it is hard to decide, on the basis of the available grammars, how many evidential choices there are, and whether these are at all obligatory, are mentioned at the end of each section.

2.1 Evidentiality systems with two choices

Systems with two choices cover:

A1. Firsthand and Non-firsthand;
A2. Non-firsthand versus 'everything else';
A3. Reported (or 'hearsay') versus 'everything else';
A4. Sensory evidence and Reported (or 'hearsay');
A5. Auditory (acquired through hearing) versus 'everything else'.

---

[2] For 'mediative', see Lazard (1957, in his analysis of Tajik dialects, and also 1999). Johanson (2000a, 2003) uses 'indirective', for basically the same concept.

An overview of the systems is under §2.1.1. Typical difficulties in analysing small evidential systems and distinguishing between them are discussed in §2.1.2.

2.1.1 *Evidentiality systems with two choices: an overview*

We will now present a brief overview of evidential systems with just two choices. Of these, A1–A3 are widespread worldwide, while A4 and A5 occur rarely. The latter are somewhat problematic, since neither of them has been attested in a fully spoken living language.

A1. Firsthand and Non-firsthand. The firsthand term typically refers to information acquired through vision (or hearing, or other senses), and the non-firsthand covers everything else. Examples 2.1–2, from Jarawara, illustrate an A1 system. The meaning of non-firsthand may be more diversified. Cherokee (Iroquoian: Pulte 1985) distinguishes 'firsthand' and 'non-firsthand' past.[3] To use the firsthand suffix, the speaker must have perceived the action or state described by the verb with one of the senses. They may have seen it, as in 2.3, or heard it, as in 2.4.

Cherokee

2.3 wesa   u-tlis-ʌʔi
     cat   it-run-FIRSTH.PAST
     'A cat ran' (I saw it running)

2.4 un-atiyohl-ʌʔi
     they-argue-FIRSTH.PAST
     'They argued' (I heard them arguing)

They may have felt it, as in 2.5; or smelled it, as in 2.6. In these cases also, the firsthand suffix is appropriate.

2.5 uhyʌdla   u-nolʌn-ʌʔi
     cold   it-blow-FIRSTH.PAST
     'A cold wind blew' (I felt the wind)

2.6 uyo   ges-ʌʔi
     spoiled be-FIRSTH.PAST
     'It was spoiled' (I smelled it)

The non-firsthand past suffix covers information acquired in some other way. It occurs if the statement is based on someone else's report, as in 2.7.

---

[3] This distinction is described as 'experienced' and 'nonexperienced' by Pulte (1985).

2.7   u-wonis-**eʔi**
       he-speak-NON.FIRSTH.PAST
       'He spoke' (someone told me)

This same suffix is used for inferences of any sort. In 2.8 all the speaker saw was the result rather than the rain itself.

2.8   u-gahnan-**eʔi**
       it-rain-NON.FIRSTH.PAST
       'It rained' (I woke up, looked out and saw puddles of water)

If the statement is based on logical assumption, the same suffix is appropriate:

2.9   guso-ʔi   u-wonis-**eʔi**
       Muskogee-at   s/he-speak-NON.FIRSTH.PAST
       'She spoke at Muskogee' (I knew she planned to speak on Sunday. It is now Monday, and I assume that she spoke as planned.)

Yukaghir employs the firsthand to mark information acquired through any appropriate sense, be it seeing or hearing (Maslova 2003: 222–3), just like Jarawara in 2.1–2. During a hunting trip the speaker HEARS the sound of something bursting (the sound of a shot)—hence the firsthand form in the second clause. He INFERS that his fellow hunter (whom he cannot see) fired a bullet— hence the non-firsthand in the first clause.

Yukaghir
2.10   [. . .] aji:-**ľel**-u-m,   šar   **qoha-s'** [. . .]
                shoot-NON.FIRSTH-O-TR:3   something   burst +FIRSTH-INTR:3sg
                ' . . . (then) he shot (I infer), something burst (I heard). . .'

The non-firsthand form describes things inferred from visible traces, as in 2.11.

2.11   taŋ   me:me: naha: motlorqo-j-ben=ŋo:-**ľel**
       that   bear   very   thin-ATTR-NOMN=COP-NON.FIRSTH(INTR:3sg)
       'That bear was very thin [as can be seen from his traces]'

The same form marks information obtained through hearsay, as in 2.12.

2.12   mieste-ge   alaŋcin   aŋil'-ge   nodo   nojdi:-t
       place-LOC   Alanchin   mouth-LOC   bird   watch-SS:IMPF
       modo-**ľel**-ŋi
       sit-NON.FIRSTH-3pl:INTR
       '[As people who once roamed together with him in their youth told,] they were sitting at a place called Alanchin mouth, watching for birds'

These systems are found in a variety of North and South American Indian languages, and in a number of languages in Eurasia, including Northeast Caucasian and Finno-Ugric. The distinction often, but not always, is made just in the past tense (see §8.4, on the correlations between evidentiality and tense). This is the case in Tsez (Bokarev 1967: 413; Bernard Comrie p.c.). In Godoberi (Northeast Caucasian: Dobrushina and Tatevosov 1996: 94–7) the firsthand and non-firsthand forms are distinguished in the perfect (both present and past). Hewitt (1979) mentions reconstruction of firsthand ('witnessed', marked by -rā) and non-firsthand ('nonwitnessed', marked by -nă) in proto-Nax.

In a number of languages from the Finno-Ugric family one of the past tenses (usually the one with perfect meaning, if the perfect/imperfect distinction is available) has a non-firsthand meaning, and the other one refers to firsthand information, as in Mari (Permic, Finno-Ugric: Perrot 1996: 160, Alhoniemi 1993). Both Komi and Udmurt have two past tenses—one usually described as firsthand ('witnessed') past, the other as non-firsthand ('unwitnessed') past (this form is based on a past participle: Leinonen 2000: 421); see examples 10.32–3.[4]

In Kalasha (Dardic: Bashir 1988: 48–54) past tense forms have an obligatory distinction between firsthand (called 'actual', that is, 'personally witnessed' and/or 'having long standing in one's conceptual repertoire': p. 58) and non-firsthand (called 'inferential', covering assumed, inferred, new information, and mirative; see §5.1). In Khowar (Dardic: Bashir 1988: 54–7) the opposition of firsthand and non-firsthand ('actual vs. inferential') is available in all tenses. Tibetan (DeLancey 1986: 210–11) distinguishes between firsthand and non-firsthand information within the perfective system (also see §8.4).

In South America, firsthand and non-firsthand (called visual and non-visual) are distinguished in Yanam, a dialect of Yanomami (Gomez 1990: 97), and in Secoya (West Tucanoan: Terry Malone p.c.). Similar distinction appears to occur in Mangap-Mbula, one of the few Oceanic languages with evidentiality (Bugenhagen 1995: 132–3).[5]

The semantic breadth of each evidential differs, depending on the language. In Cherokee and Yukaghir, a non-firsthand refers to reported information.

---

[4] For Mari, Kovedjaeva (1966) describes the meaning of the 'evidential' past (past I) as referring to a recent action 'vividly imagined by the speaker who is often a participant of it'. Alhoniemi (1993: 114–15) gives 'minimal pairs' exemplifying the 'firsthand' meaning of Preterite 1, and the 'non-firsthand' meaning (which covers inference) of Preterite 2. In Komi and Udmurt the two are termed 'obvious' and 'unobvious' past tenses. Other references for Komi and Udmurt include Tepljashina and Lytkin 1976: 179–81; Tepljashina 1967: 271; Lytkin 1966a, b).

[5] The exact semantic content of 'firsthand' and 'non-firsthand' is often hard to ascertain from the description available. For instance, Gomez (1990: 93, 97) describes the two evidential particles in Yanam as simply 'witnessed' and 'nonwitnessed'. This vague gloss is simply insufficient to determine whether or not the 'non-firsthand' has the meaning of reported or of inferred, or of both.

Not so in Jarawara: this language has a dedicated reported marker which forms a subsystem independent of the firsthand/non-firsthand opposition (see §3.3). Similarly, a past tense verb in Archi (Northeast Caucasian: Kibrik 1977: 87–9, 228–31) can be marked for 'non-firsthand', whose meaning is 'speaker and/or hearer were not eyewitness to the action X before the moment of speech'. The unmarked verb implies that the speaker and/or the hearer witnessed the action. Archi has a separate reported marker (Kibrik 1977: 231–8) as a distinct grammatical subsystem. Not surprisingly, the non-firsthand term does not have the reported as one of its meanings. Further aspects of the semantic complexity of two-term evidentiality systems is discussed in §5.1.

A2. NON-FIRSTHAND VERSUS 'EVERYTHING ELSE'. The non-firsthand evidential covers a large domain of information acquired through senses other than seeing, by hearsay and by inference of all sorts. Just like A1 systems, the non-firsthand evidential may be distinguished only in past tense. This is the case in many Caucasian languages. Hunzib (Northeast Caucasian: van den Berg 1995) is reported to have a non-firsthand 'evidential' perfect which denotes 'an uncompleted, repeated or habitual (-č(o)), or completed event (-(V)n) that took place in the past and was not witnessed by the speaker'.

Evidentiality does not have to interact with tense. Abkhaz (Hewitt 1979; Chirikba 2003) has a tense-neutral non-firsthand ('inferential') evidential; it can relate to past, present, or future. The markers are -*zaap'* (occurs with present, aorist, perfect, and one of the futures) and -*zaarən* (with imperfect, past indefinite, pluperfect, and one of the future conditionals). The non-firsthand can describe inference from visible results, as in 2.13 (Chirikba 2003: 246–7): that the woman was crying is inferred from the fact that her eyes are red.

Abkhaz

2.13 a-lašă+ra-x',   a-mca-x'   d-an-aa-j-ø,
      ART-light-DIR   ART-fire-DIR (s)he-when-hither-come-AOR:NFIN
      lə-la-kᵒa   ø-q'apš̃'-ʒa   jə-q'a-n   d'ᵒɔwa-**zaarən**
      her-eye-PL   it-red-ADV   it-be-PAST   (s)he+cry-NONFIRSTH2
      'When she came up to the light, to the fire, her eyes were very red;
      apparently, she had been crying' (speaker's inference)

The same form can refer to something learnt through verbal report:

2.14 l-xᵒɔč̃'ɔ   d-anə-l-ba-ø   a-c'ᵒɔwa-ra
      her-child   him/her-when-(s)he-see-AOR:NFIN   ART-cry-DN
      d-a-la+ga-**zaap'**
      (s)he-it-begin-NONFIRSTH1
      'When she saw her child, she reportedly started crying'

How do speakers distinguish between the two meanings of the same non-firsthand form—'inferred' and 'reported'? The exact meaning is often understood from the context, as in 2.13–14. Or the speaker may choose to emphasize the precise source. In 2.15 the reported meaning of the non-firsthand is reinforced by stating exactly who gave the information to the speaker: it was 'recounted by old people':

2.15   ø-až°ə+t'ᵒ+w-aa   jə-z+l-a-r-hᵒ-wa   a-la,
        ART-old+human-PL   it-how-about-they-tell-PRES:DYN:NFIN   it-by
        a-p'ap'   jə-w+aa-hᵒ-cᵒa   a-hᵒa   øə-r-q'aa-nə,   a-la
        ART-priest   his-helper-PL   ART-pig   it-CAUS-shriek-PABS   ART-dog
        ø-r-zə-j-s̃'-**zaap'**
        it-them-for-he-kill-NONFIRSTH1
        'As it was recounted by old people, having made the pig cry, the priest reportedly killed (and served) the dog for his helpers'

Note that the non-firsthand evidentials in Abkhaz are restricted to declarative main clauses; this is why there is no evidentiality marked in subordinate clauses in any of 2.13–15 (see §8.1).

The non-firsthand in Turkish and many other Turkic languages (called 'indirective' by Johanson 2003) is semantically even broader than in Abkhaz. The information source could be a report, as in 2.16; inference, as in 2.17; or simply non-visual perception, as in 2.18 (Johanson 2003: 274–5).[6] Inference can be based on visual perception (Johanson 2003: 282).

Turkish

2.16   bakan   hasta-**ymış**
        minister   sick-NONFIRSTH.COP
        'The minister is reportedly sick' (said by somebody told about the sickness)

2.17   uyu-**muş**-um
        sleep-NONFIRSTH.PAST-1sg
        'I have obviously slept' (said by somebody who has just woken up)

2.18   iyi   çal-ıyor-**muş**
        good   play-INTRATERM.ASP-NONFIRSTH.COP
        'She is, as I hear, playing well' (said by somebody listening to her play)

A similar system has been described for Xakas, a Turkic language spoken in the area of the Sayan mountains (Anderson 1998: 35–6). Further systems of

---

⁶ For a discussion of further functions, developments, and semantic complexities within such systems, see Johanson (2003), Csató (2000), and other papers in Johanson and Utas (2000), papers in Guentchéva (1996), and §5.1.

such kind are found in Megrelian (South Caucasian: Hewitt 1979: 88), Svan (Sumbatova 1999), Mansi (Ugric, Finno-Ugric: Rombandeeva 1966: 353; Rombandeeva 1973: 137–8, 141–2; Majtinskaja 1979: 40; Skribnik 1998), Khanty (Nikolaeva 1999, and 5.4–6), and Nenets (Samoyedic: Uralic).[7] Meithei (Tibeto-Burman: Chelliah 1997: 221–4) has a marker -*ləm* which marks indirect evidence gained through a non-firsthand source, usually inference based on past or present experience.

The non-firsthand in Hare (Athabaskan: DeLancey 1990*a*) refers to information obtained through inference and hearsay. DeLancey reports similar distinctions in Chipewyan and Kato, also Athabaskan (we need further information on this as a grammatical category; see below, on a completely different system in Hupa and in Western Apache, other Athabaskan languages). A non-firsthand marker—used when 'the speaker perceives the evidence and infers the event or action that produced the evidence'—(Nichols 1986: 247) in Chinese Pidgin Russian appears to be the only obligatory, or inflectional, category of the verb.

A3. REPORTED VERSUS 'EVERYTHING ELSE'. Systems of this sort with one, reported, evidential, which covers information acquired through someone else's narration, are widespread all over the world. (Alternative terms for 'reported' are 'secondhand', 'quotative', and 'hearsay'. Of these, 'quotative' is the most unfortunate. As we will see in §2.2, it may refer to something quite distinct from an ordinary reported evidential.) According to Silver and Miller (1997: 38), in North American Indian languages, 'if there is a single obligatory evidential in a language, it is almost always the quotative, which discriminates hearsay from eye-witness reports'. The reported term is marked, and the non-reported ('everything else') term is not marked. There are no markings of the opposite sort. The reported evidential tends to be semantically rather uniform across languages (see §5.4).

Lezgian (Lezgic, Northeast Caucasian) has a reported marker -*lda* added to a finite indicative verb form. This suffix comes from recent grammaticalization (and subsequent phonological contraction) of *luhuda*, 'one says' (Haspelmath 1993: 148). In 2.19 the information is known through hearsay.

Lezgian
2.19   Baku.d-a   irid   itim   gülle.di-z   aǧud-na-**lda**
       Baku-INESS   seven   man   bullet-DAT   take.out-AOR-REP
       'They say that in Baku seven men were shot'

---

[7] In Nenets the non-firsthand (a so-called 'auditive' mood) has a paradigm of its own. It is not compatible with any moods; and is said to indicate 'that the speaker knows about the action or event in question only from hearsay' (Décsy 1966: 48). This kind of system appears to be found in a number of other Samoyedic languages (Tereschenko 1979; Kuznetsova et al. 1980).

In contrast, 2.20 specifies the authorship of the report: it is the smart people who say that knowing too much is harmful.

2.20   Gzaf   čir   x̂u-n,   aq'ullu   insan-r.i
       much   know   ANTIC-MSD   smart   person-PL(ERG)
       luhu-zwa-j-wal,   zarar   ja-**lda**
       say-IMPF-PART-MAN   harm   COP-REP
       'As smart people say, knowing too much is harmful'

In Enga (Engan family, Papuan area), reported utterances are marked with the suffix -*na* added to the last syllable of the predicate (Lang 1973: xli). Another example of a similar system is Tauya (Madang-Adelbert Range, Papuan area: MacDonald 1990*b*: 301). Potawatomi (Algonquian: Hockett 1948: 139) has a pre-verb *ʔe* used in story-telling. Or the reported evidential can be a particle, as in Cupeño (Uto-Aztecan: Hill 2005: 62–6; 85) and in Kham (Tibeto-Burman: Watters 2002: 296–300):

Kham

2.21   ba-zya   **di**
       go-CONT   REP
       'He is going (it is said)'

Simple A3 systems are found in numerous Tibeto-Burman languages, and in many languages of South America, e.g. Arabela, from the Zaparoan family in northeast Peru (Wise 1999: 329), Dâw (Makú: Martins and Martins 1999), South Arawak languages such as Terêna, Ignaciano, Waurá, Pareci, and Piro, North Arawak languages such as Resígaro (on the border between Peru and Colombia), Piapoco (in Colombia), Baniwa of Içana (on the border between Brazil, Colombia, and Venezuela), and Achagua (on the border between Colombia and Venezuela), as well as in Suruí, Karitiana and Gavião, from the Tupí family (Rodrigues 1999: 119); in the Paraguayan Guaraní (Guasch 1956: 264; Krivoshein de Canese 1983: 102); in Guahibo languages (Aikhenvald and Dixon 1999: 376 and references therein); and in Cashibo (Pano: Shell 1978: 29–31). A few Western Austronesian languages also have reported evidentials (e.g. Philippine languages: Ballard 1974; Josephine Daguman p.c.). In all these languages, evidentiality is part of the grammar of a language.

The primarily hearsay, or reported, particle *ré* or *é* in Sissala, a Gur (Voltaic) language spoken in Burkina Faso, is among the few instances of evidentiality in Africa (Blass 1989). Besides its straightforward use to mark reported information, this particle occurs in a wide variety of contexts, including passing on information attributed to general opinion; echoing traditional wisdom (for instance, in proverbs); and also to mark inference. In the latter case, it is accompanied by the expression 'it seems' (Blass 1989: 316) (see §5.4.3).

The reported evidential is marked with a special verbal form in a number of North American Indian languages. Menomini (Algonquian: Bloomfield 1962: 51–2, 161) has a quotative mode marked by the suffix *-en*. A special reported form not compatible with declarative or other mood inflection is found in Estonian, Livonian, and Latvian. In Standard Estonian, the present reported relates historically to the partitive form of the present participle, *-vat* (see Campbell 1991; and discussion in §9.1). The past reported coincides with the past participle.[8] Consider 2.22–3.

Estonian

2.22   Ta   on   aus   mees
    he   is   honest   man
    'He is an honest man'

2.23   Ta   ole**vat**   aus   mees
    he   be.REP.PRES   honest   man
    'He is said to be an honest man'

A reported particle (commonly, a clitic) features in a few Australian languages. In Mparntwe Arrernte, it occurs in traditional Dreamtime narratives which are said to 'have been handed down to the present generation from their ancestors' (Wilkins 1989: 392) (such genre-defining use is typical of reported evidentials; see §10.2.1):

Mparntwe Arrernte

2.24   Pmere   arrule-rle   **kwele**   ne-ke;   artwe   nyente . . .
    camp   long-ago   REP   be-PC;   man   one
    'A long time ago, so they (the ancestors) say, there lived a man . . .'

Reported evidentials vary in the degree of their semantic complexity. The reported evidential in Estonian and in Latvian has overtones of unreliable information (Stolz 1991: 47–9; Haarmann 1970: 60; Metslang and Pajusalu 2002). Example 2.23 may also imply that the speaker does not vouch for the man's honesty. The Mparntwe Arrernte particle *kwele* also has epistemic extensions to do with speaker's belief in how reliable the information is, and so do reported particles *kunyu* in Yankunytjatjara (Goddard 1983: 289) and *nganta* in Warlpiri (Laughren 1982: 137–41); see §5.3. In contrast, the reported evidential in Kham and in Lezgian does not have any additional overtones of uncertainty.

Rules of usage of the reported evidential vary, depending on the language. In Shoshone (Uto-Aztecan: Silver and Miller 1997: 38), in Omaha. and in Ponca

---

[8] Additional forms are perfective past (*täisminevik*) formed with the suffix *-vat* on the copula 'be' and the past participle of the main verb; and the pluperfect formed with a past participle of the copula 'be' and the past participle of the main verb.

(Siouan: Koontz 2000), every sentence in a story has to be marked with a reported evidential. In Kham, every final verb in a narrative is marked with the reported. In contrast, the reported marker in Baniwa of Içana and in Piapoco, two Arawak languages from South America, typically occurs just once, on the first sentence in a paragraph.

A4. SENSORY EVIDENCE AND REPORTED. Ngiyambaa (Donaldson 1980: 275–8) and Diyari (Austin 1981: 173–4, 184–5), both Australian, have just two evidentiality values: sensory evidence and reported. In Ngiyambaa, the enclitic *-gara* indicates that the speaker has some sensory evidence for the statement. Exactly what evidence the speaker has is likely to be clear from the context. In 2.25, *-gara* refers to information obtained visually: one can see that someone is sick.

Ngiyambaa

2.25   ŋindu-**gara**   girambiyi
        you+NOM-SENS.EV   sick+PAST
        'You were sick' (one could see this)

In 2.26, *-gara* is used for auditory information.

2.26   gabuga:-**gara**=lu   ŋamumiyi
        egg+ABS-SENS.EV=3ERG   lay+PAST
        'It's laid an egg' (by the sound of it)

In 2.27, *-gara* refers to information acquired by taste; and in 2.28 by smell.

2.27   dhagun-gir-**gara**   ŋina   dhiŋga: ga-ṭa
        earth-NASTY.WITH-SENS.EV this+ABS   meat+ABS   be-PRES
        'This meat tastes nasty with earth' (I have tasted it)

2.28   wara:y-**gara**=dhu=na   bungiyamiyi
        bad+ABS-SENS.EV=1NOM=3ABS   change.with.fire+PAST
        dhiŋga:=dhi:
        meat+ABS=1OBL
        'I have burnt my meat, so it's no good (to judge by the smell of it)'

The same evidential morpheme can mark information obtained through physical touch. The speaker has her hand in the rabbit's burrow, and can feel the rabbit there, and says 2.29. A lexical reinforcement is added: the speaker explicitly says that she can feel the rabbit.

2.29   yura:bad-**gara**   ŋidji   guṭuga-nha
        rabbit+ABS-SENS.EV   here+CIRC   be.inside-PRES
        ŋama-ṭa-baṭa=dhu=na
        feel-PRES-CATEG.ASSERT=1NOM=3ABS
        'The rabbit is in here (I can touch it), I feel it for sure'

The reported enclitic describes information obtained by hearsay, as in 2.30 (see Donaldson 1980: 276, on its allomorphs). It occurs together with irrealis, demonstrating how evidentiality is independent of the realis–irrealis opposition (see §8.3):

Ngiyambaa

2.30   bura:y-**dja**=lu   ga:-y-aga
       child+ABS-REP=3ABS   bring-CONJ.M-IRR
       'It's said that she's going to bring the children'

This reported evidential has epistemic extensions: just as in Estonian, it may be used to refer to information one does not vouch for; see examples in §5.4.3.

Diyari (Austin 1981, 1978) also distinguishes a sensory evidential (marked with suffix -*ku*) and a reported evidential (marked with particle *pinti*). The sensory evidential indicates that 'a new action, event or state or a new participant is being added to the discourse and that the speaker identifies the referent of the word suffixed by -*ku* on the basis of sensory evidence' (Austin 1978: 471). In 2.31, the suffix -*ku* indicates that the information was acquired by sight; in 2.32 it was acquired by hearing, and in 2.33 by a combination of senses (Austin 1981: 184–5).

Diyari

2.31   ṇawu   wakaṛa-yi-**ku**
       3sgnfS   come-PRES-SENS.EV
       'He is coming (I saw him)'

2.32   wadukaṭi-**ku**,   ṇawu   kanpu-ṇa-ṇa   ṇama-yi
       emu+ABS-SENS.EV   3sgnfS   boom-PROD-PART   sit-PRES
       '[If an emu comes along booming someone gets up (and says)], there is an emu making a sound'

2.33   ŋapa   ṭalaṛa   wakaṛa-ḷa   ŋana-yi-**ku**
       water   rain+ABS   come-FUT   AUX-PRES-SENS.EV
       'It looks/feels/smells like rain will come'

The reported particle *pinti* marks secondhand information, and is also used as a token of narrative genres. Similarly to Ngiyambaa it may have overtones of 'I was told, but I don't vouch for it' (Austin 1981: 175–6).

2.34   **pinti**   ṇawu   wakaṛa-yi
       REP   3sgnfS   come-PRES
       'They say he is coming'

The two markers in Ngiyambaa are in a paradigmatic relationship, while in Diyari they belong to completely different sets of grammatical morphemes. From the available literature, it is hard to tell whether either language has an obligatory evidential system and what the meaning of verbal forms unmarked for evidentiality would be.

A similar system, with just two choices—visual sensory and reported—had survived until the time Pitkin did his fieldwork on the Wintu language in the 1950s. The full system of evidentials recorded by Lee in 1930 (Pitkin 1984: 147 and Lee 1938, 1944) consisted of five terms: visual, non-visual sensory, inferential ('information inferred from logic applied to circumstantial sensory evidence': Pitkin 1984: 133–4), experiential ('information deduced from experience' which 'involves the exercise of judgement': Pitkin 1984: 134), and reported (see 2.96 in §2.4). We return to the fate of evidentials in language obsolescence, and how the restructuring of the Wintu system fares in terms of 'gain' and 'loss' in language obsolescence, in §9.3.

Of the three languages with A4 systems, none comes from a language unaffected by language obsolescence. The two Australian languages were remembered by just a few old people, while in Wintu the system arose as a result of restructuring and reduction of an earlier and larger one. We can only conclude that the typological validity of type A4 remains doubtful.

A reduced system of evidentials similar to the one discussed here is found in Latundê/Lakondê, a moribund Northern Nambiquara language (Telles 2002: 20–4). Unlike other Nambiquara languages which have multiple evidentials (see §2.4 below), Latundê/Lakondê has just two: auditory and reported (Telles 2002: 289–90), as in:

Latundê/Lakondê
2.35   ã-'pat-ho'te-'ten-'seʔ-ø-'tãn-hi
        AG-leave-for.someone-DES-AUD-3S-IMPF-NEUT
        'She is going to leave it (for me)' (I heard this)

2.36   wet-'nãw   ta'wẹn-'naw   loh   sũn-ø-ø-setaw-'tãn
        child-PL   jungle-LOC   jaguar   hit-3O-3S-REP-IMPF
        'The children in the jungle, the jaguar got them' (they say)

As is typical for a situation of advanced language obsolescence, evidentials appear to be used sporadically. They are often replaced with periphrastic expressions, e.g. 'he left, I saw (him)', or 'he left, I heard'. (See §11.2 on the lexical reinforcement of evidentials.) In 2.37, a quotative construction with the verb 'say' is used instead of the reported evidential (Telles 2002: 290).

2.37   hejn-ka-ø-'tãn   hajn-ø-'tãn
        wash-BEN-3S-IMPF   say-3S-IMPF
        'He washed (the clothes), he said'

Lakondê is spoken just by one person; only two of nineteen speakers of Latundê are monolingual. Most other speakers are bilingual in Portuguese, a language with no grammatical evidentiality. The reduced evidential system in Lakondê/Latundê may well be a consequence of language attrition.

A5. AUDITORY VERSUS 'EVERYTHING ELSE'. Such a system has been so far found only in Euchee (or Yuchi, an isolate spoken in Oklahoma by about a dozen elders: Linn 2000; Mithun 1999: 571). A typical use of auditory evidential is shown in 2.38. A sentence like 2.38 can be rephrased with a lexical verb 'hear' (see 11.4). The possibility of such rephrasing confirms the primarily auditory meaning of this evidential. (This is somewhat similar to lexical reinforcement of evidentiality, to be addressed in §11.2.)

Euchee
2.38 'ahe   'i-gō-**ke**
     here   3sg(EUCHEE).ACTOR-come-AUD.EV
     'They are coming (I hear them)'

A sentence or a clause may be left unmarked for evidentiality, and then the source of information remains simply unspecified, as in 2.39. Here, the (female) speaker may know that the man is in the woods because she saw him walking towards the woods; or because he is always out in the woods at this time, or because he said he was going to the woods, or because someone else told her. This is similar to the 'everything else' term in A2 and A3 systems.

2.39 'yapho-he   s'e-nō
     woods-LOC   3sg(EUCHEEMALE).ACTOR-be.located
     'He's out there in the woods'

The auditory evidential in Euchee does not have any epistemic overtones: it never refers to the probability of the event, or truth of the assertion (Linn 2000: 318).

Once a language is no longer actively spoken, it becomes obsolescent. This process can affect any grammatical category, and evidentials are no exception (see §9.3). Euchee is a dying language. So, could it be the case that such an unusual system is simply the result of the drastic reduction so frequently observed in the situations of language obsolescence? We do not find any mention of evidentials in previous grammars of Euchee. In fact, Wagner (1934: 325, 370), in his grammar, interpreted -*ke* as just a locative marker. Linn (2000: 318) analysed this same morpheme as polysemous, with a locative meaning 'there, far away' and as an auditory evidential referring to 'something so far away that it can only be heard and not seen'. Could an auditory evidential meaning have developed in Euchee during the last few decades while the language was still actively used? We will never know the answer.

2.1.2 *Evidentiality systems with two choices: analytic difficulties*

Analytic difficulties which typically arise with respect to small systems concern (*a*) distinguishing between primarily evidential forms and evidential extensions of other, non-evidential, categories; (*b*) distinguishing between A1 and A2 systems; and (*c*) distinguishing among A1, A2, and A3 systems. These recurrent problems are now discussed one by one.

(*a*) Distinguishing between primarily evidential forms in A2 systems and evidential extensions of non-evidential categories.
The status of forms with non-firsthand evidential meanings can be analytically ambiguous: is a form with an evidential meaning indeed evidential-only, or maybe it just has an evidential extension, and its main meaning is something else? In other words, does a language have an evidentiality strategy of a kind described in Chapter 4, or a fully fledged evidentiality? To qualify for the latter, the form should have information source as its main meaning rather than as just one of its usages. Compare Georgian and Abkhaz. In Georgian 'non-firsthand' is just one of the meanings of the perfect forms (called 'screeves' by Hewitt 1995; also see Tschenkéli 1958: 482–96 and §4.1). In contrast, Abkhaz has a dedicated marker -*zaap'* which marks non-firsthand evidentiality. See further discussion in §§4.1–2, and a summary by Chirikba (2003: 266–7).

Numerous Eurasian languages are problematic in this respect: many of them have a form often described as 'evidential perfect' with the full range of non-firsthand meanings (as shown in 2.16–18, for Turkish). Synchronically speaking, some of these forms can either be analysed as an evidential proper, or be considered an evidential strategy (§4.2). Such problematic, borderline cases include Vlach Romani (Matras 1995), some Northeast Caucasian languages, such as Avar (Friedman 1979), and a number of Iranian languages, e.g. Persian (Lazard 1985, 1999; Hadarcev 2001) and Ishkashim (Pamir: Nazarova 1998).

The answer to the crucial question of whether a language has a grammatical category of evidentiality or simply evidential meanings as extensions of another category often depends on a grammarian's analytic stance. Most grammars of Iranian languages consider a non-firsthand meaning as one of the connotations of perfect. In his grammar of Zazaki (Iranian), Paul (1998: 91–2) demonstrates that perfect forms do not necessarily have an interpretation associated with information source. This provides justification for treating them as 'evidentiality strategies' rather than evidentials proper. Windfuhr (1982) argues in favour of non-firsthand ('inferential') forms as a separate category in Persian. Lazard (1985) shows that the term 'distant past' (passé distancié) adequately describes the use of these forms in Persian, thus arguing in favour of analysing the perfect forms in Persian as primarily not associated with information source. He points out (pp. 41–2) that such an analysis is not necessarily valid for all Iranian languages—in Tajik as analysed by Lazard (1957: 148) the non-firsthand (called 'inferential') ought to be considered a separate category rather than a special usage of perfect or past.

In actual fact, the semantic extensions of evidential strategies are often strikingly similar to the extensions of the non-firsthand term in A2 systems (see §4.2 and §5.1). This similarity was captured by Paul (1998: 91–2) in his analogy between the Turkish non-firsthand forms in *-mış* and the non-firsthand uses of perfect in Zazaki, to refer to verbal report and inference. Historically many A2 systems originate in the reanalysis of evidentiality strategies (see §9.1); and this adds an additional dimension of complexity to an analysis which aims at combining a synchronic and a diachronic perspective.

Similar problems arise with forms other than past or perfect. In Western Armenian, non-firsthand evidential meanings are expressed through a set of forms which go back to perfect. Synchronically, it is an analytic construction which consists of a participle in *-er* and an auxiliary (Donabédian 1996). As expected, its meanings cover hearsay, inference, and surprise or unexpected information; it is also used in stories, value judgements, and to express temporal, aspectual, and modal nuances (p. 100). The particle *eyer*, which goes back to an *-er* participle of the verb 'be', expresses inference and hearsay; its use is comparable to a lexical strategy (except for the fact that its occurrence is associated with perfect and indirect speech) (pp. 95–6). Since it is a special verbal paradigm, it may qualify as an evidential system, which goes back to grammaticalization of a strategy (using participles in a 'non-firsthand' sense: a possibility of this interpretation was suggested by Lazard 1999). Wasco-Wishram (Silverstein 1978) is reported to have an 'evidential' passive (with inference as one of its meanings) which goes back to a locational construction. But the existing data are not sufficient to decide whether this is an evidentiality system or just an extension of passive.

(*b*) Distinguishing between A1 and A2 systems.

Languages with an A2 evidentiality system contrast between evidentially marked forms (covering non-firsthand information sources) and evidentiality-neutral forms. There is, however, a certain amount of controversy in how to interpret forms that do not contain reference to any information source.

Consider Turkish. According to Johanson (2003: 275), 'functionally marked terms expressing the evidential notions explicitly stand in paradigmatic contrast to non-evidentials'. Every form marked for evidentiality has an unmarked counterpart, e.g. *gel-miş* (come-NONFIRSTH.PAST) 'has obviously come' (the speaker may know this by inference, or hearsay) versus *gel-di* (come-PAST) 'has come/came'; and *gel-iyor-muş* (come-INTRATERM.ASP-NONFIRSTH.COP) 'is/was obviously coming, obviously comes' versus *gel-iyor* (come-INTRA) 'is coming/comes'. The unmarked term is used if 'the speaker considers the evidential distinction unessential and thus chooses not to use it'. The unmarked terms simply do *not* signal that the event is stated in an indirect way, i.e. 'acknowledged by a recipient by means of report, inference or perception' (Johanson 2003: 276). They are 'neutral': the speaker 'considers the evidential distinction unessential and thus chooses not to use it' (p. 275). This is in stark contrast to A1 systems, which have a paradigmatic distinction between firsthand and non-firsthand, without any unspecified, 'everything else' term. Johanson (2003: 275–6) emphatically points out that 'the widespread opinion that unmarked terms such as *gel-di* "has come/came" consistently signal "direct experience" or "visual evidence" is incorrect', though 'evidentially unmarked terms may suggest that the source of information is direct experience' (p. 282). This tendency towards an unmarked interpretation of the *-dI* past as that of 'direct experience' has been signalled by Grunina (1976), Aksu-Koç and Slobin (1986: 165), and Aksu-Koç (2000); also see Kornfilt (1997: 337–8), on its overtones to do with 'certainty' and commitment 'to the truth of the statement'.

Historically, individual languages tend to reinterpret the 'everything else' term as primarily 'firsthand' and 'direct experience'. Johanson (2003: 279) reports that in some Turkic languages the *-dI* past, the 'non-evidential' counterpart of the non-firsthand *-mIş*, has acquired meanings associated with 'firsthand' evidentials. Examples are Uzbek, Turkmen, Uyghur, and Kazakh.

Along similar lines, Balkan Slavic languages developed an A1 system out of an erstwhile A2 system—which, in its turn, goes back to the grammaticalization of an evidential strategy (Friedman 2003: 212). We will see in §4.1 and in §9.1 that most A2 systems result from grammaticalization of an evidentiality strategy, whereby a verbal category develops an additional, evidential meaning. This meaning gradually becomes obligatory. Later, it becomes the only meaning of these categories. Friedman (2003: 193) shows how the languages of the Balkans— in particular, Macedonian and Albanian—grammaticalize the erstwhile evidentiality strategies into obligatory categories—that is, 'a meaning which is encoded into certain paradigms cannot be avoided when those forms are used'.

Any process of grammaticalization and reinterpretation is best viewed as a continuum. Verbal forms with an evidential meaning may occupy different places on this continuum: evidentiality-neutral forms 'drift' towards acquiring the meaning complementary to their 'non-firsthand counterparts' and thus gradually become associated with 'firsthand' information. Some may even be interpreted by linguists as a variety of A1, as has been suggested for Turkish (e.g. Grunina 1976, and discussion in Aksu-Koç and Slobin 1986 and Aksu-Koç 2000).

Additional difficulties may arise if the ways in which the description of evidentials is phrased make it hard to decide whether the language has an A1 or an A2 system. The 'inferential' in Takelma (Sapir 1922: 158) 'implies that the action expressed by the verb is not directly known or stated on the authority of the speaker but is only inferred from the circumstances of the case or rests on the authority of the one other than the speaker'. That is, if a statement 'the bear killed the man' is cast in inferential, it implies that it is either inferred from 'certain facts (such as finding the man's corpse or the presence of a bear's footprints in the neighbourhood of the house)', or that 'the statement is not made on speaker's own authority'. In contrast, if one says 'the bear killed the man' stating the event 'as a mere matter of fact, the truth of which is directly known' to speaker from their or another's experience, the aorist form would be used. Notably, the inferential is not used in myths—'either because the constant use of the relatively uncommon inferential forms would have been felt as intrusive and laborious, or because the events related in the myths are to be looked upon as objectively certain'. (Such 'epistemic' extensions of evidentials will be discussed in §5.1.) The question whether the zero-marked form in Takelma can be considered analogous to firsthand evidentials in an A1 system or not remains open. If it is an evidential, the system is of A1 type. If the unmarked form is evidentiality-neutral, the system is of A2 type.

(*c*) DISTINGUISHING BETWEEN A1, A2, AND A3 SYSTEMS.
The exact boundaries between all the three commonly attested evidential systems can be blurred, and different language analysts can produce different results. Consider Cherokee; Reyburn (1954: 64) described the non-firsthand ('non-experienced') past suffix as 'reported past' marker, thus implying that 'reported information' is its core meaning. One could infer from Reyburn's discussion that Cherokee has an A3 system. However, the analysis of various contexts of the usage of two evidentials fused with past tense by Pulte (1985) demonstrated that 'the Cherokee past suffixes . . . constitute a simple evidential system distinguishing information obtained by the senses from information obtained [in] other ways', and that 'the "reported past", previously thought to be central to the system, is only a special case of the nonexperienced past'; that is, we are dealing with an A1 system. This is fully confirmed by examples such as 2.3–9 above.

Not all languages are so well served in their documentation. In Tarascan (isolate: Foster 1969: 50), the enclitic *naa* marks reported speech. Apparently, it can also be used to refer to 'what one does not know from one's own experience', marking inference, as in expressions like 'it appears that she will die'. The available descriptions make it difficult to decide whether the reported meaning is primary. The question whether Tarascan has an A2 or an A3 system remains unanswered.[9]

On a more positive note: a careful synchronic and diachronic analysis of the non-firsthand form in an A2 system can help establish the paths of its semantic evolution. Cree, Montagnais, and Naskapi—the three northernmost members of the Algonquian family which form a dialect continuum (James, Clarke, and MacKenzie 2001)—have two evidential suffixes fused with tense: *-tak* 'present tense non-firsthand' and *-shapan* 'past tense non-firsthand'. Both can be used to mark inference based on perceived results (for instance, when the speaker hears someone snoring they infer that the person is asleep). The same morphemes are also used to convey reported information, or simply 'unspecified' indirect evidence (see further examples and semantic extensions in §5.1). A cross-dialectal analysis reveals that the two suffixes originally referred to inference and were only later extended to reported information; this expansion has occurred only in some dialects. It is thus a clear case of an A2 system.

The reported term in an A3 system often develops connotations of 'disclaimer' of firsthand knowledge on the part of the speaker. In Arizona Tewa (Kiowa-Tanoan: Kroskrity 1993: 144–5), the 'reported' particle *ba* has 'the "hearsay" qualification of the assertion' as its primary meaning; it has also been extended to disclaim 'first-hand knowledge or novelty on the part of the speaker' (p. 144). (Also see §10.2.1, on how this particle is used in traditional narratives.) There is enough evidence, however, to classify it as primarily 'reported'.[10]

Importantly, in each case evidentiality is distinct from modal expressions (involving 'epistemic' meanings relating to probability and possibility). In §8.5, we return to the question of how modalities interact with evidentials.

2.2 Evidentiality systems with three choices

Three-term systems involve at least one sensory specification. Five types have been attested so far:

B1. Direct (or Visual), Inferred, Reported
B2. Visual, Non-visual sensory, Inferred
B3. Visual, Non-visual sensory, Reported

---

[9] A recent grammar of Tarascan (Purépecha) by Chamereau (2000) does not mention this clitic. The so called 'reportative' suffix *-(ü)rke* in Mapuche (an isolate from Chile) presents a similar problem (Smeets 1989: 322; Zúñiga MS).

[10] Along similar lines, the hearsay suffix in Kiowa (Watkins 1984: 174) indicates that the speaker is giving information which was not 'personally experienced'. Since most often the source of information is someone else's verbal report, the evidential can be safely classed as 'reported' and the system as A3.

B4. Non-visual sensory, Inferred, Reported
B5. Reported, Quotative, 'everything else'

All of these are attested in more than one language, but B2 and B3 systems are relatively uncommon. Analytic problems arise with respect to the expression of visually acquired information in B4 systems together with the status and interpretation of evidentiality-neutral forms. B5 systems are different from other systems discussed here but similar to A3 systems in that they provide for an 'everything else' default choice.

B1. DIRECT (OR VISUAL), INFERRED, REPORTED. Depending on the system, the first term can refer to visually acquired information, as in Qiang; or to information based on sensory evidence, usually visual or auditory, as in Shasta. Jaqi languages (Aymara: Hardman 1986) have three evidentials—personal knowledge (acquired visually), hearsay (knowledge through language), and non-personal knowledge (inferred). The semantic complexity of individual terms and their extensions are discussed in §5.2. All the Quechua languages have three evidentiality specifications: direct evidence (*-mi*), inferred (traditionally called conjectural) (*-chi, chr(a)*), and reported (*-shi*)[11] (Floyd 1997). Their semantic complexity is addressed in §5.3.

The following examples are from Wanka Quechua (Floyd 1997: 71; 1999: 48).

Wanka Quechua
2.40   Chay-chruu-**mi**   achka   wamla-pis   walashr-pis
      this-LOC-DIR.EV   many   girl-TOO   boy-TOO
      alma-ku-lkaa-ña
      bathe-REFL-IMPF.PL-NARR.PAST
      'Many girls and boys were swimming' (I saw them)

2.41   Daañu   pawa-shra-si   ka-ya-n-**chr**-ari
      field   finish-PART-EVEN   be-IMPF-3-INFR-EMPH
      'It (the field) might be completely destroyed' (I infer)

2.42   Ancha-p-**shi**   wa'a-chi-nki   wamla-a-ta
      too.much-GEN-REP   cry-CAUS-2   girl-1p-ACC
      'You make my daughter cry too much' (they tell me)

Shilluk, a Western Nilotic language of the Northern Luo subgroup (Miller and Gilley forthcoming), is the only language in Africa with a similar three-fold evidentiality system. The direct and the inferred evidentials are verbal prefixes,

---

[11] Other Quechua varieties have somewhat different allomorphs of these. Here and elsewhere I keep the morphemic gloss in the source, unless indicated otherwise.

while the reported evidential is a particle preposed to the verb. In Mosetén, an isolate from Bolivia (Sakel 2003: 266–8), the sensory evidential particle *ishtyi'* occurs if either visual or auditory evidence is available to the speaker. If the information has been obtained by hearsay, the enclitic *-katyi'* is employed. The clitic *-(a)ke* is used if the information has been inferred, and the speaker has not heard or seen the action happen (as, for instance, in a situation when somebody found a dead body and concludes that the person died).

Shasta appears to have had a fused marking of evidentiality, tense, mood, and person with three specifications (apparently, evidentials are only used with third person: Silver and Miller 1997: 38): direct evidential non-past; inferential non-past; inferential near past; inferential distant past; quotative near past; and quotative distant past (see §8.4, for correlations between tense and evidentiality).

The visual term in a three-term system may be formally unmarked. Bora (Bora-Witoto family, Peru: Thiesen 1996; Weber and Thiesen forthcoming: 254–6) has two evidential clitics *Ɂha* 'inferred' (called 'nonwitnessed') and *-bà* 'reported'. The absence of an evidential clitic implies firsthand information. The fact that the zero-marked form has an evidential value is corroborated by the observation: 'if a speaker fails to include an evidential clitic when reporting an event he or she did not witness, they may be challenged by the hearer' (see §11.2). Koreguaje (West Tucanoan: Barnes 1999: 213; Cook and Criswell 1993: 86–7; Gralow 1993) is a similar example. In this language 'if speakers were present for the event or state they are speaking of, there is no special marker. If they obtained the information from another source, they include an auxiliary verb which indicates that they are not giving a first person account. If they assume that the assertion is/was true, they use an auxiliary verb that indicates probability' (Barnes 1999: 213).

Qiang (Tibeto-Burman: LaPolla 2003a: 67–70) also has a three-way evidential system. If the event was seen, the overt visual marker *-u/-wu* can be used, as in 2.43.

Qiang

2.43 the: ʐdʐyta: ɦa-qɔ-(w)u
      3sg   Chengdu+LOC   OR-go-VIS
      'He went to Chengdu' (the speaker saw the person leave)

The visual evidential is not obligatory; in fact, it is used mostly to emphasize that the speaker actually did see the other person perform the action, as in 2.43. If no such emphasis is required, and the event was witnessed, the evidential marking can be simply omitted, as in 2.44. The default reading for a clause unmarked for evidentiality is visually acquired information; see §3.2.

2.44 Ɂū   tɕeɣun   tu-pu-ji-n
      2sg   marry   OR-do-CSM-2sg
      'You got married' (I saw you get married)

If the evidence for the statement is based on inference, the suffix -*k* is used, as in 2.45. Here, the statement is based on inference from seeing the broken pieces in the person's hands.

2.45 panə-le: fia-χɔ̌-**k**-ən
thing-DEF:CL OR-broken-INFR-2sg
'It seems you broke the thing'

Information obtained by hearsay is marked with the suffix -*i*.

2.46 the: z̦dz̦yta: fia-qɔ-**i**
3sg Chengdu+LOC OR-go-REP
'He went to Chengdu (I heard)'

A similar system has been reported for Amdo Tibetan (Sun 1993: 950). Example 2.47 implies that the knowledge was acquired through 'direct, visual perception of event'.[12]

Amdo Tibetan

2.47 tṣaçʰi=kə ʰtæ ŋu=tʰæ
Bkra.shis=ERG horse buy(COMPL)=DIR.EV
'Bkra-shis bought a horse' (speaker saw it)

Example 2.48 refers to knowledge acquired by inference, circumstantial evidence, or even hearsay, while 2.49 is an assertion made on the basis of a verbal report by someone other than the speaker.

2.48 tṣaçʰi=kə ʰtæ ŋu=**zəg**
Bkra.shis=ERG horse buy(COMPL)=INFR
'Bkra-shis bought a horse' (speaker inferred it)

2.49 tṣaçiʰi=kə ʰtæ ŋu=**tʰæ/zəg** se
Bkra.shis=ERG horse buy(COMPL)=DIR/INFR REP
'Bkra-shis bought a horse' (speaker was told about it)

Similar systems are probably found in a number of other languages of the Americas. Ponca (Siouan: Anonymous n.d. 108–11)[13] had three evidential choices (described under the cover term 'quotative mode'): 'witnessed by

[12] Along similar lines, Hopi (Hill and Black 1998: 892) appears to distinguish an inferential marker *kur* and a hearsay or quotative *yaw*; statements based on direct experience are unmarked. Potential mood marker *kya* is used as an evidential strategy to mark assumptions. At present the exact number of evidentiality distinctions are difficult to ascertain, since the status of the verb with no evidentiality marking remains unclear.
[13] The author is probably Frida Hahn; however, this cannot be known with certainty (John Koontz, p.c.).

speaker', assertion made by the speaker 'but repeating the experience of a third person', and 'hearsay'. Loos (1999: 246) mentions a three-term system—which he terms 'factual', 'reported', 'assumed'—in Capanawa, a Panoan language. Maidu has a three-term evidentiality system: visual, reported, inferred (Shipley 1964: 45). Skidegate Haida (Swanton 1911: 248, 264) distinguished 'experienced past', 'inexperienced past', and 'quotative'. Sanuma (Yanomami: Borgman 1990: 165–73) has at least three evidentiality markers—'direct' (used in present and past tenses), 'verification', by seeing evidence or by hearing from someone who has firsthand knowledge of the state or event (also with a distinction of present and past), and 'supposition' (used in present, past, or future). Reported evidentiality is marked by a combination of inferential plus an additional morpheme. The exact structure of the system requires further investigation.[14]

B2. Visual, Non-visual sensory, Inferred. Washo (Jacobsen 1964: 626–30; 1986: 8) has visual, auditory, and a marker of 'ex post facto inference with some connotation of surprise' (which Jacobsen termed 'mirative'; also see Appendix to Chapter 6). A similar system appears to be found in Siona (West Tucanoan: Wheeler 1987: 152–3), with three evidentials interacting with tense: visually acquired information (implying full participation of the speaker), partial participation (implying non-visual sensory information and lack of control on the part of the speaker), and 'total separation' of the speaker (a judgement based on inferred or on reported information).

B3. Visual, Non-visual sensory, Reported. Oksapmin (isolate from Papua New Guinea, Sandaun province: Lawrence 1987: 55–6) has three evidentiality choices. If the information was acquired visually, the verb is formally unmarked, as in 2.50.

Oksapmin
2.50 yot   haan   ihitsi   nuhur   **waaihpaa**
      two   men   they:two   we   went:down
      'Two other men and I went down' (I saw it)

If the speaker acquired the information from someone else, the 'reported' clitic -*ri* is used, as in 2.51.

2.51 Haperaapnong   mahan   kuu   gaamin   tit
      Haperap:to   over.there   woman   husband.and.wife   one

---

[14] A three-term system of reported, inferred, and unmarked appears to have been used in Bahwana, a North Arawak language spoken on the Middle Rio Negro in Brazil (Ramirez 1992: 64–5). Materials on this language are, unfortunately, very limited (being based on work with the last speaker who is now dead) and it is impossible to say under what conditions an evidentiality specification was obligatory, and what its interrelations were with other grammatical systems.

pipaa-**ri**
went-REP
'A husband and a wife went (reportedly) over there to Haperap'

Events perceived through senses other than sight (hearing, tasting, smelling, or feeling) are expressed by using a verb stem (with a sequential marker) plus the verb 'do'. In 2.52 the speaker can hear the plane which is too far away to be seen.

2.52   barus   **apri-s**   **ha-h**
        plane   come-SEQUENCE   do-IMM.PAST
        'I hear the plane coming'

And 2.53 can be said by someone walking along the trail and smelling pork being cooked somewhere in the bushes.

2.53   imaah   gapgwe   na-**ha-m**   **hah-h-mur**
        pig   good:smell   to:me-do-SEQUENCE   do-IMM.PAST.SG-STATEMENT
        'Some pork is roasting (to me) (I smell it)'

The non-visual evidential is also used to refer to something felt—2.54 was produced by an old speaker of Oksapmin who was getting an injection.

2.54   gin   sur   oh   **mara-s**   **hah**
        now   needle   it   come.in-SEQUENCE   do-IMM.PAST
        'Now I feel the needle going in'

Similar systems are attested in Maricopa (Gordon 1986*a*; 1986*b*: 112–13) and in Dulong (LaPolla 2003*c*).

B4. NON-VISUAL SENSORY, INFERRED, REPORTED. Nganasan and Enets, of the Samoyedic branch of Uralic, distinguish non-visual sensory (traditionally called 'auditive'), inferential, and reportative ('renarrative') forms. (See §§5.2.1–3, for further semantic overtones of each term.) The auditive marks what can be heard and not seen. Examples 2.55–60 are from Nganasan (Gusev forthcoming: 4).

Nganasan
2.55   Nogutə-**munu**-t'i   mii?a
        come.close-AUD-3Du   here
        'The two of them are coming close' (one can hear them come)

The non-visual sensory evidential can refer to any sort of non-visual perception. In 2.56 it refers to a smell, and in 2.57 to tactile sensations.

2.56   Ma-tənu   hihiə   koli̯   ńeluaj-**münü**-t'u
        house-LOC   boiled   fish   feel/smell-AUD-3sg
        'There is a smell of boiled fish in the house'

2.57 . . . kobtᵘa   ŋatə-**munu**-t'u   nənd'i-tiə   maʔ
      . . . girl   found-AUD-3sg   stand-PART.PRES   house
      . . . 'a girl (who has left her house during a snowstorm and cannot see
      anything) felt (i.e. found by feeling) a standing house'

The inferential is used to mark inferences made on the basis of visual evidence, as in 2.58.[15] The speaker infers that a fox had been walking around the abandoned settlement and that it had broken a tooth—a broken-off piece of the tooth is lying on the ground.

2.58 Tərədi'-ʔ   maʔad'ə-mənu   tunt̲i-rə
      this-GEN.PL   abandoned.settlement-PROL.PL   fox-2sg
      d'oðür-**hᵘatu** . . .   t'imi-mti   ləhəra-**hᵘaðu**.   T'imi
      go.round-INFR   tooth-ACC.3sg   break-INFR   tooth(-GEN)
      ləhumuə   d̲ü̲b̲ə̲ə̲-̲t̲i̲   məu   ńini
      piece   lie-PRES   ground(-GEN)   on
      'A fox must have been going round by these abandoned
      settlements . . . it must have broken a tooth—a (broken-off) piece of
      tooth is lying on the ground'

Inference can be made on the basis of reasoning, as in 2.59. That the men did brake when their master told them to implies that he is an authority for them.

2.59 T'eliʔimid'i-ʔə-ʔ   baarbə-ðuŋ   huntə-ðuŋ   i-**hᵘaðu**
      brake-PERF-3pl   master-3pl   authority-3pl   be-INFR
      'They braked (following the master's order); (one infers that) their
      master was an authority for them'

A reported evidential marks any secondhand information. It can come from some specific person, as in 2.60, or from hearsay in general. The main character, by the name of Sünəð̲i̲ʔ Nəniku̲, instructs the girl to ask her brother for permission to go away with him.[16]

2.60 Munə-ʔ: "Sünəð̲i̲ʔ   Nənikü   mənə   kontu-nantu-**baŋhu**"
      say-IMP   (name)   I(-ACC)   take.away-VOL-REP
      'Say (to your brother): "Sünəð̲i̲ʔ Nənikü wants to take me away,
      reported" '

---

[15] Forms -*hᵘatu* and -*hᵘaðu* are allomorphs of the inferential marker -*hatu*.
[16] Similar examples from Enets are in Künnap (2002).

The three evidentials in Retuarã (Central Tucanoan: Strom 1992: 90–1; Clay Strom, p.c.) form a similar system. If one can hear people talking, one says 2.61, with the auditory evidential.

Retuarã

2.61 peta-rã   põʔĩbāhā-re   ĩbā-**ko**-yu
      downriver-LOC   people-TERM   be-AUD-PRES
      'There are people downriver (I can hear them talking)'

The assumed evidential *-rihi* indicates that the statement is based on assumption. Since the child is small, I assume that he must be one year old.

2.62 kũpahĩ-ki   ki-ĩbẽ   weheherāka
      small-masc   3masc.sg-be   year
      ki-eya-waʔ-ri-**rihi**-yu
      3masc.sg-reach-AWAY-EP-ASSUM-PRES
      'He is small; he must be one year old (I assume this)'

If the speaker learnt the facts from someone else, the reported evidential would be used.

2.63 limon   eʔe-rĩ   yi-aʔ-yu   dā-re   ki-ã-rape-**re**
      lemon   get-PURP   1sg-go-PRES   3pl-TERM   3masc.sg-say-PAST-REP
      ' "I am going to get lemons", he is reported to say to them'

Whereas B1, B2, and B3 systems consisted of just three terms, B4 systems have three marked terms and allow for the possibility of not using an evidential marker. The unmarked situation is, however, not to be regarded as a fourth evidential value, although it may be used for visually acquired information, in both Nganasan and Retuarã. If one saw the people downriver, the correct way to say this in Retuarã would be 2.64 (Clay Strom, p.c.). In Retuarã, visually acquired information is one of the readings for the verb not marked for evidentiality.

2.64 peta-rã   põʔĩbāhā-re   iba-rape
      downriver-LOC   people-TERM   be-PAST
      'There are people downriver (I see them)'

In Nganasan (Gusev forthcoming: 2–3), a verb without any evidential morpheme may be interpreted as describing visually acquired information, as in the last clause of 2.58, or information of which the speaker is certain. (The unmarked verbal forms are underlined. Also see 3.6 and 5.25.) An unmarked verb form in both languages allows for multiple interpretations. If may indicate that no evidential specification is being offered if the speaker deems it unnecessary to specify the information source (Gusev forthcoming: 3, 11). Myths recounting events which happened in times immemorial are told using unmarked forms. Or the evidential value may be clear from the context (see 5.25). (This is in sharp contrast to many other evidentiality systems where the reported evidential is a recurrent feature of mythical narratives; see §9.2.1.) Verbs unmarked for evidentiality may occur together with all three evidentials in one sentence, without any meaning difference (see §3.2.2, example 3.6 and discussion there). Zero-marked forms in Retuarã appear in procedural discourse (see texts at the end of Strom's 1992 grammar) and generally if the source of information is unknown or unimportant. This shows that a formally unmarked verb in B4 systems is evidentiality-neutral (also see Usenkova forthcoming: 11, on the ambiguity of unmarked verb forms in Nganasan).

I conclude that 'visual' evidentiality is not a special term in B4 systems. If the verb is unmarked for evidentiality, it may refer to visual information, but does not have to. This interpretation is consistent with a general tendency for information acquired visually to be less formally marked than the information acquired through any other source, as will be shown in §3.2.2.

B5. REPORTED, QUOTATIVE, AND 'EVERYTHING ELSE'. Only reported information requires a special marker, similarly to A3 systems with only a reported evidential. The reported evidential in A3 systems has a wide range of meanings. It may refer to information reported by someone from an unspecified source, and also to information acquired from a specified person, that is, as quotative (see §5.4.1). The reported proper and the quotative are formally distinguished in a few North American Indian languages.

Comanche (Uto-Aztecan: Charney 1993: 188–91) has a narrative past particle *ki*, which marks narrative 'that lies outside the speaker's personal knowledge— both folktales and events that the speaker learned of from others'. The quotative particle *me* occurs when there is a direct quotation, as in 2.65.

Comanche

2.65   hãã   **me**-se   sutɨ⁼   patsi
        yes   QUOT-CNTR   that.one   older.sister
        'The older sister said, "yes"'

The reported and the quotative evidentials can appear together, if a quotation happens to occur in a text told in narrative past.

2.66   sutɨ⁼-se   'yes'   **me-kɨ**
        that.one-CNTR   yes   QUOT-NARRATIVE.PAST
        'He (Coyote) said "yes", it is said'

'Reported' and 'quotative' are distinguished in Dakota (Siouan: Boas and Deloria 1939: 106–7). The particle *śk'a'* indicates 'statements known by hearsay', and 'when the statement or thought of a definite person is quoted, the quotation may end with *lo* (*le*), *ye*, *c'e* (or *k'ụ*). The first is used for the present or future; the second for an obligatory future; the third for the past'.

These two types of reported evidential show similarities to how C3 systems—with four evidentials altogether—distinguish between reported and quotative (see §2.3).

The difference between two reported evidentials may be of another sort: one may be a simple reported, the other a token of narrative genre for myths or stories acquired from someone else. Tonkawa (Hoijer 1933: 105–6) has two suffixes glossed as 'quotatives'. The suffix *-no'o* means 'one hears that', or 'it is being said that'. It does not appear to be restricted to any particular genre. The suffix *-lakno'o* occurs in myths, indicating that the events recounted happened a long time ago. It is added to every verb in a story, unless the clause is a direct quotation.

Chemehuevi (Uto-Aztecan: Munro 1978: 162–3) also has two quotatives (as opposed to evidentiality-neutral forms), but the semantic distinction between the two is quite different. One, *(m)aykani*, marks quotations, reported speech, and complement clauses of verbs like 'hear', 'wonder', or 'think'. Historically, it developed from *ay/may* 'say'. Another quotative-like element, *ayk'a*, possibly related to *(m)aykani*, appears only in Coyote's speech. This is to do with a tendency of marking speech characteristics of animals, tricksters, and other characters widely attested in North American Indian languages (cf. Sapir 1915, on Nootka; and Jane Hill, p.c.).

2.3 Evidentiality systems with four choices

Four-term systems involve one or two sensory specifications. Three types have been attested:

   C1. Visual, Non-visual sensory, Inferred, Reported
   C2. Direct (or Visual), Inferred, Assumed, Reported
   C3. Direct, Inferred, Reported, Quotative

Four-term evidentiality systems, which involve just one sensory specification, mark inference and assumption (C2), or two kinds of verbal report (C3).

C1. Visual, Non-visual sensory, Inferred, Reported. Systems of this kind are found in a number of East Tucanoan languages spoken in the multilingual area of the Vaupés in northwest Amazonia—Tucano (Ramirez 1997, vol. II; my field data), Barasano (Jones and Jones 1991), Tatuyo (Gomez-Imbert 1986),

Siriano (Criswell and Brandrup 2000: 400–1), and Macuna (Smothermon, Smothermon, and Frank 1995). In these languages evidentiality specification is fused with person, number, and gender and there are dependencies with tense (see §8.4 below and Malone 1988). Traditional Tariana used by older speakers also had a system of this kind. A five-term system—which we have seen in 1.1–5—has developed comparatively recently.

Seeing the dog drag the fish from a smoking grid, one says 2.67 in Tucano, with a visual evidential fused with recent past tense.

Tucano
2.67 diâyɨ   wa'î-re   yaha-**ámi**
     dog   fish-TOP.NON.A/S   steal-REC.P.VIS.3sgnf
     'The dog stole the fish' (I saw it)

If one heard the noise of a dog messing around with the smoking grid, or of the fish falling down, one uses a non-visual evidential, as in 2.68.

2.68 diâyɨ   wa'î-re   yaha-**ásɨ̃**
     dog   fish-TOP.NON.A/S   steal-REC.P.NONVIS.3sgnf
     'The dog stole the fish' (I heard the noise)

If the owner of the fish comes into the kitchen area, and sees that the fish is gone, there are bones scattered around, and the dog looks happy and satisfied, the inferred evidential is appropriate.

2.69 diâyɨ   wa'î-re   yaha-**ápɨ̃**
     dog   fish-TOP.NON.A/S   steal-REC.P.INFR.3sgnf
     'The dog stole the fish' (I inferred it)

And if one learnt the information from someone else, the reported evidential is the only correct choice.

2.70 diâyɨ   wa'î-re   yaha-**ápɨ'**
     dog   fish-TOP.NON.A/S   steal-REC.P.REP.3sgnf
     'The dog stole the fish' (I have learnt it from someone else)

Eastern Pomo (Pomoan: McLendon 2003: 101–2) also has an evidential system of a similar kind, with four terms: a visual or direct knowledge evidential (2.71), a non-visual sensory evidential (2.72), an evidential covering logical inference from circumstantial evidence (2.73), and a reported (2.74).

Eastern Pomo
2.71 mí·-p-al   Pʰa·bé-k-**a**
     3.sg.-male-PATIENT   burn-PUNCTUAL-DIRECT
     'He got burned' (I have direct evidence, e.g. I saw it happen)

2.72 bi·Yá   pʰa·bé-kʰ-**ink'e**
      hand   burn-PUNCTUAL-SENSORY
      'I burned my hand' (I feel the sensation of burning in my hand)

2.73 bé·k-al   pʰa·bé-k-**ine**
      3pl-PATIENT   burn-PUNCTUAL-INFERENTIAL
      'They must have gotten burned' (I see circumstantial evidence—signs of a fire, bandages, burn cream)

2.74 bé·k-al   pʰa·bé-kʰ-·**le**
      3pl-PATIENT   burn-PUNCTUAL-REPORTED
      'They got burned, they say' (I am reporting what I was told)

The direct evidential (termed 'indicative' in McLendon's earlier work: McLendon 1975, 1996) indicates that the speaker has direct knowledge of the event because they 'performed or experienced the action, process or state'. This evidential occurs where there is visual evidence. However, unlike the visual evidential in Tucano, it has a wider meaning—that of firsthand experience. This evidential has an epistemic extension of 'certainty': if something had disappeared, and 'one knows for sure who took it', 2.75 would be appropriate (see §5.3.1).

2.75 bé·kʰ   pʰu·dí-yaki-**ya**
      3pl.AGENT   steal-PL-DIRECT
      'They stole it'

Ladakhi (Tibeto-Burman: Bhat 1999: 72–3; Koshal 1979: 185–201) appears to have a similar system: evidential suffixes cover reported, 'direct observation', experienced (e.g. by speaker feeling), and inferred (e.g. 'he will die-inferred' on the basis of his being very sick). These occupy the same slot as mood markers. In addition, there are a number of suffixes which specify type of inference: whether it is based on sounds or habitual occurrence, or whether it has to do with 'observations not remembered correctly', or 'inferred from unobserved partial or vague knowledge', or simply 'guessed'. Whether all these are really evidentials, and how they correlate with other verbal categories requires further studies.

Goddard (1911: 124) reported a similar four-term evidential system for Hupa (Athabaskan). The choices are visual ('the object or act is within the view of the speaker'); non-visual sensory ('when the act is perceived by the sense of hearing or feeling'); inferred from evidence; and an additional inferred evidential, which differs from the other one 'in the fact that evidence is more certain'. Victor Golla (p.c.) reports that there may have been a number of other markers (for instance, a reported evidential).

A four-term evidential system in Shibacha Lisu (Tibeto-Burman: Yu 2003) also involves visual, non-visual, inferred, and reported, all expressed with particles.

C2. DIRECT (OR VISUAL), INFERRED, ASSUMED, REPORTED. Systems of this type vary in the semantic content of the sensory evidential. The sensory evidential may refer just to information acquired by seeing, or to any sensory perception. The inferred evidential typically refers to inference based on visible or tangible results, or direct physical evidence. The assumed evidential is to do with assumption, or general knowledge.

In Tsafiki (Barbacoan: Dickinson 1999: 37–8; 2000: 407–9; 2001), if an event was 'directly' witnessed—which appears to imply seeing—the verb is morphologically unmarked.

Tsafiki

2.76 Manuel   ano   **fi-e**
      Manuel   food   eat-DECL
      'Manuel ate' (the speaker saw him)

If information was obtained by inference from direct physical evidence, 2.77 would be used.

2.77 Manuel   ano   fi-**nu**-e
      Manuel   food   eat-INFR-DECL
      'Manuel ate' (the speaker sees the dirty dishes)

A nominalization followed by the verb class marker is employed if the inference is made on the basis of general knowledge. This is the assumed evidential.

2.78 Manuel   ano   fi-**n-ki**-e
      Manuel   food   eat-NOMN-VCLASS:do-DECL
      'Manuel ate' (he always eats at eight o'clock and it's now nine o'clock)

Other examples of this evidential discussed in Dickinson (2001) could be interpreted as involving assumption based on reasoning. These include 'the warmth of the child must be what is causing her to sleep so long', and 'three or four or five, (I think) he must have killed five'.

The reported evidential—marked with the suffix *-ti*—indicates that the information was obtained from someone else. We will see in §3.5 that it can occur together with any of the other three evidentials, and can even be repeated to distinguish between secondhand and thirdhand report.

The sensory evidential in a C2 system can refer to firsthand knowledge acquired through any physical sense, be it vision, hearing, smell, taste, or touch, as in Shipibo-Konibo (Valenzuela 2003: 35–7). In 2.79 the 'direct' evidential *-ra* (which is a second position clitic: see §3.1) refers to something the speaker could see (and of which he was also a participant: see §7.1).

Shipibo-Konibo

2.79   westíora   nete-n-**ra**   ka-a   iki   nokon yosi   betan
        one   day-temp-DIR.EV   go-PP2 AUX   POSS1 elder CONJ
        e-a,   piti   bena-i . . .
        1-ABS   fish:ABS search-SSSI
        'One day my grandfather and I went to look for fish . . .'

In 2.80 the direct evidential refers to non-visual sensory perception. The speaker can smell and hear that the fish is being fried, but he cannot see it.

2.80   shee   a-**rá**-kan-ai   yapa
        ONOM:frying do.TR-DIR.EV-PL-INC fish:ABS
        'Fish is being fried' (I smell it and hear it, but cannot see it)

The inferential *-bira* encodes inference based on observable evidence or on reasoning. Someone hears a baby crying and says 2.81 to the mother.

2.81   mi-n   bake   pi-kas-**bira**-[a]i, oin-we!
        2-GEN   child:ABS eat-DES-INFR-INC see-IMP
        'Your child must be hungry (inferred on the basis of him crying), come and see!'

The evidential *-mein* indicates that the information is based on assumption and speculation. If someone knocks on the door, one would use *-mein* to ask oneself 'who could this be?'

2.82   tso-a-**mein**   i-ti   iki
        who-ABS-SPECL be-INF AUX
        'Who could it be?'

If 'one is watching a soccer match on TV and sees that a player suddenly falls to the ground and others come to his help', one would use *-bira* saying 'He must have twisted his ankle', as in 2.83 (see §3.5 on how evidentials in Shipibo-Konibo can occur together).

2.83   oa-**ra**   taské-**bira**-ke
        DIST:ABS-DIR.EV sprain-INFR-COMPL
        'He must have sprained his ankle'

The assumed evidential *-mein* 'would be preferred if one simply sees an unknown person on the street walking with difficulty' (Valenzuela 2003: 47).

There is also a reported evidential, -*ronki*. (An additional reported marker -*ki* is almost synonymous with -*ronki*.) The reported can be used when the source of information is general hearsay; or when the speaker is quoting someone (Valenzuela 2003: 39).

2.84   a-**ronki**-a   iki
       do.TR-REP-PP2   AUX
       'It is said that s/he did (it)' or 'S/he says that s/he did (it)'

In Pawnee (Caddoan: Parks 1972) the visual is formally unmarked; there is a prefix marking hearsay (also used for folklore), a prefix marking inference from results, and another prefix for unspecified indirect inference. Four evidentiality specifications—visual, inferred, assumed, and reported—are described for Xamatauteri (Yanomami: Ramirez 1994: 169–70, 175, 296, 316–17.).

Whether the only sensory evidential in a C2 type system can be strictly non-visual is problematic. The only putative example found so far is Wintu (Wintun) as described by Schlichter (1986). However, Schilchter's analysis leaves it unclear as to how visual information is marked. Pitkin (1984), in his full grammar of Wintu, postulates five evidentiality choices; see discussion under §2.4 below.

A four-term system similar to C2 above was described by Kroeker (2001: 62–5), for Mamainde (Northern Nambiquara), with the following choices: visual ('I am telling you what I saw the actor doing'); inference on the basis of visual evidence ('I am telling you my deduction of an action that must have occurred because of something that I saw/see'); assumption on the basis of general knowledge ('the speaker knows this to be true from what always happens that way'); and reported ('I was told that a certain action has occurred').

Mamainde

2.85   wa³kon³-∅-na²hẽ³-la²
       work-3sg-VIS.PAST-PERF
       'He worked (yesterday; I saw him)'

2.86   wa³kon³-∅-nũ²hẽ³-la²
       work-3sg-INFR.PAST-PERF
       'He worked (yesterday; I inferred this based on visual evidence)'

2.87   ti̱³ka³l-a²   kai³l-a²   yain-∅-te²ju²hẽ³-la²
       anteater-DEF   ant-DEF   eat-3sg-GENERAL.KNOWLEDGE.EV-PERF
       'The anteater habitually eats ants (I know this as general knowledge)'

2.88   wa³kon³-∅-ta¹hxai²hẽ³-la²
       work-3sg-REP.PAST-PERF
       'He worked (I was told)'

If both the speaker and the addressee saw, inferred, or were told about the action, a special set of evidentials is employed; see discussion in §7.3.1.

2.88a wa³kon³-Ø-ta¹tẽxti²tu³-wa²
work-3sg-REP.PAST-PERF
'He worked (you and I were told)'

C3. DIRECT, INFERRED, REPORTED, QUOTATIVE. The semantics of the two reported evidentials in C3 systems may involve a distinction between reported and quotative. Cora (Uto-Aztecan: Casad 1984; Willett 1988: 68–9) distinguishes direct evidential (marked with a clitic *ku*, as in 2.89) and an inferred evidential marked with *séin* (as in 2.90), in addition to two reported evidentials. The visual evidential has an epistemic connotation—emphasizing the veracity of a statement.

Cora
2.89 a'acǔ   **ku**   rí 'ɨ   na-a-rí 'h
somewhat   DIR.EV   well   me-COMPL-do
'It made me a little better'

2.90 ah   pú-'i   há'a=hi-(y)a'-a-káa-va-cɨ   **séin**
then   SUBJ-SEQ   be=NARRATIVE-away-outside-down-fall-PAST   INFR
ɨ   tʸaška
ART   scorpion
'Apparently the scorpion dropped down from there'

Events on which secondhand report is available are marked with the particle *nū'u*. This particle also occurs in folklore, as in 2.91 (Casad 1984: 179).

2.91 ayáa   pá   **nú'u**   tyú-hu'-u-rí h
thus   SUBJ   QUOT   DISTR-NARR-COMPL-do
'This is, they say, what took place'

In addition to this, Cora has another particle, *yée*, which marks 'secondhand direct discourse' (Casad 1984: 179; 1992: 152). In other words, they function as quotatives—this is illustrated in 2.92[17]—from a story (itself marked with a reported evidential *nú'u*).

2.92 y-én   peh   **yée**   wa-híhwa   mʷáa,
here-top   you:SUBR   QUOT   COMPL-yell   you:sg
yáa   pú   nú'u   hí   tʸí-r-aa-ta-hée
PROCOMP   SUBJ   REP   SEQ   DISTR-DISTR:SG-COMPL-PERF-tell
' "From right up on top here, you will call out loud and clear", that is what she called on him to do'

[17] Casad (1984: 179) mentions additional quotative particles, *wí* (analysed as an emphatic in Casad 1992), and *yéewi*, a combination of *yée* and *wí* (Casad 1992: 153).

This particle goes back to a Proto-Uto-Aztecan verb of saying (Munro 1978; Casad 1992: 154); its semantic extensions are to do with expressing inference and other kind of information which the speaker acquired through indirect experience. These semantic extensions are reminiscent of the non-firsthand in A2 and of reported in A3 systems—we return to these in Chapter 5.

Northern Embera (Chocó family, Colombia: Mortensen 1999: 86–7) distinguishes between a reported and a quotative evidential. This language also marks inference or 'conjecture', and what appears to be 'direct' evidential. A quotative evidential *-pida* means that the speaker is repeating exactly what the other person said.

Northern Embera

2.93   o-sʰi-**pida**
       make-PAST-QUOT
       '[He$_i$ said] he$_i$ made one'

The reported evidential *-mana* is used as a general hearsay; it frequently occurs in legends.

The distinction between two reported evidentials can be of different nature. Southeastern Tepehuan (Willett 1991: 161–6) has four evidentials. The particle *dyo* marks information that was personally witnessed by the speaker, visually or through one or more physical senses. The particle *vac* marks all sorts of inference. There are also two reported evidentials: if the reported evidence was not previously known to the speaker, the particle *sap* is used, as in 2.94. The report can be based on something heard from a particular person, or on general hearsay.

Southeastern Tepehuan

2.94   oidya-'-ap   gu-m   tat.
       go.with-FUT-2sg   ART-2sg   father
       Jimi-a'   **sap**   para   Vódamtam   cavuimuc
       go-FUT   REP.1   to   Mezquital   tomorrow
       '(You should) accompany your father. He says he's going to Mezquital tomorrow'

This particle is also used in folklore, with an implication that the story comes from a reliable source, and in quotative formulas. If part of the information was previously known to the hearer, the particle *sac* is used, as a way of reminding the hearer of the information they should already be aware of, as in 2.95.

2.95   va-ji pir   gu-m   bi   na-p   **sac**   tu-jugui-a'
       REL-get.cold   ART-2sg   food   SUB-2sg   REP2   EXT-eat-FUT
       'Your food is already cold. (You said) you were going to eat'

Is this particle a true evidential or a marker of 'old' knowledge (cf. Chapter 6)? This question remains open.[18]

There could be further kinds of evidentiality systems with three or four choices. However, the existing descriptions are too sketchy to be able to evaluate them. Kwakiutl (Boas 1911*b*: 496) distinguishes four evidential suffixes: 'reported' ('it is said'), 'as I told you before', 'seen in a dream', and 'evidently, as is shown by evidence'. Salish languages (Thompson 1979: 744) appear to distinguish several specifications, to do with 'assumption' and 'observed situation', besides the ubiquitous quotative. Lillooet (Salish: van Eijk 1997: 200–7) has a variety of enclitics which look like evidentials, including _an' meaning 'the speaker concludes something from circumstantial evidence', _kʷuʔ 'quotative', and _qaʔ 'presupposed knowledge'. The Thompson language (Salish: Thompson and Thompson 1992: 140–2, 157) has a variety of particles with evidential-like meanings—reportive, conjectural, perceptual, presumptive; and a few other markers with similar meanings, such as 'apparent' and 'recognitional'. In either case, there is not enough detailed discussion to be able to fully evaluate this information. Along similar lines, the exact number of evidentiality choices in Bella Coola (also Salish) is difficult to ascertain. Saunders and Davis (1976) discuss numerous ways in which a Bella Coola speaker can convey evidence for the information and how certain he or she is of its veracity; there are a number of dubitative constructions employed when the event was not acquired visually. The absence of these implies that 'the evidence for the assertion is the speaker's witnessing of the event' (p. 35). In addition, there is a clear reportative marker k^w (pp. 40–2), used both in quotative constructions (such as 'Jeff said that Snac wiped the boat-reported') and in general reported structures (such as 'Snac wiped the boat-reported'). But are the dubitative markers evidentials, or do they express different degrees of doubt or certainty, and thus can only qualify as evidential strategies? At present, the available descriptions simply do not allow us to make a decision.

The difficulties of analysis are often to do with the status of a zero-marked term. Few authors go to the same length as Gusev (forthcoming), for Nganasan, in their analysis of various functions of the unmarked term. Wichita (Caddoan) appears to have a non-visual, an inferential, and a reported evidential;

---

[18] In his overview of evidentiality systems, Willett (1988: 68–9) mentioned the possibility of distinct marking for secondhand reported and for thirdhand reported. Examples given included Cora and Southeastern Tepehuan; however, the analysis and examples discussed by Casad (1984, 1992) clearly show that Willett was incorrect as regards Cora; see examples 2.91–2 above. In his grammar (1991: 164, n. 53), Willett acknowledges that the Southeastern Tepehuan data ought not to be analysed as secondhand and thirdhand. I have been unable to find any other examples of secondhand and thirdhand information marked with distinct morphemes (see §5.4.2). In some languages, third- and fourthhand information can be simply expressed by repeating the reported evidential—see 3.29–30 from Tsafiki.

the absence of evidential marking appears to correlate with having personally observed the event (Rood 1976: 92; also see §3.3). Whether this unmarked term is indeed a zero-marked evidential or not remains unclear.

2.4 Evidentiality systems with five or more choices

Systems which contain five evidentiality choices may have two sensory evidentials, one inferred and one assumed evidential, and also one reported marker. Rather few systems of this sort have been clearly analysed.

A five-term system of D1.VISUAL, NON-VISUAL SENSORY, INFERRED, ASSUMED, and REPORTED was illustrated in 1.1–5, from Tariana. The most frequently cited example of a similar system comes from Tuyuca, an East Tucanoan language (Barnes 1984) spoken in the same area as Tariana. A similar system is found in Desano, also East Tucanoan (Miller 1999: 64–8). Epps (2005) describes a very similar system in Hupda, a Makú language spoken in the same area.

Traditional Wintu (Pitkin 1984: 147, 183, based on materials collected by Dorothy D. Lee in 1930) also distinguished a five-way contrast in evidentials. The meaning 'he is chopping/chopped wood' could be expressed in the following ways, depending on how the information was acquired:

Wintu

2.96   k̓upa-**be·** 'he is chopping wood (if I see or have seen him)': VISUAL
k̓upa-**nt^he·** 'he is chopping wood (if I hear him or if a chip flies off and hits me)': NON-VISUAL SENSORY
k̓upa-**re·** 'he is chopping wood (I have gone to his cabin, find him absent and his axe is gone)': INFERRED
k̓upa-**ʔel·** 'he is chopping wood (if I know that he has a job chopping wood every day at this hour, that he is a dependable employee, and, perhaps, that he is not in his cabin)': ASSUMED (EXPERIENTIAL)
k̓upa-**ke·** 'he is chopping wood (I know from hearsay)':REPORTED

Complex evidentiality systems may involve further terms. Kashaya (Pomoan: Oswalt 1986: 34–42) has at least the following:

- 'Performative' (- *ŵela/-mela*) signifies that 'the speaker knows of what he speaks because he is performing the act himself or has just performed it' (it is used only with first person).
- 'Factual/visual' pair - *ŵă*, -*yă* (the two forms correspond to imperfective and perfective) signifies 'that the speaker knows of what he speaks because he sees, or saw, it'.
- 'Auditory' -*ûnnă* signifies that 'the speaker knows of what he speaks because he heard the sound of the action, but did not see it'.

- 'Inferential' -*qă* marks 'an inference based on circumstances or evidence found apart, in space or time, from the actual event or state'. An additional inferential -*bi*- could be a distributional variant of -*qă* (p. 40; also see McLendon 2003: 125).
- 'Quotative' -*do* marks that the information was learned from somebody else.

There are two further terms in the system: 'personal experience' -*yowă*, which can replace any evidential—except for quotative—when employed in a narrative construction, and remote past -*miyă*, an archaic suffix used to mark descriptions of personal experiences in remote past. To what extent these are indeed evidentials is not clear from the analysis available.

This system is similar to the one in Tuyuca in that it distinguishes visual and non-visual sensory. Kashaya has an additional distinction within the 'visual', or 'direct' (the 'factual').

Further complex systems include Central Pomo (Mithun 1999: 181). Evidentials cover general knowledge, visual, non-visual sensory, reported, inferential, 'personal experience of one's own actions', and a further one referring to 'personal affect'.

Nambiquara languages, with the most complex evidentiality system in southern Amazonia (Lowe 1999: 275–6), seem to have a comparable set of specifications. Southern Nambiquara has an obligatory marking on the verb for whether a statement is (1) eyewitness (implying that the speaker had seen the action they are reporting), (2) inferred or (3) assumed ('the speaker's claim . . . based either on seeing an associated simultaneous action and making an interpretation therefrom, or on seeing a set of circumstances which must have resulted from a previous action and making an inference; different suffixes mark these two options'), (4) reported ('the speaker is simply passing on information they have heard from another speaker'), and (5) 'internal support' ('the speaker reports their "gut feeling" that which they assert must be so'). An additional complication in the system lies in the fact that each evidential is fused with the marker of either new or old information. More information is needed on this elaborate system (which appears to be rather different from the system in Mamainde, a Northern Nambiquara language: Kroeker 2001: C2 above and 2.85–9).

Another complex system, with six terms, was reported for Foe, a language of the Kutubuan family spoken in the Southern Highlands of Papua New Guinea (Rule 1977: 71–4). 'Participatory' or factual evidential implies that the speaker is participating in the action, or is making a statement of a generally known fact, as in 2.97.

Foe

2.97   na   mini   wa-**bugege**

      I   today   come-PRES.PARTICIPATORY.EV

      'I am coming today' (PARTICIPATORY EVIDENTIAL)

Visual implies that the action was seen.

2.98   aiya bare   wa-**boba'ae**

      air plane   come-VIS.EV

      'An airplane is coming' (can see it: VISUAL)

Non-visual ('sense perception') indicates that the action was perceived by hearing, smelling, feeling, or understanding.

2.99   aiya bare   wa-**bida'ae**

      air plane   come-NONVIS.EV

      'An airplane is coming' (can only hear it: NON-VISUAL)

Mental deduction implies an inference based on something for which the speaker has evidence perceived with his senses (for instance, hearing a hen cackling and deducing by the type of sound that she must have laid an egg), or as in 2.100.

2.100   Kabe   Irabo   wa-**ada'ae**

      Mr   Irabo   come-DEDUCTIVE.EV

      'Mr Irabo is coming' (can hear him speaking and can recognize his voice)

Visible evidence implies inference based on the visible results (such as an empty trap, or footprints), as in 2.101.

2.101   Agu   amena   wa-**boba'ae**

      Agu   men   come-VIS.EVIDENCE.EV

      'The Agu men are coming' (can see the smoke rising on the Agu track)

Previous evidence describes, for instance, an event the evidence for which the speaker had seen, but cannot see at the moment of speech (Rule 1977: 71–4).

2.102   Kabe   Maduane   minage   wa-**bubege**

      Mr   Maduane   still   come-PREVIOUS.EVIDENCE.EV

      'Mr Maduane is still coming' (both left together, but the speaker came faster than Maduane, and so he knows he's still on the way)

Fasu (Kutubuan, Papuan: May and Loeweke 1980: 71–4), distantly related to Foe (Franklin 2001), appears to have an even more sophisticated system.

Declarative 'independent clause' suffixes provide a number of specifications which cover: (1) visual ('seen'), (2) non-visual sensory ('heard'), (3) reported, and also (4) heard from an unknown source, or thirdhand, (5) heard from a known source, such as the original speaker, (6) statement about something in which the speaker participated directly, and a number of further specifications which are reminiscent of 'inferred': 'statement about a thought', 'deduced from evidence', as well as 'obvious to the speaker'. However, the description is too sketchy to be able to evaluate the exact semantics of information source in each case. Karo (Tupi: Gabas Júnior 1999, 2002) has a complex system of evidential-like particles which encode visually acquired information, reported informa-tion, and eight more specifications based on different kinds of inference. However, it is not quite clear whether evidentiality in Karo constitutes one grammatical system.[19]

In some languages a wide variety of evidential meanings may be expressed in different slots of the verbal word or within a clause. Each evidential has its own restrictions on co-occurrence with other categories. At least some of these markers can be optional. In contrast to the systems discussed so far, different evidentiality specifications are 'scattered' throughout the grammar, and by no means form a unitary category. Examples of this sort cover heterogenous eviden-tials in Makah, and in Eskimo languages (also see de Reuse 2003: 97, on Western Apache). This 'scattered' coding of evidentiality will be addressed in §3.3.

2.5 Information sources throughout the world: a summary

We have established five kinds of systems with two evidential choices, and five types with three choices. Evidential systems with four choices can be of three kinds. Only one type of five-term system has been found in more than one lan-guage. Semantic parameters employed in languages with grammatical eviden-tiality cover physical senses, and several types of inference and of verbal report. The recurrent semantic parameters are:

   I. VISUAL: covers information acquired through seeing.

  II. NON-VISUAL SENSORY: covers information acquired through hearing, and is typically extended to smell and taste, and sometimes also to touch.

 III. INFERENCE: based on visible or tangible evidence, or result.

 IV. ASSUMPTION: based on evidence other than visible results: this may include logical reasoning, assumption, or simply general knowledge.

---

[19] Hixkaryana (Carib: Derbyshire 1985: 255) has six 'verificational' particles, two of which convey evidentiality-like meanings (hearsay and deduction, while visual, or 'eyewitness', if contrasted to hearsay, is zero-marked). These require further analysis.

V. HEARSAY: for reported information with no reference to those it was reported by.

VI. QUOTATIVE: for reported information with an overt reference to the quoted source.

No language has a special evidential to cover smell, taste, or feeling. 'Feeling by touch' is treated differently by different systems. The 'sensory' evidential in Ngiyambaa (A4) can be used to refer to information one acquires by feeling something (e.g. a rabbit in its burrow: 2.29). Similarly, in Shipibo-Konibo (with a C2 system) the direct evidential covers a variety of senses (including touch). This is not the case in every system: in Tariana (D1) the sensory evidential does not refer to touch if the speaker touches something on purpose, for instance, touching a piece of cloth to check if it is dry. The assumed evidential is used then. The non-visual can be used if 'touch' is not controlled by the speaker— that is, if someone steps on one's dress, as in 5.34, or gets bitten by a mosquito as in 5.37. (This is similar to how one describes getting an injection in Oksapmin (B3), in 2.54.) We return to this in Chapter 5.

The domain of 'inference' is subdivided differently in different systems. A major distinction appears to exist between an inferred evidential covering inferences made on the basis of visible or tangible results, and an assumed evidential involving general knowledge and assumption based on reasoning. Examples 2.77 and 2.78 from Tsafiki (C2) illustrate these. We return to the semantic complexity of inferred evidentials in §5.3.2.

A few languages of C3 type distinguish between hearsay and quotative. We will see in §5.4 that the hearsay and the quotative evidentials may differ in terms of how they correlate with a particular genre, and which epistemic extensions they may have (see, for instance, Casad 1992, on how the quotative *yée* in Cora has acquired epistemic overtones and can also be used to express inference).

Table 2.1 summarizes the semantic parameters attested in languages with grammatical evidentiality. The names used here for each evidential appear in the columns. As shown in this table, a number of these six parameters can be subsumed under one evidential specification. Some parameters may not be expressed at all. No systems have been found with all six specifications expressed.

The semantic parameters (I)–(VI) are operational in different kinds of systems: those which have a default 'everything else' specification: non-firsthand versus 'everything else' (A2); reported versus 'everything else' (A3); auditory versus 'everything else' (A5); and reported and quotative versus 'everything else' (B5). Since these systems are organized in different ways from those without an 'everything else' term, they have not been included in Table 2.1.

TABLE 2.1 Semantic parameters in evidentiality systems

		I. VISUAL	II. SENSORY	III. INFERENCE	IV. ASSUMPTION	V. HEARSAY	VI. QUOTATIVE
2 choices	A1	firsthand				non-firsthand	
	A1	firsthand			non-firsthand		
	A1	firsthand			non-firsthand	different system or <no term>	
	A4	<no term>	non-visual		<no term>	reported	
3 choices	B1	direct		inferred		reported	
	B2	visual	non-visual	inferred		<no term>	
	B2	visual	non-visual	inferred		reported	
	B3	visual	non-visual		<no term>	reported	
	B4	<no term>	non-visual	inferred		reported	
	C1	visual	non-visual		inferred	reported	
4 choices	C2	direct		inferred	assumed	reported	
	C3	direct		inferred		reported	quotative
5 choices	D1	visual	non-visual	inferred	assumed		reported

The 'evidentiality-neutral forms' will be discussed in §3.2.3, within the perspective of markedness in evidential systems.

Semantic parameters group together in various ways, depending on the system. The most straightforward grouping is found in B1 systems—where sensory parameters (I and II), inference (III and IV), and verbal report (V and VI) are grouped together. This corresponds to Willett's tripartite 'central domains' of evidentiality (1988): 'attested evidence' (which, for him, covers visual, auditory, and other sensory evidence), 'inferring evidence', and 'reported evidence'. However, this is not the end of the story. Visually acquired information can be marked differently from any other, and so can non-visual sensory. And inference and verbal report can be grouped together under one term. Alternatively, several inferential choices can be available.

The exact semantic details of each evidentiality specification may vary. For instance, inference based on other than result may involve general knowledge; however, in quite a few languages generally known facts are cast in visual evidential (see §5.3). Different evidentials may or may not acquire epistemic and mirative extensions. We return to this in Chapters 5 and 6.

3

How to mark information source

Evidentials can be expressed in a variety of ways: with affixes, clitics or particles, or special verbal forms. §3.1 contains an overview of these morphosyntactic techniques. Markedness in evidentiality systems is addressed in §3.2. In that section we also look at default interpretations of formally unmarked or 'evidentiality-neutral' forms. This book is focused on evidential systems taken 'to be a paradigmatic set of [. . .] forms' (Johanson 2003). But is evidentiality—a grammaticalized information source—always expressed as one paradigmatic set of forms, and always one grammatical category? Evidentiality may not form a uniform category. Instead, evidential meanings could be 'scattered' all over the grammar. This is discussed in §3.3. And, as we will see in §3.4, a language can combine two or more evidentiality subsystems.

Unlike many other categories, evidentiality can be expressed more than once in a clause, to refer to different interacting information sources. This is discussed in §3.5. This is different from the multiple occurrence of the same evidential in a clause, dealt with in §3.6. The scope of evidentiality and the time reference of evidentials are discussed in §§3.7–8. And §3.9 provides a brief summary.

3.1 Grammatical means for evidential marking

As we saw in Chapter 2, evidentials come in a variety of morphological expressions. In Wintu (Pitkin 1984), Eastern Pomo (McLendon 2003), Yukaghir (Maslova 2003), and Qiang (LaPolla 2003*a*) evidentials are inflectional suffixes. They can then be mutually exclusive with other morphemes which occupy the same slot in the verbal structure. For instance, in Yukaghir the evidentiality marker is not compatible with the prospective future. In Abkhaz, the evidential suffix occupies the rightmost place in the verb form, and is compatible with most tenses and moods (except for one future and future conditional: Chirikba 2003: 249–50).

Evidentials are often fused with tense. This is the case in Jarawara (examples 2.1–2), Tariana (1.1–5), Tucano (2.67–70), and Tuyuca (Barnes 1984). Evidentiality is expressed by a term within a tense-aspect paradigm in Turkic, Iranian, and Finno-Ugric languages, e.g. Mari, Udmurt, Komi, and Ob-Ugric languages. In Estonian and Livonian (and also in Latvian and Lithuanian) the special paradigm of reported evidential forms is traditionally known as 'oblique mood'. These are not compatible with any moods; historically, at least some go back to participles (see §9.1).

Contrary to some scholars (e.g. van der Auwera and Plungian 1998), evidentiality is often fully independent from mood and from modality. In quite a few languages, e.g. Yukaghir and Ngiyambaa (2.30), evidentials are compatible with irrealis (see §8.3, on correlations between evidentials and non-indicative modalities). In Menomini and in Samoyedic languages evidentiality markers are mutually exclusive with moods. This does not make evidentiality part of the mood system since in these languages moods differ from evidentials in a number of properties (including the ways in which they interact with person: see §7.2.2).

Evidentials may be marked with clitics which do not always attach to the verb, and yet they have scope over the whole clause, as in Tariana (Aikhenvald 2003*d*) and Hupda (Makú: Epps 2005). In Shipibo-Konibo evidentials are second position clitics, attaching to the right of the first major sentence constituent. In 2.80, the direct evidential -*ra* happens to occur on the verb, while in 2.79 it appears on the locational, 'one day'. In 3.1, -*ra* occurs at the end of a relative clause (Valenzuela 2003: 36; clause boundaries are in square brackets).

Shipibo-Konibo

3.1 [e-n   atsa   meni-ibat-a   joni]-**ra**
     I-ERG   manioc:ABS   give-YESTERDAY.PAST-PP2   person:ABS-DIR.EV
     moa   ka-ke
     already go-COMPL
     'The person to whom I gave manioc yesterday already left' (I saw it)

In Quechua, evidentials are second position enclitics which attach to the first constituent in a sentence, as in 3.2. See the discussion of their status as clitics in Lefebvre and Muysken (1988: 83–9).

Quechua

3.2 huk-**si**   ka-sqa   huk   machucha-piwan   payacha
     once-REP   be-SD   one   old.man-WITH   woman
     'Once there were an old man and an old woman'

Alternatively, the evidential enclitics can occur on a focused constituent, as in 3.3.

3.3   Pidru   kunan-**mi**   wasi-ta   tuwa-sha-n
       Pedro   now-DIR.EV   house-ACC   build-PROG-3sg
       'It is now that Pedro is building the house'

Evidential meanings are often expressed with particles. This is the case in Australian languages Yankunytjatjara, Mparntwe Arrernte, and Warlpiri, and also in Hopi (Uto-Aztecan), in Arizona Tewa (Kiowa-Tanoan), in Kamaiurá (Tupí-Guaraní), and in Akha and Lisu (both Tibeto-Burman). In numerous other Tibeto-Burman languages (such as Lhasa Tibetan and some other Tibetan dialects) evidentials are expressed with copulas and auxiliary verbs (cf. DeLancey 1986). A complex predicate involving a nominalization marks an inferred evidential in Tsafiki (see 2.78). A complex verb, consisting of the main verb and an auxiliary 'do', expresses non-visual evidentiality in Oksapmin (see 2.53). In a number of cases, evidentials go back to compounded verbs. In East Tucanoan languages (Malone 1988), and in Tariana (Aikhenvald 2003*b*), evidentiality markers must have arisen from the final verb in compounds: the verb 'see' developed into the marker for visual evidentiality, and 'hear' into non-visual. 'Evidential' passive in Wasco-Wishram (Silverstein 1978) could be an example of a derivational form used as an evidential. This goes together with the fact that nominalizations and participles often acquire evidential overtones, come to be used as evidentiality strategies, and may then develop into evidentials proper (see §4.4 and §9.1).[1]

Evidentials may derive from biclausal structures. This can happen via grammaticalization of an erstwhile independent verb 'say', as described for Maricopa (Gordon 1986*a*: 86) and for numerous Uto-Aztecan languages (Munro 1978). Evidentials may arise via de-subordination of erstwhile dependent clauses. The best-known example is Standard Estonian, where participle forms were used to mark a reported speech complement, and then came to express reportative evidential as main clause predicates (see Campbell 1991, and further details in §9.1). Also see §9.1, on the origins of two evidentials—non-firsthand ('inferential') and quotative—from different auxiliary structures in Jamul Tiipay.

That is, there are hardly any morphological limitations on how evidentials can be expressed.[2] The hierarchy in Scheme 3.1 below accounts for the relative formal markedness of individual terms.

---

[1] Evidentials also develop from derived nominalizations. In Komi, the non-firsthand past forms are based on a past participle (Leinonen 2000: 421). All this goes against Anderson's premature claim (1986: 275) that evidentials cannot be expressed with compounds, or derivational forms.

[2] The fact that I have not found any examples of evidentiality expressed with vowel apophony or internal change, or with consonant mutation, simply has to do with the fact that these processes happen

There may be language-specific restrictions as to where an evidential can or cannot occur. In Shipibo-Konibo, a vocative is not treated as a constituent of a clause. Consequently, the evidential cannot occur on a vocative, 'skipping' it (Valenzuela 2003: 36, 43). In Quechua, evidentials cannot occur on postverbal constituents (Muysken 1995: 383, 385).

If evidentials constitute part of the verbal paradigm, as in Abkhaz, Yukaghir, Jarawara, East Tucanoan languages, Wintu, and many more, they form one (or part of one) obligatory inflectional system. If evidentiality is expressed with particles, the rules for their occurrence may be less rigid, depending on the individual system. In many A3 systems, with a distinction between reported and 'everything else', the reported evidential is obligatory in every clause. In Shoshone (Uto-Aztecan: Silver and Miller 1997: 38), in Omaha and Ponca (Siouan: Koontz 2000), and in Arizona Tewa (Kroskrity 1993) every sentence in a story has to take a reported evidential. In contrast, in Baniwa of Içana the reported marker appears just in the first sentence in a paragraph. In such systems, evidentiality is not strictly obligatory. (Incidentally, neither is tense, or most other verbal categories.) In §3.2.4, we address the issue of the omission of evidentials in the languages which allow it.

3.2 Markedness in evidentiality systems

Evidentiality systems vary as to the relative markedness of terms. There is a fundamental distinction between two kinds of markedness—formal and functional. A formally unmarked term will be the only one in its system to have zero realization (or a zero allomorph). Functional markedness relates to the context of use—the marked term(s) may be used in a restricted, specifiable context, with the unmarked term being used in all other circumstances. Formal and functional markedness do not necessarily coincide—a term from a system that is functionally unmarked need not be formally unmarked, and vice versa (see Aikhenvald and Dixon 1998a: 60; Dixon 1994: 56–7).

Functional markedness in an evidentiality system is illustrated in §3.2.1. In §3.2.2, we discuss formal markedness among evidentials.

What is the status of a form with no evidentiality marking in languages with grammatical evidentiality? The answer to this question depends on the type of

___

not to occur in languages for which evidentiality has been described so far. That I have not found any convincing examples of evidentials expressed with serial verb construction may be accidental. Particles marking evidentiality in isolating Tibeto-Burman languages most probably derive from serial verb constructions (Randy LaPolla, p.c.). Also see §9.1.1, for compounded verbs as a source for evidentials in some South American languages.

system. The status of forms unspecified for evidentiality is considered in §3.2.3. In §3.2.4 we look at conditions under which evidentials can be omitted.

3.2.1 *Functional markedness in evidentiality systems*

A useful summary of criteria relevant to markedness was provided by Greenberg (1966: 25–30); also see Croft (1990: 71). These include (Aikhenvald 2000: 50–1):

(i)   The unmarked value of the form will refer to either value (marked or unmarked) in certain contexts—e.g. the unmarked term can be used for a supercategory which covers all the terms.
(ii) In certain grammatical environments, only the unmarked value will occur.
(iii) The unmarked category is realized in neutralized contexts.[3]

Formal markedness and functional markedness may correlate, but they do not necessarily always go together (see Aikhenvald 2000: 50). The only clear example of a functionally (but not formally) unmarked term in an evidentiality system so far comes from Jarawara.[4] Here, the immediate past non-firsthand is the only term that functions, in certain contexts, as neutralization of the three past tenses and two evidentiality values. So, for instance, dependent clauses can only take immediate past non-firsthand. In this context all other tense and evidentiality values are simply neutralized; the whole system is represented by the immediate past non-firsthand in the dependent clause. Consider 3.4 (Dixon 2003: 173–4). The main clause is marked with far past non-firsthand tense-evidential (masculine form, to agree with the pivot of the sentence: the man), -*himata*, plus the reported suffix -*mone*. But the dependent clause simply takes the immediate past non-firsthand marker. In its meaning, it is evidentiality-neutral.

Jarawara

3.4   hi-we-**himata-mona**-ka,
      Oc-see-FP.NONFIRSTH.m-REP.m-DECL.m
      ka-maki-**no**-ho
      be.in.motion-FOLLOWING-IMM.P.NONFIRSTH.m-DEP
      '(She) saw him, as he was following (along the road)'

---

[3] The unmarked category may also be the one most frequently used (or the one that is used at least as frequently as each marked one). See Croft (1996) and Andrews (1990) on further issues concerning markedness relations. When grammatical categories have more than two values, one value is marked relative to another (cf. Croft 1990: 66; 1996).

[4] In Mỹky (Monserrat and Dixon 2003: 240), the visual evidential appears to be functionally unmarked: it is the specification required by the mirative 'mood'.

Evidentiality and tense are neutralized in a similar way in content questions, where immediate past non-firsthand is the only possible choice.

3.5   Safato!,   hika   kosi$_o$
        name   where   urucuri(m)
        ti-jaba-ri-**ni**?
        2sgA-pick-CONTENT.INTER.f-IMM.P.NONFIRSTH.f
        'Safato! Where did you pick the urucuri (fruit)?'[5]

In a language with obligatory evidentiality, one evidential may be used as 'default'. If a speaker of Shipibo-Konibo (with a C2 system) is asked to translate a sentence taken out of its context, chances are they will use the direct evidential *-ra* without asking about the source of information (the basic assumption behind this being that they might have witnessed what is being talked about) (Valenzuela 2003: 37). It is, however, debatable whether this is a truly functionally unmarked form, rather than a general preference to assume that if someone talks about something they must have seen it: visually acquired information is usually treated as the most valuable (see §10.1).[6]

In numerous languages—including Quechua, Tucanoan languages, and Eastern Pomo—evidentials do not occur in dependent clauses (see §8.1). This, however, is different from having a functionally unmarked term in the evidentiality system: evidentiality is simply not expressed at all in a given grammatical context.

3.2.2 *Formal markedness in evidentiality systems*

In evidentiality systems of most types the formally unmarked verb implies that the speaker saw what is being talked about (cf. DeLancey 2001: 379: 'the unmarked form in an evidential system typically represents information which the speaker knows from firsthand, visual perception'). We have seen in Chapter 2 that visual evidentials are marked by zero in Bora and Koreguaje, with a three-term evidential system of B1 type; in Oksapmin, with a B3 system (2.50), and in Pawnee and Tsafiki, with a C2 system (2.76). In Hupda, with a D1 system (Epps 2005 and §2.4), the visual evidential is formally unmarked. The unmarked verb in Yukaghir (2.10) and in Archi (Kibrik 1977: 89) implies that the speaker witnessed the action with an appropriate sense. Qiang (see §2.2) employs a special visual evidential to emphasize the fact that the event was seen. This marker may be

---

[5] Personal pronouns in Jarawara are cross-referenced as feminine (Dixon 2004).

[6] A somewhat different situation has been described for Wanano, an East Tucanoan language. According to Stenzel (2003), Wanano has a special evidential form employed when none of visual, non-visual, inferred, or reported can be used. The possibility of treating this as a functionally unmarked—or perhaps a 'default'—option in the system requires further investigation.

omitted. Then, person-marking suffixes with no evidentiality marking are sufficient for a default reading of visually acquired information.

A similar principle is at work in languages where evidentiality does not seem to form one coherent grammatical category. In Hixkaryana (Derbyshire 1985: 255), absence of any 'verificational particle'—which expresses some evidentiality-related meanings—specifically marks 'eyewitness' when contrasted to 'hearsay'. This suggests visual perception and/or direct (firsthand) witness as 'default'.

Cross-linguistically, direct perception—which involves visual and sensory—tends to be less marked than any other type of evidence. In Tariana (D1), the visual evidential is the least formally marked (see 1.1–5, and Aikhenvald 2003e). The following hierarchy accounts for the relative markedness of terms in evidentiality systems:

SCHEME 3.1 Formal markedness in evidentiality systems

Visual	Other sensory	Other types of information source
←--→		
the least likely to be formally marked		the most likely to be formally marked

According to Scheme 3.1, if a language has a formally unmarked evidential, it is likely to be either visual, or visual and other sensory (if there is one term for both).[7]

An analytic problem that arises in these cases is whether the unmarked form should be considered a term in the system, or whether the system (with no zero term) allows for evidentially neutral forms. An informed decision between these alternatives can be made only on language-internal grounds. If zero-marking has a specific semantic connotation, then it should be looked upon as part of the system. This is the case in Yukaghir (§2.1.1) where zero-marked forms are interpreted as witnessed in an appropriate sense by the speaker, as opposed to a marked non-firsthand for which the source of information lies elsewhere. Similarly, in Tsafiki (Dickinson 2000: 407), a morphologically unmarked verb is used to code directly witnessed events, and is in paradigmatic opposition to an inferred, an assumed, and a reported evidential.

The situation in Qiang is different. Here an unmarked clause is 'assumed to represent knowledge that the speaker is sure of, most probably, but not

---

[7] The only problematic issue remains Euchee, with an A5 system: here the auditory evidential is marked. However, as was pointed out in §2.1.1, the system in Euchee is unclear in a variety of ways: for one thing, the language is no longer actively spoken.

necessarily, from having seen the situation or event firsthand' (LaPolla 2003*a*: 65). The 'firsthand' interpretation of a formally unmarked verb is just a tendency. Similarly, the absence of an evidential marker in Western Apache (de Reuse 2003: 83) only tends 'to imply that the speaker was an eyewitness of the event'. But this interpretation is by no means compulsory, and the absence of an evidential particle remains semantically ambiguous. In these cases, zero-marking is not a special term in the evidential system.

The status of zero-marked forms can be determined only in the context of a whole system. In Nganasan (B4: Gusev forthcoming: 3) indicative forms do not combine with any of the three evidential markers: auditory, inferred, or reported. They occur 'if the speaker does not consider it necessary to specify the information source'. A verb without any evidential can be interpreted as referring to visually acquired information, or information of which the speaker is certain (Gusev forthcoming: 3, and the last clause in 2.58). As shown in §2.2, in Nganasan forms with no evidential markers can occur next to evidentially marked forms in texts, without any change in meaning. Their evidentiality value can be easily inferred from the context (cf. §3.2.4).

In 3.6 the indicative form unmarked for evidentiality ('she laughs': underlined) occurs together with a form marked for auditive ('she says-auditive') (Gusev forthcoming: 4). Its evidentiality value is understood from the context: it is non-visual sensory (auditory) because the next verb form is overtly marked for this value.

Nganasan

3.6   Maðə   kunsi̯-ni̯   sigiʔ-iniʔa   ńüə-ti̯
       house[-GEN]   inside-ADV.LOC   cannibal-old.woman   child-GEN3sg
       nanu   hid'i̯-ti-ʔ.   ńemi̯-ðiŋ   munu-**munu**-t'u
       with   laugh-PRES-3pl   mother-3pl   say-AUD-3sg
       '[Having come outside, the daughter of a Nganasan woman came to the cannibal's house and started listening.] Inside the old woman cannibal is laughing with her children . . . Their mother says (one can hear it)'.

In 3.7 a reported evidential is used alongside a verb unmarked for evidentiality (Gusev forthcoming: 11). This extract comes from the speech of a shaman. Typically for a shaman's account of what he had learnt from the spirits, the speech is cast in reported evidential (see §5.4, on the semantics of reported in Nganasan). However, not every sentence is marked—the future indicative (underlined) is used instead of the expected future reported.

3.7   Talu   ŋanuə,   maagəl't'ə-gətə   kuəðaŋku   d'ali̯   i-śüðə
       tomorrow   real   any-ABL   sunny   day   be-FUT

ŋanuə,	koürüðaŋku.	Tərədi	koürüðaŋku	d'ali̱-təni̱
real	sunny.	Such	sunny[-GEN]	day-LOC

kab¹a-ńə		ŋonəi-''	śerə-**biahi̱**-m.
shamanic.attire-ACC.PL.1sg		one.more-GEN.PL	put.on-REP-1sg

Əmə	ńemi̱ʔa	taaniə	kəi-tə	mənə
This[-GEN]	big.river[-GEN]	other[-GEN]	side-LAT	I[-ACC]

bəuru-tə-**baŋhu**-ru?
take.across-FUT-REP-2pl

'[The shaman said, performing his shamanism], tomorrow will be a warm, hot, sunny day. On this warm day I will put my shamanic attire on again (I am told). And you must take me across the river (I am told) . . .'

In all these examples, zero-marked forms do not have an evidential value of their own. This is why we prefer not to consider them on a par with other evidentials (see similar arguments for Retuarã in §2.2). Along similar lines, in Mỹky (or Irantxe, an isolate from Central Brazil) zero-marking has no positive value but simply covers 'everything else'. Consequently, it is not treated as a term in the evidentiality system (Monserrat and Dixon 2003).

Existing descriptions may not provide enough detail to decide whether the system has a formally unmarked zero-term, or whether evidentials are just optional. Latundê (Telles 2002: 288–90) marks auditory information and reported information (as shown in 2.35–6); little is known about the status of the unmarked form. Similarly, in Lakota (Rood and Taylor 1996: 474–5), the absence of an evidential only appears to imply 'eyewitness'. Forms unmarked for evidentiality may have a 'firsthand evidence' interpretation in Takelma (§2.1.2; Sapir 1922: 158); see the mention of a similar situation in Wichita under §2.3. In all these cases we just cannot make an informed decision.

3.2.3 *Evidentiality-neutral forms*

Most evidentiality systems consist of several terms marked with respect to one another. These cover two-term systems A1 and A4 (§2.1), three-term systems B1-B4 (§2.2), four-term systems C1-C3 (§2.3) and all large systems (§2.4).

The remaining systems follow a different principle. They have one overtly marked evidential in opposition to a default, 'everything else' form where the information source is left unspecified. The most frequent systems of such kind are reported versus 'the rest' (A3), and 'non-firsthand' versus 'the rest' (A2). (There is also one instance of auditory information versus 'everything else', A5.) B5 systems have a reported and a quotative, again contrasted to 'everything else'.

What is the status of the 'everything else' form? The ways in which languages express number provide a useful analogy. Number is an obligatory nominal category in most European languages. In a language like Russian, English, German, or Portuguese every noun has to be either singular (which is often formally unmarked) or plural. In Australian languages the situation is quite different. In Dyirbal, the noun *yarraman* means 'horse' or 'horses': 'one does not have to specify number on nouns in Dyirbal, as one is forced to do in English' (Dixon 1980: 22, 267; 2002: 77). It is however possible to add an optional number suffix if necessary (*yarraman-jarran* (horse-DU) means 'two horses', and *yarramanyarraman* (horse:REDUPLICATED.PLURAL) means 'many (more than two) horses'. Number in Dyirbal is a category. However, it follows different principles from those of its English counterpart. Similar systems are found in quite a few Amazonian languages (see Aikhenvald 1999*b* and 1998).

Along similar lines, in a language with an unspecified 'everything else' option a speaker has a choice of either using a specific evidential form to express the required meaning—which is either reported (A3 systems) or non-firsthand (A2 systems)—or to employ an evidentially unspecified, or evidentially neutral, form (this can be accompanied by an optional lexical item meaning 'reportedly', or 'evidently'). The two options are almost synonymous. Example 3.8, from Estonian, contains a reported evidential. Example 3.9 does not (note that it does contain an optional adverb meaning 'reportedly'). The two are said to be synonymous (Metslang and Pajusalu 2002: 99).

Estonian

3.8   Fillmore   tule-**vat**   Eesti-sse   loenguid   pida-ma
       Fillmore   come-REP.PRES   Estonia-ILL   lecture.PL.PARTVE   hold-INF
       'Fillmore is said to be coming to Estonia to give some lectures'

3.9   Fillmore   tule-b   kuuldavasti   Eesti-sse
       Fillmore   come-IND.PRES.3sg   reportedly   Estonia-ILL
       loenguid   pida-ma
       lecture+PL.PARTVE   give-INF
       'Reportedly Fillmore is coming to Estonia to give lectures'

Another option is a subordinate clause, again without any reported evidential.

3.10   Räägi-takse,   et   Fillmore   tule-b   (kuuldavasti)
       say-IMPERS.PRES   that   Fillmore   come-IND.PRES.3sg   reportedly
       Eesti-sse   loenguid   pida-ma
       Estonia-ILL   lecture+PL.PARTVE   give-INF
       'They say that Fillmore is (reportedly) coming to Estonia to give lectures'

In Svan, with an A2 system, evidentials do not have to be used 'if the speaker just wants to tell a story, without any special stress on its "secondhand" origin' (Sumbatova 1999: 71). Sumbatova reports that the speaker may begin a story with evidentials, but then 'forgets' them and uses evidentiality-neutral forms, and 'then, at the beginning of a new episode, or after mentioning the source of the story, the speaker may remember again that the story is not of his own' and employ an evidential. An evidential may also occur at the very end of the story 'to remind the reader of its "reported" status'.

Other systems like Tariana (in 1.1–5), Tucanoan languages, Cherokee, Jarawara, or Yukaghir present speakers with no such option: evidentiality is an obligatory term within the inflectional system, and there is no neutral form available.

Evidentiality systems with one specification contrasted to 'everything else' share the following properties.

(i) Reported evidentials in numerous A3 and also B5 systems are often expressed with optional particles or clitics (often recently grammaticalized out of verbs of speech) rather than a special inflection.[8] (Special inflections also occur: we can recall that Menomini (Algonquian) has a quotative mood: §2.1; while Tunica (Haas 1941: 117–18) has a postfix with the meaning of 'reported'.)

(ii) Many of them have been recently grammaticalized out of an erstwhile evidentiality strategy. A prime example of this is found in Baltic and Balto-Finnic languages, each with an A3 system. The reported evidential in Standard Estonian in its present form has developed comparatively recently (see Fernandez-Vest 1996, on the impact of language reforms). In addition, Estonian dialects use different forms of completely different origin (see the overview in Wälchli 2000, and Metslang and Pajusalu 2002, on South Estonian dialects). The functionally similar form in Lithuanian is considered part of the verbal paradigm in some grammars, but not in others (cf. Peterson 1955 and Mathiassen 1996). For many A2 systems, controversies arise as to whether they ought to be analysed as evidentials, or as evidential extensions of another form, frequently a perfect. See, for instance, Friedman (2003), for an incisive discussion of the languages of the Balkans, and also discussion of 'evidential' uses of perfect in Georgian by Hewitt (1995), and in various Iranian languages (e.g. Nazarova 1998 and Hadarcev 2001). Along similar lines, the A2 system in Svan is one of the most recent developments in the verbal morphology (Sumbatova 1999: 89).

(iii) In addition, A2 systems tend to develop into A1 type, with a binary distinction of firsthand and non-firsthand. This has been documented

---

[8] If we adopt a strict stance that only obligatory grammatical systems of evidentiality are to be included, these optional specifications could be at best considered marginal.

by Johanson (2003: 279–80) for a number of Turkic languages. (Some scholars tend to interpret A2 systems as a variety of A1: see discussion in Johanson 2003: 276.) And we have also seen in §2.1.2 what analytic difficulties can arise in distinguishing between A2 and A1 systems.

Evidentiality-neutral forms are quite different from the situations whereby an evidential is simply omitted but can be recovered from the context. Omission of evidentials is discussed in the next section.

3.2.4 *Omission of evidentials*

If a language has obligatory evidentiality, leaving out an evidential results in a grammatically awkward 'incomplete' sentence (cf. Valenzuela 2003: 34). In Tuyuca and in Tucano every verb has to have an evidential (fused with tense); otherwise the form will be ungrammatical. In Kamaiurá, sentences without evidentiality markers come out as unnatural, 'something artificial, sterile, deprived of colour' (Seki 2000: 347; my translation).

However, even if evidentiality is obligatory, the markers may sometimes be omitted if they can be recovered from the context. In Shipibo-Konibo the evidential markers do not have to appear in every clause or every sentence. Evidentiality is obligatory 'in the sense that the evidential value of the information has always been grammatically marked in the foregoing discourse and is clear to native speakers' (Valenzuela 2003: 39).

In polysynthetic languages with rich morphology, tense–evidentiality may not be compatible with some moods and aspects; for instance, in Tariana the aspect marker -*sida* 'yet' cannot be followed by an evidentiality marker, possibly because of its implicit future reference, as in *nu-nu-sida* (1sg-come-YET) 'I am yet to come; I will still come'. (We will see in §8.4 that Tariana is among numerous languages where future and evidentiality are not compatible.)

If evidential markers are clitics which can go onto any focused constituent, they may be omissible, under certain conditions. The tense–evidentiality enclitics in Tariana can be omitted in narratives if the time-and-evidence frame is set in the previous or in the following clause, or is clear from the context. Consider the following extract from the Tariana origin myth, in 3.11. The first and the second clauses are marked with the evidential -*sina* 'remote past assumed' (this is conventionally used in origin myths if one can observe the traces of the things that are assumed to have happened—rapids where the ancestors passed, or stones they had thrown). The third clause (under c) does not have any evidentiality marking: it elaborates on (b), and the evidentiality has simply been omitted. In the fourth clause, (d), the evidential is present: it marks a new turn of events.

Tariana

3.11 (a) makara-pusita-nuku   makara-**sina**   nema
         dry-clearing-TOP.NON.A/S   dry-REM.P.ASSUM   3pl+stand

     (b) ne-**sina**   na-ruku   na-nu
         then-REM.P.ASSUM   3pl-descend   3pl-come

     (c) te   pa:-ri   na-musu   na-nu   ãdaru-ari
         until   IMP+say-NOMN   3pl-go.out   3pl-come   parrot-RIVER
         na:-ni-pua-nuku   na-musu   na-nu
         3pl+call-PASS-CL:RIVER-TOP.NON.A/S   3pl-go.out   3pl-come
         nema
         3pl+stand

     (d) diha-pua-naku   na-musu-**sina**   na-nu
         this-CL:RIVER-TOP.NON.A/S   3pl-go.out-REM.P.ASSUM   3pl-come
     '(All the Tariana) dried (themselves) on a clearing; then, they went descending to what's its name, to the rapid called 'the river of parrot', they went out to stay at this rapid; they went out to this rapid'

Along similar lines, a sentence without an evidential in Quechua can be understood as having the same evidentiality value as other sentences in the same texts. Thus, if 3.12 were encountered in the context of reported information (marked with the reported evidential *si*), it would have been understood as part of reported information (Faller 2002: 23).

Cuzco Quechua

3.12 Pilar-qa   t'anta-ta   mikhu-rqa-n
     Pilar-TOP   bread-ACC   eat-PAST-3p
     'Pilar ate bread'

In actual fact, Quechua speakers vary in how easily they omit evidentials recoverable from the context (see Weber 1989: 423, for some examples from Huallaga Quechua).

Needless to say, omission of evidentials occurs only in connected speech. This presents a special problem for linguists who work with artificially obtained elicited data.

In languages where evidentiality is fused with tense, or with tense-aspect, the option of omitting an evidential is dependent on whether the corresponding tense or tense-aspect is obligatory or not. In Jarawara evidentiality is obligatory within an optional tense system. If the speaker chooses not to mark tense, they automatically choose not to express an evidential. This is different from the situation in Kalasha and Khowar, or in Northeast Caucasian languages where tense-aspect marking fused with evidentiality simply has to be there.

3.3 Scattered coding of evidentiality

A language may have grammatical expression for a number of evidential meanings but the actual markers may not form one coherent category. The morphemes then occur in different slots of the verbal word, enter in different paradigmatic relationships with non-evidentials, and have different restrictions on co-occurrence with other categories. The expression of evidentiality may itself be obligatory—but different evidentiality specifications 'scattered' throughout the verbal system by no means make up a unitary category. They still, however, qualify as grammatical evidentials; but their status is different from the systems we saw in Chapter 2.

Jacobsen (1986) demonstrated that, although Makah (Wakashan) does have obligatory evidentiality marking, this is 'scattered' among suffixes of different orders. Each forms one paradigm with other (not necessarily evidential) affixes. That is, evidentiality is simply not a morphologically unitary category, or not even a distinct category.

A similar state of affairs has been described for other Wakashan languages (Jacobsen 1986).[9] In such instances the evidential meanings expressed can be rather numerous. Markers of inference from physical evidence—evidence obtained from hearing or feeling, and uncertain visual evidence—are in paradigmatic relationship with a large set of modal affixes, such as conditional and counterfactual. Another set often includes quotative, 'inferred probability', and 'past inferential'; yet another set includes inference based on visual evidence (e.g. tracks) and evidence based on appearance; together with an additional formative suffix used in describing taste and smell. Some of these markers often provide 'merely a kind of epistemological orientation' (p. 25); whether they ought to be analysed as evidentials proper or not remains an open question.

Different kinds of suffixes and enclitics in Eskimo languages offer an even wider variety of meanings—some seemingly 'evidential', some more modal. In West Greenlandic Eskimo (Fortescue 2003) evidential meanings are expressed with several kinds of verbal derivational suffixes, plus a quotative enclitic and an adverbial particle. These affixes do not form a category of evidentiality—they are in opposition to other derivational suffixes, most of which have nothing to do with information source. Such sentential suffixes include -*gunar*- 'it seems that' (from sensory information or logical inference); and -*sima*- 'apparently' (inferred from verbal report or visual evidence left from the event). Non-sentential suffixes include -*(r)palaar*- 'one can hear something', *(r)pallaC*- 'one can hear something; reported information', and also -*(r)paluC*- 'look like, sound

---

[9] For instance, Nootka has quotative counterparts of non-indicative modes; there is an additional quotative or inferential particle: see Sapir (1924) and Jacobsen (1986: 18).

like, etc.', plus a number of others—reporting someone else's words and stating objective or quasi-objective facts.

A 'scattered', heterogeneous expression of meanings more or less related to information source implies that evidentiality is not one grammatical system. That is, semantic and other correlations between evidentials which apply within grammatical systems of evidentiality discussed under §§2.2–4 may not be operational.

Japanese is another example of a language with different possibilities for marking source of information, but without evidentiality as a unitary grammatical category (Aoki 1986). The so-called evidentials in Japanese include one reported form (marked with a nominalizer *soo* followed by a copula *da*—see 3.47–8 below), and three 'inferential' forms: *yoo da* is used when the speaker has some 'visible, tangible, or audible evidence collected through his own senses to make an inference' (Aoki 1986: 231), *rasi -i* is used 'when the evidence is circumstantial or gathered through sources other than one's own senses', and *soo da* is used to talk about events which are imminent and when 'the speaker believes in what he is making an inference about' (p. 232). The morphemes *soo* and *yoo* are nouns, while *rasi* is an adjective; the evidential specification does not appear to be obligatory. There are a few other ways to refer to how information has been obtained. For instance, a 'marker of fact' (*no* or *n*) is 'used to state that the speaker is convinced that for some reason what is ordinarily directly unknowable is nevertheless true'. This morpheme can be interpreted as referring to validation of information rather than the way it was obtained. Since 'hearsay' in Japanese can co-occur with other so-called evidentials, it could be considered a separate system on its own; in this case we could just say that Japanese has an A3 system.[10] A similar claim can be made for West Greenlandic. Systems of such kinds are somewhat problematic and thus only marginally relevant for the present study of evidentiality.

Along similar lines, evidentiality in Western Apache is expressed with a number of optional particles which by no means form a 'neat' system. Particles with evidential meanings include the non-visual sensory, and three kinds of inferentials: one based on reasoning with overtones of surprise, one based on assumption, and another one based on physical appearance. One further particle qualifies the information as 'reported' (see 3.31). These evidential particles in fact are part of a larger system of clause-final particles (which include epistemic and deontic modals, presentationals, and tense markers). As a result, Western Apache evidentials are somewhat tangential to a study of

---

[10] However, since marking information source in Japanese is a speaker's choice, it could be argued that Japanese has a range of optional devices for marking reported information, rather than grammatical evidentiality.

grammaticalized evidentiality in its own right. However, their semantics shows striking similarities with grammatical evidentiality proper; this is why they are useful for cross-linguistic comparison.

The status of evidentiality as a category can be complicated by additional factors. Evidentiality specifications may enter into paradigmatic relations with morphemes of different sorts. In Mỹky, the reported and the inferred evidentiality markers occur in the same slot as negation. In Ladakhi (Bhat 1999: 86–7), Yukaghir, Abkhaz, and most Samoyedic languages, evidentiality markers occupy the mood and modality slot in a verbal word, and are thus mutually exclusive with conditional, imperative, interrogative markers, and so on. However, this does not imply that evidentiality is a kind of mood or modality; see §8.3.

Polysynthetic languages with rich verbal morphology—such as Eskimo languages, other North American languages, such as Wakashan, or South American languages, such as Jarawara—present another problem: most verbal affixes are optional, and the traditional distinction between obligatory inflection and optional derivation is not useful (see Fortescue 2003 and Dixon 2003). An informed decision concerning the categorial status of evidentiality and what exactly is a grammatical category in these cases can be made only on the basis of language-internal criteria.

3.4 Several evidentiality subsystems in one language

In numerous languages studied thus far, all evidential markers occur in one slot, forming one paradigm, as in Wintu (2.96) or Ngiyambaa (2.25–30). Not infrequently, different evidential specifications acquire different grammatical marking. In Diyari (A4), the sensory evidential is a suffix, and the reported is a clitic (examples 2.31–4). That different evidentials are marked in different ways indicates that they could form different subsystems.

In Nganasan (B4), the three evidential specifications differ in their morphological properties. They do not occur together. The auditive, or sensory evidential, is a non-finite form (where person is marked with possessive suffixes: Gusev forthcoming), while the inferred and the reported evidentials are in a paradigmatic relationship with mood. Or evidentials may differ in their correlations with other categories. For instance, the inferred and reported in East Tucanoan languages (C1 and D1) have no present tense. In Nganasan the reported evidential is the only one to distinguish present and future. In each of these cases, evidentials are likely to form distinct subsystems.

Evidential oppositions can differ in the restrictions on their co-occurrence. In Mỹky (Monserrat and Dixon 2003), the visual and non-visual evidentiality opposition is fused with pronominal marking on the verb, while the reported and the inferred evidentials occur in a different, optional slot within the verbal word.

Different subsystems can be independent of each other. Or they may be in a hierarchical relationship. Different evidentials can occur together in one clause, to further define the source of information for an evidential, or to refer to several sources of information. If evidentials can co-occur, this means that they may well be treated as distinct subsystems. In §3.5 we look at the languages which mark more than one information source.

If a language has two coexisting systems, one of them is usually reported versus 'everything else' (A3 type). For instance, Archi (Northeast Caucasian) distinguishes firsthand versus non-firsthand (A2) in the past (Kibrik 1977: 228–32). There is also a reported marked with a different morpheme (*-er*, termed 'commentative' by Kibrik 1977). It is a distinct system of A3 type, since it combines with various moods and with any tense. Similarly, the non-firsthand ('inferential') suffix *-kex* in Jamul Tiipay (Yuman: Miller 2001: 192–3; Langdon 1970: 161) marks statements based on inference from visually obtained information. It does not refer to reported information. Reported information is marked with a clitic (Miller 2001: 200), outside the verbal inflection.

If two evidentials can occur together, they may well be considered as belonging to different subsystems. In Bora (Thiesen 1996: 97; Wise 1999: 329, ex. 33; Weber and Thiesen forthcoming; see discussion under B1 in §2.2) a 'non-witnessed' and a reported evidential can co-occur in one verb (see §3.5). The 'non-witnessed' evidential determines the source of reported information. The Bora system can be analysed as a combination of two systems, including one A1 (firsthand and non-firsthand) and one A3, rather than a three-term system. A somewhat different situation applies in Kewa (Engan, Papuan: Franklin 1971: 50, 123), where a visual/non-visual distinction is made just within the reported evidential (being fused with it).

The reported evidential is distinct from other terms in Tsafiki, with a C2 system. Examples 2.76–8 illustrate the use of visual, inferred, and assumed evidential. The reported evidential can occur on its own (often accompanied by the verb 'say'), as in 3.13 (Dickinson 2001: 7).

Tsafiki

3.13   toda-to   ka-de   ka-de   su
       explode-SS   get-ASSOC.MOT get-ASSOC.MOT   feet.off.ground
       ja-man-**ti**-e   **ti**-e
       go-sit-REP-DECL   say-DECL
       'Exploding it (the monster fish) came running to grab (him), grab (him)'
       (it is said)

The reported evidential may occur with another evidential. In 3.14, the reported specifies the source of information the 'reporter' had: the report was based on inference from physical evidence:

3.14   Manuel   ano   **fi-nu-ti-e**
       Manuel   food   eat-INFERENCE.PHYSICAL.EVIDENCE-HEARSAY-DECLARATIVE
       'He said/they say Manuel has eaten (they didn't see him, but they have direct physical evidence, e.g. dirty dishes)'

Evidentials in Qiang form two subsystems, since the reported evidential and the visual evidential can occur together with the inferred (LaPolla 2003*a*: 64).

Jarawara has three coexisting evidentiality systems. Firsthand versus non-firsthand are distinguished in past tenses for main clauses (A1 system). There is also a reported marker within the tense–modal system which typically combines with far past non-firsthand (it cannot be used with firsthand past tenses). This is a kind of A3 system; see 3.15 and 3.19 below. Kamo's father-in-law said 3.15 since he had not witnessed Kamo kill a tapir.

Jarawara
3.15   Kamo$_A$ awi$_o$ naboe-**himonaha**   Faha.biri   jaa
       Kamo(m)   tapir(m)   kill-REP.m   Fahabiri   AT
       'Kamo is reported to have killed a tapir at Fahabiri'

The reported in Jarawara can be used as a quotative; that is, the author of reported speech may be overtly stated. In 3.16, a clause with a reported suffix is followed by a clause with the verb 'say'.

3.16   Izaki$_A$ Nanatoboto$_o$ mera   kejehe-**mona,**   Tioko$_S$
       Izaki(m)   Nanatoboto(m)   3nsgO   trick-REP.m   Tioko(m)
       hi-na-hare-**ka**
       Oc-AUX(say)-IMM.P.FIRSTH.m-DECL.m
       'Izaki is reported to have tricked Nanatoboto's people, Tioko said'

In addition, an auxiliary-type secondary verb feminine *awine*/masculine *awa* marks inference based on physical appearance (translated as 'it seems/appears' or 'in my opinion' or 'I think'). This can only occur with non-firsthand, not with firsthand, past tenses (if the tense is at all marked: note that it is not marked in 3.17). It has not been attested in the same predicate as the reported suffix. When Dixon (2003: 182) displayed his rechargeable electric razor to the Jarawara, explaining that it has a motor, just like a motorboat, they agreed, saying:

3.17   moto$_o$ kiha   **awine**-ke
       motor(m)   have+f   seem.f-DECL.f
       'It appears to have a motor'

Both the reported and the 'inferential-like' secondary verb in Jarawara can co-occur just with the non-firsthand past. All in all, for a clause with past time reference (and marked tense), Jarawara offers the following choices (Dixon 2003: 186):

SCHEME 3.2 Evidentiality subsystems in Jarawara

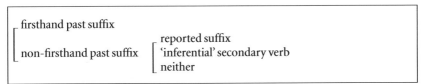

The three evidentiality subsystems differ in their restrictions on co-occurrence with tense: the inferential secondary verb can occur with future, unlike any other evidential. Both the reported suffix and the secondary verb can occur without any past suffix.

Xamatauteri (Ramirez 1994: 169, 170, 317; see C2 under §2.3) has four morphemes with primarily evidential meanings. These include two prefixes, conjecture *manaxi-* (based on indirect proof) and reported *horā-* (which may go back to an incorporated noun 'noise of'), and two suffixes, visual *-i* and inferred *no+ . . . -xi.* The latter is compatible only with one of the pasts (pre-today's past) and refers to 'unverified situation which is supposed to be true'. Inferred and conjecture can co-occur in one form (see 3.24 below). We hypothesise that Xamatauteri combines three evidentiality subsystems: visual and non-visual, and reported and 'conjecture', all having a marking of their own.

In all these instances, the coexisting subsystems of evidentials in one language somewhat differ in their distribution. We have seen that in Jarawara the three subsystems differ in whether they are actually restricted to just past tense, and whether they require a past tense marker.

Different evidentiality subsystems may be in complementary distribution depending on clause type. In Tucano the choice between a two-term system, a three-term system, and a four-term system depends on clause type as shown in Table 3.1. A four-term system of type C1 is distinguished in declarative clauses,

TABLE 3.1 Subsystems of evidentials in Tucano depending on clause types

TYPE OF SYSTEM	TERMS IN THE SYSTEM	CLAUSE TYPE
C1	Visual, Non-visual sensory, Inferred, Reported	Declarative
B2	Visual, Non-visual sensory, Inferred	Interrogative
A3	Reported (versus everything else)	Imperative

a three-term one of type B2 in interrogative clauses, and a simple A3 system in imperative clauses (see §8.1).

In Tariana, the subsystems of evidentials depending on clause type operate on the same principle, except that Tariana has a D1 system in declarative clauses.[11] In addition, purposive clauses have an A1 distinction, visual versus non-visual (see §8.1.3). Both interrogative and apprehensive ('lest') clauses have a B2 system—albeit with different marking. Interrogative evidentials overlap with declarative evidentials, while the apprehensive evidentials are completely distinct. See Table 8.2 (and Aikhenvald 2003b). Other clause types have no evidentiality distinctions (see §8.1).

The evidence in favour of neutralization of reported and inferred in interrogative clauses in Tariana and in Tucano comes from the 'conversation sustainer' question–response pattern. In the languages of the Vaupés, there is the following common strategy of showing the listener's participation in conversational interaction.

When A (speaker) tells a story, B (listener) is expected to give feedback, after just about every sentence, by repeating the predicate (or the last verb within a serial verb construction) accompanied by an interrogative evidential and interrogative intonation. For Tariana and Tuyuca, the correspondences are as shown in Diagram 3.1 (Malone 1988: 122). Tucano and a few other East Tucanoan languages employ the inferred evidential in questions as a correspondent for the reported evidential in statements.[12]

DIAGRAM 3.1. Correlations in question—response: Tariana and Tuyuca

A: visual	B: visual
A: non-visual	B: non-visual
A: inferred	B: inferred
A: assumed	B: inferred
A: reported	B: inferred

Consider the following dialogue, from Tariana:

Tariana

3.18   A: duha   Kumatharo   duka   du-nu-**pidaka**
                ART:FEM   Kumatharo   3sgf+arrive   3sgf-come-REC.P.REP
                'Kumatharo has arrived, they said (recently)'

---

[11] Traditional Tariana, still spoken by older people, has a Tucano-like system of C1 type. See the discussion in Aikhenvald (2002; 2003a, b).

[12] See full discussion in Aikhenvald (2002), and a brief mention of this strategy in Tucano in Ramirez (1997, vol.I: 144).

B: duka   du-nu-**sika**
      3sgf+arrive   3sgf-come-INFR.INTER.REC.P.REP
      'Has she?'

That is, in Tuyuca and in Tariana one interrogative evidential covers apparent, reported, and assumed: a five-term D1 system in declarative sentences 'collapses' into a three-term type B2 system.

We have seen so far that if a language has more than one evidentiality subsystem, then type A3, reported versus 'everything else'—is likely to be one of them. This is consistent with reported evidentiality and A3 systems being the most widespread across the globe.

In addition, different evidentiality subsystems within one language may be of a different origin. In the case of Tariana, only the reported system is genetically inherited from the Arawak proto-language. The rest are acquired from a variety of sources through areal diffusion (§9.2.2).

Having different evidentiality subsystems is comparable to what happens with other grammatical categories. Quite a few languages have two gender systems, a nominal and a pronominal one, with different semantic oppositions and distinct formal properties (see Heine 1982; Aikhenvald 2000: 68), or different subsets of classifiers, the choice of which depends on the modifier type (see Aikhenvald 2000).

In each of these cases the question of whether evidentiality is one category, or more, remains open for language-specific discussion. The grammaticalization of different groups of evidentials as different subsystems is consistent with the fact that evidence for any event can be acquired simultaneously in many different ways (see §10.1, on preferred evidential choices). Double marking of information source, discussed in §3.5, opens additional dimensions to evidentiality.

3.5 Double marking of information source

Some grammatical categories can be marked more than once in a constituent or in a clause. Multiple number marking usually implies the expression of the same morphosyntactic category, with the same meaning, more than once in one form, thus creating redundancy (Anderson 1993; also Chapter 7 of Aikhenvald 2003*d* and 2003*e*, for Tariana). Double case consists in marking several clausal functions on one noun phrase (for Australian languages, see Dench and Evans 1988; Dixon 1998, 2002: 147–52; see Aikhenvald 1999 for a similar phenomenon in Tariana). Double marking of gender may involve agreement with several different heads marked within the same noun phrase (Aikhenvald 1999*a*).

Marking evidentiality more than once is different from the multiple expression of any other category: it is never semantically redundant. Having several evidentiality markers in one clause allows speakers to express subtle nuances relating to types of evidence and information source, either interrelated or independent of one another. The instances found so far are discussed under (i)–(iv).

(i) TWO DIFFERENT EVIDENTIALS MARK INFORMATION ACQUIRED BY THE AUTHOR OF THE STATEMENT IN DIFFERENT WAYS FOR DIFFERENT CONSTITUENTS OF A CLAUSE. E(vidential)1 appears on the predicate and E(vidential)2 on a noun phrase (core or oblique).

Example 3.19, from Jarawara, illustrates this. Jarawara has an obligatory firsthand versus non-firsthand distinction in all past tenses, and also a reported evidential. The oblique noun phrase in 3.19 is marked for reported evidentiality: the speaker knows just by hearsay that the place where the day dawned was the mouth of the Banawá river. The story itself relates the personal experience of the speaker which took place a long time ago, and is thus cast in remote past firsthand (marked on the verb) (R.M.W. Dixon, p.c.). Constituents are in square brackets.

Jarawara

3.19   [[[Banawaa   batori]-tee-**mone**]   jaa]   faja   otaa
      Banawá   mouth-CUST-REP.f   AT   then   1nsg.EXC.S
      ka-waha-**ro**   otaa-ke
      APPL-become.dawn-REM.P.FIRSTH.f   1nsg-DECL.f
      'Then the day dawned on us (FIRSTHAND) (lit. we with-dawned) at the place REPORTED to be (customarily) the mouth of the Banawá river'

Such differential marking of information source on different clausal constituents is reminiscent of nominal tense-marking whereby the time reference of a noun or a noun phrase may be different from that of the clause, as in Tariana *waha panisi-pena alia-ka* (we house-NOMINAL.FUTURE exist-REC.P.VIS) 'there was our future house (which we saw in the recent past)'. For a typological account of nominal tense-marking, see Nordlinger and Sandler (2004).

(ii) INFORMATION ACQUIRED BY THE AUTHOR OF THE STATEMENT COMES FROM TWO SOURCES, ONE MARKED BY E(VIDENTIAL)1 AND THE OTHER BY E2. E1 and E2 either confirm or complement each other.

Qiang has visual, inferred, and reported evidentials (B1 system). The visual evidential can occur together with inferred if visual information were used to confirm the statement made on the basis of an inference. The situation described in 3.20 is as follows: the speaker first guessed that someone was playing drums next door, and then went next door and saw the person holding a drum or drumsticks. The combination of two evidentials has 'the sense of "as I had guessed and now pretty-well confirm" ' (LaPolla 2003*a*: 69–70).

Qiang

3.20 oh,   the: z̧bə   z̧ete-**k-u**
     oh   3sg   drum   beat-INFR-VIS
     'Oh, he WAS playing a drum!'

If one opens the door and sees that the other person is still playing drums, first person marker can be used to emphasize the fact of seeing something happen right now (see similar examples in §7.2). Note that the actor is third person. Adding the first person marking marks the information in the clause as obtained through direct visual perception by the speaker. This is a curious instance of 'double' marking of the person of the observer.

3.21 oh,   the: z̧bə   z̧ete-**k-u-ŋ**
     oh   3sg   drum   beat-INFR-VIS-1sg
     'Oh, he IS playing a drum!' (I, the speaker, see it)

Shipibo-Konibo has a direct evidential (which covers information acquired with any physical sense, including visual or auditory), and also an inferred, an assumed, and a reported (C2 system). The direct evidential can combine with an inferred evidential, to indicate that the reasoning or speculation is based upon evidence coming from the speaker (Valenzuela 2003: 44–6). Unlike in Qiang, the speaker uses the inferred evidential as a way of interpreting the evidence acquired visually, rather than a visual evidential to confirm one's inference. In 3.22, the woman hears a child cry (hence the direct evidential), and infers that its mean relatives have buried the boy alive (here she uses the inferred evidential -*bira*). The two evidentials appear on different constituents within the same clause (within the first clause in 3.22; the two clauses in 3.22 are separated with a comma).

Shipibo-Konibo

3.22 koka-baon-**ra**   jawe-**bira**   miin-ke,
     maternal.uncle-PL:ERG-DIR.EV   what:ABS-INFR   bury-CMPL
     bake-**ra**   sion   i-t-ai
     child:ABS-DIR.EV   ONOM   do.INTR-PROG-INC
     'What could your uncles have buried (direct evidence as a basis for inference), a boy is crying (direct evidence: the speaker can hear him cry)'

The inferred evidential can also combine with the reportative -*ronki*. In 3.23, the narrator comments on the meaning of a possibly archaic word *benta*. The reported evidential is used to refer to the source of information on *benta* (which is hearsay: this justifies the use of the reported -*ronki*). The inferred -*bira* refers to the speaker's inference in an attempt to guess what the meaning of the word could be. Later, it turned out that the speaker did have a good guess as to the meaning of *benta*: it means 'sexual partner'.

3.23   jawe   joi-**ronki**   i-**bira**-[a]i   benta   ja-boan
       what   word-REP   do.INTR-INFR-INC   benta   3-PL:ERG
       ak-á   joi-bi-ribi
       do.TRANS-PP2   language-EMPH-also
       'What could *benta* (which I learnt of by hearsay) have meant in their language (that I could infer)?'

Xamatauteri (Ramirez 1994: 317) has four evidentials (visual, inferred, 'conjecture', and reported). By their morphological status, they appear to form three subsystems (see §3.4). The marker of conjecture implies an inference based on general assumption. It can combine with the inferred marker which implies inference which is based on visual evidence. The combination of the two evidentials indicates the existence of additional evidence for an assumption. For instance, an assumption that someone was bitten by a snake is confirmed by the fact that the speaker did see the wound caused by a snake bite. This is shown in 3.24.

Xamatauteri
3.24   oru   ki-ni   pë   a   **manaxi**   tuyë-rarei
       snake   MASC.CL-ERG   3   one   CONJECTURE   bite-TELIC+DYN
       no   ku-rore-**xi**
       AUX.INFR   be-PRETODAY.PAST-INFR
       'The snake must have bitten him' (confirmed by the wound)

(iii) INFORMATION IS ACQUIRED BY THE AUTHOR OF THE STATEMENT FROM DIFFERENT BUT INTERCONNECTED SOURCES. E1 marks the fact that the information was reported to the narrator; E2 marks the source of reported information.

In Tsafiki, with a four-term evidential system of C2 type, a combination of a non-firsthand with a reported evidential specifies the source of reported information. Reported evidential can combine with any of the other three, indicating 'the type of information the original informant had for the assertion'. In 2.77, those who told the speaker that Manuel has eaten had direct physical evidence of this happening (such as dirty dishes). In 3.25, the basis of

inference (for the 'reporter') is the appearance of the canoe when he found it
(Dickinson 2001: 7).

Tsafiki

3.25   kanowa=ka   dilan=tala   ka-to   ke   ere-ka
      canoe=ACC   turn.over=DIR   get-S   throw   send-PERF
      jo-**nu-ti**-e   ti-e
      AUX.BE-INFR-REP-DECL   say-DECL
      'The canoe must have been grabbed and turned over it is said'

A similar example comes from Bora (Bora-Witoto: Thiesen 1996: 97; Wise
1999: 329, ex. 33), a language with three evidentiality distinctions (B1 type).
The inferred and the reported evidentials can co-occur in one clause. Then,
the reported evidential indicates that the speaker was told about the event by
somebody else. The non-firsthand evidential implies that the one who told the
speaker about the event had not seen it.

3.26   Hotsée-**βá-ʔhá-pʰe**   ɯmiβá   khɯɯβá-ʔóó-ha-tɯ
      Joseph-REP-NONWITNESSED-PAST   escaped   dark-room-house-from
      'Joseph escaped from jail a while back (the one who told me was not
      a witness)'

In all these cases, the position of individual evidential markers is language-
specific. In Tsafiki, the final evidential in a string refers to the source of
information for the speaker who produces the actual utterance. In Bora, the
evidential with the same type of reference comes first in the string.

(iv) INFORMATION CAN BE ACQUIRED FROM SEVERAL DIFFERENT INDEPENDENT
SOURCES BY DIFFERENT RECIPIENTS. Eastern Pomo (McLendon 2003) combines
double evidentiality marking of types (iii) and (iv), depending on the evidential.
The language has four evidentials: direct knowledge, non-visual sensory,
inferred, and reported. Reported can combine with non-visual sensory or with
inferred in myths where reported is the basic evidential. The semantic effect is
different.

A mythological narrative is typically cast in reported evidential (see §10.2.1).
This use reflects the institutionalized way in which the storyteller acquired the
information. It can then occur together with the non-visual sensory. The non-
visual sensory evidential refers to the way the information was obtained by the
main character. In this case, both the sources and the recipients of information
are different. Example 3.27 illustrates this. The non-visual sensory *-(i)nkʼe* refers
to the fact that the blind old villain could hear the hero walk out. The reported
-·le is the evidential used in traditional narratives.

Eastern Pomo

3.27   bá·=xa=khí
        then=they.say=3person.agent
        xówaqa-**nk'e-·e**
        outwards.move-NON-VISUAL.SENSORY-HEARSAY
        'Then he started to walk out, it is said (the old man villain, who is blind,
        heard the hero start to walk out)'

When the reported and the quotative evidentials occur in one clause in
Comanche (B5), the semantic effect is the same. In 2.66, the reported evidential marks the genre of the story. The quotative evidential marks what a participant said.

The reported evidential in Eastern Pomo can occur together with the
inferred evidential, and the effect is not the same. The inferred evidential
reflects the narrator's inference. In contrast, the reported indicates that the
narrator acquired the story from someone else. This is a clear case of (iii) above:
the two evidentials highlight the two ways in which the information was
acquired by the same person, the narrator. An example is 3.28, from a story
about the Bear who killed his daughter-in-law, the Deer. Such examples also
imply that 'the narrator is not quite certain as to what happened at this point in
the narrative, perhaps because he/she didn't recall exactly what was said by the
person from whom he/she had heard the narrative' (McLendon 2003: 111–12).

3.28   ka·lél=xa=kʰí   ma·ʔóral   q'á·-**ne-·e**
        simply=they.say=3pAgent   daughter.in.law   leave-INFR-REP
        'He must have simply left his daughter-in-law there, they say'[13]

In summary, evidentiality is rather unique in the ways in which it can be
marked more than once in a single clause. Double evidential marking of type
(i) is comparable to nominal and verbal tense. But there is no analogy to (ii–iv)
for any other grammatical category.

The four possibilities of double marking for information source depend on
the scope of evidentiality, and on how the two information sources relate to
each other. These are summarized in Table 3.2. Evidentials 1 and 2 can refer
to information acquired through different sources (e.g. one visual, one
reported), with a different scope (as in Jarawara), or the same scope (as in
Eastern Pomo). Alternatively, the information sources for Evidentials 1 and 2
can confirm each other, as in Qiang and a few other languages; or E2 may
specify the source for E1.

---

[13] The difference between the clitic =xa 'they say' and the reported evidential is unclear.

TABLE 3.2 Double marking of information source: a summary

	NATURE OF INFORMATION SOURCE FOR E1 AND E2	SCOPE	EXAMPLES
(i)	Different sources	Different	Jarawara
(ii)	Two different sources confirm or complement each other		Qiang, Shipibo-Konibo, Xamatauteri
(iii)	Different interconnected sources: E2 marks the source of E1	Same	Tsafiki, Bora, Eastern Pomo
(iv)	Different sources: E1 marks the source of information of a character, E2 marks that of the narrator		Eastern Pomo, Comanche

The co-occurrence of evidentials described above presents a piece of evidence in favour of several distinct evidentials forming different systems. In all these cases, it is the reported or the inferred evidential that forms a system distinct from others, since one of them can occur with some other evidential. If a language has two sensory evidentials, one would not expect them to belong to different subsystems. See §3.4 above.

Can a language mark more than two sources of information in one clause? So far, only one such example has been found. Tsafiki (Dickinson 2000: 408) allows the reported marker to be repeated to indicate up to three sources 'between the speaker and the original event'. Each source is connected to the previous one. Two sources are indicated in 3.29, and three in 3.30.

Tsafiki

3.29 tsachi-=la   jo-la-jo-**ti**-e   **ti**-e
      person-PL   be-PL-VCL.BE-REP-DECL   say-DECL
      'They say he said they were people'

3.30 Man-to=ka   ji-**ti**-e   ti-**ti**-e   ti-e
      other-earth=LOC go-REP-DECL   say-REP-DECL   say-DECL
      'They say that they say that they say that he went to Santo Domingo'

One should bear in mind that some instances of the co-occurrence of several evidentials may be of a different nature from those discussed in (i)–(iv) above. In Western Apache, when two morphemes with primarily evidential meanings happen to co-occur, only one of them keeps its evidential meaning (de Reuse 2003: 83–4). The language has one experiential evidential (describing something acquired through firsthand experience, but heard or felt rather than seen), three inferred-type, and two reported-type markers. One inferred, *lāā̧,* has an additional mirative meaning (that is, describing surprising new information; see DeLancey 1997; and Chapter 6). This morpheme can combine with a reported evidential, as illustrated in 3.31. Then it marks only surprise, and not inference.

Western Apache

3.31 ishikín   nakih   n'í   dáła'á   dayits'isxį̄į̄
      boys   two   the.former   one   3pl+3sg.PERFV.kill
      lā̧ā̧   ch'in̄ī̄
      MIR   REP
      'They killed one of those two boys surprisingly, it is said'

Kamaiurá (Tupí-Guarani: Seki 2000: 344–7) has six evidential particles. Two of them, reported (*je*) and 'attested by the speaker' (or firsthand) (*rak*), express source of information. The meaning of the other four has to do with type of evidence, direct or indirect. Direct evidence is either visual (*ehe/he*) or previously existent and now gone (*heme*). Indirect evidence (or inference) can be based on visible traces of an event (*inip*), or on the speaker's opinion or deduction (*a'aŋ*). Markers of source of information and of type of evidence can co-occur in one sentence. In 3.32, the firsthand evidential *rak* occurs because the speaker saw the snake who bit a man. Since the snake had already gone by the time the sentence was produced, *heme* 'previously existent direct evidence' must also be added.

Kamaiurá

3.32 moĩ-a   **rak**   ij-u'u-me   **heme**-pa
      snake-NUCLEAR.CASE   FIRSTHAND   3-bite-GER   PREV.DIR.EV-MALE.SPEAKER
      'It was a snake that bit him (the speaker saw it but the snake is gone now)'

The information has been acquired from the same type of source; the two evidentials differ with respect to the time of its acquisition.

Alternatively, the co-occurrence of evidential morphemes may have to do with other language-specific requirements. The reported suffix in Jarawara (Dixon 2004: Chapters 6, 10; 2003) emphasizes that the information source was hearsay. The reported can be used on its own, as in 3.15. Ninety per cent of all occurrences of far past non-firsthand (the preferred tense for traditional stories) are followed by the reported suffix. An example is given in 3.33.

Jarawara

3.33 mee   tabori-**mete-mone**   jokana   boto
      3nsg   home+f-FP.NONFIRSTH.f-REP.f   real   clearing(f)

joro   ni-kimi-ne-ke
sit(du.S)   AUX-TWO-CONT.f-DECL.f
'The two clearings of their reported past villages are there'

Tense in Jarawara—immediate past, recent past, and remote past—is fused with evidentiality. Tense is not obligatory on the clause level. If the speaker decides to overtly specify tense within a traditional story (cast in reported evidential), a choice in evidentiality needs to be made. For obvious semantic reasons, reported is not compatible with firsthand evidentiality (also see Scheme 3.2). The only choice that remains is non-firsthand. Thus, what looks like double evidentiality is in fact a result of the requirement to mark tense (already fused with one evidential) and reported evidentiality separately.

3.6 How one evidential can occur more than once

One evidential morpheme may occur several times in the same clause. Typically, the reasons for this are pragmatic. In Tariana, any verbal enclitic can be repeated to mark contrastive focus. In 3.34, the remote past reported evidential, typical in story-telling, occurs twice: first on the connective *ne* 'then' and then on the verb. The focus is on an unusual and unexpected occurrence <u>then</u>: a large canoe arriving. This is why the enclitic occurs on the connective. It is also repeated on the verb, to focus on the event itself. (Similar examples are discussed in Aikhenvald 2003c: Ch. 25.) All Tariana clitics behave this way.

Tariana
3.34 ne-**pidana**   diha   ita-whya-ne   disa
      then-REM.P.REP   ART.NF   canoe-CL:CANOE-FOC.A/S   3sgnf+go.up
      di-nu-**pidana**
      3sgnf-come-REM.P.REP
      'And then (guess what), the canoe came . . .'

Along similar lines, the reported enclitic *-pida* can be repeated on the sentence-initial element in Baniwa if there is something unusual happening. Example 3.35 comes from a story about a crab behaving in a weird way.

Baniwa
3.35 kadzu-kadana-**pida**-ni   ɾi-kapa-**pida**
      thus-NOMN-REP-3gsnfO   3sgnf-look-REP
      'He (crab) was looking like that (sideways, not normally)'

The reported morphemes in Baniwa and Tariana, from the same family, are cognates. Unlike Tariana, Baniwa has simply an A3 system (see §9.2.2 on the genesis of a D1 system in Tariana as a consequence of language contact).

Multiple evidentials in Arizona Tewa behave differently. In everyday speech, the reported evidential *ba* occurs just once per sentence. But in traditional stories (of a genre called *pɛ́:yú*) it may occur several times within one sentence, as in 3.36.

Arizona Tewa

3.36 'í-wae   **ba,** di-powá-dí   **ba,** 'ó:bé-khwó:li-ma:k'a-kant'ó-dí
      there-at REP   3plSTA-arrive-SUB REP   3pl/3.INV-fly-teach-INTENTIVE-SUB
      'From there so (*ba*), having arrived so (*ba*), they were being taught
      to fly'

The multiple use of the evidential is thus a kind of 'genre marker' (Kroskrity 1998: 28, 30–1; §10.2.1). The neighbouring Hopi also employs multiple evidentials in traditional stories of a similar genre. The emergence of this pattern in Arizona Tewa is the result of language contact (see §9.2.2).

3.7 Scope of evidentiality

An evidential usually has the whole clause within its scope. This is the case in Maricopa, in 3.37 (Gordon 1986*a*: 85). The evidential suffix is added to a negative verb (note that negation involves discontinous marking *waly- . . . -ma*):

Maricopa

3.37 waly-marsh-ma-'-**yuu**
      NEG-win+DUAL-NEG-1sg-VISUAL
      'They didn't win (i.e. they lost), I saw it'

The evidential itself cannot fall within the scope of negation. To say 'They won, I didn't see it', one has to use an independent verb 'see':

3.38 marsh-m   waly-'-yuu-ma-k
      win-DUAL+DIFFERENT.SUBJECT   NEG-1sg-see-NEG-ASPECT
      'I didn't see them win' (lit. they winning, I did not see)

Along similar lines, Kibrik (1977: 229) explicitly states that if non-firsthand forms in Archi are negated, the scope of negation is the action, and not the source of information (and see Broadwell 1991: 416, on Choctaw).

In other systems, an evidential can be within the scope of negation (pace Willett 1988 and de Haan 1999). In 3.39, from Akha (Tibeto-Burman; see Hansson 1994: 6; and discussion by Egerod 1985: 104), a negated evidential particle implies that the speaker cannot figure out from the photo what is happening. That is, visual perception (marked with the particle *ŋa*) is within the scope of negation. A similar example is under 8.38.

Akha

3.39 ɛ́   náa,   hə   à,   àdj ɛ́   ə   ṁmjɔ̀ djáŋ
      then   this noun.part what noun.part thing   make
      ə   mà   **ŋá**   é,   hə   bə
      verb.part not   EV:NONPAST.VIS.PERCEPTION FINAL.PART this one
      'Then, as (for this photo), what kind of things they are making (I don't
      know: negated visual experience), this one'

The scope of negation can be ambiguous: it can be either the information source or the whole statement. One such example comes from Warlpiri, with the reported *nganta* (Mary Laughren, p.c.). Consider the following situation. A person comes to a group of people who have gathered around someone who has obviously been attacked by someone else. The newcomer asks someone from the group:

Warlpiri

3.40 Ngana-ngku **nganta** paka-rnu
      who-ERG   REP   hit-PAST
      'Who do they say hit him/her?'

The answer may be:

3.41 ngana-ngku mayi   **nganta** paka-rnu
      who-ERG   don't.know REP   hit-PAST
      'I do not know who they reckon hit her'

When a question is formed on a clause marked for evidentiality, the action or state may be questioned, rather than the information source, as in Qiang (LaPolla 2003*a*: 73). But in other systems, the information source (that is, the evidential) can be questioned. Consider the following dialogue, from Wanka Quechua (Floyd 1999: 132). M. queries the source of information R. has, and the appropriateness of the reported evidential:

Wanka Quechua

3.42 R. wasi-i-ta   am-**shi**   yayku-llaa-la-nki
          house-1p-ACC you-REP   enter-LIM-PAST-2p
          'They say you entered my house'

3.43 M. mayan-taa   ni-n
          who-SCORN   say-3p
          'WHO says that?!'

R. answers, referring to a different information source:

3.44 R. nuna   lika-a-niki ka-ña   achka-**m**
          person see-AG-2p   be-NONPAST   much-DIR
          'There are lots of people who saw you'

The direct evidential in the last sentence is a good indicator that the speaker knows who these people are: we will see in §5.2.1 that the direct evidential is used when the speaker saw the event happen and also is certain of it. (A similar example from Bora is given by Weber and Thiesen forthcoming: 256.)

Semantically an evidential is very much like a predicate. Examples of how to tell a lie in Tariana show how one can distinguish the truth value of an evidential and that of the actual event. One can deliberately use a wrong evidential with the correct information. This is summarized in Table 3.3 (examples are referred to by their numbers). No instances of wrong evidentials with false information have been attested in my corpus.

An example of a lie is 3.45. The facts are correct, but the evidentials are deliberately wrong. The woman was annoyed that her husband had gone to look for caraná palm leaves though she had told him not to. Two days later he has not come home, and so she says to his friends:

Tariana

3.45 i-kesini   pune   ka-kaɾi-ka-**pida**
      2pl-relative caraná REL+go-PAST.MASC-DECL-PRES.REP
      hyukade-**naka**   diha ñamu   nihya-**sika**-niki
      not.appear-PRES.VIS he   evil.spirit 3sgnf+eat-REC.P.ASSUM-COMPL
      di-na   nese-nuku   na-yena-ka   na-ya-**ka**
      3sgnf-OBJ there-TOP.NON.A/S 3pl-abound-DECL 3pl-live-REC.P.VIS
      ñamu
      evil.spirit
      'Your friend is the one who had gone (to look for) caraná leaves (REPORTED:FALSE). He is not here (VISUAL). The evil spirit has eaten him (ASSUMED). There have been many evil spirits there (VISUAL)'

TABLE 3.3 How to tell a lie in a language with obligatory evidentiality: Tariana

STATEMENT	EVIDENTIAL	EXAMPLE
true	correct	1.1–1.5
true	wrong	3.45
false	correct	3.46
false	wrong	not found

In the first clause, she uses the present reported evidential. Such a form is normally employed to refer to information one has just learnt from someone else's report (see §3.8, on the time reference of evidentials). According to the story, the woman had in fact seen her husband go out to look for caraná, so she ought to have used visual evidential. In addition, she has known for two days that he had gone. So using present reported is also inappropriate: she ought to have used recent past. She is in fact using the wrong evidential with wrong time reference—as if she was quoting something she has just learnt—in order to distance herself from the whole business. This verbal behaviour is unusual and suspicious. Then she goes on to say that an evil spirit must have eaten him, using an assumed evidential. Her assumption is based on a generally known fact that there are many evil spirits in the jungle. However, by then using a visual evidential to talk about evil spirits (whom only shamans can 'see'—see Chapter 11), she betrays herself. From here on, it should be quite transparent to the hearers of the story that it is she, the daughter of a powerful evil shaman, who must be to blame for the misfortune (the man was actually eaten by a spirit).

The other option is wrong information accompanied by the correct evidential. In 3.46, a man tells a deliberate lie to an evil spirit pretending not to know what day of the week it was. In fact, he did know that it was Good Friday, when, according to modern Tariana beliefs, one is not supposed to go hunting. The non-visual evidential is always used with verbs of knowledge in such contexts (and it is also the preferred evidential option in negative clauses).

3.46 ma-yekade-**mahka**   nuha
      NEG-know+NEG-REC.P.VIS   I
      'I didn't know (what day of the week it was)'

In all these cases evidentials behave similarly to predications in their own right, unlike most other grammatical categories. In this way, evidentials resemble negation, whose marking is not infrequently achieved through a fully or partially inflected negative verb (Payne 1985: 207–22). A negative verb may take the rest of the clause as a sentential complement, as is the case in numerous Oceanic languages, yielding a structure like 'it is not the case that X'. Or there can be a negative auxiliary, as in Tungusic and numerous Finnic languages. However, negation lacks another feature characteristic of some evidential systems—a time reference of its own. See §3.8 below.

3.8 Time reference of evidentials

The time of verbal report about something happening may coincide with its actual happening, or the two may be different. That is, the time reference of an evidential does not have to coincide with that of the event.

The tense on the verb often refers to the time when the action took place (which may, or may not be the same as the time when the speaker acquired the information). This is the case in Japanese (see §3.4 and §3.7; Aoki 1986: 231).

Japanese

3.47 Kare wa   daigakusei   da-tta-**soo da**

       he   TOPIC.MARKER   university.student be-PAST-HEARSAY

       'They say he was a university student'

3.48 Kare wa   daigakusei   da-**soo da**

       he   TOPIC.MARKER   university.student be-HEARSAY

       'They say he is a university student'

The tenses (present, recent past, and remote past) of visual, non-visual, and inferred in Tariana combine reference to the time of the action and to the time when the information was acquired—this is illustrated with 3.49. That is, the time of the action and the time when the information was acquired always coincide.[14]

Tariana

3.49 iya   di-nu-ka-**naka**

       rain 3sgnf-come-DECL-PRES.VIS

       'The rain is coming' (it is coming now and I see it now)

In contrast, the reported evidential refers to the time when the reporter learnt about the event.[15] Reported evidentials in Tariana distinguish three tenses.[16] Present or very recent past refers to something reported right now, or from a minute ago to a day ago. Recent past refers to something learnt a couple of days ago, and remote past is used in all other circumstances; it is also the conventional evidential used in story-telling. The tense of the reported evidential refers exclusively to the time of the report, the time of the actual event being

---

[14] Along similar lines, the time reference of some evidentials in Tuyuca appears to relate to the time at which the information was acquired, and not to that of the action. According to Barnes (1984: 265), tense in visual, non-visual, and reported evidentials 'tells when the speaker got his information'. In contrast, tense in inferred and in assumed evidentials relates the 'assumed time of the state or event to the time of utterance'.

[15] Another example of an evidential which combines the reference to the time of event and the time when the information was acquired could be the 'immediate' evidential in Amdo Tibetan (Sun 1993: 950), which indicates that 'the speaker's basis for his assertion comes solely from perceptible evidence directly present in the immediate speech-act situation'.

[16] We have mentioned that one morpheme in Tariana typically marks tense and evidentiality. In actual fact, in some evidential morphemes tense markers are clearly segmentable: ø for present (as in -*pida* 'present reported'), -*ka* for recent past (as in -*pida-ka* 'recent past reported'), and -*na* for remote past (as in -*pida-na* 'remote past reported'). In others, the morpheme boundaries are less clear, e.g. -*mha* 'present non-visual' and -*mahka* 'recent past non-visual'. The question of segmentability of tense–evidentiality markers and of their origin is addressed in Aikhenvald (2003c: 285–9) and (2003e).

irrelevant. Present reported is often used to repeat what someone else has just said, as a sort of quotative.

Consider 3.50. The Tariana village chief had just heard on the radio the news about the untimely death of an indigenous politician, and announced it (in Tucano); Olívia Brito repeated it for my sake, in Tariana, as 3.50. Tiago had in fact died the previous day, so recent past would have been appropriate if the time reference of the actual event were at all relevant.

3.50 Tiago   di-ñami-**pida**
     Tiago   3sgnf-die-PRES.REP
     'Tiago has died' (the speaker has just learnt it)

The next day she was reporting the same piece of news to a visitor from another village, and used recent past reported (since she had learnt the information the previous day).

3.51 Tiago   di-ñami-**pidaka**
     Tiago   3sgnf-die-REC.P.REP
     'Tiago has died' (the speaker learnt about it the previous day)

A speaker who learnt the same information a long time ago would say:

3.52 di-ñami-**pidana**
     3sgnf-die-REM.P.REP
     'He died' (the speaker learnt about it a long time ago)

With a reported evidential, a clause in Tariana can acquire a 'double time' marking. If a reported action is said to be about to happen in the future, the verb is marked with a purposive and an evidential corresponding to the time when the speaker acquired the information as in the examples below:[17]

3.53 du-a-kaɾu-**pida**
     3sgf-go-PURP-PRES.REP
     'She will come reportedly' (the speaker has just acquired the information)

3.54 du-a-kaɾu-**pidaka**
     3sgnf-go-PURP-REC.P.REP
     'She will come reportedly' (the speaker has learnt the news a few days prior to the utterance)

3.55 du-a-kaɾu-**pidana**
     3sgf-go-PURP-REM.P.REP
     'She will come reportedly' (speaker learnt about it a long time ago)

---

17 This is shared with Tucano; see Aikhenvald (2002: 122–3), on the diffusion of this phenomenon.

A different time reference and the possibility of double tense-marking with the reported evidential provide an additional indication in favour of the reported as a separate evidentiality subsystem in Tariana (see §3.4).

A language can have an option for an evidential either to be within the scope of the clausal tense or to fall outside it. In 3.56, from Western Apache (de Reuse 2003: 91–2), the evidential is within the scope of past tense (to reflect this in the translation, both the source of information and the actual event are cast in past tense).

Western Apache

3.56 Izee   baa   gowąhyú   óyāā   ch'inīī
     medicine about.it home.to   3sgPERF.go.off REP
     ni'
     ASSERTED.PAST
     'I heard she went to the hospital'

In contrast, in 3.57, the asserted past tense marker *ni'* provides past reference just for the verb. The evidential is not within its scope. Note the different tense-marking on the source of information and on the main verb in the translation.

3.57 Dakīī baa   ch'inkai   lą̄ą̄   ni'
     they to.him 4PL.PERF.come INFER/MIR ASSERTED.PAST
     'It appears that they came to visit him'

The difference between 3.56 and 3.57 is not in tense-marking; it is in the scope of tense.

In numerous systems inferred evidentials have a semantic nuance of 'deferred realization'. The inference can be made simultaneously with the event—as in 2.10, from Yukaghir. Or it can be made later, after the event had happened. Some illustrative examples come from speakers' descriptions of their own actions (Maslova 2003: 223–4). In 3.58, the speaker did take part in fishing, but the fish were counted after the event. This is why he describes his own actions with the non-firsthand evidential (we can recall, from §2.1.1, that the non-firsthand evidential in Yukaghir has 'inferred evidence' as one of its meanings).

Yukaghir

3.58 ataq-un   kun'il-get ningo: i:die-l'el-d'i:l'i
     two-ATTR ten-ABL   lots.of catch-NONFIRSTH-INTR:1pl
     'It turned out (later) that we had caught more than twenty (fish)'

A similar example is in 5.7: the speaker had drunk tea without knowing that the lair of a bear was so close; he noticed the lair later.

These facts demonstrate the relative independence of evidentials—which behave, in a number of ways, as predications in their own right.

3.9 Expression of evidentials: a summary

Evidentials can be expressed with a wide array of morphological mechanisms and processes. There are very few examples of a truly functionally unmarked form in an evidentiality system. A clear-cut tendency exists as to which term tends to be less formally marked. As shown in Scheme 3.1, we expect the visual, or a combined visual and auditory evidential, to be less formally marked than any other term. Evidentiality-neutral terms are a property of a few systems where one evidential is opposed to 'everything else'. Examples are A2, A3, and B5 systems. This is quite different from omitting an evidential, which may be done either if the information source is clear from the context or if evidentials cannot be used in a particular grammatical context.

If a language has several distinct evidentiality subsystems, the reported is most likely to be set apart from others. Co-occurrence of different evidentials in one clause, and different morphological statuses of evidentials, provide tools for distinguishing evidentiality subsystems within one language. The information source can be marked more than once in a clause (see Table 3.2). This is different from simple repetition of an evidential for pragmatic reasons (see §3.6). Two sources of information can be different, with two different evidentials having different clausal constituents in their scope, as in Jarawara. Two different sources may confirm or complement each other, as in Qiang, Shipibo-Konibo, and Xamatauteri. Two sources can be different, but somehow linked together, as in Tsafiki and Bora. Or they can be fully distinct, as in Eastern Pomo. Evidentiality is thus different from any other verbal category, and rather similar to a predication in its own right. Further arguments to the same effect include:

- An evidential may be within the scope of negation, as in Akha (see §3.7).
- An evidential can be questioned, as in Wanka Quechua (see §3.7).
- The 'truth value' of an evidential may be different from that of the verb in the clause (see Table 3.3, on the various possibilities to this effect).
- And finally, evidentials can have their own time reference, distinct from the time reference of the event talked about (see §3.8).

The historical origins of evidentials confirm their similarities with independent predicates. We will see in §9.1 that the development of an independent verb into an evidentiality marker is a frequently attested grammaticalization path in the history of evidentials. And, as shown in §11.2, evidentials can be rephrased with verbs, to strengthen or to disambiguate their meanings.

4

Evidential extensions of non-evidential categories

Mood, modality, tense, person, nominalizations, and complement clauses can develop overtones similar to some semantic features of evidentials. The conditional in French can be used for information obtained from a questionable secondhand source for whose veracity the speaker refuses to take responsibility. This does not mean that this conditional has 'become' an evidential. Rather, it has acquired a semantic extension to do with evaluating an information source. Categories and forms which acquire secondary meanings somehow related with information source are called evidentiality strategies. They are distinct from evidentials proper, whose primary—and not infrequently exclusive—meaning is information source.

Evidentiality strategies include non-indicative moods and modalities (including conditional and irrealis) and future (§4.1), past tenses, resultative and perfect (§4.2), passive (§4.3), nominalizations (including participles and infinitives) (§4.4), complementation (§4.5), and person-marking (§4.6). Even demonstratives may encode auditory and visual information (see §4.7). Every language has some way of reporting what others said. Functionally reported speech is comparable to grammaticalized reported and quotative evidentials. Reported speech and quotations are discussed in §4.8. A language can use several evidentiality strategies in different contexts and with different overtones; see §4.9. Just like evidentials themselves, evidentiality strategies may, or may not, have 'epistemic' extensions of their meanings (that is, refer to the probability or possibility of something happening). A brief summary is in §4.10.

Typical meanings found among evidential extensions of non-evidential categories are remarkably similar to 'non-firsthand' (in A1 and A2 types), 'firsthand' (in A1), 'reported' (in A3), as well as inferred evidentials of several kinds. Evidentiality strategies are a frequent historical source for evidentials. We return to this in §9.1.

Every language is likely to have modal expressions indicating speaker's attitude to information, or its veracity. Should every modal expression be treated as a kind of evidentiality strategy? This is discussed in §4.11.

4.1 Non-indicative moods, modalities, and future

Non-indicative moods and modalities often develop a meaning comparable to that of a non-firsthand evidential (in A1 or A2 systems).

CONDITIONALS can acquire an additional meaning to do with the evaluation of a non-firsthand information source. French *conditionnel de l'information incertaine* is a case in point (also known as *conditionnel de l'information hypothétique, conditionnel de la rumeur, conditionnel de l'information prudente*, etc.; see Dendale 1993). This is frequent in newspaper reports, as in 4.1. Here and throughout this chapter forms with evidential extensions are underlined.

French
4.1   La flotte britannique <u>aurait quitté</u> ce matin le port de Portsmouth.
       'The British Navy would have left the port of Portsmouth this morning (we are told)'

The conditional has a variety of other meanings—future in the past, conditional, and counterfactual. It often expresses potential condition (Liddicoat 1997: 769). The conditional may also imply 'attenuation of a wish or desire', 'an imaginative use that moves events into the realm of fiction', and, most importantly for us here, it may serve 'the expression of a doubtful event, particularly hearsay' (Liddicoat 1997, Grevisse 1980).

Used in main clauses, the conditional has the following semantic features:

  (i)   firstly, it expresses 'uncertainty' concerning the information conveyed;
  (ii) secondly, it indicates that the information has been taken from some other source; and
  (iii) thirdly, the speaker/writer takes no responsibility for the information.

The second and the third meanings are reminiscent of the non-firsthand evidentials in the A1 and A2 systems discussed in §2.1. The third meaning also occurs as an extension of the reported evidential in A3 systems—see especially 2.23, from Estonian. This shows similarities between the evidential-like use of conditional and a grammatical evidential.[1]

The frequency of the evidential-like use of the French conditional varies depending on the genre. It appears to be quite frequent in scientific texts,

[1] In some semantic analyses, the non-firsthand information value is considered primary (see Dendale 1993: 175, who calls it *conditionnel d'emprunt*). A functionally similar form with similar semantic extensions has been reported in Eastern Quebec Cree; see James (1982: 386). Conditional and subjunctive moods can acquire other meanings related to the evaluation of information. In Spanish journalistic discourse, past subjunctive is used 'to mark information which can be assumed to be known to readers' (Lunn 1995: 432–4). Conditional and other non-indicative moods are often used for unreliable information (e.g. in Even: Malchukov 1995: 16; also see Haarmann 1970: 77; in Evenki: Nedjalkov 1997: 265–6; also see Haarmann 1970: 77). However, these meanings appear to remain within the limits of epistemic modality, and have no evidential extensions.

especially in the reporting of interpretations of other researchers.[2] However, this is never the only meaning of the conditional. In addition, it stresses the tentative character of one's conclusion, and interpretations of which the researcher is not quite sure. That is, the conditional combines epistemic meaning 'perhaps' with an evidential extension (Liddicoat 1997).

The German conditional also occurs in a number of contexts, one of which is to report what someone else had said. Consider 4.2 (Feuillet 1996: 79).

German

4.2 Er   sagte   ihr   ernst,   die   Einstellung
    he   said   she+DAT   seriously   ART.DEF.fem.sg   opinion
    ihr-es   Vater-s   zu   ihm   hab-e   ihn
    her-GEN father-GEN   to   he+DAT   have-COND.PRES he+ACC
    in   allerhand   Schwierigkeiten   gebracht
    in   all.kinds   difficulties   brought
    'He said to her seriously that her father's opinion about him had brought him all sorts of difficulties'

A reported speech complement in German can appear on its own as a 'de-subordinated' main clause. This type of construction is known as 'free indirect speech' (also see §4.8).[3] The conditional in such a 'de-subordinated' clause is shown in 4.3 (the clause is in square brackets). There is no overt marking of reported speech. It is the conditional that makes it clear: the sentence in square brackets is what was claimed by Miks (Feuillet 1996: 80).

4.3 Miks   bestritt   natürlich   alles.   [Von   dem
    Miks   disputed   of.course   everything.   Of   ART.DEF.masc.sg+DAT
    Bock   wiss-e   er   nichts.   Er   hab-e   nur
    goat   know-COND.PRES   he   nothing. He   have-COND.PRES only
    Krähen   schießen   wollen,   und   das   könn-e   unmöglich
    crow   shoot   want   and   this   can-SUBJ.PRES   impossible
    ein   großes   Verbrechen   sein]
    ART.INDEF   big+NEUT.SG   crime   be

[2] Consider the following example (Liddicoat 1997: 773): 'T. A. Quillam (1966) croit lui aussi que cet organe, fondamentalement tactile, **pourrait détecter** d'autres types de stimulus. Le corpuscule dermique **réponderait** à des vibrations et **serait** une "sonde vibratoire" qui **donnerait** à l'animal des "renseignements télétactiles préalables sur l'état du sol"' (T. A. Quillam (1966) also believes that this fundamentally tactile organ **could detect** other types of stimuli. The dermic cells **would react** to vibrations and **would be** a "vibratory sounding" that **would give** the animal "preliminary teletactile information about the state of the soil"').

[3] In German grammatical terminology, present conditional (or subjunctive) is called 'Konjunktiv I' and past conditional is known as 'Konjunktiv II'; see ten Cate (1996), for a brief description of their use. Also see Feuillet (1996) and ten Cate (1996) on how indicative can replace the conditional in reported speech as subordinate or main clause, depending on their semantics.

'Miks disputed everything, of course. [(According to him), he <u>knew</u> nothing about the goat. He <u>had</u> only <u>wanted</u> to shoot crows, and this <u>could not</u> possibly <u>be</u> a big crime]'

The conditional often marks reported speech in journalistic discourse 'mainly to distinguish reported speech from utterances by the reporter' (Starke 1985: 165; ten Cate 1996: 202). However, the indicative remains an alternative to it, depending on the author's attitude to the information. According to Starke (1985: 165), 'when the reported speech contains viewpoints which are considered correct and adequate by society as a whole, the indicative is preferred. In this way, the journalist expresses approval of the content of the speech he reports'. The use of the subjunctive creates a 'distancing' effect: the author does not vouch for the veracity of the statement. Not surprisingly, the subjunctive forms are extremely rare with first person: in ten Cate's words, 'there are not too many reporters who will want to distance themselves from their own words'.

A similar 'distancing' effect (*non-engagement*: Feuillet 1996: 83) is achieved by using the French conditional in cases like *Un accident s'est produit sur l'autoroute A 10. Il y'aurait dix morts.* (An accident occurred on route 10. (It is reported that) there are ten dead). It is not that the speaker doubts that ten people died. The speaker simply cannot vouch for this, since the information was not acquired firsthand. This is strikingly similar to the 'distancing' effect described for the non-firsthand in small evidentiality systems—see Chirikba (2003: 264–5). We return to this in §5.1.

Similarly, the presumptive mood in Romanian can be used with overtones of non-firsthand (Friedman 2000), while in Albanian the admirative mood developed overtones similar to the non-firsthand term in A1 and A2 systems (Friedman 2003: 205–6). In Northern Iroquoian languages the optative mood can be extended to express information source (Mithun 1986: 93–7).[4]

IRREALIS can be used in a similar way. In Mangarayi, an Australian language with a realis/irrealis contrast, one use of irrealis is to encode the event as hypothetical. Past irrealis forms are used if the speaker is 'unable to vouch for the factuality of the event because he lacks direct evidence of it (usually, did not experience it himself)'; consequently, past irrealis forms are translated as 'supposedly', 'allegedly' (Merlan 1981: 182). Merlan gives an example from a story about the flight of Aborigines from a station worker. The narrator was very young at the time, and was carried by her relatives as they fled. This explains the use of the irrealis verb form *a-ŋila-man-bub* (IRREALIS-1EXCLUSIVE-run-AUXILIARY) 'we supposedly ran', since it 'sums up the speaker's presentation of the narrative as reported from hearsay'; this goes together with various

---

[4] The abilitative verb forms in Hungarian can have inferential overtones depending on constituent order, and also intonation (Kiefer 1986 and p.c.).

indications that the speaker was not old enough to have been fully aware of what
was going on.

Irrealis forms in Semelai (Aslian, Mon-Khmer: Kruspe 2004: 281–91) usually
express hypothetical and conditional meanings. They may acquire additional,
evidential-like extensions, marking inference based on indirect evidence, and
recollections of a speaker's direct experience of past states and events. Similarly,
in Bukiyip Arapesh (Papuan: Conrad 1987), irrealis marks both inferences and
reported speech.

FUTURE indicative forms develop extensions to do with inference and
speculation. This extension arises out of overtones of uncertainty and prediction
associated with future. In Afghan Persian dialects, the periphrastic future may
develop non-firsthand meanings (Perry 2000: 243). Simple future in Andean
Spanish has a distinct non-firsthand meaning, rather similar to that of French
and German conditionals. In 4.4, the speaker knows that the children are not well
fed (and uses present tense). She then infers that their parents do not have
enough money to buy food for them. This is where the simple future appears.

Andean Spanish

4.4 los   niños   están   mal   alimentados no
    ART.DEF.pl.masc children   are   bad   fed   not
    tendrán   para   un   tarro de leche para
    have+3plFUT   for   one.masc.sg   can   of   milk for
    una   libra   de   carne
    one.fem.sg   pound   of   meat
    'The children are not well fed. They must not have enough for a can of
    milk, for a pound of meat.'

A future can occasionally develop into a non-firsthand evidential. This is
what happened in Abkhaz (Chirikba 2003: 262–4, and §9.1).

INTERROGATIVE verb forms may also acquire an additional meaning related
to information source. In Fox (Algonquian: Dahlstrom forthcoming: 117–18),
the 'plain interrogative' paradigm can be employed to indicate that the speaker is
deducing after the event what must have happened. In 4.5, the speaker did see
the victim's tracks and the tracks of a bear in the snow; there were 'also signs of
struggle and that the man had been killed and eaten. The plain interrogative is
appropriate here because the speaker did not witness the killing himself, but
rather deduces that it happened on the basis of available evidence.'

Fox

4.5 nese̲kokwe:ni̲=ma·hi·='na   mahkwani
    kill.3'.to.3/INTER=AFTER.ALL=THAT.ANIM   bear.OBV
    'A bear (obviative) must have killed that guy (proximate)'

Recent studies in Estonian grammar (Erelt 2002*a*) have demonstrated that the form homophonous with third person imperative ('jussive') marked with -*ku/gu* for all persons is employed as an evidentiality strategy. This form appears in a variety of contexts, one of which is reported speech. A jussive can also occur in a main clause, similarly to 'free indirect discourse' and rather like the German conditional. The implication then is that the source of information is someone other than the speaker. However, the main meaning of the jussive is command. Similar examples are found in Serbian, Croatian, and Slovene (Gvozdanović 1996: 67–9): here, the subordinator *da* 'that' can be added to a periphrastic third person imperative, to express that someone else is responsible for the order (or for the illocutionary value).

All these examples involve de-subordination. That is, a dependent clause comes to be employed as an independent main clause. Along similar lines, a narrative in Nyangumarta (Australian: Sharp 2004: 186) can consist of a series of imperatives as part of de-subordinated reported speech. Example 4.6 comes from a story where a dog is commanding a child to do a number of things. The verb of speech does not have to be overtly present.[5]

Nyangumarta

4.6 pala-ja   yapan   <u>ma-rra,</u>   yirti   <u>ngarta-la</u>   makanu,
     that-ABL   hot.stones get-IMPV   stick   break-IMPV   long
     wika   <u>tili-ji-li</u>
     fire   flame-AFF-IMPV
     'And after that (he told him) to get the hot stones, a cooking-stick, and to break up the firewood to make a fire'

De-subordinated structures do not appear to have any further evidential meanings. They are rather similar to other strategies used for reported speech (see §4.8).

The development of evidential extensions for non-indicative moods in main clauses can be viewed along the following lines:

SCHEME 4.1 Evidential extensions for non-indicative moods in main clauses

---

Stage 1. Unreal or potential event (marked with conditional, dubitative, potential, or irrealis), and/or an event concerning which only prediction or 'educated guess' is possible (future)
↓
Stage 2. Assumption and inference one cannot vouch for
↓
Stage 3. General range of non-firsthand meanings with epistemic overtones

---

[5] Karatjarri, also Australian, employs future forms in the same function (Janet Sharp, p.c.).

Examples of Stage 1 cover conditionals, subjunctives, and most other non-indicative moods across the languages of the world. Stage 2 and Stage 3 are interconnected. These are exemplified by Semelai, Mangarayi, Abkhaz, and Andean Spanish.

Evidential extensions for non-indicative moods in subordinate clauses, especially in complement clauses of verbs of speech, involve de-subordination, whereby an erstwhile complement clause comes to function as a main clause, with a meaning of reported speech, as in German (examples 4.2–3). The pathway of development can be schematically represented as follows:

SCHEME 4.2 Evidential extensions for non-indicative moods in non-main clauses

> Stage 1. Complement clause of a speech verb used as a main clause, meaning 'reported speech'
> ↓
> Stage 2. Meaning 'reported speech' acquires overtones of 'distancing', and facts one does not vouch for
> ↓
> Stage 3. General range of non-firsthand meanings with epistemic overtones

Stage 1 has been exemplified by Nyangumarta. The imperative used in 'de-subordinated' direct speech complements has no further non-firsthand extensions. Again, just like in Scheme 4.1, Stages 2 and 3 are linked. Examples include German, Estonian, and possibly also French. Similar extensions have been observed for a reported speech marker, and now a particle, *dizque* (lit. says-that) in Colombian Spanish; see §4.8.4. In §4.4, we discuss 'de-subordination' and the emergence of the reported evidential in Estonian.

Non-indicative moods and modalities both in main and in non-main clauses develop a range of meanings covered by the non-firsthand term in A1 and A2 systems. Before non-indicative forms can develop these meanings in an erstwhile dependent clause, this clause has to acquire an independent status; that is, it must come to be used as a main clause.

Can a non-indicative mood develop into a grammatical evidential (whose primary meaning is information source)? The presumptive mood in Daco-Romanian has developed strong overtones of inference and is comparable to the non-firsthand in A2 systems. So is the probabilitive mood in the Bulgarian dialect of Novo Selo (Friedman 2003: 191–2, 211–12). Since these moods have no other uses, they could be synchronically viewed as evidentials, of a modal origin. South Estonian reported evidential marked with -*na* could have arisen from the erstwhile potential mood (Metslang and Pajusalu 2002: 106). Occasionally, evidentials go back to future markers. We return to this in §9.1.

4.2 Perfect, resultative, and past tenses

Perfect aspect and other forms with a completive and/or resultative meaning can be extended to information source. The ensuing meaning is often similar to that of the non-firsthand in A1 and A2 systems. The semantic connection between perfect and non-firsthand goes along the following lines. The primary meaning of perfect is to focus on results of an action or process, thus relating a past event to present time.[6] In other words, an event or a process is viewed as completed in the past but still relevant for the present. An inference is made based on some traces or results of a previous action or state. Hence there is a semantic link between a non-firsthand evidential and a perfect (also see Comrie 1976: 110; and Johanson 1971, 2000b). Perfects and resultatives may extend their non-firsthand meanings to cover verbal reports.[7]

Non-firsthand extensions of perfects are found in many Caucasian and Iranian languages. The 'distanced past' in Persian, based on the perfect series of forms, covers several related meanings, such as actions which take place in the remote or distant past, or actions presented as the result of an indirect experience (hearsay, inference, or presumption) (cf. Lazard 1985).[8] Tajik (Lazard 1996: 29) seems to be developing a series of forms with non-firsthand meanings in past and present, thus being on the way to developing an evidential system out of an erstwhile strategy (also cf. Kerimova 1966: 224). Perfect in Scandinavian languages also has a distinct non-firsthand nuance (see Haugen 1972, especially examples from Ibsen's *Hedda Gabler*).

Analytic difficulties in distinguishing between an evidential extension of a perfect and an evidential proper (made in past or in perfect: see §8.4) were

---

[6] A similar defintion for the term 'perfect' was given by Nedjalkov and Jaxontov (1988: 15). This is different from PERFECTIVE aspect which specifies that the event is regarded as a whole, without respect for its temporal constituency (even though it may be extended in time). IMPERFECTIVE focuses on the temporal make-up of the event. For instance 'John baked the cake (perfective) while Mary was sleeping (imperfective)' (Dixon forthcoming; cf. Aikhenvald and Dixon 1998a). The semantic connection between non-firsthand evidentials, resultatives', and anteriors was mentioned by Bybee, Perkins, and Pagliuca (1994: 95–7). This analogy was drawn without distinguishing between languages with evidentiality as an obligatory grammatical meaning (as in Udmurt) and evidentiality as an extension for another category (as in Georgian). In their terminology, 'anterior' implies the same as 'perfect' (that is, an action in the past which continues to be relevant for the present). The term 'experiential perfect' discussed by Comrie (1976: 58–9) refers to a concept radically different from any evidential. 'Experiential' perfect indicates 'that a given situation has held at least once in the past leading up to the present' (Comrie 1976: 58; other examples are in Geniušienė and Nedjalkov (1988: 379–80) and Kozinceva (1988: 459).

[7] There are a few examples of similar developments for past tenses. According to Matras (1995), Romani employs simple past forms as a discourse strategy to distinguish between 'personal' and shared knowledge.

[8] Windfuhr (1982: 281) defines its meaning as follows: 'conclusion/assumption and absence of speaker/second-hand knowledge and reminiscence'. According to Windfuhr (1982: 282–3), some scholars equate these forms with the 'non-firsthand' -*miş* found in Turkish and other Turkic languages;—see §2.1, and Paul (1998: 91–2), for Zazaki.

discussed in §2.1.2. One example is perfect in Georgian, considered as primarily evidential by some linguists (see Boeder 2000).

The Georgian perfect—whose traditional name translates as 'first evidential' (or 'apparential')—is employed 'when the speaker is referring to a past action which he did not himself witness but assumes took place on the basis of some present result (e.g. wet ground suggests the past occurrence of rain) or because someone had told him that it did' (Hewitt 1995: 259). In such uses the perfect may be accompanied by the particle *turme* 'apparently' (Hewitt 1995: 259, 93). An example of such non-firsthand use of perfect is in 4.7.

Georgian
4.7 varsken-s   ianvr-is   rva-s   p'irvel-ad
    Varsken-DAT January-GEN   8-DAT   first-ADV
    (ø-)u-c'am-eb-i-a   šušanik'-i
    (he-)ov-torture-TS-PERF-her   Shushanik'-NOM
    'Varsken apparently first tortured Shushanik on 8th January'

This is neither the only context in which perfect is used, nor is this its primary use (cf. Hewitt 1979: 88). Perfect can be employed similarly to the present perfect in English, in sentences like 'How many deer have I and your grandfather killed?' It also occurs in negated past statements (whose positive equivalent would contain the aorist). And it can be used to refer to present, to future, or as a kind of imperative or optative. Such 'non-evidential' uses of the Georgian perfect (amply exemplified by Hewitt 1995: 260) point in one direction—that in Georgian perfect has non-firsthand meaning as an extension of its major meaning, that of result.[9] That is, the Georgian system is more adequately interpreted as an evidentiality strategy rather than evidentiality proper. This is in stark contrast to Svan (see §5.1) where the non-firsthand evidential is a separate category, with a number of distinct paradigms, only some of which historically go back to perfect.

Along similar lines, in Ishkashim (Pamir subgroup of Iranian: Nazarova 1998: 23–4) perfect forms are used to report information acquired from someone else, and for non-firsthand and assumption concerning something which has already taken place. These meanings are just extensions of the main,

[9] Tschenkéli (1958: 493) lists similar uses of the perfect in Georgian, starting with its 'non-firsthand' meaning, and then going on to illustrating its other nuances. Most sources treat the Georgian perfect as simply 'evidential', including Harris (1985: 296–306) who concentrates on diachronic perspectives rather than synchronic analysis. Unlike other Kartvelian languages, and the neighbouring Abkhaz, evidential meanings in Georgian are found only with the perfect tense group (perfect and pluperfect: Hewitt 1979; Chirikba 2003: 267), very much like the neighbouring but genetically unrelated Armenian. In Svan, Megrelian, and Laz evidential meanings are attested throughout other tense paradigms—see Hewitt (1979: 87–8), and also Sumbatova (1999).

resultative, meaning of perfect (and this is how they are analysed in Nazarova's grammar). In Dogon a non-firsthand overtone is associated with a resultative form (Plungian 1988: 491; 1995: 24), but this is not its main meaning.

In the Spanish of La Paz, spoken in contact with Aymara, 'it is relevant whether the knowledge of facts is direct or indirect' (Martin 1981: 205). The pluperfect is used to indicate 'indirect knowledge', as in 4.8. The main function of the pluperfect in Spanish of La Paz is 'past with respect to past' (Laprade 1981: 223); evidential usage is just one of its extensions.

Spanish of La Paz

4.8	Hoy día	había	llegado	su	mama	de	él
	today	had	arrived	his	mother	of	he

'Today his mother arrived' (but I didn't see her arrive)'

Preterite tends to indicate 'direct knowledge', something the speaker has seen.

4.9	Hoy día	llegó	su	mama	de	él
	today	arrive:PRET	his	mother	of	he

'Today his mother arrived' (and I saw her arrive)'

In the context of first person, the pluperfect in La Paz Spanish refers to uncontrolled, unintentional actions (see §7.2) and may then have overtones of surprise (see §6.3) (Laprade 1981: 225). Another past form, the preterite (which does not have a perfect meaning) is employed to refer to something witnessed. This can be looked at as a firsthand versus non-firsthand opposition in the making. Most probably, the pluperfect has acquired its evidential overtones as a result of Aymara substratum (see §9.2). A similar use of pluperfect, to express meanings close to those of a non-firsthand in A2 systems, has been reported for Istanbul Judezmo (Spanish Jewish language: Friedman 2003: 190) where it is considered a calque from Turkish.

In Modern Persian (Hadarcev 2001: 119) the perfect continuous can also acquire the non-firsthand meaning, and the imperfective may refer to information acquired firsthand. This is shown in 4.10. The first sentence in the direct speech part is marked with imperfective: the speaker was eyewitness to the fact that the master used to recite poetry loudly. That is, in a special context, the imperfective can be used to refer to 'firsthand' information. When the lady's words are being retold by the speaker in the last sentence, the perfect continuous is used as a marker of reported (also underlined).

Persian

4.10	"Tuye	xâne-yemân	ke	kâr
	In	house-PRON:1pl	SUB	work

mikard   hamĩše šĕ'r   <u>mixând"</u>.
do:IMPF:3sg always   poetry   recite:IMPF:3sg
Boland boland   <u>mixândeast</u>
loudly loudly   recite:PERF.CONT:3sg
'[The neighbour's wife said] "When he worked at our place, he always
recited poetry (IMPERFECTIVE: FIRSTHAND READING)". (According to her),
he recited (poetry) very loudly (PERFECT: NON-FIRSTHAND READING)'

Since perfect refers to an action whose traces are still relevant, or perhaps still
there before the speaker's eyes, why cannot it acquire a meaning close to that of
the firsthand term in an A1 system? Such extensions have been attested in a few
languages where perfect and resultative are expressed in distinct ways. Then the
resultative acquires non-firsthand extensions, and the perfect may imply that
the speaker actually saw what had happened. In Agul (Northeast Caucasian:
Maisak and Merdanova 2002), the resultative focuses on the end state, while the
perfect refers to an action in the past which carries on being relevant for
the present (this covers a variety of other meanings, including simple past).
The perfect may have had resultative meanings in the past, but these are now
lost. According to Maisak and Merdanova (2002: §2.1), 'the perfect indicates
that the person is reporting the events he himself observed', while the resultative has a whole range of non-firsthand meanings.

If a language has two perfects, one with resultative overtones, and the other one
without them, the two may extend to cover different kinds of inference. In Newari
(Genetti 1986) the verb *tọl*, meaning 'put, keep' by itself, has developed into
a marker of perfect, with an implication of 'lasting consequences of the event'.
This is similar to a resultative in that it 'denotes the resultant state'. In contrast, the
verb *dhun(-k)-*'finish', which has also grammaticalized into a perfect, does not
have such implications: it simply focuses on 'the end point of the event' (p. 64).
An additional semantic distinction between the two lies in their evidential
extensions: the resultative *tọl* implies that the speaker witnessed the resulting state
(not the event itself); it thus marks inference based on visible results, as in 4.11.
The non-resultative perfect *dhun(-k)-*marks inference of any kind.[10]

Newari

4.11   mọste-sõ̃   mhitọy-a   tọl-ọ
       children-ERG   play-PART   keep-PAST.DISJ
       'The children have played' (I can tell because the room is all messed up)

---

[10] Whether the same perfect form can encode both inference and direct witness is problematic. Such
an account for the varied semantic overtones of perfectives in Sinitic languages was provided by Chappell
(2001: 68). Whether or not these are indeed evidential extensions, or just a possible interpretation of the
idea of completion in various contexts requires reassessment.

The emergence of evidential extensions for perfects and resultatives can be viewed along the following lines:

SCHEME 4.3 Evidential extensions for perfects and resultatives

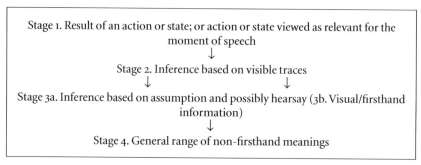

Stage 1. Result of an action or state; or action or state viewed as relevant for the moment of speech
↓
Stage 2. Inference based on visible traces
↓   ↓
Stage 3a. Inference based on assumption and possibly hearsay (3b. Visual/firsthand information)
↓
Stage 4. General range of non-firsthand meanings

If a language differentiates perfects and resultatives, the latter are likely to acquire the non-firsthand meaning extension. Perfects and resultatives as evidential strategies may develop epistemic extensions if they acquire the full range of non-firsthand meanings (similarly to non-indicative moods such as conditional, dubitative, and so on, with their meanings of probability and doubt). Perfects, resultatives, and past tenses with perfective meanings often give rise to small evidentiality systems of A1 and A2 types (see §9.1).

Past tense forms can develop into an evidentiality strategy similar to reported evidentials. Special narrative past tense forms may become markers of particular genres of story-telling (cf. §10.2.1). Takelma (isolate) (Sapir 1922: 296) had a narrative past, used in stories and independent from evidentiality marking. Sierra Miwok (Freeland 1951: 87) had imperfect and perfect narrative forms in formal story-telling (alongside perfect and present tense forms also employed in stories: p. 63). And Itelmen (Jacquesson 1996: 216–20) has a set of verbal forms restricted to myths. Narrative past tenses typically have no epistemic extensions. (Also see Longacre 1990, for a discussion of tenses and aspects as tokens of narrative genres in a number of African languages.)

4.3 Passives

A prototypical passive involves focusing attention on the original object (the subject of the clause that is passivized) and also focusing on the state it is in, as a result of the action (Dixon and Aikhenvald 1999: 8; Dixon 1994: 149). As a consequence, passives often have resultative connotations (also see Haspelmath 1994: 157–62, on the links between resultative and passive participles). Not unexpectedly, passives acquire the same evidential extensions as do resultatives.

The impersonal passive in Lithuanian (Timberlake 1982; called non-agreeing passive by Gronemeyer 1997: 97–100, 102–6) is a case in point. It is used when some direct physical evidence is available for the statement; the inference is based on visible results. Lithuanian also has a reported evidential (formed on the basis of active participles: see Mathiassen 1996: 134–5, §3.1, and §8.1).[11]

Lithuanian

4.12   čia   žmoni-ų   gyven-ta
        here   people-GEN.PL   live-PASS.PAST.NOM.NEUTER
        'People have evidently been living here'

The impersonal passive covers a wide range of modal meanings like supposition, possibility, and doubt (Timberlake 1982: 510 and Gronemeyer 1997: 106) as well as inference. The impersonal passive is often used as a resultative (Ambrazas 1990), and is formed with the past passive participle (with an optional copula), which in Lithuanian has a typical perfect meaning, marking past actions still relevant to present.[12] Its evidential extensions are similar to those expected for a perfect or a resultative.

A connection between a passive and a non-firsthand has been noted by Kendall (1976: 28–30) for the marker -o- in Yavapai. This form translates into English as a 'get'-passive with a non-firsthand meaning. It is used if the speaker has observable evidence for the statement (such as seeing a person with a rash, or lying down, and then saying: 'He or she is sick').

One of the two passives in Wasco-Wishram (Silverstein 1978) implies an inference or an assumption (the example given is 'they must have boiled'). We do not have enough data to decide whether this is an evidentiality system or 'just' an extension of passive. The 'evidential passive' goes back to an erstwhile locational construction. According to Silverstein (1978: 246), 'the passives of evidence originally entered Wasco-Wishram idiomatic speech as forms pointing out where such-and-such an action took place, as a conversational equivalent to referring to the evidence for that action'. An evidential extension here lies in the deictic nature of the construction: the focus is on the visible and tangible evidence for the event.

4.4 Nominalizations

Nominalizations with a resultative meaning or past tense reference often develop non-firsthand overtones, in the same way as perfects and resultatives discussed in §4.2. Deverbal nominals of all sorts, including deverbal nouns,

---

[11] Impersonal passives in Lithuanian may be formed on transitive and intransitive verbs (Timberlake 1982: 522).

[12] See Holvoet (2001: 378–9) on the history of Lithuanian passives.

participles, gerundives, gerunds, converbs, and infinitives, can all acquire evidential overtones. The term 'nominalization' has been chosen here to cover a wide variety of non-finite deverbal forms.[13]

Nominalizations develop evidential extensions when used as (*a*) head of predicate, or as (*b*) part of a complex predicate.

(*a*) NOMINALIZATIONS AS HEAD OF PREDICATE

In Nenets folklore, past participles are employed as a narrative technique (Perrot 1996: 163; Tereschenko 1973: 144). Similarly, in Purépecha (Tarascan) (Chamereau 2000: 256–7), using an infinitive as predicate head is a widespread device in traditional narratives (alongside an inflected verb). Past participles in Mansi (Ob-Ugric: Perrot 1996: 158) are sometimes used for describing processes or actions in which the speaker has no direct involvement (e.g. hearsay, or non-firsthand), as in 4.13. (Skribnik 1998 considers these as a special evidential paradigm.)

Mansi

4.13   ta   xontl-unkwe   patiyla-m-ot
        there   fight-INF   start-PAST.PART-3pl
        'They started fighting there, they say'

Resultative nominalizations in Panare (Payne and Payne 1999: 48–9, 116–8) are used as evidential strategies in a somewhat different way. The past participle in -*jpë* refers to the result of a past action; when used as the predicate head it describes an inference from visible results. When one can see that a tree is gone, and just its stump remains, 4.14 is appropriate.

Panare

4.14   yï-kïtë-jpë   mën
        3-cut-PART.PAST.INFER   INAN
        'It's (apparently) been cut'

The past participle in -*sa*' refers to a result of an action; so if the speaker observes 'firsthand' that the tree has been cut, 4.15 is used.

4.15   yï-kïtë-sa'   mën
        3-cut-PART.PERF   INAN
        'It's been cut' (it's a cut thing)

The two nominalizations each have a variety of other meanings, both as heads of noun phrases and as modifiers, and as predicate heads. For instance, the -*sa*' nominalization expresses passive and also perfect aspect, while the -*jpë*

---

[13] A detailed semantic classification of nominalizations is in Comrie and Thompson (1985); Haspelmath (1994) provides a useful overview of participles or deverbal adjectives.

nominalization refers to past actions whose effects are no longer apparent. The Panare nominalizations show some similarity to a two-term A1 system.

Past participles gave rise to the past forms of reported in Standard Estonian. A past reported is under 4.16. This is a typical beginning of a folk tale.

Estonian

4.16 **ela-nud** kord eit ja taat
live-PAST.REP(=PAST.PART) time old.woman and old.man
'Once upon a time there lived an old man and an old woman'

This same participle is used in a variety of other ways, e.g. as a modifier and as past imperative (Erelt 2002*a*: 115–16). The past reported could have developed as a result of omission of the copula in perfect forms used as erstwhile evidential strategies for reported speech (see Künnap 1992: 209). (Further discussion is in Wälchli 2000: 193; also see Tuldava 1994: 262.) And see Muižniece, Metslang, and Pajusalu (1999) for other possible ways of 'finitisation' of the past participle. In Estonian—unlike other languages discussed in this section—the past participle has become a firmly established component of the reported paradigm (see §9.1).[14] In Lithuanian, the reported evidential goes back to an active participle.

(*b*) NOMINALIZATIONS AS PART OF A COMPLEX PREDICATE

A nominalization with perfect meaning as part of a complex predicate can acquire an evidential extension similar to that found for perfects and resultatives. Tucano has an evidential strategy used when the speaker's statement is based on having seen the result of the action and not the actual thing happening. The construction involves a perfective or resultative nominalization of the main verb and the auxiliary *niî* 'be, do' which takes a visual evidential specification (see Ramirez 1997, vol. I: 140–1, 291–2; West 1980: 75–6 calls this 'verificational construction'). A speaker who has received a letter from his mother would say 4.17. He did not see his mother write the letter, but the result of her writing—the letter—is a visual enough result for him (West 1980: 75).

Tucano

4.17 yi'î pako <u>ohá-ko</u> <u>niá-mo</u>
I mother write-NOMN.PERF.3sgfem be-PRES.VIS.3sgfem
'My mother has written the letter' (I did not see her write it, but the letter constitutes the proof)

---

[14] The ways in which the Estonian system has been shaped were partly conditioned by the activities of language reformers—for instance, Johannes Aavik (see Perrot 1996: 159). The paradigm of four tenses given by Fernandez-Vest (1996: 172) is as follows (the verb *tule-*'come'): present reported: *tule-vat*; simple past *tul-nud* (=PAST.PART); perfect or completed past *ole-vat tul-nud* (be-PRES.REP come-PAST.PART); pluperfect *ol-nud tul-nud*. Viitso (1998: 141) cites somewhat different forms for simple past: *sööt-nu-vat* (feed-PAST.PART-PRES.REP). These forms were introduced during the Estonian language reform in 1922, but not uniformly accepted.

This construction is often used when telling someone else about one's personal experience, since the visually obtained information and inference based on visible results is highly valued in the Vaupés culture. (Also see Aikhenvald 2002: 123.)[15]

Nominalizations may combine epistemic meanings ('it is possible that') with reference to the source of information. Qiang, a Tibeto-Burman language with a three-term evidentiality system (LaPolla 2003a: 72), also uses nominalizations with a copula to express epistemic meanings which imply some kind of assumption, as in 'it might rain', 'to make a strong statement of certainty, or of information that was not recently discovered'. This is in addition to a three-term evidential system.

Compound verbs can develop other evidential-like meanings. Bashir (1988: 53) reports that Kalasha employs compound verbs consisting of the perfective participle and a finite form of verbs 'go' or 'put'. Compounds with 'go' are associated with the semantics of 'prepared mind' (which is typical for firsthand evidentials) and are used to describe undesirable situations of which one has premonitory awareness. Compounds with 'put' are to do with 'unprepared mind': something one is not aware of, or something one really understands only after it had happened. The semantics of 'unprepared mind' is typically associated with non-firsthand evidentials.

Nominalizations used to mark an erstwhile complement clause can develop into a reported evidential once the dependent clause starts being used as a main clause. This scenario has been documented for present reported in Standard Estonian and a number of Estonian dialects (see §4.5 below and discussion in §9.1.3).

4.5 Complementation

Subordinating morphemes which introduce complement clauses can distinguish meanings related to information source and speaker's degree of belief in—or degree of commitment to—the proposition (see Givón and Kimenyi 1974 and also Givón 1982 on the choice of complementizers with cognition verbs in Kinyarwanda; similar phenomena in Chadic languages were described by Frajzyngier 1991: 227; 1995; Frajzyngier and Jasperson 1991; and Frajzyngier 1996: 105–200). Verbs of perception and cognition in English take several kinds

---

[15] A similar analytic construction, with the verb 'be' and a visual evidential, is used in Desano (Miller 1999: 64) and Wanano (Waltz and Waltz 1997: 38; and also Malone 1988: 135). These constructions have grammaticalized into 'inferred' evidentials for other Tucanoan languages, such as Tuyuca. The Tucano evidential strategy has influenced the emergence of the inferred evidential in Tariana, exemplified in 1.3.

of complement clauses. A *that* complement clause 'refers to an activity or event or state as a simple unit, without any reference to its internal constitution or time duration' (Dixon 1995: 185). In contrast, an *-ing* complement clause contains reference to an activity 'as extended in time, noting the way in which it unfolds'. As a result, different complement clauses may serve to distinguish an auditory and a hearsay meaning of some verbs, for instance, *hear*. Saying *I heard France beating Brazil* implies that I actually heard how this happened. It would be an appropriate thing to say if I had actually been listening to the match on the radio, and did hear, say, the description of the winning shot. Saying *I heard that France beat Brazil* implies that I have heard the results of the match, that is, the information was reported to me. (Along similar lines, Kirsner and Thompson 1976 distinguish between 'direct perception of a situation' and 'deducing a situation' in their analysis of complements of sensory verbs in English.)

Russian achieves a similar effect by choosing different complementizers with verbs of perception and cognition. The conjunction *kak* implies direct perception (Barentsen 1996: 24), while the conjunction *čto*, a general complementizer, implies that what the speaker actually perceives is a clue, or basis of an inference which may give give an idea about the situation. Example 4.18 can only be used if Len saw Margie playing.

Russian

4.18 Len   videl,   kak   Mardži igraet
      Len   see+PAST+sg.masc   how/that   Margie play+PRES+3sg
      v   kroket
      in   croquet
      'Len saw Margie play croquet'

Example 4.19 implies that all he saw was some indications that she had played—her mallets, balls, and so on.

4.19 Len   videl,   čto   Mardži igraet   v
      Len   see+PAST+sg.masc   that   Margie play+PRES+3sg   in
      kroket
      croquet
      'Len saw that Margie played croquet'

With the verb 'hear', *kak* marks information acquired by actual hearing, while *čto* implies information obtained through hearsay. Example 4.20 means that I was at the hostage scene and heard what was happening—shouts, gun shots, and the like.

4.20   ja   slyshal,   kak   chechency   vzjali
       I   hear+PAST+sg.masc   how/that   Chechens   take+PAST+pl
       zalozhnikov
       hostages+ACC.PL
       'I heard the Chechens take the hostages'

Example 4.21 implies that I heard the information from someone else.

4.21   ja   slyshal,   čto   chechency   vzjali
       I   hear+PAST+sg.masc   that   Chechens   take+PAST+pl
       zalozhnikov
       hostages+ACC.PL
       'I heard that the Chechens took the hostages'

Boumaa Fijian has a similar strategy. Here, the difference between a clausal NP and a *ni* complement corresponds to the distinction between a firsthand and a hearsay source of information (Dixon 1988: 38). In 4.22, a clausal noun phrase complement means that I heard the match. The clauses are in square brackets.

Boumaa Fijian

4.22   au   aa   rogo-ca   [a   o-dra   qaaqaa   a   cauravou   yai]
       1sg   PAST   hear-TR   ART   CL-3pl   win   ART   youth   this
       'I heard these youths winning'

And in 4.23, all I heard was a verbal report.

4.23   au   aa   rogo-ca   [ni+ra   qaaqaa   a   cauravou   yai]
       1sg   PAST   hear-TR   THAT+3pl   win   ART   youth   this
       'I heard that these youths had won'

Complement clauses as evidentiality strategies tend to be restricted to verbs of perception and cognition. If the choice between several complement clauses correlates with evidential-like distinctions, the following predictions can be made:

(i)   Complement clauses marked with the most frequently used general complementizer are likely not to have any perceptual overtones, as is the case in English, Fijian, and Russian.

(ii) Clausal noun phrase complements, or nominalizations, tend to convey perceptual overtones, as in Fijian. In Japanese (Dik and Hengeveld 1991: 242–4) complementizers *no/koto*, which nominalize the clause, have evidential overtones, while the general complementizer *to* does not.

Complement clauses to verbs of saying can give rise to evidentials through their reanalysis as main clauses. One of the paradigmatic forms of reported evidential in Standard Estonian developed as a result of such reanalysis.[16] The present reported in Estonian came from the partitive case form of the active participle originally used in complement clauses (cf. Ikola 1953; Campbell 1991; Harris and Campbell 1995: 99; Wälchli 2000: 194–6). This is a clear instance of how a verbal form whose only meaning is evidential developed out of an erstwhile strategy (see §9.1). A similar development probably took place in Livonian, also Balto-Finnic. Here, the marker of reported is *-ji*, used to derive agent nouns, and as a present participle (Laanest 1975: 155; 1982: 239). And see Wälchli (2000: 194–5), on similar processes of reanalysis of complement clauses as main clauses in the history of Latvian and Lithuanian reported evidentials.[17]

4.6 Person-marking

When making a statement, it is up to the speaker to establish the information source. If a speaker was involved in the action, he or she may be expected to have direct evidence available. A story told in first person often recounts what happened to the narrator, that is, things he or she experienced directly. In languages with grammatical evidentiality, one may expect different possibilities for evidentiality marking depending on person. We will see in Chapter 7 how some languages have restrictions on the use of first person with reported or inferred evidentiality. Alternatively, a non-visual or a reported evidential with first person has additional meanings; such 'first person effects' are also found for some evidentiality strategies (§7.2). An evidential can combine reference to speaker and to addressee and also to information source (see example 2.88a, from Mamainde, in §2.3; and §7.3.1).

The choice of person-marking itself may correlate with information source, and the speaker's attitude to it. This is the case in languages with the so-called disjunct and conjunct participant marking (also known as congruent–non-congruent). In these languages statements which contain a first person

[16] For an up-to-date account of the forms of reported evidential paradigm in Estonian, see Fernandez-Vest (1996), Perrot (1996), and also Laanest (1975: 155–6) and Tauli (1973–83). Somewhat different forms are in Viitso (1998) (these forms could have come from Võru dialect: Bors Lees, p.c.). For an overview of dialectal variants, see Metslang and Pajusalu (2002).

[17] A complementizer may be chosen depending on the degree of certainty the speaker has (see, for instance, Akatsuka 1978, 1985 on the choice of complementizers in Japanese; and further examples in Noonan 1985). This is only tangentially relevant to evidentiality inasmuch as some evidentiality specifications can have meaning extensions to do with evaluating the probability or the certainty of the event (see Chapter 5). Further epistemic and evaluative connotations of complement clauses, equally tangential to the analysis of evidentials, are discussed by Thompson (2002).

participant are marked differently from those which do not; and in questions the second person is marked in the same way as first person in statements. This type of system is also known as 'locutor' versus 'non-locutor': 'locutor' refers to first person in statements and to second person in questions, and 'non-locutor' covers second or third person in a statement, and first or third person in a question. Classical examples come from Tibeto-Burman languages—these were described by Hale (1980) for Newari and Schöttelndryer (1980) for Sherpa (also see Woodbury 1986: 192). They are also found in a few Barbacoan languages from South America (an overview is in Curnow 2002*b*).

Conjunct–disjunct participant markers can acquire additional meanings related to the source of information and a speaker's participation in the action. Tsafiki, a Barbacoan language spoken by the Tsachi (Dickinson 2000), has two construction types. One appears with first person in statements and requires 'conjunct' marking, as in 4.24.

Tsafiki

4.24   tse   Tsachi   jo-y̱o-e
        1.FEM   Tsachi   be-CONJ-DECL
        'I am a Tsachi'

The other one occurs in all other contexts and requires 'disjunct' marking; see 4.25.

4.25   ya/nu   Tsachi   jo-Ø-e
        3/2   Tsachi   be-(Ø.DISJ)-DECL
        'He/you are a Tsachi'

In questions, the conjunct marking typically occurs with second person; see 4.26.[18]

4.26   nu   seke   tera   ki-y̱o-n
        you   good   dance   do-CONJ-INTER
        'Did you dance well?'

Woodbury (1986: 192), in his study of Sherpa, a Tibeto-Burman language with a similar system, explains it this way: 'second person forms in questions anticipate the use of first person in the answer'.

---

[18] Tsafiki has a special disjunct marking for first person in questions:

(i)   la   seke   tera   ki-i-n
      1M   good   dance   do-DISJ-INTER
      'Did I dance well?'

Disjunct and conjunct forms contrast in meaning if used with a 'wrong' person. When disjunct forms are used with first person in statements, they may indicate that the speaker did something unintentionally, without being in control. In 4.27, the pig was killed intentionally, and the speaker uses the conjunct marking.

4.27 la   kuchi=ka   tote-yo-e
      1M   pig=ACC   kill-CONJ-DECL
      'I killed the pig' (intentionally)

In 4.28, disjunct marking is used: the speaker did not mean to kill the pig.

4.28 la   kuchi=ka   tote-i-e
      1M   pig=ACC   kill-DISJ-DECL
      'I killed the pig' (unintentionally)

Disjunct forms with first person may indicate a speaker's surprise, that is, have mirative overtones (see §6.3, and the discussion of Lhasa Tibetan there), or be used ironically. Example 4.29 is a simple statement of a fact; as expected, conjunct marking is used (Dickinson 2000: 388). The pronoun is omitted.

4.29 unila   jo-yo-e
      man   be-CONJ-DECL
      '(I) am a man'

A distinct overtone of irony is present in 4.30: this was uttered in a situation when a woman was complemented for her prowess in soccer. Someone said she played like a man, and she said 4.30, with a shrug of her shoulders.

4.30 unila   jo-i-e
      man   be-DISJ-DECL
      '(I) am a man, indeed!'

Example 4.31 is a normal way of saying 'I have money'. The conjunct marking appears, as expected. The personal pronoun is omitted: first person reference is understood, based on the marking on the verb.

4.31 kala   ta-yo-e
      money   have-CONJ-DECL
      '(I) have money'

If the speaker suddenly discovers to his surprise he has some money which he did not think he had, the disjunct marker would be used.

4.32   kala   ta-i̱-e
        money   have-DISJ-DECL
        '(I) have money!' (what a surprise!)

Conjunct markers can in turn be used with third person subject. Then the implications are that the speaker is a knowing participant. Such constructions are used to refer to something the speaker knows firsthand: in 4.33 the conjunct marker indicates that the speaker is a knowledgeable member of the group (despite the fact that the sentence contains a third person subject).

4.33   amana   tsachi=la   fi-tu-min=la   jo-yo̱-e
        now   Tsachi-PL   eat-NEG-NOMN=PL   be-CONJ-DECL
        'Nowadays, we, the Tsachi, do not eat snakes' (lit. the Tsachi do not eat snakes)

Person-marking in this and other conjunct–disjunct systems codes the degree of congruence of the information with the speaker's general knowledge, and thus is indirectly connected with the way of obtaining information. The conjunct marking—especially when used with third person—has an overtone of information integrated into the person's knowledge. The disjunct marking when used with first person produces the effect of unintentional action, surprise, or irony. That is, in conjunct–disjunct systems, the choice of person-marking acquires an additional evidentiality connotation in that it can be used as an evidentiality strategy.

We can recall that Tsafiki also has a four-term evidentiality system (C2 in §2.3; visually acquired information is formally unmarked as in the examples above). There is a certain degree of semantic agreement between the person-marking (conjunct or disjunct) and the evidential choice. The two non-first-hand evidentials require disjunct marking when used with first person; conjunct marking would be ungrammatical. This is hardly surprising, given that non-firsthand evidentials with first person in Tsafiki can only describe an unexpected event which the speaker infers after it had happened. In 4.28 the disjunct person marker indicates that the speaker did not mean to kill the pig— he could have run over it with his car. In 4.34, the inferred evidential implies that the pig was killed accidentally, and that the speaker is inferring from some (visual) evidence what must have happened (he may have given the pig some medication and inadvertently caused its death—Dickinson 2000: 412–13).

4.34   la   kuchi=ka   tote-i̱-nu-e
        1M   pig=ACC   kill-DISJ-INFR-DECL

'I must have killed the pig' (unintentionally, and realized this based on physical evidence)

Thus, the non-firsthand evidentials and disjunct first person marking have a combined semantic effect of lack of intention and lack of control on the part of the speaker.

The Tsafiki system displays striking similarities with the conjunct–disjunct system in copular verbs in Lhasa Tibetan (DeLancey 1986, 1990*b*, 1992, 1997, 2003: 278–9; Tournadre 1994, 1996). Lhasa Tibetan has two conjunct and two disjunct copulas; see Table 4.1.

The conjunct forms of a copula occur with first person subject in statements, and with second person subject in questions. Disjunct forms occur elsewhere. Example 4.35 is equivalent to Tsafiki 4.31.

Lhasa Tibetan (DeLancey 2003: 279)

4.35 nga-r   dngul   tog=tsam   yod
     I-DAT   money   some   EXIST/CONJ
     'I have some money' (lit. some money is to me)

Just like 4.32 in Tsafiki, the disjunct copula is used in Lhasa Tibetan with an implication that the speaker has just discovered money he thought he did not have.

4.36 nga-r   dngul   tog=tsam   'dug
     I-DAT   money   some   EXIST/DISJ
     'I have some money!' (what a surprise!)

Conjunct–disjunct person-marking systems are not evidential in nature (see DeLancey 1986: 206–10 and Caughley 1982: 84–5 for Chepang, also Tibeto-Burman). They may, however, be similar to evidentials in their semantic extensions, and also in their interaction with evidentials proper (if the language happens to have them).

Evidential-like meanings developed by conjunct–disjunct person-marking are similar to non-firsthand evidentials in A1 and A2 systems in the way they

TABLE 4.1. Conjunct and disjunct copulas in Lhasa Tibetan

	CONJUNCT	DISJUNCT
Equational copula	*yin*	*red*
Existential copula	*yod*	*'dug*

correlate with person. If used with first person, the disjunct marking implies unintentional action of which speaker takes no responsibility. We return to these 'first person' effects of evidentials in §7.2.

The opposition between locutor (first person in statements, second person in questions) and non-locutor (the rest) can be expressed in yet another way, extending to further ways of obtaining information. In Japanese a locutor versus non-locutor distinction is made for a subgroup of predicates which deal with feelings and sensations. These predicates can be used with first person subject reference, as in 4.37, since only the experiencer is supposed to have access to information regarding his or her internal state. The same form can be used with second person in questions.

Japanese
4.37   Atu-i
        hot-NON.PAST
        'I am hot'

When the subject is third person, a non-firsthand marker *-gar* 'display symptoms of being...' must be used as in 4.38 (Aoki 1986: 226-7).

4.38   kare   wa   atu-gatteiru
        he   TOPIC   hot-*GAR*+GERUNDIVE+NON.PAST
        'He is hot' (that is, he displays symptoms of being hot)

The marker *-gar* does have an evidential-like meaning since it marks information about other people's states and feelings—which cannot be acquired directly. This marker is used to describe feelings and sensations of a first person experiencer as well as those of a third person if 'there is a shift in time away from the time of speaking' (Aoki 1986: 226), and in neutral, 'non-reportive' style; the same marker also has the meaning of 'acting as if', as in 4.39 (p. 227).

4.39   Sonnani   atu-garu   na
        so.much   hot-*GAR*   NEG.IMPV
        'Do not act so hot' (it cannot be that hot)'

Similarly, 'sensory' adjectives in Korean operate on a conjunct–disjunct basis. They denote what Sohn (1994: 99) calls 'an unobservable internal state of mind' and occur only with first person subject in statements and second person subject in questions, as in 4.40–1.

Korean
4.40   na-nun   Nami-ka   pwulep-ta
        I-TOP   Nami-NOM   envy-DECL
        'I envy Nami'

4.41 ne-nun   Nami-ka   pwulep-ni
      you-TOP   Nami-NOM   envy-Q
      'Do you envy Nami?'

A sentence like 4.42 is ungrammatical: one cannot make statements about someone else's internal feelings. It can be acceptable only if 'the speaker makes a dogmatic assertion, knowing or believing or pretending to know the subject referent's state of mind'.[19]

4.42 ? ne-nun   Nami-ka   pwulep-ta
         you-TOP   Nami-NOM   envy-DECL
         'You envy Nami'

To make statements about other people's feelings, one can use a variety of strategies: the expression -*(u)n moyang ita* 'appear to be', or the modal suffix -*keyss* 'maybe', or the 'indicatory verb construction' -*e hata* 'show signs of'. These possibilities are shown in 4.43a–c.[20]

4.43 a   ne-nun   Nami-ka   pwulew-un
          you-TOP   Nami-NOM   envy-MODIFYING.SUFFIX
          moyang   i-ta
          appearance be-DECL
          'You seem to envy Nami'

4.43 b   Yongho-nun   Nami-ka   pwulep-keiss-eyo
          Yongho-TOP   Nami-NOM   envy-MAY-POLITE
          'Yongho may envy Nami'

4.43 c   Yongho-nun   Nami-lul   pwulep-e   ha-n-ta
          Yongho-TOP   Nami-ACC   envy-INF   show.signs-IND-DECL
          'Yongho envies Nami' (lit. shows signs of envy towards Nami)

The primary meaning of these constructions is not information source. That is, they do not qualify as evidentials. Only marginally do they relate to how

---

[19] This restriction applies only in the present tense; in the past tense one can very well say *Yongho-nun Nami-ka pwulew-ess-ta* (Yongho-TOP Nami-NOM envy-PAST-DECL) 'Yongho envied Nami'.

[20] The so-called 'retrospective mood' in Korean (Chang 1996; Sohn 1994: 48, 341–2, 350) marked with the suffix -*teo*- also operates on the conjunct–disjunct principle. Its main function is the validation of 'past perception, observation, or experience' of the speaker in a statement, or of the hearer in a question rather than establishing the information source. Hence its semantic breadth: depending on the context, retrospective mood can refer to a directly witnessed event, inference, or reported speech. As demonstrated by Chang (1996: 193), this is not a primarily evidential form (also see Sohn 1986: 137–54). Korean has yet another strategy allowing it to distinguish between describing a character's mental state from an internal point of view, and describing it from the point of view of external observer. This is achieved through a combination of verbal derivation and nominal case marking (see discussion by Chun and Zubin 1990). However, this is not directly linked to person-marking or evidential extensions.

the information has been acquired. The distinction made between one's own feelings and states and those of the 'other' are pervasive in evidentiality systems—see §7.2–3. They often correlate with conventionalized ways of talking about the way someone feels—see §11.3.[21]

4.7 Perceptual meanings in demonstratives

Meanings related to perception may be encoded within the grammar by means other than evidentiality systems. A number of languages have a grammatical system of demonstratives with one or more terms referring to visible objects. Visibility in deictic systems may correlate with proximity to the speaker, and/or to the addressee, and/or to a third person. Kwakiutl, a Wakashan language with at least three evidentiality terms (Boas 1910, 1911b: 496), has six demonstratives, with an obligatory visible/non-visible distinction: 'visible near me, invisible near me; visible near thee, invisible near thee; visible near him and invisible near him' (Boas 1910: 527). Demonstratives in Shoshone (Uto-Aztecan: Miller 1996: 709) combine reference to proximity and to visibility of an object: its four-term system of demonstratives consists of 'near', 'not quite so near', 'far but not in sight', and 'not in sight, usually far'.

In Eskimo, demonstratives combine reference to boundedness and visibility of the objects (see Aikhenvald 2000, table 7.4, for their analysis as deictic classifiers; see Woodbury 1981: 237–8; also Denny 1979). Jarawara has a two-term demonstrative system: 'here, visible' and 'here/there, not visible'. And see Anderson and Keenan (1985: 292–3) on the distinction between 'visible' and 'invisible' deictics in Malagasy.

The exact semantic content of what is covered by 'visible' and 'invisible' varies from grammar to grammar. Palikur distinguishes objects in the speaker's hand, those near to speaker and to hearer, those far from both but visible, and those far and invisible (Aikhenvald and Green 1998). 'Visibility' of the object is often a concomitant feature of near deixis, as in Tariana *hūhī* 'this (emphatic) near you and me'.

Audibility appears to also be relevant for some demonstrative systems: 'non-visible' objects may be audible. Dyirbal (Australian: Dixon 1972) has a three-term system of noun markers: *bala*-'referent is visible and not near speaker';

---

[21] Further research may reveal other ways in which pronouns may contribute to developing evidentiality overtones. The first person dative plural pronoun in Albanian is a way of 'strengthening' the epistemic meaning of the admirative mood (used as an evidentiality strategy): it increases the sense of doubt for the statement (Friedman 2003: 208). However, since such pronominal forms have to occur together with admirative, they can hardly be considered a bona fide evidential strategy on their own.

yala-'referent is visible and near speaker'; and *ŋala-*'referent is not visible (but may be audible or remembered from the past'). Muna (Austronesian: van den Berg 1997: 199–201) has a seven-term system: 'near speaker', 'near addressee', 'away from speaker and addressee, but nearby', 'far away, lower than or level with point of speaking or orientation', 'far away, higher than point of speaking or orientation', 'not visible (may be audible), unspecified for time', and 'not visible, was in view but no longer is'. However, a two-term audible versus inaudible demonstrative system has not been recorded.

Santali (Munda: Neukom 2001: 42–4) has a special series of demonstrative pronouns (used as modifiers in a noun phrase and also adverbially) referring to what is seen, or to what is heard. Both distinguish six degrees of distance combined with emphasis. A visual demonstrative in 4.44 refers to something that can be seen.

Santali

4.44 <u>hanɛ</u>   ɲɛl-pe   tale   bagwan
     that.far.vis   see-2pS   palm   garden
     'Look at that one over there, (there is) a palm-tree garden'

An auditive demonstrative refers to something that can be heard, such as the beating of drums:

4.45 <u>ɔtɛ</u>   ṭamak-ko   ru-y-et'-kan
     that.aud   drum(sp)-3pS   beat-y-IMPF:ACT-IMPF
     'Listen, they are beating the drums' (lit. those drums you can hear)

The semantic extensions of these demonstratives are parallel to those in evidentiality systems: the visual demonstrative can refer to 'what is evident', while the auditive one may also refer to smell, taste, and feeling (Neukom 2001: 42).

Unlike evidentiality systems, visual demonstratives either combine reference to distance in space; or have additional functions where the source of information is irrelevant. Santali (Neukom 2001: 43) is a case in point. Here the visual demonstrative occurs as an anaphoric pronoun for abstract referents (e.g. 'this is just what I told you beforehand'), and as a relative pronoun in indefinite relative clauses.

Visibility and audibility distinctions in demonstratives are only superficially similar to perception meanings as encoded in grammatical evidentials. Unlike evidentials, they are likely to have additional spatial and anaphoric meaning extensions. Only occasionally (see Santali above) do they acquire a set of extensions similar to evidentials proper.

4.8 Reported speech as evidentiality strategy

Every language has some way of reporting what someone else said. The speaker can use their own words, or quote the other person verbatim. These strategies are functionally similar to reported and quotative evidentials. We first look at how languages mark reported speech (§4.8.1). Reported speech and quotations may develop epistemic and other overtones similar to those of reported evidentials (§4.8.2). Languages with reported evidentials may have other ways of marking reported speech. In §4.8.3 we will see how these relate to each other semantically. How reported speech expressions give rise to incipient evidentials is discussed in §4.8.4.

4.8.1 *Marking reported speech*

Reporting someone else's speech may involve a word-for-word quotation. Such quotations can be accompanied by a verb of speaking. They can have their own constituent order, as in the languages of the Ethiopian Plateau (Longacre 1990; Güldemann 2001: 329). In Dani (Bromley 1981: 270), a quoted utterance has to be followed by the participle of the verb 'say'. Quotations may involve juxtaposition of clauses, as in Menomini.

A 'direct speech' clause may be a special clause-type or it may behave like any other complement clause in the language. In Tikar (Benue-Congo: Jackson 1987: 100), it requires a complementizer 'that', just like any other complement clause.

Tikar

4.46 à   s̃è̃   lè   kpulu lè   [Kpulu wù   yibâ   mũ̀   ndɛm]
      he   say to   turtle that turtle you stole me   field
      'He said to the turtle (that) "You, Turtle, stole my field"'

Or a speaker may choose to report someone else's speech with their own words, recasting what was said as 'indirect speech'. Then all deictic elements—such as person or time shifters, e.g. 'now'—change to fit in with the perspective of the reporter. The defining features of indirect speech include pronoun reference, verb tense, complementizers, deictic markers, and degree of reported-speaker identity with the original speaker (cf. Li 1986; Janssen and van der Wurff 1996 and papers in the same volume; Kammerzell and Peust 2002: 293; and other papers in Güldemann and von Roncador 2002). Having an indirect speech construction is by no means universal: some languages have direct speech quotations as the only option. This is the case in Kwaza (van der Voort 2000: 291), Dyirbal and a few other Australian languages, and a few languages from Papua New Guinea (see examples in Larson 1984: 367–8).

Reporting or quoting something does not have to involve verbs of speaking. In English, motion verbs, e.g. *go*, are used to reproduce speech and sounds (Hickmann 1993: 87). In American English, *be like* in quotations is employed to 'foreground the expressive value of utterances', as in *He was like "Now I've seen everything"* '(Lucy 1993: 98). An up-to-date bibliography of reported discourse is Güldemann, von Roncador, and van der Wurff (2002). Güldemann (2001) is an exhaustive study of quotative constructions, their meanings, functions, and history in African languages. Dimmendaal (2001: 142–7) provides an overview of reported speech markers, their historical correlations with verbs of speech in Niger-Congo languages, and of complementation strategies with different verb classes.

In numerous Indo-European languages including English (see an overview in Janssen and van der Wurff 1996), the choice of tense in reported speech is often determined by temporal relations between the main clause and the dependent clause. (Other factors at play include reporter's attitude to information: see Sakita 2002.) A special mood form may be used in the same function; for instance, jussive can be used this way in Estonian and imperative in Nyangumarta. A number of African languages use logophoric pronouns as tokens of indirect speech. One of the functions of logophoric pronouns is to indicate whether the speaker and the subject or object of the reported utterance are the same person, or not. Consider 4.47–8, from Donno Sɔ, a Dogon language from Burkina Faso (Culy 1994). In 4.47 the referent of 'he' is neither Anta nor Oumar. In 4.48, 'he' is Oumar. The logophoric elements are underlined. The reported speech complement clause is in square brackets.

Donno Sɔ
4.47 Oumar [Anta wo-ñ   waa   be] gi
      Oumar Anta 3sg-OBJ seen   AUX said
      'Oumar$_i$ said that Anta$_j$ had seen him$_k$.'

4.48 Oumar [Anta <u>inyemɛ</u>-ñ   waa   be] gi
      Oumar Anta LOGOPHOR-OBJ seen   AUX said
      'Oumar$_i$ said that Anta$_j$ had seen him$_i$.'

Logophoricity can be expressed with cross-referencing on the verb, or with an affix (see Hyman and Comrie 1981: 24; and an overview by Curnow 2002c). Or a conjunct–disjunct person-marking system may be used for similar purposes. Conjunct and disjunct copulas in Lhasa Tibetan are listed in Table 4.1; see examples 4.35–6. The same copulas appear in complement clauses with verbs of speaking (and also of cognition). The conjunct copula in 4.49 shows that the 'reporter' and the author of what is being reported are the same person. The disjunct copula in 4.50 shows that they are two different people (DeLancey 1992: 43).

Lhasa Tibetan

4.49 khos   kho   bod=pa   <u>yin</u>   zer-gyis
      he+ERG   he   Tibetan   EQUATIONAL.BE/CONJ   say-IMPF
      'He_i says that he_i is Tibetan'

4.50 khos   kho   bod=pa   <u>red</u>   zer-gyis
      he+ERG   he   Tibetan   EQUAT.BE/DISJ   say-IMPF
      'He_i says that he_j is Tibetan'

   Reported speech complements can come to be used as main predications. The tense and mood choices in such constructions known as 'free indirect speech' are often different from main clauses of other kinds: the free indirect speech is recognizable by the tense forms used. An example of this is under 4.51, from French (Landeweerd and Vet 1996: 158–9). The first sentence of 4.51 introduces a speech event (it is cast in *passé simple* 'simple past', a form never used in free indirect speech discourse). The subsequent sentences in *imparfait* 'imperfect' are interpreted as representing Séverine's story. The verbs are underlined. The free indirect speech is in square brackets.

French

4.51 Alors,   très   nettement, Séverine   conta   comme quoi
      then   very   simply   Séverine   told:PS   how
      son   mari   <u>était menacé</u>   d'une
      her   husband   was threatened (IMPARF)   of.INDEF+FEM
      destituition.   [On   le   <u>jalousait</u>   beaucoup,   à cause de
      dismissal.   IMPERS him   envy:IMPARF   much   because.of
      son   métier   et   de   la   haute   protection
      his   merit   and   of   DEF:FEM   high:FEM   protection
      qui,   jusqu-là,   <u>l'avait   couvert</u>]
      which   until.then   him+have:IMPARF   cover
      'So she told him quite simply how her husband was threatened with dismissal. People (as she said) were very jealous of him because of his merit and the protection he enjoyed in high places until then' (Zola, *La bête humaine*)

   Such free indirect speech is very similar to the uses of non-indicative moods as markers of reported speech, which may be subsequently used in 'de-subordinated' free indirect discourse. An example of this is 4.3, from German. The verb form alone indicates that the information is part of a verbal report. Once this becomes the main context for the verbal form, it starts evolving into a reported evidential; see §4.8.4.

4.8.2 *Reported speech and reported evidentials: semantic affinities*

Reported evidentials and reported speech do essentially the same job: they indicate that the information was acquired from someone else. It is no wonder, therefore, that they can acquire similar semantic extensions.

Reported evidentials acquire overtones of unreliable information which one does not vouch for. Similarly, speaker's attitude to the reliability of information may be reflected in the choice of reported speech strategy (also see Hassler 2002, on how reported speech in French and Spanish can acquire epistemic extensions). In Adioukrou (Kwa: Hill 1995), reported and non-reported speech can be recognized by pronoun employment. Different kinds of speech correlate with the speaker's attitude to the information. Direct speech, with free subject pronouns, is used when the speaker 'wishes to be the guarantor of the message'. This is shown in 4.52.

Adioukrou

4.52 Jɛj   dad   eke   <u>li</u>   b'ow   l'ow
      Jej   said   that   3sg.FREE.PRONOUN   FUT   3sgFREE.PRONOUN+come
      'Jej said that he (Mel) will come' (I guarantee it)

A set of 'reporting' pronouns implies that the speaker wishes to be a simple reporter, without assuming any responsibility for the truth of the message. That is, in 4.53, where reporting pronouns are used, the speaker does not vouch for the reliability of the message.

4.53 Jɛj   dad   eke   <u>in</u>   b'ow
      Jej   said   that   3sg.FREE.PRONOUN   FUT
      <u>ow</u>
      3sgFREE.PRONOUN+come
      'Jej said that he (Mel) reportedly/supposedly will come' (I do not guarantee it)[22]

Non-firsthand evidentials may acquire a similar meaning, that of 'distancing' oneself from the event, and removing all responsibility for the information. Word-for-word quotations are often used to reconfirm what has already been said, but also, in Burridge's words (2001: 190–1), 'as a kind of verbal escape

---

[22] See Hill (1995: 95), on how reporting and free pronouns interact with logophoric marking. Logophoric markers (see above, and also Culy 1994; Dimmendaal 2001: 134) may interact with the degree of reliability of a report.

hatch for those moments when you might want to distance yourself, when you don't want to take full responsibility for your words'. A speaker may choose a direct quotation as a disclaimer: an example, from Arizona Tewa, will be given in §4.8.3 below.

A reported evidential may also be used this way. In Tariana, with a five-term grammatical evidentiality system, using the reported is a means of 'removing' responsibility from the speaker. Example 4.54 comes from a traditional story about the frog-people. A man married a frog-woman, but failed to obey her instructions not to bother the frogs when they slept. She had to tell on him to her father, which she did, using a reported evidential to show that she had no idea what was happening, no personal connections with the man, and consequently nothing to do with the wrong-doing. This is also an example of how evidentials can be manipulated as a means of giving wrong information.

Tariana

4.54 hĩ-**pidaka**   di-uka   wa-dalipa-se
      DEM:AN-REC.P.REP   3sgnf-arrive   1pl-near-LOC
      'This one (her ex-husband) has come to us, I am told'

A similar example is 3.45: the wife uses the reported evidential—where she ought to have been using a visual evidential—pretending she has nothing whatsoever to do with her husband going off to look for palm leaves. Again, this is a deliberate lie. Reported and non-firsthand evidentials may also be used this way, to create a conceptual distance between the information and the reporter. See 4.55 below, from Bulgarian, and further examples in §5.4.3. The inferred evidential in Tsafiki may imply that the speaker deliberately declares that he or she is not involved in the action. Other evidential strategies may also acquire overtones of non-controlled action, especially when used with first person. A Spanish-speaking girl from La Paz knew she had been naughty; to distance herself from the responsibility for what she had done she 'excused' herself by using pluperfect with non-firsthand overtones (see Laprade 1981 and (d) in §7.2). The indirect discourse and the reported evidential can have similar epistemic extensions in Tamil: in both, the speaker distances 'himself from the content of what is being said' (Steever 2002: 105).

Different ways of reporting speech may correlate with the degree of participation of the reporter in the original action. In his analysis of reported speech in Yoruba, Bamgboṣe (1986) distinguishes eyewitness-to-eyewitness report (usually done for some special purpose, such as reiteration, emphasis, confirmation, or reminder, and expressed with 'I said that . . .' construction); eyewitness-to-outsider report (also involving a speech complement clause); and hearsay reports. These are marked either with a generic 'they say' (*wǫ́n ní*), or a more specific 'he says'. A 'characteristic of a general hearsay report is that the reporter does not accept any responsibility for the accuracy of the report', and 'should the report turn out to be false, the reporter can take refuge in its indefinite source' (Bamgboṣe 1986: 95). This provides additional justification for frequent epistemic extensions of reported strategies and reported evidentials alike: they all refer to information one does not vouch for. See §5.4.

Quotations can be a rhetorical device. In Aguaruna narratives (Jívaro, Peru: Larson 1984: 60–84) quotations highlight participants and events: important information is often presented in the form of quoting what some other participant said about the event.[23] In Yucatec Maya a quotative verb *ki-* follows the reported direct speech, and has a variety of functions in discourse: it foregrounds the form of the quoted utterance, marks the boundary of a quotation, signals the shift of speaker, and serves various other rhetorical ends (Lucy 1993: 116).[24] We will see in §10.2.2 how evidentials can be manipulated to achieve varied stylistic effects. For instance, in Abkhaz the non-firsthand evidential is used to draw the listener's attention to a focal point in a story.

Just like reported evidentials, reported speech can be a token of certain speech genres, such as traditional stories, as in Kunama (Nilo-Saharan) and Bedauye (Cushitic) (see Güldemann 2001: 330). Comment clauses in English (which express the speaker's comments on the content of the matrix clauses) have similar functions (Sakita 2002: 188). This does not imply that having reported speech is the same as having a reported evidential. This is the topic of the next section.

4.8.3 *Reported evidential and reported speech: division of labour*

Most languages with a reported evidential combine it with some other way of marking reported speech. Reported speech and reported evidential often differ in their semantic nuances, and their function and usage.[25]

Kham (Watters 2002: 296–300) has a reported evidential which is obligatory in every narrative (see 2.21). It is a stylistic token of folk tales and narratives as a special speech genre. An alternative to the reported evidential is a direct speech

---

[23] Further discussion of rhetorical effects associated with quotations is in Larson (1984: 450–1).

[24] For discussion of further functions of reported speech, see papers in Lucy ed. (1993). Noonan (2001) provides an incisive account of the rhetorical effects of direct speech in Chantyal. Reported speech may correlate with the ways of marking grammatical relations, as shown by Merlan and Rumsey (2001).

[25] Just a few languages with an evidential which combines the functions of a reported and a quotative appear to have no additional ways of marking reported speech. Kombai (Awyu-Ndumut, West Papua: de Vries 1990) has an A3 system: the evidential *ne* functions as a reported marker, both if the author of the verbal report is not specified and as a way of marking a direct quote. This reported–quotative is used in many other contexts, including purpose and intention, reported thought, and mental processes.

complement used with one of the two utterance verbs, 'say (intransitive)' and 'say, tell (transitive)'. The reported evidential simply shows that the ultimate source of information (be it an assertion, a question, or a command) is someone other than the speaker. The choice of a direct speech complement with a verb of speech allows the speaker to express further subtle distinctions: internal cognitive processes like thinking, non-directed audible speech, or directed audible speech as part of a larger transitive speech-act.

A direct speech complement or 'direct quote' may be employed in order to specify the exact author of the information. The reported evidential in Menomini (called 'quotative mode' by Bloomfield 1962: 161) simply indicates that the information comes from a verbal report. Various quotation constructions (Bloomfield 1962: 444, 506–7) involve an explicit statement of who provided the information, as in 'That is what I said to him: "I am too busy"'. Along similar lines, in Tamil, indirect speech must contain an explicit indication of who said what; the reported evidential clitic $=\bar{a}m$ simply states that the speaker has acquired the information from someone else (Steever 2002: 105).

If the reported evidential has epistemic overtones, some other strategy could be used to report someone else's speech in order to avoid these. One of the meanings of the non-firsthand form in Bulgarian is what Gvozdanović (1996: 63) refers to as 'distance': the speaker may use the reportive if they are 'unwilling to bear the responsibility for claiming that the event has occurred'.

Bulgarian

4.55   Dumat,   zmejat   **sljazăl**   v
        think+PRES+3pl   dragon   come.down.REPORTIVE.sg   into
        našata   niva
        our   field
        'They think that the dragon would seem to have come down into our field' (not very likely)

A reported speech complement without the non-firsthand does not have any of the epistemic overtones of the non-firsthand—as in the case in 4.56.

4.56   Georgi   kaza   na   Ljubčo,   če   mu
        Georgi   say+AOR+3sg   at   Ljubčo   that   him
        poželava   uspex   na   zrelostnija   izpit
        wish+IMPERF:PRES+3sg   success   at/on   maturity   examination
        'Georgi said to Ljubčo that he wished him success at the final examination'

In languages where the choice of evidential correlates with attitude to information, a direct speech complement may be preferred to retelling someone else's speech and reinterpreting evidentials they used. The Tariana use direct

speech complements to avoid interpreting other people's sources of information. When reporting what someone else had said, the preferred strategy is
a direct speech complement, so that the speaker can avoid making a choice of
an evidential for another person and run the risk of any undesired implications
as to 'evaluation' of the other person's evidence. Thus, instead of saying, 'he
is coming-reported', the speaker would prefer saying 'he said: I am coming-
visual'. Only when talking about one's own experience does a direct speech
complement sound odd (other complementation strategies are used then).

Quoting someone verbatim can have the opposite effect. Tewa (Kroskrity
1993: 145) offers several alternatives for reporting what someone else had said. If
one uses the reported evidential, the exact 'author' of the information is left
unknown (hence the English translation with an indefinite 'they').

Tewa
4.57   **ba**   'í'í'-di   na-mɛ
       REP   there-OBL   3sgSTAT.PREF-go:PAST3
       'They say he left there'

If a speaker chooses to specify who said what, a direct quotation is used.
The construction includes the reported evidential accompanied by a complementizer:

4.58   'o-he: gi-**ba**   na-tú
       1sgSTAT.PREF-sick   that-REP   3sgSTAT.PREF-say
       ' "I'm sick", he said'

An alternative would be to use indirect speech, where the third person
prefix replaces the first person. The complementizer remains, and the reported
evidential is removed:

4.59   na-he: gi   na-tú
       3sgSTAT.PREF-sick   that   3sgSTAT.PREF-say
       'He said that he is sick'

The two alternatives are not fully synonymous. The difference between 4.58
and 4.59 lies in the speaker's attitude to the veracity of information. Example 4.58
means ' "I am sick", he is quoted as saying' and implies that the speaker does not
vouch for the information reported. That is, for the native speakers of Tewa, the
direct quotation 'lacks the reliability or facticity of its indirect counterpart'
(Kroskrity 1993: 146). In contrast, indirect speech, as in 4.59, contains fully reliable information. Indirect speech is systematically preferred to direct quotations in Tewa narratives and everyday conversations. Similar effects of direct
speech quotations have been reported for Gahuku and Usan (Deibler 1971: 105

TABLE 4.2. Reported evidential and reported discourse: division of labour

SEMANTIC FEATURES	REPORTED EVIDENTIAL	REPORTED DISCOURSE	EXAMPLES DISCUSSED HERE
Indicating the specific author of information	no	yes	Tamil, Menomini, Tewa
Epistemic extensions	yes	no	Bulgarian, Tariana

and Reesink 1986: 259), and Tauya, all from Papua New Guinea (MacDonald 1990a). In these three languages, direct quotes indicate false presupposition on the part of the speaker.

As we have seen, reported speech and reported evidentials complement each other. One may be used instead of the other to avoid unwanted epistemic or other overtones. Reported speech may allow the speaker to be precise about who told what. Both reported speech and reported evidentials may be employed as stylistic devices in discourse.

In summary, reported evidentials and reported speech strategies are hardly ever fully synonymous. Table 4.2 summarizes the ways in which they differ, both semantically and functionally.

4.8.4 *Grammaticalization of reported speech markers and incipient evidentials*

There are two basic pathways for developing a reported evidential. A speech complement can change its status: from a subordinate clause it becomes a main clause. The marking found in an erstwhile dependent clause may regrammaticalize to mark reported speech. This is how the present reported evidential evolved in Standard Estonian. The present participle (in partitive case) was first used to mark the predicate of a non-finite complement clause with verbs of speech. It then came to be used in a main clause on its own, giving rise to the reported evidential; see examples in §9.1. Similar paths of development have been suggested for Latvian and Lithuanian (see Wälchli 2000; Wiemer 1998), also spoken in the Baltic area.

Another pathway involves reanalysis of verbs of saying. A verb 'say' may be on its way to full grammaticalization as a reported evidential. In Kambera (Western Austronesian: Klamer 2002) the root *wà* 'say' in report constructions can still be analysed as a verbal root. Its grammatical properties are somewhat unusual: it has limited morphological possibilities and discourse functions, and is prosodically deficient compared to any other verb. This indicates that 'say' is on its way towards becoming a fully grammaticalized element.[26]

In some varieties of South American Spanish and Portuguese, the verb 'say' (Spanish *decir*, Portuguese *dizer*) plus the complementizer *que* appear fused into a particle *dizque* which is on its way towards grammaticalization into a reported and general non-firsthand evidential.[27] The history of *dizque* in European and in American Spanish has been briefly outlined by Kany (1944): this particle, no longer used in literary Spanish (it is 'only occasionally heard in restricted areas of Spain, but only as an archaism in familiar or jocose style'), appears to be pervasive in South America.

In Colombian Spanish, *dizque* introduces reported speech and marks information acquired by hearsay which may be fully reliable (Travis forthcoming). In 4.60, the two speakers are discussing how dangerous some areas of Colombia are said to be. Rosario is fully committed to the truth of what she is reporting: she rejects her interlocutor's attempt at correcting what she says.

Colombian Spanish

4.60 Rosario: y   eso,   **dizque**   es   peligroso   no?
               and   this   REP   is   dangerous   no
               que   atracan   y   todo .... No?
               that   they.attack and   all   No?
               'And it, it is said to be dangerous, isn't it? They attack and
               everything. Don't they?'

      David: de   noche,   parece   que   sí
               at   night   seems   that   yes
               'At night it seems that they do'

      Rosario: No,   y   que   **dizque**   hasta   de   día
               no   and   that   REP   during   of   day
               'No, and that it is said that even during the day'

In 4.60, the second token of *dizque* occurs together with the quotative *que*. This suggests that *dizque* has been reinterpreted as a reported speech marker. The form *dizque* has undergone further semantic developments, which are quite similar to those of some reported evidentials. *Dizque* may encode a range of notions to do with make-believe, unachievable goals, and uncontrollable actions. For instance, a character talks about how she would pretend to buy bread and candy with false money—this was phrased as 4.61, with *dizque*.

---

[26] A similar situation was mentioned for Aguaruna (Larson 1978: 50–1) where the inflected verb *ti*-'say' is extremely frequent in traditional legends (where it occurs at the end of every sentence). In due course it is likely to provide a historical source for a reported evidential in the making.

[27] Travis (forthcoming) mentions the existence of a related form with a similar range of functions in Galician.

4.61 yo **dizque** les   compraba   pan   y   dulce
      I   REP   to.them   used.to.buy bread and   candy
      'I would **dizque** buy bread and candy from them'

This 'pretend' usage is strikingly similar to how the reported evidential is used in Yankunytjatjara (see 5.68), in children's games. *Dizque* may have only a name within its scope; this usage also indicates that the speaker takes no responsibility for the name given, and even has their doubt about the name. Here is another example. The speaker introduces *elíxir para la eterna juventud*, 'an elixir for eternal youth', which turns out to be totally ineffective, with *dizque*. In English, one could use *so-called* with similar pejorative and sarcastic overtones. The reported evidential is often used in a similar way, to express a negative attitude, irony, and disagreement with what was said. A similar example is 5.71, from Nganasan: here the reported evidential is used ironically to talk about a man who does not behave like a father and yet is said to be the girl's father.

At least in some varieties, the development of *dizque* may have to do with the substratum of indigenous languages with highly developed grammatical evidentiality. In La Paz Spanish, the construction *dice que* (lit. says that) or *dizque*, or its variants *dice* (says) or *dicen* (they say), in the clause-final position marks the information as 'non-personal knowledge', something the speaker did not acquire firsthand and therefore cannot vouch for. In La Paz Spanish this usage is sometimes linked to the Aymara substratum (Laprade 1981: 221–2). No such information is available for Colombian Spanish.[28]

Optional reportative and quotative particles frequently come from depleted verbs of speech, e.g. Modern Greek *lé[e]i* (Friedman 2003) and Russian *mol* (Rakhilina 1996). The Abkhaz quotative particle *hᵒa* is an archaic past absolutive of the verb 'say' which underwent phonological depletion (Chirikba 2003: 258–9). Such particles provide a frequent source for the development of an obligatory reported evidential. A marker on its way towards becoming a grammaticalized reported evidential tends to develop a range of meanings characteristic of a reported and a general non-firsthand evidential. This is a typical feature of evidentiality strategies.

4.9 Several evidentiality strategies in one language

One language can use several strategies for somewhat different meanings related to information source. Different strategies can plainly have distinct

---

[28] Kany (1944) demonstrated that *dizque* as a marker of reported speech is a characteristic of most varieties of South American Spanish; at least in some instances, *dizque* carries strong overtones of doubt and 'often corresponds to our "is supposed to" ' (Kany 1944: 171).

meanings, as in Fox (Algonquian: Dahlstrom forthcoming: 116–18). Dubitative is used to express speculation while interrogative marks inference based on visible evidence (see example 4.5). The form called 'aorist conjunct' (p. 111) typically occurs in subordinate clauses; it can occur in a main clause if it is preceded by a temporal adverbial clause. It is also used in main clauses as a kind of narrative past tense, marking a traditional narrative 'as one the narrator was told, not his own lifestory'.

Meaning differences between several evidential strategies may be rather subtle. La Paz Spanish (Laprade 1981: 221–4) has two evidential strategies. Pluperfect (example 4.8) has an overtone of 'indirect' evidence—something the speaker has not seen, or does not vouch for, or takes no responsibility for. Another form, *dice* 'he/she says', can be put at the end of a clause as a reported speech marker, as well as a kind of disclaimer. A sentence like *Lorenzo está enfermo dice* (Lorenzo is sick-he/she says) implies more than just 'Lorenzo is said to be sick': there is strong nuance of 'I do not vouch for it'. The pluperfect differs from the *dice* strategy in its mirative overtones, and the ways in which it can be used with first person (see §6.3 and §7.2).

In Agul (Maisak and Merdanova 2002) both the resultative form and the compound past (formed with the auxiliary 'be' and a participle) have evidential overtones. Both can have a range of non-firsthand meaning: something the speaker had not seen, but either inferred or heard about. The resultative usually refers to inference based on visible results. It is used in a sentence like 'she has wept' (her eyes are red, and one can see traces of tears on her cheeks). In contrast, the compound past is often used to talk about a mere assumption (what Maisak and Merdanova call 'weak non-firsthand meaning'), as in 'she has probably wept—we cannot see any obvious evidence, but she is behaving in a bizarre way as if she had wept'. We can recall, from §4.2, that perfect often has firsthand overtones. This indicates that evidential extensions of various categories may tend to form semantic oppositions, very similar to small evidentiality systems of the firsthand/non-firsthand (A1) type.

An evidentiality strategy may coexist with grammatical evidentials (see §4.8.4, and Table 4.2). An evidentiality strategy differs from grammatical evidentiality in its meaning or its epistemic extensions. The two are hardly ever fully synonymous.

Agul has a reported evidential alongside three evidential strategies (Maisak and Merdanova 2002: §2.3). Of these, the resultative with its non-firsthand range of extensions can cover reported information. The grammatical evidential, but not the resultative, has an epistemic extension: it may refer to what the speaker knows by hearsay and does not vouch for.

Meithei, a Tibeto-Burman language with an A2 system (see §2.1; Chelliah 1997: 295–312), has a variety of evidential strategies, all somewhat different in their meanings:

- A nominalizer -ǰat indicates that the speaker has only indirect evidence that the action or state has occurred, such as inference or hearsay; it can indicate that something happened contrary to the speaker's expectations.

- The copula -ni with a nominalization as its complement implies an assertion of truth; another nominalizer is used when the speaker has just some knowledge supporting the truth of the complement.

- Another complementizer is used to describe an undisputed fact (consequently it cannot occur with verbs such as 'think' or 'believe' which express potentially unrealized states).

- Four complementizers mark quotations; their choice depends on how much evidence the speaker has for the proposition expressed in the complement.

- The way aspect is used in questions in Meithei also indicates what knowledge the speaker has about the topic. If the speaker chooses to use the perfect marker it implies that they already know that what is being asked about has indeed happened.

- Finally, verbal derivational markers also have evidential-like meanings: the inceptive may imply that 'the speaker is a witness to the initiation of an action' (p. 309), and the prospective may mean that 'the speaker can see or has knowledge of the culminating point of an action' (p. 310).

None of the evidentiality strategies interacts with other categories in the same way as does the non-firsthand evidential in Meithei (Chelliah 1997: 224, and see §7.2 and §8.1.2).

Different evidentiality strategies in one language often overlap in their semantic range: they typically cover non-firsthand meanings. Any further correlations between a strategy and a particular overtone appear to be language-specific.

4.10 Evidentiality strategies: what can we conclude?

Not every category discussed in this chapter has evidential extensions in every language which shows it. That is, evidential strategies are not universal. Grammatical categories and constructions which can develop evidential-like overtones include non-indicative moods, perfects, resultatives, past tenses, passives, nominalizations, complementation strategies, and person-marking. Schemes 4.1 and 4.2 above show the development of evidential extensions for non-indicative moods and modalities. Scheme 4.3 features the development of evidential extensions for perfects and resultatives. The semantic path of development of non-firsthand extensions for passives and for resultative nominalizations follows a similar path. De-subordination—whereby a dependent clause becomes reinterpreted as a main clause—is concomitant to how some non-indicative moods and modalities, and nominalizations, can develop evidential extensions, and even grammaticalize as evidentials in due course.

Conjunct–disjunct person-marking develops the same meaning extensions as a non-firsthand evidential only in the context of first person. It develops mirative, rather than epistemic, extensions (see §6.3).

Complement clauses of verbs of perception and cognition can express perceptual (that is, visual or auditory) meanings as opposed to a simple report. They do not have either mirative or epistemic extensions of meaning. If a language has several evidentiality strategies these are never fully synonymous.

Reported speech can be viewed as an alternative to a reported evidential. The two have a few features in common, but are never fully synonymous (see §4.8, and Table 4.2). Just like reported evidentials, reported speech can express information one does not vouch for. Quoting someone verbatim may allow the speaker to be precise as to the exact authorship of information. This same technique may have different overtones: quoting someone verbatim in Arizona Tewa implies that the speaker does not vouch for what he or she quotes.

When visual and auditory meanings are encoded in demonstrative systems, they interact with other, typically demonstrative, meanings—such as spatial distance and anaphora.

Evidentiality strategies tend to develop a range of meanings characteristic of reported and non-firsthand evidentials: inference and verbal report. The semantic range of the strategies described here is shown in Scheme 4.4.

Reported speech, particles derived from 'say', and de-subordinated speech complements show the direction of semantic change opposite to that of other

SCHEME 4.4 The semantic range of evidentiality strategies

inference based on results or assumption	hearsay
--→	
non-indicative moods and modalities, perfects, resultatives, passives, nominalizations	
hearsay	inference based on results or assumption
--→	
reported speech, particles derived from 'say', de-subordinated speech complements including nominalizations	

evidentiality strategies. Non-indicative moods and modalities, perfects, resultatives, passives, and nominalizations start with basic inferential meanings, and may end up getting extended to cover verbal reports. Reported speech markers may end up extended to cover inference. Demonstratives are rather different: they may evolve perceptual meanings, of visual and sensory perception. Conjunct–disjunct person-marking systems differentiate between 'self' and 'other' as information source, but do not fully match any of the semantic parameters found in evidentiality systems (see Table 2.1).

The meanings of inference and deduction are linked to the results of something already achieved. This explains why perfects and resultatives, and also resultative passives and nominalizations, tend to develop inferential overtones. They can then extend to cover reports as shown in Scheme 4.4. Non-indicative moods and modalities tend to preserve their non-evidential core meanings. In the same way conjunct/disjunct systems primarily mark speech-act participants, and demonstratives indicate spatial distance and anaphora. Table 4.3 summarizes the semantic content of evidential strategies, and the mechanisms involved.

Historically, any evidentiality strategy, except for demonstratives and conjunct–disjunct person-marking, can develop into a grammatical evidential. In §9.1 we will see numerous examples of how small evidentiality systems can arise through reanalysis of perfects, resultatives, passives, nominalizations, de-subordinated complement clauses of verbs of speech, and reported speech markers. In contrast, non-indicative modalities with 'epistemic' meanings or the future modality only occasionally give rise to an evidential (see the mention of Abkhaz in §4.1). This is a result of an independence of such meanings as probability and possibility from the semantics of 'information source' proper.

In languages with complex systems of grammatical evidentiality hardly any category acquires evidential extensions. That is, in such languages there are no evidentiality strategies. In Tariana, with a five-term system (see Aikhenvald 2003c: 156–7), no grammatical category acquires a semantic extension to do with information source. A number of modalities mark doubt, uncertainty, and condition (Table 8.3 shows how these interact with evidentiality). One can talk about one's suppositions, or opinions, using a variety of lexical means. If one is not sure whether something has happened, one can put a phrase *pa:pe di-ni-ka* (maybe 3sgnf-do-SUB) 'maybe he (or she, or they) does', and then use an inferred or an assumed evidential. Similarly, in Tuyuca (Barnes 1999: 214) if 'speakers really have no idea as to whether or not an event occurred, they will use the assumed evidential, and will preface their statements with the word /õba/ which indicates that they are not at all sure'.

TABLE 4.3. Evidentiality strategies: a summary

STRATEGY	SEMANTICS	EPISTEMIC EXTENSIONS	DE-SUBORDINATION
Non-indicative moods and modalities (§4.1)	similar to non-firsthand in A1 and A2 systems	yes	yes (Schemes 4.1 and 4.2)
Perfect and resultative (§4.2) and passive (§4.3)	(a) similar to non-firsthand in A1 and A2 systems (b) similar to firsthand in A1 systems	yes	no
Nominalizations (§4.4)	similar to non-firsthand in A1 and A2 systems	yes	yes
Complementation with verbs of cognition and perception (§4.5)	perceptual meanings	no	no
Complementation with verbs of speech (§4.5)	reported meaning	yes	yes
Conjunct–disjunct person marking (§4.6)	same semantic extensions as for non-firsthand in A1 and A2 systems	no	no
Demonstratives (§4.7)	visual or auditory	yes	no
Reported speech (§4.8)	similar to reported evidential in A3 system; overtones of non-firsthand in A1 and A2 systems	yes	yes

This shows, once again, that evidential extensions of non-evidential categories are not universal.

4.11 Modal expressions and evidentiality strategies: where to draw the line?

Lexical expressions of information source and probability have nothing to do with what this book is about—the grammatical expression of evidentiality. An analogy between English expressions like *it looks like rain*, or *this idea sounds good*, or *I hear you are getting married*, and bona fide evidential systems and even evidential extensions of, say, perfects, or conditionals, is superficial (though accepted by some authors in their attempt to include familiar Indo-European languages in discussions of evidentiality: see Fox 2001, and King and Nadasdi 1999). This is similar to how the linguistic literature on gender as a grammatical category does not discuss words for 'man' and 'woman', or 'bull' and 'cow' in each particular language. And time words—such as *yesterday, today, tomorrow*—are hardly ever included in the analysis of tense systems; to deal with these is a different task which belongs to a lexicographer. 'Evidentiality in English' has the same status as 'gender in Hungarian'. Of course, sex distinctions can be expressed in Hungarian if one wants to, but there is no grammatical category of gender. One can indicate information source in English, if necessary. But this is not grammatical evidentiality.

How do we draw a line between grammatical and lexical expression of information source? Most languages have a set of modal expressions (adverbs, particles, or others) referring to doubt, the validity of information, or used as disclaimers. (See Ramat 1996, for their analysis in an array of European languages.) Particles with predominantly modal meanings may acquire inferential extensions. The adverbial phrase *χsu-ɲi* in Qiang (LaPolla 2003a: 71–2) indicates uncertainty and may extend to assumption. In 4.62 it is glossed as 'seem'. In its meaning it is reminiscent of an evidentiality strategy. It may occur together with the reported evidential *-i.*

Qiang

4.62   the: ʐdʐyta: ɦa-qə-i   χsu-ɲi
        3sg   Chengdu+LOC   OR-go-REP   'seem'-ADV.M
        'S/he went to Chengdu, I am told' (guessing, unsure if true)

Lexical means describing information source vary in their wealth and their expression. Western Apache (de Reuse 2003: 93–4) employs a postpositional stem -*n̲ā̲ā̲ł* 'in one's presence', literally 'with one's eyes' to stress that the speaker was watching what was happening. Inference from reasoning can be expressed with the verb *nsi̲h* 'I think'. The way lexical expressions of information source correlate with categories such as person may be similar to correlations found with proper evidentials (see §7.4): in Western Apache, the verb 'think' is hardly ever used with non-first person, simply because it is considered 'culturally inappropriate to presume to know the thoughts of others' (de Reuse 2003: 94).

Chukchi has numerous modal particles of epistemic nature, e.g. *lureq* 'maybe' and *etʔəm* 'apparently' (see Fortescue 2003: 305), many of them borrowed into Central Siberian Eskimo (de Reuse 1994: 367–413). Similarly, Turkana (Dimmendaal 1996) also has numerous particles expressing personal attitude, emotional state, validity of information, and so on. The deontic particle *k ò hà* in !Xun (Northern Khoisan) has mirative extensions, and can also denote doubt (König and Heine forthcoming; Christa König. p.c.). These means are on a borderline between grammar and lexicon.[29]

What is, and what is not, an evidentiality strategy? In principle, any epistemic meaning can be stretched to cover assumption, inference, or supposition. Past tenses are frequently associated with hypothetical and uncertain information (not surprisingly, past is often seen as something remote and thus uncertain). Imperfective aspect may also be associated with a hypothetical unrealized state or action (see discussion in James 1982). Every language has some way of stating that what the speaker says is true; otherwise it won't be worth listening to. An unmarked statement may be always assumed to be true (as it is in Dyirbal: R. M. W. Dixon, p.c.). One of the common-sense principles of pragmatic theory is the assumption that the speaker's authority for the information in an utterance is a precondition for a declarative statement (cf. Hargreaves 1991: 381; Gordon and Lakoff 1971). Grice's maxim of Quality (1989) is 'try to make your contribution one that is true'. Frajzyngier (1985) convincingly showed that the inherent meaning of unmarked indicative sentences in a number of languages is to 'express what the speaker wants to convey as truth'. Every speech-act may be interpreted as containing some kind of reference to the speaker's commitment, credibility, persuasion, or doubts.

A broad stance on the notion of evidentiality strategy would be to include every linguistic expression with a potential interpretation as having to do with truth, commitment, or the speaker's authority. Such an 'all-inclusive' approach may have its merits: for instance, it focuses on some universal features of linguistic expression. At the same time, an 'anything goes' approach makes the idea of evidentiality strategy meaningless. An alternative to this is a narrower approach: a grammatical technique is an evidentiality strategy if, in addition to its primary meaning, it can acquire one or more semantic features characteristic of evidentiality proper (see §2.5). For instance, resultative nominalizations frequently acquire an additional inferential meaning (see §4.2 and §4.4). But not every resultative nominalization does so. Yukaghir is a case in point: Maslova (2003: 233) showed that resultative nominalizations may be associated with the information inferred from some observable evidence, but do not have to be.

With the exception of reported speech, none of these evidentiality strategies can be considered a universal, or even a near-universal (pace Bulut 2000: 148,

---

[29] Along similar lines, Russian has a number of 'quotatives'—adverbs and particles employed when the speaker's statement is based on the information acquired from someone else (and especially if the speaker does not vouch for it) (Bulygina and Shmelev 1997: 299–300). The choice of a marker often depends on speaker's attitude to information (also see Rakhilina 1996). This is indicative of a lexical, rather than grammatical, expression of information source.

and others). The likelihood of the development of evidential extensions for all the categories discussed here has to do with a number of different, albeit interconnected paths of semantic change (see §4.10).

Modal verbs present a separate problem. In many languages they are a closed subclass. One may wonder whether their evidential extensions, if any, should be treated on a par with lexical expression of evidentiality, or as evidentiality strategies. In German, the modal verb *sollen* 'must' may indicate that the speaker is reporting the information they acquired from someone else or that they inferred or assumed it, as shown in the following examples (Blass 1989: 303). The English *must* may have a similar meaning.

German

4.63 Er   hat   sich   das   Bein   gebrochen
      he   has   self   DEF:NEUT   leg   broken
      'He has broken his leg'

4.64 Er   soll   sich   das   Bein   gebrochen   haben
      he   must:3PPRES   self   DEF:NEUT   leg   broken   have
      'Apparently he has broken his leg'

That a modal verb can express inference does not mean that it is an evidential (also see discussion in Ramat 1996). Evidentiality is not among its primary meanings. But is this an evidentiality strategy?

The answer to this question depends on the status of modal verbs in the language—whether they are indeed a closed class, and whether they form special grammatical constructions in which they acquire additional meanings related to information source. Generally speaking, they are on the borderline between lexical evidentiality and evidentiality strategy.

One ought to make a careful distinction between lexical items to do with assumption, possibility, and hedging, and closed grammatical systems of particles which acquire evidential extensions. Take Modern Greek. It is rather unusual for a language spoken in the Balkans (Friedman 2003: 189) in that it does not have evidentiality. (As pointed out by Joseph 2003: 315, evidentials probably did not diffuse into Greek because of various socio-cultural reasons and the Greeks' attitude to their language.) The adverb *taha* 'maybe, it seems, apparently' is often referred to as a 'hesitation' marker (and treated by Ifantidou 2001: 170–1. as a 'weak' evidentiality marker: see Chapter 1). However, it has nothing to do with grammatical evidentiality or even a strategy of any kind—any language has similar lexical means expressing a speaker's hedging, doubt, and attitude to information. Greek does have a particle *lé[e]i* 'one says' meaning 'reportedly, allegedly' (this particle can also acquire mirative extensions)

(Friedman 2003: 189). At most, this could be an incipient reported evidential, comparable to Colombian Spanish *dizque* (see §4.8.4).

It is sometimes difficult to decide whether a particular particle is mostly modal or mostly evidential in nature and to draw the line between a purely epistemic meaning of a modal particle and its use to express assumption or inference (cf. the list of varied particles to do with certainty in Squamish: Jacobs 1996: 253). Whether or not such particles can be considered evidentiality strategies is a marginal issue. Such particles do not usually give rise to grammatical evidentials, and are thus tangential for the study of grammatical systems of evidentiality.

5

Evidentials and their meanings

Source of information is the semantic core of any evidential. The basic semantic parameters of evidentials across the world were summarized in Table 2.1. Individual terms in evidentiality systems may acquire various semantic extensions, including attitude to information, its probability, a speaker's certainty of the truthfulness of their statement, and their responsibility for it. That is, evidentiality may come semantically close to modalities of varied sorts—but on its periphery, not in its core. This is why it is misleading (pace Willett 1988) to classify evidentials on a par with expressions of possibility and probability (so called 'epistemic' modalities). Which evidentials acquire such an extension depends on the system they occur in. A non-visual, a non-firsthand, and an inferred evidential may each be used to describe something one does not really believe. A reported evidential may acquire overtones of doubt, but does not have to. A visual evidential can relate generally known facts and things one is sure of. But this is not the case in every system. An additional semantic extension found with some evidentials relates to new, unusual, and surprising information ('mirative'); see Chapter 6.

Semantic extensions of evidentials depend on the overall organization of the language—after all, every language is 'système où tout se tient' (a system where everything holds together), to quote Antoine Meillet's famous statement (1926: 16). If a language already has a highly developed system of epistemic modalities one does not expect a large variety of epistemic extensions for evidential terms. As a result, evidentiality systems differ in how semantically complex each term is.

Establishing the core meaning of an evidential may be a daunting task. Lexical reinforcements of evidentials (§11.2), whereby the speakers themselves rephrase an evidential with a lexical item to strengthen it, provide a useful clue. For instance, the visual evidential in Tariana can be rephrased as 'I saw it', or 'he saw it', serving as a kind of justification to an incredulous audience. Ad hoc explanations of evidentials by native speakers are another way of teasing apart the core meaning and the extensions of evidentials. For instance, actions of an evil spirit in the Vaupés area are typically talked about with non-visual evidentials. Speakers justify this use by saying 'we cannot see them'. In §11.2, we return to speakers' metalinguistic awareness of evidentials and native speakers' intuitions.

Evidentials can acquire various not quite evidential meanings. They are often used as tokens of narrative genres, and a way of making one's story-telling more effective. The non-firsthand evidential in Abkhaz narratives is a way of focusing listener's attention on a crucial part of the story. Discourse functions of evidentials are further discussed in §§10.2.1–2.

A terminological remark is in order. We have already seen, in Chapter 2, that labels used for individual terms in evidential systems are somewhat arbitrary and even misleading. They do to some extent reflect the core meaning of each evidential; but are better considered nicknames used for ease of reference. The readers ought not be misled by them, in the same way as they ought not be misled by translations of individual evidentials into English, where lexical equivalents have to be employed for what is part of another language's grammar.

We will first look at the semantics of individual terms and semantic complexity within evidential systems of two terms (§5.1), three terms (§5.2), and four and more terms (§5.3). A reported term often forms a subsystem on its own (as shown in §3.3 and §3.5). It is semantically rather uniform if looked at cross-linguistically; see §5.4. The last section, §5.5, contains a summary of evidentials and their meanings.

5.1   Semantic complexity in systems with two evidentiality choices

Systems with two evidentiality choices (§2.1) encode similar meanings. The firsthand term within an A1 type (firsthand versus non-firsthand) and the 'sensory' term within an A4 type (sensory versus reported) are typically associated with what the speaker had seen. This term often covers what was heard, smelt, or even felt, and also actions in which the speaker participated. Examples 2.1–2 from Jarawara, 2.3–6 from Cherokee, and 2.10 from Yukaghir illustrate this. In both Ngiyambaa and Diyari, each with an A4 system, the sensory evidential refers to seeing, hearing, or to a combination of senses (see 2.25–33).

In contrast, the non-firsthand evidential may refer to an action not seen by the speaker and in which they did not participate. This covers inference based on the visible results of an action, as in 2.11, from Yukaghir. It is semantically similar to the non-firsthand evidential in A2 systems. The two evidentiality values, firsthand and non-firsthand, are contrasted in one sentence in 5.1, from Kalasha, a Dardic language (Bashir 1988).

Kalasha

5.1 a aya' **a**   ågar' Zot   **ka'da**
    I here   come(PAST.FIRSTH) fire   already do(PAST.NONFIRSTH)+3
    'I came here (which I witnessed personally: FIRSTHAND), (and someone)
    (had) already made the fire (in my absence so I didn't see it being done:
    NON-FIRSTHAND)'

The firsthand evidential can be extended to visible results if the verb
describes something that cannot be seen; for instance, feelings or cognitive
processes (see §10.3). In 5.2, from Bagvalal (Maisak and Tatevosov 2001: 310),
the firsthand is used with the verb 'forget'. The speaker had visual evidence for
his statement: he had given his address to a friend, but the friend had never
written to him. After having found out what had happened, the speaker says
5.2. (The evidential is a complex verb form.)

Bagvalal

5.2 o-šu-ba   di=b   adres
    this-OBL.M-AFF   1sg.OBL=GEN.N   address
    b=ēc̃a   **b=uXXu**   **b=isã**
    N=forget   N=stay   N=found(FIRSTH)
    'He forgot my address' (as I found out) (FIRSTHAND)

Non-firsthand forms have a wide variety of meanings: from any kind of
INFERENCE to HEARSAY, as in 2.7–9 from Cherokee, 2.10–12 from Yukaghir, and
2.16–18 from Turkish. Inference based on visually obtained results is a major
meaning of non-firsthand evidentials in Mansi (Skribnik 1998: 200, 206).
A non-firsthand form may be ambiguous if taken out of context. If the speaker
runs across Ali in the forest, and sees him cutting up a bear, 5.3 would be appropriate in Bagvalal. The non-firsthand here is to do with inference: Ali, I infer,
has killed the bear. If someone else had told the speaker that Ali had killed the
bear, 5.3 would be equally appropriate. (The non-firsthand evidential is
expressed with a converbal construction.)

5.3 ʕali-r   sī k_o'ā=b=o ek_o'a
    Ali-ERG   bear kill=N=CONV   eat
    'Ali, as I infer, has killed the bear' or 'Ali, as I am told, has killed the bear'

Optional particles may disambiguate a non-firsthand evidential (also see
Donabédian 2001: 425 and §9.2.2). The non-firsthand evidential in Northern
Khanty may cover inference based on speaker's own observation. If inference is
based on common sense, no context is required. In 5.4 the speaker can see the
rotten knife; this is an obvious result of the fact that 'the knife was getting rotten' (Nikolaeva 1999: 142).

Northern Khanty

5.4   Ma   kese-m   xărŋajət-**m**-al
    I   knife-1sg   get.rotten-NONFIRSTH.PAST-3sg
    'My (wooden) knife got rotten'

The same form can cover inference based on reasoning. Then some explanation is likely to be provided, as in 5.5.

5.5   Wŭr   l∩ś   elti   ul-ti   urəŋna   ma   mŏsltə-s-əm
    blood   snow   on   be-PART.PRES   because   I   understand-PAST-1sg
    kălaŋ   mosməl-**m**-em
    reindeer   wound-NONFIRSTH.PAST-1sg
    'Because of the blood on the snow I understood that I had wounded the reindeer'

When the non-firsthand evidential has a reported meaning, it occurs together with a particle *mătti* 'they say, reportedly'. Or the source of reported information may be explicitly stated, as in 5.6.

5.6   Pilip   iki   jast-əl:...   uś   pulnawət   kema
    Philip   old.man   say-PRES   rising.fish   Obdorsk   to
    jŏxət-**m**-al
    come-NONFIRSTH.PAST-3sg
    'Grandfather Philip said: "... The rising fish has already reached
    Obdorsk"'.

The reported reading is preferred in traditional folkloric stories. We return to the issue of preferred evidentials and their genre-determined interpretations in §10.2.1.

Similarly, in Komi and Udmurt (see Winkler 2001: 50–1) the non-firsthand ('unobvious') past tense describes the result of a completed action not witnessed by the speaker and in which he or she did not participate; it covers the semantics of inferred and reported. In contrast, the firsthand ('obvious') past describes actions which took place before the speech act, and were witnessed by the speaker.

The extension from inferential to hearsay is not universal. The non-firsthand evidential in Nepali (Michailovsky 1996) does not have this extension. Neither do the non-firsthand evidentials in Jarawara, Archi, and Mỹky (we can recall that each language has a reported evidential as an independent subsystem).

'DEFERRED REALIZATION' is another notable semantic feature of non-firsthand evidentials. It implies that full information on the situation was obtained and correctly interpreted post factum, no matter whether the speaker saw it or not.

In Yukaghir, this meaning extension is particularly striking when the speaker describes their own action. In 5.7 it was not until after he had drunk tea that he had realized where he was: near the lair of a bear (Maslova 2003: 223–4).

Yukaghir
5.7   ta: ejre-t   met   me:me: abut   aŋil'-ge   ta:
      there   walk-SS:IMPF   I   bear   lair   inlet-LOC   there
      cha:j-e   o:ža:-**l'el**-d'e
      tea-ACC   drink-INFR-INTR:1sg
      'While walking there, I drank tea near the lair of a bear' (the speaker
      noticed the lair later)

'Deferred realization' and inference in general are often associated with unexpected information, and thus give rise to mirative interpretations: see Chapter 6.

In the context of a first person participant, a non-firsthand evidential may imply lack of any responsibility for a wrong action, or lack of control (see §7.2 and examples 7.3–4). Through association with 'unprepared mind', non-firsthand evidentials often acquire a secondary 'mirative' meaning (Lazard 1999; cf. also Guentchéva 1996; see §5.5), presumably linked to 'the idea of a distance between the speaker and the event s/he reports' (Lazard 1999: 94); other meanings include 'unconscious or unintentional actions' (see §6.1). In contrast, the firsthand term is often associated with the 'prepared mind' of the speaker. It goes together with a report on volitional action whereby the speaker is 'aware of the entire cause-effect chain from start to finish', as in Khowar and Kalasha (Bashir 1988) (see §7.2).

A non-firsthand evidential often has overtones of CONCEPTUAL DISTANCE. That is, it can be used if the speaker simply chooses to describe the state of affairs as if they were not direct witness of it (even if in fact they were), to make sure the audience understands that they have little to do with the whole thing. Example 5.8, from Cree/Montagnais/Naskapi, is an answer to a question: 'What did Sister (a nun) say to you?' (James, Clarke, and MacKenzie 2001: 240–3).

Cree/Montagnais/Naskapi
5.8   tshe-tshishkutama:shuin   nititiku-**shapan**
      you.go.to.school   she.told.me-NONFIRSTH
      'I think she told me to go to school'

The speaker here is talking about an incident in which she took part. She ought to have had firsthand knowledge of it. The thing is, she does not remember exactly what the Sister had said. Choosing not to present oneself as a direct witness is a stylistic option for talking about something one is unsure of. The non-firsthand evidential here has an epistemic connotation: 'she may have told me to go to school, but I am not sure'. The overtones of lack of control over the information and distancing oneself from the event (no matter whether one was directly involved with it or not) takes us into a different, albeit related, semantic domain—that of probability and uncertainty, and also non-commitment of the speaker to the truth of the utterance.

These epistemic overtones are absent from most A1 systems. As has been convincingly shown by Friedman (1986: 185), for Balkan Slavic and Albanian, and then by Lazard (1999), many A2 systems mark the source of information alongside the speaker's attitude towards it (also see Matras 1995, on similar phenomena in Vlach Romani). 'Distancing' may have an additional DISCOURSE EFFECT: the non-firsthand evidential in Cree/Montagnais/Naskapi is used to signal background rather than foreground information (see Drapeau 1996). This is similar to the 'commentative' use of the non-firsthand evidential in Abkhaz (see §10.2.2) where the non-firsthand form may provide a piece of background information or a comment which may turn out to be significant for the remainder of the narrative.

The non-firsthand evidential may relate events which are outside normal reality. In Svan (Sumbatova 1999: 75) and Yukaghir (Jochelson 1905: 400) it describes dreams. (This is not universal: in Jarawara descriptions of dreams are cast in the firsthand evidential since they are supposed to be 'seen'. Neither is the non-firsthand evidential used this way in Turkic languages; see §11.3, on evidentials in dreams and visions.)

We have seen that the non-firsthand evidential in A1 and A2 systems share quite a few semantic extensions. In addition, both are likely to develop mirative overtones (§6.1), and overtones of uncontrolled non-volitional action in the context of first person ('first person effect' described in §7.2). Evidentiality strategies discussed in Chapter 4 have similar extensions. The semantic path for these evidentials can be schematically represented as follows:

SCHEME 5.1 Meaning extensions for non-firsthand evidentials

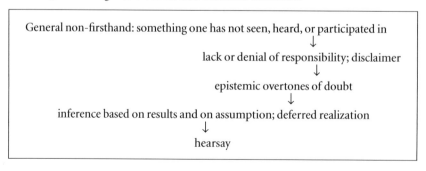

General non-firsthand: something one has not seen, heard, or participated in
↓
lack or denial of responsibility; disclaimer
↓
epistemic overtones of doubt
↓
inference based on results and on assumption; deferred realization
↓
hearsay

Firsthand evidentials are somewhat simpler. They refer to something acquired either visually or with some other appropriate sense. They hardly ever have any epistemic extensions relating to the truth or validity of what is being talked about. The firsthand evidence (in A1 systems) and sensory evidence (in A4 systems) are usually treated as conclusive. In Ngiyambaa, the sensory evidential *-gara* cannot occur together with epistemic 'belief' clitics: once the sensory evidence is there, one cannot doubt its validity (Donaldson 1980: 241).

The semantic similarities between the non-firsthand and the reported evidential may result in analytic problems. As we will see in §5.4, the reported evidential may develop the same extensions as the non-eyewitness and the non-firsthand terms in Scheme 5.1, with one difference: the direction of semantic extension goes from bottom up. As a result, the exact semantic nature of a small system may be difficult to ascertain (see (*c*) in §2.1.2; and also §4.8.2).

5.2 Semantic complexity in systems with three evidentiality choices

We will first look at the semantics of visual or direct evidentials within systems with three choices (§5.2.1). Then we discuss similarities and differences in the semantics of non-visual sensory terms (§5.2.2). Inferred evidentials will be exemplified in §5.2.3. The semantics of reported in B1, B3, B4, and of reported and quotative in B5 systems will be looked at in §5.4.

5.2.1 *Visual, or direct, evidential in systems with three choices*

Visual, or direct, evidentials in systems with three evidentiality choices (systems B1–3) show considerable semantic similarity with each other, and with the firsthand term in smaller systems (A1 and A4). Visual evidential is used to refer to something seen. It does not cover something one can hear or smell if there is a non-visual sensory to subsume these meanings (as in B2 and B3). In a system without a special non-visual sensory term, the direct evidential may extend to cover information obtained through hearing, smell, and taste.

In Quechua, the best described language group with a three-term system of type B1 (direct, reported, and inferred), the 'direct' evidential *-mi* refers to what one has 'seen', as in 2.40 and in 5.9.

Wanka Quechua (Floyd 1999: 61)
5.9   ñawi-i-wan-**mi**   lika-la-a
       eye-1p-with-DIR.EV   see-PAST-1p
       'I saw [them] with my own eyes' (DIRECT)

In 5.10, this evidential covers auditory information (Floyd 1999: 62–3).

5.10   ancha-p   ancha-p-ña-**m**   buulla-kta   lula-n
        too.much-GEN   too.much-GEN-NOW-DIR.EV   noise-ACC   make-3p
        kada   tuta-**m**
        each   night-DIR.EV
        'He really makes too much noise . . . every night' (I hear it: DIRECT)

In 5.11 the same form refers to what one can taste:

5.11   chay-chru   lurin   yaku-kuna-si   llalla-ku-n-**mi**
        that-LOC   Lurin   water-PL-also   be.salty-REF-3-DIR.EV
        'Even the water around Lurin is salty' (DIRECT)

The 'direct' evidential in Quechua covers speaker's INTERNAL EXPERIENCE which cannot be 'seen': emotions (as in 5.12), physical states (5.13), and thoughts and knowledge (5.14) (Floyd 1999: 63–4).

5.12   kushi-ku-lka-a-ña-**m**-ari   kuti-ila-ali-mu-pti-ki-a
        glad-REF-IMPF-1p-now-DIR.EV-EMPH   return-ASP-PL-AFAR-DS-2p-TOP
        'When you came back, we were happy' (DIRECT)

5.13   pata-yuu-ña-**m**-ari   ka-ya-a   ya'a
        stomach-HAVE-now-DIR.EV-EMPH   be-IMPF-1p   I
        'I sure AM pregnant' (DIRECT)

5.14   ya'a   mana-**m**   lima-pa-y-ta   yachra-a-chu
        I   not-DIR.EV   talk-BEN-IMP-ACC   know-1p-NEG
        'I don't know how to advise them' (DIRECT)

In Shasta (Silver and Miller 1997: 38), Mosetén (Sakel 2003), and Amdo Tibetan (Sun 1993: 961) the direct evidential also covers VISUAL and AUDITORY information, as well as smell. That is, for these languages and for Quechua the 'direct' evidential could be just as well called 'sensory'.

The semantic content of the only 'sensory' specification in Qiang is visual only (as in 2.44). The inferred evidential is used if one feels something in one's hand but cannot see it. If one hears a noise, such as the sound of drums, the inferred is used (LaPolla 2003a: 66):

Qiang
5.15   mi   ʐbɔ   ʐete-k
        person   drum   beat-INFR
        'Someone is playing drums' (it seems to me from hearing a noise that sounds like drums)

In both Quechua and Mosetén, the direct evidential may cover an inference the speaker considers obvious. In 5.16, from Mosetén (Sakel 2003: 267), the

speaker has heard a baby cry and immediately understands that the neighbour's baby has been born.

Mosetén

5.16 Mi'   **ishtyi'**   käedäej   nä'-ï
      3sgmasc   DIRECT.EV   baby   get.born-verb.stem.marker.masc.subj
      khin'
      now
      '(I heard it cry in the house.) The baby has been born now' (DIRECT)

And in Wanka Quechua (Floyd 1999: 62), one can say 5.17 meaning 'it is
morning now' (I see the sun, and this obviously means that it has dawned).

Wanka Quechua

5.17 lishi   kanan   wala-alu-n-ña-**m**
      Lishi   now   dawn-REC.PAST-3p-now-DIR.EV
      'Lishi, it is morning now' (the sun is already up; it has dawned; I see the
      sun) (DIRECT)

Further extensions of the direct evidential in both languages involve a
speaker's CERTAINTY. We will see below (§5.2.3) that inferred (or reported)
evidential is preferred when talking about the internal experience (emotions,
thoughts, and the like) of someone other than the speaker. Example 5.18
would be the usual way of talking about someone else being tired (Floyd
1999: 68–9).

5.18 pishipaa-shra-**chr**   ka-ya-nki
      be.tired-ATTRIB-INFR   be-IMPV-2p
      '(Sit here); you must be tired' (INFERRED)

But if the speaker is sure of how the other person feels, the direct evidential is
appropriate, as in 5.19. One can even use direct evidential to express one's
certainty concerning what another person thinks; this, however, appears to
be rare.

5.19 llaki-ku-n-**mi**
      sad-REF-3p-DIR.EV
      'He is sad' (DIRECT)

The direct evidential expresses the speaker's firm belief that what they are
talking about is true, and the speaker is in full control of the information (Floyd
1999: 69–70). By saying 5.20 the speaker does not mean to say that he has seen
his parents fail to do a particular job. This example implies that the speaker is
quite sure that his parents are unable to do it.

5.20 papaa-kaa-si   mana-**m**   atipa-n-chu   lula-y-ta
      father-DEF-also   not-DIR.EV   be.able-3p-NEG   do-IMPF-ACC
      'Our parents can't do it either' (DIRECT)

Manipulating these epistemic extensions of evidentials creates unusual effects in narratives; see §10.2.2. The use of the direct evidential implies the 'direct responsibility' of the speaker. This use correlates with the Quechua attitude towards knowledge. As Weber (1989: 421) puts it, 'only direct experience is reliable'. A Quechua speaker accepts full responsibility for something only if it is directly experienced by them. According to Nuckolls (1993) the visual evidential in Pastaza Quechua marks 'what is asserted by the speaker of an utterance' (cf. also Adelaar 1977: 79, on the association between a speaker's conviction and the use of direct evidential in Tarma Quechua). To escape the implications of taking full responsibility for something, a Quechua speaker would avoid the direct evidential (Weber 1989: 422).

The direct evidential is also used when talking about generally known facts. Example 5.21 is something every Peruvian knows.

Cuzco Quechua
5.21 Yunka-pi-**n**   k'usillu-kuna-qa   ka-n
      rainforest-LOC-DIR.EV   monkey-PL-TOP   be-3p
      'In the rainforest, there are monkeys' (DIRECT)

Visual evidentials are used this way in larger systems: visually obtained information is viewed as most reliable (see §5.3.1). Overtones of commitment to the truth of utterance, control over the information, and certainty are related to how the direct evidential in Quechua is used in questions (§8.1.1), in commands (§8.1.2), and with future (§8.4).

The direct evidential in Jaqi (Aymara: Hardman 1986) has comparable semantic extensions. Along similar lines, in Maricopa, with a B3 system, the firsthand evidential implies that the speaker is asserting something on the basis of having seen the event; both visual and non-visual sensory terms are used when the speaker 'is absolutely sure' of the facts (Gordon 1986*a*: 84–5). No epistemic extensions have been found in languages with a B1 system (e.g. Qiang, Bora, or Koreguaje).

5.2.2 *Non-visual sensory evidential in systems with three choices*

The non-visual sensory evidential in three-term systems which distinguish visual and non-visual (B2 and B3) is semantically rather uniform. It covers information obtained through senses other than sight, be it hearing, tasting, smelling or even feeling, as shown in 2.50 and 2.52–4, from Oksapmin (B3 system). No epistemic extensions have been attested.

In three-term systems without a visual evidential (B4), the non-visual term covers hearing, smell, and touch, as in 2.56–7, from Nganasan, and 2.61, from Retuarã. In 5.22, a girl left her house during a snow storm. (We can recall, from §2.2, that an unmarked verb in these languages is not to be regarded as a fourth evidential value.) She cannot see anything. She can only feel someone lift her by the crown of her head (the continuation of this example is 2.57).

Nganasan
5.22   Kuə   t'uhə-güə-nu   sil̠it̠'ə-küə-tə   ńoŋhu-gətə
       some   time-that-LOC.ADV   who-INDEF-LAT   crown-ABL
       d'ilə-ri̠-**mini̠**-t'i   d'ikar-aʔa   ńi
       lift-PASS-AUD-3sg   mountain-AUG[-GEN]   on
       'Some time later somebody lifted her by the crown of her head onto a
       mountain (she felt this)' (NON-VISUAL)

The non-visual sensory evidential describes physical states and feelings of the speaker, as in 5.23, also from Nganasan (Gusev forthcoming 5):

5.23   D'ütü-mə   d'ari-**mini**-t'i
       hand-1sg   ache-AUD-3sg
       'My hand is aching' (NON-VISUAL)

Non-visual evidentials have no epistemic extensions—in contrast to non-firsthand terms in A2 systems. Neither do they acquire mirative overtones, in contrast to non-firsthand in A1 systems. Unlike the non-visual evidential in D1, they do not have overtones of lack of control or awareness on behalf of the speaker. That is, the exact semantic content of superficially comparable terms in systems of different structure is far from identical.

5.2.3 *Inferred evidential in systems with three choices*
The inferred evidential in systems with three choices (B1, B2, and B4) covers inference based on visual evidence (as in 2.45, from Qiang, and 2.58, from Nganasan). It may imply reasoning, as in 2.59, from Nganasan, or assumption, as in 2.62, from Retuarã. The inferred evidential in Bora is used if one can see the result, but not the actual process that led to it. In 5.24, *-ʔha* 'inferred' indicates that all I saw was a burned house. I did not see it burn: it had burned before I saw it (Weber and Thiesen forthcoming: 254).

Bora

5.24 ó   áxt^hùmɨ-ʔ   tsʰà-há-ʔha^H-a^L   hà:
      I   see-(t)   that-(shelter)-INFR-REMOTE.PAST   shelter
      aíŋ-:ḅè-hà
      burn-sIn-(shelter)
      'I saw a burned house (one that had burned before I saw it)'

In Qiang (5.15) the inferred covers non-visual sensory evidence. It is not used
for an assumption. For this purpose a speaker would use the adverbial phrase
χsu-ɲi 'it seems' (LaPolla 2003*a*: 71–2), or a strategy involving a nominalized
verb with a suffix *-tan* 'appearance' or *-lahan* 'that kind, such' with a copula
(Randy LaPolla, p.c.).

An inference can be based on information the speaker acquired by hearsay.
The first sentence in 5.25, from Nganasan (Gusev forthcoming: 7), is cast
in reported evidential: the speaker says that he heard about an unusual type
of traditional house with short eaves. He then sees an unusual house and
comments, using the inferred evidential, that this must be it.

Nganasan

5.25   əuʔ,   ńenduʔ   munu-ntuə-ʔ   munu-ŋkə-ndu-ʔ:
      o!   not.without.reason speak-PART.PRES-pl speak-ITER-PRES-3pl
      ŋunirịʔa   maʔ   tənij-h^uaŋhu.   əmtị   i-h^ua∂u
      with.short.covers   house exist-REP.   This   be-INFR
      ŋunirịʔa,   təti   i-h^ua∂u təʔ?
      with.short.eaves   this   be-INFR   truly
      'O! It is not without reason that people say: there are said to exist houses
      with short eaves. (I infer that) this is a house with a short cover, this is
      it (I infer)'

The inferred evidential (marked with *-ch(i)*, *-ch(a)*, *-chr(i)* or *-chr(a)*) in
Quechua is used when a statement is based on inference or conjecture.[1] Such
an inference can be based on reasoning. Consider 5.26. A woman's house was
robbed. She has been told that her neighbour was seen working near her house
earlier that same day. She accuses her neighbour of being the thief. He denies
the accusation, and then adds 5.26. The reasoning is as follows: if the witness
saw someone and it was not this man, it must have been someone other than
him (Floyd 1999: 104).

---

[1] The choice of an allomorph depends partly on dialect area, partly on phonological context
(Floyd 1999: 94; also see Adelaar 1977, 1987, 1997).

Wanka Quechua

5.26 chay   lika-a-nii   juk-ta-**chra**-a   lika-la
      that   see-NOMN-1p   other-ACC-INFR-TOP   see-PAST
      'The witness (lit. my see-er) must have seen someone else' (I infer)

The inferred evidential in Wanka Quechua is a conventional way of talking about someone else's psychological and physical states (to which the speaker does not have 'direct' access, just like 'subjective' predicates in Japanese: see 4.37–8 and §4.6). An example is under 5.18.

Epistemic extensions of the inferred in Quechua involve probability, doubt, uncertainty, lack of personal responsibility, and the like (see Cerrón-Palomino 1976: 239; Adelaar 1977: 79; and Soto Ruiz 1976: 124, among others). But the inferred evidential does not have to imply any doubt. This is unlike, for instance, the irrealis marker -*man* as exemplified by Faller (2002: 160) whose primary function is epistemic; this marker can combine with any of the three evidentials. Whether the inferred evidential acquires an epistemic extension or not depends on the context. In 5.27, the inferred evidential occurs together with a future marker (see §8.4). This example comes from a conversation about F's daughter who has gone off to another town with her husband (Floyd 1999: 105). F's interlocutor says:

5.27 kay-lla-piita   kuti-i-mu-n'a-**chra**-a
      here-LIM-ABL   return-ASP-AFAR-3FUT-INFR-TOP
      'They will come back from this place'

This statement does not imply any doubt. Earlier on in the conversation the same speaker had pointed out that many people are going off to faraway places and then come back. The speaker is simply stating that, in his opinion, they will return (Floyd 1999: 105). An inferred evidential can even co-occur with adverbs like 'sure, very likely' in one clause, as in 5.28 (where *siguuru* is a loan from Spanish *seguro* 'sure').

5.28 waala-a   li-sha   siguuru-**chra**
      morning-TOP   go-1FUT   sure/very.likely-INFR
      'I'll surely/very likely go tomorrow'

If accompanied by the adverb *ichá* 'maybe', the inferred evidential conveys an epistemic extension of non-commitment. Taken out of its immediate context, a sentence with an inferred evidential can be interpreted as having overtones of doubt; this is why it can be translated as 'probably'. Floyd (1999: 101–3) provides an ample discussion of degrees of uncertainty and probability associated with the inferred marker.

The inferred evidential lacks the strong overtones of certainty associated with the direct evidential. If a vehement denial of having fathered a baby (as in 10.20) were cast in inferred evidential it would have left open the possibility that the man was the father. That is, the inferred evidential implies that the speaker does not commit themself to the truth of the statement. As a consequence, it is widely used in conversations as way of responding to a statement 'without being taken as gullible' (Weber 1989: 425). Hence its rhetorical effects (see §10.2.2).

A statement cast in the inferred evidential can have the force of a query, or a challenge as an answer. If the speaker's boss had read a list of those who are to go, and he is not sure whether his name was called, he could say 5.29, with a meaning 'am I to go?' (implying 'surely no!') (Weber 1989: 425).

Huallaga Quechua
5.29   noqa-**chi**   aywa-shaq-paq
        I-INFR   go-1FUT-FUT
        'I will go (am I to go?)'

Irony and sarcasm are associated with the inferred in Quechua. A flippant or sarcastic comment is often cast in inferred (see Weber 1989: 425–6; also see Floyd 1999: 115–17 for similar examples of Wanka Quechua). In 5.30, the inferred evidential implies the opposite of what is said. The girl's father is trying to persuade her to go to school, and when she continues to resist, he ironically makes fun of his daughter's assumption that she might learn by not going to school (Floyd 1999: 115).

Wanka Quechua
5.30   chay-nuu-pa-**chr**   yachra-nki
        that-SIM-GEN-INFR   know-2p
        'This is how you are supposed to learn!'

The ways in which inferred evidentials are used in questions provide further clues to their rhetorical overtones in Quechua; see §8.1.1. We will also see that an inferred evidential can acquire mirative extensions (see §6.2), as is the case in Nganasan (but not in Quechua).

5.3 Semantic complexity within larger systems

Evidential systems with four or more choices (C1–C3 and D1: §§2.3–4) show consistent semantic similarities between corresponding terms. A historical connection between a C1 and a D1 system holds for at least some languages (see §9.2.2). We first discuss the semantics of sensory evidentials (visual and non-visual in C₁ and D₁, and visual, or 'direct' in C₂₋₃ systems), and then look at types of inference encoded within large evidentiality systems.

5.3.1 *Semantic complexity of sensory evidentials*

In systems with two sensory evidentials, the visual evidential covers information acquired through seeing. The non-visual implies sensory perception other than seeing (hearing, smell, feel, and touch). Examples are 2.67–68 from Tucano, 2.71–2 from Eastern Pomo (C₁ systems), 1.1–2 from Tariana, and 2.96 from Wintu (D₁ systems).

The semantic range of the visual and the non-visual evidential is further illustrated below, with examples from Tariana. Visual evidential expresses something a person has seen, and a non-visual something they have not seen. In 5.31, the character sees an unusual white deer and comments:

Tariana

5.31 ne:ri halite ma-ka-kade-**mhana** nu-yã-ka
deer white+NCL:ANIM NEG-see-NEG-REM.P.NONVIS 1sg-stay-DECL
nuha ne:ri irite-mia-**na** nu-ka
I deer red+NCL:ANIM-ONLY-REM.P.VIS 1sg-see
nu-yã-ka nuha
1sg-stay-DECL I
'I have never seen a white deer (NON-VISUAL), I have only seen red deer (VISUAL)'

The visual evidential covers easily observable phenomena. Example 5.32 comes from a letter written by one of the speakers to the author, describing what he is doing and how everyone is at the moment of writing:

5.32 Kayumaka hĩ-tuki-**naka** nu-dana pi-na.
thus DEM:ANIM-DIM-PRES.VIS 1sg-write 2sg-OBJ.
Waha aĩ-se-nuku matʃa-**naka** thuya
We here-LOC-TOP.NON.A/S be.well-PRES.VIS all
'So I am writing this little bit to you. We here are all well'

The visual evidential is used when pointing at something. During the 2000 literacy workshop, the Tariana speakers provided captions for photographs depicting their village and themselves. The caption of the picture of the village of Santa Rosa, whose indigenous name translates as 'Salt Point', is *Iwi-taku-naka* (salt-point-PRES.VIS) 'this is Santa Rosa'. Similar examples abound in most languages with a C₁ system. When asked in Tucano who the person in a photograph was, I was instructed to say *Yi'î maki niî-mi* (I son be-PRES.VIS.3sg.masc) 'It is my son'.

In both Tariana and Tucano, the non-visual evidential covers a wide range of things one cannot see but can hear or smell, and also feeling something done to one (as one feels an injection, or a blow, but not what one feels by touch). The same range of meanings has been described for the non-visual evidential in Hupda (Epps 2005). In 5.33, from Tariana, a girl hears the noise of someone walking behind her. She cannot see him, since the man has been made invisible, and so she says, using the non-visual evidential:

5.33   patʃi-**mha**   wa-pumi   na-nu
       someone-PRES.NONVIS 1pl-after 3pl-come
       'Someone is coming after us' (I can hear it)

Her sister feels someone step on her dress and hold the dress firmly—again, the person is invisible and she cannot see him. She comments:

5.34   paita-**mha**   nuha-naku   yaɾumakasi
       one+NUM.CL:ANIM-PRES.NONVIS   I-TOP.NON.A/S   dress
       di-phua-liphe
       3sgnf-step-FIRMLY
       'Someone has stepped on my dress and is holding it firmly' (I can feel it)[2]

An evil spirit comes home from a hunting trip, smells human blood, and comments, using the non-visual evidential:

5.35   aĩ-nuku   iɾi   puisani-pu-**mha**
       here-TOP.NON.A/S   blood   smell.of.flesh-AUG-PRES.NONVIS
       'There is a very strong smell of blood here'

Similarly, the non-visual evidential in Tucano can refer to something one hears (2.68), or to something one can taste (5.36), or feel, as a mosquito bite in 5.37 (Ramirez 1997, vol. I: 131).

Tucano
5.36   ba'â-sehé   akâ+yɨ'dɨa-**sa'**
       eat-NOMN.INAN.PL   salty+very-PRES.NONVIS.nonthird.p
       'The food is very salty' (I can sense it by taste)

5.37   ãhú-pẽa   bãdî-de   dū'dî-dã'   weé-**sa**-bã
       mosquito-PL   we-TOP.NON.A/S bite-SUB.MASC AUX-PRES.NONVIS-3pl
       'Mosquitoes are biting us' (we can feel it)

The non-visual evidential is used to describe the emotions, thoughts, and physical states of the speaker, including hunger, thirst, being drunk, dizzy, and

---

[2] The non-visual evidential in Tariana is not used to describe feeling or touching something on purpose: if one checks clothes on the line, and feels that they are dry, an assumed evidential is used; see §5.3.2.

so on. Example 5.38 is a normal way of saying 'I am sick with fever'. (Other 'first person effects' of non-visual evidentials will be considered in §7.2.)

Tariana

5.38 adaki   di-nu-**mha**   nu-na
      fever   3sgnf-come-PRES.NONVIS   1sg-OBJ
      'I have fever' (lit. fever comes to me)

The non-visual evidential is employed to talk about one's own emotional state, as in 5.39, from Tucano (Ramirez 1997, vol. I: 134).

5.39 koô   etâ-kǎ   yi'î   e'katí-**asɨ**
      she   arrive-SUB   I   be.happy-REC.P.NONVIS.nonthird.p
      'When she arrived, I felt happy'

The non-visual evidential occurs with verbs of difficulty, liking, and wanting.

Tariana

5.40 uni   kada-peɾi   hui-**mha**   nuha
      water   black-NCL:COLLECTIVE   like.food-PRES.NONVIS   I
      'I like coffee' (lit. black water)

In these cases, the first person pronoun can be omitted: the first person effect of the evidential itself is enough to figure out the person value; see §7.4, on the implicit person value conveyed by evidentials.

The non-visual sensory evidential in Eastern Pomo has the same range of meanings as in other C1 and in D1 systems (McLendon 2003: 103). In 5.41, the non-visual evidential describes 'liking' and in 5.42, the state of 'being afraid'.

Eastern Pomo

5.41 mí   ma·rá·-**nk'e**
      2.sg.patient   like/want-NONVIS
      'I like you'

In 5.42, the non-visual evidential itself indicates that the speaker is talking about their own feelings. This is another example of the 'first person effect' with a non-visual evidential.

5.42 kʰéˑs̃   kʰúˑlma-**nk'e**
      lots   afraid-NONVIS
      'I am afraid (of the dark)'

In large systems with two sensory evidentials, the non-visual evidential cannot describe sensations experienced by non-first person. Similarly, the direct evidential in Quechua does not normally refer to something experienced by someone other than the speaker. To report a feeling being experienced by someone else, one has the option of using a visual evidential if one can see the state the other person is in, as in 5.43 (McLendon 2003: 104), from Eastern Pomo.

5.43   mí-p'   kʰúˑlma-k'iˑyàˑl-**a**
        3sg-MASC.AGENT   afraid-CONTROL-VIS
        'He's afraid (of the dark)' (I can see he is)

If one does not have enough visual evidence, one can make an inference about another person's feelings. In Eastern Pomo, 5.44 is an alternative to 5.43, if the speaker can make an inference based on the person's behaviour.

5.44   mí-p'   kʰúˑlma-k'iˑyàˑl-**ine**
        3sg-MASC.AGENT   afraid-CONTROL-INFR
        'He's afraid (of the dark)' (I infer from his behaviour or other evidence)

The non-visual evidential is used to describe 'stereotyped experiences' as 'unseen'. This includes the deeds of evil spirits and dreams by ordinary people (see (*A*) and (*B*) under §11.3).

The visual may have an additional epistemic extension of certainty. Example 5.45 is a statement of a fact obvious to any Tariana—that the Tariana are direct descendants of Thunder, and are hence superior to any other group of people.

Tariana
5.45   waha-wya-ka   enu   i-daki-ne-**naka**
        we-LIM-DECL   thunder   INDEF-grandchild-PL-PRES.VIS
        'We <u>are</u> grandchildren of Thunder'

Similarly, one does not need to be looking at the sun to say that it is round—this is encyclopedic knowledge. Visual evidentials cover all generally known and observable facts (Ramirez 1997, vol. I: 127).

Tucano
5.46   būhîpũu   opâ-sɨtɨ   dî-**bɨ̄**
        sun   ANAPH-CL:ROUND   be-PRES.VIS.3sg.masc
        'The sun is round'

This is very similar to the use of direct evidential in Quechua (as in 5.21). The visual evidential is associated with 'timeless' generally known facts in other Tucanoan languages of the Vaupés region with four- and five-term evidential systems (see Barnes 1984: 259, for Tuyuca).

The visual evidential is also employed if the speaker takes full responsibility for the statement (in which he or she may also be personally involved). In 5.47, the woman confronts the shaman, accusing him of killing her children who had ravaged his fruit tree. Although she did not see this, she talks as if she did. She thus takes full responsibility for what she says—as a consequence, the shaman ends up killing her.

Tariana

5.47   ma:ʧite   phya-yana   nu-enipe-nuku   pi-hña-**naka**
       bad+NCL:ANIM   you-PEJ   1sg-children-TOP.NON.A/S   2sg-eat-PRES.VIS
       'You bad one you eat my children'

The visual evidential in Eastern Pomo has a similar epistemic extension of certainty: one can say 2.75 only if one is sure who had taken the thing. So does the visual evidential in Wintu (D1): 'the speaker does not claim to be absolutely sure of anything unless he sees it right then and there' (Schlichter 1986: 54). These extensions are similar to those described for the direct evidential in three-term systems—see 5.16, from Mosetén, and 5.19–21 from various Quechua languages. But note that non-visual evidentials do not have any overtones of uncertainty.

The non-visual evidentials may refer to accidental and uncontrollable actions, especially in the context of first person. This includes things one does not mean to do and can't help doing, as in 5.48, from Tariana, or something beyond one's control, as in 5.49, from Tucano (Ramirez 1997, vol. I: 133) (see §7.2).

Tariana

5.48   wa-pika-**mhana**   wha   awakada-se
       1pl-get.lost-REM.P.NOVIS   we   jungle-LOC
       'We got lost in the jungle (without meaning to and not being able to help getting lost)'

Tucano

5.49   pũûgi-pi   bidî-diha-'**ast**
       hammock-TOP.NON.A/S   fall-go.down-REC.P.NONVIS.nonthird.p
       'I fell down out of a hammock' (without intending to: maybe while asleep)

The only sensory evidential in four-term evidentiality systems of C2 and C3 types covers any sensory perception. In Shipibo-Konibo (with a C2 system) the direct evidential -*ra* is ubiquitous in texts describing one's personal experience. It also refers to what one hears or smells, as in 2.80 (the speaker could hear and smell the fish being fried, without seeing it). In 5.50, the speaker uses -*ra* to give information about himself (this is the context where a Tariana or a Tucano speaker would also use a visual evidential).

Shipibo-Konibo

5.50   Nokon jane   **r**-iki   Inkan Soi
        POSS.I name:ABS   DIR.EV-COP   Inkan Soi
        'My name is Inkan Soi'

The direct evidential is also used to make statements about generally known
facts (Valenzuela 2003: 35–7). Similarly to the systems above, the sensory 'direct'
evidential is associated with reliable information and with certainty. This is
particularly salient in threats, warnings, and statements about habitual and
future events. The threat in 5.51 sounds very real.

5.51   jatíbi-tian-**ra**   i-nox   iki   chiní   bake-bo
        all-TEMPORAL-DIR.EV   do.INTR-FUT   (FUT)   last   child-PL:ABS
        ja-ská   ja-skát-i
        that-COMP   that-COMP-INTR
        'From now on, your children will live just like that'

Along similar lines, the direct evidential in Cora (C3) is associated with the
veracity of a statement (§2.3). In Tsafiki, with a C2 system, the visual evidential
is normally used for visually acquired information, and also for well-known
facts, if the information is part of the speaker's integrated knowledge (Connie
Dickinson, p.c.).

In addition, the evidential choice in Tsafiki correlates with the speaker's
participation in the situation, and how close the speaker is to someone he or
she is talking about. If someone asks a wife where her husband has gone, she
would be expected to use the direct evidential (formally unmarked), even if
she had not seen her husband leave, as in 5.52 (Dickinson 2000: 409–10).
A neighbour would not be able to use the direct evidential without having
seen the man leave: they would have to use either the inferred evidential
marked by -nu-, or the reported. If a neighbour does use the direct evidential in
such circumstances, he or she would be accused of being a liar or 'at the very
least very presumptuous'. (See §11.1.) The wife 'is a participant in the event in a
way her neighbour is not'—and this explains why she can use the direct evidential to describe something she has not necessarily seen.

Tsafiki: the wife speaking

5.52   ya   man-to=ka   **ji-e**
        3p   other-earth=LOC   go-DECL:VISUAL
        'He went to Santo Domingo'

The use of visual or direct evidential is not conditioned by any particular
kinship relation. People who share a household typically consider each other
close enough for this purpose (also see Dickinson 2000: 420).

If the wife uses the inferred evidential, this has additional implications: what it means is that either the husband did not discuss his plans with her or she disapproves of his actions. By using the inferred evidential, as in 5.53, she declares herself a 'non-participant'.

5.53   ya   man-to=ka   ji-**nu**-e
       3p   other-earth=LOC   go-INFR-DECL
       'He has gone to Santo Domingo' (and she does not approve)

This is rather similar to the 'distancing' effect of non-firsthand evidentials in small systems (see §5.1). Inferred evidentials may extend to cover non-participation and new non-integrated knowledge. We return to this in §5.3.2.

The extensions of sensory evidentials are summarized in Table 5.1. The main meanings related to perceptual sources are under 1 (in bold). The range of meanings of the direct evidential in C2 and C3 systems shows considerable similarity with the visual evidential in C1 and D1 systems. All it shares with the non-visual evidential is straightforward cases of sensory perception (hearing or smelling). It does not cover any of the extensions of the non-visual, either to one's own internal states or to actions or states treated as 'not seen'. Neither does it extend to uncontrollable actions: other non-evidential means are then used.

TABLE 5.1 Sensory evidentials in large systems

SYSTEMS C1/D1	INFORMATION SOURCE	SYSTEMS C2/C3
Visual	1. Information obtained through seeing, or data on events which can be observed 2. Events for which speaker takes full responsibility and/or has a personal involvement 3. Generally known (and observable) facts	**Direct**
Non-visual 'sensory'	1. Events or states which the speaker has heard, smelt, tasted, or felt but not seen 2. Events or states never seen (but perceived in some other ways, also negative clauses: e.g. I did not see) 3. Accidental uncontrollable actions for which no responsibility is taken (hence use with verbs of obligation, feeling, illness, physical process), as well as with verbs like 'be lost'; actions in dreams, descriptions of uncontrollable actions of evil spirits who cannot be seen but can be felt and heard (see §11.3)	**Other means**

5.3.2 *Semantic complexity of inferred evidentials*

Two basic kinds of inference can acquire grammatical expression in large evidentiality systems: inference based on results and assumption based on reasoning. If there is just one inferred evidential (as in C1 and C3), it combines both meanings. An inference about a dog eating a fish in 2.69 from Tucano can be based on physical evidence, such as bones scattered around and the dog looking happy. Or it can be based on the general assumption that only a dog in a household could do such a thing. Along similar lines, the inferred evidential in Eastern Pomo indicates that the statement is based on inference of any kind (McLendon 2003: 104–5). In the words of McLendon's consultant, 'if you come home and find a vase broken and only your ten year old son was home during the afternoon, you could say "my son broke the vase" with this suffix attached to the verb "break" '. The inferred evidential in 5.54 is used in similar circumstances: you know it is taken because you left it there, and now it's disappeared.

Eastern Pomo

5.54 bá·=kʰi   pʰu·di-yaki-**ne**-he
     SPEC.ANAPHORIC=3p.AGENT   steal-PL:AGENT-INFR-ANT
     'They must have stolen it'

An inference can be based on sensory evidence. In 5.55, also from Eastern Pomo, the speaker concludes that the fish must be ripe based on his interpretation of the type of smell.

5.55 šá-heʔ   mo·wós-k-**ine**
     fish-SPEC   ripe-PUNCTUAL-INFR
     'Fish must be ripe' (said when one smells that fermentation has reached the desired point)

In contrast, the non-visual sensory evidential in 5.56 tells us nothing about any interpretation of the sensory evidence; it simply asserts that there is a smell.

5.56 šá-heʔ   mi·šé-**nk'e**
     fish-SPEC   smell+PUNCTUAL-NONVIS
     'I smell the fish' (said of one's perception, not inferring the state of fish)

In none of these cases does the inferred evidential imply any uncertainty or conjecture: it describes a steadfast conclusion one makes. (Once again, the reader should be warned against relying on the English translation, which necessarily involves modal verbs.)

Languages can distinguish between inference and assumption. We have seen how inference and assumption are distinguished in Tsafiki. In 2.77 an inference is made on the basis of physical evidence (dirty dishes show that Manuel has eaten). The basis of an assumption in 2.78 is general knowledge: we know that Manuel eats at eight, and if it is nine o'clock already, we assume he has eaten. Similar examples are under 2.81–2, from Shipibo-Konibo. Tuyuca, Desano, and Tariana also distinguish inferred (based on visible results) and assumption (based on unspecified reference and/or on prior knowledge and/or experience with similar situations and general common sense: Barnes 1984: 262; Miller 1999: 67–8). In 1.3, from Tariana, we infer that José has gone to play football because there is enough visual evidence for it (his boots are missing, there is a football match planned, and so on). And in 1.4 our assumption is based on general knowledge about what José does on Sundays: he always plays football.

The assumed evidential in Tariana is employed to interpret one's non-visual experience. When one touches something to see if it is dry, one says *yarumakasi makara-sika* (clothes dry-REC.P.ASSUMED) 'the clothes are dry'. The assumed evidential also involves inference based on common beliefs. If someone sneezes, people often say: *pi-na nawada-**sika*** (2sg-OBJ 3pl + think-REC.P.ASSUM) 'They are thinking about you (I assume)'. This is based on a belief that if someone is thinking strongly about someone else, this other person would sneeze. In addition, the assumed and the inferred evidentials are used in different kinds of narratives as genre markers (see §10.2.1).

We saw in §5.3.1 that in large systems the non-visual evidential is employed to talk about one's own feelings, physical states, and emotions (in the same way that a Quechua speaker, with a three-term evidential system, would use the direct evidential for this purpose). To talk about someone else's feelings or state, one has a choice of employing an inferred evidential or a visual evidential (as in 5.43 and 5.44, from Eastern Pomo). In Tariana, the visual evidential will be appropriate if there is enough visual evidence for the statement. If not, one uses the assumed evidential. On my first lengthy canoe journey to the village of Santa Rosa, Jovino Brito was concerned about my discomfort (I did my best not to show this), since I was far too big for a narrow canoe. He said:

Tariana

5.57   maːtʃi-pu   du-ɾena-**sika**   wepa-**sika**
       bad-AUG   3sgf-feel-REC.P.ASSUM   stiff-REC.P.ASSUM
       'She feels bad, she is stiff' (I assume this because she is crouching in the
       canoe which is too narrow for her and she is not used to such journeys)

In none of these instances does the inferred or assumed evidential imply any doubt. The inference or the assumption is considered valid because there is 'proof'. This is how Tariana speakers justify the use of both inferred and assumed evidentials (see §11.2 on how people talk about evidentials in their language). Along similar lines, the inferential evidential in Kashaya does not imply any 'lack of certainty'. All it implies is a lack of visual or auditory information.

A rare instance I found of an assumed evidential with epistemic extensions is the assumed-speculative -*mein* in Shipibo-Konibo; unlike the inferred evidential, -*bira*, which marks inference, -*mein* may have overtones of doubt (see 2.82). And we saw in 5.53 that the inferred evidential in Tsafiki may imply speaker's lack of participation and distancing. This is akin to non-integrated knowledge and ensuing mirative extensions of the inferred evidential; see §6.2.

Languages are known to mark inferences of other sorts. Foe, a language with six evidentials from the Southern Highlands of Papua New Guinea (Rule 1977: 71–4 and examples 2.97–102), appears to have separate markers for statements made on the basis of mental deduction, visible evidence, and previous evidence. Hill Patwin (Southern Wintun: Whistler 1986) has five inferential suffixes: indirect evidential 'based on other than direct sensory evidence requiring no inference'; two suffixes marking 'tentative inference' ('implied insufficient grounds for certain knowledge'), one of which is used with realis and the other with irrealis; confident inference, and circumstantial inference.

Languages with scattered coding of evidentiality (§3.4) make further distinctions. Makah (Wakashan: Jacobsen 1986) distinguishes (1) inference from hearing and physical evidence such as the leftovers of food, (2) visual evidence of a second person, (3) uncertain visual evidence, and (4) logical inference from unspecified evidence (and also hearsay). And see Fortescue (2003: 292–5) for a fine-grained analysis of varied affixes in West Greenlandic which may be interpreted as having to do with inference.

None of the epistemic extensions of evidentials are universal. Tuyuca, Tariana, and Tucano evidentials have no epistemic overtones. Also see Dickinson (2000), on how epistemic modality is marked distinctly from evidentiality. (See §7.3, on how these interact with evidentials.) This is hardly surprising. Languages with large evidentiality systems tend to have rich verbal morphology. Typically, there are numerous ways of expressing doubt, uncertainty, and conjecture within the modality system. Every morpheme is highly specialized in meaning. And, consequently, evidentials acquire hardly any extensions beyond their major meaning, the information source.

5.4 Semantic complexity of reported evidentials

The reported evidential is semantically uniform throughout evidentiality systems. Typically, it covers information acquired through somebody else's report, without any claim about the exact authorship or the speaker's commitment to the truth of the statement. A reported evidential may be distinct from a quotative; see §5.4.1. A reported evidential may, or may not, refer to secondhand, thirdhand, and so on, information; see §5.4.2. It may have epistemic overtones; see §5.4.3. No language has two visual or two non-visual evidentials. It is not uncommon, however, for a language to have two reported specifications. This is the topic of §5.4.4.

5.4.1 *Reported versus quotative*

If a language has two reported-type evidentials, the most common distinction is that between reported (stating what someone else has said without specifying the exact authorship) and quotative (introducing the exact author of the quoted report). Examples are B5 systems (see examples 2.65–6 from Comanche in §2.2), and also Cora (under C3: §2.3).

The reported evidential can refer to information obtained from someone else either with or without indicating the exact source of the report. The reported evidential may simply not be used if the source of information is explicitly stated, as in Kham (see §4.8.3).[3] A sentence like 5.58, from Tucano, is vague as to the exact authorship of the information.

Tucano (Ramirez 1997: Vol. I: 142)
5.58   utî-**apo'**
          cry-REC.P.REP.3sg.fem
          'She cried' (it is said: either she told me herself, or somebody else told me)

The reported in Tariana is equally vague. The report of Tiago's death in 3.50 was in fact based on a radio announcement, so 'who told what' was clear to everyone present. The source of information can be added optionally, as a strategy of lexical reinforcement of the reported meaning. This is often done to add weight to the story (see §11.2). The present reported in Tariana has a quotative-like use: it refers to a piece of information someone has just learnt (but the source itself is not specified). Example 3.50 was uttered by a speaker immediately after the sad news was heard on the radio. During our work on Tariana placenames, José, a young speaker, would often ask his father about

---

[3] One ought to beware of the terms some authors use with respect to reported evidential; the term 'quotative' is widely used in lieu of reported by North American linguists (cf. Silver and Miller 1997) and many South Americanists. For instance, Ramirez (1994: 169–70) calls the Xamatauteri *horã* 'citatif' ('quotational'); it is, however, obvious from his discussion and from his ample exemplification that this marker does not specify the exact authorship of information, hence its translation into French as *on dit*, *le bruit court*.

a name he did not know, and then repeat it, using the present reported evidential: *popoa-kuya-pida* (arumã.vine-CL:PROMONTORY-PRES.REP) 'the name is "Promontory of the arumã vine", he has just said'.[4]

Along similar lines, the reported *-sh(i)* in Quechua never indicates who the author is. Floyd (1999: 130–1) presents an extract from a conversation where the speaker is telling his friend about the age of some pottery he saw during a trip to a museum a few hours earlier. Every sentence contains a reported evidential. At the beginning of the conversation, the speaker says that the information comes from a particular woman, a tour guide. In the following text, there is no more mention of her as being the author of information. As Floyd puts it, 'the *-sh(i)* that appears throughout the conversation is clearly understood as oblique reference to her'; the woman 'still figures prominently' in the speaker's mind as the source of information—but the reported evidential simply does not allow the inclusion of an overt 'author'. Similarly, in Tsafiki the reported evidential *-ti-* indicates that the information comes from someone else's report but does not mark quotations. The verb marked with the reported can be a complement to the verb *ti* 'say' (which gave rise to the reported evidential: Dickinson 2000: 419) indicating who the author is (see 3.13–14).

The same evidential may combine the meanings of a reported and a quotative, as in Jinghpaw (Tibeto-Burman: Saxena 1988: 377) and in Copala Trique (Oto-Manguean: Hollenbach 1992: 241). A reported evidential can be obligatory in reported speech and in quotations, as in Udihe (Nikolaeva and Tolskaya 2001: 663–4, 668), Kiowa (Watkins 1984: 84–5), Nganasan, and Latundê (Nambiquara).

A direct speech complement may be an alternative to the reported evidential (see §4.8.1), to avoid unnecessary connotations of unreliable information associated with the reported evidential. Direct speech complements in Tariana are preferred as quoting strategies: this tendency also has to do with reluctance to interpret other people's evidentials, since it is 'safer' to repeat what they said themselves (§11.3). In contrast, in Tewa a direct quotation conveys overtones of disbelief (§4.8.3).

5.4.2 *Distinguishing secondhand and thirdhand information*

If a language has one reported term, it is typically used for secondhand and thirdhand information. Whether the information is secondhand or thirdhand is known from the context only. In 5.59, from Tariana, Lion, the ruler of

---

[4] When talking about the behaviour of an animal, one may use a present reported evidential in a 'quasi-quotative' function to interpret what the animal 'means'. When we were leaving for the village of Santa Rosa, a local dog was whimpering and whining while trying to get into our canoe. The dog's 'message' was interpreted as follows, using the present reported: *di-na di-a-ka-pida wa-ine* (3sgnf-want 3sgnf-go-DECL-PRES.REP 1pl-with) 'He wants to come with us (it is said/he says)'.

animals, tells all the animals that the world is going to end if the stone falls down (as he had just learned from someone else—using the recent past reported evidential).

Tariana

5.59   ha-ehkwapi   di-disa   di-a-kaɾu-pena-**pidaka**
      DEM:INAN-CL:DAY   3sgnf-end   3sgnf-go-PURP.VIS-FUT.NOM-REC.P.REP
      wa-na
      1pl-OBJ
      '(When this stone falls) this world will end for us (I am told)'

The jaguar volunteers to stand underneath the stone to prevent it from falling. A few lines later, a coatimundi comes along and asks the jaguar why he is standing there. The jaguar answers, in 5.60, using the same evidential. He then adds where the information comes from, to give his assertion more authority: it was the Lion himself who had told him! We return to this 'lexical reinforcement' of evidentials in §10.3.

5.60   ha   hipada   di-wha-ka   di-ɾuku   di-a
      DEM:INAN   stone   3sgnf-fall-SUB   3sgnf-go.down   3sgnf-go
      ha-ehkwapi   di-sisa-kaɾu-pena-**pidaka**   wa-na
      DEM:INAN-CL:DAY   3sgnf-end-PURP.VIS-FUT.NOM-REC.P.REP   1pl-OBJ
      kayu   di-a-**ka**   di-sape   wha   wekana   leo
      thus   3sgnf-say-REC.P.VIS   3sgnf-tell   we   1pl+chief   lion
      'Here, when this (stone) falls, the world will end for us (it is said), thus our chief the lion has said'

Similar examples of a reported evidential marking secondhand and third-hand information are found in Shipibo-Konibo (Valenzuela 2003: 42–3, ex. (21)). A few languages have additional means of distinguishing 'degrees' of hearsay. In Tsafiki one can indicate up to three sources 'between the speaker and the original event' by combining the reported evidential and the verb 'say' as in 3.13 (Dickinson 2000: 408). Similarly, in some varieties of Brazilian Portuguese spoken in Northwest Amazonia, the particle *dizque* can be repeated several times to indicate the 'degree' of hearsay (see §4.8.4, on how the same particle is used in Colombian Spanish).

5.4.3 *Epistemic extensions of reported evidentials*

The reported evidential may just refer to data acquired through somebody else's report, without making any claim about the truth of the statement. A prime example of this is the reportative particle *di* in Kham (Tibeto-Burman: Watters

2002: 296–300). The reportative *-ronki* in Shipibo-Konibo (Valenzuela 2003: 37–43) does not have any overtones of low degree of reliability: it simply refers to information obtained from verbal report. The reported evidential in Nganasan ('renarrative': Gusev forthcoming: 3, 11) occurs only in narratives describing something that happened to a particular person, most often the narrator's ancestor. This evidential is also used by shamans recounting what the spirits had told them. The use of reported evidential presupposes the existence of a firsthand information source. Reported evidential in Nganasan implies that the information is highly reliable.

In other systems the reported evidential makes an implicit reference to the speaker's attitude to the information obtained from someone else. The speaker may choose to employ the reported evidential for two reasons. Firstly, to show his or her objectivity; that the speaker was not the eyewitness to an event and knows about it from someone else. Secondly, as a means of 'shifting' responsibility for the information and relating facts considered unreliable.

We saw, in 2.23, that reported evidential in Estonian has overtones of information one does not vouch for. Examples 5.61–2 illustrate the point (Ilse Lehiste, p.c., and cf. Fernandez-Vest 1996: 171). Saying 5.61 is just stating a fact (the form is evidentiality-neutral: one is not saying how one knows it).

Estonian

5.61 Ta   lõpetas   arstiteaduskonna
      he   finished   doctor.faculty.GEN
      'He completed his study of medicine' (graduated from a faculty of medicine)

Recasting this statement with a reported evidential implies that the speaker simply quotes someone else's report, and thus distances themselves from responsibility for its veracity. This holds for both present and past reported (2.23 contains a present reported form).

5.62 Ta   **olevat**   arstiteaduskonna   **lõpeta-nud**
      he   be:PRES.REPORTED   doctor.faculty:GEN   finish-PAST.PART
      'He is said to have completed his studies of medicine (but I wouldn't vouch for it)'

The reported evidential in Australian languages with an A3 system is similar. In Mparntwe Arrernte, the reported evidential *kwele* can be used 'to bring into question facts put forward by others', indicating that the speaker 'has no direct experience of the facts'; this 'leads to the logical inference that s/he is saying the facts are untrue' (Wilkins 1989: 392–3).

Mparntwe Arrernte

5.63   The   **kwele**   re-nhe   twe-ke
        1sgA   REP   3sg-ACC   hit/kill-PAST.COMPL
        'I am supposed to have killed him' (I am reported to have killed him;
        I didn't)

When used as a marker of the narrative genre of Dreamtime stories, the reported evidential does not have any epistemic extension; see §10.2.1, on evidentials as genre tokens. A similar example from Diyari is at 2.34. Besides its use as a marker of reported speech, the reported particle *kunyu* in Yankunytjatjara (Australian: Goddard 1983: 289) may imply that the speaker does not want to be held personally responsible for the information.

The reported marker *nganta* is used in a similar way in Warlpiri (Australian: Laughren 1982: 138). The speaker is merely reporting what was said by someone else.

Warlpiri

5.64   Ngaju-ku   **nganta**   ngulaju   yuwarli
        I-DAT   REP   that(is)   house
        'They say that house is for me' (but I don't vouch for it or am not sure)

Example 5.64 is a less strong claim than simply saying 'that house is for me' without an evidential, as in 5.65.

5.65   Ngaju-ku   ngulaju   yuwarli
        I-DAT   that(is)   house
        'That house is for me'

The reported marker in Warlpiri may also imply that the speaker knows (or thinks) that the statement within the scope of *nganta* is downright false. Example 5.66 comes from a mythological text about an evil old man who pretended to be blind. The storyteller uses the reported marker to 'distance himself from the proposition', since he knows it to be false; it is the old man, not the narrator, who says that he is blind. The reported marker has distinct epistemic overtones: one does not believe the old trickster's pretences.

5.66   **Nganta**-lpa   purlka   yangka-ju   Lungkarda   parntarrija—
        REP-IMPF   old.man   ANAPH-DEL   Lungkarda   crouched-PAST
        pampa   **nganta**   nyanja-wangu.   Kala   ruyu   parntarrija
        blind   REP   seeing-PRIV   but   ruse   crouch-PAST
        'That old man Lungkarda was supposedly crouching down reckoning
        he was blind—that he could not see. But he was just crouching down
        pretending'

Similarly, in Tauya (Madang-Adalbert Range subphylum, Papuan: MacDonald 1990a: 42–3) the emerging reported evidential suffix signals false presupposition. In 5.67, the scope of the evidential -ʔopa is the noun phrase which translates as 'as if it were' or 'alleged'.

Tauya

5.67   oʔosi   ni-pi-**ʔopa**   wate   mene-a-ʔa
       land   3sg-GEN-REP   NEG   stay-3sg-IND
       'His so-called land isn't his' (i.e. the land said to be his does not belong to him)

Reported evidentials in West Greenlandic and in Uto-Aztecan languages (Munro 1978: 160, 163) are used to mark sentences 'for which the speaker does not claim direct responsibility'. Along similar lines, in Maricopa (Gordon 1986a: 86) the reportative construction implies that the speaker does not vouch for the truth of the utterance. In Sochiapan Chinantec (Foris 2000: 373–4) the reported particle né?^{H} has an overtone of 'this is what I heard, but who knows if it is true' (also see §8.1.1 on its use in questions). In Jamul Tiipay (Yuman: Miller 2001: 277), the reported evidential may indicate that 'the speaker is not willing to vouch for the truth of the material contained with the preceding clause'. A similar extension is found in Cora (Casad 1992: 152). Cupeño (Hill 2005: 459–68) the reported evidential is used to challenge the validity of a statement by another. And in Yosondúa Mixtec (Farris 1992: 47–8), Jamiltepec Mixtec (Johnson 1988: 45), Ocotepec Mixtec (Alexander 1988: 190–1), and Silacayoapan Mixtec (Shields 1988: 341), all from the Oto-Manguean family, the hearsay markers function as disclaimers.

Reported evidentials often cover 'pretend' and 'make-believe' situations. The reported particle *kunyu* in Yankunytjatjara (Goddard 1983: 289) occurs in talking about children's 'pretend' games, as in 5.68 (see 4.61, for a similar use of *dizque* in Colombian Spanish).

Yankunytjatjara

5.68   nyanytju   **kunyu**
       horse(NOM)   REP
       'It's a horse according to him' (said of a boy playing 'horsies' with a dog)

In West Greenlandic the reported enclitic -*guuq* is also typical of children's 'pretend' games, whereby one child is proposing a game: 'you-quotative be a doctor and I—a patient' (Fortescue 2003: 299; the same usage is found in Central Siberian Yupik: Willem de Reuse, p.c.). The reported *nganta* is also used this way in Warlpiri (see Appendix to Chapter 11, and Edith Bavin, p.c.).

Reported evidentials can be used ironically, rather like the way the inferred evidential is used in Quechua (see 5.29–30). The reported particle *kwele* in Mparntwe Arrernte expresses criticism when used in a statement that both the speaker and the hearer know to be true. If a person is behaving in an unacceptable manner, this is a way of reminding them that they probably only know the norm by hearsay—but in fact, the norm is known to everyone, hence the stylistic, almost sarcastic effect. In 5.69, a husband is scolding his wife who had not looked after the baby properly while he had been away hunting. In Mparntwe Arrernte society the woman's role is to look after the children. The husband found the baby sick and scratched all over (Wilkins 1989: 394), and said:

Mparntwe Arrernte

5.69 Unte **kwele** ampe kweke arntarntare-me
      2sgA REP child small look.after-NONPAST.PROGR
      'You, so they say, are meant to look after the baby' (but I have seen no
      evidence of it myself, in fact I have evidence to the contrary)

The reported *nganta* in Warlpiri can also be used ironically. If someone claims to be beautiful, the reported can be used to mark disagreement. This is similar to the 'pretence' meaning of reported illustrated in 5.68 above (for Yankunytjatjara) (Laughren 1982: 141). The nearest English equivalent to 5.70 is 'As if she is beautiful!' The speaker does not hold to the truth of the proposition that the referent is beautiful. The claim is made by the referent herself (Mary Laughren, p.c.).

Warlpiri

5.70 Yuntardi **nganta!**
      beautiful REP
      'She is beautiful indeed! As if she is beautiful!'

The reported evidential in Nganasan may also express a negative attitude to and disagreement with what was said. Example 5.71 (Gusev forthcoming: 12) is about the despicable behaviour of the child's father who had abandoned her. The reported evidential in the sentence 'he is reported to be (her) father, as if he is her father!' stresses that he does not behave like a proper father (like referring to a father who is not behaving in a very father-like way as 'her so-called father'). A similar example is under 7.18 (it involves a reported evidential with first person).

Nganasan

5.71 d'esi̯ i-**bahu**
      father be-REP
      'He is reported to be her father' (and yet he abandoned her, and she left
      her home)

We have seen in 3.45 how the reported evidential in Tariana may imply that the speaker does not want to have anything to do with the situation. The wife of a man who had gone off to the jungle on his own disapproved of this. She used the reported evidential to tell his friends about her husband's trip as a way of saying 'this is what I am told, but I dissociate myself from the whole business'.

A reported evidential can be used ironically (in combination with intonation or a gesture) even if it does not have any overtones of unreliable information. In 5.72, from Shipibo-Konibo, the reported evidential is used this way (Valenzuela 2003: 41). The speaker simply does not believe what he is reporting.

Shipibo-Konibo

5.72 Nato oxe-**ronki** mi-a sueldo nee-n-xon-ai apo-n,
     this moon-REP 2-ABS salary:ABS go.up-TR-BEN-INC chief-ERG
     oin-tan-we!
     see-go.do-IMP
     '(It is said that) this month the president will raise your salary. Go see it!'
     (I am sure this is not true)

Not every reported evidential implies that the information is unreliable. In Ngiyambaa, the reported marker itself does not carry such overtones. To refer to something one does not vouch for and to make one's statement tentative, one can use the hypothesis-marking clitic -*gila* in addition to the 'ignorative' -*ga:*, together with the reported evidential -*DHan* (Donaldson 1980: 277), as in 5.73.

Ngiyambaa

5.73 ŋindu-gila-ga:-**dhan**   guɽuŋa-y-aga
     you+NOM-HYPOTH-IGNOR-REP   swim-CM-IRR
     'I gather that perhaps you are going to swim' (lit. 'from what's been said, I guess, (but) don't know, (that) you are going to swim')

If one is sure of what is being reported, an assertive clitic is used, as in 5.74.

5.74 waŋa:y-baga:-**dhan**=du   ŋudha-nhi
     NEG-COUNTER.ASSERTION-REP-2NOM   give-PAST
     'But rumour has it you didn't give (anything)'

The reported itself does not imply that one does not vouch for the information provided. The 'belief' clitic imparts this. In this way, the reported evidential is markedly different from the sensory evidential which cannot co-occur with a belief clitic. Once the sensory evidence is there, it is conclusive, and one cannot doubt its validity (Donaldson 1980: 241). Unlike the sensory evidential, the reported simply allows a leeway for doubt.

Reported evidentials, with their overtones of unreliable information and inference, may develop a range of meanings similar to the non-firsthand evidential in A2 systems (see Scheme 5.1, and the discussion at the end of A3 in §2.1). The reported particle in Sissala (a Gur language from Burkina Faso) and the reported evidential in Tewa (Kroskrity 1993: 144–5) can be extended to information for which no firsthand evidence is available. In these and other instances the primary reported meaning of the evidential is obvious. In other cases either the available descriptions or the actual data do not allow us to decide which meaning is primary. We discussed these difficulties in §2.1.2. For instance, the analysis of the enclitic *naa* in Tarascan (Foster 1969: 50) as primarily reported or primarily non-firsthand remains problematic simply for lack of data.

Further extensions of reported evidentials include mirative (§§6.1–2). When reported occurs with first person this may imply that the speaker does not remember that something had happened to him or her (see §7.2).

5.4.4 *Two reported evidentials in one language*

If a language has two reported-type evidentials, the most common distinction is that between reported and quotative. Such systems seem to be common in North American Indian languages.

In some languages the two reported evidentials are almost synonymous. The reported evidentials—-*ronki* and -*ki* (possibly, diachronically a short form of -*ronki*: see Valenzuela 2003: 37–43)—in Shipibo-Konibo are almost identical in meaning. The form -*ki* appears to be more frequent in stories: unlike -*ronki*, -*ki* does not have to occur after the first major constituent in a clause and may even occur more than once in a sentence (Valenzuela 2003: 41–2, and p.c.). Just -*ki*, not -*ronki*, can be used in commands (§8.1.2). The reported evidential suffix -·*le* in Eastern Pomo (McLendon 2003: 118–20) frequently occurs together with a hearsay clitic =*xa* as in 3.28. In some examples—as in 2.74—the reported suffix occurs on its own. The difference between these is hard to ascertain.

Languages with scattered coding of evidentiality (§3.3) may have several synonymous reported evidentials. For instance, West Greenlandic (Fortescue 2003: 295–6) has a reportative sentential affix, an enclitic, and a particle. The differences in meaning are rather subtle: the sentential suffix -*nirar-* 'say that someone/something VERBS' is the only one not to have any epistemic overtone. In contrast, reports with the enclitic -*guuq* suggest 'displaced reponsibility' rather than downright doubt in the veracity of the statement. The particle has a 'gossipy' flavour to it; and has mirative overtones (see §6.2). Similarly, Western Apache has two particles with the function of reported. One is reported only.

The other one refers to something a speaker saw but could only interpret later ('deferred realization'), and is also used in story-telling as a means of allowing storytellers to emphasize that they cannot be held responsible for the story (de Reuse 2003: 87–8). It is also linked to mirativity (see §6.2).

Several synonymous ways of marking a statement as 'reported' may reinforce each other. As mentioned in §4.8.3, Abkhaz has a non-firsthand evidential which can refer to reported information (2.15). In addition, information acquired through someone else may be marked with the impersonal reportative verb 'it is said'. Both have epistemic extensions of 'unreliable' information. The two can occur together, with a cumulative 'distancing' effect: the speaker does not take any responsibility for the veracity of information. An additional quotative particle, $h^{o}a$ (Chirikba 2003: 258–62), can be used to introduce direct speech or simply reported discourse. (The particle and the reportative verb are of the same origin: see §9.1.) Having the quotative particle, the reportative verb, and the non-firsthand evidential together in one sentence emphasizes the speaker's 'lack of commitment'.

5.5 Evidentials and their meanings: a summary

Evidential markers may indicate a speaker's attitude towards the validity of certain information (but do not have to). Evidentials are part of the linguistic encoding of epistemology in the sense of how one knows what one knows, but they are not part of linguistic encoding of probability and possibility (or 'epistemic modalities' which reflect the degree of certainty the speaker has). The meanings and extensions of individual terms depend on the system. The simpler the system, the more semantic complexity of terms we expect. There is here similarity to vowel systems. In a small system, with just three or four members, each vowel is likely to cover a considerable phonetic space, while in a large system each vowel is likely to have a restricted range of phonetic realizations.

We now briefly summarize the semantic content of each evidential term, depending on the system.

Semantic extensions of evidentials in small systems are summarized in Table 5.2. The main meaning is given first. Examples are in §5.1. The FIRSTHAND term in two-term systems typically refers to visual and often other sensory information, and can be extended to denote the direct participation, control, and volitionality of the speaker. The sensory evidential in A4 systems refers to sensory perception of any kind, without any other overtones.

The NON-FIRSTHAND terms in A1 and A2 systems each mean the opposite of FIRSTHAND. They often imply lack of participation, lack of control, nonspecific evidence (or no evidence at all), inference, and hearsay. An extension to hearsay is not found in some systems.

There are hardly any epistemic extensions in A1 evidentiality systems with two choices. Occasionally, epistemic overtones of uncertainty are found in some A2 and A3 systems. Languages tend to have other ways of expressing probability and possibility (as we noted in §4.1, non-indicative moods and modalities, such as dubitative in some Algonquian languages, may, in their turn, develop evidential overtones).

The major difference between A2 and A3 systems on the one hand and other small systems on the other lies in the existence of an evidentiality-neutral 'everything else' term. Unlike A1 systems, A2 (and A3) systems offer an opportunity of not marking any information source (see §3.2.3).

Semantic extensions of evidentials in systems with three choices are summarized in Table 5.3. Examples are in §5.2. The meanings of terms in evidentiality systems with three choices are rather similar to those in small systems, but not identical. Languages with B1 systems have just one sensory evidential. There is a major difference between representatives of B1 type: while in Qiang the only sensory evidential refers exclusively to things seen, in other systems (e.g. Quechua and Shasta) such a term covers information acquired by any appropriate sense—hearing, smelling, touching, or 'internal experience'. The VISUAL evidential in languages with two sensory evidentials (B2 and B3) refers to visually acquired information.

The VISUAL evidential may have epistemic extensions of certainty and commitment to the truth of the proposition. It also carries overtones of the speaker's conviction, and their responsibility for the statement, and is used to talk about generally known facts. It is used to refer to the speaker's internal states. Epistemic extensions of the direct evidential in B1 systems are not universal—they are not found in Qiang, Bora, and Koreguaje.

The NON-VISUAL SENSORY evidential in B2, B3, and B4 systems refers to information acquired by hearing, smell, touch, or feeling (such as an injection). There are no epistemic extensions—with the possible exception of Maricopa (B3), where both visual and non-visual evidential are said to assert something 'which truly happened in the past' (Gordon 1986a: 84).

The INFERRED evidential in B1, B2, and B4 systems covers inference of all sorts: based on visual evidence, on non-visual sensory evidence, on reasoning, or on assumption. It is also used to refer to someone else's 'internal states'—feelings, knowledge, and the like. Due to its links with inference based on conjecture, the inferred evidential may acquire epistemic overtones of doubt and non-committal in some systems—such as Quechua (but not any of the others exemplified in §5.2.3), especially if the sentence already contains some formal marking of doubt. Examples like 5.27–8 demonstrate that by itself the inferred evidential has little to do with doubt. Additional uses of the inferred include ironic and sarcastic observations.

TABLE 5.2 Semantic extensions in evidentiality systems with two choices

TWO EVIDENTIAL CHOICES	TERM	MEANINGS	EPISTEMIC EXTENSIONS
A1	Firsthand	• Actions or states seen or perceived with appropriate senses • Statements based on visible results • Speaker's participation, control, intentional action, 'prepared mind'	None
A4	Sensory	• Actions or states seen or perceived with appropriate senses	
A1	Non-firsthand	• Actions or states not seen or otherwise perceived	None
A2	Non-firsthand	• Inference based on results or reasoning • Deferred evidence • Reported information • Speaker's lack of participation and control, non-intentional action, 'unprepared mind' (see §6.1) • Distancing	Possible extension to unreliable information

The semantic complexity of sensory evidentials in large systems (C1–3 and D1) is summarized in Table 5.4 below.

The VISUAL evidential in C1 and D1 systems and the DIRECT evidential in C2 and C3 systems cover what is seen. These terms often have overtones of reliable information for which the speaker takes personal responsibility, and an epistemic extension of certainty. They also refer to generally known facts. The DIRECT evidential occurs in statements describing information obtained by senses other than feeling—that is, its semantic breadth is similar to that of the direct in a B1 system (as in Quechua). In Tsafiki (C2), the direct evidential implies the speaker's participation in the action. In Tariana (D1), the visual evidential also has this meaning (see Table 5.1).

The NON-VISUAL sensory evidential covers what is not seen, but is perceived by hearing, smelling, or feeling. This does not include purposeful touching: the non-visual evidential has overtones of non-volitionality and non-control. This is especially salient in the context of first person participants. We return to this in §7.2. The non-visual evidential is used to talk about one's own internal states and processes interpreted as not really 'seen' (such as dreams or actions of evil spirits—see examples in §11.3). Only straightforward perceptual meanings of the non-visual are covered by the direct evidential in C2 and C3 systems—see Table 5.1.

The INFERRED evidential in C1 and C3 systems is used to describe all kinds of inference and also to talk about other people's internal states. C2 and D1 systems distinguish inference based on visible results and assumption mainly based on reasoning. The latter is used to describe other people's internal states in some D1 systems. Further types of inference can be based on previous evidence, uncertain visual evidence, physical appearance, and so on; most of these choices occur in languages with scattered coding of evidentiality where it does not form one grammatical category.

Similarities between individual evidentiality terms across systems go along the following lines.

I. The firsthand and sensory terms in A1 and A4 systems subsume the meanings encoded with visual evidentials in B2–3, C1, and D1; non-visual sensory evidentials in B2–4, C1, and D1; and direct evidentials in B1, C2, and C3.

Unlike the visual evidentials in B2–3, C1, and D1, and direct evidentials in B1, C2, and C3, firsthand specifications do not have epistemic extensions.

II. The non-firsthand in A1 and A2 systems typically subsumes the meanings of the inferred term in B1–2 and B4, and inferred and assumed terms in C1–2 and D1. The non-firsthand evidential may be used for reported information. Only some systems develop epistemic extensions for a non-firsthand evidential.

TABLE 5.3 Semantic complexity of evidentials in systems with three choices

SYSTEMS WITH THREE CHOICES	TERM	MEANING	EPISTEMIC EXTENSION
B1	'Visual' or 'direct'	• Strictly visual information (Qiang) • Information acquired through any appropriate sense (Quechua) and speaker's internal states (e.g. emotions and knowledge) • Direct responsibility of the speaker • Generally known facts	Certainty and commitment to the truth of the utterance (not found in some B1 systems)
B2, B3	Visual	• Strictly visual information	None (with the exception of Maricopa)
B2, B3, B4	Non-visual sensory	• Information acquired through organs: hearing, tasting, smelling, or feeling (touch) • One's own internal states	
B1, B2, B4	Inferred	• Information acquired by means other than seeing or verbal report (Qiang) • Inference of all sorts: based on visual evidence, on non-visual sensory evidence, on reasoning, or on assumption • Another person's internal states • Irony and sarcasm	Overtones of conjecture, doubt and lack of commitment in appropriate contexts (Quechua only)

TABLE 5.4 Semantic complexity of evidentials in systems with four and five choices

SYSTEMS WITH THREE CHOICES	TERM	MEANING	EPISTEMIC EXTENSION
C_1, D_1 and other large systems	Visual	• Information obtained through seeing, or events which can be observed • Events for which speaker takes full responsibility and/or has a personal involvement • Generally known facts • Speaker's participation (Tariana)	Certainty
C_2, C_3	Direct or visual	• Information acquired through any appropriate sense and speaker's internal states (e.g. emotions and knowledge) • Speaker's participation	None
C_1, D_1	Non-visual sensory	• Information acquired through organs: hearing, tasting, smelling, or feeling (touch) • One's own internal states • Accidental uncontrollable actions for which no responsibility is taken, as well as with verbs like 'be lost'; actions in dreams, descriptions of uncontrollable actions of evil spirits who cannot be seen but can be felt and heard (see §11.3).	
C_1, C_3	Inferred	• Inference based on results, visual evidence, or reasoning • Another person's internal states	
C_2, D_1	Inferred	• Inference based on visual evidence	
C_2, D_1	Assumed	• Inference based on reasoning and general knowledge • Another person's internal states (D_1 only)	

We will see, in §7.2, that the non-firsthand, some inferred and even reported evidentials can develop a 'first-person effect'. These terms are also likely to develop mirative extensions—as shown in Chapter 6.

III. The visual evidential in three- and four-term systems always refers to strictly visual information. Its epistemic extensions include the speaker's certainty and possibly also commitment to the truth of the statement. Its further extensions include the speaker's responsibility and generally known facts.

This is consistent with the preferred status of visually acquired information. We will see in §10.1 that such information is considered the most valuable.

IV. The non-visual evidential in three- and four-term systems covers information obtained by any sensory perception (which can also be metaphorical; we will see, in §11.3, how the actions of evil spirits in Tariana, with a D1 system, are described with a non-visual evidential). In four-term systems these evidentials also refer to accidental and non-controllable actions, and produce a 'first person effect' (see §7.2). Non-visual can be extended to refer to one's own or other peoples' states or feelings—as in Tariana and Tuyuca, where these states are regarded as being perceived by senses other than 'seeing'. They never have any mirative or epistemic extensions. In no language of the world is taste or smell the primary meaning of a non-visual term.

V. The direct evidential in B1, C2, and C3 systems spans the domain of visual and non-visual evidentials under III and IV above. It is similar to visual (III) in its epistemic extensions, to cover the speaker's responsibility, certainty, commitment to the truth of the statement, and generally known facts.

VI. The inferred evidential in B1, B2, and B4 systems covers all inferential meanings (which may each have a separate term in larger systems). Inferred evidentials have no epistemic extensions. In the absence of a non-visual sensory, an inferred evidential can develop a 'first person' effect, as is the case in Tsafiki. The inferred evidential in three-term systems may acquire epistemic extensions of uncertainty and probability. The non-visual acquires epistemic extensions in (some) four-term systems, since this may imply that the speaker is not in control.

Just in Shipibo-Konibo, the assumed evidential has overtones of doubt. In contrast, the assumed evidential in other C- and D-type systems does not have any epistemic connotations. In fact, many multiterm systems require subtle precision in indicating how the information was obtained, which leaves little leeway for uncertainty; consequently, epistemic meanings are not expressed through evidentials.

Languages with multiterm evidential systems generally tend to have a multiplicity of other verbal categories, especially ones that relate to modalities. The larger the evidential system, the less likely are the evidential terms to develop epistemic extensions.

The types of inference most often grammaticalized in evidential systems distinguish inference based on results (usually visible, or acquired in a direct way by the speaker) and inference based on reasoning and assumption.[5]

Evidentials can be used in different ways to describe cognitive states and feelings. In the three-term system in Quechua visual is used to talk about one's own feelings. Tariana and the Tucanoan languages with four-term systems use non-visual for this. Assumed evidentials are preferred when speaking about a third person—there is no way of *perceiving* that such a state exists inside another person, one can really only assume it. This usage may correlate with cultural stereotypes (yet to be investigated). We return to these in subsequent chapters (in particular, §10.3 and §11.3).

The REPORTED evidential is the most semantically uniform in systems of all types. Its core meaning is marking that information comes from someone else's report. The reported evidential may have the following extensions:

1. A reported evidential can be used as a quotative, to indicate the exact authorship of the information, or to introduce a direct quote. A special quotative evidential is found just in B5 systems.
2. A reported evidential can be used for secondhand and thirdhand report. Only some C3 systems distinguish secondhand and thirdhand evidentials.
3. A reported evidential can develop an epistemic extension of unreliable information, as a means of 'shifting' responsibility for the information to some other source one does not vouch for. Such extensions are not universal. They are found in Estonian, and in a number of Australian languages (Mparntwe Arrernte, Yankunytjatjara, Warlpiri, and Diyari), as well as in Maricopa, Jamul Tiipay, Tauya, and a number of Uto-Aztecan languages, but not in Ngiyambaa, Kham, Shipibo-Konibo, or Nganasan.

A non-firsthand term in a two-way system, or an inferred term in a three-term system, tends to subsume all sorts of information acquired indirectly. This includes inference (based on direct evidence, or general knowledge, or no information), as well as indirect participation, and new knowledge. These evidentials may then evolve mirative extensions. This is the topic of the next chapter.

---

[5] A distinction between 'synchronic' and 'retrospective' evidence made by Plungian (2001) is not substantiated by the language facts. Inference based on observed results is usually made after the event, and is thus bound to be retrospective (this is linked to deferred realization; see example 5.7 and §6.2). This is corroborated by correlations between past tenses and inferentials, and by the absence of present tense forms in inferentials in such languages as Tariana and Tucanoan. We have not found any substantiation for a claim concerning the putative 'synchronic' evidence as part of evidential systems. Lack of control or 'non-volitionality' can occur as an extension of an evidential, but never as the core meaning of any evidential (despite the importance attached to it by some authors).

6

Evidentiality and mirativity

Mirativity covers speaker's 'unprepared mind', unexpected new information, and concomitant surprise. DeLancey (1997) was the first scholar to demonstrate that though mirativity is often connected with evidentiality there is enough data to postulate it as a distinct semantic and grammatical category. (Later, Lazard 1999 suggested that mirativity can in many cases be regarded as an extension of the category of 'mediativity' which covers the non-firsthand in A1 systems and the non-firsthand in A2 systems: see §1.3. In fact, these evidentials often do have mirative extensions, but they are not the only ones to acquire them.) Cross-linguistically, mirative meanings do not always have to be expressed through evidentials. That is to say, mirativity can be a separate grammatical category in its own right, rather than a simple extension of another category. In this section I discuss mirative extensions of evidentials in systems of different types. Further examples of mirativity as a separate category are in the Appendix to this chapter. Categories other than evidentials can acquire mirative extensions; this is also taken up in the Appendix.

In small systems with two evidentials, the non-firsthand evidential may extend to cover new, unusual, and surprising information—that is, develop mirative overtones. In larger systems, the inferred evidential may acquire a similar range of meanings. A reported evidential may occasionally acquire a mirative meaning in an evidential system of any kind. A firsthand or a visual evidential hardly ever does. We discuss these in §§6.1-2. Mirative extensions often occur if there is a first person participant (we return to this in Chapter 7). Due to their semantic similarities to small evidentiality systems, evidentiality strategies may also acquire mirative nuances; see §6.3. Terms in evidentiality systems with more than four choices typically have no mirative overtones; there are often other ways of expressing such meanings. Some of these are mentioned in the Appendix to this chapter. Evidentials with mirative connotations discussed here can be viewed as 'mirativity strategies'; see the summary in §6.4.

6.1 Mirative extensions in systems with two evidentiality choices

The non-firsthand evidentials in small systems (A1 and A2) often cover things one has not seen, heard, or taken part in (see Scheme 5.1 in §5.1). Consequently, one may not take any responsibility for such events. One may even not be aware of them happening. They may be perceived as beyond one's control, unexpected, and consequently 'surprising' to the speaker. This is how mirative extensions come about (DeLancey 1997 called this complex of meanings 'unprepared mind'). Consider 6.1, from Abkhaz (Chirikba 2003: 248–9). The Prince of Abkhazia is visiting a peasant who is entertaining him as well as he can. All of a sudden the prince hears a child crying. He is surprised since he was not aware of the child's presence, and says:

Abkhaz

6.1 sa+ra   jə-s-ajha+bə-w   a-wa+jº-dəw-cʹºqʹ′a   abra
     I   it-me-elder-PRES:STAT:NFIN   ART-man-big-really   here
     də-qʹa-**zaapʹ**
     (s)he-be-NONFIRSTH
     'It turns out (unexpectedly) that there is really a great person here who is more important than me!'

Although he has firsthand knowledge of the child's existence (having seen the child), the non-firsthand suffix is used in a mirative sense, to express the Prince's surprise.

The non-firsthand evidential in Northern Khanty also acquires a mirative extension if one discovers something unexpected, or new (Nikolaeva 1999: 148). In 6.2, those who were building the house did not think that the poles would be made of iron. They were surprised to find this out.

Northern Khanty

6.2 śi   x∩t-ən   wer-lə-ŋən   pa   xŏti   ul-lən
     so   house-3du   make-PRES-3du   and   so   pole-3du
     kurte-t   ul-**m**-el
     iron-PL   be-NONFIRSTH.PAST-3sg
     'So they are making the house, and the poles turned out to be iron'

If the speaker has just become aware of something they did not expect, the non-firsthand evidential is appropriate in Turkish (Johanson 2003: 285).

Turkish

6.3 büyü-**müş**-sün!
     grow-NONFIRSTH-2sg
     'You have grown!'

Further examples of 'mirative' as a semantic extension of the non-firsthand term in A2 system can be found in Lazard (1999). They have been described for Mansi (Skribnik 1998: 206–7), for Turkic languages (also see Slobin and Aksu-Koç 1982), and also for Tajik, Nepali, Albanian, and a number of Balkan Slavic languages. Hare (Athabaskan: DeLancey 1990*a*: 154) has an optional non-firsthand marker; with first person it means 'inadvertent action' (see §7.2), and is also employed to cover new information; that is, it is related to mirative.

The mirative meaning is often associated with the first person participant (see §7.2, on further 'first person effects'). Then, the use of a non-firsthand evidential implies the lack of control and, more generally, the 'unprepared mind' of the speaker. In Northern Khanty (Nikolaeva 1999: 147) first person can be used with the non-firsthand evidential only in the mirative sense. On waking up, the man says 6.4. He did not realize he had slept and 6.4 shows how surprised he is.

Northern Khanty

6.4 takan   wŏjǝmp-**t**-ew
     deeply   sleep-NONFIRSTH.PRES-1pl
     '(Apparently) we have been sleeping deeply'

Similar examples abound in Turkish (Aksu-Koç and Slobin 1986: 160). Upon waking over one's books one may exclaim:

Turkish

6.5 uyu-**muş**-um
     sleep-NONFIRSTH-1sg
     'I must have fallen asleep!'

Along similar lines, in Kalasha (Dardic: Bashir 1988: 48–54)—where a distinction is made between firsthand and non-firsthand—the non-firsthand with a first person agent 'gives a sense of unconscious or inadvertent action' (Bashir 1988: 53–4) and ensuing 'surprise'. And in Chinese Pidgin Russian, the non-firsthand evidential with first person describes 'a more or less spontaneous reaction to a "new, salient, often surprising event" ' (Nichols 1986: 248).

A non-firsthand evidential may acquire a mirative extension independently of the choice in the tense-aspect system, as in Northern Khanty (6.2 is cast in past tense, and 6.4 in the present). Or a mirative extension can be restricted to just one choice in the tense-evidentiality system. In Jarawara, with an A1 system, only the immediate past non-firsthand has a mirative extension. Okomobi thought he was being given a cup of cane whisky. When he raised the cup to his lips he discovered that it was just water; the surprise he experienced was coded by using immediate past non-firsthand.

Jarawara

6.6 Okomobi   faha   hi-fa-**hani**   ama-ke
     Okomobi   water   Oc-drink-IMM.P.NONFIRSTH.f   EXT-DECL.f
     'Okomobi (to his surprise) drank water'.

The story from which 6.7 is taken is told in far past firsthand. It is a personal reminiscence by the narrator about how he and his companions had gone up a strange river and come across a patch of forest full of game animals. Their surprise is expressed by 6.7—this is achieved with the immediate past non-firsthand marking (Dixon 2004).

6.7 bani_s   mee   wina-tee-**hani**
     animal(m)   3non.sg   live-HAB-IMM.P.NONFIRSTH.f
     'There were surprisingly many animals'

One may be surprised at an ongoing process, or at an inference made on the basis of some visible evidence. In Svan, these effects are achieved by using different aspectual forms. An unexpected and surprising situation which holds over time (that is, has a general present reference) is described with the imperfective non-firsthand present. In 6.8, the speaker hears a friend play the guitar. He did not expect him to be able to play it, and says:

Svan
6.8 si   gitara-ži   **lumšwemin**-xi!
     you   guitar-up   play+IMPF.NONFIRSTH-2sg
     'You (surprisingly) can <u>play</u> the guitar!'

An unexpected inference is marked with perfective non-firsthand (Sumbatova 1999: 76–7). In 6.9, the speaker hears his friend play the guitar, and infers that, to his surprise:

6.9 isgowd   xočāmd   **oxwtorax**
     your:TRANSFORM   good:TRANSFORM   teach:PERF.NONFIRSTH:3sg.S/3pl.O
     gitara-ži   lišwme
     guitar-UP   play:NOM
     'You (apparently) have been well taught to play the guitar!'

A mirative extension can be limited to just one semantically defined subclass of verbs. In Yukaghir, talking about internal properties, such as being clever or bad, has to be based on some visible manifestation.[1] If such a property is acknowledged by the speaker for the first time as new and surprising information, the non-firsthand is used. If a property has been previously established, the firsthand form is appropriate. Example 6.10 comes from a story about the

---

[1] Skribnik (1998: 207–8) showed that in Mansi, non-firsthand evidentials formed on resultative verb forms do not have a strong mirative meaning. Also see 6.17, from Qiang where the mirative sense of the inferred evidential is primary with stative verbs. These correlations require further cross-linguistic study.

speaker's first hunting expedition. His elder brother who was supervising him makes an encouraging statement (6.10), just after the hunting was finished (Maslova 2003: 229).

Yukaghir

6.10 qal'it'e   o:-**l'el**-d'ek
      best.hunter   COP-NONFIRSTH-INTR:2sg
      'You proved to be a real hunter!'

And then he says 6.11. Since he has already stated that the speaker is a real hunter the firsthand form is appropriate: it marks established knowledge and, in DeLancey's words, 'prepared mind'. This difference between non-firsthand and firsthand is akin to that between new, non-integrated knowledge and old knowledge.

6.11 qal'it'e   o:-**d'ek**
      best.hunter   COP+FIRSTH-INTR:2sg
      'You are a real hunter'

The non-firsthand evidential in an A2 system is likely to have mirative overtones, even if the language has special admirative forms for marking new knowledge and surprise. In Tsakhur (Tatevosov and Maisak 1999*a*: 232–3), the non-firsthand evidential may acquire a mirative connotation if something happens contrary to the speaker's expectation and much to their regret. The speaker has told his son not to go to a wedding. Nevertheless, the son is going to go. The speaker did not expect his son to disobey, and says 6.12:

Tsakhur

6.12 Ru   š̃ā-qa   **ulq̄-a**   **wo=r**
      you.1   there-ALL   1.go-IMPF   be=1(NONFIRSTH)
      'So you are still going there!'

A mirative extension may imply new knowledge and surprise for both the speaker and the hearer. In Archi (A1) the non-firsthand marker *li* (Kibrik 1977: 230–1) can be used if the speaker participated in a situation the meaning of which is unknown to the hearer, and turns out to be unexpected for the hearer (also see §7.3.1).

A mirative meaning can be strengthened by an additional, often optional, marker: Abkhaz (Chirikba 2003: 249) employs an emphatic particle or an emphatic interjection. Northern Khanty has a number of expressions meaning 'it turns out, apparently'. Lexical expression of mirativity is a different issue, for a separate informed analysis.

We have no clear-cut examples of mirative extensions of the reported term in A4 systems.[2] However, in Lithuanian and Estonian, the use of reported evidential with first person implies surprise, or a 'non-deliberate' action over which the speaker claims no control (Gronemeyer 1997: 100). We return to this in §7.2.1 in a discussion of the 'first person' effect of evidentials (see 7.17).

An evidential can be ambiguous between a primarily reported sense and a primarily non-firsthand with a mirative extension. In Mapudungun (isolate from Chile: Zúñiga 2000: 52, MS; and Salas 1992: 149) the marker *-rke* covers verbal report, as in 6.13.

Mapudungun

6.13   aku-**rke**-y
        arrive-REP-IND
        'S/he arrived, they say'

The same form can also express an unexpected and surprising 'discovery':

6.14   Fey   ti chi   domo   kalko-**rke**
        that   ART   woman   witch-MIR
        'This woman turned out to be a witch (surprisingly)'

At present, it appears impossible to decide which meaning is primary (see Zúñiga MS). We will see in §6.2 how a reported evidential in a larger system can have overtones of challenge and new unexpected knowledge; that is, surprise or mirativity.

6.2 Mirative extensions in other evidentiality systems

If a language has three or four evidentials, mirative overtones are likely to be associated with either the inferred or the reported term. The inferred evidential acquires mirative readings in many three-term systems. The inference made by the speaker implies a discovery of something new, unexpected, and therefore surprising for the speaker. In 6.15, from Nganasan (B4 system), the information is new and unexpected for the character.

Nganasan

6.15   ńaa   ma-tə   t'ii-ʔə,   səŋüli-ʔi-də.
        Nganasan   house-LAT   enter-PERF   look.around-PERF-3sg

---

[2] Austin (1978, 1981) notes the association in Diyari between the use of the sensory evidential suffix *-ku* and the indication of a new participant or a new state or event. This could reflect an erstwhile mirative extension, which is all the more interesting since Diyari is one of the three rare cases of an A4 system (with a sensory and a reported evidential). However, since Diyari was an obsolescent language at the time of fieldwork, this hypothesis cannot be further substantiated.

Ma-tənu   s<u>il</u>i̱-gəlit'ə   d'aŋguj-**h^uatu**
house-LOC   who-EMPH   be.absent-INFR
'The Nganasan man came into the house and looked around. (It turned
out that) there was no one in the house'

A connotation of new information and 'surprise' can be reinforced with an
exclamatory marker, as in 6.16 (Gusev forthcoming: 8). The ways in which the
inferred evidential in questions is used in Nganasan also correlate with surprising
discovery and new information (see §8.1.1).

6.16 əlü-**h^ua∂u**-ŋ   tə-əuʔ
    be.weak-infr-2sg   truly-EXCLAM
    'You are weak, as it turns out!'

The inferred evidential in Qiang often refers to new and surprising information. This 'mirative' sense is primary if the statement refers to a state or the
result of an action, as in 6.17. If it is an action, the inferential sense is primary, as
in 3.20 ('he was playing a drum (inferred)!': LaPolla 2003a: 67).

Qiang
6.17 the: çtçimi z̞dz̞i-**k**!
      3sg   heart   sick-INFR
      'He's unhappy!'

In Washo (B2), the inferred evidential has the meaning of 'ex post facto
inference with some connotation of surprise' (Jacobsen 1986: 8).
    Of languages with four-term evidentiality systems, mirative extensions have
been noted for Shipibo-Konibo and Tsafiki (both C2). The evidential *-mein*
in Shipibo-Konibo refers to assumption and speculation. This evidential
may be used when 'the speaker is confused or surprised because what he
experiences is totally unexpected or contradicts his knowledge of the world'
(Valenzuela 2003: 48). Whether the evidential *-mein* has mirative overtones
or not depends on the context. There are a number of other ways to mark
surprise: an emphatic suffix, a contrastive suffix, and a periphrastic 'mirative'
verb form.
    In Tsafiki (C2) the evidential marking inference from visible traces can
also indicate surprise. We have seen this evidential in its primary inferential
meaning in 2.77. In 5.53 the inferred evidential implies that the speaker wishes
to act as if she did not have visual evidence (when in fact she does). In 6.18,
the same evidential reflects the speaker's 'unprepared mind'. The speaker
heard the noise and thought that it was a car approaching. When he saw what

it was he realized, to his surprise, that it was a motorcycle, and said 6.18 (Dickinson 2000: 411).

Tsafiki

6.18   moto   jo-**nu**-e
         motorcycle   be-INFR:MIR-DECL
         'It's a motorcycle!'

The speaker's surprise comes as a result of 'deferred realization'. This is a post-factum inference made on the basis of something that the speaker had previously witnessed but only later could realize what it had meant. We saw in §5.1 (especially 5.7, from Yukaghir) how 'deferred realization' can be part of the semantics of a non-firsthand evidential.

A reported evidential can also acquire connotations of 'surprise' and 'after-the-fact' realization. In his incisive analysis of the use of the reported evidential in Quechua riddles, Floyd (1996a: 919) pointed out a link between mirativity and 'after-the-fact' realization. A typical Quechua riddle has a formulaic structure. It consists of a question cast in reported evidential and followed by a somewhat obscure description of the object. This description is not to be taken at face value—to give the correct answer, one needs to make the right metaphorical connections. The answer to 6.19 is 'scissors'.

Wanka Quechua

6.19   Ima-lla-**sh**   ayka-lla-**sh**.
         what-LIM-REP   how.much-LIM-REP
         Chraki-n   chay-chru   ñawi-yu.   Ishkay   tupshu-yu   uma-n-chru
         foot-3p   there-LOC   eye-having two   beak-having head-3p-LOC
         'What could it be, what could it be? Its feet have eyes. Its head is two beaks'

A reported evidential within such a riddle has a twofold role. First, it is a token of a genre. Quechua folk tales, traditional narrative, and riddles are typically passed from person to person by word of mouth, and always contain the reported evidential as a genre marker (see §10.2.1). Secondly, riddles contain puzzling information which goes against normal expectations. That is, they presuppose the addressee's surprise. Hence their mirative overtones.

A somewhat similar meaning is found in what Floyd calls 'challenge construction', a formulaic expression involving the particle *maa* 'let's see' followed by an interrogative pronoun plus the reported evidential, and then the verb marked with what Adelaar (1977: 98) calls 'sudden discovery tense'. In 6.20, the parents are discussing a situation in which their son has borrowed money from their neighbour under false pretences; and the neighbour now wants the parents to pay it back. The parents decide to recover the money. The father then says to the mother:

6.20   maa   mayan-man-**shi**   chay   illay-kuna-a-ta
       let's.see   who-GOAL-REP   that   money-PL-DEF-ACC
       u-ña
       give-NONPAST(SUDDEN.DISCOVERY)
       'Let's find out who he gave the money to'

This 'challenge' ought to be understood as an invitation for the addressee to join the speaker. The reported evidential does not overtly refer to any verbal report. Rather, it evokes a 'circumstance which involves some sort of impending revelation' (Floyd 1999: 150). What riddles and the challenge construction share is the anticipation of result or 'revelation'. The result is unexpected—hence an overtone of surprise, or mirativity, reinforced by the use of 'sudden discovery' form. (We will return in §8.1.1 to further ways in which evidentiality in Quechua questions reflects the source of information available to speaker and to addressee; cf. Floyd 1999: 146.) Along similar lines, in Jaqi the remote past reported marker which typically occurs in myths and legends of all sorts may also indicate surprise (Hardman 1986: 130).

Reported evidentials may develop a mirative flavour in other languages where evidential concepts do not form a unified category. At first sight, the morpheme *lẹ́k'eh* in Western Apache is a typical reported evidential. It occurs at the end of every sentence in any traditional narrative. For a Western Apache speaker, a story without the sentence-final *lẹ́k'eh* is not recognizable as a story (see §11.2). In non-narrative genres, however, *lẹ́k'eh* has a somewhat different meaning: it is to do with 'past deferred realization' (de Reuse 2003: 87) whereby the speaker was not aware of the event when it occurred, but realized what it was later on. In 6.21 the speaker had no personal recollection of the fact that they had been to the store (he could have been unconscious, or temporarily lost his memory). He realized it later—he could have been told about it, or inferred it (de Reuse 2003: 86).

Western Apache
6.21   Yáhwạhyú   nashāā   **lẹ́k'eh**
       store+at   1sg.IMPF.ASP.be.around   REP/DEFERRED.REALIZATION
       'I was at the store' (but was not aware of it at the time)

In another story quoted by de Reuse (2003: 84), a family is returning from a dance. On the way home they grow tired and spend a night in an unknown place, not realizing what it was. They are constantly disturbed by something touching them; so finally, they leave. When it becomes light, they look back at the place where they could not get to sleep—and realize that they had tried to sleep in a graveyard! In this very last sentence, *lę́k'eh* is used.

Employing *lę́k'eh* in a traditional narrative indicates that the evidence is not firsthand. At the same time it emphasizes that the storyteller is aware of their authority as narrator and often as author. This awareness can be considered a facet of the 'deferred' realization meaning of the particle *lę́k'eh* and provides a bridge between its two seemingly distinct meanings—as a marker of a narrative genre and as an indicator of post-factum realization of what the witnessed thing actually was (see further discussion in de Reuse 2003: 87–8).

Whether 'deferred realization' always has to involve surprise remains an open question. One of the inferential evidentials, *-biw*, in Kashaya (Oswalt 1986: 42) describes events or states perceived by some means and which have become interpretable later—for instance, if a woman saw a man approaching but could not recognize him until he arrived, she could say 'it is-*biw* my husband'. We hypothesize that whether a newly discovered piece of information is indeed surprising or not may well depend on the context.

No mirative extensions have been found in other multiterm systems. (At least some of the languages with a D1 evidentiality system have mirative as a distinct grammatical category; see Appendix to this chapter.)

6.3 Mirative extensions of evidentiality strategies

Evidentiality strategies are similar in meanings to non-firsthand and reported evidentials. They frequently develop mirative extensions, as in Georgian (Hewitt 1995; DeLancey 1997), or Persian (Lazard 1985: 28–9). In Sunwar, Tibeto-Burman (DeLancey 1997: 41–4), mirativity is encoded into the system of existential copulas whose primary meaning is the contrast between old knowledge and new knowledge (see Table 4.1). In a number of Tibeto-Burman languages—e.g. Lhasa Tibetan, Akha, Chepang, and Newari (DeLancey 1997: 44), as well as in Tsafiki (Barbacoan)—the alternation between conjunct and disjunct person-marking (§4.6) is employed to mark new information and surprise, especially in the first person contexts. The disjunct person-marking indicates something out of the speaker's control, unexpected, and thus surprising. See examples 4.32 from Tsafiki and 4.36 from Lhasa Tibetan. Aspects as evidentiality strategies can acquire mirative overtones. As noted by DeLancey (1997: 38–40), perfective aspect may be associated with inference, and imperfective with 'new knowledge'. This is the case in Hare (Athabaskan) and Sunwar (Tibeto-Burman).

The pluperfect form in La Paz Spanish is often used to indicate that the speaker did not see the action take place—they either inferred it from some evidence or heard it from someone else. This form can also be used to indicate a speaker's surprise 'upon encountering an unknown or something seen for the first time or something that occurred without one realising it. The meaning of this form is that the event occurred in the past with respect to the present or in the past with respect to the moment when the speaker becomes aware or became aware of the event. The speaker had no personal awareness of the event until after it occurred' (Laprade 1981: 223). That is, pluperfect as an evidential strategy has overtones of lack of awareness and 'deferred realization' (on which see below). Examples include *habías estado trabajando fuerte* 'You have been working hard!' (to my surprise) and *había sabido hablar Aymara muy bien* 'It turned out he *did* know how to speak Aymara very well'. With first person, the pluperfect marks accidental and unintentional actions, again, very similarly to a non-firsthand evidential (see §7.2).[3] In the Spanish of Quito—and Ecuadorian Highland Spanish in general—a similar mirative extension is a feature of present perfect employed as an evidentiality strategy (Bustamante 1991: 203–4; Olbertz 2003).

In Lithuanian, a passive form used as an evidentiality strategy with inferential meaning acquires a mirative reading in the context of first person (see the discussion in §4.3 and 4.12). In 6.22 (Gronemeyer 1997: 107), the speaker has just realized, to his surprise, that he is sick. The mirative interpretation goes together with lack of control and 'inadvertent' action, typical for inferential evidentials in the context of first person (see §7.2, on 'first person effects').

Lithuanian

6.22 Mano   <u>serga-ma</u>!?
      I.GEN   sick-PASS.PRES.NOM.NEUT
      'Evidently I am sick!?'

Mirative overtones may come about as the result of manipulating narrative strategies, such as narrative forms in West Tibetan and other Tibetan languages to signal a climax in a story, marking an unexpected arrival of a new participant, or mark an unexpected outcome of an event (Zeisler 2000).

We have seen in §4.8.4 how a morpheme, on its way towards evolving into a grammaticalized reported evidential, may develop semantic overtones similar to those of a true reported evidential. The reported particle *dizque* (literally, '(it) says that') in Colombian Spanish is a case in point. An erstwhile marker of reported speech, it developed a variety of epistemic meanings covering information one does not vouch for, 'make-believe', and pretence (see 4.61). That is, semantically it has become similar to the non-firsthand in A1 and A2 systems.

---

[3] This use is found in other areas of Bolivia, and in Peru (Willem Adelaar and Pilar Valenzuela, p.c.).

No wonder *dizque* can also refer to non-volitional and uncontrollable actions which go against the speaker's expectations.

An example of this mirative extension is at 6.23 (Travis forthcoming). The speaker has been given a job cleaning bathrooms, to his disgust. He lists a number of ways in which he is unsuitable for the job because he is over-sensitive about cleanliness. He expresses his disbelief at finding himself in this position. This is where he uses *dizque*. In this example, *dizque* does not mark reported speech. Rather, it indicates that the speaker has no control over the situation. In Travis's words, 'it also expresses an element of surprise, as though he has all of a sudden found himself in this terrible situation'.

Colombian Spanish

6.23   ... yo, que incluso algunas veces limpié la taza que otro había chapoteado para que quien usara el baño después de mí no fuera a pensar que el descarado había sido yo; yo, por Dios, *dizque* a limpiar baños
'... me, who even sometimes wiped the toilet bowl that someone else had splattered so that whoever used the bathroom after me wouldn't think that the shameless one had been me; I, for God's sake, <u>dizque</u> to clean bathrooms'

In another situation observed by Travis, a speaker of Colombian Spanish made a comment on her own actions *Me puse a hacer **dizque** el almuerzo* 'I started to make *dizque* lunch'. She knew she should have been studying but instead she was wasting time making lunch. This example carries an overtone of uncontrollability and surprise at one's own actions: the speaker found herself doing something she had not consciously chosen to do.

Along similar lines, *diz que* 'it is said that' in the Portuguese of northwest Amazonia can be extended to cover all non-firsthand evidentiality specifications (see §9.2.3, on how evidentiality emerges in contact languages). Some speakers of this variety also employ *diz que* to talk about uncontrolled and surprising actions. A girl in the Vaupés area in northwest Amazonia in Brazil (who speaks no language other than the regional Portuguese) hardly ever cooked or did any other household jobs. But once she decided to try and do some cooking. I was surprised to see her pottering at the stove, and asked her what she was doing. The answer was *tou fazendo bolinho diz que* 'I am making pancakes *diz que*'. Here *diz que* expressed the girl's surprise at her own endeavour, and lack of control over what she was doing—she was not sure anything worthwhile would come of her enterprise.

These overtones of evidentiality strategies are consistent with their semantic similarities to evidentials in small systems and their historic development (see §9.1, on how evidential extensions give rise to grammatical evidentials).

6.4 Evidentials as mirative strategies: a summary

Every language has some way of expressing what is new and unexpected for the speaker or for the hearer, and of indicating surprise. This does not mean that every language has grammatical mirativity. Evidentials may have mirative meanings as part of their semantic extensions (cf. Zeisler 2000: 73). However, no evidential has mirativity as its main meaning (in agreement with Lazard 1999). Categories other than evidentials may have mirative overtones: examples 4.32 and 4.36 show how conjunct–disjunct person-marking can encode surprise. In some languages, however, mirativity is a category in its own right; see Appendix to this chapter.

'Mirative' extensions are typical of non-firsthand evidentials, where they often go together with 'lack of control' on the part of the speaker, and of inferred and sometimes reported evidentials. Table 6.1 summarizes mirative extensions in evidentiality systems of various types (discussed in §§6.1–2).

A mirative extension of an evidential may be weaker or stronger, depending on a language. As noted by Valenzuela (2003: 48), the mirative uses of assumed evidentials are heavily context-dependent; just as in other languages with large evidentiality systems and rich verbal morphology, a variety of other means serve to express surprise if necessary. A mirative meaning can be strengthened with an additional, often optional, marker (see §6.1).

TABLE 6.1 Mirative extensions of evidentials: a summary

EVIDENTIALITY CHOICES	TYPE OF SYSTEM	TERM WITH MIRATIVE EXTENSION	EXAMPLES
Systems with two choices	A1	Non-firsthand	Yukaghir, Jarawara, Archi
	A2	Non-firsthand	Abkhaz, Turkish, Northern Khanty, Tsakhur
	A3	Reported	Lithuanian (in the context of first person only)
Systems with three choices	B1	Reported	Quechua (reinforced by the 'sudden discovery' tense)
	B1 B2 B4	Inferred	Qiang Washo Nganasan
Systems with four choices	C2	Inferred	Tsafiki
	C2	Assumed	Shipibo-Konibo

TABLE 6.2 Restrictions on mirative extensions of evidentials depending on other categories

Categories	Type of restriction	Example languages
Person	First person	Lithuanian
Verbal semantics	'Internal' physical and mental states, or result of an action	Yukaghir (A1) Qiang (B1)

Mirative extensions can be limited to some fixed contexts. In Quechua, these are found in riddles and in 'challenge' constructions. The presence of a special 'sudden discovery' tense marker (called mirative by Willem Adelaar, p.c.) reinforces the mirative reading of these constructions.

Evidentials may not have any mirative extensions; other means can be used to express the meanings of 'unprepared mind' and subsequent surprise (see the discussion of Shilluk at the end of the Appendix to this chapter).

Mirative extensions may be independent of any other category. This is the case in Abkhaz, Northern Khanty, Tsakhur, and Turkish. Alternatively, a mirative extension may arise in the context of a particular choice of person, tense-aspect, or verb class. If a mirative extension depends on person, it is likely to develop in the context of first person participants. Verbs particularly susceptible to mirative extensions cover mental and physical states, or resulting states which the speaker cannot control. A summary is in Table 6.2.

Several interconnected semantic paths give rise to mirative readings of evidentials. The first path is shown under Scheme 6.1.

SCHEME 6.1 Mirative extension of an evidential (I)

> (I) lack of firsthand information → speaker's non-participation and lack of control → unprepared mind and new knowledge → mirative reading

This path explains the frequent link between non-firsthand specification, on the one hand, and new information and 'unprepared mind' on the other. We have seen in the examples above that mirative overtones are often interconnected with the speaker's lack of control and lack of awareness of what's going on. The 'lack of control' and lack of awareness is a characteristic effect of the use of first person with non-firsthand evidentials in small systems (see §7.2). This is why mirative extensions frequently occur in first person contexts (see 6.1 from Abkhaz, 6.4 from Northern Khanty, and 6.5 from Turkish). In Lithuanian, they appear to be limited to first person.

An alternative semantic path is shown under Scheme 6.2.

SCHEME 6.2 Mirative extension of an evidential (II)

> (II) Speaker's deliberate non-participation → distancing effect → presenting the information as new, unexpected, and thus 'surprising'

Speaker's deliberate non-participation is part of the semantics for some inferred evidentials, as in Tsafiki (5.53). A deliberate 'distancing' effect of an inferential evidential creates the possibility of presenting information as new and thus 'surprising'. The paths presented in Schemes 6.1 and 6.2 are interconnected: the main difference between them is whether the speaker does or does not exercise deliberate distancing or non-participation.

Scheme 6.3 involves the concept of 'deferred realization'—whereby the speaker gives a post-factum interpretation to what they may have observed in some way. Deferred realization is an integral part of mirative meanings in all systems where mirativity is associated with inference. Deferred realization does not, however, necessarily imply a mirative reading (Maslova 2003: 224). And it is also possible that in some languages—such as Western Apache, where evidentiality is not a single grammatical category—'deferred realization' is a special semantic category overlapping with a putative evidential.

SCHEME 6.3 Mirative extension of an evidential: deferred realization (III)

> (III) Deferred realization: speaker sees or learns the result but interprets it post factum → the newly understood result is unexpected and thus surprising

None of these paths is unique to any particular evidentiality system discussed here, with the exception of the 'deferred realization' path (Scheme 6.3). This path explains the semantic connection between inferred evidentials and their mirative extensions in three- and four-term systems, in particular, for instance, where mirative readings are restricted to results, as in Qiang (cf. 6.17).

We saw in §6.3 that evidentiality strategies with meanings similar to those of non-firsthand in A1 and A2 systems also develop mirative extensions. This is in full accord with a general tendency for evidentiality strategies to follow a semantic path similar to evidentials.

Appendix. Mirativity: grammaticalized 'unprepared mind'?

Mirativity is a grammatical category whose primary meaning is speaker's unprepared mind, unexpected new information, and concomitant surprise. Linguists have long known that languages employ various means to express 'surprise' and new information.

The mirative overtones of Turkish non-firsthand -*miş*- have been discussed by Slobin and Aksu-Koç (1982; Aksu-Koç and Slobin 1986). Bashir (1988: 51) recognized the mirative extensions of a non-firsthand evidential in Kalasha. The inferential evidential as a marker of 'surprise' was described by Jacobsen (1964) for Washo. But it was not until DeLancey's seminal paper (1997) that mirativity was 'put on the map' as a cross-linguistically valid, independent category in its own right, rather than an extension of an evidential. A full typological study of grammaticalized mirativity—a rather rare category, as pointed out by Lazard (1999: 107)—is a matter for future research.[4] One purpose of this Appendix is to present examples demonstrating that mirativity can be independent of any other category. Its other purpose is to show that mirative extensions can be found with categories other than evidentials (thus providing a background for the discussion above which focused on mirative extensions of evidentials).

The term '(ad)mirative' is sometimes used for categories which may have nothing to do with Delancey's and Lazard's semantics of mirativity. Thus, for Archi 'admirative' (Kibrik 1977: 238–9) has the following semantics: 'someone becomes eyewitness of an action or of its result'. 'Admirative' mood in the languages of the Balkans is a term for non-firsthand evidential (see Friedman 2003: 191): it can have a mirative extension, just like any other non-firsthand specification, but this is not its major meaning.

We have seen in this chapter that any evidential except for visual and firsthand, can acquire mirative extensions. These extensions are a frequent feature of the non-firsthand form in small systems, and of inferred in larger systems. (Reported evidentials also have them, albeit examples are scarce.) The emerging correlation is intuitively right: new and unexpected knowledge appears to be interconnected with something one makes inferences about but has not witnessed or hardly has under control. On the other hand, new and unexpected knowledge may also be acquired visually or as direct firsthand experience. That is, inference or any other information source is not necessarily the underlying motivation for mirative as a separate category (see Watters 2002: 288).

Hardly any mirative extensions have been noted for evidentials in larger systems. We will see in a little while that some languages with five or more evidentials have a special verbal form indicating surprise.

A major argument in favour of mirative meanings as independent from evidentials and information source comes from languages where mirative extensions are characteristic of categories other than evidentials. We have shown above that evidentials have a propensity to become 'mirativity strategies'. Similarly, other categories can be employed in this way.

Perfect, with its focus on the current relevance of past event to the moment of speech, may acquire a mirative nuance even if not employed as evidentiality strategy.

In Semelai, irrealis or hypothetical mood has a mirative extension 'in contexts resulting from direct perception, marking it as an unanticipated observation counter to

---

[4] We can recall, from Chapter 1, that Lazard (1999) sees a categorical difference between multiterm evidential systems (which he calls 'evidentials') and small systems (which he calls 'mediative') which are likely to have mirative extensions. We have seen that 'mirative' extensions can be found in both (see §§6.1–2).

expectation or normality' (Kruspe 2004: 286). The mirative extension is restricted both in person and in type of predicate: it occurs in first and third person with predicates of perception and cognition. For predicates of 'affective states', mirative overtones are restricted to first person. In (1), a child (nicknamed Mischievous Bear) who is normally a chatterbox is unusually quiet. His grandmother teases him, saying (Kruspe 2004: 288):

Semelai
(1) daʔ   ma=ʔyəŋ   cəŋ   cɒkɒp   bɔ̃n.trɛ̃k
    NEG   IRR=hear   at.all speak   bear:mischievous
    '(To my surprise), I haven't heard Mischievous Bear speak at all'

In Ladakhi (Tibeto-Burman: Bhat 1999: 72–3), a language with four evidentiality specifications—reported, observed, experienced (e.g. by feeling), and inferred—'surprise' (for second person subjects only) is marked with a narrative mood but not with an evidential.

None of these languages has a special grammatical category with 'mirativity' as its primary meaning. Mirative meanings are extensions of other categories (none of which is evidentiality).

The inferential evidential in Tsafiki has a mirative extension (see 6.18). In addition, disjunct form with first person reference indicate speaker's surprise, as in 4.32 (also see DeLancey 2001 on how conjunct–disjunct person-marking interacts with mirativity in Tibetan, and example 4.36). That is, a language can have several strategies for expressing mirativity, only one of them to do with evidentiality.

We will now look at some examples of mirativity as a separate category.

A mirative construction in Kham (Watters 2002: 288–93) involves the auxiliary use of the existential copular verb 'be' in third person singular (both main and copula verb are nominalized). The following examples illustrate the contrast between the unmarked form (2) and the mirative (3):

Kham
(2) ba-duh-ke-rə
    go-PRIOR-PERF-3p
    'They already went/left'

(3) ya-ba-duh-wo   **o-le-o**
    3p-go-PRIOR-PERF.NOMN   3sg-be-NOMN(=MIR)
    'They already left!'

The necessary semantic component of the Kham mirative is 'not the source of the speaker's knowledge, but rather that the information is newly discovered—not yet integrated into the speaker's store of knowledge' (Watters 2002: 290). The mirative is used to convey the speaker's discovery of the fact. This can happen post factum when all the speaker observes is the result; then, surprise is based on inference. Consider (4). The speaker's dog went missing, and he suspects a leopard has taken him. Coming across the carcass of the dog, he infers that this is what must have happened and says (4) to his friend—the mirative indicates that the newly discovered information is surprising:

(4) e   babəi, a-kə   zə   o-kəi-wo   **o-le-o**
     hey   man   prox-LOC EMPH   3sg-eat-NOMN 3sg-be-NOMN(=MIR)
     'Hey man, he ate him right here!'

In (5) the speaker sees the leopard in front of him: he uses the mirative to convey his surprise at having discovered a leopard:

(5) nə-kə   zə   ci   syã:-də   u-li-zya-o
     DIST-at EMP   COUNTEREXP   sleep-NF   3sg-be-CONT-NOMN
     o-le-o   sani
     3sg-be-NOMN(=MIR)   CONFIRMATIVE
     'He's right there sleeping!'

Mirative in Kham has overtones of 'deferred realization' (see §6.2): the event occurred in the past but it was only later that the speaker realized what had happened (Watters 2002: 293). Example (6) comes from the same story as (4) and (5), about the speaker's hunt for a leopard that killed one of his sheep dogs; (6) is said at the beginning of the narrative, 'at a time in the story before anyone knew what was responsible for the missing dog'. Only later on he discovers the dog's remains (see (4)) and then sees the leopard (see (5)). Then the speaker fully realizes that a leopard was to blame.

(6) ri-lə   te   ge-ka:h   la:-ye   bəi-də
     night-IN FOC   1pl-dog   leopard-ERG   take-NON.FINAL
     o-ya-si-u   **o-le-o**
     3sg-give-2pl-NOMN   3sg-be-NOMN(=MIR)
     'In the night a leopard took our dog away on us!'

This use of the mirative is nicely captured by the term 'hindsight': that it is not until later that the speaker gains full understanding of the previous event, and this understanding is new and unexpected. Compare 5.7 from Yukaghir, 6.18 from Tsafiki, and 6.21 from Western Apache: in all these cases 'deferred realization' expresses basically the same thing.

Interestingly, reports on recent events in Kham are also marked with mirative—as new information which has not yet become part of established integrated knowledge. This agrees with Slobin and Aksu-Koç's analysis (1982, Aksu-Koç and Slobin 1986) of the use of the non-firsthand evidential in Turkish: once the reported information becomes part of general knowledge, the evidential is not used. Narratives other than reports on recent events in Kham are marked with the reported evidential (particle *di*), devoid of any mirative or epistemic overtones.

Whether or not the mirative here is similar to reported evidential or any other evidential is highly debatable. The mirative and the reported do share one feature: the event was not known to the speaker when it first occurred. Despite some semantic overlap with the reported in Kham, mirative is definitely a separate category. Mirativity is also a separate grammatical category in a number of other Tibeto-Burman languages; see DeLancey (1997).

Along similar lines, the mirative clitic $=(a)m$ in Cupeño (Hill 2005: 66) is distinct from evidentials. In (7), the mirative refers to new discovery and surprise. The example comes from a traditional story in which Coyote has unexpectedly arrived, uninvited, at a church service conducted by birds (to whom the Coyote is potentially dangerous). One of the birds recognizes him:

Cupeño

(7) Mu=ku'ut   "Isi-ly=**am**",   pe-yax=ku'ut
    and=REP   Coyote-NPOSS.NOUN.MIR   3sg-say=REP
    'And it is said, "It's Coyote!", he (the bird) said it is said'

The reported enclitic $=ku'ut$ occurs twice in this sentence: it usually occcurs in traditional stories as a 'genre marker' (see §10.2.1).

The 'sudden discovery' tense in Central Peruvian Quechua (including the Tarma and Junín varieties) can be considered a mirative marker: its main meaning is 'surprise' and sudden realization (Willem Adelaar, p.c.; Adelaar 1977: 97–8).

Tariana expresses a whole range of mirative meanings (including surprise and unexpected information) with a complex predicate of the following structure: lexical verb+suffix *-mhe*+auxiliary verb *-a* 'go, say, let, give'. Both the lexical verb and the auxiliary receive the same subject cross-referencing, and no constituent can intervene between them. Stative verbs cannot be used in mirative, and mirative cannot be negated. The form is not at all frequent, and is mostly used with verbs of perception (*-ka* 'see, look', *-hima* 'hear'). We can recall that Tariana has five obligatory evidentiality terms (D1), none of which has mirative overtones. In (8), the mirative construction is used to express pleasant surprise.

Tariana

(8) Oli yaɾu-si   ma-weni-kade-ka **du-ka-mhe**   **du-a-ka**
    Oli thing-NPOSS   NEG-pay-NEG-SEQ 3sgf-see-MIR   3sgf-AUX-REC.P.VIS
    'Olívia was surpised at things being cheap' (lit. Olívia, things being cheap, looked (at this) in surprise)

In (9), the surprise is rather unpleasant:

(9) **nu-ka-mhe**   **nu-a-mahka**   na-ĩtu-nipe-nuku
    1sg-see-MIR   1sg-say-REC.P.NON.VIS   3pl-steal-NOMN-TOP.NON.A/S
    'I was unpleasantly surprised by the theft' (which I heard but could not see)

The mirative construction can combine with any evidential, except for present visual. The evidential choice depends on the information source: in (8) Olívia saw the facts that caused her surprise, and in (9) she did not see them. These examples demonstrate independence of evidentiality and mirativity as separate grammatical categories.

Makah (Wakashan: Davidson 2002: 276, apud Jacobsen 1986) has a special verbal form called 'realizational'. The form indicates that 'the speaker has only belatedly perceived, learned, or realised a fact . . .', and it also refers to facts 'generally surprising and unexpected in some way'. For Choctaw, -*chih* 'wonder' is considered as a separate term in the so-called 'evidentiality' system (Broadwell 1991). Wichita (Caddoan: Rood 1996: 589) has an exclamatory tense used to express 'surprise'; this form appears to be independent of evidentiality choices in the language.

Languages with mirative extension of an evidential can also have mirative as a separate category. In Tsakhur (Northeast Caucasian: Tatevosov and Maisak 1999*a*: 233), forms with an auxiliary—which have an inferential or non-firsthand meaning—can have an additional meaning of counterexpectation, marking 'mirative'. In addition, two further markers have counterexpectation and mirativity as their primary meaning (Tatevosov and Maisak 1999*b*: 289–91).

A language may have a morpheme with 'surprise' as its main meaning; but its status as that of 'mirative' as a category may still be problematic. The morpheme -*kun* in Korean marks surprise and new information independently of inference and hearsay (DeLancey 1997: 46). But morphologically it appears to be a member of a large set of final particles, a kind of 'utterance qualifier' rather than an expression of an independent category (see the discussion and references in Lazard 1999; also see Sohn 1994).

Mirativity can be expressed with other means. Hone (Central Jukunoid: Storch 1999: 136–7 and p.c.) has a set of pronouns consisting of a pronominal base and the conjunction *bé* 'with'. These pronouns follow the finite verb in the perfective aspect, indicating that the fact that the subject performed the action was unexpected, as in (10).

(10)   ku-yak   **bóà**
        3sg-go   MIR.PRON.3sg
        'She or he went away' (even though this was not wanted or expected).

Shilluk (Miller and Gilley forthcoming), with a B1 evidential system, employs a variety of means to express mirative meanings—a special set of third person pronouns, and the transitive subject (A) constituent being postposed to the verb with the ergative marker being omitted. Once again, information source and mirativity are marked independently of each other.

The key semantic components of mirativity—'surprise' and 'new information'—can be expressed by lexical means. Many languages have an interjection meaning 'Wow!'. Just as having lexical expression of evidentiality does not mean that there is any grammatical evidentiality, 'mirative' interjections are not grammatical mirativity.

Intonation is frequently the only clue to the mirative overtones of a sentence (see DeLancey 2001: 377–8). Whether this marking is enough for postulating mirativity as a distinct category in a language is an open question.

In summary, the answer to Lazard's question (1999: 106) 'Are there, in some languages, GRAMMATICAL categories that may be called evidential and mirative?' is yes. Evidentiality is well-established cross-linguistically. And there are a scattering of instances, across the world, which demonstrate the existence of a GRAMMATICAL category expressing surprise, new information, and 'unprepared mind' in general.

Delineating the exact semantic content of 'mirative' is another matter. Nambiquara languages have special marking for new information (independent of evidentiality marking: Lowe 1999: 275). Is this mirativity? Note that new information need not necessarily be associated with surprise. Since mirativity often goes together with unexpected information, does this imply that any marker of counterexpectation qualifies as 'mirative'? How uniform is the semantic and pragmatic content of mirativity as a category across languages? Is it possible that the cover term 'mirativity' subsumes a number of distinct categories rather than always one? To answer these questions, we require further in-depth studies of how languages mark new information and surprise in their grammars.

7

Whose evidence is that?
Evidentials and person

7.1 Evidentiality and nature of observer

Evidentials reflect the ways in which information was acquired. But whose perception and whose evidence do we have in mind when we talk about information source? The 'perceiver' can be 'I' (the speaker), 'you' (the hearer, or the audience), or someone else, a 'third' person. The ways in which evidentiality systems interact with the person of the participants are different from how evidentials interact with other grammatical categories and meanings (see Chapter 8). Some evidentials seem to presuppose that the observer is 'I'. It appears counterintuitive to use a non-firsthand evidential when talking about one's own actions. And it is precisely in this context that evidentials develop unusual overtones, involving lack of intention, awareness, control, and volition.

We saw in Chapter 6 that evidentials may acquire mirative extensions to do with new, unexpected, and generally surprising information if first person is involved (as in 6.4–5, from Northern Khanty and from Turkish respectively, where the speakers are surprised that they had fallen asleep). In §7.2 we discuss this within the context of the 'first person effect' of evidentials. Interaction of second and third person with evidentials is the topic of §7.3.

Given the ways in which evidentials interact with person, do evidentially marked sentences provide any clues as to whom the observer is? That is, do evidentials contain implicit reference to the person whose information source is reflected in their choice of an evidential? The answer is yes. Given that this is so, whose evidence is this: the speaker's, the addressee's, or both? We will see in §7.4 how evidentials can be tantamount to person markers as a side outcome of the 'first person effect'. Correlations between evidentials and person are summarized in §7.5.

Two further observations are in order.

- Firstly, I won't distinguish between the behaviour of first person singular and first person non-singular arguments with evidentials, since no significant differences or dependencies between evidentials and number have been found so far.

- Secondly, our discussion will include all first person participants, without limiting this to one particular grammatical function, such as 'subject' (e.g. Curnow 2003a). What is important is the person of the participant rather than its surface realization as a 'subject' or 'object' or 'oblique'. What is marked as a first person object[1] produces a similar effect to what is marked as 'subject'. If I am talking about my physical state—say, a toothache—in Tucano, the experiencer ('I') takes the object marking: 'tooth aches to me' (see 7.35). In Nganasan, the same experiencer is cast as possessor ('my hand aches'). But in Tariana a stative verb requires the experiencer as a subject, as in 7.14 ('I am sad'). In 5.37, from Tucano, 'I' is marked as the object of a mosquito bite: 'my' feelings are cast in non-visual. In Jarawara (7.5), a physical state, 'a bad cold', literally 'finds me'; and this is cast in non-firsthand. Notwithstanding the surface differences in grammatical function, the principles of evidential choice follow similar lines: if I am talking about my feelings or about states that I do not control, I choose the non-visual or the non-firsthand evidential. The concern of this chapter is semantics, and the semantic consequences of having a first person participant involved. We will see in §8.5 that the correlations between evidentials and grammatical relations found so far are very few, and hardly any of them depend on person.

Finally, if the observer is different from the participant, the person of the observer may acquire independent marking. We saw in 3.21, from Qiang, how adding the first person marker to a clause marked for third person can indicate that the information was acquired by the speaker (rather than by the agent). This is akin to marking several different information sources in one clause which reflect different 'observers' (see §3.5 and Table 3.2, especially examples from Jarawara, Eastern Pomo, and Comanche).

One further analytic difficulty is worth mentioning. Differences in interpreting evidentials depending on person may be more or less clear-cut. An evidential may have a clearly different meaning in first person context. We saw, in §6.1, that the non-firsthand evidential with first person in Northern Khanty always has a mirative meaning, covering surprise and unprepared mind of the speaker. The same holds for reported with first person in Lithuanian. In other cases, interpretation differences could be better treated as semantic extensions rather than fully separate meanings. For instance, the reported evidential in

---

[1] See Dixon and Aikhenvald (1999a), on how core and oblique participants may be grammatically distinguished.

Tucano occurs with first person only if the speaker cannot remember what had happened to them. Different interpretations can be explained by pragmatic inferences and common sense, rather than by strictly grammatical context. A number of languages have grammatical restrictions on evidentials with first person (see §7.2.2). This shows how what can be conceived as pragmatic, or common sense, may in fact become part of the language's grammar.

A special meaning of an evidential in the context of first, second, or third person may be limited to a semantic subclass of predicates. We saw in §§5.2–3 that languages have preferences for using direct or non-visual evidential to talk about speaker's 'internal states' (emotions, physical states, and the like). A language like Nganasan, with just one sensory evidential—non-visual sensory—employs it in similar contexts (see 5.23). Someone else's internal state is described using a different evidential (unless some special effect is implied)—see 5.18–20 from Wanka Quechua, and 5.41–4 from Eastern Pomo. We can recall, from §4.6, that even in languages without any evidentiality, expressions which refer to speaker's internal, 'unseen' states may acquire similar connotations. If the meaning of the verb implies something negative, using it with first person may have special overtones of inadvertent action or 'wrong-doing'. In 5.48, from Tariana: the verb *-pika* means 'get lost' and also 'become wayward' and 'go mad'. When it occurs with first person the connotation is 'I or we did not mean to do it, it just happened out of our control': people are not expected to consciously do something to their own detriment. Specific overtones of evidentials in these contexts go beyond 'first person' effect. Rather, they reflect an interaction between evidentiality and lexicon (see §10.3) and may mirror the culturally conventionalized relationships between 'self' and 'other' expressed in a language (see §11.3).

7.2 Evidentiality and first person

Evidentials may develop additional semantic overtones in the context of first person participants. So may evidentiality strategies; see §7.2.1. If a language has restrictions on the use of evidentials, these are likely to involve first person. Some evidentials may occur just in the first person context, or not occur there at all; see §7.2.2.

7.2.1 *'First person' effects in evidentials*

Evidential marking often reflects the information source of the speaker. The choice between firsthand and non-firsthand can depend on whether the event is perceived by the speaker or by someone else. The firsthand evidential in 7.1, from Jarawara (Dixon 2004), indicates that the speaker could smell the white-lipped peccaries he and his companions were hunting.

Jarawara

7.1 [hijara   mee   mahi]ₛ   kita-**hare**-ke
    peccary(m)   PL   smell+f be.strong-IMM.P.FIRSTH.f-DECL.f
    'The peccaries' smell was strong' (I could smell it)

The non-firsthand evidential in 7.2, from a little later in the same text, shows that the peccaries rather than the speaker smelt the smell. The speaker does not have any sensory perception of his and his companions' smell.

7.2 faja   [otaa maho]ₒ   mee   hisi   na-**ni**-ke
    then   1excl smell+m   3PL   sniff AUX-IMM.P.NONFIRSTH.f-DECLf
    fahi
    THERE.NON.VISIBLE
    'Then they (the peccaries) sniffed our smell there'

If the speaker is talking about themself, certain evidentiality choices appear counterintuitive: how can I talk about something I myself did using a 'non-firsthand' or 'non-visual' evidential? This is where an evidential acquires additional overtones. If one of the participants is 'I', a non-firsthand or a non-visual evidential may gain a range of additional meanings, to do with the first person participant not quite 'being all there'. Their actions are then interpreted as non-intentional, non-volitional, and generally lacking in control or awareness of what is happening. Not infrequently, these are linked to overtones of new information, unprepared mind, and surprise (see Chapter 6, on mirativity).

This range of meanings is what is meant by 'first person effect'. This has been attested for (a) the non-firsthand evidentials in A1 and A2 systems, (b) the non-visual evidentials in C1 and D1 systems, and for (c) reported evidentials in any system. Similar effects have been observed for (d) some evidentiality strategies which, as we saw in Chapters 4, 5, and 6, generally develop the range of meanings found for A1 and A2 systems.

In contrast, the firsthand evidentials in A2 systems, as well as visual and even non-visual evidentials in larger systems, may develop the opposite meaning—that of control and assertion about the utterance; see (e). In some Tibeto-Burman languages a visual evidential may imply that the action was unintentional; see (f). Inferred and assumed evidentials with first person are examined in (g).

(a) FIRST PERSON EFFECT WITH NON-FIRSTHAND EVIDENTIALS IN A1 AND A2 SYSTEMS
The non-firsthand evidential in the context of a first person participant implies lack of control on behalf of the speaker, resulting in an inadvertent action the speaker is not fully responsible for or even aware of.

The non-firsthand evidential with first person in Jarawara implies lack of control and the diminished responsibility of the speaker. Examples 7.3 and 7.4 illustrate the contrast between firsthand and non-firsthand evidentials (Dixon 2003: 170). If a person deliberately got drunk and is fully aware of what they did, the firsthand evidential is used.

7.3   o-hano-**hara**   o-ke
      1sg.s-be.drunk-IMM.P.FIRSTH.f   1sg-DECL.f
      'I got drunk (deliberately)' (FIRSTHAND)[2]

But if the speaker woke up drunk, with a hangover and no memory of what he had done the previous night, 7.4, cast in non-firsthand evidentiality, will be appropriate.

7.4   o-hano-**hani**   o-ke
      1sg.s-be.drunk-IMM.P.NONFIRSTH.f   1sg-DECL.f
      'I got drunk (and don't recall it)' (NON-FIRSTHAND)

Uncontrollable events—such as catching a cold —are cast in non-firsthand. The way of saying 'I caught a bad cold' is 'a bad cold found me-non-firsthand'. Note that this example contains a first person object.

7.5   ito   owa   wasi-hani-ke
      bad.cold(f)   1sgO   find-IMM.P.NONFIRSTH.f-DECL.f
      'A bad cold found me' (i.e. I got a bad cold) (NON-FIRSTHAND)

'Going to sleep' takes non-firsthand evidentiality, as in 7.6; one is not aware of how this happens.

7.6   amo   o-waha-**ni**   o-ke   waha
      sleep   1sg.S-NEXT.THING-IMM.P.NONFIRSTH.f   1sg.S-DECL.f   NEXT.THING
      'The next thing was I fell asleep' (NON-FIRSTHAND)

In Jarawara, if 'I' touch someone in the dark, the firsthand evidential would be used 'if this was done deliberately while awake'. The non-firsthand will be used if I inadvertently put out my arm while asleep and touched something (Dixon 2004: Chapter 6).

Along similar lines, first person non-firsthand in Yukaghir always implies inadvertent action over which one has hardly any control, as in 7.7 (Maslova 2003: 229). This goes together with speaker's unprepared mind: hence a mirative reading of similar examples in 6.4, from Northern Khanty, and in 6.5, from Turkish.

---

[2] First person pronouns in Jarawara are cross-referenced as feminine.

Yukaghir

7.7   modo-t   taŋdiet   mala-j-**l'el**-d'e
       sit-SS:IMPF   then   sleep-PERF-NONFIRSTH-INTR1sg
       'I was sitting and then somehow fell asleep'

If the speaker was a participant in a situation, using non-firsthand with first person in Yukaghir may produce a 'deferred realization' reading, as in 5.7 (where the speaker had had tea next to the bear's lair, but did not realize it until later). In both 7.7 and 5.7, the speaker was not aware of what was happening until after the event. The interpretation of 7.7 as 'inadvertent action' or as 'deferred realization' may have to do with the choice of the verb, rather than with any special semantics of first person in the context of non-firsthand evidentiality.

A non-firsthand form with first person often has an overtone of unconscious and inadvertent action, as in 7.8, from Kalasha.

Kalasha

7.8   a   åga'   ne   **hu'la him**
       I(NOM)   aware   not   become(PAST.NONFIRSTH)+is
       'I didn't remember (to get up and make your breakfast, although I had intended to)'

In Khowar, the non-firsthand form with first person 'conveys a sense of inadvertency or nonvolitionality' (Bashir 1988: 55), or implies that the action was mistaken or wrong. Similar examples come from Archi (Kibrik 1977). The use of non-firsthand forms with first person in Western Armenian (Donabédian 1996: 94) has the implication of an involuntary action, and also surprise at what one is (inadvertently) doing. In Hare (DeLancey 1990a: 154) the non-firsthand with first person means 'inadvertent action'. And the non-firsthand with first person in Tsez may imply that the subject was drunk (Bernard Comrie, p.c.).

Using a non-firsthand evidential with first person in Abkhaz covers 'such situations as dreams, actions carried out under the influence of alcohol, or when the speaker's actions have been performed without their control and come to them as a surprise' (Chirikba 2003: 251–2). A combination like this may produce an additional stylistic effect: 'even when directly and consciously involved in a certain situation', a speaker may use the non-firsthand evidential with first person to make 'a comment on their own action(s) as if observed or judged by an outside observer'. In 7.9, the speaker was involved in a fight. And yet he is talking about the event as if it was beyond his control.

Abkhaz

7.9   ha+ra   h-nə-(a)j+ba-r-c'ºa-wa-**zaap'**
       we   we-thither-together-CAUS-exterminate-PROG-NONFIRSTH
       'We are apparently killing each other'

This goes together with a 'distancing' effect of non-firsthand evidentials. In some languages, such as Salar (Turkic: Dwyer 2000), a first person statement can be marked as non-firsthand to indicate 'speaker's distance from the topic'. In §10.2.2 we return to how non-firsthand evidentials can have overtones of 'distancing'.

(*b*) First person effect with non-visual evidentials in C1 and D1 systems

The primary meaning of the non-visual evidential is that the action or state was not seen (it could have been heard, or smelt, or felt). In addition to this, the non-visual evidential in Tariana and Tucano, when used with any verb in first person, can refer to unintentional and uncontrolled action, just like the non-firsthand specifications in Abkhaz and Jarawara discussed above. Consider 7.10, from Tucano, and 7.11, from Tariana (Ramirez 1997, vol. I: 133). The speaker did not mean to break the plate. This sentence could also mean that he could not see this happening or that he had had no control over it: the plate was near the edge of the table and slipped off before he could stop it. Or it could have cracked in his hands. This illustrates, in a nutshell, the whole array of meanings a combination of a non-visual evidential and a first person can acquire. Whether the action was not controlled, or non-intentional, or non-volitional, or whether the speaker simply did not look the right way can only be resolved by context and with additional lexical means as necessary.

Tucano
7.10   bapá   bopê-**asɨ**
       plate   break-REC.P.NONVIS.nonthird.p
       'I have broken a plate unintentionally'

Tariana
7.11   karapi   nu-thuka-**mahka**
       plate   1sg-break-REC.P.NONVIS
       'I have broken a plate unintentionally'

A similar example, also from Tucano, is under 5.49. Here, the speaker fell out of a hammock—without intending or wanting to, or because of being dizzy and having lost control of his limbs, or simply because he could not see in the dark.

In contrast, if the speaker was doing something consciously, intentionally, and could see what was happening, they would use visual evidential. This is shown in 7.12 and 7.13.

Tucano
7.12   bapá   bopê-**apɨ**
       plate   break-REC.P.VIS.nonthird.p
       'I have broken a plate intentionally' (e.g. I was angry or hated the plate)

Tariana

7.13   kaɾapi   nu-thuka-**ka**
        plate   1sg-break-REC.P.VIS
        'I have cracked a plate intentionally' (e.g. I was angry or hated the plate)

This is similar to the use of firsthand in 7.3 in Jarawara, where the speaker deliberately got drunk; he then uses the firsthand evidential. In contrast, the non-firsthand evidential in 7.4 implies that the speaker got drunk without being aware of what he was doing. A non-visual or a non-firsthand evidential is thus in a paradigmatic relationship with the corresponding visual or firsthand evidential as far as the 'first person' effect is concerned. One implies non-intentional, uncontrolled, and non-volitional action. The other means the opposite. Lack of control, of volition, intention, and awareness constitute one semantic package. Only in a given context can one tell for sure which precise semantic interpretation is the most appropriate one.

Feeling something (as one feels a mosquito bite: see 5.37, from Tucano) and deliberately touching something can be differentiated with evidentials. If I feel something that happens to me, I use the non-visual evidential. Once again, the non-visual evidential presupposes lack of conscious participation. If I consciously need to know whether some clothes are dry and touch them to check, the inferred evidential will be appropriate (see §5.3.2).

A non-visual evidential is used when talking about oneself if the verb itself describes a non-controlled state of mind or body, including a feeling of any kind. In Tariana, one says 'I have fever-non-visual' (literally, 'fever comes to me', as in 5.38 and in 7.15). A similar example is 5.39, 'I felt happy', in Tucano. And the expression for 'I am sad' in Tariana is 7.14.

7.14   kawalikupeda-**mha**   nuha
        be.sad-PRES.NONVIS   I
        'I am sad, I feel sad'

Saying *kawalikupeda-**naka** nuha* (be.sad-PRES.VIS I) 'I am sad', with the visual evidential, implies that it is a generally known fact that I am a gloomy, sad person. Visual, inferred, or assumed evidential can all be used to talk about someone else being sad (depending on whether one sees, infers, or assumes the other person's state, since one can only feel one's own state).

The semantics of the verb overrides the first person effect: if the verb implies an uncontrollable state, the choice of non-visual evidential automatically goes with first person. For verbs of other semantic groups, a combination of non-visual evidential and first person implies lack of intention, control, or volition on the part of the speaker.

In Tariana, if I am talking about myself being sick, I have to use non-visual evidential, as in 7.15: 'fever came over me-non-visual'. In this context the non-visual does not have overtones of lack of control. It cannot mean 'fever overcame me and I could not help it (for instance, despite my shamanic powers)'. The meaning 'I could not help it' would have to be expressed lexically.

7.15   adaki   nu-na   di-nu-**mahka**-niki
        fever   1sg-OBJ   3sgnf-come-REC.P.NONVIS-COMPL
        'Fever has come over me' (NON-VISUAL)
        (Not: 'Fever has come over me and I could not help it')

In fact, the evidential choice can be a sort of person indicator; see §7.4. In §10.3, we return to the correlations between the choice of evidentials and semantic classes of verbs.

Similarly, if a certain experience (say, dreams) requires a choice of an evidential, this convention overrides the first person effect. As we will see in §11.3, dreams by ordinary human beings in Tariana and in Tucano are cast in non-visual evidential. Once again, 7.16, from Tariana, cannot mean 'I called my wife unintentionally in the dream'. Lack of intention can be expressed with means other than evidentials.

7.16   nu-sa-do-nuku   nu-wana-**mhana**   tapuli-se
        1sg-spouse-FEM-TOP.NON.A/S   1sg-call-REM.P.NONVIS   dream-LOC
        'I called my wife (NON-VISUAL) in the dream'
        (Not: 'I called my wife unintentionally in the dream')

No first person effects have been attested for non-visual evidentials in systems of other types (B2, B3, or B4 systems); see (*f*) below on first person and visual evidentials in some B1 systems.

(*c*) FIRST PERSON EFFECT WITH REPORTED EVIDENTIALS
A reported evidential in an A3 system with first person implies overtones of lack of control and subsequent surprise on behalf of the speaker; an example is 7.17 (Gronemeyer 1997: 1990).

Lithuanian
7.17   aš   pa-raš-ęs   nauj-ą   knyg-ą!?
        I:NOM   PERF-write-ACT.PAST.NOM.sg.masc=REP   new-ACC   book-ACC
        'It seems as if I have written a new book!?'

The reported evidential with first person in Estonian produces a similar effect: one can say *ma olevat seda teinud* (I:NOM be + REP this:ACC do + PAST.PART), meaning ' "I am reported to have done this", but I am surprised or denying that I did' (Aet Lees, p.c.).

A reported evidential with first person can have strong overtones of irony, surprise, and disagreement with what was said about the speaker. Example 7.18, from Nganasan (Usenkova forthcoming: 7), implies the speaker's vehement disagreement with what was said about them. This is similar to a range of other ironic uses of the reported evidential (see, for instance, 5.71, also from Nganasan).

Nganasan

7.18 **djacüxüaŋxumu**
make.noise+REP+1.PL.S
'We are said to make a lot of noise!' (at night and at day time when we tell stories—which is absolutely not true)

Adding the hearsay particle to a verb marked with a first person pronominal affix in Shilluk has a similar effect: the speaker then states that they have been wrongly accused of performing an action (Miller and Gilley forthcoming: 14–15).

In evidentiality systems with four or five terms, the reported evidential may be used with first person if the speaker does not remember what they did. The speaker could have been drunk, or too young to remember, and had to learn the facts about themselves from someone else's report. Examples 7.19–20 are from Tucano (Ramirez 1997, vol. I: 142).

Tucano

7.19 yɨ'î   utî-**apa'do**
I   cry-REC.P.REP.nonthird.p
'They say that I cried' (I do not remember because I was drunk)

7.20 yãbî+deko   yɨ'î   bahuá-**pa'do**
night+middle   I   cry-REM.P.REP.nonthird.p
'They say that I was born at midnight' (I cannot possibly remember this)

In Shipibo-Konibo, a reported evidential can be used with first person to talk about what took place while the speaker was drunk. If the speaker recalls what had happened, the direct evidential would be used; if they were told about what happened, reported would be acceptable (Valenzuela 2003: 41). Similar examples are found in Eastern Pomo (Sally McLendon, p.c.), and in Wintu (Schlichter 1986: 49). In Wichita, the reported evidential[3] with first person implies that 'the subject was somehow unaware of what he was doing (or temporarily insane)' (Rood 1976: 93).

---

[3] Wichita has three or four evidentials (non-visual, inferred, and reported at least); see §2.3.

The reported evidential with first person may not have any of these over-tones. In Kiowa (Watkins 1984: 173–6) it simply implies that the information about the speaker comes from another source. In 7.21, the speaker was told that he had a particular disease.

Kiowa

7.21 t'ɔ́·dè   ę́-k'ɔ́·dè-**hèl**;   cɔ̂·   dɔ́ttè·
      gall bladder   2,3sg/agent:1sg/patient:sg/object-bad-REP   thus   doctor
      nɔ́·-ì·   ę́-tél-**hèl**
      my-son   3sg/agent:du/object-tell-REP
      'The doctor told my sons (du) that my gall bladder isn't good', or ' "My gall bladder reportedly isn't good", that's what the doctor told my sons' (reported)

Similarly, in Ngiyambaa (Donaldson 1980: 276) the reported evidential can be used with first person if the speaker makes a statement simply based on 'linguistic evidence previously supplied by someone else'. If a speaker says *Nadhu-**dhan** wiri-nji* (I + NOM-REP cook-PAST) 'I am supposed to have cooked', she might have been told by someone that she was to cook, or 'word might have gone round that it was her turn to cook'. No examples of the reported and the quotative with first person in B5 systems have been found in the available literature.

(*d*) FIRST PERSON EFFECT WITH EVIDENTIALITY STRATEGIES
The meanings of evidentiality strategies are similar to those of non-firsthand evidentials in A1 and A2 systems. When used with first person, they develop meanings of uncontrolled, unconscious, and unintentional actions. We can recall that the pluperfect in La Paz Spanish has an array of non-firsthand meanings while the simple perfect tends to be interpreted as 'firsthand' (see 4.8–9: 'His mother arrived'). With a first person subject, a 'non-firsthand pluperfect' has an overtone of accidental or unintentional action, as in 7.22.

La Paz Spanish

7.22 me había cortado mi dedo
      'I cut my finger!' (pluperfect: I hadn't realized)

In contrast to the pluperfect, the perfect in the same context implies a volitional and intentional action.

7.23 me he cortado mi dedo
      'I cut my finger' (present perfect: I was aware of what I was doing)

When children know that they have been naughty but want their parents to think that they were unaware of their doing anything wrong, they would employ a pluperfect form. Laprade (1981: 224) tells a story about a girl who was 'instructed not to go downstairs to play with other children until her father returned home. Unable to resist temptation, however, she did go down, only to be confronted by her father shortly thereafter. In all innocence she offered the excuse: *me había bajado* (literally, I went downstairs-pluperfect)'. It was her way of 'washing her hands of personal responsibility for her action: "The devil made me do it"'. This is an instance of the speaker stylistically manipulating the 'first person effect' of the pluperfect with an evidential overtone.

This is strikingly similar to the first person effect of non-firsthand evidentials discussed above. Along similar lines, the impersonal passive as an evidentiality strategy in Lithuanian indicates surprise at something one did not realize before when used with first person. One can only say 6.22 ('evidently I am sick!?') if one is surprised (Gronemeyer 1997). Similar 'mirative' overtones of evidentiality strategies were discussed in §6.3 (also see 6.23, for a similar example of *dizque* in Colombian Spanish, where the speaker expresses his surprise and disgust at being told to clean bathrooms).

An evidential strategy does not have to have a first person effect, or a mirative overtone: Maisak and Merdanova (2002, especially note 4) report their virtual lack in Agul, a Northeast Caucasian language.[4]

(*e*) FIRSTHAND AND VISUAL EVIDENTIALS WITH FIRST PERSON: INTENTIONAL ACTIONS
If I use a visual or firsthand evidential to talk about my own actions, the implication is that I was aware and in control of what I was doing, and performed them intentionally. This was illustrated in 7.12–13. An evidentiality strategy with first-hand overtones may produce a similar effect—see 7.23. This is consistent with the epistemic extension of visual evidential to cover certainty and commitment to the truth of the utterance on the part of the speaker, as summarized in Table 5.4.[5] The direct evidential may, however, produce a different effect in languages marking just one sensory information source. This is discussed below.

(*f*) VISUAL OR DIRECT EVIDENTIALS WITH FIRST PERSON: UNINTENTIONAL ACTIONS
In a few Tibeto-Burman languages, the visual evidential with first person agent implies that the action was unintentional or mistaken. We can recall,

[4] 'The 'first person effect' may differentiate evidential extensions of a particular category from its other extensions. In Dargwa (Northeast Caucasian: Tatevosov 2001*a*: 450), the perfect may have a purely resultative or an anterior meaning; or it may be interpreted as non-firsthand. The 'first person effect' only occurs when the perfect has a non-firsthand extension.

[5] The use of visual and non-visual sensory evidentials with first person subject in Maricopa (Gordon 1986*a*: 85) implies a strong assertion about the truth of the utterance and thus has a strong epistemic force: the natural inference of these evidentials is that 'something truly happened in the past'. Both evidentials when used with first person have 'less an evidential meaning than a strong assertiveness about the actual occurrence of the action expressed by the verb' (Gordon 1986*b*: 112). The first person context accentuates the epistemic extension of 'certainty' which the visual or direct evidential has in many—though not all—large systems.

from §3.2.2, that the formally unmarked verb form in Qiang—with three evidentials: visual, inferred, and reported (B1 system)—can be used for visual evidence and general statements. If the actor is third person singular (and is zero-marked), the first person marker can be added on to a verb which contains a visual evidential. This is done to emphasize that the speaker did see the person perform the action, as in 7.24 (LaPolla 2003*a*: 66). Another example of 'double' person marking is at 3.21 ('he is playing a drum—I, the speaker, see it') (§3.5).

Qiang

7.24   the: jimi   de-se-ji-**w**-<u>D</u>
       3sg   fertilizer   OR-spread-CSM-VIS-1sg
       'She spread the fertilizer' (<u>I</u> saw her spread it)

If the same form is used when the actor is first person singular, the clause describes something done accidentally, as in 7.25. The context for this example was 'the speaker having hit the person while leaning back and stretching his arms back without looking behind him'.

7.25   qD   the: tD   de-we-ʐ-**u**-<u>D</u>
       1sg   3sg   LOC   OR-have/exist-CAUS-VIS-1sg
       '<u>I</u> hit him (accidentally)'

A combination of the inferred and visual evidentials with first person actor (described by LaPolla 2003*a*: 69–70 as 'I had guessed and now pretty-well confirm'—see §3.5) implies that the action was unintentional and just discovered. Example 7.26 also indicates that the action was a mistake.

7.26   qD   Dpǝ-tçǝ-iantu-le: tsa   tçy-**k**-**u**-<u>D</u>
       1sg   grandfather-GEN-pipe-DEF+CL   here   bring-INFR-VIS-1sg
       '<u>I</u> mistakenly brought grandfather's pipe here'

In Amdo Tibetan, whose evidentiality system is similar to that of Qiang (§2.3), the direct evidential normally used for visual or sensory perception (see 2.47) marks non-volitional acts when used with first person. These include yawning or smelling something, and also accidental actions, such as breaking a dish (Sun 1993: 961–6). Inherently non-volitional predicates—such as 'fall asleep', 'snore', 'forget'—which describe things speakers do unconsciously, require the inferred evidential (called 'indirect' by Sun; cf. 2.48). Unmarked sentences express intentional and purposeful acts.

Consider the following pair of examples. The unmarked verb in 7.27 describes something I did on purpose.

Amdo Tibetan

7.27 ŋə   der   tɕag=taŋ
      I(erg)   dish   break=aux
      'I broke the dish (on purpose)'

The verb with the direct evidential describes something that happened accidentally.

7.28 ŋə   ma   sæm   sʰæ   ni   der   tɕag=taŋ=tʰæ
      I(erg)   NEG   think   place   LOC   dish   break=aux=DIR.EV
      'I broke the dish by accident' (literally: when I was 'at a non-thinking place')

Sun (1993: 961) argues that the direct evidential in examples like 7.28 indicates that the speaker was 'merely a passive participant or witness of the portrayed events'. All the speaker has is 'direct perceptual knowledge of the event itself, but not the antecedent intention or volition'. In contrast, the unmarked forms 'represent direct knowledge of the volition as well as the event parts of a causal chain'. This semantic property of the direct evidential in Amdo Tibetan and in Qiang is thus markedly different from direct and visual evidentials in other multiterm systems.

(*g*) INFERRED AND ASSUMED EVIDENTIALS WITH FIRST PERSON

These often have the same meaning as with any other person (in B1, B2, B4, C1–3, and D1 systems). Example 5.28, from Wanka Quechua, has the usual inferential meaning ('I will surely go tomorrow-inferred'). So does 7.29, from Tucano (Ramirez 1997, vol. I: 139). This statement is cast in inferred evidential: the fact that the Tucano have the possession of their lands is a good enough reason for an inference that their grandparents bequeathed them to them.

Tucano

7.29 bãdî   yẽkɨsɨ-mɨ́ a   dãâ   bãdî-de   a'té+di'ta-di
      we   grandparents   they   us-TOP.NON.A/S   these+land-PL
      kũû-pã
      leave-REM.P.INFR.3pl
      'Our grandparents left us these lands' (INFERRED: we infer this on the
      basis of the fact that we still have these lands)

Along similar lines, in Tariana the inferred and the assumed evidentials occur with first person in the same circumstances as with other persons. An inferred evidential with first person may have additional overtones of irony, as in 5.29, from Huallaga Quechua ('Am I to go?—surely not!').

First person inferences in Wanka Quechua may be similar to rhetorical questions: they are often used if the speaker 'infers' something he or she knows is false, mocking their interlocutor. Consider 7.30 (Floyd 1999: 118–21), which describes the same situation as 5.26. The woman's house was robbed, and she accused the man of theft. She then claims he cannot think of doing anything other than stealing. He replies with 7.30. The inferred evidential is intended to prompt the addressee to revise her assumption about the man being the thief: 'If I can't think of anything but stealing, why do I have to hoe? So, if I do have to hoe (and I do), you have to rethink your ideas about me'.

Wanka Quechua

7.30 nila   talpu-ku-na-a-paa-**chra**   chakma-ka-yaa-mu-u
      so   plant-REF-NOM-1p-PURP-INFR   break.ground-REF-IMPF-AFAR-1p
      'So then (I suppose) I break up the ground (i.e. hoe) in order to plant'

Such ironic uses of the inferred evidential are not restricted to first person (cf. 5.30, with second person: here the father addresses an ironic comment to his daughter who refuses to go to school). They do appear to be preferred when one is forced to make inferences about one's own actions.

In no system does an inferred or an assumed evidential by itself have the 'first person effect' described for the non-firsthand and non-visual evidentials in (*a*) above. We saw in §4.6 that conjunct and disjunct person-marking correlates with whether 'I' did something intentionally or not. In 4.27 from Tsafiki, with conjunct marking, I meant to kill the pig. In 4.28, with disjunct marking, I did not mean to kill it. The disjunct marking can occur together with the inferred evidential, as in 4.34.[6] In this example, I also killed the pig without meaning to. The difference between 4.27 and 4.34 lies in the time frame (Dickinson 2000: 412). The inferred evidential is only used if the speaker takes time to infer from the visual evidence available that something had occurred for which the speaker could have been to blame: 'perhaps the speaker gave the pig some medication that inadvertently caused his death'. The 'first person' effect—similar to that of non-firsthand and non-visual evidentials—is achieved by a combination of inferred evidential and person marker.

7.2.2 *Restrictions on evidential use in first person contexts*

First person participants show more restrictions when used with specific evidentials than any other person (cf. Guentchéva et al. 1994). In a few languages with small evidentiality systems, evidentials do not occur with first person at

---

⁶ When the inferred evidential in Tsafiki is used with first person, the connotation is that of unexpected information. The required person marking is disjunct, as in (i) (Dickinson 2000: 412).

(i) tse   lowa=bi   ne=chi   keere-i-**i-nu**-e
     1p.fem   bed=LOC   from=LOC   throw-become-DISJ-INFR/MIR-DECL
     'I must have fallen out of bed' (I'm on the floor)

all. This is the case in Hunzib (van den Berg 1995: 103). According to Prokofjev (1935: 69–70), 'auditive' in Selkup has no first person forms (also see Perrot (1996: 160 and examples therein). Komi languages have no first person form of non-firsthand past (Tepljashina and Lytkin 1976: 179–81, cf. Serebrjannikov 1960). That is, it is in first person that evidentials show gaps in their paradigms. Mỹky (Monserrat and Dixon 2003) has no first person firsthand or non-firsthand. Similarly, in Tuyuca (Barnes 1984: 258, 261) present inferred is not used with first person. We are not aware of any such restrictions in other languages with large evidentiality systems.

In Koasati (Muskogean), the reported ('auditory') -hawa- (position 11 in the verbal structure) is 'rarely if ever used with verbs having a first or a second person subject' (Kimball 1991: 206). Similar restrictions apply in Kham (Tibeto-Burman: Watters 2002: 296–9).

Similarly, evidentiality strategies whose meanings are similar to non-firsthand may be restricted to third person only. The perfect in Georgian has a variety of 'non-firsthand' meanings (see §4.2) with any person except first (Hewitt 1995: 259). In Vlach Romani (Matras 1995) participles acquire non-firsthand overtones with third person only.

Ladakhi (Koshal 1979: 186–7), a language with at least four evidentials (§2.3), has a different restriction: the visual evidential (employed in statements made on the basis of seeing something) is not used with first person subjects. According to Koshal (1979: 186), 'one cannot see himself but can see only others'. This is markedly different from most other systems—where the visual evidential explicitly implies seeing what one, or other people are doing (see §11.2, on metalinguistic explanations of evidentials). In Ladakhi, the visual evidential can be used with first person subjects if one sees oneself in a mirror or in a dream. We have seen (under (f)) how in related Tibeto-Burman languages Qiang and Amdo Tibetan the direct evidential with first person implies an accidental action. Since Koshal's description (1979) does not provide further examples or explanations, one can only tentatively infer that the visual evidential in Ladakhi—just like in Amdo Tibetan—indicates that the speaker was 'merely a passive participant or witness of the portrayed events' (Sun 1993: 961) and thus cannot be used if the speaker describes their own, consciously undertaken activities.

Alternatively, in a large evidentiality system, an evidential may occur exclusively with first person subjects or first person affected participants. Central Pomo (Mithun 1999: 181) has a number of evidential markers which cover general knowledge, visual, non-visual sensory, reported, inferential, and two more markers: one used to mark 'personal experience of one's own actions' and the other one referring to 'personal affect'. Similarly, performative evidential suffixes in Kashaya (also Pomoan family: Oswalt 1986: 34–6) imply that the speaker 'knows of what he speaks because he is performing the act himself or has just performed it'.

The reason for these attested restrictions on evidentials with first person lies in the nature of 'I' as a primary 'observer'. In other systems, this primary observer is accorded a special, first-person-only evidential. Alternatively, 'I' can be extended beyond the speaker, to include the addressee. Evidentials and other person values are the topic of the next section.

7.3 Evidentials and 'others'

'First person' can be looked on as 'primary observer', the ultimate source of perception. But is first person always first person only? In fact, an evidential in the first person context may include the addressee as well as the speaker; see §7.3.1. Evidentials with second and third persons may also develop semantic nuances of their own; see §7.3.2.

7.3.1 When 'I' involves 'you'

An evidential with first person can combine reference to both the speaker and the addressee. We can recall from §5.1 that non-firsthand forms in Archi can be used with first person, if the speaker did see the actions happen but was unaware of or not responsible for what took place. It is also employed if the speaker observes the result of something that happened in their absence and is unexpected for them (§6.1; Kibrik 1977: 230–1).

The non-firsthand with first person can have yet another meaning: if the speaker participated in a situation the meaning of which is unknown to the addressee, and is unexpected and surprising. For instance, the speaker may say 'I hate you-non-firsthand', since the addressee does not know that he hates her, and the use of firsthand emphasizes information new to the addressee. Similarly, if a man says 'I brought these people to help you-non-firsthand', this implies that the addressee does not know why the people were brought to them. All such examples involve first person (the second person does not have to be mentioned).

The non-firsthand evidential with a first person actor in past or present in Meithei (Tibeto-Burman: Chelliah 1997: 222–3) is somewhat similar. It shows that, while the speaker has evidence about the statement, the addressee does not; that is, the speaker assumes the perspective of the hearer (similarly to 'perspective' questions in Sherpa, another Tibeto-Burman language when the speaker 'takes the perspective of the hearer in order to establish empathy with the hearer': Chelliah 1997: 222). Example 7.31 is grammatical only if the speaker accepts the perspective of the addressee. See §8.4, for an example of a different semantic effect of the same evidential with future.

Meithei

7.31 əy čák čá-ləm-lə-e
      I   rice eat-NONFIRSTH-PERF-ASSERT
      'I have eaten' (for you to know)

In both Archi and Meithei first person non-firsthand transmit information about the speaker which is unknown and new to the addressee, effectively covering two observers ('you' and 'me'). Nambiquara languages of Southern Amazonia are unusual in having a set of evidentials which contain reference to the source of information available to the speaker and to the addressee simultaneously (see Kroeker 2001: 62–5 and 2.88a, for Mamainde (Northern Nambiquara), and Lowe 1999: 275–6, for Southern Nambiquara). These evidentials are distinct from those where the speaker is the only observer. This is an extreme case of differentiation between the information source as 'mine' or 'ours'.

7.3.2 *Second and third persons with evidentials*

Most descriptions of evidentials are predominantly based on sentences with third person participants. Just occasionally, evidentials can develop special meanings or conventionalized usages with second or third person. The reported suffix in Jarawara (Dixon 2003: 178) can be used to remind someone of their own words, as in 7.32.

7.32 ti-fimiha-**mone**,   ti-na
      2sgS-be.hungry-REP.f 2sgA-AUX(say)f
      'You were hungry, you said'

In Salar, one uses the non-firsthand evidential with second person to indicate politeness or deference (Dwyer 2000: 57). In Shilluk (Miller and Gilley forthcoming: 14–15), using the second person marked just with a pronominal suffix on the verb form—which expresses inferred evidentiality and is accompanied by a hearsay marker—implies that the addressee has been wrongly accused of doing something, according to the speaker. Mah Meri (Aslian, Mon-Khmer: Nicole Kruspe, p.c.) has a particle which is used with first person to express internal feelings, such as 'I am hungry', 'I am fed up'. When used with third person it refers to reported information. The 'first person effect' described in §7.2.1 effectively differentiates first person from other persons. This brings us to the implicit person value of evidentials; see §7.4 below.

7.4 Evidentials as implicit person markers

We have seen that in some languages, an evidential choice presupposes a particular person value. The visual or the firsthand evidential is typically used for autobiographical accounts and for talking about the speaker's own experiences, almost like a marker of a genre (see §10.2.1), thus containing an implicit 'first person'. This is comparable to how in Qiang the first person marker can be added to a verb already marked for third person, to stress that the speaker indeed saw it happen—see 3.21 ('he is playing the drum—I, the speaker, see it') and 7.24. The person marker indicates the perceiver, not the agent.

In Eastern Pomo (McLendon 2003: 113) all four evidential suffixes mark the speaker's source of information, and imply first person involvement. This is particularly obvious from the ways in which speakers translate sentences with evidentials into English. In 5.56, the perceiver is 'I'. There is no first person in view—but it is understood from the evidential choice. The English translation involves first person ('I smell the fish'). In the absence of any overt first person marking it is the non-visual sensory evidential *(i)nk'e* that produces this effect. The unmarked recipient of information is first person. Along similar lines, in Maricopa (Gordon 1986*b*: 113), if a verb is marked with an evidential suffix, the addressee and/or the recipient is assumed to be first person.

The fixed choice of evidential with verbs of 'internal state'—cognition, feelings, and so on—may simply correlate with a default person reading. This works in the following way. East Tucanoan languages have three persons in their pronouns, but just a third/non-third person distinction in verbal cross-referencing. Evidentiality is fused with tense and person-marking. That is, in Tucano *apê-samo* (play-PRES.NONVIS.3sg.fem) means 'She is playing' (I hear her); *apê-sami* (play-PRES.NONVIS.3sg.masc) means 'He is playing' (I hear him), and *apê-sa-ma* (play- PRES.NONVIS.3pl) means 'They are playing' (I hear them). One form *apê-sa'* (play-PRES.NONVIS.nonthird.p) covers the rest: it means 'I/you/we/you pl play' (non-visual). The ambiguity can be resolved by adding a personal pronoun, or by the context.

We saw in §5.3.1 (example 5.39) that the non-visual sensory evidential with verbs of internal states is used to describe the speaker's own condition. That is, with the full pronoun omitted, the statement in 7.33 has a default first person reading.

Tucano

7.33   do'âti-gi'   weé-**sa'**
       be.sick-NOM.MASC   do/be-PRES.NONVIS.nonthird.p
       'I am/feel sick' (non-visual)

When talking about someone else, visual or inferred evidential will be used, as in 7.34. The overt subject does not have to be mentioned (this is why 'Pedro' is in parentheses).

7.34   (Péduru)   do'âti-gi'   weé-**mi**
       (Pedro)   be.sick-NOM.MASC   do/be-PRES.NONVIS.3sg.masc
       '(Pedro) is sick' (I can see he is)

The default person reading includes the subject, as in 7.33, and also an experiencer (marked as an indirect object).[7] In 7.35, the first word, 'to me', can be omitted: the evidential itself indicates that the 'sufferer' is the first person.

7.35   (yi'î-re)   upîka   pũrí-**sa'**
       (I-TOP.NON.A/S-OBJECT)   tooth   ache-PRES.NONVIS.nonthird.p
       'A tooth is aching' (to me)

In Tariana, just as in Tucano, verbs of internal state require non-visual evidential when first person is involved. Person is marked with prefixes, obligatory on all active verbs. But stative verbs, many of which refer to internal states, do not take prefixes. A non-visual evidential with such a verb implies first person (one can only feel something that is happening to oneself). Examples are *amiri-mha* (be.drunk-PRES.NONVIS) '(I) am drunk'; *khenolena-mha* (feel.like.vomiting-PRES.NONVIS) 'I feel like vomiting'; and also 'I am sad' in 7.14. If my eyes are watery because I have been peeling onions, I can well say *cebola dhe-mha nu-thida-se* (onion 3sgnf+enter-PRES.NONVIS 1sg-eye-LOC) 'Onion has affected me', literally, 'onion enters my eye'. I do not have to say all that—if I simply say *Cebola-**mha*** (onion-PRES.NONVIS) the meaning is the same—'it was onion (non-visual) that hurt my eye'. An evidential is enough to show whose perception this is.

Any other evidential—visual or inferred—implies non-first person. One says *amiri-sika* (be.drunk-REC.P.ASSUM) 'He, she, you, we, or they must be drunk' (judging by the mess the person's clothes are in; or if the beer is gone and the culprit was the only person in the house). Saying *amiri-naka* (be.drunk-PRES.VIS) means 'He, she, you, we, or they is/are drunk' if one sees the person in question staggering or vomiting. A similar example, from Tariana, is 'I am sad' at 7.14. There, too, the pronoun can be omitted, and the predicate has no person-marking. The person value is likely to be understood based on the evidential.

The implicit person reference of evidentials in Tariana helps to distinguish two meanings of the polysemous pronoun *pha*: the 'impersonal' ('one') meaning, and the first person inclusive 'us, including you, that is, the addressee'

---

[7] If topical, direct and indirect objects in Tucano are marked in the same way.

meaning. With a non-visual evidential and a verb of 'internal state', *pha* can only be understood as having first person reference, as in 7.36. (The chosen meaning is underlined in each case.)

Tariana

7.36 nhesiɾi-pu-**mha** pha
  like-AUG-PRES.NONVIS one/<u>we</u>
  'We (including you) like (this course) very much'

With any other evidential, the 'impersonal' reading is appropriate.

7.37 nhesiɾi-pu-**naka** pha
  like-AUG-PRES.VIS <u>one</u>/we
  'One likes it'

Person-marking can be used as an evidential strategy; see §4.6. As just shown, evidentials, in their turn, may become an extra strategy for marking person.

7.5 Information source and the observer: a summary

An evidential can reflect the information source of any person—'I', 'you', or third person. Not infrequently, the firsthand, the visual, and the non-visual evidential reflect the way the speaker perceives what is happening. This is not to say that these evidentials always reflect the speaker's perception. We saw in §3.5 how perception by multiple observers can be marked in one clause.

When the observer is first person, certain seemingly counterintuitive evidential choices develop specific overtones which I refer to as 'first person effect'. Non-firsthand evidentials in A1 and A2 systems, non-visual evidentials in larger systems, and reported evidentials in many systems of varied types may acquire additional meanings of lack of intention, control, awareness, and volition on the part of the speaker. This complex of meanings correlates with the speaker's 'unprepared mind', sudden realization, and ensuing 'surprise', thus resulting in mirative extensions (see §6.4). With firsthand and visual evidentials, first person marking may acquire the opposite meaning: the action is intentional and the speaker is fully aware of what they are doing. In none of the instances investigated is it possible to distinguish between 'control', 'volition', and 'intention' as separate semantic components. This group of meanings is realized as a bundle. In contrast, in a number of Tibeto-Burman languages, the combination of first person with direct evidential implies accidental uncontrolled action of which the speaker was merely a passive participant. A summary of first person effects with evidentials is given in Table 7.1.

TABLE 7.1 First person effects in evidentials

TYPE OF SYSTEM	EVIDENTIAL	MEANING	LANGUAGES EXEMPLIFIED
A1	non-firsthand	unintentional, uncontrolled, non-volitional action	Jarawara, Yukaghir, Archi
	firsthand	opposite of the above	
C1, D1	non-visual	unintentional, uncontrolled, non-volitional action	Tariana, Tucano
	visual	opposite of the above	
A2	non-firsthand	unintentional, uncontrolled, non-volitional action	Abkhaz
A3	reported	action the speaker does not remember new information, surprise, denial	Tucano, Wintu, Eastern Pomo, Lithuanian, Estonian, Nganasan
B1	direct (or visual)	accidental uncontrolled action	Qiang, Amdo Tibetan
A1, A2	non-firsthand	speaker's information is new to the addressee	Archi, Meithei

Assumed and inferred evidentials have hardly any first-person-specific extensions. When used with second and third person, evidentials may occasionally develop overtones of politeness.

First person marking with a non-firsthand evidential may transmit information about the speaker which is new to the addressee. It then includes two observers, 'you' and 'me'. Examples of such 'inclusive' evidential use come from Archi and Meithei. There tend to be more restrictions on evidentiality choices with first person than with second or third. Some languages have evidentials used just to refer to information acquired by first person.

Verbs covering internal states may require obligatory evidential choice depending on person. As a result of these correlations, evidentials acquire the implicit value of person markers. They could then be treated on a par with person-marking strategies.

Correlations between evidentiality and person may follow another direction. The frequency of an evidential may interact with person. Even if there are no absolute restrictions as to the co-occurrence of evidentials with different persons, statistical tendencies may be significant. A representative corpus of Wanka Quechua (Floyd 1997: 246–7) displays such correlations—over 53 per cent of all the occurrences of the direct evidentials are with first person and over 84 per cent of the reported are with third person. However, this could well be an 'artefact' of the type of materials on which a grammar is based. As we will see in §10.2.1, reported evidentials are typical 'tokens' of traditional stories. Historical narratives are usually told in third person. Autobiographical accounts tend to be cast in first person. And finding a whole text told in second person may not be that easy. Whether a given statistical correlation is a genuine tendency in a language or just a side effect of the database is an open question. A study of evidentials in terms of their overall frequency has not yet been undertaken for any language.

8

Evidentials and other grammatical categories

In the preceding chapter we saw how evidentials interact with person. Evidentials interrelate, in different ways, with most other grammatical categories. Different evidentials may be available in a statement, in a question, or in a command. Which evidential is used may depend on whether a clause is positive or negative (that is, on choices made in the polarity system). The form or the semantics of an evidential may depend on tense-aspect or on mood.

How evidentials expressed by a verbal affix interrelate with other categories may depend on the slot they occupy in a verbal word and on their place within the verbal paradigm. Evidentials in Samoyedic languages (Selkup, Nenets, Enets, and Nganasan), in Yukaghir, in Archi, and in Mao Naga are in a paradigmatic relationship with the mood system (cf. Tereschenko 1973: 145–6, Kuznetsova et al. 1980: 240–3, 247; Tereschenko 1979: 220–1; Décsy 1966: 48; Perrot 1996: 162–3). Consequently, they are mutually exclusive with any non-indicative moods. Similarly, in Wakashan languages, imperatives are in a paradigmatic relationship with tense, aspect, mood, and evidentiality; for this reason, evidentials are not expressed in commands. In Yanam (Gomez 1990: 98), evidentials are in paradigmatic relationship with aspect. And in Takelma, the inferential evidential (A2 system) is one of six tense-mode systems; and so it is mutually exclusive with aorist, future, potential, and present and future imperatives.[1] In Abkhaz evidentials are mutually exclusive with some modalities but not with others (see §8.3).

We first look at correlations between evidentiality and clause types (§8.1), then at negation (§8.2), non-indicative modalities (§8.3), tense and aspect (§8.4), and then at a few other categories (§8.5). A brief summary is given in §8.6.

---

[1] In all these cases a question may arise: is there a special category of evidentials or is it just a choice within a mood system? This problem should be solved on the basis of language-internal criteria.

8.1 Evidentials and clause types

So far we have only discussed evidentials in declarative clauses. In an overwhelming majority of languages more evidential choices are available in statements than in any other clause type. In the case of questions and commands, the choice of an evidential may reflect the source of information available to the speaker and/or to the addressee. We first discuss evidentials in interrogative clauses (§8.1.1), then in commands (§8.1.2), and then in dependent clauses and other clause types (§8.1.3).

8.1.1 *Evidentials in questions*

An evidential can be within the scope of a question (see examples 3.42–3, from Quechua, where what is queried is the authorship of a report marked with a reported evidential). Evidentials may not be used in questions at all, as in some languages, including Abkhaz, Baniwa, Mỹky, Retuarã, and Jarawara.[2]

The same set of evidentials can occur in questions and in statements, as in Quechua, Eastern Pomo, Nganasan, Tsafiki, and Qiang. Fewer evidentiality choices are likely to be available in questions than in statements. This is discussed in (A) below.

Evidentials used in questions may differ in their semantics and pragmatic connotations from their counterparts in declarative clauses. In a question, an evidential may relate to the source of information available to the addressee, or to the speaker, or to both; see (B). Evidentials in questions may acquire mirative overtone; see (C). When in questions, evidentials may be used in yet other ways (for instance, as rhetorical questions and as speech formulae); see (D).

(A) Reduced systems of evidentials in questions
A language can have several evidentiality subsystems depending on clause type (see §3.4). This is the case for East Tucanoan languages and for Tariana.[3] In Tucano the choice between a two-term system, a three-term system, and a four-term system depends on clause type (see Table 3.1). A full four-term system of type C1 is distinguished in declarative clauses, a three-term system of type B2 in interrogative clauses, and a simple A3 system in imperative clauses. Tariana has a five-term D1 system in declarative clauses, a three-term system of the B2 type in interrogative and in apprehensive clauses, and two-term systems of A3 type in imperatives and A1 in purposive clauses (see Table 8.2).

---

[2] As we saw in §3.2.1, Jarawara has a functionally unmarked tense–evidentiality combination, immediate past non-firsthand, which can be used as an evidentiality-neutral choice. This form also occurs in content questions—but it does not impart any evidentiality value since its firsthand counterpart cannot be used (Dixon 2003: 175).

[3] In Hupda (Epps forthcoming), a language with five evidentials (D1 type) spoken in the same area, all evidential choices are allowed in interrogative and declarative clauses.

The evidence in favour of neutralization of reported and inferred in interrogative clauses in Tariana and in Tucano comes from the 'conversation sustainer' question–response pattern. In languages of the Vaupés region, there is the following common strategy of showing a listener's participation in conversational interaction.

When A (speaker) tells a story, B (listener) is expected to give feedback, after just about every sentence, by repeating the predicate (or the last verb within a serial verb construction) accompanied by an interrogative evidential and interrogative intonation. For Tariana and most East Tucanoan languages, the correspondences are as shown in Diagram 3.1[4] (and also see Malone 1988: 122, for a similar pattern in Tuyuca). In Tariana and in Tuyuca one interrogative evidential covers the inferred, the reported, and the assumed, and in Tucano it covers the inferred and the reported. In both cases a four- or a five-term system in declarative sentences 'collapses' into a three-term B2 system. Example 3.18 showed how this works in a dialogue from Tariana.

In an evidentiality system with three terms, just one may occur in questions. The only evidential used in interrogative clauses in Shipibo-Konibo (C2) is the marker of assumed evidence *-mein*. Its meaning in questions differs somewhat from the one it has in statements. In both statements and in questions, it expresses speculation and assumption based on 'poor' evidence—in contrast to the inferred evidential *-bira* employed for inference based on direct evidence (Valenzuela 2003: 47–9; and examples 2.81–3). The assumed evidential in questions is a token of politeness, and it can also indicate involvement on the part of the speaker (cf. (D) below). A polite question-request with *-mein* is illustrated in 8.1.

Shipibo-Konibo

8.1 Mi-n-**mein**   e-a   nokon wai   oro-xon-ai?
     2-ERG-ASSUM   1-ABS   POSS.1   garden:ABS   clear-BEN-INC
     'Would you please/perhaps clear my garden for me?'

This use is rather similar to the way modal particles are used as politeness markers in commands in many languages of the world (Aikhenvald forthcoming). We can recall that the assumed evidential *-mein* implies doubt (an epistemic extension not attested with most other inferred evidentials—see §5.3.2), and thus comes close to being a modal marker.

In Bora, with a three-term system of B3 type, only the reported evidential appears to occur in questions (Weber and Thiesen forthcoming: 254–6). In contrast, in Eastern Pomo all evidentials except for reported have been attested in interrogative clauses (McLendon 2003: 114–16).

---

[4] Aikhenvald (2002: 125–6) provides a discussion of this technique and how it was calqued from Tucano into Tariana. This strategy in Tucano is mentioned by Ramirez (1997, vol. I: 144).

(B) Whose source of information does the evidential reflect?
The use of evidentials in interrogative clauses may reflect either (i) the information source of the speaker, or (ii) assumptions the speaker has about the information source of the addressee. The first possibility appears to be somewhat rarer. A reported evidential in an interrogative clause may reflect (iii) the information source of a third party.

(i) Evidentials in an interrogative clause reflect the information source of the speaker. In Yukaghir, the non-firsthand evidential in questions indicates that the speaker has not witnessed what they are asking about: in 8.2 the speaker did not see people going away from where he is at the moment of speech, and so he asks (Maslova 2003: 228):

Yukaghir
8.2   qodo   ti:-t   kebej-nu-**l'el**-ŋi?
      how   here-ABL   go-IMPF-NONFIRSTH-3pl:INTR
      'How do people go away from here?' (the speaker did not see them)

Evidentials in questions in Eastern Pomo also cover the information source of the speaker rather than that of the addressee. The non-visual sensory evidential in 8.3 implies that the speaker heard the sound, but is wondering who produced it (McLendon 2003: 114–16). (All evidentials, except for the reported, can occur in questions.)

Eastern Pomo
8.3   ki·yá·=t'a   ʔéč̃-**ink'e**?
      who=INTER   sneeze-NONVIS
      'Who sneezed?' (I heard, but don't know who sneezed)

The inferred evidential in 8.4 occurs in a question asked when the speaker has enough evidence to make an inference.

8.4   k'e·héy=t'a   mí·   ka·dá-k-k'-**ine**?
      self=INTER   2sg.PATIENT   cut-PUNCTUAL-REFL-INFR
      'Did you cut yourself?' (When seeing bandages, or a bloody knife, etc.)

A reported evidential in a question in Bora presupposes that the speaker got the information from someone else.

Bora
8.5   à-**bà**   ǘ   phè-é-ʔí
      INTER-REP   you   go-FUT-VERB.TERMINATING.CLASSIFIER
      'Are you going (as I was told)?'

Alternatively, an evidential in a question presupposes the addressee's information source.

(ii) EVIDENTIALS IN AN INTERROGATIVE CLAUSE REFLECT THE INFORMATION SOURCE OF THE ADDRESSEE. In Tsafiki, all four evidentials can be used in questions; questions are said to relate to 'the source of the addressee's information' (Connie Dickinson, p.c.). A similar situation obtains in Nganasan (Gusev forthcoming: 5; Usenkova forthcoming: 10) and Central Pomo (Mithun 1999: 181). In Wintu (Lee 1938: 92), the visual interrogative evidential 'assumes that the questionnee has been an eye-witness', and the non-visual evidential 'shows the expectation of auditory evidence from the questionnee' (also see Pitkin 1984: 147). According to Comrie (p.c.), for Tsez (with a two-term A1 system), 'in questions the relevant factor is whether or not the addressee witnessed the event'; since 'it implies that if the event took place then the addressee witnessed it'.

In Quechua (Floyd 1996b, 1999: 85–111; Faller 2002: 229–30) any of the three evidentials (direct, inferred, and reported) can be used in questions. The direct evidential in a question implies that the addressee has 'directly acquired' information about the event. Consequently, a question marked with the direct evidential places a strong obligation on the addressee to provide an informed answer, as in 8.6.

Wanka Quechua

8.6   imay-**mi**   wankayuu-pi   kuti-mu-la
      when-DIR.EV   Huancayo-ABL   return-AFAR-PAST
      'When did he come back from Huancayo?'

Along similar lines, Cerrón-Palomino (1976: 108) states that a question marked with the direct evidential is not very polite and implies that the speaker does not have much confidence in the addresse.[5]

An evidential in Tariana and Tucano questions refers to the addressee's information source (see Aikhenvald 2003b: 144–5; 2003c: 311–20; Ramirez 1997, vol. I: 144). If a question is cast in visual evidential, it implies that the addressee must have seen what they are being asked about. In 8.7, the evil spirit asks his wife 'Who came here?' He uses the visual evidential; she has been at home all the time, and she must have visual information about who came to the house while she was there.

Tariana

8.7   kwana-**nihka**   nawiki   na:ka?
      who-REC.P.VIS.INTER   people   3pl+arrive
      'What kind of people have been here?' (VISUAL: the addressee saw them)

---

[5] Other authors offer different interpretations of the direct evidential for other Quechua dialects. Faller (2002: 229–30) notes that the direct evidential in a question in Cuzco Quechua may be 'anchored to the speaker', as well as to the hearer, and is thus 'evidentially ambiguous', while the inferred evidential in a question is 'always anchored to the person who provides the answer'. (She does not provide any textual or conversational examples to support her claim.) In his analysis of Tarma Quechua, Adelaar (1977: 255) suggests that the direct evidential in questions is 'virtually meaningless'.

A visual evidential in questions has additional connotations: the speaker is sure the addressee has visual information even if the addressee denies this. The addressee of a question cast in visual evidential is held responsible for their actions. A question in visual evidential can sound as an accusation, as in 8.8 where the shaman is plainly accused of telling a lie.

8.8   kwe-**nihka**   pi-ni   pi-mayẽ   wa-na?
       why-PAST.VIS.INTER   2sg-do   2sg-lie   1pl-OBJ
       'Why have you lied to us?' (VISUAL: you are held responsible for this)

In Tucano and in Tariana, a question cast in non-visual evidential presupposes the addressee's access to non-visual information—they may have obtained their information by hearing, smell, or internal feeling.[6] A typical example of such inter-action comes from Tucano (Ramirez 1997, vol. III: 63). The question in 8.10 is cast in non-visual evidential: the addressee is supposed to have non-visual information about their own sickness (see §5.3.1, on how non-visual evidentials in C1 and D1 systems describe one's own 'internal states': emotions, pain, and the like).

Tucano

8.9   Father speaking:
       Makí,   do'âti-gi'   weé-**sa'**
       son   ill-NOMN.MASC.SG   AUX-PRES.NONVIS.nonthird.p
       'Son, I am sick' (NON-VISUAL: refers to speaker's internal state)

8.10   Son speaking:
       Yẽ'e   nohó   niî-**sa**-ri?
       what   kind   be-PRES.NONVIS-INTER
       'What is it?' (NON-VISUAL: refers to addressee's internal state)

The assumed evidential in a question in Tariana and the inferred evidential in Tucano questions imply that the addressee has no firsthand information to provide an answer. After a mysterious animal (which later turned out to be an evil spirit) has disappeared, the speaker asks everyone (including himself) the question in 8.11—neither he nor anyone else has a clue.

Tariana

8.11   kani-**sika**   di-a   diha   ma:tʃite?
       where-REC.P.INFR.INTER   3sgnf-go he   bad+NCL:ANIM
       'Where has this bad one gone?' (INFERRED: None of us have a clue)

Such question may imply that the addressee is not knowledgeable enough and is thus potentially offensive. The semantic connotations of evidentials in ques-tions are summarized in Table 8.1 (adapted from Table 5, Aikhenvald 2003c: 145).

---

[6] This is also the case in Hupda (Epps forthcoming: 6).

TABLE 8.1 Semantics of evidentials in interrogative clauses in Tariana and in Tucano

TERM	SEMANTICS
Visual	1. Addressee saw something which the speaker did not (or did) see 2. Speaker is sure the addressee saw the fact and knows it 3. Addressee is held responsible for the action: accusation
Non-visual	1. Addressee has not seen it (they may have heard it, or smelt it) 2. Addressee may not know 3. Addressee may not be really responsible
Assumed	1. Addressee does not have any firsthand information about it 2. Addressee is not knowledgeable (they do not know enough)

Evidentials in questions have epistemic connotations lacking from their counterparts in declarative clauses. Asking a question involves making assumptions about the source of the other person's information. This is potentially dangerous (see §11.3–4, on evidentials and cultural conventions). As a result it is not culturally appropriate to ask too many questions in Tariana. One asks a question if one is sure the addressee can provide the desired information. Otherwise, asking a question may presuppose the 'questioner's' insistence—which is readily interpreted as implying that they suspect that something is wrong.

In Quechua, the inferred evidential in questions does not have overtones of the addressee's ignorance and incompetence. Rather, it implies that the speaker 'sets the stage' for conjecture on the part of the addressee. Such questions may not even require a response: the speaker does not expect the addressee to be knowledgeable enough to answer. In 8.12 and 8.13 the parents are wondering what their son could have done with the money he had borrowed under false pretences (Floyd 1999: 113). Neither of them has any answer.

Wanka Quechua

8.12   Father speaking:
    may-chruu-**chra**   gasta-y-pa   paawa-alu-n?
    where-LOC-INFR   spend-NOMN-GEN   finish-ASP-3p
    'I wonder where he spent it all?' (lit. Where did he spend it-INFERRED)

8.13   Mother speaking:
    kanan   ima-nuy-**chra**   ka-shrun
    today   what-SIM-INFR   be-1.to.2.FUT
    'Now what will we do?' (lit. Today how will we be-INFERRED)

In Tariana, Tucano, or other East Tucanoan languages the reported evidential is not used in questions. A reported evidential in a question in Quechua implies that the addressee is expected to provide secondhand information, as in 8.14 (Faller 2002: 230; cf. also Floyd 1999: 127).

Cuzco Quechua

8.14 pi-ta-**s**   Inés-qa   watuku-sqa?
      who-ACC-REP   Inés-TOP   visit-PAST2
      'Who did Inés visit?' (speaker expects hearer to have reportative
      evidence for his or her answer)

(iii) EVIDENTIALS IN INTERROGATIVE CLAUSE REFLECT THE INFORMATION SOURCE OF A THIRD PARTY. A request for information using a reported evidential can come from a third party. This is unlike any other evidential in questions. A reported evidential in an A3 system and a non-firsthand evidential in an A2 system (if they can be used to refer to secondhand information) can be used in questions asked on behalf of someone else. This is rather similar to how reported evidentials are often used in commands (§8.1.2): marking an order on behalf of another person. In 8.15, from Kham (Watters 2002: 300), the question is directed by the speaker to the addressee (second person), but it 'has its origin outside the speech act situation': the author of the question is 'he or she'.

Kham

8.15 karao   **di**
      why   REP
      '(He or she wants to know) why'

In Warlpiri (Laughren 1982: 140), 'if a woman is publicly accusing someone of hitting her son, one spectator might ask another the question' in 8.16. It is obvious from the context who is making the claim about the culprit.

Warlpiri

8.16 Ngana-ngku   **nganta**   pakarnu?
      who-ERG   REP   hit+PAST
      'Who does she say hit him?'

Similar examples are found in Turkic languages (see Johanson 2003: 286). In all these cases the use of evidentials in questions has nothing to do with the speaker's assumptions about the addressee. According to Faller (2002: 230), 8.14, from Cuzco Quechua, also can be interpreted as a question on behalf of someone else. No evidential other than reported can be used this way in a question—one does not ask about something which a third party (not the speaker or the addressee) had seen, or heard, or inferred.

The meaning of an evidential in a question may depend on what kind of question it is. In Western Armenian (Donabédian 1996: 103–4) the use of the non-firsthand evidential in polar questions requests confirmation of the fact that the information was acquired in some indirect way—that is, it might be interpreted as presupposing some assumption about the addressee on the part of the speaker. A non-firsthand evidential in a content question does not have this effect. In other languages, no differences have been noted as to the use of questions in polar and content questions.

(C) MIRATIVE OVERTONES OF EVIDENTIALS IN QUESTIONS

Evidentials in questions may carry overtones of surprise (see §6.4). In Sochiapan Chinantec (Foris 2000: 373–4) the reported particle *né?^{H}* implies that the speaker is puzzled by something overheard, and expects further discussion of the matter. In 8.17, the speaker heard the information from someone else, and the speaker expects positive response; use of the 'quotative' implies the speaker's surprise and the desire to discuss the matter further. This 'mirative' overtone of the reported evidential may be reflected in the way it marks the point of climax in the storyline in narratives (§10.2.2).

Sochiapan Chinantec (raised letters indicate tones)

8.17   ?í^H ka^L-hĩe?^{LM} **né?^{H}**   ?ué^{LM} ?ŋo^{L}hmáï^M dí^H
       QUERY   PAST-shake.it   REP   and   Mexico.City   INDUBITATIVE
       'Did Mexico City have an earthquake (as I/we have heard)?'

The reported evidential in Quechua has mirative overtones, in two kinds of constructions: riddles and the 'challenge construction'. Both involve questions; see 6.19–20 in §6.2.

The auditory evidential in yes–no questions in Euchee has similar connotations: the speaker 'is showing more excitement or surprise that they are coming rather than needing information' (Linn 2000: 317–18). Unlike in Chinantec above, the information source is that of the addressee, rather than of the speaker.

Euchee

8.18   'ahe   'igō   'le-**ke**?
       here   3sg(EUCHEE).PATIENT+come   QUESTION-AUD.EV
       'Are they coming (you hear them?)?' (women's speech)

(D) OTHER MEANINGS OF EVIDENTIALS IN QUESTIONS

When used in questions, evidentials often acquire rhetorical value. In Quechua questions cast in inferred evidential do not require an answer. Examples like 8.12 and 8.13 may be understood as rhetorical exclamations rather than information-seeking devices. The reported evidential is frequent in rhetorical questions in Sissala (Blass 1989: 318–19). Example 8.18, from Euchee, is also a rhetorical question which requires no factual reply. A similar example is 8.1, from Shipibo-Konibo: this rhetorical question has the force of a mild command. If questions are used in speech formulae, evidentials may also occur. We discuss these in §10.3.

8.1.2 Evidentials in commands

An overwhelming majority of languages with evidentials do not use them at all in imperative clauses. Examples include Sochiapan Chinantec, Jarawara, Eastern Pomo, Qiang, Yukaghir, Abkhaz, Wakashan, and Turkic languages, and in Quechua and Aymara (an overview is in Aikhenvald forthcoming).

A few languages have a secondhand imperative meaning 'do something on someone else's order' marked differently from evidentiality in declarative clauses. This is the case in Nganasan, Cavineña (Tacanan: Guillaume 2004), Cora, and Lak. The reported enclitic -guuq in West Greenlandic is also used in commands on behalf of someone else (Fortescue 2003: 295–6). Secondhand imperatives are a typical feature of Tucanoan languages (see Barnes 1979 on Tuyuca, Ramirez 1997, vol. I: 144–7 on Tucano, and further references in Aikhenvald 2002). Such an imperative can occur with any person. An example is under 8.19.

Tucano
8.19   āyu-**áto**
        good-REP.IMPV
        'Let them stay well (on someone else's order)!'

A secondhand imperative form can be part of the evidential paradigm, as in Tariana. The reported marker -pida- is also used in declarative clauses (albeit with obligatory tense marking: see §8.4 and §3.8). This indicates the relatively late origin of the Tariana evidentials (see further arguments in Aikhenvald 2003e and §9.2.2).

Tariana
8.20   pi-hña-**pida**
        2sg-eat-REP.IMPV
        'Eat on someone else's order!'

In Shipibo-Konibo, only one of the two otherwise synonymous reportatives is used in imperatives (Valenzuela 2003: 42). The meaning is of a command on someone else's behalf.

Shipibo-Konibo
8.21   onpax-**ki**   be-wé!
        contained.water:ABS-REP   bring-IMPV
        '(S/he says that you must) bring water!'

The reported evidential nganta in Warlpiri is commonly used to attribute a command to someone else other than the speaker (Laughren 1982: 140). In 8.22 it is clear from the context that the original command comes from the police. Similar examples are in Yankunytjatjara (Goddard 1983: 289).

Warlpiri
8.22 Kulu-wangu **nganta**-lu nyina-ya yurrkunyu-kujaku
       fight-PRIV REP-3pl be-IMPV police-AVERSIVE
       'Don't fight or you will be in trouble with police (on the order of the police)'

In Mparntwe Arrernte, the reported evidential in a command can have somewhat different overtones (Wilkins 1989: 393). It provides softening by 'falsely indicating that the order is only being passed on through the speaker from some unnamed "commander" ', as in 8.23.

Mparntwe Arrernte
8.23 Arrantherre **kwele** ntert-irr-Ø-aye!
       2plS REP quiet-INCH-IMPV-EMPH
       'You mob are supposed to be quiet' (lit. Someone else has said that you mob have to shut up!)

The reported evidential in Warlpiri may also attenuate an order. The sentence is then pronounced with a question intonation (Laughren 1982: 138).

Warlpiri
8.24 marna-lu ma-nta, **nganta**?
       spinifex-3pl get-IMPV REP
       'Pick up the spinifex grass, won't you?'

Other evidentials only rarely occur in commands. The auditory evidential in an imperative clause in Euchee (Linn 2000: 318) refers to the source of information the addressee is commanded or is invited to use.

Euchee
8.25 khōkhō **ke**
       blow:REDUPLICATION AUD.EV
       'Hear the wind blowing!'

When used in a command, the non-firsthand evidential in Meithei implies that the speaker expects the order to be carried out in their absence (Chelliah 1997: 223).

Meithei
8.26 nəŋ əy lak-tə-li-pə ŋay-**ləm**-u
       you I come-NEG-PROG-NOMN wait-NONFIRSTH-IMPV
       'Wait till I come'

This is quite different from the meaning of this same evidential in declarative clauses (see §2.1).

Most languages have more evidential choices in declarative than in any other clause type. Nivkh is the only language I have found so far which makes a distinction between 'observed' and 'non-observed' events just in the 'apprehensive' imperative, with the meaning 'lest' (called preventive by Gruzdeva 2001: 70). There are no evidentiality distinctions elsewhere in the language. We return to a special subsystem of evidentials in apprehensive clauses in Tariana in §8.1.3.

Occasionally, evidentiality choices in imperatives differ from those in declarative clauses. Maidu (Shipley 1964: 51) has two imperatives with an evidential-like distinction. One, marked with -*pi*, is used 'when the action of the order is to be carried out in the presence of the speaker or when there is no interest in the place of the ordered action', as in 'Look! I am dancing'. The other imperative, -*padá*, is used 'when the ordered action is to be carried out in the absence of the speaker', as in 'when you have gotten to my house and have sat down, drink a beer!'. Note that Maidu has a three-term evidentiality choice in affirmative clauses—visual, reported, inferred (Shipley 1964: 45; see §2.2). Visual and non-visual distinctions in Nivkh are restricted to the apprehensive used for warnings (see §9.3). There are no other evidentials in the language.

Declarative sentences may be used as commands (see Aikhenvald forthcoming, on these as 'imperative strategies'). Evidentials in Quechua are incompatible with imperatives. In Wanka Quechua, evidentials in declarative clauses may be used as commands, with additional overtones. The direct evidential -*mi* in Quechua has an epistemic extension: it may indicate 'the speaker's certainty that the event *will* take place' even in the absence of any visual or sensory evidence (Floyd 1996b: 84 and §5.2; also see §8.4 on its use with future tense). In agreement with this, clauses with direct evidential can be used as strong suggestions to the addressee. The speaker expects that the suggestion will be carried out. Commands cast as declarative clauses with the direct evidential remain suggestions. This is to say that they do not sound as authoritative as true imperatives. The imperative in 8.27 sounds stronger than the suggestion in 8.28, where it is accompanied by the direct evidential.

Wanka Quechua

8.27   shramu-y
        come-IMPV
        'come!'

8.28   shramu-nki-**m**
        come-2p-DIR.EV
        'You will come' (directive: strong suggestion)

A clause marked with an inferred evidential, -*chra*, can also be used to tell somebody to do something. It is, however, understood as milder than 8.28 'in its potential manipulative effect' (Floyd 1996b: 85).

8.29 shramu-nki-**chr**
      come-2p-INFR
      'You might come' (mild suggestion)

Along similar lines, the assumed evidential -*mein* in Shipibo-Konibo
questions may in fact function as a polite request—'could you perhaps clear my
garden for me', as in 8.1. The occurrence and the manipulative force of evidentials in non-imperatives used as commands require further investigation.

8.1.3 Evidentials in dependent clauses and other clause types

Dependent clauses cover relative clauses, complement clauses, and subordinate
clauses of other types. Such clauses never have more evidentiality choices than
main declarative clauses. They may have none at all, as in Abkhaz (2.13–15),
Eastern Pomo, Turkic languages, Baniwa, and Fasu. In Chinese Pidgin Russian
the evidential marker *est'* is restricted to main clauses (Nichols 1986: 246). So
are the evidentials in Quechua (Muysken 1995).

If evidential marking is fused with tense and person, and if dependent
clauses allow only a reduced tense choice, one expects them to have fewer evidentiality choices than main clauses, or none at all. For this reason dependent
clauses in Panare have no evidentials. In Jarawara, only relative clauses can
take a full set of past tense–evidentiality markers; other dependent clauses take
one functionally unmarked term which coincides with the immediate past
non-firsthand (see §3.2.1). In East Tucanoan languages most dependent clauses
are nominalizations and are not compatible with the fused tense–person–
evidentiality markers.

Just one clause type in Tucano allows a reported evidential, in its 'imperative'
form (illustrated in 8.19). Purposive 'so that' clauses contain a reported imperative as the complement of the nominalized verb 'say', literally meaning 'saying:
may they (not) do such and such on the speaker's order', as in 8.30 (Ramirez
1997, vol. I: 147).

Tucano
8.30 wi'bágo-re   utî-ti-kã'-**ato**   dîi-gi'   bũbî
      girl-TOP.NON.A/S   cry-NEG-DECL-REP.IMPV   say-NOMN   lolly
      o'ô-**api**
      give-REC.P.VIS.nonthird.p
      'I have given a lolly to the girl so that she shouldn't cry' (lit. saying 'may
      she not cry on someone elses's order')

Tariana also uses the reported imperative -*pida* (see 8.20) in 'so that' clauses
(see Aikhenvald 2002: 164–5, on how Tariana borrowed the 'so that' clauses

from East Tucanoan languages). The same marker is used in purposive clauses, to mark negative purpose.

Tariana

8.31 Yapiɾikuɾi hi-nuku   pi-na   wa-sata   ne   kawhi
      God   this-TOP.NON.A/S   2sg-OBJ 1sg-pray   NEG   flour
      [ne   pethe   mhaîda-**pida**   hñakasi di-sisa]
      NEG   manioc.bread PROHIB-REP.IMPV   food   3sgnf-finish
      'Let's pray to the Lord so that flour and manioc bread are not exhausted'

The reported evidential in Ngiyambaa occurs in dependent clauses which 'explain' the content of the main clause in terms of 'the personal intention or conscious reason which motivates it' (Donaldson 1980: 277, 284):

Ngiyambaa

8.32 mayiŋ-gu   wi: bangiyi   [girbadja-**dha**=lu
      person-ERG   fire+ABS   burn+PAST   kangaroo+ABS-REP=3erg
      wiriŋ-giri]
      cook-PURP
      'The person burnt a fire [expressly] so that she could cook a kangaroo'

Positive purposive clauses in Tariana are unusual. They cannot take the five evidentiality markers exemplified in 1.1–5. Instead, they distinguish visual and non-visual (thus forming a simple A1 system). The visual purposive -*kaɾu* refers to something the speaker, the addressee, or the protagonist can see, hear, or smell, as in 8.33.

Tariana

8.33 ha-hinipu   pi-uma   pi-dia-**kaɾu**   pi-a
      DEM:INAN-CL:ROAD   2sg-try   2sg-return-PURP.VIS   2sg-go
      'You try in order to return by that road' (which you can see)

The non-visual purposive -*hyu* is used to talk about something which cannot be seen, including future and projected events.

8.34 ha-hinipu   pi-uma   pi-dia-**hyu**   pi-a
      DEM:INAN-CL:ROAD   2sg-try   2sg-return-PURP.NON.VIS   2sg-go
      'You try in order to return by that road' (which you cannot see)

Apprehensive 'lest' clauses in Tariana are a special clause type, distinct from both declaratives and imperatives. They do not combine with any tense–evidentiality markers in main clauses. Instead, they have evidentials of their own, of B2 type: visual, non-visual, and inferred. The enclitic -*ñhina* marks the non-visual apprehensive, as in 8.35.

8.35   pi-wha-**ñhina**
       2sg-fall-APPR.NONVIS
       'You might fall! (Take care) lest you fall!' (You cannot see because it is
       far; or you are not looking)

The enclitic -*da* marks visual apprehensive:

8.36   pi-wha-da
       2sg-fall-APPR.VIS
       'You might fall! (Take care) lest you fall!' (Both you and I can see where
       you are going)

The complex predicate consisting of the main verb plus -*da* followed by 'say'
and the subordinating enclitic -*ka* occurs if the speaker does not have firsthand
information. The whole predicate has the meaning of an inferred evidential.

8.37   awakada-se   matʃa   pi-ni   mawali   **di-ñha-da**   **nu-a-ka**
       jungle-LOC   proper   2sg-do   snake   3sgnf-eat-APPR   1sg-say-SUB
       'Be careful in the jungle lest a snake eats you up' (lit. snake might eat you
       up me saying)

We can recall that Nivkh also has an A1 evidentiality subsystem (with a
visual–non-visual opposition) in apprehensives. In contrast, Tariana distinguishes three values in the same clause type.

TABLE 8.2 Subsystems of evidentials in Tariana depending on clause types

TYPE OF SYSTEM	TERMS IN THE SYSTEM	CLAUSE TYPE
D1	Visual, Non-visual sensory, Inferred, Assumed, Reported	Declarative
B2	Visual, Non-visual sensory, Inferred	Interrogative Apprehensive
A3	Reported (versus everything else)	Imperative; 'so that' clause; Negative purposive
A1	Visual, Non-visual	Purposive
no evidentials	—	Conditional; Relative clauses; Complement clauses; Temporal subordinate clauses

Conditional clauses, complement clauses, temporal subordinate clauses, and relative clauses have no evidentials. All in all, Tariana has five evidentiality subsystems depending on clause types; this is summarized in Table 8.2.

The same set of evidentials can be used in main and in dependent clauses in Shipibo-Konibo (Valenzuela 2003: 35), and in a number of languages with an A3 system, including Estonian and Kombai (de Vries 1990: 295). Alternatively, different kinds of dependent clause may behave differently. Relative or conditional clauses in Qiang (LaPolla 2003a: 74–5) have no evidentiality marking. In contrast, direct speech complements tend to take the same set of evidentials as declarative clauses (see §4.8.3; example from Qiang is in LaPolla 2003a: 74). Complement clauses can also occur with any evidential.

8.2 Evidentials and negation

Evidentials can be within the scope of negation; see 3.39 in §3.7 ('as (for this photo), what kind of things they are making I don't know (negated visual experience)') and 8.38 below, from Akha. In both examples the visual experience and not the verb itself is being negated (Hansson 2003: 249). This property makes evidentials in Akha look similar to verbs. In actual fact, they differ from verbs in their morphosyntactic properties.

Akha

8.38	àjɔ̀q	áŋ	dì	ə	àshú yà	mà	ŋá
	he	NOUN.PARTICLE	beat	VERBAL.PARTICLE	who	not	VIS

'I do not know/can't see who is beating him'

In many languages the information source cannot be negated (de Haan MS and 1999 erroneously lists this among definitional properties of evidentials). Kibrik (1977: 229) explicitly states that if non-firsthand forms in Archi are negated, the scope of negation is the action, and not the evidential (see also Broadwell 1991: 416, on Choctaw; LaPolla 2003a: 75, on Qiang; Chirikba 2003: 251, on Abkhaz; and 3.37–8, from Maricopa: Gordon 1986a: 85).

Evidentiality choices in negative and in positive clauses may be the same, as in Eastern Pomo or Quechua. Or there may be fewer evidentiality choices in negative clauses than in positive ones. This means that certain evidentiality contrasts may be neutralized in negative clauses. In Mỹky all four evidentiality choices—visual, non-visual, inferred, and reported—are neutralized in negative clauses (Monserrat and Dixon 2003); that is, negation and the four evidentials form one paradigm. In Shilluk (Miller and Gilley forthcoming: 6), the opposition of inferred and visual evidentiality is neutralized in negative clauses. This is similar to how negative clauses in other languages have a reduced choice of tense and aspect. A general dependency between polarity and all other categories was established in Aikhenvald and Dixon (1998a): one expects fewer grammatical categories in negative clauses than in corresponding positive clauses.

A language may have a preference for a particular evidential under negation. Any evidential can be used in Tariana negative clauses; however, the non-visual evidential is a preferred option for something which the speaker did not see, or know, or do, as in 5.31. Along similar lines, in positive clauses in Jarawara verbs such as 'see' and 'know' generally take firsthand evidentials; but when negated, the non-firsthand is used (Dixon 2003: 176). A similar tendency to use the non-firsthand term in negative clauses was noted for Macedonian (Friedman 2003: 203–4). This choice is intuitively appropriate, though in most cases it reflects a tendency rather than a strict grammatical rule.

8.3 Evidentials and non-indicative modalities

In many languages with obligatory evidentiality, evidentials co-occur with non-indicative modalities of all sorts, covering such diverse meanings and functions as conditional, dubitative, probabilitative, and irrealis in general. Anderson's claim (1986: 277) that evidentials are not distinguished in irrealis clauses does not hold cross-linguistically. The very possibility of such co-occurrence demonstrates that irrealis and information source are different categories. This is a strong argument against grouping evidentiality under the umbrella term of 'modality', or referring to it as 'epistemic', or linking it to varied 'degrees of certainty' (as does Frajzyngier 1985: 250). The reader is referred to de Haan (1999), for a discussion of how to set boundaries between evidential and 'epistemic' meanings.

Combining an irrealis and an evidential marker can be fairly straightforward: in 5.73, from Ngiyambaa, the reported marker in combination with irrealis, with the hypothesis-marking clitic, and with the 'ignorative' marker implies that the speaker does not vouch for the reported information. In 2.30, from Ngiyambaa, the reported evidential with irrealis marks a report about a future event ('It's said that she's going to bring the children'). Or a combination of an irrealis and an evidential can produce a special semantic effect. In Jamul Tiipay, the inferential marker -*kex* with the irrealis (Miller 2001: 192–3) expresses an inference about something that has not yet happened, as in 8.39. The irrealis morpheme is underlined.

Jamul Tiipay

8.39 xu'maay-pe-ch   nya-xemii   kush-x̱-**kex**
      boy-DEM-SJ   WHEN-grow   be.tall-IRR-INFR
      'That boy is going to be tall when he grows up' (the boy is already tall for his age; the inference is made about the future)

The non-firsthand irrealis forms are rare in Yukaghir natural discourse; they occur within stretches of discourse told in non-firsthand (for instance, if the whole text is based on hearsay: Maslova 2003: 227). An example is given in 8.40.

Yukaghir

8.40   tamun-gele   el-l'uö-**l'el**-ŋi   juö-**l'el**-ŋide
        that-ACC   NEG-see-INFR-3pl:INTR   see-INFR-SS:COND
        m-<u>et</u>-aji:-nu-**l'el**-ŋa
        AFF-IRR-shoot-IMPF-NONFIRSTH-3pl:TR
        '[Two swans passed by (NON-FIRSTHAND).] They did not see that (NON-FIRSTHAND). If they had seen it, they would be shooting at them (IRREALIS + NON-FIRSTHAND)'

'Epistemic' modality is more often than not marked distinctly from evidentiality. Tsafiki (Dickinson 2000) has a system of epistemic modalities separate from evidentiality. The same holds for Jarawara, Baniwa, Bora, Makah, Kashaya, and numerous other languages with complicated verbal morphology. In Quechua, all three evidentials occur with any modality (Adelaar 1977: 98–9, and p.c.). In particular, the 'conjecture' evidential -*cha* is 'often found together with the potential mode or future tense, which implies insecurity about the possible realisation of what is said' (Dedenbach-Salazar Sáenz 1997b: 161). Unlike Estonian (where there is no conditional reported), Latvian has a debitive form of the reported (Fennel and Gelsen 1980: 1100–1).

In other languages, we find fewer evidential choices in non-indicative modalities than in declarative clauses. The non-firsthand evidential in Turkic languages can occur together with the necessitative and debitive, but not with optative (Johanson 2003: 286). In Abkhaz, the non-firsthand evidential does not combine with some modalities (such as conditional, optative, intentional, and subjunctive), simply because their respective markers occupy the same slot. The evidential can occur together with others, including potential in 8.41 and debitive in 8.42 (Chirikba 2003: 252–4). (The modality markers are underlined.)

Abkhaz

8.41   jə-s-<u>z</u>-aj+lə-m-k'+aa-**zaap'**
        it-I-POT-PREV-not-understand-NONFIRSTH
        'Apparently I could not understand it' (I infer this)

8.42   jə-ga-<u>t'ˤə</u>-**zaap'**
        it-carry-DEB-NONFIRSTH
        'Apparently it must be taken' (I infer this)

In Tucano, with a four-term evidentiality system, all the evidentials can co-occur with the declarative and frustrative mood and with 'dubitative' modality (Ramirez 1997, vol. I: 156–9). The conditional mood occurs just with the inferred and non-visual evidentials (Ramirez 1997, vol. I: 192–3). In Hupda (Epps 2005: 632), the inferred evidential occurs together with the epistemic modality marker, 'for expressions of inference or speculation when no evidence is on hand, or when the evidence is too vague to be very conclusive'. This is shown in 8.43. The element of doubt comes from the epistemic marker (underlying form = *ʔũh*) and not from the evidential (=*sud*).

Hupda

8.43 hup   kəwəg   pog=suʔn'uh
        person   eye   big=INFR+EPISTEMIC
        'It must have been that big-eyed one (who ate my fruit)'

In Tariana the declarative-assertive, frustrative, intentional, and admirative modalities occur with all the five evidentials. The dubitative marker, the counterexpectation marker, and the epistemic complex predicate meaning 'probably' can co-occur with any evidential except for present visual. Only the conditional does not occur with any evidentials.

Stating that something is probable—that is, establishing one's epistemic stance—is independent of expressing the information source. This can be seen from the way in which the dubitative occurs together with evidentials. In 8.44, Olívia says that she had already told me a story (using visual evidential). But she is not quite sure she did, and she adds the dubitative -*da*. Then she definitely remembers she had—and this explains the lack of -*da* in the second clause.

Tariana

8.44 nu-kalite-tha-**ka**-sita-<u>da</u>   diha-misini
        1sg-tell-FR-REC.P.VIS-ALREADY-DUB   he-TOO
        nu-kalite-**ka**-sita   pi-na   heku
        1sg-tell-REC.P.VIS-ALREADY   2sg-OBJ yesterday
        'I probably did tell this already (VISUAL, but I am not quite sure), I did tell you this yesterday (VISUAL: I saw this)'

In 8.45, another speaker talks about what they could hear on a tape: they could hear it, hence the non-visual evidential, but they could not quite understand what it said.

8.45 Manaka-taku   di-a-tha**ma**-<u>da</u>
        açai.fruit-point   3sgnf-say-FR+PRES.NONVIS-DUB
             'He said "Manakataku"(lit. point of açai fruit) (I heard him say it but I am not sure whether it really was Manakataku)'

TABLE 8.3 Co-occurrence of evidentials with modalities in Tariana

MODALITY	EVIDENTIALITY SPECIFICATIONS USED
Non future indicative	
Declarative-assertive	
Intentional	all evidentials
Frustrative	
Dubitative	all evidentials except present visual
Counterexpectation	all evidentials except present visual
Conditional	none
Admirative	all evidentials
Epistemic 'probably'	all evidentials except present visual
Indefinite 'whatever'	all evidentials except present visual

Table 8.3 summarizes how evidentials occur together with modalities in Tariana. Evidentiality and modalities, especially epistemic ones, are plainly different categories. Present visual appears to be the one specification having most restrictions on its co-occurrence—with meanings related to uncertainty, doubt, and so on. Presumably this has to do with the intrinsic certainty of immediately available visual evidence.[7]

Epistemic expressions may accompany evidentials. In Tuyuca, the 'assumed' evidential is used when there is no reason to assume that an event did not occur, or is not occurring (Barnes 1999). If speakers really have no idea as to whether or not an event occurred, they will use the assumed evidential, and will preface their statements with the word /ōba/ which indicates that they are not at all sure. Tariana uses an epistemic *pa:pe* 'maybe' with future (where there are no evidentiality specifications) and with non-visual and inferred, to reinforce the 'probability' meaning (see §10.3).

Non-indicative modalities can be used as evidential strategies; see §4.1. Examples of evidentials developing out of a non-indicative modality are not at all widely attested (see §9.1).

---

[7] This is in fact similar to the meaning of a morpheme in Amdo-Tibetan termed the 'immediate' evidential by Sun (1993) which indicates that 'the speaker's basis for his assertion comes solely from perceptible evidence directly present in the immediate speech-act situation'.

8.4 Evidentials, tense, and aspect

Correlations between tense, aspect, and evidentiality involve two separate issues. One concerns the expression of evidentiality within tense and aspect systems (or vice versa) and possible dependencies therein. The other concerns the time reference of evidentials. We have seen in §3.8 that evidentials may have time reference of their own: the time when the information was acquired can be marked differently from the time of the action. This shows that evidentials may behave, to a certain extent, as predications in their own right. We have already seen in §3.7 that an evidential can be within the scope of negation (see 3.39 and 8.38, both from Akha), and that the truth value of the information source does not have to coincide with that of the verb.

The general tendency in languages with evidentials is never to have more evidentiality choices in a non-past tense than in a past tense. Tense, aspect, and evidentiality can be (A) independent systems; or (B) evidentials can be distinguished in some tenses but not in others. It is far from uncommon for a language not to distinguish evidentiality in future at all. Another possibility, (C), is for different evidentials to each have a different set of tense distinctions.

(A) TENSE/ASPECT AND EVIDENTIALITY AS INDEPENDENT SYSTEMS
If a language has tense/aspect and evidentiality as independent systems, the full set of evidentiality choices is available in each tense and/or aspect. Evidentials in Estonian have a full set of tenses (see Fernandez-Vest 1996: 172; also see note 14 to Chapter 4). The same applies to Khowar (Bashir 1988: 54), Quechua (Weber 1986, 1989; Floyd 1997), Hupda (Epps 2005: 636–7), and Shipibo-Konibo (Valenzuela 2003).

Even if any evidential can be used with any tense, future evidential forms may be rarer than their non-future counterparts, as noted for Abkhaz (Chirikba 2003: 249–51). Alternatively, evidentials with future are likely to develop additional overtones: a direct evidential in future cannot indicate first-hand evidence of the event which has not yet occurred. And so, for instance, in Shipibo-Konibo (Valenzuela 2003: 35), the direct evidential -*ra* with future indicates certainty rather than firsthand evidence.

The exact meaning of a direct evidential with future may depend on person. In Wanka Quechua, the direct evidential with third person future implies the speaker's certainty that the event will take place. In 8.46, a speaker who is worried about his daughter's trip to a far-away town recounts a neighbour's comment. A sentence like 8.46 (Floyd 1999: 75) encourages the addressee not to worry about what is going to happen.

Wanka Quechua

8.46   kuti-mu-n'a-**m**
        return-AFAR-2p.FUT-DIR.EV
        '(When brother Luis arrived he said to me) She will return'

The direct evidential with first person future implies the speaker's definite
intention and determination to do something, as in 8.47 (Floyd 1999: 75–6).
Interestingly, in 60 per cent of the cases in Floyd's corpus in which the direct
evidential occurred with future, the speaker was the grammatical subject. We
return to this in §8.5.

8.47   agulpis-si   ya'a   ma'a-shrayki-**m**
        hitting-even   I   beat-1>2p.FUT-DIR.EV
        'I'll even beat it [the truth] out of you'

And when used with second person future, the direct evidential does not
mark a prediction or certainty; rather, it expresses a strong directive (similarly
to 8.28, with no future marking). This is why 8.48 can be interpreted as a command (Floyd 1999: 82–3).

8.48   wik   punta   punta   muula-p   linli-n-ta-**m**   lika-nki
        yonder   first   first   mule-GEN ear-3p-ACC-DIR.EV   see-2p
        'Look at the ears of that very first mule over there' (Lit. You will look at
        the ears ...)

In contrast, the inferred evidential *-chra* is normally used with future to
make inferences, or conjectures, about future events (Floyd 1999: 74).

8.49   paaga-llaa-shrayki-**chra**-a
        pay-POLITE-1>2p.FUT-INFR-EMPH
        'I suppose I'll pay you, then'

The meaning of an evidential in a small evidentiality system may depend on
tense and on the verb's semantics. Yukaghir distinguishes non-future and
future (Maslova 2003: 227). The combination of future and the non-firsthand
evidential expresses hypothetical modality with any verb. This combination
can encode hypotheses about the present, as in 8.50, and about the past, as
in 8.51.

Yukaghir

8.50   a:che   chuge-ge   jo:dude-t   ejrie-**l'el**-te-j
        deer   track-LOC   turn-SS:IMPF walk-NONFIRSTH-FUT-INTR:3sg
        'He is probably walking along deer tracks'

8.51   locil-ŋin   lebie-d   emej-ŋin   tadi:-nu-**l'el**-te-m
       fire-DAT   soil-AT   mother-DAT   give-IMPF-NONFIRSTH-FUT-TR:3sg
       'Probably, he used to give it to the Fire, to Mother of the Earth'

The epistemic meaning of this combination ('probably' in the English translation) is imparted by the future suffix. The non-firsthand suffix by itself has nothing to do with expressing probability (Maslova 2003: 225–7).

The reading of non-future evidential forms as present or as past depends on their aspect, in agreement with Table 8.4.

In contrast, a combination of future with non-firsthand evidential in Chinese Pidgin Russian (Nichols 1986: 248–9) results in 'predictive' future: 'the speaker confidently infers future event from present evidence'.

In Meithei the non-firsthand evidential with a first person actor in past or present tense (Chelliah 1997: 222–3) indicates that while the speaker has evidence about the statement the addressee does not (see §7.3.1 and 7.31). When the same evidential is used with first person future, the speaker predicts that an action will take place and that the addressee will not see the action happen. With other persons, the non-firsthand evidential expresses the speaker's inference based on their past experience which allows them to predict a future event.

(B) EVIDENTIALITY DISTINCTIONS MADE ONLY IN SOME TENSES OR ASPECTS
Many languages do not distinguish evidentiality in future. Examples include Qiang, Eastern Pomo, Mỹky, Kalasha, Tariana, and East Tucanoan languages. (See §3.8 for events reported to happen in the future, in Tariana.) This restriction may have to do with the fact that future is not quite a 'tense', since it involves prediction and even probability. It may be treated as inherently related to epistemic modality. Since—as we have shown in §8.3—fewer evidentials (if any at all) typically occur with different non-indicative modalities, we would expect fewer evidentials—if any at all—in future.

In two-term systems evidentiality is often distinguished just in past and/or perfect. This is the case in most Northeast Caucasian, Finno-Ugric languages,

TABLE 8.4   Evidentials, aspect, and tense in Yukaghir

ASPECTUAL VALUE OF VERB	FIRSTHAND	NON-FIRSTHAND
Perfective	past	
Habitual	past/present	past
Continuous	past/present	

in Svan, and in Jarawara. In Tibetan (DeLancey 1986: 210–1) the 'true' evidentiality system (firsthand versus non-firsthand) is only found in perfective. In Jarawara firsthand and non-firsthand evidentials are distinguished only in the three past tenses. Similarly, in the languages of the Balkans evidentiality is restricted to the past (Friedman 2003: 206). Among A2 type systems, Chinese Pidgin Russian is unusual in that the non-firsthand is not a past tense category.[8]

An explanation for this connection between perfective or past and evidentiality has been suggested by Comrie (1976: 110): 'the semantic similarity (not, of course, identity) between perfect and inferential lies in the fact that both categories present an event not in itself, but via its results, and it is this similarity that finds formal expression in languages like Georgian, Bulgarian and Estonian'. A similar tendency has been described by Nichols (1986: 254–6); also see Johanson (2000b). Also see §4.2, on the connection between past tenses and perfects, on the one hand, and information source on the other, as a basis for the development of past tenses into evidentiality strategies.

(C) DIFFERENT EVIDENTIALS CAN HAVE DIFFERENT TENSE DISTINCTIONS

In small systems, a non-firsthand specification may distinguish fewer tenses than others. Bulgarian (possibly, A2) also has a grammatical system combining tense and aspect; nine choices are available in non-reported but just five in reported evidentiality (see Friedman 1986). The reported evidential may have more tense distinctions than others in a three-term system. In Nganasan (Gusev forthcoming), the non-visual and inferred evidentials do not distinguish tense, while the reported evidential has future and non-future (while the

---

[8] Aikhenvald and Dixon (1998a) described this phenomenon as a dependency: Tense > Evidentiality. Another dependency is Evidentiality > {Tense and Aspect}. We have no example of a dependency Aspect > Evidentiality, but predict that one may be found as more languages with Evidentiality systems are described. This is the only gap in our data which illustrate that there can be dependencies in either direction between any pair of Tense, Aspect, and Evidentiality. Other, more complex dependencies are Evidentiality > {Person and Number}. In Estonian, verbs in a clause with non-reported evidentiality distinguish person and number of subject. However, in a reported clause, no persons or numbers are distinguished, the two systems being neutralized. Another dependency is {Tense and Evidentiality} > Person. In Udmurt (from the Permian subgroup of Uralic), verbs show neutralization of second and third persons (in both singular and plural) in past tense, non-firsthand evidentiality, and positive polarity (Tepljashina and Lytkin 1976: 179). There may be some dependencies between tense, person, and evidentiality in Japanese (see Aoki 1986: 233 on the restrictions on occurrence of the reported *soo da* with tense and predication type, and on the co-occurrence of the three inferential markers with first person).

Another dependency is {Polarity, Tense, and Evidentiality} > {Person and Number}. In Udmurt all three persons and both numbers are neutralized in past non-firsthand within a negative clause. Komi, a closely related language, maintains distinct forms for all persons and numbers in past non-firsthand for positive polarity, but has one form covering second and third person in the plural in a negative clause. Here we get person neutralization depending on a combination of Tense, Evidentiality, and Polarity (Tepljashina and Lytkin 1976: 179).

indicative mood distinguishes at least present, past, and future). In Bora, with a B1 system, the inferred evidential always occurs together with one of the two past tense markers, unlike the reported evidential which is not restricted to any tense.

Large evidentiality systems in Tucanoan languages and in Tariana show more complex correlations with tense. As already mentioned, Tuyuca (Tucanoan: Barnes 1984) has five evidentiality choices—visual, non-visual, inferred, assumed, and reported—in past tense. In present tense there are just four choices (no 'secondhand evidence'). No evidentials occur in the future tense. Having no reported evidential in present tense is a typical feature of other Tucanoan languages (see Miller 1999: 64, for Desano, and Ramirez 1997, vol. I: 120, for Tucano). Neither the assumed nor the inferred evidential in Tariana has a present form. Tucano does not have a present tense form for the inferred evidential. This gap is filled by the non-visual evidential if one wishes to make inferences about ongoing events. Visual and non-visual specifications have thus more tense distinctions than any others. Correlations between tense and evidentiality in Tariana and Tucano are summarized in Table 8.5.

The absence of the present inferred evidential in Tariana and Tucano, and of the present assumed evidential in Tariana, can be accounted for by the fact that an inference ought to be based on a fait accompli. An event must have taken place before the moment of speech; only then can it be used as basis for an inference or an assumption. However, neighbouring East Tucanoan languages do not have this restriction—this just shows that, though frequent, the restriction is far from universal.

TABLE 8.5 Tense and evidentiality in Tariana and Tucano

TENSE	EVIDENTIALITY	TARIANA	TUCANO
Present	visual	yes	yes
	non-visual	yes	yes
	inferred	**no**	**no**
	assumed	**no**	—
	reported	yes	**no**
Recent past and remote past	visual	yes	yes
	non-visual	yes	yes
	inferred	yes	yes
	assumed	yes	—
	reported	yes	yes

Different evidentials may distinguish different aspects.[9] Kiowa (Watkins 1984: 173–6), with an A3 system, distinguishes an unmarked and an imperfective reported evidential form. The imperfective form is used to report a continuous, repeated, or habitual event known to the speaker through someone else, as in the second clause of 8.52. Here, the speaker is reminding the addressee of a doctor's instructions which were received not directly from the doctor but through the addressee. The imperfective reported attaches to the imperfective future. That is, the aspectual values of the evidential and of the verb must match.

Kiowa

8.52 dɔ́ttè·   gyát-kɔ́m-**hêl**   déòp
      doctor   x/agent:2sg/patient:p1/object-indicate-REPORTED   at+times
      èm-cą̀·n-ì·t'ɔ́·-**dè·**
      2sg-arrive-IMPF/FUT-IMPF.REPORTED
      'You are to be coming at times the doctor indicated to you' (I am told)

The unmarked reported means just that the information was reported to the speaker by someone else; there is no reference to duration of the event, as in the first clause in 8.52 and in 7.21 ('my gall bladder reportedly isn't good'). Verbal aspect can also correlate with a mirative interpretation of an evidential—we have seen examples from Svan in 6.8–9.

In summary: more evidential choices are likely to be available in past tenses than in other tenses. If a language has a small evidentiality system of A1 or A2 type, evidentiality is likely to be distinguished in past tense only. This correlates with the nature of the semantics of evidentials in these systems. The non-firsthand term often develops an inferential meaning. An inference is usually made on the basis of something that had happened before the moment of speech. That is, inference is inherently anchored to the past. If evidentials can occur with future at all, they often have non-evidential meanings (as in Quechua and Yukaghir).

Different evidentials may differ in the number of tenses they distinguish. However, the evidence as to whether assumed, inferred, or reported evidentials are likelier to have fewer tense distinctions than sensory evidentials is inconclusive. We have seen that in Nganasan and Selkup, the sensory evidentials have fewer tense distinctions than reported. In East Tucanoan languages it is the other way round: reported evidentials do not have present tense. Nor does the inferred evidential in Tucano or the inferred and the assumed in Tariana. These correlations are summarized in Table 8.6.

---

[9] Kashaya has restrictions on the use of aspects with different evidentials; for instance, AUDITORY -v̂nnǎ signifies that 'the speaker knows of what he speaks because he heard the sound of the action, but did not see it' (Oswalt 1986: 37), and INFERENTIAL 1, -qǎ, marks 'an inference based on circumstances or evidence found apart, in space or time, from the actual event or state'; these distinguish no aspects. The data are hard to interpret because there is a possibility that different evidentials form different subsystems.

TABLE 8.6 Correlations between tense and evidentiality

EVIDENTIALITY AND TENSE	PARTICULAR FEATURES	EXAMPLES
(A) All evidentiality choices available in all tenses	• Special meaning of an evidential in future • Different tense reference depending on verb semantics	• Direct evidential in Shipibo-Konibo • Direct evidential in Quechua (depends on person) • Non-firsthand in Yukaghir (Table 8.4)
(B) Fewer evidentiality choices in some tenses	• No evidentials in future • Evidentials only in past tense(s)	Qiang, Eastern Pomo, Myky, East Tucanoan, Tariana Jarawara, Svan, Northeast Caucasian, some Finno-Ugric
(C) Different evidentials have different tense systems	• More distinctions in reported than in sensory evidentials • Fewer distinctions in reported than in other evidentials • Fewer distinctions in reported and inferred than in others • Fewer distinctions in inferred and assumed than in others	Nganasan, Selkup Desano and Tuyuca (no present reported: full tense distinctions in others) Tucano (no present reported and no present inferred; full tense distinctions in others: Table 8.5) Tariana (no present inferred and assumed; full tense distinctions in others: Table 8.5)

8.5 Evidentials and other categories

Evidentiality may interact with other predicate categories. Aoki (1986: 235) describes correlations between the use of evidentials and POLITENESS in Japanese: the use of conjectural and inferential specifications is considered more polite. Along similar lines, in Wanka Quechua a clause marked with an inferred evidential is used as a polite command (see 8.29); a question cast in direct evidential is 'less polite' than the one without (Cerrón-Palomino 1976: 108). In Shipibo-Konibo, the assumed evidential in questions is a token of politeness (as in 8.1). The combination of the non-firsthand evidential with second person in Salar expresses politeness (see §7.3.2).

Evidentials may correlate with pragmatic categories. In Quechua, they combine reference to information source and to marking focus. Evidential markers are enclitics which go onto a focused constituent (see Muysken 1995, and Adelaar 1997, and Examples 3.2 and 3.3). As we will see in the Appendix to Chapter 11, Quechua evidentials appear to be first acquired by children as focus markers and only later as evidentials proper. If no constituent is focused, an evidential occurs on the first constituent of the clause (Muysken 1995: 381–2). A sentence with an evidential attached to the first constituent is consistently ambiguous; it may indicate that there is (*a*) no contrastive focus at all and (*b*) focus on the first constituent. A sentence like 8.53 can be understood in two ways.

Quechua
8.53   Pidru-**n**   wasi-ta   ruwa-n
        Pedro-DIR   house-ACC   make-3p
        (a) Pedro builds a house—no constituent is focused
        (b) It is Pedro who builds the house—the first constituent is focused

Evidential clitics in Quechua can thus be viewed as portmanteau morphemes combining reference to focus and to information source.

Evidentials may interact with less common categories. Oksapmin, with a B3 system (Lawrence 1987), has an unusual category of 'viewpoint' which interacts with the three evidentials—visual, non-visual sensory, and reported. A story can be told from the point of view of the subject, or from the point of view of another participant. 'Viewpoint' is obligatorily distinguished only in past tenses. An alternative is to use a zero-marked form, called 'omniscient viewpoint' (Lawrence 1987: 60); then no evidentiality distinctions are made. There are a number of correlations between the choice of a viewpoint and other categories: if the story is in first person, the subject viewpoint is obligatory. A different language, Southern Nambiquara, appears to have fused expression of evidentiality with the marking of new or given information (Lowe 1999: 274–6).

The choice and meaning of evidentials can correlate with the semantic properties of predicates. Predicates of internal states require fixed evidentiality choices. Volitionality and non-volitionality as semantic characteristic of the predicate are crucial for the choice of evidential in Amdo Tibetan (Sun 1993: 960–6) (here the inferred evidential is used with inherently non-volitional acts, such as 'fall asleep', 'snore', and so on; verbs of other semantic groups would require a direct evidential instead—see (*f*) in §7.2.1). Active and stative predicates may develop additional differences in evidential uses. The inferred evidential in Qiang (see §6.2 and 6.17) tends to have a mirative meaning with states, and an inferential meaning with verbs referring to actions. (Also see §10.3.)

In Jarawara, the evidential choice interacts with pivot assignment and verb class. If the speaker is pivot (that is, grammaticalized topic: Dixon 1994: 11–14) for a clause with a verb of perception, the firsthand value is likely to be used (Dixon 2004: chapter 6). This is the case in 8.54 where the A argument is the pivot and the agent. Tense and mood markers show agreement with the A argument (*o*-'first person singular' takes feminine cross-referencing as do all pronouns).

Jarawara

8.54 [afiao   ati]ₒ   o-mita-**ra**   o-ke
     plane(m)   noise   1sgA-hear-IMM.P.FIRSTH.f   1sg-DECL.f
     'I heard the plane's noise' (I was listening for it; 'I' is the pivot)

But if the thing perceived functions as pivot, the non-firsthand evidential is more likely to occur. Example 8.55 has the 'plane' as its discourse pivot. Tense and mood markers agree with 'plane' (which is masculine).

8.55 [afiao   ati]ₒ   o-mita-**no**-ka
     plane(m)   noise   1sgA-hear-IMM.P.NONFIRSTH.m-DECLm
     'I heard the plane's noise' (unexpectedly; 'plane' is the pivot)

There appear to be hardly any interactions between evidentiality and grammatical function. As mentioned in §8.4 above, in 60 per cent of cases in the Wanka Quechua corpus where the direct evidential occurred with future, the speaker was grammatical subject (Floyd 1999: 75–6). In Tariana, over 80 per cent of sentences in autobiographical stories cast in visual evidential have first person subject. This putative correlation between statistical frequency of first person subject and visual evidential needs further investigation.

An evidential form may require a non-canonical case-marking pattern. In Svan (Sumbatova 1999) evidentials in perfective aspect require a dative-marked subject. This is an outcome of their origin from a type of resultative construction. Imperfective evidentials originate from a resultative construction of a different structure, and consequently they require a nominative subject.

The choices available in the person and number system may depend on the choice made in the evidentiality system. In Estonian, verbs in a clause not specified for reported evidentiality distinguish person and number of the subject, while no person and number are distinguished in the reported evidential. Passives can be used as an evidential strategy (see §4.3), but I have not found any correlations between voice and evidentiality.

No interactions have been found between evidentials and nominal categories, such as gender or classifiers. However, evidentials may interrelate with gender and number in verbs inasmuch as these are fused with person marking. The frequency of the non-firsthand evidential can correlate with a speaker's sex: in Salar, women tend to use more non-firsthand forms than men (Dwyer 2000: 57). We return to this in §10.2.2.

8.6 Evidentials and other grammatical categories: a summary

Evidentials interrelate with clause types and grammatical categories of mood, modality, negation, and tense and aspect in the following ways. (There are hardly any correlations between evidentials and any other categories.)

I. The maximum evidential distinctions are made in declarative main clauses.

II. The most frequent evidential in commands is reported ('do what someone else told you to'). The choice of an evidential in questions may contain reference to the source of information available to the speaker, to the addressee, or to both. As a result, the meaning of evidentials in interrogative clauses and in declarative clauses can be rather different; see Table 8.1.

III. Fewer evidentials may be used in negative than in positive clauses.

IV. Non-indicative modalities (conditional, dubitative, and so on) tend to allow fewer evidential specifications than indicative.

V. The maximum number of evidential specifications is expected in past tenses. There are often no evidentiality choices at all in future which tends to be, by its nature, a kind of modality. This can be accounted for by the nature of evidentiality, and its relations to temporal settings of events. The evidence for an event is often based on its result, hence the link between firsthand/non-firsthand, on the one hand, and past, perfect, and perfective aspects on the other. Not uncommonly, past tenses and perfects develop evidential overtones and evolve into evidentials (which are still restricted to past tense only). This is the topic of the following chapter.

9

Evidentials: where do they come from?

Evidentials come from various sources, some from grammaticalized verbs, others from evidential strategies. Evidentials in large systems are often hetero-geneous in origin. In §9.1 we discuss these sources and the evidential systems they produce. Evidentials easily diffuse from one language to another. Having evidentiality is a property of quite a few linguistic areas. Emergence and loss of evidentials is often due to intensive language contact. Not infrequently, evidential meanings make their way into a contact language. This is the topic of §9.2. Evidentials in obsolescent languages are discussed in §9.3. There is a summary in §9.4.

9.1 Origins of evidentials

Evidentials often come from grammaticalized verbs, as illustrated in §9.1.1 (pace Willett 1988, this is not a universal mechanism). Evidential markers may also develop out of deictic and locative markers, see §9.1.2. A small eviden-tiality system may evolve via grammaticalization of one or more evidentiality strategies (outlined in Chapter 4): (i) non-indicative modalities, (ii) perfect, resultative, and past tenses, or (iii) participles and often nominalizations; see §9.1.3. De-subordination of speech complements is a frequent mechanism for evolving reported evidentials; see §9.1.4. Evidentials may come from the reanalysis of a copula construction discussed in §9.1.5. Other sources for evid-entials are discussed in §9.1.6. An evidentiality system may be etymologically heterogenous: see §9.1.7. A brief summary is under §9.1.8.

9.1.1 *Grammaticalized verbs as source for evidentials*

Different evidential specifications come from (A) verbs of speech, (B) verbs of perception, and, more rarely, from (C) verbs of other semantic groups.

(A) VERBS OF SPEECH AS SOURCE FOR EVIDENTIALS
Markers of reported evidentiality in any system and quotative evidentials (in B5 systems) often come from a grammaticalized verb of speech. This is the

case in Lezgian (Haspelmath 1993), Tauya (MacDonald 1990*a*), Tibetan (Tournadre 1994: 152), Maricopa (Gordon 1986*a*: 86), Akha (Thurgood 1986: 221), and Cora (Casad 1992: 154–6). Munro (1978) provides an exhaustive account of verbs of saying grammaticalized as reported evidentials in Uto-Aztecan languages; also see Saxena (1988) for the development of reported and quotative evidentials from verbs of saying in Tibeto-Burman languages. The adverbial reported particle *unnia* in West Greenlandic is derived from verb stem *unnir-* 'say (that)' (Fortescue 2003: 301). Further examples of quotative markers developing from verbs of speech are in Heine and Kuteva (2001: 267–8), Klamer (2000), and also Harris and Campbell (1995: 170–2).

A verb of speech can be grammaticalized as a reported speech marker in its third person form, as in the case of the incipient reported marker in Modern Greek *lé[e]i* 'one says' (Friedman 2003: 189). The quotative particle *hºa* in Abkhaz is an archaic past absolutive of the verb 'say' (Chirikba 2003: 258–9). Two quotative particles in Georgian involve different forms of the verb 'say'. The particle *metki* contains 'say' and its subject: historically it comes from the sequence *me* (I) *vtkvi* (first person singular subject aorist indicative of 'say') 'I said (it)'. The particle *tko* contains the same root without subject marking; diachronically, it is derived from the form *tkva* of the root *tkv* 'say' (see discussion in Harris and Campbell 1995: 168–72). The two particles, which have a very similar meaning, differ in their position in the clause. (There is another, more archaic, quotative particle *o*, of a different origin.) Alternatively, an evidential can come from a derivation based on a verb of speech. In Udihe (Nikolaeva and Tolskaya 2001: 461), one of the variants of the reported evidential, *gum(u)*, could be an old passive form of the verb *gun* 'say'. Another variant, *gun-e*, goes back to a habitual form of the same verb. A further variant, *gun-e-i*, is a habitual present participle of the same verb 'say'.[1]

The following three mechanisms can be involved in the development of reported and quotative evidentials via grammaticalization of lexical verbs of speech.

(i) REANALYSIS OF A BICLAUSAL QUOTATION OR REPORTATIVE CONSTRUCTION WITH A COMPLEMENT CLAUSE. A matrix clause with the verb 'say' and a complement clause of this verb become a single clause via the loss or reinterpretation of the subordinator.

---

[1] The following 'universal' of the 'quotation-to-quotative transition in languages with hypotactic structure' was suggested by Harris and Campbell (1995: 171): 'a quotative particle is formed from some combination of the following: (i) the verb "say", (ii) its subject, (iii) the pronoun "it", and (iv) the complementizer'. As can be seen from the examples mentioned here, this statement is incomplete, and far from being a universal.

(ii) REANALYSIS OF A BICLAUSAL QUOTATION OR REPORTATIVE CONSTRUCTION
CONSISTING OF TWO JUXTAPOSED INDEPENDENT CLAUSES, ONE OF WHICH
CONTAINS THE VERB OF SAYING AS ITS PREDICATE. This pathway is found in
Abkhaz, Lezgian, and numerous other languages—including Kham,
where the reported evidential *di* is probably connected to the verb of
speech (Watters 2002: 296–300).

Both mechanisms appear to be at work in Tonkawa (Hoijer 1933:
105–6), with its two reported evidentials (see §2.2): *-lak-no'o* 'narrative
reported' and *-no'o* 'non-narrative reported'. Both contain the third
person form of the declarative past of the theme *new-* 'say, tell'. The
formative *-lak* of the narrative reported is possibly cognate with the
nominal accusative suffix. This evidential goes back to a reanalysed and
grammaticalized direct speech construction involving a case marker as
a subordinator (see (i) above). The other evidential probably goes back
to a juxtaposed structure (see above).

(iii) REANALYSIS OF A COMPLEMENT CLAUSE OF VERB OF SPEECH AS MAIN CLAUSE. A
reported evidential may develop out of reanalysis of a complement clause
which then becomes the main clause. The verb of saying is simply omitted, and no grammaticalization of a lexical item is involved. See §9.1.4.

If a language has more than one reported evidential, their emergence may
involve different mechanisms—as in Tonkawa (see §2.3). In Jamul Tiipay the
quotative can be marked in at least two, synonymous, ways (Miller 2001: 200,
276–7). A quotative construction involves one of the two verbs of 'saying'
(*-i* 'say:intransitive' or *-a* 'say:transitive') and a complement containing the
auxiliary *yu* 'be'. Or the verb of saying *-i* may appear without inflectional
prefixes but fused with *yu*, yielding a clitic *yúi* 'quotative'. That is, the language
displays different stages of grammaticalization for what appears to be
essentially the same construction.

(B) VERBS OF PERCEPTION AS SOURCE FOR EVIDENTIALS
Markers of sensory evidentiality (visual and non-visual) may derive from
verbs of perception (see Matlock 1989: 219–22, for the role of metaphor in such
development). In Maricopa (Yuman: Gordon 1986a) the visual evidentiality
suffix has developed from the lexical verb 'see'. In Wintu (Schlichter 1986: 49;
Pitkin 1984: 148), the non-visual sensory evidential *nt^hEr* goes back to a passive
form based on the verb 'hear' (followed by the inferred evidential) (also see the
discussion in de Haan 2001: 101; and Matlock 1989). Non-visual marker *-mha* in
Tariana goes back to the verb *-hima* 'hear, feel', while the present visual *-nuka,
-naka* could go back to the first person singular form of the verb *-ka* 'see'
(Aikhenvald 2003e). The non-visual evidential in Hupda and in the closely

related Yuhup (both from the Makú family) is the result of grammaticalization of the verb 'produce sound' (Epps 2005: 628; Ospina Bozzi 2002: 182).

Verbs meaning 'seem, be perceived, feel' often participate in developing non-visual evidentials in East Tucanoan languages (see Aikhenvald 2003e on shared grammaticalization paths in the genesis of non-visual evidentials in the Vaupés area where East Tucanoan languages and Tariana are spoken). Desano uses a compounded verb *kari-* (accompanied by tense and person markers homophonous with those for visual evidentials) to indicate 'that the speaker obtained his information from senses other than the visual' (Miller 1999: 65). According to Malone (1988: 132), the Tuyuca non-visual present marker could have evolved from 'a relic auxiliary verb' 'seem' or 'be perceived'. In all these cases, grammaticalization must have taken place in compounded verbs (other examples of grammaticalization of the second part of a verbal compound in all the languages of the Vaupés area—including East Tucanoan, Arawak, and Makú—are discussed in Aikhenvald 2002: 136–43).

Occasionally, a verb of perception may give rise to a quotative evidential. In Biansi (Tibeto-Burman) a past non-finite form of *run* 'cause to hear' marks quoted speech (Trivedi 1991: 26). In Shibacha Lisu (C1: Yu 2003) all evidentials come from grammaticalized verbs: the visual evidential comes from the verb 'see', the non-visual and the reported come from the verb 'hear' (following different paths of phonological change), and at least one inferred evidential comes from the verb 'listen'. This is a remarkable example of an etymologically homogenous system; it is in stark contrast with evidentials in other large systems where various terms come from formally different sources.

(C) VERBS FROM OTHER SEMANTIC GROUPS AS SOURCE FOR EVIDENTIALS
Verbs referring to location and existence may give rise to inferred and assumed evidentials. The inferred evidential -*ʔel* in Wintu (Schlichter 1986: 52) probably goes back to a verbal element meaning 'exist' (also see §9.1.5 below, on the development of copulas into evidential markers). In Hupda, one inferred evidential comes from a grammaticalized verb meaning 'be located inside something else', and the other one comes from the verb 'exist' (Epps 2005: 632, 638–40).

Grammaticalization of a verb of motion as an evidential may go together with its grammaticalization as a tense marker. The verbs for 'come' and 'go' in Dulong (LaPolla 2003c: 679) have undergone polygrammaticalization, as direction markers and as tense–evidentiality markers. Bot *jǐ* (from *jì* 'go') and *lŭŋ* (from *lùŋ* 'ascend') are used for recent past actions, with one difference: *lŭŋ* marks an unseen action and *jǐ* marks something the speaker had seen. This is similar to how a verb 'complete' or 'finish' may grammaticalize into a marker of perfect, and then become an evidentiality strategy (see §4.2; 4.11, from Newari, and further examples in Genetti 1986).

Grammaticalization of a verb as an evidential may involve a change in its status, from main to secondary, rather than transforming it into a bound morpheme. The secondary verb *awine/awa* 'seem' in Jarawara now marks inference as part of a complex predicate. It is likely to go back to a biclausal construction involving verb -*awa*- 'see, feel', which later on fused into one predicate (Dixon 2003: 184–5).

9.1.2 *Deictic and locative markers as sources for evidentials*

The source of evidence is established by the speaker, at a specific time and place. This is similar to tense which can be present, past, or future in relation to the time of speaking. Just like tense, evidentials can be considered deictic in character (also see de Haan 2001: 102–3). So, primarily deictic elements may evolve into evidentials. An evidential category can be polysemous with a spatial deictic. What Golla (1996, p.c.) considers the visual evidential in Hupa is also used as 'there, at that point in view', and as 'right' (as in 'the rock fell right there'). The source for the 'assumed experiential' evidential -*?el* in Wintu is the proximal demonstrative root -*?E* and a derivational suffix -*l* (see 2.96, and Pitkin 1984: 175).[2] The primarily hearsay, or reported, particle *ré* or *έ* in Sissala, a Gur (Voltaic) language spoken in Burkina Faso, developed from the locative-demonstrative *ré* 'here', 'this' (Blass 1989: 303).

We can recall, from §4.7, that demonstratives may have evidential-like meanings. Not surprisingly, demonstratives and third person pronouns give rise to evidentials of all sorts. A number of evidential particles in Hakha Lai (Tibeto-Burman: Peterson 2003: 416) go back to deictics and demonstrative pronouns. A similar example from Lega, a Bantu language, was discussed by Botne (1995).

Locative and directional markers also give rise to evidentials. The inferential -*ləm* in Meithei is an erstwhile directional suffix (Chelliah 1997: 224). Its directional meaning, lost from modern Meithei, survives in many other Tibeto-Burman languages. This suffix comes from the grammaticalization of a Proto-Tibeto-Burman noun **lam* 'road, way' (details are in Matisoff 1991: 389–90). The auditory evidential marker -*ke* in Euchee is cognate with the locative suffix *ke* meaning 'yonder', 'way over there' (Linn 2000: 318). According to Linn, the semantic connection between the two is to do with distance: 'the action is so far away that it can only be heard and not seen'.

Wasco-Wishram (Silverstein 1978) has a passive with a non-firsthand ('inferential') meaning which goes back to a locational construction (with no tense

---

[2] An evidential may be superficially similar to another morpheme in the language. The 'witnessed present' in Sanuma (Borgman 1990: 167) is homonymous with the verb 'be'; however, at present, no definitive statement can be made as to their etymological affinity (pace de Haan 2001: 99).

specification). Its meaning is: 'as can be surmised based on evidence, X has been V-ed'. The suffix which developed into the marker of this 'passive of evidence' construction goes back to an adverbial-forming suffix with locational verbs (pp. 242–3). Silverstein (1978: 246) concludes that 'the passives of evidence originally entered Wasco-Wishram idiomatic speech as forms POINTING OUT where such-and-such an action took place, as a conversational equivalent to referring to the evidence for that action'. This could be an example of an evidentiality strategy developing out of a basically deictic category.

9.1.3 Evidentiality strategies as source for evidentials

Evidential extensions of non-evidential categories, or evidentiality strategies, are similar to evidentials in their semantics (see Chapter 4). An evidentiality strategy can evolve into grammatical evidentiality, with information source as its main meaning. This can be the case for (i) modalities, (ii) perfect, resultative, and past tenses, and (iii) nominalizations of all sorts, including participles. Cross-linguistically, participles and nominalizations not infrequently give rise to perfects and past tenses. At what stage each of these develop evidential connotations depends on the language (and establishing any relative chronology of changes is a daunting task). Participles and nominalizations are often employed as complementation strategies. When a complement of a verb of speaking acquires the status of a main clause, its predicate then develops into a reported evidential via de-subordination (see §9.1.4).

Whether any of the other evidentiality strategies discussed in Chapter 4 can give rise to grammatical evidentials is not fully clear. The use of passives as evidential strategies (see §4.3) may be linked to their resultative semantics and focus on the object. However, I have found no clear examples of passive markers giving rise to evidentials. Neither have I found any example of a conjunct–disjunct system of person-marking (§4.6) developing into grammatical evidentiality. This may constitute an additional piece of evidence in favour of conjunct–disjunct and information source as categorically different notions. We saw, in §9.1.2, how a deictic marker can develop into an evidential term (usually, in a largish system). There are, however, no examples of an evidentiality system having evolved exclusively out of demonstratives.

(i) MODALITIES AS SOURCE FOR EVIDENTIALS.   Non-indicative modalities may develop evidential overtones similar to a non-firsthand evidential (see §4.1). Consequently, they may give rise to evidentials (though examples are not frequent).

The development of a non-firsthand evidential may involve future, which, by its nature, is close to a non-indicative modality. A future typically includes an element of prediction concerning something unwitnessed and of subsequent lack of certainty. It can easily come to be associated with a description of events which the speaker has not witnessed personally, and of which they can only talk on the basis of an educated guess, an inference, as well as assumption or hearsay.[3] The non-firsthand evidential in Abkhaz goes back to the future marker (Chirikba 2003: 262–4; Hewitt 1979; and also §4.1). In the closely related Circassian, the non-firsthand evidential suffix *-*ya-n* is a combination of perfective -*ya* with future marker -*n* (Chirikba 2003: 264; also see §3.1). (This is unlike most Caucasian languages where evidentials come from perfects: see (ii) below.)

Similar examples are found in few other languages. In Hill Patwin, the 'indirect' evidential -*boti*/-*beti* (Whistler 1986: 69–71) comes from a combination of the auxiliary *bo*/*be*'be (locational)' followed by the definite future suffix (see §9.1.5 on copula constructions as a source for evidentials). The original future sense of this suffix is still preserved in some examples, but in most cases it has been generalized to cover present and past tenses, where a claim is made in the absence of any direct (typically, visual) evidence. Along similar lines, two non-sensory evidentials in Akha developed from two future markers: 'assumptive' future and 'speculative' future (Thurgood 1986: 221–2). And we saw in §4.1 that the simple future in Andean Spanish has evolved a non-firsthand evidential meaning, probably under influence from Quechua (Escobar 1997: 81–8); see 4.4. Friedman (2003: 211–12) argues that the presumptive mood in Daco-Romanian and the dialect of Novo Selo (Vidinsko) spoken in northwestern Bulgaria near the Romanian and Serbian borders can be considered on a par with a non-firsthand evidential.

An interesting, albeit somewhat inconclusive piece of evidence in favour of a reported evidential originating from a non-indicative mood comes from South Estonian. The reported evidential in South Estonian dialects, marked with the suffix -*na*, may be related to the potential mood marker -*ne*. The following example (Metslang and Pajusalu 2002: 101) illustrates this reported evidential, whose marking is strikingly different from that in Standard Estonian and in Northern Estonian dialects—see discussion under §9.1.4 below. Similarly to Standard Estonian, their past tense counterparts come from past participles (illustrated under 4.16).

---

[3] Cf. Hewitt (1979: 91): '[i]f an action is inferred to have occurred, to be occurring or to be likely to occur, the possibility remains that the inference may be proved wrong by the subsequent acquisition of more information. This is precisely and necessarily the case with each and every pronouncement concerning an event in the future; the same lack of certainty attaches to statements about the future which attaches to descriptions of events not witnessed, or being witnessed, by the speaker personally'. This excerpt captures nicely the main semantic extensions of the formally marked term in small evidentiality systems; see §5.1.

South Estonian

9.1 sis   na   ol-**na**   julge, sis   murd-**na**-va   inimese
     then   they   be-REP   bold   then   break-REP-3pl   human:GEN.SG
     ka   ära
     even   down
     'Then they are said to be bold, then they can kill even humans'

The arguments in favour of linking the reported -*na* to the potential mood are compelling (see Metslang and Pajusalu 2002: 104–7). Firstly, the potential mood has been lost in dialects where the -*na* suffix marks reported evidentiality. Secondly, some potential forms in Old Written South Estonian appear to have had a reported meaning, as in *mis tennes* (what do + POT + 3sg) 'what could he do; what is he said to do'. Thirdly, the phonological change from -*ne* to -*na*/-*nä* (with the two variants conditioned by vowel harmony) is plausible. (The only aspect which is hard to explain is the loss of third person marker -*s*.)

An alternative etymology links the -*na* marked forms with the past participle marker -*nu*. Firstly, the development of participles into evidentiality markers is typical for Baltic languages. We can recall that past participles gave rise to the past tense of the reported evidential in Standard Estonian (see §4.4, and Example 4.16). Secondly, in some South Estonian dialects participles are marked with -*ne* rather than -*nu*. Two aspects of this etymology remain problematic. Firstly, how did a past participle lose its past reference? And secondly, the phonological change from -*nu* to -*na* is hardly plausible.

Mestlang and Pajusalu conclude that the -*na* marked reported evidential is likely to have developed from the -*ne*-marked potential mood. This process could have been influenced by an independent development of reported use of the -*nu*-marked past participle (pervasive in the Standard variety).

In Cree/Montagnais/Naskapi, conjunct dubitative forms have developed non-firsthand evidential meanings in contexts which prohibit the non-firsthand markers proper, for instance, under negation (see James, Clarke, and MacKenzie 2001: 230, 254–7; and Drapeau 1984 and 1996). Since the non-firsthand meaning 'has become conventionalised as a new meaning for dubitative suffixes in appropriate contexts', we hypothesize that an erstwhile evidential strategy is on its way towards becoming an evidential in itself.

Declarative and assertive markers may give rise to direct and visual evidentials. In Shipibo-Konibo, the direct evidential -*ra* may have come from the declarative–indicative marker reanalysed as an evidential at a later stage of language evolution (Valenzuela 2003: 43). In Tariana, an erstwhile declarative marker -*ka* (which survives in this function in closely related Arawak languages) was reanalysed as recent past visual evidential (Aikhenvald 2003e). And also see de Haan (2001: 94, and McLendon 2003), for a putative link between 'indicative', 'factual', and 'direct' (or 'visual') evidentials in Pomoan languages.

(ii) Perfect, resultative, and past tenses as source for evidentials. Perfect aspect, past tenses, and other forms with a completive and/or resultative meaning can acquire an additional meaning related to information source (§4.2). This meaning is similar to a non-firsthand in small evidentiality systems. These same forms often give rise to evidentials proper. Then information source becomes their main meaning. As Friedman (2003: 209) puts it, 'both Balkan Slavic languages and Albanian developed evidential strategies using native past forms, and as the contextual variant meanings became invariant the strategies became grammaticalised'. The non-firsthand evidential in Turkic languages originates in anterior and perfect forms (called 'postterminal' by Johanson 2003: 287). A similar path has been attested for neighbouring Iranian languages. In Tajik (Lazard 1996: 29) a series of forms with non-firsthand meanings has developed out of a perfect.

Finno-Ugric languages show the same line of development. Serebrjannikov (1960: 59, 66) traces the 'unobvious' past to perfect in both Komi and Mari. Similarly, evidentials in Northern Khanty developed out of a perfect in its resultative sense (Nikolaeva 1999: 141, 156). And in Cree/Montagnais/Naskapi, the non-firsthand evidential marker *-shapan* goes back to a Proto-Algonquian perfect (James, Clarke, and MacKenzie 2001: 247). Complex resultative constructions (involving perfective converbs and a copula 'be') gave rise to non-firsthand evidentials in Dargwa and Archi (Tatevosov 2001*a*: 460–1). Whether a non-firsthand meaning is just one of the meanings of a perfect, or whether it is its main meaning, may be hard to decide (see §4.2, on Georgian).

The connection between perfect (or anterior) in its resultative meaning and a non-firsthand evidential is a typologically widespread tendency (see Bybee, Perkins, and Pagliuca 1994: 95–7, Comrie 1976: 109–10, and Dahl 1985: 153, among others).[4] This path of development is summarized in Scheme 9.1, which is similar to Scheme 4.3:

Scheme 9.1 The development of non-firsthand evidentials out of perfects and resultatives

Stage 1. Result of an action or state; or action or state viewed as relevant for the moment of speech
↓
Stage 2. Inference based on visible traces, assumption, and possibly hearsay
↓
Stage 3. General range of non-firsthand meanings

---

[4] In the Balkan area, this tendency was reinforced by language contact; see §9.2.

Resultatives give rise to non-firsthand evidentials, and thus to A2 systems. In languages with A1 systems, different terms may develop from different verbal aspects and tenses, in paradigmatic opposition to each other. Balkan Slavic languages have developed an A1 system. The simple preterite acquired the 'firsthand' meaning and the old perfect became associated with the array of non-firsthand meanings.[5]

The emergence of A1 and A2 systems within the same area suggests two possible paths for the grammaticalization of evidentials. One involves a simple non-firsthand (what Friedman calls 'nonconfirmative') on the basis of a perfect or a resultative. The other one involves an additional development of a firsthand evidential (Friedman's 'confirmative'). This term may develop out of a simple past. Once a firsthand has been developed, a non-firsthand will follow suit, giving rise to an A1 system. This results from the non-existence of evidentiality systems which distinguish a firsthand evidential versus everything else. The development of firsthand overtones for simple preterites in Balkan Slavic triggered the emergence of a corresponding non-firsthand within the perfect paradigm (Friedman 2003: 212).

In some languages with an A1 system, the two terms developed through different grammaticalization paths. Bagvalal, a Northeast Caucasian language, is a case in point. The perfect forms (which consist of a perfective converb and the verb 'be') have evolved a full range of non-firsthand meanings (Tatevosov 2001*b*). The preterite forms are evidentially neutral (they have no evidentiality value). The firsthand forms are composed of a converb, or a participle, followed by the verb 'turn out to be, appear'.

We have little clear evidence of perfectives or resultatives giving rise to evidentials in larger systems. The Tuyuca non-visual present marker may have evolved from an older perfect aspect construction (Malone 1988: 132). The emergence of the inferred evidential in Tariana involved the reanalysis of the anterior aspect marker -*nhi* accompanied by the visual evidential (reinforced by grammatical accommodation: see end of §9.1.7). A somewhat different pattern emerges from McLendon's analysis of evidentials in Pomoan languages (2003: 125): the visual evidential marker in some Pomoan languages corresponds to the perfective marker in others (further speculations concerning the origins of Pomoan visual evidentials in perfective/imperfective aspect markers are in de Haan 2001: 94–5).

Several past tenses may develop into different evidentials. In Kamaiurá, *je* 'reported' and *rak* 'attested' have clear cognates in past tense markers in other Tupí-Guaraní languages: the 'attested' evidential goes back to a recent past

---

[5] This is in contrast to Albanian. Here the so-called inverted perfect became the basis for a new set of non-firsthand evidentials (Friedman 2003: 209), with an ensuing A2 system.

marker and the 'reported' to a remote past marker (Seki 2000: 344). The ways in which past markers have developed different evidentiality values require further investigation.

(iii) PARTICIPLES AND OTHER NOMINALIZATIONS AS SOURCE FOR EVIDENTIALS. Participles and other nominalizations are often used as evidentiality strategies (§4.4), with the meaning of non-firsthand or reported evidential. They can develop into a separate paradigm of evidentials (as was the case in Mansi: see Skribnik 1998: 197). In Nenets (Décsy 1966: 48; Perrot 1996) the non-firsthand ('auditive') forms probably come from nominalizations. The non-firsthand past in Komi is based on a past participle (Leinonen 2000: 421). In Estonian the present and the past participles have become part of the paradigm for the reported evidential (see Muižniece, Metslang, and Pajusalu 1999, on how past participles developed evidential meanings). In Lithuanian, the reported evidentials developed out of active participles; see 9.2 (Gronemeyer 1997: 93), where the participle form of 'hunt' is in fact a reported evidential.

Lithuanian
9.2 Vyr-ai   **medžio-dav-ę**   mišk-uose
    men-PL.M.NOM hunt-ITER-ACT.PAST.PL.M.NOM(=REP) forest-LOC.PL
    'It is said that men used to hunt in the woods'

Similarly, in Latvian an erstwhile participle construction which is used to convey reported meaning can now be considered a separate 'reported' paradigm (see Wälchli 2000). The process whereby a complement clause of a verb of speech becomes a main clause in its own right is discussed under §9.1.5.

A non-firsthand evidential may develop from a nominalization or another kind of non-finite verb (e.g. converb, used for adverbial subordination) with a perfective meaning in a copula construction. Then, the development involves a combination of structures: a non-finite verb form in a perfective meaning and a copula, as in Dargwa (Tatevosov 2001a: 461). In some Turkic languages (including Uyghur, Salar, and Tuvan) non-firsthand evidentials go back to periphrastic constructions consisting of a converb and an auxiliary 'stand' (Johanson 2003: 287).

9.1.4 *Speech complements as source for evidentials*

The development of evidentiality marker out of a complementation strategy involves 'de-subordination' of an erstwhile subordinate clause. That is, a complement clause of a verb of saying can acquire the status of a main clause. Then, if the verb in such a dependent clause had a special form, this form takes on the status of a reported evidential. This scenario has been reconstructed for present reported evidentials in Standard Estonian (see §4.5; and also Ikola 1953; Campbell 1991: 285–90; Harris and Campbell 1995: 99; Wälchli 2000: 194–6).

For similar developments in Livonian, see Laanest (1975: 155; 1982: 239). Wälchli (2000: 194–5) suggests similar processes at work in the creation of Latvian and Lithuanian reported evidentials.[6]

Estonian, just like many other Balto-Finnic languages, had a number of constructions available for complement clauses of speech act and mental state verbs. Two constructions were, we hypothesize, available simultaneously:

(*a*) MAIN VERB *et* (complementizer) FINITE VERB, and
(*b*) MAIN VERB ACTIVE PARTICIPLE

The (*a*) construction is shown in 9.3, and the (*b*) construction in 9.4. The two are almost synonymous.

Estonian

9.3 sai   kuulda,   et   seal   üks   mees
     get.3sg.PAST   hear+INF   that   there   one:NOM.SG   man:NOM.SG
     ela-b
     live-3sgPRES
     'One learned (lit. 'got to hear') that a man lived there'

In 9.4 the active participle and its subject are in the singular partitive form. They are treated as objects of the verb in the main clause.

9.4 sai   kuulda   seal   ühe   mehe
     get.3sg.PAST   hear+INF   there   one:GEN.SG   man:GEN.SG
     ela-vat
     live-PRES.PART.PARTVE.SG
     'One learned (lit. 'got to hear') that a man lived there'

By extension of participle forms, a third construction evolved, consisting of:

(*c*) MAIN VERB *et* (complementizer) ACTIVE PARTICIPLE

This new construction is exemplified in 9.5. The participle keeps its partitive form, but its subject is marked with nominative. In addition, the complementizer is now optional. The meaning of this construction is very similar to those discussed above.

9.5 sai   kuulda,   (et)   seal   üks   mees
     get.3sg.PAST   hear+INF   (that)   there   one:NOM.SG   man:NOM.SG
     ela-vat
     live-PRES.PART.PARTVE.SG
     'One learned (lit. 'got to hear') that a man lived there'

---

[6] According to Skribnik (1998: 205–7), similar processes could have been at work in developing non-firsthand evidentials in Mansi.

What was a non-finite verb form could now occur in a main clause. The construction *sai kuulda* 'learn, get to hear' can be omitted altogether, and the resulting structure is at 9.6. The only indication that the information comes from someone else is the present participle in partitive case. This form is now a reported evidential.

9.6   seal   üks   mees   **ela-vat**
       there   one:NOM.SG   man:NOM.SG   live-PRES.PART.PARTVE.SG = REP.PRES
       'A man lived there (it is said)'

A similar pathway can be constructed for past participles which gave rise to past reported (as in 4.16; see footnote 14 to Chapter 4, and also (*a*) under §4.4, for a complete paradigm of reported evidential in Standard Estonian). The grammaticalization of 'reported' in Standard Estonian (see Mürk 1991: 227; Kask 1984) was sped up by deliberate language planning starting from 1922, especially by Johannes Aavik, the leading figure of the Estonian language planning movement (Perrot 1996: 159).[7]

In summary, the emergence of reported evidential in Estonian involved

(i)   extension of complementation constructions,
(ii) reanalysis of subordinate clause as main clause, and
(iii) reinterpretation of the forms used in subordinate clauses as main clause predicates with the meaning of 'reported' information.

9.1.5 *Copula constructions as source for evidentials*

Reanalysis of a copula construction may result in the creation of a non-firsthand evidential. These constructions often involve an existential verb; they may have resultative meanings, and follow the same path of development as do resultatives and perfectives. This is the case in Chinese Pidgin Russian (Nichols 1986), which has an A2 system. The present existential copula *est'* follows the verb root, just like any other postverbal auxiliary. See 9.7.

Chinese Pidgin Russian
9.7   Ljudi   **pomiraj**   **est'**
       person   die   EXIST.COP=NON.FIRSTHAND
       'The man's died' (the presence of crows makes the speaker infer that the man has died)

---

[7] Somewhat different pathways of grammaticalization took place in other dialects. South Estonian dialects diverge most from the Standard Estonian pattern. The Võru dialect marks present tense reported with a form homophonous with the nominative form of the active participle. The Western Tartu dialect has a form which goes back to a genitive/accusative; and the Mulgi dialect developed a special form based on the present participle of monosyllabic verbs (further details are in Metslang and Pajusalu 2002: 100–1).

Copula constructions are involved in the formation of evidentials via their role in the formation of perfects (as in Dargwa, see under (ii) in §9.1.3). Individual terms in complex evidential systems also develop in this way. In Patwin (Whistler 1986) the auxiliary (the locational 'be') marks a 'direct' sensory evidential. In Jamul Tiipay (Yuman: Miller 2001: 193), the non-firsthand evidential derives from an auxiliary construction involving the verb 'be'; also see Langdon (1978: 119–20). In Akha (Thurgood 1986: 218–21), 'nonsensorial' evidential particles developed from copulas. The reported enclitic -*guuq* in West Greenlandic has probably arisen from the verbalizing affix -*(ng)u-* 'it is so that' and third person singular indicative inflection, that is, 'be it so that' (Fortescue 2003: 301).

9.1.6 *Other sources for evidentials*

Evidentiality systems may arise as the result of a number of reanalysis processes. The emergence of an evidentiality system in Lhasa Tibetan appears to have resulted from a variety of diachronic processes (Saxena 1997) which involved the reanalysis of the tense-aspect system and the reanalysis of an original copula as an evidential marker: '*dug*, an erstwhile existential copula, now marks 'actual visual knowledge' (DeLancey 1986: 205).

Evidentials rarely come from nouns. However, in Xamatauteri (Ramirez 1994: 170) the reported evidential *hora* comes from a noun meaning 'noise'; its grammaticalization may have involved noun incorporation (a productive process in Xamatauteri). The marker of the non-visual sensory in Northern Samoyedic languages Nganasan, Nenets, and Enets goes back to a noun with the meaning 'voice' (Künnap 2002: 149; Gusev forthcoming: 17). The reported particle *omen* in Basque also occurs as a noun meaning 'rumour, fame, reputation' (Jacobsen 1986: 7). The Arrernte reported evidential *kwele* could have come from the locative form of the noun meaning 'arm' (Gavan Breen in prep. and p.c.).

Other word classes can be reinterpreted and reanalysed as evidentiality markers. The reported adverb 'they say' in Paumarí, an Arawá language, is likely to have developed out of the noun meaning 'news'; a cognate adverb subsequently grammaticalized as a verbal suffix in the Madi dialect complex which includes Jarawara (Dixon 2003: 180).

In a few cases separate morphemes with epistemic meanings develop into evidentials. The reported evidential in Wintu probably came from a morpheme meaning 'maybe, potentially' (see 2.96, and discussion in Schlichter 1986: 50). The assumed evidential in Tariana arose as a result of the reanalysis of a dubitative marker -*si*, or -*sika* (still employed as a marker of doubt and speculation in Piapoco, a language closely related to Tariana and spoken outside the Vaupés area: Aikhenvald 2003*e*). In West Greenlandic, the inferential suffix *-gunar-* derives from a Proto-Eskimo morpheme meaning 'probably' (Fortescue 2003: 292, 299).

Various morphemes with evidential value in Makah and related Wakashan languages come from a variety of suffixes, and nominal, verbal, and descriptive markers. An evidential suffix referring to a dream in Kwakiutl could be related to a formative suffix in Makah meaning 'have a dream' (Jacobsen 1986). An evidential with a meaning 'it seems' has cognates in a lexical suffix 'similar, like in appearance'. Further possibilities have been described for Akha. Here, the 'expected' non-visual sensory particle *mí-a* probably developed from a concessive particle followed by the third person pronoun. The visual evidential may have originated from a first person pronoun (Thurgood 1986: 217; also see de Haan 2001: 100).

9.1.7 *Etymologically heterogenous evidentials*

The few available studies of the genesis of large systems (such as Wintu: Schlichter 1986) show that, by and large, they are etymologically heterogenous. That is, different terms come from different sources. Of the evidentials in Wintu, three came from independent verbs, and one from a particle. We have seen above that the non-visual sensory in Nganasan, Nenets, and Enets prob- ably derives from a noun. Both inferred and reported evidentials in these languages contain a formative *-bi-* which is most probably related to a past tense or a past participle marker (see Künnap 2002: 151 for further details).

Table 9.1 illustrates the combination of strategies employed in the evolution of the partly fused tense and evidentiality system in Tariana (adapted from Aikhenvald 2003*e*).

The system in Tariana is of a relatively recent origin. We will see, in §9.2 below, how it matches the patterns found in neighbouring East Tucanoan lan- guages. The scenario for the historical development of the tense–evidentiality paradigm involves a variety of mechanisms. Data from related Arawak languages indicate that, before intensive language contact with the East Tucanoans, Tariana is likely to have had an optional reported evidentiality specification. The marker, *-pida-*, is shared with closely related Baniwa. After Tariana came into contact with East Tucanoan languages (see Aikhenvald 2003*c* for the available historical information), the optional tense and mood system was reanalysed as obligatory tense-marking with present as a formally unmarked member (the markers are *-ka* for recent past and *-na* for remote past). The existing reported specification came to be reanalysed as unmarked present reference, and the newly evolved tense markers were added to it: hence the emergence of forms *-pida* 'present reported', *-pida-ka* 'recent past reported', and *-pida-na* 'remote past reported'. The assumed specification arose as the

TABLE 9.1. Strategies employed in the development of the tense-evidentiality system in Tariana

CATEGORY	REANALYSIS AND REINTERPRETATION
Tense: present	unmarked; reanalysed as a tense marker
Tense: recent past	reanalysis and reinterpretation of declarative *-ka*
Tense: remote past	reanalysis of past/perfective *-na* as an obligatory tense
Evidentiality: visual	marker recent past and remote past: formally unmarked; present: unknown; could be grammaticalization of the form *nu-ka* 'I see'
Evidentiality: assumed	reanalysis and reinterpretation of *-si-* or of *-si-ka* 'dubitative'; then combination of *-si-* with tense markers
Evidentiality: reported	reanalysis and reinterpretation of optional reported marker *-pida* (from Proto-Baniwa-Tariana) as unmarked present; then combination of *-pida* with tense markers
Evidentiality: non-visual	combination of the result of grammaticalization of compounded verb *-hima* 'hear, feel, seem, perceive' with already established tense markers
Evidentiality: inferred	reanalysis and reinterpretation of a combination *-nhi* 'anterior' and past tense visual evidentials as a new evidential

result of the reanalysis of a dubitative marker *-si-* or *-si-ka*. The non-visual specification developed as the result of the grammaticalization of a verb of non-visual perception, *-hima* 'hear, feel, seem, perceive'. The visual specification is formally unmarked. An additional term, the inferred evidential, has evolved under the massive impact of the Tucano language. This involves reanalysis of an anterior marker homophonous with a marker of the corresponding construction in Tucano; here, grammatical accommodation goes together with reanalysis and reinterpretation.

Hupda, a Makú language also spoken in the Vaupés area, has developed five evidential specifications, similar to those in Tariana. The visual evidential is formally unmarked, and the non-visual and the two inferred evidentials are derived from grammaticalized verbs (see §9.1.1 above). The reported evidential does not come from a grammaticalized verb; its form is cognate to the reported enclitic found in other Makú languages. Of these, two—Yuhup and Dâw—are spoken in the Vaupés area (see Martins 1994: 106), and one—Nadëb—is spoken outside this area (Epps 2005: 640–2).

This is in contrast to a system like Shibacha Lisu, where all the evidentiality specifications appear to have developed from grammaticalized verbs (see §9.1.1).

9.1.8 *Sources for evidentials: a summary*

Evidentials evolve from a variety of sources. These are:

- grammaticalization of forms from open classes (mostly verbs, more rarely nouns) and from closed classes (deictic markers, pronouns, locationals); and
- reinterpretation and reanalysis of evidentiality strategies, whereby a grammatical device for which information source was a secondary meaning acquires it as its primary meaning.

We hypothesize that the semantic mechanisms at play in the development of evidential meanings by grammaticalized forms from open and from closed classes involve metaphors as the underlying driving force of the occurring semantic changes. Rather few examples have been found of modalities and lexical items with purely 'epistemic' meanings developing into grammatical evidentials.

Small evidentiality systems often have their roots in the reinterpretation of evidentiality strategies. Reanalysis of subordinate clauses as main clauses results in the creation of reported evidentiality. Large evidentiality systems tend to be etymologically heterogenous: their terms come from different sources.

What are the exact mechanisms involved in the development of grammatical evidentiality? We have seen that, in many instances, evidentials originate in lexical items. It is, however, not at all true that all evidentials derive from lexical items (also see Joseph 2003: 317 who offers incisive criticism of the claim that all affixes have 'a prior lexical history'). A number of evidential affixes in Eskimo languages are reconstructible as affixes for Proto-Eskimo-Aleut, with no obvious or even likely lexical sources (Fortescue 2003: 300–1). Similarly, no lexical source can be reconstructed for the reported evidential in Hupda or in Baniwa-Tariana.

When evidentials develop via grammaticalization and reinterpretation of open or closed classes, do they necessarily have to go through a phase in which they function as evidentiality strategies? That is, is it the case that the information source gradually becomes the central meaning of a form, or forms, which develop into an evidential paradigm? To answer this question, we need to know what intermediate stages of grammaticalization of evidentials look like.[8] Since we do not have enough information on these, the question remains open.

Why and how do languages acquire evidentials? In §9.2 we will see how language contact provides an answer to this question.

---

[8] These questions involve more general issues related to the universal validity and mechanisms of grammaticalization (see Joseph 2003), and the creation of 'emergent grammar' (as per Hopper 1987). These are outside the scope of this book.

9.2 Evidentials and language contact

The emergence and the loss of evidentials is often due to intensive language contact. Evidentials are a property of several linguistic areas (§9.2.1). Evidentials can be gained as a result of one language influencing the other, or lost if the neighbouring languages happen to have no evidentials (§9.2.2). Contact languages spoken by those whose first language has evidentials may also mark information source (§9.2.3).

9.2.1 Evidentiality as an areal feature

A linguistic area (or Sprachbund)[9] is generally taken to be a geographically delimited area including languages from two or more language families, sharing significant traits. Most of these traits are not found in languages from the same families outside the area (also see Aikhenvald 2002, definitions by Emeneau 1956; Sherzer 1973: 760; and discussion in Tosco 2000). A number of well-established linguistic areas have evidentiality among their defining features. The distribution of evidentiality systems across the world is roughly outlined on the Map in this book.

THE BALKANS are probably the best known example of a linguistic area with evidentiality. 'Classic' Balkan languages include Slavic (Bulgarian, Macedonian, and Serbian), Romance (Daco-Romanian and various dialects, including Aromanian), Albanian, and Greek. Balkan Slavic languages form a dialectal continuum.

All these languages—with the exception of Greek—have small evidentiality systems. Balkan Slavic languages have an A1 system (firsthand and non-firstand), while Albanian and Megleno-Romanian have an A2 system (non-firsthand evidentials versus everything else). The Romanian 'presumptive mood' is in the process of becoming a non-firsthand evidential in its own right. Evidential paradigms have, by and large, developed out of the reanalysis of past tenses and perfects. (Also see Matras (1995), on the spread of evidentiality into Gypsy (Romani) dialects.) By the time of the Ottoman invasion of the Balkans, the A2 evidentiality system in Turkish appears to have already been established. In all likelihood, what could have been evidentiality strategies in medieval Slavic evolved into full-fledged evidentials under Turkish influence. The impact of Turkish as the dominant language in urban areas may have contributed to the grammaticalization of already pre-existing evidentiality strategies. This

---

[9] Here I follow the traditional approach whereby the terms Linguistic Area and Sprachbund are treated as synonyms. An alternative approach advocated by Thomason and Kaufman (1988) involves distinguishing Linguistic Areas (with mostly unilateral diffusion) and Sprachbund (where diffusion is multilateral). See Aikhenvald (2002), on types of diffusion and the ensuing linguistic areas.

influence did not involve morpheme-by-morpheme translations and structural isomorphism; see Friedman (1978), on the complex mechanisms of the development of evidentials out of native past tense forms. Bulgarian and Macedonian, both Balkan Slavic, developed an A1 system—synchronically different from a typical Turkic A2 system found in other Balkan languages (see §9.1 above).[10]

The area borders on Turkey, with Turkish as the main language. Turkic languages are generally considered to be the 'epicentre' of diffusion of evidentiality in Central Asia. Small systems (A1 and A2 types) are widespread in Iranian languages (cf. Bulut 2000: 147, on their origins in contacts with Turkish), including Tajik and Kurdish. Small evidentiality systems in the Dardic languages Kalasha and Khowar has been described by Bashir (1988). Similar systems are found in Finno-Ugric languages (Permic and Mordva branches), where their emergence could also be due to Turkish influence. The spread of evidentiality cannot always be accounted for by one source of diffusion. The development of evidentiality in Armenian can be partly explained as a result of contacts with both Iranian and Turkic languages (Kozintseva 2000: 414; Donabédian 2001). Evidentials in Svan did not arise as a result of straightforward influence from Turkish. The evidentials in this language evolved under the influence of Megrelian, another South Caucasian language, which, in its turn, could have acquired a small A2 evidentiality system under Turkish influence (Boeder 2000: 275–7; Friedman 2000: 357; Sumbatova 1999).

The situation in West Caucasian languages is rather different. An evidential category is likely to have been in place before any contact with Turkic languages (Chirikba 2003: 266–7). Evidentiality can be reconstructed for Proto-Abkhaz and Proto-Circassian. These proto-languages are thought to have been spoken around the eighth and ninth century AD.[11] This suggests the independent development of an evidentiality system (A2 type), predating the spread of Turkic languages. Small evidentiality systems are a feature of numerous Northeast Caucasian languages; however, the exact direction of diffusion remains to be ascertained.

---

[10] The exact mechanism of diffusion is still a matter for discussion. The firsthand ('confirmative') terms may have developed first, and this entailed the development of matching non-firsthand forms (Friedman 2003: 212). An alternative scenario (Comrie 2000: 8) could have involved markedness inversion, whereby the old 'non-firsthand' ('nonconfirmative') 'was reinterpreted as unmarked', with the form originally unmarked for evidentiality becoming a marked, 'firsthand' term.

[11] Contacts with Turkic languages (Kypchak, Crimean Tatar, or early Karachay-Balkar) are thought to have been negligible. According to Chirikba (2003: 266), 'any discernible Turkish presence in Abkhazia can be traced back to a period not earlier than 16th century, when Ottoman Turkey had established its hegemony over the Caucasian Black Sea coast.' However, one cannot exclude influence from other Turkic languages such as Bulgar (starting from the end of the fifth century BC), Western Türk (from the sixth century BC), and Khazar (from the seventh century BC) (Lars Johanson, p.c.). The Bulgarian evidentiality system is thought to have been influenced by Turkic languages prior to the Ottoman Turkish impact (Johanson 1998).

Having a small evidential system is thus an areal feature of a largish 'evidentiality belt' spreading across the Balkans, the Caucasus, and Central Asia into Siberia.[12] The marking of evidentiality differs from language to language and from subgroup to subgroup. But the systems and their usage are very similar. We have seen above that Ugric languages (Khanty and Mansi) have small evidential systems (A1 and A2) (see Skribnik 1998 and Nikolaeva 1999). Samoyedic languages have larger systems (up to three terms, as in Nganasan). Yukaghir, spoken in the Yakut republic in northeast Russia, has a small A1 evidential system. Eskimo-Aleut languages have evidentiality scattered through their grammar (Fortescue 1998: 69). That is, evidentiality 'spreads' across the Balkans into Asia (see Haarmann 1970, for a suggestion that non-firsthand evidentials are a diffusional feature found in numerous languages of Eurasia; also see Skribnik and Ozonova forthcoming). Only a small number of languages have no, or almost no, evidentiality—these include Chukotko-Kamchatkan (Fortescue 1998: 69), Ket, and Nivkh.[13]

Throughout the preceding chapters, I have frequently mentioned structural and semantic similarities of the reported evidential in THE BALTIC REGION—Estonian and Livonian (Balto-Finnic) on the one hand, and Latvian and Lithuanian (Baltic branch of Indo-European) on the other. In all these languages, the reported evidential comes from active participles (see §9.1.4) which developed into a special paradigm. This type of construction with reported meaning may go back to Common Baltic (Holvoet 2001: 379); or it may be an innovation (Balode and Holvoet 2001: 43). It is shared with Estonian and Livonian, the two Balto-Finnic languages, which may have acquired it through prolonged contact. Whether this happened as a result of direct influence of Latvian on Estonian, or whether the development occurred in several dialect areas of Estonian remains open to debate—see the discussion in Künnap (1992: 209); also see Stolz (1991). (The use of agentless passive participles as evidentiality strategy in Lithuanian (see §4.4) is likely to be an independent innovation.)

According to Fortescue (1998: 78), evidentiality spread from Eurasia into adjacent areas across the Bering Strait (his Map 31 shows a degree of distribution of evidentials across the Bering Strait, with the proviso that evidentials are not really distinguished from attitudinal and modal markers).

Evidentials are considered an areal feature for a number of regions in North America (see Jacobsen 1986: 7–8 and Sherzer 1976). Evidentials are defined as

---

[12] There is hardly any evidence for the existence of evidentials in any of the ancient languages of the Middle East, Mesopotamia, or Anatolia. Joseph (2003: 320–1) discusses the origins of the quotative enclitic in Hittite, Luvian, and Palaic. Its emergence may have been influenced by the Hatti substratum (Slava Chirikba, p.c.).

[13] See Jacquesson (1996) for an alternative view of Chukotko-Kamchatkan languages.

a 'central areal trait' in the Northwest Coast area (including numerous Salish, Wakashan, and Chimakuan languages, and a few others: Sherzer 1976: 78, 230), the Great Basin (with Washo and Northern and Southern Paiute (both Uto-Aztecan): Sherzer 1976: 163–5, 245–6), and the Plains (with Cheyenne and Arapaho (Algonquian), Siouan, Caddoan, Kiowa (Kiowa-Tanoan), Apache (Athabaskan), and Tonkawa: Sherzer 1976: 183–5, 248). It is interpreted as a 'regional areal trait' of northern-central California (including Hupa and Kato, both Athabaskan; Maidu, Wintu, Miwok, and Yokuts) and a Papago-Apachean-Tanoan region of the Southwest (Sherzer 1976: 125, 128, 147, 238). Evidentiality is considered a family feature of Wakashan, Salish, and Siouan languages, and possibly also Athabaskan, Chimakuan, Uto-Aztecan, Algonquian, Hokan, and Penutian (Sherzer 1976: 78, 125, 183, 198). Languages such as Yana in California, Washo in the Great Basin, and Kiowa and Tonkawa in the Plains are thought to have acquired evidentiality via areal diffusion (Sherzer 1976: 125, 130, 163, 166, 183). This statement of areal distribution is highly preliminary; as pointed out by Jacobsen (1986: 8), the broad areal picture drawn by Sherzer may be somewhat vitiated by his failure to distinguish various kinds of evidentials and evidential systems. For instance, the term 'narrative' may in fact refer to a tense-aspect term; and what is called 'quotative' is not necessarily the same as a reported evidential.[14]

Simple evidential systems are found in some languages of Mexico (Chinantecan: see Foris 2000; Mixtecan: see, for instance, Farris 1992, Hollenbach 1992, and Shields 1988; and some Uto-Aztecan and Mayan: see Haviland 1987 and Lucy 1993).

Turning back to Eurasia, evidentials are found in quite a few Tibeto-Burman languages (LaPolla 2003*b*: 35), where the systems vary from two terms (as in Dulong-Rawang) to three or more terms (as in various dialects of Tibetan, and in Newari, Qiang, and Akha); also see Bickel (2000) for an overview of evidentials in Himalayan languages. Indic languages typically have no evidentials (with the exception of Nepali which has developed a non-firsthand evidential: Michailovsky 1996 and Peterson 2000). Reported evidentials appear to be a feature of India as a linguistic area (Saxena 1988: 375; cf. Kuiper 1974: 146). Areal impact from neighbouring Indo-Aryan languages may have contributed to the wealth of quotative and reported constructions in Tibeto-Burman languages (see the arguments in Saxena 1988).

Very few evidentiality systems have been decribed for African languages. The only examples known so far include Sissala (Gur, Upper Volta), Lega (Bantu), and Shilluk (Nilotic).

---

[14] To his credit, Sherzer defines evidentiality as 'information source', rather than stretching this notion to cover modalities of all varieties.

According to Aikhenvald and Dixon (1998b), grammatical evidentiality has been independently innovated in at least six places in Amazonia. Four of these are south of the Amazon river and include (1) Kamaiurá, a Tupí-Guaraní language on the Upper Xingu River; (2) Nambiquara, on the headwaters of western tributaries of the Madeira River; (3) the Madi group of Arawá languages (covering Jarawara, Jamamadí, and Banawá), close to the Purús River; (4) Panoan languages and South Arawak (which include Terêna, Ignaciano, Waurá, Pareci, and Piro). A careful analysis of evidential marking in Panoan languages shows that evidentiality must have evolved only recently, since not a single marking or category can be securely reconstructed for the proto-language (Valenzuela 2003: 56–7). Of other Tupí-Guaraní languages, Paraguayan Guaraní (Guasch 1956: 264; Krivoshein de Canese 1983: 102) has a reported evidential.

The remaining two are north of the Amazon—(5) Yanomami and (6) Tucanoan languages. Reported evidentials in a number of North Arawak languages in northwest Amazonia, northern Peru and adjacent areas of Colombia (Resígaro, Achagua, Piapoco, and Baniwa of Içana) could have been diffused from Tucanoan languages. Evidentiality in Bora-Witoto languages in northeastern Peru (and possibly in other Peruvian languages, such as Arabela, a Zaparoan language) could be of the same contact-induced origin. The East Tucanoan evidentiality system has been diffused into Tariana, replacing an original optional reported evidential marker with an obligatory and intricate grammatical system (see §9.2.2).[15] Complex evidential systems have also diffused into Hupda and Yuhup, two Makú languages spoken in the Vaupés area.[16] Dâw, a Makú language spoken in the same area, has only a reported evidential, and so does Nadëb, also Makú, but spoken outside the Vaupés River Basin. Epps (2005) hypothesizes that reported evidentiality could be reconstructed for Proto-Makú.

ANDEAN languages shows a significantly different typological profile from Amazonian languages (see Aikhenvald and Dixon 1998b). However, one feature that is found in both areas is evidentiality. Since Amazonian languages with evidentiality are not in geographical contact with Andean languages, the most likely scenario is that evidentials evolved in the Andean area independently of what was happening in Amazonia. But it is not absolutely impossible that there

---

[15] The origin of evidentiality in other families requires further study. Among Carib languages, evidentiality developed out of a non-finite verb form in Trio and probably in Wayana (Carlin 2002: 70–2). In Hixkaryana and maybe also in Wai Wai, particles mark various evidentiality distinctions (Derbyshire 1985; Hawkins 1994). Further analysis of these and other languages may reveal presence of further evidential systems in Amazonia.

[16] The structure of the evidentiality system in Yuhup is very similar to that in Hupda (Patience Epps, p.c., and Ospina Bozzi (2002: 181–2).

was some category diffusion (in either direction—especially if we remember that the Tucanoans state that they came from further to the west, and there could conceivably have been contact in the not-too-distant past). Evidentiality in Tsafiki (Barbacoan) spoken on the western side of the Andes and in some Choco languages on the Pacific side (see Mortensen 1999: 86–7) could be an off-shoot of this category in the Andean area.

In New Guinea, evidentials are found in languages of the Engan family and a few other, geographically contiguous languages in the Southern Highlands Province (Foley 1986: 166). Isolated 'pockets' of languages with evidentiality include Oksapmin, in West Sepik province, and Tauya, in the Upper Ramu Valley, Madang province. Mangap-Mbula, an Austronesian language from Papua New Guinea, appears to have an A1 (firsthand versus non-firsthand) evidentiality system (Bugenhagen 1995: 132–3). Reported evidentials are found in some Western Austronesian languages (see Ballard 1974, on Philippine languages, and Klamer 2000).

A particle marking reported evidentiality is found in four contiguous languages in Central Australia—the Western Desert language (Yankunytjatjara: *kunyu*); Warlpiri (*nganta*); Arrernte (*kwele*); and Warluwarra (Breen, p.c.). The forms are different; but their semantics is strikingly similar; see examples in §5.4.3.

We have seen that evidentials are easily spread through areal diffusion in language contact. But even if evidentiality is a prominent feature in a given linguistic area, not every language acquires it. Greek—one of the 'classic' languages of the Balkan area—is a case in point (see, however, Friedman 2003: 189–90, on *lé[e]i* 'one says' as an emerging reported particle). According to Joseph (2003: 315), reasons for not developing evidentiality may have to do with speakers' attitude to their language as an obstacle to areal diffusion—the 'literary tradition of Greek, the identification of Greek with religion and the importance of religion in identity formation among Greeks, and the like'. Numerous Romani dialects in the Balkan area also failed to develop evidentiality. Here, the explanation could be different: there is no mutual bilingualism, since the Gipsies are often considered outcasts and outsiders. In this case, social factors may have played a role in creating an atypical situation. In other regions, relevant social factors may be rather difficult to establish. Ubykh, a West Caucasian language squeezed between Circassian and Abkhaz (both with evidentiality of A2 type), has no evidentials. Ubykh is known to have served as a 'bridge' between Circassian and Abkhaz-speaking areas (Chirikba 2003: 267), and the majority of Ubykhs were bi- or even tri-lingual. And yet the language has acquired no evidentials. The question 'why' remains open.

9.2.2 Gain and loss of evidentials in language contact

Evidentiality often spreads from one language to another if they are in contact. An evidential marker can be borrowed. This is known as direct diffusion. Or the evidential forms may be different, but their meanings and usage match those in another language. This is known as indirect diffusion, or diffusion of categories (see Aikhenvald 2002: 3–7). A language can develop a system of evidentials out of its own formal resources to match the existing categories in a language with which it is in contact.

Borrowing an evidential marker (known as 'direct diffusion') is not too common. This is part of a general tendency not to borrow grammatical morphemes. (That this is only a tendency has been demonstrated in Aikhenvald 2002: 264–78.) Soper (1996: 59–61) mentions instances of borrowing the non-firsthand marker -*miş* from Uzbek into Tajik. In the Romani dialect of Silven, the -*l* marker of the Bulgarian evidential past has been reanalysed as an evidential particle -*li* which is suffixed to indigenous past tense forms (Friedman 2003: 193).

A clear-cut example of calquing the whole system of obligatory evidentiality specification under the impact of areal diffusion is found in Tariana, spoken in the Vaupés area; see Table 9.1 in §9.1.7 and the discussion in Aikhenvald (2003*b*, *e*; 2003*c*: 293–322, and 2002: 117–29). Similarities go beyond simple matching of a system. Diagram 3.1 shows almost identical patterns in question–response. The ways in which evidentials are used in commands are also remarkably similar; see §8.1.2. The origins of some evidential terms are also similar. The non-visual evidential in Tariana is most probably the result of grammaticalization of compounded verb 'hear, feel, seem, perceive'. This is similar to what happened in Desano and Tuyuca, both East Tucanoan.

The only term in the Tariana system that has a cognate with a closely related North Arawak language Baniwa of Içana is reported (Baniwa -*pida*, Tariana -*pida*-, with corresponding tense specifications). We showed in §3.8 that the reported evidential in Tariana differs from all other evidentials in that it can have a time reference of its own, different from that of the verb (Examples 3.50–5). Since this is probably the only term inherited from the protolanguage, its distinct synchronic status is corroborated by its different origin.

In spite of their common origin, the reported evidentials in Tariana and in Baniwa are used differently. Every clause in Tariana must contain an evidential, thus matching the East Tucanoan pattern. In Baniwa only every chunk of text has to be marked with an evidential.

Language contact can affect the ways evidentials are used in discourse. Arizona Tewa and Hopi are both spoken in the Pueblo area in North America

(Kroskrity 1998). Examples 3.36 (§3.6) ('from there so (*ba*), having arrived so (*ba*), they were being taught to fly') and 10.15 ('And then (*ba*) so, again so (*ba*), as one stood up again so (*ba*), they started to sing') show multiple occurrences of the non-firsthand evidential *ba* in Arizona Tewa. This evidential is characteristic of a specific narrative genre for traditional Pueblo stories. Almost identical patterns have been observed in the corresponding narratives in Hopi. This is illustrated in 9.8, another example with multiple evidentials.

Hopi

9.8 noq **yaw** 'ora:yvi 'atka   ki:tava   **yaw** piw
     and REP   Oraibi   below:south   from:village REP   also
     tɨcvo ki'yta
     wren   sg:lives
     'And wren also lives below Oraibi, south of the village' (it is said)

The form of evidentials in the two languages is different, but their functions are very similar. Both are closely associated with a traditional genre (Arizona Tewa *pę́:yu'u* and Hopi *tutuwutsi*). Kroskrity (1998) compares patterns found in Arizona Tewa with Rio Grande Tewa, genetically related but spoken in different linguistic areas. Multiple occurrences of the evidential particle in Rio Grande Tewa are far less frequent than in Arizona Tewa, though the meaning of the evidential particle is the same. The convergence between Arizona Tewa and Hopi is not complete. Hopi narrators use the evidential particle in sentence-initial position, impossible in Tewa narratives.

Stable societal multilingualism in both Hopi and Tewa, enhanced by generations of intermarriage, is characterized by intense indirect diffusion (and very little borrowing of actual forms) and shared discourse patterns. Kroskrity (1998: 32) reports that 'over the past two centuries at least, Tewa children have heard Hopi traditional narratives from their paternal kinsmen' who were Hopi-speakers, following the norm of intermarriage of the Tewa with the Hopi. As a result, narrators used to be able to perform traditional narratives in both languages. It is thus no wonder that the two narrative traditions show dramatic convergence not only in the themes but also in genre-specific evidentiality marking. The convergent pattern of usage includes the 'elevation' of the Tewa evidential to the status of a genre marker, to match its Hopi counterpart (see §10.2.1).

Diffusion of evidentials thus goes together with diffusion of narrative genres and narrative techniques (see Chapter 6 of Aikhenvald 2002, on the spread of narrative techniques in the Vaupés area; and Haig 2001, for further examples). Tariana shares the use of the assumed evidential as a marker of a narrative genre with the East Tucanoan languages, Tucano (Ramirez 1997, vol. I: 140) and

Desano (Miller 1999: 67). This extreme diffusibility of evidentiality goes alongside the spread of cultural attitudes and stereotypes associated with it. We return to this in §11.4.

Evidentials can be lost, or significantly reduced, in other language-contact situations. Tucanoan languages spoken outside the Vaupés area have a rather reduced system of evidentials. Retuarã, from the Central Tucanoan subgroup, is spoken in Colombia next to Yucuna, a language from the North Arawak subgroup that only has a reported evidential. Yucuna is the dominant language in this region, with speakers of Retuarã being bilingual in it. As a result of Yucuna influence, Retuarã has lost the high unrounded central vowel *i* and simplified the system of classifiers (Gomez-Imbert 1996, and p.c.). Its system of evidentials is also reduced. Yucuna has just one optional evidential: reported *-le* (Schauer and Schauer 1978: 43). Retuarã has three evidentials, all of which are optional: strictly auditory information, assumed information, and reported (Strom 1992: 90–1; Barnes 1999: 213). This is in contrast to East Tucanoan languages, which have either four or five obligatory evidentials (see Aikhenvald 2002: 129).

Turkic languages in contact with Indo-European languages tend to lose the non-firsthand evidential. Examples include Karaim spoken in Lithuania, and the Turkish dialects in the Trabzon province on the east Black Sea coast, in contact with Greek (Johanson 2003: 288–9).[17]

A dialect of a language within a linguistic area with evidentiality may develop evidentials, while its dialects spoken outside such an area remain without any evidentiality. This is the case with Albanian: the pre-sixteenth-century diaspora dialects spoken in Italy (Arbëresh) and in Greece (Arvanitika) have no evidentiality. In contrast, evidentiality is a prominent category in the Albanian varieties spoken in the Balkans (Friedman 2003: 193, 209).

9.2.3 Evidentials in contact languages

Evidentials are a salient feature in languages which have it. Expressing one's information source becomes a speech habit. And it is very often a cultural requirement. One has to be precise about how one knows something, or else one could be accused of lying, or worse, of sorcery. Hardman (1986: 133) reports how difficult it is for Jaqi speakers to imagine that there are languages which do not mark the information source. It took Hardman and her colleagues 'a great deal of persuasion and illustration to lead [their Aymara assistants] to the belief that we really are not lying when we use an unmarked sentence to relate the

---

[17] A study of how evidentials develop into other categories would be a fascinating enterprise. For the time being, no such information is available.

material we have not personally experienced. As when I might say, "Whorf was the student of Sapir"—"No, I did not know them,—but no, I am not lying,—and no, I don't have to say that I read it" '. And she adds: 'To some degree we find ourselves having to adjust our English'.

According to Friedman (2003: 210) 'speakers of Turkic and Balkan languages have reported feeling the absence of a nonconfirmative (i.e. non-firsthand—A. Y. A.) verb form when speaking English', and he adds 'I have felt this same lack myself when I have returned to the US after spending several months in Macedonia'. Indians of the Vaupés area, when asked to translate into Portuguese what they had just said in one of their languages, complained that Portuguese was not good enough, and the elaborate expressions came out 'too short'.

Since lack of evidentials is perceived as a gap, speakers of contact languages are likely to 'make up' for it by using an array of lexical and other means. Evidentiality is pervasive in Andean languages—in numerous varieties of Quechua and Aymara. The local Spanish has come to mark evidentiality by reinterpreting certain tenses (Silver and Miller 1997: 262–3). The pluperfect in La Paz Spanish has an array of non-firsthand meanings while the preterite tends to be interpreted as 'firsthand' (see 4.8–9). If used with first person subject, the pluperfect acquires nuances of uncontrolled, unintentional, and accidental action. If the speaker had accidentally fallen asleep, they would say *Me había dormido*, with a pluperfect. If they had intentionally taken a siesta, they would say *Me he dormido* with the simple perfect (Laprade 1981). The non-firsthand pluperfect can also have overtones of surprise, marking a new, unexpected piece of information, or turn of events (see §6.3). With a first person subject, a 'non-firsthand pluperfect' has an overtone of accidental or unintentional action, as in 7.22. This is again in contrast to the present perfect which implies a volitional and intentional action (in 7.23). This is strikingly similar to the first person effect of non-firsthand evidentials discussed in §7.2. The 'first person effect' is not found in Quechua or Aymara; it is, however, an almost universal semantic development typical for a small evidentiality system and for a corresponding evidentiality strategy.

For the time being, such uses of pluperfect are evidential strategies rather than evidentials (since the pluperfect retains other functions unrelated to information source: see §4.2). Along similar lines, the present perfect in Ecuadorian Highland Spanish is developing an additional meaning of a non-firsthand evidential (Olbertz 2003; and also Bustamante 1991: 222–3, on how this phenomenon could have partly resulted from Quechua influence). The Spanish varieties influenced by Quechua and Aymara are in the process of developing a firsthand–non-firsthand (A1) evidentiality system out of their past tenses (this could be considered similar to how A1 systems were developed in Macedonian and Bulgarian in the Balkans).

These developments make the Andean and other Latin American varieties of Spanish markedly different from other 'Spanishes'. Misunderstandings often arise, usually without speakers realizing it (Silver and Miller 1997: 262); see §11.1.

Speakers of Vaupés Portuguese, whose mother tongue is an East Tucanoan language, use an array of lexical markers for different evidentiality specifications (Aikhenvald 2002: 315–16). Statements referring to information obtained visually are usually accompanied by a phrase *eu vi* 'I saw', or (if contrasted to something else) *eu tenho prova* 'I have proof', or, more rarely, *eu tenho experiência* ('I have experience'). Information obtained by hearing or by other sensory experience can be accompanied by *eu escutei* 'I heard' or *eu senti* 'I felt'. Talking about someone else, one could use third person (*ele viu* 'he saw', *ele sentiu* 'he felt', and so on). The way of marking inferred information is by saying *parece* 'it appears, it seems'. And *diz que* 'it is said that' is a conventional way of marking a reported evidential.

The formula *diz que* 'it is said' can be extended to cover all non-firsthand evidentiality specifications. Thus, an Indian who has read an announcement may talk about it using *diz que* (which sounds bizarre for speakers of Standard Portuguese, since for them this conveys a tinge of incredulity). The use of these expressions makes Vaupés Portuguese sound somewhat obsequious and hedging, and is often judged as weird by monolingual Brazilians from other areas. In Tariana, inferred evidentiality is used in translations and in rendering what one has just read. It sounds bizarre to native speakers of Standard Portuguese when an Indian who has just read an announcement about a football match in the Mission centre says: 'There is a football match on, it appears'. Silver and Miller (1997: 36–7) mention that if an outsider says, 'I'm from California', a Jaqi speaker would be likely to reply in Andean Spanish: 'You say you are from California'. For the Jaqi speaker this means simply stating the information source, but for the English-speaking outsider such a reply may sound offensive: they may feel they have been accused of lying. Similarly, overuse of 'lexical evidentials' by the Vaupés Indians usually does not impress the local non-Indians.

Speakers of Southern Paiute (Uto-Aztecan) and Verde Valley Yavapai (Yuman) face a similar problem when they communicate in English. Evidentials are obligatory in their own languages, and they do their best to express them in their English. However, they opt for a different solution (Bunte and Kendall 1981). When Paiute and Yavapai bilinguals converse among themselves in English, they simply add their native words with evidential meanings. A Paiute speaker would say *Minnie is pregnant ʔikm* or *The car's brakes need greasing ʔikm.* A Yavapai speaker would say *Calvin is going to Nevada* **aik** or *He's crying* **aik**.[18] Speakers are aware of this language mixing, and they do their best to avoid such insertions while speaking to Anglos. If non-indigenous people are present, they would use the nearest possible English equivalent—the phrase 'they say': *Minnie is pregnant* **they say** or *The car's brakes need greasing* **they say**. A Yavapai speaker would say *Calvin is going to Nevada* **they say** or *He's crying* **they say**. However, this 'literal translation' often results in miscommunication. The English speakers understand the Paiutes and the Yavapais to mean exactly what other speakers of standard English mean by the phrase. Their impression is that 'those Indians sure say "they say" a lot when they don't mean it'. This can be explained by the range of meanings *ʔikm* and *aik*. Both markers can be used in a variety of contexts, from hearsay (where they are equivalent to 'they say' in English) to inference. 'Now imagine that you are inside a house and you hear a crash and run outside to see a single person kneeling over the body of an unconscious child who has had some kind of accident involving a bicycle. You ask the person: "What happened?" He or she replies "He fell off his bike they say." This is very hard to process as normal English usage' (Bunte and Kendall 1981: 5). And it is hardly 'normal' English usage: the phrase 'they say' is a means to fill a gap in English, acutely felt by the first-language learners of Yavapai and Paiute.

How stable is evidentiality in contact languages? If the dominant language in the community—such as English or Portuguese—has no evidentials, the speakers will eventually have to assimilate to it, and lose their speech character-istics which are perceived as 'aberrant' by the more prestigious and dominant norm (see Joseph 2003: 315). As soon as speakers of Vaupés Portuguese acquire the standard language, they stop using lexical evidentials. In Andean Spanish the situation appears to be different: the evidential-type distinctions are part of the norm and not an exception (Silver and Miller 1997: 263; Bustamante 1991; Olbertz 2003). They are therefore best treated as an established feature of this variety of Spanish.

9.3 Evidentials and language obsolescence

Language obsolescence, whereby a language starts 'retreating, contracting, as it gradually falls into disuse' (Dixon 1991*b*: 199), is often associated with straight-forward language simplification and degeneration (e.g. Grinevald 1997). In actual fact language obsolescence is a complicated set of processes, mostly to do with the restructuring of an endangered minority language to fit in with

---

[18] Gavan Breen (p.c.) reports similar uses of the reported *kwele* in the English spoken by the Arrernte.

the patterns found in the majority language to which it gradually succumbs. The difference between language change in 'healthy' and in endangered or obsolescent languages often lies not in the SORTS of change, which may be, by and large, the same. Rather, it lies in the QUANTITY of change, and in the SPEED with which the obsolescent language changes (see Schmidt 1985: 213 on the Dyirbal language-death situation). Very few scholars have addressed the issue of the effects of language obsolescence on evidentiality systems. This is in sharp contrast with other grammatical categories, such as genders and classifiers, whose treatment in language obsolescence has been frequently discussed in the literature (see the overview in Aikhenvald 2000: §13.7.1).

Evidentials may become lost in language obsolescence. Nivkh once had a visual versus non-visual opposition in the apprehensive (preventive) mood (Gruzdeva 2001). Krejnovich (1934, 1979) worked on this language in the thirties when it was still actively spoken, and discussed this opposition at some length. The language is now severely endangered: speakers of Nivkh are shifting to Russian. By the time of Gruzdeva's work with Nivkh speakers, the visual versus non-visual opposition in apprehensives had been lost from the language.

A similar situation appears to obtain in Sm'algyax (Tsimshian). The traditional language once had a reported enclitic -gat (Boas 1911c: 348–9). Stebbins (1999), who worked with the remaining semi-speakers of the language in the 1990s, reports that this and a few modal enclitics were considered archaic and did not feature in her data. Further evidence in favour of the reduction of evidentiality systems comes from Selkup. Contemporary work on Selkup (Kuznetsova et al. 1980: 242) shows that the reported evidential (with a variety of meanings, from inference to reported speech) is expanding at the expense of the non-visual sensory evidential ('auditive'). Along similar lines, semi-speakers of Estonian in Australian immigrant communities do not seem to know how to use the 'reported' form. This could be considered concomitant to general morphological reduction characteristic of semi-speakers' competence.

We have seen, in §2.1 above, that Wintu drastically reduced its evidential system between the 1930s (when Dorothy D. Lee did her fieldwork) and the 1950s when Pitkin did his (Pitkin 1963: 105). The system of evidentials recorded by Dorothy D. Lee had five terms: visual; non-visual sensory, inferential based on logic, inferential based on personal experience, and reported (see 2.96 in §2.4). A system with just two choices—visual and reported—had survived in the spoken language by the time Pitkin did his fieldwork on the Wintu language in the 1950s (other evidentials were used just in narratives). The visual evidential replaced the non-visual in descriptions of one's feelings: talking about a headache in 1930 would have involved the non-visual sensory -$nt^h er(e)$, whereas a quarter of a century later the same statement involved a visual evidential; see 9.9 and 9.10 (Pitkin 1984: 150).[19]

Traditional Wintu

9.9   pʰoyoq   kuya·-binthida
        'I have a headache (I feel it)' (contains {nthere} 'non-visual sensory')

Innovative Wintu

9.10   pʰoyoq   kuya·   ʔibi·da
        'I have a headache ('(I vouch for it being entirely true on the basis of sen-
        sory evidence' (contains {be·} 'visual sensory')

The reduction of the evidential system involves restructuring rather than downright 'impoverishment'. In the traditional language, the visual evidential implied the strong personal responsibility of the speaker, thus being clearly associated with first person. By contrast, the reported evidential was almost a disclaimer of the speaker's responsibility for the truth of the statement. The change, from five evidentials to just two, implies that the category of evidence has been simplified. However, at the same time the category of person has become more elaborate. In the earlier system visual evidential was associated with the first person marker -*da*. In the later system, this marker acquired its place in the three-term person paradigm which grew to be separate from the evidentiality system. The evidentials which 'survived' were the most prominent ones: the visual, associated with full certainty, and the reported, with its opposite connotation of uncertainty. Thus, the system started shifting towards marking epistemic distinctions rather than evidentiality, independently of a newly acquired clear-cut three-person system. The shift may have occurred under pressure from English. This goes together with the fact that endangered languages tend to restructure their grammatical systems to 'match' those of the dominant majority language which is gradually replacing it.

As a result of language obsolescence, an evidential may become less frequent. We will see in §10.2.1 that evidentials can be an obligatory feature, or a token, of a narrative genre. When a language becomes obsolescent, speakers tend to forget narratives and the stylistic conventions associated with them; this is known as stylistic reduction (Aikhenvald 2002: 257). If an evidential was a salient feature of such a forgotten genre, it will cease to be used as often once the genre disappears. For instance, Tariana narratives about the travels of ancestors whose traces can be seen are marked with the assumed evidential. Younger people no longer know them; this results in reducing the overall frequency of this evidential.

---

[19] No interlinear gloss is given in the original; this is why the examples are not glossed.

9.4 Where do evidentials come from: a summary

Evidentials often come from grammaticalized verbs. The verb of 'saying' is a frequent source for reported and quotative evidentials, and the verb 'feel, think, hear' can give rise to non-visual evidentials in large systems. Closed word classes—deictics and locatives—may give rise to evidentials, in both small and large systems.

Evidentiality strategies involving past tenses and perfects, and nominalizations, can develop into small evidentiality systems (A1 and A2). The creation of a reported evidential may involve the reanalysis of subordinate clauses (typically, complement clauses of verbs of speech) as main clauses. Non-indicative moods and modalities may give rise to a term in a large evidentiality system; however, there are no examples of a modal system developing into a system of evidentials. This confirms the separate status of evidentiality and modality. Large evidential systems tend to be heterogenous in origin.

Evidentiality is a property of a significant number of linguistic areas. It is highly diffusible: languages acquire evidentials through contact, and also lose them when confronted by neighbouring languages with no evidentials. Categories, rather than forms, tend to be borrowed. Not infrequently, evidentials make their way into contact languages. Their stability then depends on whether or not a particular variety of a contact language becomes the norm.

When a language becomes obsolescent, it may lose its evidentials as part of its general simplification and readjustment to a dominant language. Alternatively, an erstwhile evidential system may get readjusted to the system in a dominant language, just as evidentials in Wintu have become reinterpreted as epistemic markers under the encroaching influence of English.

Evidentials Worldwide: Areal Distribution

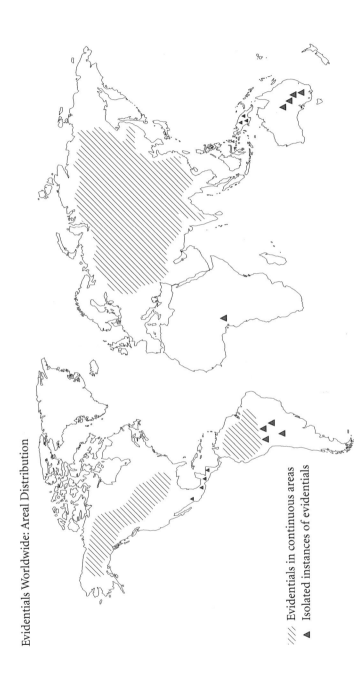

/// Evidentials in continuous areas
▲ Isolated instances of evidentials

NOTE TO THE MAP: The Purpose of this Map is to give a rough picture of the loci of major concentration of evidentials throughout the world. It is schematic because of the lack of precise information in many instances, and debatable interpretations of existing systems. A more precise map can only be done once we learn more about the types of systems in numerous languages of South and North America, Mexico, Eurasia (especially Tibeto-Burman speaking area), New Guinea, and Africa.

10

How to choose the correct evidential: evidentiality in discourse and in lexicon

In a language with grammatical evidentiality, an evidential value has to be selected. More often than not, evidence comes from a variety of sources. One can see and hear something at the same time. Once it is seen and heard, an inference can be made about it. With more than one option available, a problem arises—which evidential to use? The ways in which evidentials are chosen involve 'preferred evidentials'; see §10.1. Alternatively, a particular narrative genre may require a certain evidential. An unconventional and unexpected evidential is likely to produce an unusual effect. These issues are discussed in §10.2. The choice of an evidential may partly depend on the lexical class of a verb. There may be correlations between evidentials and the organization of the lexicon; see §10.3. Choices of evidentials dictated by genre requirements and verb subclasses tend to be obligatory, and may override the 'preferred evidential' hierarchy. These and other principles involved in choosing an evidential are summarized in §10.4.

10.1 Preferred evidentials

When relating an event in a language with obligatory evidentiality, the speaker has to select an evidential. What if the same event was seen and heard simultaneously? What if one has enough visual evidence to make an inference, and enough common sense for an assumption?

In all such cases, visually obtained information is preferred over any other information source. This means, in Janet Barnes's words (1984: 262), that 'it does not matter what evidence the speaker later sees or what information he receives; if, at any point, he saw or is seeing the state or event he reports it using a visual evidential'. The same applies to Tariana. When a drunken Makú man was bitten by a dog, Olívia—who was sitting next to the window—saw this happen and simultaneously heard the noise. She could have said 10.1 or 10.2; she chose 10.1 since to have seen something is more important than to have heard it.

Tariana

10.1 Valteir   ite   tʃinu   nihwã-**ka**   di-na
      Valteir   POSS+NCL:ANIM   dog   3sgnf+bite-REC.P.VIS   3sgnf-OBJ
      'Valteir's dog bit him' (VISUAL)

Olívia's brother José was sitting further away from the window; he heard the noise and commented on it using 10.2.

10.2 Valteir   ite   tʃinu   nihwã-**mahka**   di-na
      Valteir   POSS+NCL:ANIM   dog   3sgnf+bite-REC.P.NONVIS   3sgnf-OBJ
      'Valteir's dog bit him' (NON-VISUAL)

The bitten man came inside to show us his wound and José commented on his state saying 10.3 with a visual evidential (see similar examples in Barnes 1984: 263). José explained this usage to me saying that he could see the man was drunk, and could smell whiskey on his breath, plus his drunken behaviour was obvious enough (though he had not seen him drink). If it had been just the smell, he would have used non-visual evidential, but since sight was involved in obtaining evidence, he had chosen the visual evidential.

10.3 yanaka   di-kama-**ka**   diha   kayumaka
      whiskey   3sgnf-get.drunk-REC.P.VIS   he   this.is.why
      'He got drunk on whiskey, this is why (the dog bit him)' (VISUAL)

Another speaker did not have access to visual information but could observe the result—the traces of dog's teeth on the hand of the bitten man. He used the inferred evidential to comment. Having seen the visual result enabled him to use this form.

10.4 Valteir   ite   tʃinu   nihwã-**nihka**   di-na
      Valteir   POSS+NCL:ANIM   dog   3sgnf+bite-REC.P.INFR   3sgnf-OBJ
      'Valteir's dog bit him' (INFERRED)

A man who did not see any of it, but just heard the information from someone else, would use a reported evidential, as in 10.5.

10.5 diha   tʃinu   nihwã-**pidaka**   di-na
      the   dog   3sgnf+bite-REC.P.REP   3sgnf-OBJ
      'The dog bit him' (REPORTED)

It is not uncommon to talk about an event using the inferred evidential, as in 10.4, even if one acquired information through someone else, but had already seen sufficient evidence of it. In the situation described here, José's elder brother Jovino was not present at the scene; he was told about what had happened, and then observed the Makú man staggering along in the distance. This was good enough evidence for him to say 10.4 while telling the news to his other relative. We saw in §5.4.3 that the reported evidential in Tariana has an overtone of information one does not vouch for (since one does not have one's own evidence). As soon as any evidence is available, the inferred evidential is preferred since it implies access to some visually accessible information.

The assumed evidential would only be appropriate if the statement were based on no visual or other evidence, just a general assumption. When Jovino's relative heard the news, his reaction was 10.6—it is logical to assume that the Makú man must have been drunk. The Makú people do indeed drink a lot, and are perceived as somewhat inferior by most other Indians in the area.

10.6   di-kama-**sika**   diha   mẽdite-pu
        3sgnf-get.drunk-REC.P.ASSUM   he   useless + NCL:ANIM-AUG
        'He got drunk the useless one' (ASSUMED on basis of general knowledge)

The following hierarchy of preferred evidentials suggested for Tuyuca (Barnes 1984: 262–4) also works for Tariana:

DIAGRAM 10.1. Hierarchy of preferred evidentials in Tuyuca and Tariana

Visual < Non-visual < Inferred < Reported < Assumed

This reflects the primary importance of visual evidence, and firsthand evidence in general. One's own non-visual report (which means reporting an event or state that the speaker had heard, smelt, or tasted) is preferred to inferred, reported, or assumed, in this order. The inferred evidential, which implies inference on the basis of direct visual observation, is preferred to reported, and reported is preferred to assumed, which is used only when there is no information about the event and the speaker has to base their statement on a general assumption (prior knowledge about the state of affairs or general 'behaviour patterns'). If a speaker has access to direct evidence of something happening, he or she would prefer an inferred evidential. This is considered a better choice rather than reporting what they heard from someone else.

A hierarchy for the choice of preferred evidentials in Kashaya given by Oswalt (1986: 43) follows a similar principle: sensory evidence is given preference to all else; see Diagram 10.2. According to Oswalt, 'someone speaking of an act he himself is performing, or has performed, would not normally attribute knowledge of that event to a lower type of evidence'. Performative and factual-visual in Kashaya are only distinguished in the 'spontaneous' mode and merge in other modes (this is why they are in square brackets in Diagram 10.2).

DIAGRAM 10.2. Hierarchy of preferred evidentials in Kashaya

[Performative < Factual-visual] < Auditory < Inferential < Quotative

Similarly, in Maricopa (Gordon 1986*a*: 85), 'if an event is both seen and heard (probably, the most commonplace situation), then the sight evidential is used; the hearing evidential is used only when the event is witnessed but not seen'.

Diagrams 10.1–2 show that everything else being equal, the visual evidential is preferred as the functionally unmarked choice in these languages. We can recall, from §3.2.1, that the direct evidential may be considered functionally unmarked in Shipibo-Konibo (Valenzuela 2003: 37); when a speaker is asked to translate a sentence taken out of context, they are likely to use the direct evidential *-ra*. This goes together with a tendency to leave visual evidentials formally unmarked (see §3.2.2): vision is the default kind of perception.[1]

In a language with a small A1 system (firsthand versus non-firsthand), like Jarawara, or Yukaghir, the evidential is chosen depending on whether the event was witnessed or not. For instance, in 10.7 the speaker could not see the cartridges were inside the bag—this is why the non-firsthand evidential is used. In the second clause, he took them out—he could see this, and the firsthand occurs (similar examples are 2.1–2) (Dixon 2003: 169).

Jarawara

10.7 kataso   ka-foja-**ni**, . . .   o-wa-kiti
      cartridges(f) APPL-be.inside-IMM.P.NONFIRSTH.f 1sgA-APPL-take.out
      o-na-**hara**   o-ke
      1sg-LISTING.VERB-IMM.P.FIRSTH.f 1sg-DECL.f
      'The cartridges were inside (the bag) (NON-FIRSTHAND), I took them out
      (FIRSTHAND)'

Those who misuse an evidential get corrected. One morning Dixon went 'into the forest with a Jarawara friend and saw a tree which had just fallen over'. He tried to comment on this using the immediate past firsthand suffix, but was immediately corrected and told to say 10.8 (Dixon 2003: 178), since he himself did not SEE it fall.

10.8 awa   ka-so-**hani**-ke
      tree(f) APPL-fall-IMM.P.NONFIRSTH.f-DECLf
      'The tree has recently fallen down (and I did not see it fall)'

---

[1] We have no information on how competing sources of information are treated in other systems, or languages other than the ones discussed here.

If used on its own, a firsthand form implies seeing. As we noted in 2.2, the firsthand evidential can also cover something that is heard. However, in Jarawara this 'earwitness' sense is restricted to cases where an explicit noun (*ati*) refers to the noise. If this noun is absent, the speaker has a choice. They can use the non-firsthand, as in 10.9 (continuation of 2.2, where *ati* was present).

10.9   moto   ka-time-**no**
       motorboat(m)   be.in.motion-UPSTREAM-IMM.NONFIRSTH.m
       'The motorboat was coming upstream (although it could not yet be seen)'

Alternatively, they can use the firsthand, as in 10.10 where it was the dog, and more specifically, the dog's barking that woke the speaker.

10.10 owa   na-tafi-**are**-ka
       1sgO   CAUS-wake.up-IMM.P.FIRSTH.m-DECL.m
       'It (the dog's barking) did waken me'

Similarly, when the firsthand evidential refers to a 'smell', the word for smell must be present (see 10.30 below). But there is no noun for 'touch' to accompany a non-firsthand evidential describing what one can feel by touching. If one sees something, no word for 'sight' is required. That is, seeing something with one's eyes is the preferred interpretation for a firsthand evidential.

The non-firsthand evidential in Jarawara has overtones of surprise (as in 6.6). If such an effect is to be achieved, a non-firsthand evidential is preferred over a firsthand. Intrinsically uncontrollable events require non-firsthand—such as catching a cold (as in 7.5: in Jarawara, a bad cold FINDS one), or going to sleep, as in 7.6. Along similar lines, the hierarchies in Diagrams 10.1–2 operate with a proviso: any conventionalized choice of an evidential may take preference over the hierarchy. In Tariana and in Tucano dreams require a non-visual evidential (see §11.3). If a speaker had dreamt about a dog biting someone, 10.2 would have been the only option, no matter exactly what happened in the dream. And if they had been translating a story from Portuguese, they would have used the assumed evidential (typically used in translations: see §11.3). A preferred evidential as a genre marker in a narrative also precludes any further choices; see §10.2.1. Along similar lines, conversation-sustainer patterns illustrated in Diagram 3.1 offer speakers no choice as to what evidentials to use. Speech formulae discussed at the end of §10.3 are also fixed in the evidential choices they offer. In §10.4, we return to an overall hierarchy of evidential choices, as dictated by various conventions and the lexicon. Further principles of evidential choices determined by pragmatic and stylistic factors are addressed in the next section.

10.2 Evidentiality and discourse

Languages with obligatory evidentials develop conventions concerning evidentiality choices in discourse genres; see §10.2.1. In §10.2.2, we look at how manipulating evidentials produces additional stylistic effects.

10.2.1 *Evidentials and narrative conventions*

Evidentials are often conceptualized as genre markers, or 'tokens' of a narrative. There is then an expectation that a story describing a particular kind of knowledge will contain an established, conventionalized evidential. In A3 systems traditional stories about the creation of the world, the origin of humankind, animals, and so on, are typically cast in reported evidential (see Bloomfield 1962; Munro 1978; Güldemann 2001; Mithun 1999: 181–3 and many others). In Mparntwe Arrernte and in Yankunytjatjara, highly traditional and culturally significant Dreamtime stories have to contain the reported particle. The reported particle *di* in Kham (Watters 2002: 299–300) is widely used in folk tales, and must appear on the final verb in every sentence. The reported marker is associated with the entire genre, and not with individual statements: no speaker's choice is involved. Similar conventions abound in A3 systems; examples include Baniwa, Achagua, and Piapoco (North Arawak). The reported enclitic -*guuq* is typical of the traditional narrative genre in West Greenlandic (Fortescue 2003: 299). And in Potawatomi (Hockett 1948: 139), the reported evidential preverb 'is the mark of a certain style, namely that of story-telling and the like, in contrast to statements made about what has happened in reality to the speaker'.

Reported specification tends to be the unmarked choice for narratives in larger systems as well—examples are Bora and Shipibo-Konibo (Valenzuela 2003). Similarly, in Pawnee (C2: Parks 1972)—where the visual ('direct evidence') term is formally unmarked—the reported evidential prefix is generally used in folkloric texts. The same applies to narratives in Kashaya (Oswalt 1986: 41), in Wintu (Schlichter 1986: 49), and in Qiang (LaPolla, p.c.).

If the evidentiality choice is linked to a choice made in a tense system, or if evidentiality marking is fused with tense, the combination of a tense plus an evidential marker becomes a typical feature of a narrative. In Estonian, past reported is a salient feature of folk tales and legends. A typical beginning of a folk tale is *elanud kord* (live-PAST.REP(=PAST.PART) time), which sounds as formulaic as 'once upon a time' (cf. 4.16) (see Tuldava 1994: 262 and Wälchli 2000).[2] A similar formula, containing the non-firsthand evidential, is the

---

[2] The formulaic nature of this expression gives special flavour to Künnap's discussion (1992) of the origins of evidentiality systems across the Uralic family: the formula is in the title of his article.

standard beginning of Turkish fairy tales: *bir var-mış, bit yok-miş* (one be-NONFIRSTH not.be-NONFIRSTH) 'there was and there was not' (Bulut 2000: 161; Johanson 1971: 79–80; also see Johanson 2003: 287). Traditional stories in Tuyuca are couched in remote past reported. In Jarawara traditional tales normally employ far past non-firsthand, and about 90 per cent of the occurrences of these are followed by the reported suffix (Dixon 2004).

In languages with A2 and A1 systems, the non-firsthand is typically employed in traditional stories and in folklore (cf. Lazard 1999; Donabédian 2001; and the papers in Guentchéva 1996). In Meithei (Tibeto-Burman: Chelliah 1997: 224) the non-firsthand marker is used for 'the narration of past events'. In Macedonian the non-firsthand ('non-confirmative') *l*-past is the usual tense for folk tales (Friedman 2003: 207). The narrative can switch into the firsthand ('confirmative') for 'vividness', and this may result in striking effects (see §10.2.2). In Yukaghir, the non-firsthand is commonly used in historical and mythological narratives (Maslova 2003: 231). In Godoberi (Kibrik et al. 1996: 255–78) the non-firsthand evidential is used in ancestors' stories.

Different kinds of stories may require different narrative conventions. In Tariana, Tucano, and Desano, folk tales and animal stories are typically cast in remote past reported evidential. (This similarity is part of an overall convergence in all aspects of evidential usage in the Vaupés linguistic area.) Example 10.11, from Tariana, is the typical beginning of an animal story.

Tariana
10.11   pa:-piu-**pidana**   paita   neri
        one-CL:TIME-REM.P.REP   one+NUM.CL:ANIM   deer
        'Once upon a time there was a deer' (REPORTED)

The assumed evidential is employed in stories about events in Tariana history based on recoverable evidence—such as caves and stones that the ancestors left behind.[3] A very similar use of assumed evidential was reported for Desano (Miller 1999: 67). Example 10.12 comes from the origin story which describes how Indians and White people came about. The assumed evidential is then used.

10.12   di-yeda   na-miña-**sina**   yalana
        3sgnf-downstream   3pl-emerge-REM.P.ASSUM   White.people
        di-yekwe-se   wha   yeposana   wa-miña-**sina**
        3sgnf-upstream-LOC   we   Indians   1pl-emerge-REM.P.ASSUM
        'White people emerged from downstream, we Indians emerged from upstream'

[3] An inferred evidential in systems of other kinds may be used differently. In Xamatauteri, the inferred evidential frequently occurs at the end of myths and legends, indicating that the information 'has not been verified by the narrator' (Ramirez 1994: 317).

Narratives involving narrators' personal experiences are cast in remote past visual, as shown in 10.13.

10.13   nuha   nu-emhani-**na**   Wepi-se
        I   1sg-go.around-REM.P.VIS   Wepi-LOC
        'I went around in the area of Wepi river'

Types of experience stereotyped as 'unseen'—such as encounters with evil spirits, or dreams—are cast in non-visual. Example 10.14 comes from a long description of a dream about a plane trip. Every verb is marked with the non-visual evidential (independently of person: the first verb in 10.14 takes first person subject, while the second verb is third person).

10.14   nese-nuku   nuha   nu-sadu   nu-enipe-tupe
        then-TOP.NON.A/S   I   1sg-wife   1sg-children-DIM:PL
        waka-**mhana**   karakawhya   di-uka-**mhana**
        1pl+arrive-REM.P.NONVIS   plane   3sgnf-arrive-REM.P.NONVIS
        'Then I, my wife and my small children, we arrived (at the airport: in my dream), the plane arrived (in my dream)'

This can be viewed as a type of evidential convention. If an account of a dream occurs within a traditional story cast in reported evidential, the dream will also be cast in the reported evidential. That is, overall narrative conventions override the particular conventionalized evidentials chosen for various types of experience. Further evidential requirements for varied types of experience will be discussed in §11.3. Diagram 10.3, in §10.4, shows the hierarchy of conventionalized evidential choices.

The inferred evidential has a particular rhetorical force in story-telling: it is used if one has enough visible evidence for a claim. Jones and Jones (1991: 87) report the same use of the inferred for Barasano, an East Tucanoan language spoken in the same area as Tariana, also with a five-term evidentiality system.

Salar displays intricate patterns of interaction between the non-firsthand evidential and the unmarked form in different genres (Dwyer 2000: 52–7). The non-firsthand is the default choice in narratives (but an unmarked form can be used for a sudden change of state; see §10.2.2 on further alternations between firsthand and non-firsthand, to do with the foregrounding and backgrounding of information). In formulaic wedding speeches the firsthand is preferred. The less conventionalized the discourse, the more freedom speakers have to choose between firsthand and non-firsthand: it is in conversations that context-sensitive choices are usually made.

Connotations of an evidential may depend on a genre. When the reported evidential is a 'token' of a narrative genre, it has no epistemic overtones, as in

Mparntwe Arrernte (see §5.4.3). In Arizona Tewa, semantic differences between the use of evidentials in traditional stories and in everyday speech go together with subtle contrasts in their morphosyntax.

The evidential particle *ba* in Arizona Tewa marks a genre of traditional stories. In the everyday language, this particle (Kroskrity 1993: 144–63; 1998: 27–8) is often used to disclaim firsthand knowledge on the part of the speaker: the narrator is simply 'speaking the past', repeating 'prior text'. Unlike in everyday speech, *ba* in traditional Pueblo narratives assumes the role of 'genre-marker'. Example 10.15 is a typical example of multiple occurrence of *ba*.

Arizona Tewa

10.15 'ihaedám **ba,** huwa **ba,** wi' huwa 'i-wínu-di   **ba,**
then:FOC   EV   again EV   one again 3sgREFL-stand-SUB   EV
dí-khaw-kaenu
3plACTIVE-sing-start
'And then (*ba*) so, again so (*ba*), as one stood up again so (*ba*), they started to sing'

A 'non-narrative rendering' of such a sentence would simply eliminate all but one of the occurrences of *ba*. This narrative convention was probably influenced by similar patterns of the multiple use of the evidential particle *yaw* in Hopi, an unrelated language spoken in the same area (Kroskrity 1998: 30–1; see §9.2). Along similar lines, in West Greenlandic, where the 'heavy use' of the reported particle *-guuq* is a property of traditional stories, this particle often occurs more than once 'for stylistic rather than informational purposes' (Fortescue 2003: 299).

The reported evidential *-shi* is widely used in Quechua folk tales as a genre token. Even when consultants made up their own original stories, they marked them with reportative. This evidential also occurs in conversations if the information was acquired from someone else; however, the marking is different. Floyd (1999: 135) reports that a conversational text of some 245 sentences contained only sixteen occurrences of the reported evidential. The reason for this could be a tendency to avoid redundancy: once the information source has been established, speakers do not repeat the evidential in every sentence. In folk tales, however, evidentials occur in every sentence. The difference in how the reported evidential is used in folk tales and in conversation reflects the basic difference in its function as an indicator of a genre, or as an individual choice referring to a particular verbal report.

The reported evidential in Sochiapan Chinantec is pervasive in fables and legends. It typically occurs near the beginning. It also appears 'at points of climax in the storyline' (Foris 2000: 375). This use is similar to the commentative function of the non-firsthand evidential in Abkhaz; see §10.2.2.

Alternatively, the very absence of a reported evidential may indicate the climax in a story. The reported evidential clitic *-ku'ut* in Cupeño (Hill 2005: 459–68) is a genre-defining feature of traditional narratives (see Example 7 in the Appendix to Chapter 6). It is absent when 'the context is in the "build to peak" of an episode, often at moments of highest tension in the narrative'.

Narrative conventions as to the use of evidentials vary from language to language. In Wintu (Schlichter 1986: 49), the reported evidential does not have to be suffixed to every verb in a story (unlike other evidentials, or, as it appears, the same evidential when used outside such stories). A sentence like 10.16 establishes the frame for the whole story.

Wintu

10.16   le·ndada   suke   kila**ke**
         long.ago   stand   COND.AUX + REP
         'Long ago they lived' (I am told) (frequently used to begin a myth)

The reported evidential does not have to occur at the end of a narrative, since there is a set of fixed expressions to finish a story, thus 'completing' the frame. Other evidentials may be used within a text to refer to evidence 'adduced' by participants. Similar conventions have been noted in Eastern Pomo folk tales (McLendon 1982).

The use of reported evidential as a marker of a narrative genre is by no means universal. Typical verb forms used in myths and folk tales in Nganasan are evidentiality-neutral. The reported evidential ('renarrative': Gusev forthcoming: 3, 11) is restricted to narratives describing something that the narrator learnt from particular people, most often the narrator's ancestors. This evidential is also used by a shaman recounting what spirits had told him. Unlike in many other languages, the use of reported evidential presupposes the existence of a firsthand information source.

Neither is the reported marker used in traditional stories in Warlpiri (Laughren 1982, and p.c.). The reason is quite different from Nganasan. The reported marker *nganta* in Warlpiri 'implies uncertainty and doubt on the part of the speaker' (Mary Laughren, p.c.): since in story-telling speakers usually emphasize the veracity of the story, this would be incompatible with using *nganta*. This is in stark contrast to a number of other Australian languages, such as Mparntwe Arrernte and Yankunytjatjara, where the reported evidential is used as a narrative genre-marker, notwithstanding its overtones of 'unreliability'; see §5.4.3. In Cree/Montagnais/Naskapi (Algonquian languages) the non-firsthand evidential has a primarily inferential meaning, and is not a genre token (see James, Clarke, and Mackenzie 2001: 247–8 for an explanation). In Tsez firsthand past is used in the body of traditional texts, probably comparable to the historic present for past narration in English (Bernard Comrie, p.c.).

The frequency of an evidential may simultaneously correlate with genre and with the sex of a speaker. As mentioned in §8.5, female speakers of Salar tend to use more non-firsthand forms than male speakers. In narratives told by women, even direct quotations are cast in non-firsthand, while men favour the firsthand form (Dwyer 2000: 57). Partly, this has to do with what the stories told by men and by women are about. Men often talk about important things like history and legends, which 'they may have perceived as relatively factual, direct, and based on reliable information'—hence the preference for firsthand. In contrast, women tend to tell 'tales of fantasy, which they in turn may have perceived as so far beyond immediate experience' that they have to be couched in non-firsthand. This could well be due to the existing cultural stereotypes and the conventionalized perception of stories and narratives.

Different kinds of stories are told by different groups of people in other parts of the world. None of the Tariana women I ever worked with considered herself knowledgeable enough to tell a story about the ancestors (which would have to be cast in remote past assumed evidential). In contrast, anyone could tell an animal story, or any other folk tale (cast in remote past reported). Salar appears to add a further complication: even when men tell fairy tales, they still use more firsthand forms than do women; conversely, when women talk about local history, they use more non-firsthand forms than men would. One can hypothesize that this has to do with assertiveness and authority associated with the firsthand evidential on the one hand, and the conventional 'macho' stereotypes of the Salar culture (in the same vein as further correlations between cultural stereotypes and evidentials discussed in §10.3). This is a topic for future exploration.

The narrative conventions described here reflect the conceptualization of a link between an evidential and traditional knowledge. The ways in which evidentials become conventionalized largely depend on different kinds of cultural experience, both traditional and newly introduced. The assessment of the evidential status for a particular statement in discourse is 'a culturally mediated statement that no doubt also reflects immediate communicative needs and contextual factors' (Beier et al. 2002: 133). These requirements dictated by context and by tradition coexist with grammaticalized rules and lexical conventions (summarized in §10.4). How evidentials reflect the conceptualization of different kinds of cultural experience is discussed in §11.3.

10.2.2 *Manipulating evidentials in discourse*

When an evidential is used in an unexpected way, this achieves a stylistic effect, backgrounding or foregrounding the speaker's participation or the information itself.

In small systems of A1 and A2 types, manipulating evidentials in discourse is linked to a speaker's perspective (see the discussion in Lazard 1996, and 1999: 93–6): when speakers choose the non-firsthand term, they choose to talk about the event 'mediately . . . without specifying how it happened, and in doing so they are placing themselves, so to speak, at a distance from what they are saying'. We have seen that in many small systems, the non-firsthand evidential often has a 'distancing' effect. When the speaker chooses to relate their personal experience—for which the non-firsthand or the reported ought to be unacceptable—they make a point of presenting themselves as an outside observer, rather than a participant.[4] This distancing effect is independent of existing narrative conventions. In 10.17, from Salar, a non-firsthand evidential is used to mark the speaker's personal experience. This is an answer given by a ninety-year-old woman interviewed by a younger Salar man whom she had not previously met; the man asks her whether or not she used to cover her head many years ago when she was young. The woman responds using the non-firsthand: she did so in order to distance herself from the old-time practice, possibly because most Salar women nowadays consider it shameful not to cover their head (Dwyer 2000: 51–2).

Salar

10.17   daxən   **ixua**
    wear   NOT+NONFIRSTH
    'No, we didn't wear (the veil)'

In 5.66, from Warlpiri, a reported evidential is used in a similar way: here, it implies not just distancing, but mistrust (the old villain pretends to be blind—and this is marked with *nganta* 'reported'). Other, similar examples, involving different genres, are 5.8 from Cree/Montagnais/Naskapi—here a little girl says 'I think she told me to go to school' (but she is not really sure)—and the discussion of Pastaza Quechua below (also see Leinonen 2000: 429, for similar examples from Komi, and Tatevosov 2001*b* and Maisak and Tatevosov 2001 on Bagvalal, and Tatevosov and Maisak 1999*a, b* on Tsakhur). In Abkhaz, folkloric texts are introduced with a non-firsthand form 'signalling the fact that the narrator heard the story from somebody else and does not vouch for its actual truth' (Chirikba 2003: 255). There is thus a distinct semantic overlap between the distancing function of an evidential and its epistemic extension to cover information one does not really vouch for.

In its 'distancing' function, the non-firsthand evidential may serve to differentiate backgrounded and foregrounded information, that is, distingushing

---

[4] In various studies on Caucasian languages within the Russian tradition, this phenomenon is known as 'effect otstranenija', literally, the effect of moving away.

what is concomitant rather than vital to the main thread of a story, as in Cree/Montagnais/Naskapi (Drapeau 1996). In Abkhaz, an aside comment is cast in a non-firsthand evidential. Example 10.18 comes from a story about a man who gained power over a mermaid by cutting off and hiding a lock of her hair. Throughout the story, the verb forms are evidentiality-neutral until the narrator remarks that in fact the man's little daughter had seen where the father had hidden the mermaid's hair. This 'aside' is marked with the non-firsthand (Chirikba 2003: 247–8).

Abkhaz

10.18   a-x°ɔč̆''ə   jə-l-ba-**zaap'**
        ART-child   it-she-see-NONFIRSTH1
        'The child, as it turned out, saw it'

This background information turns out to be crucial: the mermaid tricks the child into telling her where the lock is hidden, gets it, kills the child, and disappears.

Manipulating firsthand and non-firsthand evidentials is a prominent stylistic device in the languages of the Balkans. The non-firsthand past tense is the unmarked choice for a Macedonian folk tale. The narrative may switch into the firsthand for 'vividness'. The firsthand past can also be used for well-established historical facts; but its abuse may produce a negative reaction. A striking example of how the choice of an evidential affects the perception of the text by the readers comes from comments on a book on Alexander the Great by Vasil Tupurkovski, a Macedonian politician. Friedman (2003: 207) reports that many Macedonians 'saw the book as a nationalist ploy' and criticized the excessive use of the firsthand (confirmative) past. The effect of an 'overuse' of these forms 'was felt to be bombastic, as if he were trying to present himself as the direct heir of Alexander the Great'. Macedonian newspapers even have 'house styles' which differ in their evidential choices: a relatively independent paper uses far more non-firsthand forms than one which is government owned. In Albanian internet news reports, the non-firsthand ('admirative') is used only if the author wishes to cast doubt on the information (such as accusations and other items from Serbian sources).

Similarly, in Yukaghir, if a story is told in non-firsthand the narrator may switch to firsthand form for a couple of episodes, 'most often when the speaker goes into vivid details of some episode (as if they were an actual witness of the situation)' (Maslova 2003: 232). Johanson (2003: 287) mentions the 'discourse-propulsive' functions of non-firsthand evidentials in various Turkic languages. In Turkish, the non-firsthand evidential 'covers high degrees of focality, including cases where a property of a subject is focussed on' (Johanson 2000*a*: 75; and also see Bulut 2000: 161, on the correlations between focality and the non-firsthand evidential in Kurmanji Kurdish). The non-firsthand evidential in Abkhaz is often used as a way of focusing on any activity (witnessed or not: Chirikba 2003: 255–6).

Manipulating evidentials in systems with three or more terms also serves various pragmatic functions. Unexpected evidentiality choices in Quechua may be made to achieve additional discourse effects. A number of pragmatic implications of the direct evidential in Quechua were discussed in §5.2.1. Example 10.19 comes from a story cast in reported evidential, about how the speaker's father got a deformed foot; halfway through the narrative, the speaker says 10.19, with the direct evidential. This information was obviously not obtained by her through personal experience of any sort. The direct evidential here indicates that the rest of the story presents a true and valid reason for the deformity.

Quechua

10.19   Chay-pii-**mi**   papaa-nii-si   chraki   palta-n
         this-ABL-DIR.EV   father-1p-ALSO   foot   palm-3sg
         nana-y-ta   allayku-yku-la . . .
         ache-INF-ACC   begin-ASP-PAST
         'This is why/when the sole of my father's foot started aching . . . '

The direct evidential does not imply that the speaker observed the event personally: within the context of the story, it suggests the speaker's personal corroboration of the fact stated. A speaker can even use direct evidential to impose their conviction upon others. A man who has been accused of having fathered a child denies this vehemently, and says:

10.20   mana-**m**   chay   ya'a-pa-chu
         not-DIR.EV   that   I-GEN-NEG
         'That [the child] is not mine'

The man should have used inferred evidential, since the identity of the child's father is, strictly speaking, a matter of inference (Floyd 1999: 73). An inferred evidential would have left open the possibility of the man actually being the father. The direct evidential does not allow any such alternative.

The ways in which evidentials are used in Quechua accounts of community history illustrate a similar point. In an account of the foundation of his home town, a speaker used the direct—rather than the reported—evidential in almost every clause (Floyd 1999: 70). However, the speaker could not have seen or otherwise witnessed any of it since it all happened before his lifetime. The direct evidential is used throughout the whole text, and not just in an aside (as in 10.19). Its effect is not so much stressing the validity of the information, or the speaker's certainty that this is right; rather, the direct evidential makes the whole account sound personal. As suggested by Floyd (1989), 'the community and its history are construed as metaphorical extensions of the speaker's own personal domain'. 'The speaker's strong personal association with his community outweighs the fact that the story is technically second-hand information' (Floyd 1999: 71–2). The facts—learnt through someone else— acquire a high degree of 'psychological proximity' (using a term from Slobin and Aksu-Koç 1982: 196), so that they become an integral part of speaker's own cultural experience and inherent knowledge. The original 'prompt' for the narrative, the question under 10.21, supports this hypothesis. The person is being asked about their own experience—the use of the direct evidential in a question presupposes one in the answer (see discussion in §8.1.1, and 8.6).

Wanka Quechua

10.21 ima-nuy-**mi**   piwas-pa   mila-y-nin   ka-la
       what-SIM-DIR   Piwas-GEN   increase-NOMN-3p   be-PAST
       'What is the history of Piwas?' (literally: How did the increase of (the
       village of) Piwas occur?': Willem Adelaar, p.c.)

Thus, a narrative cast in the direct evidential presupposes the speaker's personal involvement which may be just as good as personal experience. This is corroborated by further instances. A story about a condor fiesta was couched in the reported evidential—the reason for this being that the fiesta is no longer celebrated in the way reported, and is thus foreign to the speaker's experience. In Floyd's words (1999: 72), the reported *-sh(i)* 'capitalises on the inherent "other-ness" of the reportative construal'. There has, however, to always be a culturally appropriate justification for marking the experience as 'personal' and thus employing the direct evidential. Those who overuse it are at risk of losing their credibility; see §11.4, and the quote from Weber (1986: 142) there.

The 'self' versus 'other' contrast has been shown to be important in constru- ing narratives in Pastaza Quechua (Nuckolls 1993). The choice of an evidential specification in a narrative often depends on the perspective of the speaker. The choice between the reported *-shi* and the direct *-mi* may have to do with the speaker's point of view. Telling about a type of tree bark whose resin can be used to relieve toothaches, a speaker reported what someone else had told her: that the foam from the resin kills worms living inside the teeth. She used *-mi* in a statement about a foam that emerges, marking her own assertion. Since someone else told her about the worms, she used the reported in the statement 'It kills-reported the worms in the teeth'. The use of reported does not imply any doubt of the statement—it simply states that the speaker is not the author. In narratives, the alternation between *-shi* and *-mi* is indicative of a shift in perspective. If an event is represented from the perspective of the speaker, they would use the direct *-mi*. The reported *-shi* could be used 'as a way of focusing an assertion from someone else's perspective', to distance oneself from the event (Nuckolls 1993: 249).

In Huarochirí texts—the oldest known source written in Quechua—manipulating evidentials is also a stylistic device. The link between the narrative type and the evidential choice is transparent. The reportative suffix 'characterises a genre of story-like texts removed from the narrator in time and frequently situated in a non-defined space; the characters often belong to the mythical sphere'. This suffix also 'serves to mark events that happened in a not very remote past connected with historical persons, or events not witnessed by the narrator'. In contrast, the visual *-mi* is typical of personal accounts and 'of a descriptive genre of rituals and ceremonies'. It is also used 'in connection with certain supernatural beings, probably marking their integration into human lived experience' (Dedenbach-Salazar Sáenz 1997b: 164).

Just as in Pastaza Quechua, the choice between the direct and the reported evidential may have to do with the narrator's stance. In Dedenbach-Salazar Sáenz's words (1997b: 153–4), 'whenever the narrator takes an explicit position in a story—that is, when he comments on what he has told', he changes from the reported to the direct evidential. By switching to the direct evidential, the narrator 'gives a personalised presentation of the event' (Howard-Malverde 1988: 128). The narrator's familiarity with the spatial location of the narrated events also influences the choice of evidential: the direct evidential often occurs in descriptions of geographical features and socio-political divisions of the region. Space, and familiarity with it, are thus important dimensions of the personal witness category involved in the choice of the direct evidential.

In other words manipulating evidentials allows the narrator of the Huarochirí texts to express their personal knowledge or ignorance and degree of participation in the event, 'thereby conveying some information about how he wants to be seen by the addressee' (Dedenbach-Salazar Sáenz 1997b: 159).

The choice made in the evidentiality system correlates with the narrator's attitude towards the information. The narrator 'automatically uses the appropriate evidentiality suffix to testify his personal knowledge or ignorance of a phenomenon; on the other hand, he employs this linguistic means in order to deny or confirm his knowledge of certain events he relates, thereby conveying some information about himself and about how he wants to be seen by the addressee' (Dedenbach-Salazar Sáenz 1997b: 159). For instance, the narrator tends to use the 'direct' (visual) evidential *-mi* to describe feasts and rites which he seems to have witnessed; but he switches to reported *-si* 'to deny personal knowledge of' 'barbarian' customs; that is, 'in order to document the non-witnessing of an event and/or to deny having witnessed it' (Dedenbach-Salazar Sáenz 1997*b*: 160). The detailed analysis of the use of evidentials in this text shows 'a combination of the evidential aspect (how the narrator obtained his knowledge) with the validational aspect (the narrator's commitment with respect to the truth of the narrated account)'. Artful use of evidentials creates the effect of polyphony—'there is more than one voice to be heard'. The narrator may be different from 'the commentator who puts the story into the overall framework of the collection, and may be different again from a redactor who may have been responsible for putting the texts together and writing them down' (Dedenbach-Salazar Sáenz 1997*b*: 164).

We can thus establish a link between evidential use, conventionalized types of knowledge, and the narrator's experience and the perspective he wishes to take with regard to the event. Along similar lines, the assertiveness of a speech by a warrior ancestor in a Kalapalo story discussed by Basso (1990: 137) is reflected in his choice of evidentials: the most assertive and imposing part is marked with distant past firsthand evidential (p. 140), and 'the tone is something like, "I bear witness"'.

Similarly to Quechua, the direct (visual) evidential in Eastern Pomo narratives is a way of making a passage particularly dramatic by emphasizing one's personal experience. We saw in 2.75 ('they stole it: direct evidential') that the direct evidential in Eastern Pomo has epistemic overtones of certainty. A speaker may use the visual evidential to emphasize the direct knowledge they had of an event. In Ralph Holder's retelling of his grandfather's account of the visit of the McKee expedition to Clear Lake in California to negotiate a treaty, almost every verb is suffixed with the reported evidential—this is typical for a story learnt from someone else (McLendon 2003: 107–8). Towards the end, Ralph Holder describes how his grandfather—then a teenager—was attacked by a jealous white man and how he fought him to a bloody draw. Then his grandfather ran to McKee's camp, where the soldiers met him. The speaker describes this passage using the direct evidential:

Eastern Pomo
10.22   bá-ya   xól-dí-yaki-qan
        there-LOC   fire.towards-bring-PL.AGENT-then.SWITCH.REF
        mi·kʰí-yi'=kʰi   té·tel-a . . .
        McKee-PATIENT=3AGENT   tell-DIR.EV
        'Then [the soldiers] brought him to camp [i.e. where the fire is] and he
        told McKee . . . [what the white man had done to him]'

The direct evidential here emphasizes the direct knowledge Ralph Holder has of what had happened to his grandfather. In addition, the direct evidential here 'is clearly dramatically effective': it highlights a climactic event—whereby a native teenager did a particularly brave thing, going right into the camp of powerful and dangerous strangers and telling their boss how one of his soldiers had attacked him. McKee's response is also cast in direct evidential, to emphasize the intentionality of his actions. He says: 'I'm going around teaching/instructing people . . . [to be good, to get along]' (direct evidential).

The double marking of information source in Eastern Pomo was discussed in §3.5. In 3.27 ('then he started to walk out, it is said (the old man villain, who is blind, heard the hero start to walk out)'), the non-visual sensory evidential -*ink'e* reflects the information source of the protagonist (the blind old villain who could only hear the hero walk out). The reported suffix -*le* marks the narrative as a genre; this is the evidential typically used in traditional narratives. The co-occurrence of non-visual sensory with the reported evidential reflects the multiple voices within the narrative: in McLendon's words (2003: 113), 'it takes the listener inside the narrative action, giving the performance drama and realism, just as the use of direct quotes allows the narrator to take on different voices or speech mannerisms for each character, turning a narrative performance into something more like a play or a novel'. When the inferred evidential occurs together with the reported, the opposite effect ensues, 'drawing the listener's attention to the speaker's feelings (or reservations) about the narrative action'.

We have seen that evidentials are frequently a feature of a genre. Deviations from a conventionalized pattern of evidential use create an additional effect. This may convey the narrator's standpoint, or reflect the polyphonic nature of the narrative.

Cross-linguistic conventions as to how evidentials are used in day-to-day communication—which is less regimented than, say, traditional stories—have been studied in much less detail than evidentials as genre tokens. The reported evidential is not appropriate as a direct response to the addressee (there is no reason to inform the addressee that what they have just said is secondhand information). In Huallaga Quechua, the inferred evidential never initiates a conversation (Weber 1986: 143–52). It is often employed as a challenge, and may have the rhetorical force of a negative, sarcastic, haughty, or flippant remark (see Example 5.29: 'Am I to go-inferred—surely not!'). The inferred evidential has overtones of irony and sarcasm in B1, B2, and B4 systems (see 5.30 ('this is how you are supposed to learn-inferred—by not going to school!') from Wanka Quechua). The reported evidential can also be used this way, as in Shipibo-Konibo (5.72: 'It is said that this month the president will raise your salary. Go see it!' (I am sure this is not true)), Arrernte (5.63: 'I am supposed to have killed him' (I am reported to have killed him; I didn't), and Warlpiri (5.70: 'She is beautiful indeed! As if she is beautiful!'). The assumed evidential in Tariana may bear overtones of incredulous response. When Leo Brito found himself a wife, a Cubeo woman whose language he did not know, his relatives reacted to the news with an incredulous *Kaya-sika* (thus-REC.P.ASSUM) 'This is so then'.

In small systems, the non-firsthand evidential may have connotations of irony or sarcasm (mentioned by Chirikba 2003: 255, for Abkhaz). The non-firsthand evidential in Armenian often has overtones of mild irony mixed with reproach (Donabédian 2001: 425–6 calls this 'argumentative' value). A mother-in-law comments on her daughter-in-law whom she has just seen asleep in the afternoon.

Armenian

10.23   Paṙk-**ac**   ē
        lie.down-NONFIRSTH   be-3sg
        'She is lying down' (understood: it's shocking how lazy she is)

Donabédian (2001: 432–9) demonstrates that about 30 per cent of utterances marked with the non-firsthand evidential in a corpus of spoken Armenian have the 'argumentative value' of reproach tinged with irony or contrastive value. They typically go against what the other person has just said. The evidential is employed as a way of arguing, and not solely indicating the information source.

The choice of an evidential in spontaneous speech may depend on the genre. It may create a special stylistic effect, be it distancing, or making the narrative more vivid, backgrounding or foregrounding some piece of information, or producing an aside comment, or an ironic remark. As Aksu-Koç and Slobin (1986) pointed out for Turkish, the interpretation of an utterance out of context may be ambiguous. An example of the multiple interpretation of a non-firsthand evidential comes from Donabédian (2001: 425), from a novel.

Armenian

10.24   norēn   č'očowx   mə   ownec'-**er**   es?
        again   child   ART.INDEF   have-NONFIRSTH   AUX.2sg
        '(Petros silences him and says with feigned serenity: 'So, Hratch, tell me is this the kind of thing one does?') You've had another child: NON-FIRSTHAND'

The context suggests the interpretation of the evidential as ironic or reproachful; but it could also be inference or hearsay. As Gumperz (1982: 330) pointed out, 'any single utterance is always subject to multiple interpretations'. Taken out of context, an evidential can be interpreted in many ways, and its semantics presented as a continuum of values, with the non-firsthand information source being the default one.

Evidentials can be conventionalized in other ways. Their use as 'conversation sustainers' in the languages of the Vaupés area was discussed in §8.1.1 above.

Similarly, in Hixkaryana, one of the strategies for feedback in conversation (called 'echo responses') consists in repeating one or more elements of the speaker's sentence, followed by the 'deduction' particle (Derbyshire 1985: 72).

Languages with an evidentiality strategy often also manipulate it in discourse in order to highlight some kinds of information and background other kinds. Vlach Romani has two pasts—one which goes back to an adjectival past participle 'denoting a state which is the result of an action' (Matras 1995: 98), the other (the inflected preterite) 'referring to the action itself and its agent'. Matras (1995) shows how these are used to manipulate the information in discourse. The non-firsthand participle is used to mark information for which 'the speaker needs to resort to circumstantial evidence in order to maintain assertive authority' (p. 104), while the inflected form is used 'as if speaker and hearer were witnessing' the activity. The non-firsthand forms are also used in pre-planned discourse to prepare 'the immediate information background', consolidating 'interactional authority' (p. 118).

Perfect as an evidentiality strategy in Georgian can also be used with overtones of irony and sarcasm, similarly to non-firsthand evidentials (Boeder 2000: 289; cf. Chirikba 2003: 255, for Abkhaz). Along similar lines, the perfect in Georgian is often used in narratives, indicating that the speaker follows a tradition (Boeder 2000: 290) which is similar to using a non-firsthand evidential to indicate the narrative type or genre.[5]

This goes together with the general semantic similarities between small evidentiality systems and evidentiality strategies, and is further confirmed by a historic link between them.

10.3 Evidentials and the lexicon

Evidentials can interrelate with the lexicon in several ways. The choice and the meaning of an evidential may depend on the lexical class of a verb. Fixed expressions can allow restricted evidentiality choices. How all these interrelate with evidentials and narrative conventions is the topic of the next section.

I. EVIDENTIALS AND VERB CLASSES
We have seen throughout the preceding chapters that certain classes of verbs may require certain evidentiality choices. Verbs of 'internal states' which cover

---

[5] Lexical expressions with the meaning 'it seems' may develop overtones similar to the reported evidential, as shown by Mushin (2001b), on the material of Japanese conversational corpus. As we have seen in Chapters 2 and 5, this development is fairly typical in small evidentiality systems and in evidentiality strategies which follow essentially the same semantic path (cf. Travis forthcoming on *dizque* in Colombian Spanish). Mushin's results are tainted by her lack of differentiation between grammatical and lexical evidentiality.

physical states, emotions, feelings, evaluations, desires, cognition, and so on require different evidentials depending on person (see §5.2.1 and §7.2). In Quechua these verbs of feeling and cognition require the visual evidential if used with first person, and inferred if used with another person (5.18–19; 5.26). Only if one is absolutely certain about the other person's feelings can the direct evidential be used to talk about someone else's feelings, or knowledge (as in 5.19, 'he is sad'). Along similar lines, in Nganasan these verbs require the non-visual sensory evidential (see 5.23, 'my hand is aching').

In Tariana and the East Tucanoan languages the non-visual evidential is used to describe one's own feelings or states. Other people's feelings are typically cast in inferred or in visual evidential, depending on the kind of evidence one has. For instance, if a statement is made on basis of the physical appearance of a sick person, a sentence 'he is sick' may be cast in visual. If it is based on inference or reasoning, an inferred or an assumed evidential is appropriate. As a result, evidentials can acquire the reading of 'default person markers'—this was illustrated in 7.33–4 ('I am sick'; 'Pedro is sick'), from Tucano, followed by similar examples from Tariana. Similar principles operate in Tuyuca (Malone 1988: 131).

An evidential may develop a mirative meaning just with verbs of psychological states. In Chinese Pidgin Russian, the non-firsthand evidential with first person of 'psychological' verbs contributes an 'immediate' meaning, as a more or less spontaneous reaction to a 'new, salient, often surprising event' (Nichols 1986: 248). This agrees with the tendency for first person marked as non-firsthand to develop mirative connotations, as outlined in §6.1.

In languages with small evidentiality systems, the non-firsthand evidential is also preferred when one talks about 'invisible' internal states. We can recall that in Bagvalal (Maisak and Tatevosov 2001: 310) the firsthand evidential can be used with verbs denoting feelings or cognitive processes only to describe visible results, as in 5.2. These correlations are remarkably similar to how conjunct–disjunct person-marking is used in Barbacoan languages to distinguish the feelings and cognitive states of 'self' and 'other'. Verbs of state in Japanese and Korean operate on a similar principle. The way I talk about my own state is different from the way I am allowed to talk about someone else. See §4.6. This by no means implies that any of these strategies are grammatical evidentiality. What it does indicate is the existence of a cross-linguistically valid semantic group of verbs of internal states which tends to show consistent correlations with the person of the 'experiencer'.

The 'internal states' are often characterized by speakers of languages with evidentials as something one cannot 'see' (cf. §11.2 on how speakers conceptualize evidentials).

Further semantic features of the verb which correlate with evidential uses involve volitionality and controllability (or, to use Sun's term (1993: 964), 'consciousness'). Verbs denoting inherently 'uncontrollable' and non-volitional actions are likely to occur with non-firsthand or non-visual evidentials, especially in combination with first person. We saw examples of this in §7.2.1; for instance, in Jarawara 'catching a bad cold' (7.5). Whatever a person does when asleep is cast in non-firsthand: an action in one's sleep is involuntary.[6] If I touch something while asleep, the correct way of phrasing this would be (R. M. W. Dixon, p.c.):

Jarawara

10.25 [jama   soki   jaa]   maki   bojo
       thing(f)   dark   AT   man   touch/feel
       o-ne-**hino**-ka
       1sgA-AUX-IMM.P.NONFIRSTH.m-DECL.m
       'At night I touched a man (while I was asleep)'—NON-FIRSTHAND

If I were awake, the same action of touching someone would be described as 10.26, with a firsthand evidential.

10.26 jama   soki   jaa   maki   bojo
       thing(f) dark   AT   man   touch/feel
       o-na-**hare**-ka
       1sgA-AUX-IMM.P.FIRSTH.m-DECL.m
       'At night I touched a man (while I was awake)'—FIRSTHAND

Falling asleep is non-firsthand in Jarawara, as in 7.6 (7.7, from Yukaghir, illustrates the same point). 'Waking up' is firsthand, as in 10.27 (Dixon 2003: 169).

10.27 manakobisa   jama   siri-maki   jaa
       later   thing(f)   be.cold-FOLLOWING+NOM   AT
       o-tafi-**ara**   o-ke
       1sgS-wake-IMM.P.FIRSTH.f   1sg-DECL.f
       'Later, when it was cold (in the middle of the night), I woke up'—
       FIRSTHAND

In Amdo Tibetan, the direct evidential, used for visual or sensory perception (see 2.47: 'Bkra-shis bought a horse' (speaker saw it)), marks inherently non-volitional acts, such as yawning or smelling something. Unmarked sentences express intentional and purposeful acts (Sun 1993: 962–3). Once again, volitionality as a semantic feature of a verb correlates with corresponding overtones of evidentiality.

---

[6] Dreams are an exception since one 'sees' things in a dream; see §11.3.

If a verb can be interpreted as either volitional or not, an evidential may help disambiguate these meanings. In Tariana, the verb -*maña* (variant -*mañe*) means 'get something wrong, forget' and also 'tell a lie, cheat'. In the meaning of 'forget' or 'get something wrong unintentionally', it occurs with a non-visual evidential—as in 10.28.

Tariana

10.28   nu-mañe-**mahka**   di-pitana-nuku
        1sg-get.wrong/forget-REC.P.NONVIS   3sgnf-name-TOP.NON.A/S
        'I forgot his name'

With a visual evidential, the same verb means 'tell a deliberate lie, cheat on purpose'. In 10.29, the man is vehemently denying that he could have lied to the evil spirit.

10.29   nu-mañe-**naka**   ma-ni-kade   nhua
        1sg-lie-PRES.VIS   NEG-DO-NEG   I
        'I am NOT lying'

The verb -*pika* means 'get lost' when used with a non-visual evidential. When used with a visual or an inferred evidential, its meaning is 'go mad'. The verb -*himeta* means 'think; say something in one's mind; feel (sad, scared, etc)'. When used with non-visual evidential and first person it always refers to 'feeling'. With a visual evidential, it is normally interpreted as referring to 'talking to oneself in one's mind'. So, the expression *kapemani nuhmeta-mhana* (ashamed 1sg+feel,think-REM.P.NONVIS) containing a non-visual evidential means 'I felt shame'. The expression *mhaisiki nuhmeta-mhana* (hunger 1sg+feel,think-REM.P.NONVIS) means 'I felt hungry'. In contrast, the phrase *nu-kale-se nuhmeta-na* (1sg-heart-LOC 1sg+feel,think-REM.P.VIS), with a visual evidential, means 'I said in my heart'.

Evidentials describe the ways in which information was perceived. They inevitably show some semantic overlap with verbs of perception. And verbs of perception can have their preferred evidential choices. The verbs 'see', 'hear', and 'know' in Jarawara generally take firsthand evidentials unless negated (Dixon 2003: 176). The presence of an overt noun referring to a physical sensation may trigger the use of an evidential: when something is heard or smelt, the statement is to be cast in firsthand if there is an overt noun *ati* 'noise', as in 2.2, or *maho* 'smell', as in 10.30 (Dixon 2003: 171).

Jarawara

10.30   jao   bete   maho   kita-**hare**-ka
        sloth(m)   rottenness   smell+m   be.strong-IMM.P.FIRSTH.m-DECL.m
        'The smell of the rotten sloth was strong'

Verbs referring to noise and speech have a preferred evidential in Nganasan: they take the non-visual sensory evidential (Gusev forthcoming: 4). Such verbs include 'shout', 'talk softly', 'talk in a thundering voice', and 'sound'.

Nganasan

10.31   Təti, təti!   ńüə-d'üm   munu-**munu**-t'u
      here, here!   child-which   speak-NONVIS-3sg
      ' "Here, here!" said the son'

Along similar lines, verbs of speech and sound in Tariana—such as 'speak', 'talk', 'call', 'shout', 'mutter'—often occur with non-visual evidential.

A semantically defined subclass of verbs may not require an evidential at all. In Euchee, the auditory evidential marker *ke* does not have to be used with verbs of sound (Linn 2000: 318). No evidential occurs then.

The interpretation of an evidential may depend on the inherent aspectual semantics of a verb. In Chinese Pidgin Russian the same marker has a non-firsthand meaning for verbs with punctual semantics and immediate meaning for non-punctuals (Nichols 1986: 255–6).

The inherent aspectual value of a verb correlates with the meaning of an evidential in Komi Zyryan. The non-firsthand past forms of telic verbs (which imply achieving a result) has a resultative interpretation without evidential connotations (Leinonen 2000: 423–5). This is often the case in impersonal constructions, and intransitive and reflexive structures where the focus is on the salient resulting state of the subject, as in 10.32.

Komi Zyryan

10.32   Körtön   **ez̆öma**   ödzössö
      iron+with   cover+NONFIRSTH+3sg   door+ACC
      'The door was covered with iron'

In contrast, in transitive clauses with overt subject and object, the default interpretation of the non-firsthand past is to do with the way in which the information was acquired. The speaker infers that Vera hasn't forgotten him since she has brought him food.

10.33   Vera   köt'   abu   na   **vunödöma**   menö
      Vera   at.least   not   yet   forget+NONFIRSTH+3sg   I+ACC
      'At least Vera hasn't forgotten me yet' (NON-FIRSTHAND: inference)

We saw in §6.1 that mirative extension of the non-firsthand evidential in Yukaghir is attested only for stative verbs. Similarly, the inferred evidential in Qiang has a mirative meaning with verbs referring to states (see §6.2). See Table 6.2.

In summary: only a fine-grained semantic analysis of verbal semantics in languages with evidentiality will enable us to produce an exhaustive account of how various parameters interrelate with evidential choices, and with their extensions. So far, we have seen that:

- Verbs of cognition, emotions, mental, and physical states show cross-linguistically similar correlations between evidentials and person. Experiences undergone by 'self' and by 'other' consistently require different evidential choices (see §11.3).
- Verbs whose semantics involves lack of controllability and volition also have restricted evidential choices.
- Verbs of perception ('see' and 'hear') whose semantics overlaps with that of evidentials may have preferred evidentials: see above, on evidentials with verbs of seeing and hearing in Jarawara.
- If an action is typically perceived in just one way, the verb denoting it may have a restricted evidential choice, as in Nganasan where verbs of speech and noise require the non-visual evidential. Telic and atelic verbs, and punctual and nonpunctual verbs, can also have evidential preferences of their own.

II. RESTRICTED EVIDENTIAL CHOICES AND 'LEXICALIZED' EVIDENTIALS
Limited evidential choices are typically available in speech formulae—greetings, farewells, and so on. In both Tariana and Tucano greeting formulae contain visual evidentials. A morning greeting in Tucano is:

Tucano
10.34 wã'ka-**tí**,   mɨ'î̵
        be.awake-PRES.VIS.INTER   you
        'Are you awake?'

And the answer is:

10.35 wã'ká-'
        be.awake-PRES.VIS.non.third.p
        '(I) am awake'

When seeing a person in the middle of the day, it is customary to ask:

10.36 āyu-**tí**   mɨ'î̵
        good-PRES.VIS.INTER   you
        'Are you well?'

And the conventional answer is:

10.37   ãyú-'
         good-PRES.VIS.non.third.p
         '(I am) well; (it) is well'

Visual evidentials are common in greetings and formulaic replies to them in both Kalapalo (Basso 1990: 138) and Huallaga Quechua (Weber 1989: 441). In Tucano, 10.37 is used nowadays as a functional equivalent of 'thank you'.

A preferred evidential may become the only choice in a construction type where its usage cannot be easily explained by its erstwhile evidential semantics. For instance, in Kiowa (Watkins 1984: 174), the reported evidential is required in telling traditional stories and transmitting reported information; there are a number of particles, e.g. *béthɔ̀ˑ* 'unknown', that also require it, as a grammatical rule. This is shown in 10.38.

Kiowa
10.38   béthɔ̀ˑ   èm-kò·dó-ɔ̀ltʰɔ̀-kʰɔ̀p-ɔ̀mdè-**hèl**
         unknowing   [2sg]-very-head-hurt-become-REP
         '(I) didn't know you had gotten a bad headache'

In Warlpiri, the reported particle *nganta* occurs in conjunction with two other particles with which it synchronically forms a single unit (Laughren 1982: 144–50). One is *kari-**nganta*** (ASSERTION-REP) 'declarative particle' (whose meaning appears idiomatic). The other is *kula-**nganta*** (NEG-REP), which means that 'the proposition over which it has semantic scope is believed and claimed to be false by the speaker, but that either the speaker or another had previously believed it be true'. Again, the meaning of the whole is hardly derivable from that of its parts. In Ngiyambaa, the sensory evidential -*gara* occurs within the standard greeting *yama-**gara*** (dubitative-SENS.EV), 'How are you feeling' (literally, 'Yes or no, by sensory perception') (Donaldson 1980: 242; also end of §2.1.1). It is also used as an attention-getting device, something like 'Well?' A delocutive verb *yamagara-ba-y* 'greet' is derived from this sequence of particles. In these cases, evidentials are virtually lexicalized.

An evidential can survive just in a few fixed expressions. Sakel (2003: 267) reports that in Mosetén, a Bolivian isolate, the 'deductive evidential', which used to refer to information inferred on the basis of heard or seen evidence, today appears only 'in place names and other lexicalised items' and is hardly ever used productively.

An additional question is: does having an evidential imply having a vast array of verbs of perception and mental processes? In other words, does having an evidential system impact on the wealth of lexical items to do with perception, inference, reasoning, and so on? At present, this question remains open.

10.4 How to choose the correct evidential: a summary

Every evidential has its core meaning. These meanings were described at some length in Chapter 5. Various additional principles regulate the ways in which evidentials are employed, including: (*a*) narrative conventions, whereby the genre of a text determines the choice of an evidential, and (*b*) lexical conventions, which include preferential evidential choices for different classes of verbs.

Evidentials may also have varied semantic effects depending on person; see Chapter 7 and a summary in Table 7.1. Something can be seen, heard, and inferred simultaneously. If a language offers a choice between visual, non-visual, and inferred evidential, the visual source is given preference to other sources of evidence; see Diagrams 10.1 and 10.2.

We are thus confronted with a few principles of evidential choices. In what order—if any—do they apply? Choosing an evidential is quite unlike automatically applying steadfast rules accounting for deviations from a core meaning. The pragmatics of evidential choice has to do with various competing factors, depending on which aspect of the situation the speaker wishes to highlight. Diagram 10.3 shows the ways in which these choices can be and usually are restricted, and which one is preferred over the other, everything else being equal.

DIAGRAM 10.3 How to choose the correct evidential: restrictions and preferences

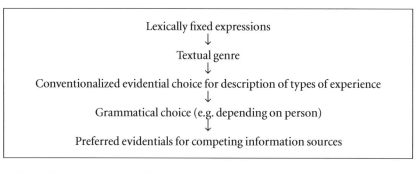

An evidential in a lexically fixed expression—such as a speech formula, or a fully lexicalized form (as in the examples from Warlpiri and Kiowa in II under 10.3 above)—does not allow for variation.

Narrative conventions override requirements dictated by the semantic class of a verb. If the genre of a story requires that it be cast in reported evidential, the reported evidential must be used no matter what semantic class the verbs belong to or what other conventions there are which may require a particular evidential choice.

Similarly to narrative conventions, evidential conventions associated with a particular type of experience override the conventions associated with a semantic verb class. It was mentioned in §10.2.1 that in Tariana and Tucano, dreams by common people are cast in non-visual evidential. The verb 'see' tends to occur with visual evidential. If used in describing a dream, it will take non-visual evidential.

We saw in §7.2.1 that the semantics of a verb overrides the 'first person effect'; if the verb implies an uncontrollable state, the choice of non-visual evidential automatically goes with first person and does not have any further implication of lack of control (see 7.14, 'I feel sad-non-visual', and 7.15, 'Fever has come over me' (NON-VISUAL) and not: 'Fever has come over me and I could not help it'). And we saw in 7.16 ('I called my wife in the dream' (NON-VISUAL), and not 'I called my wife unintentionally in the dream') that if a certain experience (say, dreams) requires a choice of an evidential, this convention overrides the semantic effect imposed by the choice of person. If a verb of cognition is used in a description of a dream, it will be cast in non-visual evidential independently of what person it relates to. An account of a dream cast in non-visual evidential cannot be interpreted as unintentional. If there are competing information sources, and everything else is equal, one applies the principle of the preferential status of visually acquired data.

The hierarchy in Diagram 10.3 roughly accounts for the pragmatics of evidentiality choices. The genre as a macro-convention typically overrides other preferences. Narrative conventions thus serve to narrow down the polysemy of evidentials depending on person and other factors.

11

What are evidentials good for? Evidentiality, cognition, and cultural knowledge

In languages with evidentiality as part of grammar, marking one's information source is a 'must'. The concepts expressed by evidentials cover the ways in which information was obtained. They only marginally relate to truth, speaker's responsibility, and reliability of information. To speakers of languages with obligatory evidentials, European languages appear lacking in precision, with statements being too vague, or too short. Speakers of European languages have an opposite impression, when confronted with attempts by Paiute, Yavapai, or Tariana Indians to express evidentials with lexical means: Indians' ways of speaking sounds unpleasant, incredulous, and generally weird (see §9.2.3). What it is that makes evidentials so important for human communication, interaction, and cognition is the topic of §11.1. Speakers of languages with evidentials are highly aware of this grammatical category. Metalinguistic perception of evidentials further corroborates their impact on the ways in which people communicate. We discuss this in §11.2.

Evidentials are associated with different kinds of knowledge and experience, and with conventionalized ways of talking about them. Cultural practices and lore may acquire their own stereotyped evidential uses: the way of talking about supernatural phenomena may differ from how one talks about a fishing trip. The advent of European innovations brought about a whole array of new ways of acquiring information in traditional communities—reading, radio, television, the telephone, and so on. The ways in which these new avenues acquire their own, preferred evidential choices reflect the adaptability and semantic nuances of the system. Correlations between evidentials, types of knowledge, and traditional and newly emerging cultural stereotypes are examined in §11.3.

And finally, why are languages with evidentiality the way they are? Do evidentials have any correlates in the known cultural and social practices of those who must mark the information source whenever they speak? In §11.4, I offer hypotheses concerning some putative cultural and cognitive correlates of evidentials. A brief summary is given in §11.5.

Most languages with large evidentiality systems are spoken by small groups of indigenous peoples which have not yet been affected by global tendencies or diluted by 'Standard Average European' or other stereotypes. In this chapter I will focus on these groups whose unique, individual features—alien to European routines and conventions—may provide new insights into the cognitive and cultural underpinnings of evidentiality.

11.1 Evidentials, communication, and cognition

The function of evidentials is to signal where information comes from. Having obligatory evidentials implies the necessity of being precise about the information source. This is a major requirement for successful communication, and an efficient way of avoiding potential misunderstandings. Example 11.1 comes from a Jarawara story told in firsthand evidential. In the middle of the story, the speaker switches to reported evidential. This indicates that he did not LOOK into his father's future grave. He was present during the grave-digging (hence the firsthand in the rest of the story), but learnt about the water inside the grave from other people.

Jarawara
11.1   faha   kasiro-tee-**hamone**
       water(f)   be.a.lot-HABITUAL-REPORTED.f
       'There was a lot of water' (in the grave, it is said)

In a language without evidentials, information source either is left vague or may be viewed as part of implicature. Having no grammatical evidentials in their language does not prevent speakers from maintaining efficient communication. Communicative efficiency is based on cooperation between speakers and addressees. As Grice (1989: 26) puts it: 'Our talk exchanges do not normally consist of a succession of disconnected remarks, and would not be rational if they did. They are characteristically, to some degree at least, cooperative efforts; and each participant recognizes in them, to some degree at least, a common purpose or a set of purposes, or at least a mutually accepted direction.' This is the 'Cooperative principle', which underlies four supermaxims of human communication. By the supermaxim of Quantity speakers are supposed to make their 'contribution as informative as required'. The supermaxim of Quality states that speakers are not expected to say what they believe is false and only say things for which they have adequate evidence. The supermaxim of Relation requires that only what is relevant should be said. Finally, the fourth supermaxim, of Manner, speakers are expected to avoid obscurity of expression and ambiguity, and to be brief and orderly.

These maxims are achievable in every language. The question is, how? Having grammatical evidentials relegates the task of fulfilling the requirements of at least the supermaxims of Quantity and Manner to the grammar. Since the information source has to be specified, the speaker's contribution is bound to be informative, based on adequate evidence, and unambiguous in this respect.

In a language with evidentials, asking 'how do you know this?' makes little sense. It is all there, in the speaker's contribution. As we saw in §3.7, one can question the validity of the other person's evidence. One can even give false evidence and false information source (see Table 3.3). The information source simply cannot be left vague. Accuracy in getting one's information source right is crucial for successful communication and for the speaker's reputation (see Hardman 1986: 133, and §9.2.3).[1]

The obligatory marking of one's information source is perceived as universal by the Jaqi speakers also because—as we saw in §9.2.3—evidentiality has become part of the local Andean variety of Spanish. This diffusibility of evidential conventions further confirms the cognitive importance of being precise in stating one's information sources. The Aymara had been living in the area of modern Bolivia for centuries before the Spanish occupation. There is no doubt that nowadays Spanish is the dominant language, and that the Spanish influence on Aymara has been greater than the Aymara influence on Spanish (Laprade 1981: 207). One of the few Aymara categories that found their way into the local Spanish is evidentiality. As a result, outsiders who speak different varieties of Spanish, or learners of Aymara who disregard the evidential system, are at a disadvantage. At best, they are perceived as unreliable and, at worst, as outright liars. 'A missionary's statement as personal knowledge that Adam ate the apple is interpreted as a claim of having been present in the Garden of Eden. If a Peace Corps volunteer, reading from a book, states as personal knowledge that certain seeds yield good crops, the perception, again, is of someone trying to deceive' (Silver and Miller 1997: 36). Similarly, if a Shipibo-Konibo man says 11.2 (Valenzuela 2003: 41) using the reported evidential when he actually saw the act of stealing, there is no mistake: the man is a liar.

---

[1] Hardman (1986: 133) reports how difficult it is for Jaqi (Aymara) speakers to imagine how one can speak a language which does not mark the information source . Finally she and her colleagues had to 'adjust their English' and always specify how they knew things, so as not to upset their Jaqi-speaking friends.

Shipibo-Konibo

11.2   Ja-**ronki**   yometso-iba-ke

        3:ABS-REP   become.thief-YESTERDAY.PAST-COMPL

        '(I heard that) he stole it'

Those who come into Jaqi communities from outside and 'state as personal knowledge . . . facts which they know only through language (e.g. things they have read in books) are immediately categorised as cads, as people who behave more like animals than humans and, therefore, ought to be treated like animals, specifically, through the loss of linguistic interchange' (Hardman 1986: 133). Getting one's evidentials right is important for one's status and credibility. As Hardman (1986: 131) puts it, 'the skilful and accurate use of the data-source discourse devices at their command is highly esteemed by the Jaqi people; minimum competent use is a prerequisite to a claim to human status'. People who cannot use the evidentials correctly are not worth talking to.

The Aymara concern for precise data source often results in misunderstandings and cultural 'clashes'. Miracle and de Dioz Yapita Moya (1981: 53) mention incredulous responses of the Aymara to statements in some written texts like 'Columbus discovered America'; 'was the author actually there' to see? They react with incredulity to 'new (unseen) ideas' such as astronauts visiting the moon. This creates an image of socio-cultural conservatism. And, as a result, some Western writers see the Aymara as 'negative, unimaginative, suspicious, and skeptical'.

Misunderstandings arise when evidential distinctions are 'forced' upon languages which do not have them. Overusing English expressions like 'I am told', 'they say' creates a variety of negative impressions: the speaker either may be considered obnoxious or may be seen as lacking trust. We can recall, from §9.2.3, that if an outsider says to a Jaqi person, 'I'm from California', a Jaqi speaker would be likely to reply in Andean Spanish, or in Jaqi: 'You say you are from California'. The outsider is then likely to feel that they are being accused of telling a lie. And yet for a Jaqi speaker the issue is simply one 'of accuracy' and not of 'morality' (Silver and Miller 1997: 36–7). Once again, evidentials help to put Grice's conversational maxims into practice, rather than being concerned with undisputable 'truth values' and 'speaker's commitment'.

Evidentials are just as important in the Tariana- and Tucano-speaking milieus. One's status in the Tariana community correlates with one's ability to speak the language correctly and be articulate in it. In a society where the language one inherits from one's father is the main mark of a person's identity, it is natural that only those who are the most articulate and proficient speakers should be called 'true Tariana'. A major token of 'correct' Tariana is the ability to use evidentials in the right way (see details in Aikhenvald 2002: 213–20). Good speakers of Tariana distinguish three reported evidentiality terms: present (*-pida*), recent past (*-pida-ka*), and remote past (*-pida-na*). One of the village elders uses just one marker of reported evidentiality (*-pida*) disregarding the tense forms. As a result, he is not considered a fully competent speaker of the language, nor is he treated with full respect. Behind his back, people call him *mẽdite* (in.vain + NCL:ANIM) 'useless one'.

Evidentials are a powerful means for manipulating discourse (see §10.2.2). They help to achieve a variety of subtle effects. Knowing which evidential to use, and when, provides an important way of imposing one's authority. We saw in §10.2.1 that the frequent use of a firsthand evidential by a Kalapalo chief reflects the 'assertiveness' of his discourse (Basso 1990: 137). (Similar examples were discussed by Bendix 1992, for Newari.) But those who overuse an evidential without enough reason are in danger of others doubting their competence. Excessive use of the direct evidential *-mi* in Quechua may sound 'incautious with respect to the information' conveyed. According to Weber (1986: 142n.), this may even imply that the author is 'not a member of a Quechua speaking community which values his stature'. An unauthorized use of the direct evidential can be interpreted in even stronger terms. In Weber's words, 'TCV [Weber's consultant] knows a man (referred to by his neighbours as "loko" ['crazy']) who constantly uses *-mi*. TCV reports that no one believes what he says because he "always speaks as though he had witnessed what he is telling about" '. To this, Weber adds: 'At best he is an argumentative braggart and from TCV's description I would guess that he is mentally ill.' Breaching evidential conventions appears to be a good enough reason for an amateur psychiatric diagnosis.

This high demand for precision in stating one's information source results in the perception of languages without evidentiality as somehow inadequate. It was mentioned in §9.2.3 how speakers of languages with evidentiality complain that languages which lack such distinctions are somehow less expressive and 'deficient'. Even speakers of languages without evidentials wish they had been compelled to always be so precise. In Palmer's (1996: 200) words, 'what a lot of breath and ink this might save us in English if we had evidential suffixes that we could use in the courtroom. Using the Wintun suffix, we might say, for example, "The defendant shoplift-*be* [*be* is a visual evidential: A.Y.A.] the compact disc", thereby eliminating the need to ask the inevitable question: "Did you actually see her take it?" '

Unmarked statements in English (as well as numerous varieties of Spanish and Portuguese) are evidentially vague. This may give rise to cross-linguistic and cross-cultural misunderstandings. If a speaker of English says 'it is raining', we do not know whether he or she 'heard the rain on the roof, saw it out of the window, heard that it was raining from a third party, or has inferred that it is raining from other evidence, like wet tracks on the floor' (Hill and Irvine 1992: 18–19). Speakers of any language can express the information source lexically if they need to. But such lexical explanations may produce additional illocutionary effects. A long explanation such as 'It is probably raining, since that is what it does most of the time' (in this place) sounds unpleasantly precise. We can recall, from the beginning of §9.2.3, how Victor Friedman, a fluent speaker of Macedonian, mentioned that he himself had felt the absence of evidentiality in his native English after having spent several months in Macedonia (Friedman 2003: 210). He goes on to say that 'although adverbs such as *apparently* in English carry the same type of distancing semantics lexically, their use is felt to be gross and intrusive compared to selecting a verb form'. Insisting on one's information source—'this is what it is, I have seen it'—may sound defensive. And querying the other person's information source can sound as an insult: asking 'how do you know it?' implies 'I don't believe you'.

Disregard for obligatory marking of information source in preparing information booklets on agriculture in Aymara led to their rejection by the people. A primer prepared by a German linguistic team in 1980 suffered the same fate for the same reason (Hardman 1986: 135). Those who speak Bolivian Spanish, which distinguishes evidentiality, despise or reject literature written in other varieties, including European Spanish: in actual fact, this variety has to be explained to them and even translated into their Spanish (Hardman 1986: 136).

Throughout the world, visually acquired information is considered highly valuable and reliable, perhaps more so than information acquired through any other means. What is inferred or learnt through verbal report is likely to be considered less reliable. Hence the development of epistemic connotations of reliability for visually obtained data, and doubt and lack of certainty for inference or verbal report. The cognitive importance of visual perception underlies other grammatical categories besides evidentials. Classifiers categorize entities primarily in terms of their visual features; there is no noun categorization by smell, sound, or temperature (cf. Adams and Conklin 1973: 8; Aikhenvald 2000: 337–9). These considerations may 'justify' the central role of the visual evidential in evidentiality systems. However, we need much more information than we have at present to establish the perceptual correlates of other evidential specifications.[2]

All this confirms the importance of evidentials and their impact on people's perception of the world around them, of other languages, and of their speakers.

---

[2] The linguistic behaviour of physically handicapped people, for instance, blind speakers of languages with an obligatory visual evidential, could provide interesting clues to evidentials' semantics and usage. At present, no such information is available.

Their significance in daily life is reflected in the ways people talk about them, and how conscious they are of the conventions underlying the 'correct' choice of evidentials; see §11.2. The perception of external and internal experience is interwoven with evidential conventions in various languages, as discussed in §11.3. Last but not least, evidentials correlate with a variety of cultural attitudes; see §11.4.

The ways in which children acquire evidentials is a potential source of significant insight into human cognition, and the development of cultural and cognitive stereotypes. Yet very few studies have been accomplished so far— these are discussed in the Appendix to this chapter.

11.2 Metalinguistic perception of evidentials

Speakers' awareness of the need to be precise in marking information source manifests itself in numerous ways. The importance of evidentials is reflected in how people talk about information sources. Aymara has an array of proverbs used in teaching children the significance of correct use of evidentials: 'Seeing, one can say "I have seen", without seeing one must not say "I have seen" '.[3] The following proverb in Jaqi stresses the importance of visually acquired information: 'Seeing, speak; without seeing, do not speak.' These same proverbs are used in disputes, to revile the statements of an opponent. Children are immediately corrected if they make a mistake in choosing an evidential (Hardman 1986: 132).

Languages with obligatory evidentiality often have a lexical way of referring to someone who just cannot get their evidential right. The Tsafiki term *nene pun* translated as 'liar' (Dickinson 2000: 420) is a case in point. In actual fact, this term covers those who misuse the evidential system, as well as intentional lies, white lies, and any kind of misinformation (no matter whether done on purpose or not). The Tariana verb *-anihta* 'be unreasonable, not think' describes someone who draws a wrong inference and does not use evidentials correctly. This is the nearest equivalent in the language to 'crazy'.

Speakers of languages with evidentiality feel a need to express it with lexical means when they have to switch to a contact language with no evidentiality (see §9.2.3). When the Tucano and the Tariana speakers use their Portuguese to report something they heard from someone else, the source is always included. This is another way of expressing their metalinguistic awareness of evidentials.

---

[3] Aymara *Uñjasaw [uñjt] sañax, jan uñjasax jani [uñjt] sañakiti,* Jaqi *Illush arma, ish illshuq jan artatxi* (Hardman 1986: 132–3).

Evidentials can be paraphrased and reinforced with lexical items corresponding to the information source. This 'lexical reinforcement' provides additional semantic clues for determining the core meaning of an evidential. A visual evidential can be followed by a lexical comment as 'I saw it', and a non-visual as 'I heard it' or 'I felt it'.[4] Such 'lexical reinforcement' of evidentiality (an instance of redundancy for emphatic purposes) has a rhetorical effect. Example 11.3 comes from a nostalgic story about the good old days when people lived well, no one quarrelled, and no one was hungry, told by Américo, the oldest living speaker of Tariana. The story was cast in visual evidential—this was Américo's personal experience. Now and again he inserted a phrase 'I saw it-visual', stressing his unique visual experience of this paradise lost. The phrase reinforces the source of evidence, and is underlined here.

Tariana

11.3 hiku-**na**   na-ni   na-yā-**na**   nu-kesi-do
      be.thus-REM.P.VIS   3pl-do   3pl-live-REM.P.VIS 1sg-relative-FEM
      pedale-pe-se   nhuaniɾi-pe-se.   Nha   kayu   na-ni-ka,
      old.people-PL-LOC   1sg+father-PL-LOC they   thus   3pl-do-SUB
      <u>nu-ka-**na**</u>   nuha,   yanape-ka   <u>nu-ka-**na**</u>   mẽda
      1sg-see-REM.P.VIS   I   be.child-SUB   1sg-see-REM.P.VIS   UNEXPECTED
      'This is how they lived, my female relative, in the old people's times, in our fathers' times. I saw them do it, when I was a child I did see (it)'

Américo felt the need to reinforce his visual source of information about the paradise on earth he was describing since he was aware that for most people his story sounded like a fantasy tale. In his other story about a traditional ritual no one but him had actually seen, he also judged appropriate to insert the phrase 'I saw it' (+remote past visual), strengthening the value of his unique, visually obtained information.

To add flavour to his story, a narrator may finish it by explicitly stating that he had learnt it from 'the horse's mouth'. A story in a reported evidential may finish with 'this is what old people told me-visual' (further examples of such 'lexical reinforcements' of evidentials are in Aikhenvald 2003b: 157). The narrator does so to make sure his audience realizes that he got his story from the most reliable source imaginable, thus adding weight to the narrative.

As an alternative to lexical reinforcement, speakers of a language with evidentiality may rephrase an evidential with a lexical item. The auditory evidential in Euchee (Linn 2000: 317) can be rephrased with the verb 'hear' (see §2.1.1): 11.4 is an alternative to 2.38 ('they are coming: I hear them'), which has an evidential on the verb.

---

[4] Cross-linguistically, these two meanings are often expressed with one lexical root.

Euchee

11.4 'ahe   'i-gō
     here   3pl(EUCHEE).ACTOR-come
     do-ch'wē
     1sg.ACTOR/PLUS.PARTICIPANT.VALENCE-hear
     'I hear them coming'

In Latundê (Nambiquara) evidentials are frequently rephrased with lexical items such as 'he left, I saw (it)/I did not see it/I heard/I did not hear', etc. In 2.37 ('he washed (the clothes), he said'), a quotative construction with the verb 'say' is used instead of the reported evidential (Telles 2002: 290).

If an evidential is polysemous, a lexical explanation may disambiguate it unless the exact source is clear from the context, as in 5.3, from Bagvalal ('Ali, as I infer, has killed the bear' or 'Ali, as I am told, has killed the bear'; see §5.1). The sensory evidential in Ngiyambaa covers information obtained by seeing, hearing, or touching. In 2.29 ('The rabbit is in here (I can touch it), I feel it'), the speaker explains exactly how she had acquired the sensory information about a rabbit in the burrow: she could feel it by touch. The exact type of non-firsthand information—whether inferred or reported—in Northern Khanty (§5.1) is made explicit by additional explanation. In 5.5 ('Because of the blood on the snow I understood that I had wounded the reindeer') the blood on the snow allows the speaker to INFER that the deer was wounded, while 5.6 ('Grandfather Philip said: " ... The rising fish has already reached Obdorsk" ') explicitly states who told what to the speaker.

Speakers of languages with evidentiality can explain why one evidential is appropriate, while another is not, much in the spirit of 'naive linguistic explanations' exemplified by Dixon (1992). This happens when correcting mistakes made by linguists as language learners. We can recall, from 10.8, how Dixon was corrected by Jarawara speakers when he attempted to use the first-hand evidential to talk about a tree that he had not seen fall. If one uses a direct evidential to talk about someone else's internal state or feelings, this could be taken as an intrusion (unless one has culturally valid reasons to do so: see under (*C*) in §11.3) (Silver and Miller 1997: 36). Such 'internal states' are often charac-terized by speakers of languages with evidentiality as something one cannot 'see'. And we can recall, from §2.2, that in Bora, 'if a speaker fails to include an evidential clitic when reporting an event he or she did not witness, they may be challenged by the hearer' (Weber and Thiesen forthcoming: 254–6).

Evidential conventions—see §11.3—can be given a similar, metalinguistic justification. The conventionalized use of the non-visual evidential to describe the actions of evil spirits was explained to me, by the Tariana (first in

Portuguese, and later on, in Tariana), as 'one cannot see him, or else one would die'. Speakers can be equally aware of evidentials as tokens of a genre (as shown in §10.2.1). As de Reuse (2003: 87) put it for Western Apache, 'if one reads a story without the sentence-final *lék'eh* [one of the reported markers—A. Y. A.], my consultants react that it is no longer recognisable as a story: "*lék'eh* brings you back to the fact that this is a story" '. Turkish-speaking children (Aksu-Koç 1988: 157) can provide verbal justification for the use of evidentials, as they acquire them, in the spirit of 'he can't say anything because he did not see the event happen': see the Appendix to this chapter.

In a language where being precise in stating one's information source is indispensable, reinterpreting what other people say about their information source may be dangerous. To avoid this, Tariana and Tucano speakers prefer quoting exactly what the other person had said (that is, using direct speech complements) to reporting it indirectly, and thus running the danger of upsetting the other person (see §5.4.1; and Ramirez 1997, vol. I: 370, on Tucano). We saw in §8.1.1 that evidentials in questions presuppose the information source of the addressee. This is potentially dangerous: a question may sound like an accusation if the addressee turns out to have a different information source from what the speaker had thought it to be. As a result, being too inquisitive and asking too many questions in Tariana is frowned upon. Quoting a statement verbatim is a safer option than recasting it in some other way. By itself, this does not convey any incredulity, unlike in Arizona Tewa (see §5.4.1). The verb of speech is marked with frustrative mood if one quotes something one only half-believes. This is what Olívia Brito did: 11.5 is her comment on Américo's account of the ritual. She was incredulous about the validity of his experience, and employed the frustrative marker (underlined).

Tariana

11.5   [nu-ka-**na**   thuy-niki]   di-a-<u>tha</u>-**na**
       1sg-see-REM.P.VIS   all-COMPL   3sgnf-say-FR-REM.P.VIS
       'He said (in vain, in front of me), "I had seen it all" ' (but I have my doubts)

This shows, once again, how evidentials are independent of the expression of doubt or disbelief: such an expression is achieved using other means.

In summary, speakers of languages with evidentials tend to be aware of their importance. This awareness transpires in the ways native speakers are social-ized, in how they talk about evidential use, and in the strategies they employ when rephrasing evidentials with lexical items in their own language. Last, but not least, speakers of languages with evidentials are aware of the lack of this category in other languages. We can recall, from §9.2.3, that speakers of Turkic and Balkan languages feel the absence of evidentials in a language like English. Jaqi speakers find it hard to believe that one can adequately communicate in a language which does not mark the information source. And the Indians of the Vaupés area complain that when non-Indians speak Portuguese they are not explicit enough and often 'lie'.

This awareness is akin to the ways in which people can be aware of what they consider particularly unusual phenomena in their languages. Lindström (2002: 193) reports that speakers of Kuot, the only non-Austronesian language of New Ireland, are very aware of their grammatical gender, a distinctive feature absent from the neighbouring languages. The Manambu of East Sepik are equally aware and proud of their gender system associated with shape: whatever is long is masculine; whatever is short and squat is feminine. The Thai are highly aware of the complexities in their pronominal system and of the varied politeness levels (Tony Diller, p.c.), and of the multiplicity of classifiers which 'allow us to understand and visualise features of the preceding noun' (Phosakritsana 1978: 13), so that 'as such, we should preserve them as part of our linguistic identity'.

Linguistic awareness may have its roots in a special effort one has to make to learn a particular distinctive grammatical phenomenon, and so one ends up being proud of it (this is probably the case with varied speech styles in Thai). Or it may be something people find truly lacking in surrounding languages, and yet communicatively useful and even essential in their own. Evidentiality appears to fall into the latter category. The alacrity with which speakers of languages without evidentiality recognize its usefulness points in the same direction—see the quote from Palmer (1996: 200) above. As Boas (1942: 182) put it, 'we could read our newspapers with much greater satisfaction if our language would compel them to say whether their reports are based on self-experience, inference, or hearsay!' The ways in which evidentiality is ingrained in speech habits and conventions—whose breach may result in losing face and reputation—testify to this.

11.3 Evidential conventions and knowledge

Each evidential is associated with a specific information source: seeing; hearing, smelling, and feeling; reasoning; inference; and so on. Different kinds of knowledge come to be associated with the information source typically used for its acquisition. For instance, a traditional story is typically acquired through someone else's verbal report. The type of knowledge encoded in such a story will then be marked with a reported evidential, which, in its turn, becomes a token of the narrative genre (see §10.2.1). Actions of supernatural beings, or one's internal states, can be treated as 'unseen'. Some of these evidential conventions are the topic of this section.

As pointed out by Hill and Irvine (1992: 17), ' "knowledge" is . . . a social phenomenon, an aspect of the social relations between people'. It is indeed 'misleading to think of evidentiality in the strictly cognitive or epistemological terms preferred by "personalist" accounts' (also see arguments by Du Bois 1986, to the same effect). Unlike epistemic modality (intrinsically related to probability and possibility), obligatory evidentiality is only tangentially relevant to the 'human awareness that truth is relative' (Chafe and Nichols 1986: vii). As Silver and Miller (1997: 37) put it, in the use of evidentials the issue is not morality, or truth—it is accuracy. And it is often a matter of speech habits and practices based on typical conventionalized avenues of information acquisition.

Consequently, types of knowledge heavily depend on the cultural conventions and traditions in each particular society. They interrelate systems of belief and models of the outside world. For instance, in numerous indigenous societies shamanic knowledge differs from that of ordinary humans. The way one talks about the spiritual world obviously depends on conventionalized ideas concerning its structure and the existing cultural stereotypes: that, for instance, different evil spirits have different kinds of power. Ideally, we ought to discuss conventions of evidential usage for all and every type of cultural knowledge. This can hardly be achieved, given the gaps in what we know about these. Here, I will concentrate on conventionalized evidential choices in a number of situations which are typically addressed by linguists and anthropologists. They can be viewed as representative of existing cultural stereotypes in presenting knowledge obtained through these avenues.

These focal points are (A) what one sees in dreams, (B) supernatural phenomena (including spiritual world and people with supernatural powers), and (C) the internal states and feelings of someone other than the speaker. As a result of new avenues for information acquisition—writing, radio, television, internet, and the like—new conventions are introduced which shed light onto the subtle tinges of meaning of evidentials and the ways in which their semantic scope can be subject to expansion; this is discussed under (D).

(C) Evidentials in dreams

The treatment of dreams varies from culture to culture. For some, this is a type of experience that bears little relation to the actual outside world, belonging to the realm of the supernatural or unreal. For others, dreams are a continuation of day-to-day life. Dreams 'constitute a sort of intermediate or cross-cutting category between internal and external experience' (Floyd 1999: 64): on the one hand, they are not an event in the real world, on the other hand within the world of dream, the dreamer as a participant can be viewed as an objective observer. In different languages, recounting a dream requires different evidentials.[5]

Some languages treat dreams on a par with ordinary, directly observed experience. In Jarawara (Dixon 2004) descriptions of dreams are cast in first-hand evidential since they are supposed to be 'seen'. In contrast, all other activities performed when one is asleep are non-firsthand (e.g. 'touching someone in one's sleep' in 10.26), since these activities are non-volitional and not controlled by the person. In Turkic languages dreams are never cast in non-firsthand evidential. Similarly, in Wanka Quechua the direct evidential is used in recounting dreams, as if it were part of 'everyday experienced reality' (Floyd 1999: 64–5). The direct evidential *-mi* in an account of one's dream is shown in 11.6.[6]

Wanka Quechua

11.6 ya'a   suyñu-ñaa   ka-a   anyan   tuta   katarpillar
      I   dream-PAST   be-1p   yesterday   night   tractor
      karritiira-a-ta   trabaja-shra-nchik-kaa-ta-**m**
      road-DEF-ACC   work-NOM-1 + 2-DEF-ACC-DIR.EV
      'Last night I dreamed about when we worked on the road with the
      tractor'

As Floyd (1999: 65) puts it, this implies that 'an event marked with the direct evidential can be grounded to realms other than the speaker's current or conscious reality'. Similarly, in Amdo Tibetan dreams are cast in direct evidential, while all the other activities which occur when one is asleep take the indirect evidential (Sun 1993: 966–7). The activity of dreaming is thus treated 'as a kind of subconscious visual experience', distinct from 'truly subconscious activities'. Along similar lines, in Tuyuca and Tatuyo (East Tucanoan), dreams are cast in visual evidential: speakers rationalize this evidential choice by saying that dreams are 'seen' (Janet Barnes, p.c.).

In other languages dreams are cast in non-firsthand evidentials. They are represented as unconsciously acquired information, outside reality, and therefore not 'seen' in the same way one sees objects and activities in real life. The non-firsthand evidential is frequently used in Cree/Montagnais/Naskapi to describe dreams, as in 11.7. In such contexts, the non-firsthand marker *-shapan*

---

[5] Kwakiutl (Boas 1910: 496) is reported to have a special evidential meaning 'see in a dream'. According to Jacobsen (1986: 24) this evidential suffix could be related to a formative suffix in Makah meaning 'have a dream'. This meaning is labelled 'revelative evidence' by Jakobson (1957).

[6] Whether an account of someone else's dream could be cast in direct evidential without any additional overtones requires further investigation (Floyd 1997: 95).

occurs in combination with the affix *ka-* . . . *-ua* whose main meaning is that the whole assertion is the speaker's mental construct (James, Clarke, and MacKenzie 2001: 243).

Cree/Montagnais/Naskapi

11.7   pepunit   ma:k   eku   peua:tat   ne   na:peu   ekute   anite
         in.winter   and   then   he.dreamt   that   man   that's   there
        eukuannua   <u>ka</u>-utiniku**shapan**-<u>ua</u>:   ishineu
        that's.the.one   <u>ka</u>-he.was.taken + NONFIRSTH-<u>ua</u>   he.dreamt
        'In winter the man dreamt that the person was taken (i.e., abducted), he dreamt'

In Yukaghir, dreams are cast in non-firsthand (see Jochelson 1905: 400). In Svan (Sumbatova 1999: 75) dreams are also treated as not real-world events, and thus require a non-firsthand evidential form. Similarly, a non-firsthand form is used to talk about dreams in Modern Eastern Armenian (Kozintseva 2000: 411): dreams are something from a pretend or make-believe world. The non-firsthand evidential can occur when reporting a dream in Macedonian and in Abkhaz to create a distancing effect between the real world and the pretend 'dream-world' (Friedman 2003: 210; Chirikba 2003: 251–2).

In a larger system a similar 'out-of-this-world' effect can be achieved with the reported evidential, as in Shipibo-Konibo.

Shipibo-Konibo

11.8   E-a-**ronki**   i-wan-ke   ani   aros   wai
         1p-ABS-REP   do.INTR-EARLIER.TODAY.PAST-COMPL   large   rice   garden
        napo   chankat-a
        centre   stand-PP2
        'I was standing in the center of a large rice garden (in a dream)'

The reported evidential—rather than the direct evidential—signals that what one experienced in a dream is not part of reality (Valenzuela 2003: 51). This is in contrast to shamanic hallucinations under the influence of the hallucinogenous substance *ayahuasca* which are cast in direct evidential (see (B) below).

In Tariana and in Tucano, accounts of dreams by ordinary humans are couched in non-visual. Dreams are not treated on a par with conventional visual experience, since they belong to an unreal imaginary world. In 10.14 ('Then I, my wife and my small children, we arrived (at the airport: in my dream), the plane arrived (in my dream)'), from Graciliano's description of a dream in Tariana, every verb takes the non-visual evidential. To make sure the audience realizes that what he is talking about was a dream, a speaker may insert a lexical reminder, 'in a dream' (as in 7.16: 'I called my wife in the dream'). This lexical 'reminder' is akin to the lexical reinforcement of evidentials in §11.2. Dreams by ordinary humans in Tucano, with which Tariana is in constant contact, are also typically cast in non-visual evidential, as in 11.9 (further examples are in Ramirez 1997, vol. II: 79).

Tucano

11.9 niˈkaá yami-re   miˈî-re
      today   night-TOP.NON.A/S   you-TOP.NON.A/S
      kẽ'e-**ási**
      dream-REC.P.NONVIS.nonthird.p
      'Last night I dreamt of you' (NON-VISUAL)

In contrast, Tariana shamans have prophetic dreams, which are part of their supernatural experience. Accounts of such dreams are cast in visual evidential. Shamans are omniscient and their dreams are tantamount to statements about what they see. In 11.10, a shaman sees his grandfather in a dream and says upon waking up:

Tariana

11.10 wa-hweɾi-ne   ikasu-nuku   matʃi-pu-**naka**   diha
       1pl-grandfather-FOC.A/S now-TOP.NON.A/S bad-AUG-PRES.VIS   he
       'Right now our grandfather is in a bad way'—VISUAL

Needless to say, the rest of the story confirms that he was right: while he was dreaming, an evil spirit came and devoured their grandfather. When I expressed my surprise at this use of evidentials, Jovino Brito explained it to me saying 11.11—'the shaman sees it all'. This is another example of rephrasing an evidential with a lexical item.

11.11 matʃa di-ka-**na**   thui-niki
       well   3sgnf-see-REM.P.VIS   all-COMPL
       'He had seen it all through and through'—VISUAL

This perception of prophetic visions by shamans as tantamount to true visual experience is intrinsically related to the shaman's capacity of seeing what ordinary humans cannot. The fact that shamans are traditionally considered omniscient could provide additional reason why shamanic speech is usually cast in visual evidential, as in 11.10. Also see Gomez-Imbert (1986), on similar examples from Tatuyo, and §5.3.1 on the association between omniscience, generally known facts, and the visual evidential in multiterm systems. We will now discuss some conventionalized information sources for supernatural phenomena.

(B) SUPERNATURAL PHENOMENA AND EVIDENTIALS

The supernatural world of magic can be viewed as an extension of the real world. Or one's experience in dealing with it may be interpreted as something which one cannot see. In Tariana and in Tucano tradition, evil spirits are not 'seen'; their actions are perceived as 'non-visual' experience. An example is under 11.12.

Tariana

11.12 ñamu   wa-na   matʃa-**mahka**   di-hña-niki
       evil.spirit 1pl-OBJ be.well,real-REC.P.NONVIS 3sgnf-eat-COMPL
       'The evil spirit has well and truly eaten us up'—NON-VISUAL

When talking about supernatural healing powers of shamans non-visual evidential is the right choice; these powers cannot be seen with an eye of an ordinary human.

Tariana

11.13 kanapada   herenasi naha na-pusua-**mha**
       whichever   illness   they 3pl-suck-PRES.NONVIS
       nheta-niki
       3pl+take.away-COMPL
       'They (shamans) suck any illness and take it away'—NON-VISUAL

Along similar lines, the non-visual evidential is used in Wintu for 'any kind of intellectual experience of "sixth sense" ' (besides hearing, feeling, taste, smell, and touch), and when talking about the supernatural (Schlichter 1986: 47; also see Lee 1941).

As mentioned above, in Shipibo-Konibo, shamanic visions and experiences under the influence of the hallucinogenous *ayahuasca* are cast in direct evidential. This is in contrast to dreams by ordinary humans cast in reported, as we saw under 11.8. In the Shipibo-Konibo world-view, when the great shaman takes *ayahuasca*, he 'travels to another layer of reality and relates with beings that cannot be seen by the non-specialist' (Valenzuela 2003: 51). With the help of *ayahuasca*, 'the shaman sees designs or knots on a patient's face and body, and consults with his allied spirits to arrive at a diagnostic and determine the appropriate treatment'. Consequently, when a shaman diagnoses a patient, he uses the direct evidential.

Shipibo-Konibo

11.14 mi-a-**ra**   koshoshka-nin   yoto-a   iki
       1p-ABS-DIR.EV   river.dolphin-ERG hit.with.blowpipe.dart-PP2 AUX
       'The river dolphin hit you with an (imagined) blowpipe-dart'

In summary, beings with supernatural magical powers can 'see' things other people cannot 'see'. As a result, their powers and actions are referred to with a non-visual evidential by ordinary humans, and with a visual evidential by themselves. As Valenzuela (2003: 58) puts it, 'the use of direct evidential when describing events experienced under the influence of *ayahuasca,* as opposed to the reportative when narrating one's own dream, is very revealing of Shipibo worldview. While *ayahuasca* visions are part of reality, dreams are not, and this distinction is encoded in the system.'

Other evidentials also occur in shamanic revelations. We can recall, from §5.4.3, that in Nganasan these are cast in reported evidential: the shamans are recounting what the spirits told them (Gusev forthcoming: 3, 11). The reported evidential in Nganasan presupposes learning something from 'the horse's mouth'. That shamans use it implies that they communicate directly with spirits—this makes their announcements highly reliable and authoritative. Once again, evidential conventions are rooted in the speakers' beliefs.

A further note on evidential conventions is in order. Many of the tribal societies with large evidential systems have been, or are being, Christianized. Very little is known concerning the impact this has on the evidential use. The Tariana (where the impact of Catholicism has been very strong since the 1920s) have adapted Catholic festivities and restrictions on what to do and what not to do into their belief system. This is reflected in hunting stories. If a man ventures out hunting on Good Friday, the evil spirit of the jungle comes along, tells him off, and punishes him. Jesus is equated with the traditional Creator called *Yapi-riku-ri* (lit. bone-on-REL: 'the one on the bone') and the term for Good Friday is 'the day when Yapirikuri died'. When the Tariana talk about Jesus and Virgin Mary, they consistently employ visual evidentials, just as they would do for omniscient shamans. Whether this usage is to do with calquing the existing Bible translations into Tucano, or whether everything concerning Christianity is treated on a par with visually marked 'common knowledge' requires further investigation.

(C) 'OTHER' VERSUS 'SELF': INTERNAL STATES AND FEELINGS OF SOMEONE OTHER THAN THE SPEAKER

One perceives one's own feelings, states, and emotions in one way; feelings, states, and emotions of other people are perceived differently. This difference between one's own internal experience and someone else's feelings is often reflected in the choice of evidentials. These tendencies have been mentioned numerous times throughout this book. In Quechua, the direct evidential is employed to refer to what the speaker feels, or knows, or suffers (see §5.2). In Nganasan, the non-visual sensory evidential is appropriate. In Tariana and

East Tucanoan languages, as well as in Eastern Pomo, the non-visual evidential is employed in the same circumstances (see §5.3.1 and §10.3). In Tuyuca (Malone 1988: 131), non-visual evidentials are preferred when speakers refer to their own cognitive states (e.g. knowing or understanding).

When it comes to the same feelings, sensations, and emotions for other people, one ought to make a different choice: a Quechua speaker will use the inferred evidential (as in 5.18: 'you must be tired' (INFERRED)), while in Tariana and East Tucanoan languages one uses either visual or inferred evidential (as in 7.34: 'Pedro is sick: I can see he is'). In Sun's words (1993: 968), Amdo Tibetan verbs of internal states 'convey inner situations that are inaccessible for direct observation and can only be inferred subjectively by onlookers on the basis of tangible clues'. That is, for the semantic class of verbs referring to internal states evidentials almost always serve to distinguish between 'self' and 'other people' and their personal domains.

Altered states of mind—that is, speech behaviour under the influence of alcohol or drugs—behave just like verbs of 'internal state'. Since being drunk implies not being in control and not having complete knowledge of what one is doing, this is expressed with non-firsthand, as in Abkhaz (Chirikba 2003: 251), or non-visual evidential, as in Tariana and Tucano.

The ways evidentials can be used with such verbs is somewhat dependent on how the speaker understands and expands his or her 'personal' domain (this makes them akin to 'shifters', in the sense of Jakobson 1957; cf. Broadwell's discussion (1991) of 'speaker' and 'self' as reflected in the evidential system of Choctaw). We saw in §5.3.1 that the 'right' to use the visual or the direct evidential to talk about other people's states may be reserved. This relationship is something negotiated by the people: Dickinson (2000: 420) reports that she can use direct evidential forms in Tsafiki when she speaks of the activities of the family she lives with; and they can use direct forms when they speak of her (though they are not related). I was instructed to use visual evidential in Tariana, to comment about my son's fever. Not only could I see the symptoms of fever; I was sufficiently close to him to be able to know exactly what the matter was. If the speaker feels empathy for the hearer, they can employ the non-visual evidential to talk about the feelings of their interlocutor as if they were talking about their own feelings. Such statements have strong overtones of 'I know exactly what it feels like for you' and may sound rather patronising.

What types of kinship and other relationship allow such extensions? How does this correlate with other social interactions and networks in a society? These are among the many questions that require further investigation, in order to fully evaluate the ways evidential conventions reflect 'other' and 'self' in each society.

(D) EVIDENTIALS AND CULTURAL INNOVATIONS

As a result of spreading cultural innovations, new avenues of information acquisition have become available to many communities. As Boas (1942: 183) put it, 'when changes of culture demand new ways of expression, languages are sufficiently pliable to follow new needs'. Further insights on evidentials can be obtained from the ways in which evidentials are used to describe newly emerging cultural practices. Once again, 'under modern conditions culture controls the growth of language' (Boas 1942: 183).

One such practice is READING. Speakers of Shipibo-Konibo use the reported -*ronki* for the information they read in a book, or in a newspaper because 'the newspaper says it'. Similarly, a reported evidential in Wintu was used to refer to facts one learns from newspaper reports (Lee 1938: 92). The reported evidential in Shipibo-Konibo also describes what one gets on the internet (simply reading, without watching images: we will see below that seeing something—for instance, on television—requires the direct evidential -*ra*). The reported -*ronki* is ubiquitous when talking about Peruvian history in bilingual elementary schools (Valenzuela 2003: 52).

Shipibo-Konibo

11.15	No-n	reken	Inka-**ronki**	ik-á	iki	Manco	Capac
	1pl-GEN	first	Inka:ABS-REP	be-PP2	AUX	Manco	Capac

'Our first Inka was Manco Capac' (it is said: REPORTED)

Reading involves reporting; seeing an actual picture, even a symbol on a map, is akin to visual experience. A Shipibo geography teacher explained that if someone reads in a book about where a given place is, the reported -*ronki* will be appropriate, as in 11.16.

11.16	Alemania-**ronki**	Holanda	patax	iki
	Germany:ABS-REP	the.Netherlands	next.to	COP

'Germany is next to the Netherlands' (I read it in a book: REPORTED)

But if the same information was obtained from a map, the direct evidential -*ra* would be the preferred choice.

11.17	Alemania-**ra**	Holanda	patax	iki
	Germany:ABS-DIR	the.Netherlands	next.to	COP

'Germany is next to the Netherlands' (I saw it on a map: DIRECT)

Literate Tariana speakers use the assumed evidential rather than the reported when retelling stories they have read in books or newspapers. This evidential also occurs when translating Catholic prayers, or acting as Bible translators during church services. We can recall that the assumed evidential marks information derived from reasoning and common sense. This use of evidential may be due to the fact that the reported evidential in Tariana has connotations of 'unreliability' and distancing oneself from the source. In contrast, the assumed evidential does not have any epistemic connotation and can be safely used for information transmission. Talking about locations on the map is different from retelling something one read in a paper. Just as in Shipibo-Konibo, locating something on a map involves pointing to a dot, or to a river: the visual evidential is the only option. This concerns any map—whether a printed map of the world, or a rough map of the area compiled by the author together with the Tariana.

Information obtained through watching TELEVISION, or listening to the RADIO and TAPE RECORDER can be treated in a variety of ways. A speaker of Cherokee (Pulte 1985) would use the firsthand (called 'experienced past'), if an action or state was seen on television or heard on a tape recorder, as shown in 11.18 (see other examples from Cherokee in §2.1: 2.3–9).

Cherokee

11.18   u-wonis-ʌʔi

she-speak-FIRSTH.PAST

'She spoke' (I saw her speech on television or heard a tape recording of the speech later)

For a Shipibo-Konibo, watching something on television also implies 'experiencing the event oneself, since one actually "sees" what is happening'. (Valenzuela 2003: 52). While watching a soccer match, the ongoing events and the result will be described using the direct evidential -*ra*.

Shipibo-Konibo

11.19   Penal   r-iki

penalty:ABS   DIR.EV-COP

'It is a penalty' (I am watching it on television: DIRECT)

But if one hears the match on the radio, the reported -*ronki* must be used: the speaker interprets radio as tantamount to 'being told' about the events.

11.20   Penal-**ronki**   iki

penalty:ABS-REP   COP

'It is a penalty' (I am hearing it on the radio: REPORTED)

A consultant explained that 'if one hears the news on television without watching images', the reported rather than the direct evidential would be appropriate (Valenzuela 2003: 52). Along similar lines, Tariana and Tucano speakers consider televised images on a par with any other visual information, and consequently, retell what they have just seen on TV using visual evidential.

In contrast, a Qiang speaker would use reported to tell about something he or she saw on television (Randy LaPolla, p.c.). In West Greenlandic the reported evidential -*guuq* is used to talk about what one has heard on the radio and seen on television, but it would not be normally used in reporting something one has read in a newspaper (unless it was quoted speech: Fortescue 2003: 301)[7]— again, unlike Shipibo-Konibo.

The reported -*ronki* is used in Shipibo-Konibo to talk about something one heard on the phone. Tariana speakers consistently use the non-visual evidential for what they hear on the radio, or on a tape recorder. An interesting development has been noticed over the years, since Tariana speakers began to talk on the phone for the first time. When they first had this experience in 1999 they described what they had heard with the non-visual evidential. By and by they became more used to telephone conversations, and started speaking Tariana on the phone. In 2001, the phone was installed in the mission centre where numerous Tariana speakers reside. Since then, reports of our phone conversations have been cast in visual evidential—the speakers are now used to this medium of communication and perceive it as equivalent to face-to-face interaction.

In summary: the impact of new technical innovations and new information avenues may affect evidential conventions in two ways. One option is to simply project previously existing traditional evidential conventions onto modern means of communication in much the same way as one would expect in traditional oral communication. That is, whatever is seen is cast in visual evidential. The other option is to develop new evidential conventions for newly emerging communication means, thus adding new semantic complexity to evidentials. All the examples documented so far combine both. What is seen on television is often treated as 'visually acquired'. In Qiang it is considered 'reported' instead. A sign on paper—such as a mark on the map—can be considered tantamount to seeing something, as in Shipibo-Konibo and Tariana. What is read or heard on the radio is hardly ever treated as equivalent to visual. In some systems it is cast in reported evidential (as in Shipibo-Konibo and in Quechua), while in Tariana the preferred evidential is assumed, the choice that allows speakers to avoid the epistemic connotations associated with the reported choice. After the Tariana got used to communicating by phone, they started treating this avenue as the same as face-to-face interaction, which requires visual evidential. A new metaphorical extension to the visual evidential has emerged, due to a new practice. The meaning of an evidential has

---

[7] The suffix -*sima*- meaning 'apparently' (Fortescue 2003: 292, 301–2) can be used in reporting information acquired from TV, radio, or newspaper (Michael Fortescue, p.c.).

been extended to accommodate an extralinguistic reality (much in the spirit of Boas 1942: 183).

We saw, in §10.2.2, that evidentials constitute a powerful and versatile means of manipulating one's discourse: by choosing an evidential one indicates the information source and, if the evidential has an epistemic extension, also what one thinks of the information. This is what happens in Macedonian: people are aware 'that television is used as a propaganda device and that the same footage is used for different news stories'. As a result, the evidential choice depends on the 'trust of the reporter' (Friedman 2003: 211)—we can recall that the non-firsthand evidential in Macedonian has an overtone of information one does not vouch for, while the information cast in firsthand is fully reliable. Example 11.21 sums it up.

11.21 Nad   Kumanovo **puk-a-a**   ili
       above   Kumanovo shoot-IM-3pl(FIRSTHAND)   or
       puka-l-e,   zavis-i   dali
       shoot-L-PL(NON-FIRSTHAND)   depend-PRES+3sg   Q
       veruv-a-ŝ   vo   televizijsk-i   slik-i   ili   ne
       believe-PRES-2sg   in   television-PL   picture-PL   or   not
       'Above Kumanovo they were shooting (FIRSTHAND) or they were allegedly shooting (NON-FIRSTHAND), it depends whether you believe television pictures or not'

No such awareness has yet made its way into small communities, such as the Tariana or the Tucano of the remote Upper Negro area in the state of Amazonas in Brazil. People appear to believe everything they see on television—visually acquired information is the most reliable. In due course, we may expect new epistemic extensions for propaganda devices when these are recognized for what they are.

So far, we have only scratched the surface in looking at correlations between conventionalized information sources and evidential stereotypes. Languages with elaborate multiterm evidential systems tend to be spoken in small tribal societies. As we learn more about their cultural knowledge and stereotypes and how they are adapting to the modern world, we will no doubt acquire further insights into the existing and the developing evidential conventions. One such additional issue in evidential conventions concerns the differences in how men and women use evidentials. Salar-speaking women use more non-firsthand evidential forms than men (Dwyer 2000: 57, and §10.2), possibly because they are traditionally more subdued and less assertive. Further studies are necessary in order to investigate these—and possibly many other—additional conventions and tendencies in evidential usage across the world.

11.4 Cultural and cognitive correlates of evidentials: some speculations

An important question that linguists hardly ever venture to ask is: why is the grammar and the lexicon of a language the way it is? Why are languages with evidentiality systems the way they are? Why do some languages have only one or two evidentials, and others many more? When told about the wonders of precision one can achieve when speaking a language with evidentiality, English speakers often lament—why don't we have that in our language? Wouldn't it be good if our politicians were obliged to say exactly how they learnt so-and-so? And yet English—like many other European languages—simply does not have this grammatical category. When necessary, it makes do with bulky lexical expressions like 'John allegedly (or apparently) killed Paul'. Complex evidential systems, in their vast majority, are confined to languages with a smallish number of speakers, spoken in small, traditional societies. (Quechua and Aymara with a few million speakers each, and a system of three evidentials, are rather exceptional.) If evidentiality is so important for our cognition, and could even facilitate our daily interaction, why does not every language have it?

Given the importance of evidentials for human cognition and status in the community, and their role in conventionalized knowledge, to what extent does their presence in a language and their semantics confirm the Sapir-Whorf hypothesis—that 'through the analysis of a language one can show the viewpoint of a people' (Denny 1979: 117, n.1)? Using Whorf's words (1941: 77), can evidentials be treated on a par with other 'grammatical patterns as interpretations of experience'?

An array of factors combine to determine why a language is, synchronically, the way it is (see Aikhenvald and Dixon 1998*b*: 253–5). These factors include:

1. GENETIC INHERITANCE. A language may maintain the grammatical categories and forms found in its ancestor language. That is, if a category was present in a proto-language, the chances are that it will be there in the daughter languages. This is the case with gender inherited from Proto-Indo-European into most modern Indo-European languages, and with evidentiality inherited by individual Tucanoan languages from Proto-Tucanoan.

2. LANGUAGE CONTACT AND LINGUISTIC DIFFUSION OF CATEGORIES. When languages come in contact with each other, they borrow grammatical categories as well as forms (see Aikhenvald 2002: 3–14). In quite a number of cases one language acquires evidentials under the influence of another, as a result of linguistic diffusion. Numerous examples were discussed in §§9.2.1–3. The reverse can also occur: evidentials are often lost if a language is dominated by another language which does not have them; see §9.2.2.

3. TYPOLOGICAL TENDENCIES.   A certain kind of grammatical system, X, may tend to co-occur with another type of system, Y, and be seldom found in the same language as a further type of system, Z. If a language has X it is likely to develop Y, and unlikely to develop Z. If a language does acquire Z (say, in a language contact situation), it is likely to lose X. For instance, serial verbs and switch-reference marking are predominantly found in languages with accusative (not ergative) syntax. Alternatively, the existence of a value of a category may presuppose another value: if a language has trial number it is likely to have dual as well. Or if a language distinguishes gender in second person it is also likely to distinguish gender in third person (see Aikhenvald 2000: 243–8). Languages with evidentials vary widely in their typological profiles, and no such correlations have so far been established for languages with evidentiality.

4. FACTORS RELATING TO THE SPEAKERS AND THEIR ENVIRONMENT.   Some possible factors include:

(*a*)GEOGRAPHICAL ENVIRONMENT. For instance, languages which make a grammatical distinction 'up/down' in their demonstratives, and/or in other parts of the grammar, are typically spoken in hilly country.

(*b*)SOCIAL ORGANIZATION, LIEFESTYLE, POLITICAL, AND ECONOMIC SYSTEMS. Systems with obligatory grammatical marking of politeness are only found in languages whose speakers have a strongly articulated social hierarchy (e.g. Japanese, Korean, and Balinese). If a language is spoken in a desert, it is unlikely to have a numeral classifier used for counting canoes. It is hardly surprising that a language like Nivkh, whose speakers are experienced fishermen, had special numeral classifiers for counting various arrangements of fish.

(*c*)BELIEFS, MENTAL ATTITUDES, AND BEHAVIOURIAL CONVENTIONS OF THE SPEAKERS.   Myth and belief principles in the semantic organization of noun classes and genders (Dixon 1972; 1982) may account for semantic extensions in these categories. In Dyirbal, birds belong to feminine gender by mythological association since women's souls are believed to enter birds after death. In the Western Torres Strait language all nouns denoting males are masculine, with the remainder being feminine. But the moon is masculine, since it appears as a man in myths (Bani 1987).

The parameters under 4 have scarcely been studied in any depth. Many attempts to establish some connections between grammar and physical environment sound, at best, dubious if not utterly ridiculous. It has been suggested that people who live in damp areas tend to 'select sounds requiring minimal lip opening', or that people who inhabit mountains might well develop 'sounds characterized by large expense of air from enlarged thoracic capacity' (see Brosnahan 1961: 19). Attempts to establish correlations between beliefs, mental attitudes, and the structure of language include unfounded 'explanations' of ergativity as resulting from the passive and subservient character of people who speak ergative languages (Dixon 1994: 214–5).

Notwithstanding such crackpot theories, investigating the correlations between mental attitudes and linguistic categories remains a worthwhile task. Take the use of third person pronouns in English. Up until recently, the masculine pronoun *he* was used as a generic term for any human being, no matter what sex. Recently, with the rise of equal rights for women, this usage has been branded as 'sexist' (cf. for instance, Baron 1982: 193–5).[8] A common convention is to use the unmarked generic pronoun 'they'. That is, cultural pressure against what was conceived as 'male chauvinism' reflected in pronominal usage resulted in semantic change. This shows, in a nutshell, that a study of putative correlations between beliefs, mental attitudes and behavioural conventions, and linguistic phenomena could be potentially rewarding. It may suggest fruitful lines of explanation for why some languages are the way they are. In particular, these correlations may shed light on why some languages have grammatical evidentiality while many lack it.[9]

Being precise in defining one's information source goes together with cultural conventions which appear to be particularly strong in languages with evidentials. Such conventions may include:

(i) whether one should be as specific as possible when speaking, or whether a high degree of vagueness is a normal social expectation, and

(ii) attitudes to the communication of information—whether one should tell people what they want to know, or whether 'new information' is regarded as prized goods, only to be disseminated for some appropriate return (see Keenan and Ochs 1979: 147–53).

As we saw above, in many linguistic communities with evidentiality being as specific as possible about what one has to say is a 'must'. In §§11.1–2, we saw the caution exercised by Aymara speakers with respect to how they know things. Those who do not obey the cultural conventions of evidential usage are not to be

---

[8] This association can be easily falsified: the few languages where the feminine pronoun is used to cover both sexes are spoken in male-dominant societies (see Alpher 1987 and Aikhenvald 2000: 54–5).

[9] Other, more successful attempts have been made to relate cultural and cognitive patterns to other grammatical categories. Amazonian languages are known for a special grammatical category of 'frustrative', with the meaning of 'I want to but I can't'. At the end of an incisive account of this category in Amahuaca and other Panoan languages, Sparing-Chávez (2003: 12) attempts to provide a culture-specific correlate for this category in the Amahuaca society: 'The Amahuaca people are shame oriented and it seems to me that the frustrative helps them to save face by covering up their own shortcomings. They blame others, natural forces, or circumstances. It also helps them to express disagreement or carefully accuse someone without having face-to-face confrontation.'

trusted. Quechua cultural postulates summarized by Weber (1986: 138) point in the same direction. These are:

1. (Only) one's own experience is reliable.
2. Avoid unnecessary risk, as by assuming responsibility for information of which one is not absolutely certain.
3. Don't be gullible. (Witness the many Quechua folktales in which the villain is foiled because of his gullibility.)
4. Assume responsibility only if it is safe to do so. (The successful assumption of responsibility builds stature in the community.)

That is, one should provide the information required, and be specific about it. In a similar vein, McLendon (2003: 113) reports: 'Eastern Pomo speakers from whom I have learned Eastern Pomo since 1959, remembered that when they were children their grandparents constantly reminded them to be careful how they spoke. They were told to be especially careful to speak well to, and about, other people, because if they didn't the person spoken about, or to, might be offended and try to "poison" them, that is, use ritual or other means to bring them misfortune, illness, or even death. Evidentials which distinguish non-visual sensory experience, inference, memory, and knowledge seem a useful means of speaking with care, asserting only what one has evidence for, and making one's evidence clear.'

In the context of Amazonian societies, the requirement to be precise in one's information sources may be related to the common belief that there is an explicit cause—most often, sorcery—for everything that happens. So as not to be blamed for something that in fact they had no responsibility for, a speaker is careful always to be as explicit as possible about what they have done. This relates to the desirability of stating the evidence for everything that is said, visually obtained information being the most valuable. The speaker is also careful not to impute their assumption and their information source onto another person. This could be potentially dangerous: if the speaker is perceived as having access to how other people know things, they may well be regarded as a sorcerer. In a society where sorcery is the most dangerous crime of all, to be accused of it is hardly desirable.

The requirement to mark information source in Western Apache (with scattered evidentiality: de Reuse 2003: 96) may go together with 'Athabaskan attitudes about the autonomy of the person . . . resulting in a reluctance to speak for another person, or to impute feelings to another person.'

Attitudes to truth—that is, whether or not telling lies is an accepted social practice—appear to be irrelevant to the ways in which evidentials are employed, since evidentiality is not about truth or validity of information. We saw in §3.7 that a language with evidentials allows one to lie in rather sophisticated ways: one can provide the right facts with false evidentials, or get the right information source and false information.

These correlations between the requirement to be precise in one's information source imposed by the grammar, and cultural conventions, are very tempting, but highly tentative. Moreover, the same requirements and conventions appear to hold in languages with no grammatical evidentiality. Neither Tuvaluan (Besnier 1992; 2000) nor Weyewa (Kuipers 1992) have grammatical evidentials. And yet what was said above applies to speakers of these languages, too.

Being specific in one's information source appears to correlate with the size of a community. In a small community everyone keeps an eye on everyone else, and the more precise one is in indicating how information was acquired, the less the danger of gossip, accusation, and so on. No wonder that most languages with highly complex evidential systems are spoken by small communities. On the other hand, why is it so that some languages spoken in small closed communities have only a reported evidential? Fortescue (2003: 301) is also convincing when he speculates that 'presumably life in very small, scattered Arctic communities, where everyone is likely to know of everyone else's doings and where rumours spread easily, is such as to make being VAGUE [emphasis mine] about one's source of information . . . a generally sensible strategy'.

When we look for extralinguistic explanations for linguistic categories, we should avoid the danger of being circular. Do Tucano or Quechua have an elaborate system of evidentials because of a cultural requirement to be precise about one's information source lest one is accused of sorcery? Or is the explanation the other way round? At this point in time, I do not have a sensible answer.

At present, all that can be suggested is that some communities in some areas—for instance, in the Amazonian area, and those in the adjoining Andean region—in some way share a common set of beliefs, mental attitudes, and behavioural conventions, as well as discourse genres; and that these are compatible with the independent development of evidential systems with their requirement to be as precise and as specific as possible about information source. This could help explain why evidentiality has independently evolved in at least six (possibly, more) places in Amazonia, and also why it is so susceptible to being diffused in language contact.

We need many more cross-cultural studies of societies which speak languages with evidentiality before any cross-linguistically valid conclusions can be formulated. We can only hypothesize that, because of the way in which such small communities act and think, they welcome specification of the nature of evidence for a statement. Their languages are thus open to the introduction of grammatical marking of this evidence.

11.5 Evidentials in culture and cognition: a summary

Having obligatory evidentials implies being precise in stating one's information source. The diffusibility of evidentials further confirms their importance
for human cognition, and the ways in which people organize their thoughts
through the language they speak. Failure to demonstrate one's competence
in the use of evidentials or a breach of evidential conventions may inflict a blow
to the speaker's reputation and stature as a proficient and trustworthy speaker,
as well as as a responsible and valued member of the community. Evidentials
are thus a category which, once obligatory, influences perception and possibly
even 'subconscious thought' (Hardman 1981: 11) and plays an important part
in speakers' understanding of other people and of the world. Those who speak
a language with evidentiality find it hard to adjust to the vagueness of
information source in many familiar European languages—such as English,
Portuguese, and varieties of Spanish other than those spoken in the Andes.

Speakers are aware of evidentials and their functional load. This awareness is
metalinguistically reflected in the ways people can discuss evidentials and
explain why one evidential and not another was used in a particular circumstance. This involves rephrasing evidentials with lexemes. If a speaker feels that
their evidential choice may appear unjustified to the audience, they may choose
to reinforce an evidential by an explanatory sentence: for instance, a visual evidential can be accompanied by 'I saw it'. Metalinguistic awareness of evidentials
is realized through proverbs, and the ways in which people teach children to
always be precise about saying how they know things.

Each evidential is associated with a certain information source. Different
types of traditional knowledge and experience come to be associated with
conventionalized sources. For instance, dreams can be treated on a par with
directly witnessed observed reality (as in Jarawara, Quechua, Tuyuca, and
Tatuyo). Or they can be represented as being outside conscious reality, and cast
in reported or in non-firsthand evidential (as in Shipibo-Konibo, Yukaghir,
Cree, and Modern Eastern Armenian). The choice of evidential in a dream may
depend on who the dreamer is: dreams by ordinary humans in Tucano and
Tariana are cast in non-visual evidential—such dreams are something not
'seen' in the same way as what one sees while awake. However, shamanic
dreams are couched in visual evidential. Shamans are traditionally considered
omniscient and they 'see' what other humans do not. Similarly to dreams, the
supernatural world of magic and fairy tales can be viewed as an extension of
the ordinary world. These realms can be conceived as not really 'seen'. In
Tucano and in Tariana, evil spirits are not seen: they are 'perceived' in other
ways; for that reason, the non-visual evidential is preferred when talking about

them. But when powerful shamans talk about themselves and their powers, they employ visual evidentials. In Shipibo-Konibo, shamanic visions under the influence of *ayahuasca*, a powerful hallucinogenic substance, are cast in direct evidential—unlike dreams experienced by humans. Such visions are part of a tangible reality: the shaman 'sees' what others do not.

The distinction between 'self' and 'other' is typically reflected in the choice of evidentials: one talks about one's own feelings, states, and emotions differently from the ways in which one talks about someone else's. The degree of proximity and empathy between the speaker and the 'other' may influence the evidential choice: in Tariana, I can talk about my son as if he were myself. What social and other relationships underlie these conventions remains a topic for future studies.

An important issue in the semantics of evidentials and their correlations with cultural knowledge is how new cultural practices get incorporated and what evidentials they require. Introducing reading, television, and radio into the daily life of traditional communities has affected the ways in which evidentials are employed. Previously existing evidential conventions have often been simply extended to cover modern avenues of communication: what one sees on the television screen is marked as visual information. New conventions have been developed for other avenues: for instance, information acquired through reading is never reported in 'visual' evidential. It may be treated on a par with a verbal report—as in Shipibo-Konibo or Quechua, where the reported evidential is then used. The Tariana use the assumed evidential, since the reported evidential has an undesirable overtone of untrustworthy information. Evidentials can acquire new metaphorical extensions with the introduction of innovative means of communication: phone conversations in Tariana are now retold in visual evidential, just like any face-to-face communication.

Evidentials are a powerful and versatile avenue for human communication. Once again, their similarity to Grice's conversational maxims (see §11.1) is striking. What evidentials do is provide grammatical backing for the efficient realization of various maxims within Grice's 'cooperative principle'.

Speaking a language with obligatory evidentials implies adhering to strict cultural conventions. Beliefs, mental attitudes, and patterns of behaviour appear to correlate with these. Exactly how this happens remains to be investigated on the basis of cross-cultural studies of traditional societies. Thus far, I have only been able to offer a few speculations, to be confirmed or refuted by future research.

As Heine (1997: 14–15) put it, 'the way people in Siberia or the Kalahari Desert experience the world around them can immediately be held responsible for the way they shape their grammars. Although conceptualisation strategies are perhaps the main driving force for linguistic categorisation, conceptualisation is not the only force that can be held responsible for why grammar is structured the way it is. . . . Another, equally important, force is communication.' The importance of evidentials for successful communication is what underlies their relevance for human cognition.

Appendix. How children acquire evidentials

The ways in which evidentials are acquired by children could provide invaluable insights into cognitive development and the evolution of cultural and cognitive stereotypes. Yet the investigation of this issue on the basis of a wide variety of cross-linguistic data is in its infancy.

As Joseph (2003: 320) puts it, 'studying the acquisition of evidentials by children is a fertile testing ground' for their various tinges and extensions of meanings: 'When, for instance, does a child learn to talk about his/her dreams? Are there changes in the way children talk about them—or other "sensory-based knowledge"—at different stages of their cognitive development?' At present, these questions remain an area for future research.

According to the preliminary results of a study of the acquisition of the direct evidential -*mi* in the Cuzco-Collao variety of Quechua undertaken by Courtney (1999), young children aged between 2.5 and 2.6 years do not use any evidentials. They first start using the direct evidential in responses to questions. They also employ it as a focus marker (we can recall, from §8.5, that the evidential clitics in Quechua also function as focus markers). It is not until the end of the learning process that children work out the information source marking function of the direct -*mi* and its contrastive use with the inferred evidential (their use as evidentials was recorded in a three-year-old child). No data is available for the reported evidential.

In her seminal study of the acquisition of Turkish past tense forms, including evidentials, Aksu-Koç (1988: 189) found that the 'indirect' evidential -*MIŞ* is first acquired as a tense-aspect marker, and then soon gets extended to mark resultant states and new information. To be able to use the indirect evidential at all, the speaker must differentiate between (i) the time at which the event took place, (ii) the time at which the non-firsthand reporter acquires information about the event based on its result, or on hearsay, and (iii) the time of speech. That is, the correct use of an evidential would require an ability to coordinate at least three different spatio-temporal points. At an early age (about 3.7), this 'informational perspective' is not recognized at all as a factor of any importance. At the age of about 4.6, children only consider the perspective of a direct observer as valid, and disregard all other possibilities. Moreover, the mere possibility that 'an indirect experiencer can make a statement about the event appears contradictory to the existing beliefs of children at this stage and is denied with the claim: "he can't say anything because he did not see the event happen"'. It is not until the age of five and a half that children acquire the underlying rule that 'although the event was not witnessed, the end-result was observed, therefore one can talk about it'. And, as a result, they start using the non-firsthand evidential correctly (Aksu-Koç 1988: 157).

In her most recent publication on how children acquire Turkish evidentials, Aksu-Koç (2000) concludes that monolingual Turkish-speaking children within the age range of 1.3–2.6 years first acquire the past tense–perfective aspect marker -*DI* and the present tense–imperfective aspect marker -*Iyor* to indicate direct experience. These occur in statements about the situation 'here-and-now', paradigmatically opposed to imperative and optative for expressing intentions and requests. That is, the very first distinction relevant for young children is in terms of mood. The non-firsthand 'indirect' evidential -*MIŞ* is first acquired with stative predicates. It is then used to comment on 'locative and physical states which are presented as "novel experience" in discourse' (p. 25). This is remarkably similar to the correlations between verb class and new experiences or mirative readings of evidentials in languages such as Qiang and Yukaghir (see §§6.1–2).

The emergence of an evidential in child's speech heavily depends on the input they get. Aksu-Koç (2000: 25) remarks that 'in all cases the semantic and pragmatic patterns of use observed in adult speech to children, which in turn is coloured by modifications made to adjust to the child interlocutor, play a determining role'. Edith Bavin (p.c.) reports similar patterns underlying the acquisition of Warlpiri by three year olds. They appear to use the reported evidential *nganta* only in its meaning of 'pretend' and 'make believe' (compare 5.68 from Yankunytjatjara: 'It's a horse according to him' (said of a boy playing 'horsies' with a dog)), as in playing at hunting with toy animals rather than real hunting. She further notes that a boy nearly three years old used *nganta* this way, and that this usage was based on how his grandmother employed this evidential marker.

It is possible that, given the elaborate correlations between evidentiality, cultural practices, and stereotyped knowledge, children do not fully acquire all the intricacies of an evidential system until late. This is similar to Carpenter's 'later rather than sooner' principle in the acquisition of classifiers in Thai; just as various stages in the acquisition of classifiers are best characterized as 'stages of organising knowledge' (Carpenter 1991: 108–9),[10] so there may be various stages in acquiring the correct use of an evidential, with all its overtones and extensions, before the children actually have the linguistic and the extralinguistic experience to know what are the 'right' (i.e. the conventionalized grammatical) correlates of an extralinguistic category of information source.[11] Child language acquisition of the whole plethora of evidential uses and meanings, especially in large systems, requires further in-depth investigation.

---

[10] For instance, even ten-year-old Thai children got only 89 per cent of their classifiers right (Carpenter 1991: 98).

[11] A systematic study of how Tucano-speaking children acquire evidentials is a matter for future investigation. During my stay with Tucano-speaking families, I observed that children aged between four and five appear to have fully mastered the tense–evidential system in its daily usage.

12

What can we conclude?
Summary and prospects

Evidentiality is a grammatical means for marking information source. The correct use of evidentials is linked to categorizing ways in which information is acquired. Just as the function of classifiers is 'to place objects in classes to do with human interaction with the environment' (Denny 1976: 130; Aikhenvald 2000: 337–40), so the function of evidentials is to indicate how one has learnt about something, and how to categorize the sources of knowledge

Evidentials across the world share a common semantic core. Their expression varies. Evidentials may be distinguished only in the past. They may be mutually exclusive with some other category; for instance, mood or negation. Evidentials may develop overtones of attitude to information and its probability. None of these features, however, justifies treating evidentials as a kind of tense, aspect, mood, or modality. Evidentials occur together with markers of probability, possibility, and irrealis. Throughout this book I have presented ample evidence in favour of evidentiality as a cross-linguistically valid category in its own right, with information source as its core meaning. Evidentiality only marginally relates to truth value, reliability of information, speaker's responsibility, and epistemic meanings (related to possibility and probability). Consequently, such notions as 'epistemic scale' and certainty are tangential to evidentials.

Evidentiality as a grammatical category is not to be confused with evidential extensions of other grammatical categories. Non-indicative modalities, perfective aspect, nominalizations, and the like can occasionally imply reference to an information source without this being their main and primary meaning. These 'evidentiality strategies' provide historical sources for grammatical evidentials. So sometimes do lexical ways of referring to how one knows things. However, the analysis of lexical expressions for information source lies outside the scope of this study.

This final chapter contains a précis of this book. It recapitulates the general themes and principles which have emerged from the cross-linguistic study of grammaticalized information source, starting with an overview of the types of evidential systems found so far, their expression, their semantics and pragmatics, and their interactions with other grammatical categories. It goes on to discuss the major kinds of evidentiality strategies and summarize the attested historical sources for evidentiality systems, alongside the relationships between evidentials, cultural conventions, and communication. In the last section I suggest further problems and routes of investigation for evidentiality across the world's languages.

12.1 Cross-linguistic properties of evidentials: a summary

Cross-linguistic properties of evidentials cover:

   (I)   organization of systems (Chapter 2);
  (II)   expression of evidentials (Chapter 3);
 (III)   evidential extensions of non-evidential categories (Chapter 4);
 (IV)   semantics of terms within systems of various kinds (Chapters 5 and 6);
  (V)   correlations of evidentials with other grammatical categories (Chapters 7 and 8);
 (VI)   origins of evidentials (Chapter 9);
(VII)   the use of evidentials in discourse and their pragmatic implications (Chapter 10); and
(VIII)   evidentials and cultural conventions (Chapter 11).

(I) Organization of systems

Evidentiality systems are known to make from two to more than five choices. Small systems with just two choices include:

A1. Firsthand and Non-firsthand;
A2. Non-firsthand versus 'everything else';
A3. Reported (or 'hearsay') versus 'everything else';
A4. Sensory evidence and Reported (or 'hearsay');
A5. Auditory (acquired through hearing) versus 'everything else'.

Of these, A1 and A4 are clear-cut two-term systems. In contrast, A2, A3, and A5 include an 'everything else', or evidentiality-neutral term. A4 and especially A5 systems are somewhat problematic in that they have only been described for highly endangered languages. In one case (Wintu), an A4 system arose out of a more complex five-term system as a result of language restructuring due to obsolescence.

   Systems with three choices are:

B1. Direct (or Visual), Inferred, Reported;
B2. Visual, Non-visual sensory, Inferred;
B3. Visual, Non-visual sensory, Reported;

B4. Non-visual sensory, Inferred, Reported;
B5. Reported, Quotative, 'everything else'.

In some B4 systems, the evidentiality value of the unmarked term is typically recoverable from the context.

Four-term systems cover:

C1. Visual, Non-visual sensory, Inferred, Reported;
C2. Direct (or Visual), Inferred, Assumed, Reported;
C3. Direct, Inferred, Reported, Quotative.

Both three-term and four-term systems involve at least one sensory specification. This could be visual, non-visual, or 'direct' (either visual or covering any sensory information).

If there is just one sensory evidential, additional complexity in a four-term system may arise within evidentials based on inference (C2). Then, one evidential refers to inference based on visible results, and the other one to inference based on reasoning and assumption. Additional choices between reported evidentials involve distinguishing reported and quoted information (C3). The reported and the quotative evidentials may differ in terms of how they correlate with a particular genre, and which epistemic extensions they have.

The only type of multiterm system found in more than one language involves:

D1. Visual, Non-visual sensory, Inferred, Assumed, and Reported.

Systems with five or more terms have just two sensory evidentials, and a number of evidentials based on inference and assumption of different kinds.

Semantic parameters employed in languages with grammatical evidentiality cover physical senses and several types of inference and of report. The recurrent semantic parameters are:

I. Visual which covers evidence acquired through seeing;
II. Sensory which covers evidence through hearing, and is typically extended to smell and taste, and sometimes also touch;
III. Inference based on visible or tangible evidence or result;
IV. Assumption based on evidence other than visible results: this may include logical reasoning, assumption, or simply general knowledge;
V. Hearsay, for reported information with no reference to whom it was reported by; and
VI. Quotative, for reported information with an overt reference to the quoted source.

No language has a special evidential to cover smell, taste, or feeling (see summary in Table 2.1). No systems have been found with all six specifications expressed. Semantic parameters group together in various ways, depending on the system. Some of the six parameters can be covered with one term. The most straightforward grouping is found in B1 systems—where sensory parameters (I and II), inference (III and IV), and reported (V and VI) are grouped together. This roughly corresponds to Willett's (1988) tripartite 'central domains' of evidentiality: 'attested evidence' (which for him covers visual, auditory, and other sensory evidence), 'inferring evidence', and 'reported evidence'.

However, this three-fold subdivision, does not exhaust the actual situation. Visually acquired information can be marked differently from any other, and so can non-visual sensory. Inference and report can be grouped together under one term. The exact semantic details of each evidentiality specification may vary. For instance, assumption may cover general knowledge. In contrast, in systems with three terms or more, generally known facts may be cast in visual evidential. Different evidentials may or may not acquire epistemic and mirative extensions—see (III) below.[1]

(II) Expression of evidentials
Evidentials can be expressed with a wide array of morphological mechanisms and processes. There is no correlation between the existence of evidentials and language type. Even Pidgins and Creoles are known to have had evidentials (see Nichols 1986, on Chinese Pidgin Russian). No evidentials have as yet been found in any Sign Language (Ulrike Zeshan, p.c.). Examples of a truly functionally unmarked form in an evidentiality system are rare. The visual, or a combined visual and sensory, evidential tends to be less formally marked than any other term (see Scheme 3.1, repeated below as Scheme 12.1 for easy reference).

SCHEME 12.1 Formal markedness in evidentiality systems

Visual	Other sensory	Other types of information source
← -- →		
the least likely to be formally marked		the most likely to be formally marked

Evidentiality-neutral terms are a property of a few systems where an evidential is opposed to 'everything else' (these are A2, A3, A5, and B5). This is quite different from omitting an evidential, whether because the information source is clear from the context, or because evidentials are mutually exclusive with some other morpheme.

---

[1] Rephrasing Denny (1976: 131) on classifiers, 'a particular advantage of a semantically-based theory' of evidentials 'is that it enables the essential commonalities [. . .] to be perceived across the enormous variety in their morphology from language to language'.

Co-occurrence of different evidentials in one clause and the different morphological status of evidentials provide tools for distinguishing evidentiality subsystems within one language. If a language has several distinct evidentiality subsystems, the reported is most likely to be set apart from others.

Evidentials differ from other grammatical categories in a number of ways. The information source can be marked more than once in a clause (see Table 3.2). Two sources of information can have different scope, as in Jarawara. Or two different sources may confirm or complement each other, as in Qiang and Shipibo-Konibo. Alternatively, two sources can be different, but somehow linked together, as in Tsafiki and Bora. Or they can be fully distinct, as in Eastern Pomo (see §3.5). (This should not be confused with repeating an evidential, for pragmatic reasons or as a genre marker; see §3.6.) These features make evidentiality similar to a predication in its own right. Further arguments to the same effect include:

- An evidential may be within the scope of negation, as in Akha; see §3.7.
- An evidential can be questioned, as in Wanka Quechua; see §3.7.
- The 'truth value' of an evidential may be different from that of the verb in the clause; see Table 3.3 on how evidentials can be manipulated to tell a lie.
- And finally, an evidential can have its own time reference, distinct from the time reference of the event talked about; see §3.8.

(III) Evidential extensions of non-evidential categories

Grammatical categories and constructions which can develop evidential overtones include non-indicative moods and modalities, futures, perfects, resultatives, past tenses, passives, nominalizations, complementation strategies, and person-marking. Schemes 12.2 and 12.3 (repeated from Schemes 4.1 and 4.2) show the development of evidential extensions for non-indicative moods and modalities.

SCHEME 12.2 Evidential extensions for non-indicative moods in main clauses

Stage 1. Unreal or potential event (marked with conditional, dubitative, potential, or irrealis), and/or an event concerning which only prediction or 'educated guess' is possible (future)
↓
Stage 2. Assumption and inference one cannot vouch for
↓
Stage 3. General range of non-firsthand meanings with epistemic overtones

SCHEME 12.3 Evidential extensions for non-indicative moods in non-main clauses

Stage 1. Complement clause of a speech verb used as a main clause, meaning 'reported speech' ↓ Stage 2. Meaning 'reported speech' acquires overtones of 'distancing', and facts one does not vouch for ↓ Stage 3. Further development of a range of non-firsthand meanings with epistemic overtones

Scheme 12.4 (repeated from Scheme 4.3) features the development of evidential extensions for perfects and resultatives.

SCHEME 12.4 Evidential extensions for perfects and resultatives

Stage 1. Result of an action or state; or action or state viewed as relevant for the moment of speech ↓ Stage 2. Inference based on visible traces ↓   ↓ Stage 3a. Inference based on assumption and possibly hearsay (3b. Visual/firsthand information) ↓ Stage 4. General range of non-firsthand meanings

The semantic path of development for non-firsthand extensions for passives and for resultative nominalizations is essentially the same. De-subordination—whereby a dependent clause becomes reinterpreted as a main clause—is concomitant to how some non-indicative moods and modalities, and nominalizations, can develop evidential extensions, and even grammaticalize as evidentials in due course. The development of evidential extensions by perfective and resultative nominalizations is similar to that of perfectives and resultatives. This holds for nominalizations both as heads of predicates and as parts of complex predicates.

Complement clauses of verbs of perception and cognition can express perceptual (that is, visual or auditory) meanings as opposed to a simple report. They do not have either mirative or epistemic extensions of meaning. If a language has several evidentiality strategies they are never fully synonymous.

None of the evidentiality strategies is universal, with one exception. Just about every language has some way of reporting what someone else had said.

Reported speech can be viewed as a universal evidentiality strategy and as an alternative to a reported evidential. The two have a few features in common, but are never fully synonymous (see §4.8, and Table 4.2). Just like reported evidentials, reported speech can express information one does not vouch for. Quoting someone verbatim may allow the speaker to be precise as to the exact authorship of information. This same technique may have different overtones in different languages: quoting someone verbatim in Arizona Tewa implies that the speaker does not vouch for what he or she quotes.

When visual and auditory meanings are encoded in demonstrative systems, they interact with other, typically demonstrative meanings—such as spatial distance and anaphora.

Evidentiality strategies typically develop a range of meanings characteristic of reported and non-firsthand evidentials: inference and verbal report (see Scheme 12.5, repeated from Scheme 4.4, for an outline of the semantic range of evidentiality strategies).

SCHEME 12.5 The semantic range of evidentiality strategies

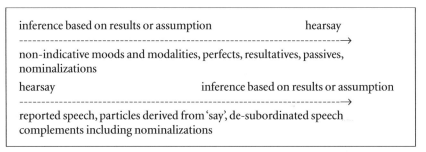

Just occasionally, evidentiality strategies distinguish firsthand and non-firsthand information sources. No language has been found to have a special evidentiality strategy for each of the evidential meanings which can be expressed in a multiterm evidential system.

Non-indicative moods and modalities, perfects, resultatives, passives, and nominalizations start with basic inferential meanings, and may end up getting extended to cover verbal reports. Reported speech constructions, particles derived from 'say', and de-subordinated speech complements (including nominalizations in this function) start as markers of reported speech and may extend to cover inference. Demonstratives are rather different: they may evolve perceptual meanings, of visual and other sensory origin. Conjunct-disjunct person-marking systems differentiate between 'self' and 'other' as information source, but do not fully match any of the semantic parameters found in evidentiality systems (see Table 2.1).

The meanings of inference and deduction are linked to the results of something already achieved. This explains why perfects and resultatives, and also resultative passives and nominalizations, tend to develop inferential overtones. Non-indicative moods and modalities preserve their non-evidential core meanings. In the same way conjunct/disjunct systems primarily mark speech-act participants, and demonstratives indicate spatial distance and anaphora. Table 4.3 summarizes the semantic content of evidential strategies, and the mechanisms involved.

Historically, most evidentiality strategies develop into grammatical evidentials. Small evidentiality systems can arise through the reanalysis of perfects, resultatives, passives, nominalizations, de-subordinated complement clauses of verbs of speech, and reported speech markers (see §9.1). In contrast, non-indicative modalities can only occasionally give rise to an evidential, while conjunct/disjunct person systems and demonstratives never do. This could be explained by the semantic path involved in the emergence of evidential overtones in various categories.

Languages with complex systems of grammatical evidentiality have few if any evidentiality strategies at all.

(IV) Semantics of terms within systems of various kinds
Different evidentials have different semantic extensions, depending on the system and its structure. Evidential markers may indicate a speaker's attitude towards the validity or probability of certain information (but do not have to); this is why evidentiality is not part of epistemic modality. The simpler the system, the more semantic complexity of terms we expect.

Semantic extensions of evidentials in small systems are summarized in Table 5.2. The main meaning is given first. The FIRSTHAND term in two-term systems typically refers to visual and often other sensory information, and can be extended to denote the direct participation, control, and volitionality of the speaker. The sensory evidential in A4 systems refers to sensory perception of any kind, without any epistemic or other overtones.

The NON-FIRSTHAND term in A1 and A2 systems means the opposite of firsthand. These terms often imply lack of participation, lack of control, non-specific evidence (or no evidence at all), inference, and hearsay. An extension to hearsay is sometimes found but is not universal.

There are hardly any epistemic extensions in A1 evidentiality systems with two choices. Occasionally, epistemic overtones of uncertainty are found in some A2 and A3 systems. Languages tend to have other ways of expressing probability and possibility.

A typologically universal tendency is operational for evidentiality strategies based on perfects and nominalizations as well as on reported particles: they develop similar overtones to non-firsthand evidentials.

In other, larger systems the visual evidential usually covers information acquired through seeing, and also generally known and observable facts. It may be extended to indicate certainty. The inferred evidential may acquire an epistemic extension of 'conjecture', uncertainty, and lack of control in three-term systems, but not in larger systems, while the non-visual sensory evidential—but not the inferred term—may acquire similar extensions in four-term systems.

The major difference between A2, A3, and A5 systems on the one hand and other small systems on the other lies in the existence of an evidentiality-neutral 'everything else' term. Unlike A1 systems, A2 systems offer an opportunity of not marking any information source (see §3.2.3).

Semantic extensions of evidentials in systems with three choices are summarized in Table 5.3; examples are in §5.2. The meanings of terms in evidentiality systems with three choices are rather similar to those in small systems, but not identical. Languages with B1 systems have just one SENSORY evidential. There is a major difference between representatives of B1 type: while in Qiang the only sensory evidential refers exclusively to things seen, in other systems (e.g. Quechua and Shasta) such a term covers information acquired by any appropriate sense— hearing, smelling, touching, or 'internal experience'. The VISUAL evidential in languages with two sensory evidentials (B2 and B3) is restricted to visually acquired information.

The VISUAL evidential may have epistemic extensions of certainty and commitment to the truth of the proposition. It may also carry overtones of the speaker's conviction and responsibility for a statement, and is commonly used to talk about generally known facts. It is used to refer to the speaker's internal states. Epistemic extensions of the direct evidential are not universal—for example, they are not found in Qiang, Bora, and Koreguaje (B1 systems).

The NON-VISUAL SENSORY evidential in B2, B3, and B4 systems refers to information acquired by hearing, smell, touch, or feeling (such as an injection). There are no epistemic extensions—with the possible exception of Maricopa (B3), where both visual and non-visual evidentials are said to assert something 'which truly happened in the past' (Gordon 1986a: 84).

The INFERRED evidential in B1, B2, and B4 systems covers inference of all sorts: based on visual evidence, non-visual sensory evidence, reasoning, or assumption. It is also used to refer to someone else's 'internal states'—feelings, knowledge, and the like. Due to its links with inference based on conjecture, the inferred evidential may acquire epistemic overtones of doubt and non-commitment in some systems—such as Quechua (but not any others exemplified in §5.2.3), especially if the sentence already contains some indication of doubt. Examples like 5.27–8 ('They will come back from this place' and 'I'll surely/very likely go tomorrow') demonstrate that by itself the inferred evidential has little to do with doubt. Additional uses of the inferred include ironic and sarcastic observations.

The semantic complexity of sensory evidentials in large systems (C1–3 and D1) is summarized in Table 5.4.

The VISUAL evidential in C1 and D1 systems and the DIRECT evidential in C2 and C3 systems cover what is seen. This term often has overtones of reliable information for which the speaker takes personal responsibility, and an epistemic extension of certainty. It also refers to generally known facts. The DIRECT evidential occurs in statements describing information obtained by senses other than feeling—that is, its semantic breadth is similar to that of the direct evidential in a B1 system (as in Quechua). In Tsafiki (C2), the direct evidential implies the speaker's participation in the action. In Tariana (D1), the visual evidential has this meaning (see Table 5.1).

The NON-VISUAL SENSORY evidential covers what is not seen but is perceived by hearing, smelling, or feeling. This does not include purposeful touching: the non-visual evidential has overtones of non-volitionality and non-control. This is especially salient in the context of first person participants (see §7.2). The non-visual evidential is used to talk about one's own internal states and processes interpreted as not really 'seen' (such as dreams or the actions of evil spirits; see examples in §11.3). Only straightforward perceptual meanings of the non-visual are covered by the direct evidential in C2 and C3 systems; see Table 5.1.

The INFERRED evidential in C1 and C3 systems is used to describe all kinds of inference and also to talk about other people's internal states. C2 and D1 systems distinguish two types of inferred evidentials: inference based on visible results (inferred) and assumption based on reasoning. The latter is used to describe other people's internal states in some D1 systems. Further types of inference can be based on previous evidence, uncertain visual evidence, physical appearance, and so on; most of these occur in languages with scattered coding of evidentiality where it does not form one grammatical system and different evidential specifications are expressed in different parts of the grammar.

The REPORTED evidential is semantically uniform in systems of all types. Its core meaning is to mark that information comes from someone else's report. The following extensions have been attested:

(*a*) A reported evidential can be used as a quotative, to indicate the exact authorship of the information, or to introduce a direct quote. A special quotative evidential is found only in B5 and C3 systems.

(*b*) A reported evidential can be used for secondhand and for a thirdhand report. Only some C3 systems distinguish secondhand and thirdhand evidentials.

(*c*) A reported evidential can develop an epistemic extension of unreliable information, as a means of 'shifting' responsibility for the information to some other source one does not vouch for. Such extensions are not universal. As Valenzuela (2003: 57) remarks for Shipibo-Konibo, the selection of reported evidential over the direct evidential 'does not indicate uncertainty or a lesser degree of reliability but simply reported information'.

Similarities between individual evidentiality terms across systems cover:

1. The firsthand and sensory terms in A1 and A4 systems subsume the meanings encoded by visual evidentials in B2–3, C1, and D1, non-visual sensory evidentials in B2–4, C1, and D1, and direct evidentials in B1, C2, and C3.
2. The non-firsthand evidentials typically subsume the meanings of the inferred term in B1, B2, and B4, and inferred and assumed terms in C2 and D1. The non-firsthand evidential may be used for reported information. Only some systems develop epistemic extensions for a non-firsthand evidential.
3. The visual evidential in three- and four-term systems always refers to strictly visual information. Its epistemic extensions may include the speaker's certainty and possibly also their commitment to the truth of the statement. Its further extensions include the speaker's responsibility and generally known facts.

   These extensions are consistent with visually acquired information being considered the most valuable (see §10.1).
4. The non-visual evidential in three- and four-term systems covers information obtained by any other sensory perception. In four-term systems these evidentials also refer to accidental and non-controllable actions, and produce a 'first-person effect'. Non-visual can be extended to refer to one's own or to other peoples' states or feelings.
5. The direct evidential in B1, C2, and C3 systems spans the domain of visual and non-visual sensory evidentials under (1.) and (4.) above. It can be similar to visual (3.) in its epistemic extensions, which cover the speaker's responsibility, certainty, commitment to the statement, and generally known facts.
6. The inferred evidential in B systems covers all meanings to do with inference and assumption (which may each have a separate term in larger systems). Inferred evidentials have no epistemic extensions. The inferred

in three-term systems may acquire epistemic extensions of uncertainty and probability. The non-visual acquires epistemic extensions just in some four-term systems. In fact, many multiterm systems require subtle precision in indicating how the information was obtained, which leaves little leeway for uncertainty; consequently, epistemic meanings are not expressed through evidentials.

Some evidentials have epistemic extensions. But this does not make evidentials into modal or epistemic markers. In Shipibo-Konibo, the direct evidential has overtones of certainty and the inferred has overtones of probability. If these were primarily epistemic, a combination of direct and inferred evidential would have yielded meaningless combinations such as 'I am sure that I doubt' Valenzuela (2003: 57). Since the evidential meanings and not those of probability or certainty are primary, combining the two evidentials makes sense (see examples in §3.5).

Languages with multiterm evidentials generally tend to have a multiplicity of other verbal categories, especially ones that relate to modalities. The larger the evidential system, the less likely are the evidential terms to develop epistemic extensions.

A non-firsthand term in a two-term system, or an inferred term in a three-term system, tends to subsume all sorts of information acquired indirectly. This includes inference (based on direct evidence, or general knowledge, or no information), as well as 'indirect participation' and new knowledge. These evidentials may then evolve mirative extensions (to do with unexpected information, 'unprepared mind' of the speaker, and speaker's surprise). No evidential has mirativity as its main meaning (in agreement with Lazard 1999). Categories other than evidentials may also have mirative overtones. In some languages, however, mirativity is a category in its own right (this is discussed in the Appendix to Chapter 6). 'Mirative' extensions are typical of non-firsthand evidentials (where they often go together with 'lack of control' on behalf of the speaker), and of inferred and sometimes of reported evidentials. See Table 6.1, for a summary. Mirative extensions can also depend on tense-aspect and the semantic class of the predicate. We saw that in Qiang these are found with verbs to do with the result of an action. Mirative extensions can arise through the speaker's lack of firsthand information, non-participation, and lack of control and awareness. This non-participation can be deliberate or not. Mirative overtones can also be linked to 'deferred' realization, whereby the speaker gives a post-factum interpretation to what they may have observed in some other way.

Evidentiality strategies with meanings similar to those of non-firsthand in A1 and A2 systems also develop mirative extensions. This is in full accord with the general tendency for evidentiality strategies to follow a semantic path similar to evidentials.

(V) Correlations of evidentials with other grammatical categories

Meaning and occurrence of an evidential interrelate with various grammatical categories. Evidentials interact with the person of the participants and observers.

An evidential can reflect the information source of any person 'I', 'you', or a third person. Not unfrequently, the firsthand, the visual, and the non-visual evidential reflect the way the speaker perceives what is happening. This is not to say that these evidentials always reflect the speaker's perception. We saw in §3.5 how perception by multiple observers can be marked in one clause. In 3.27, from Eastern Pomo, the non-visual sensory evidential refers to the perception by a blind character who could only hear the hero walk out. The reported *-le* is the evidential used in traditional narratives. The two occur together in one clause.

When the observer is first person, certain seemingly counterintuitive evidential choices develop specific overtones which I refer to as 'first person effect'. Non-firsthand evidentials in A1 and A2 systems, non-visual evidentials in larger systems, and reported in many systems of varied types may acquire additional meanings of lack of intention, control, awareness, and volition on the part of the speaker. This complex of meanings correlates with a speaker's 'unprepared mind', sudden realization, and ensuing 'surprise', resulting in mirative extensions (see §6.4). With firsthand and visual evidentials, first person may acquire the opposite meaning: the action is intentional and the speaker is fully aware of what they are doing. In none of the instances investigated is it possible to distinguish between 'control', 'volition', and 'intention' as separate semantic components. This group of meanings is realized as a bundle. Evidentiality strategies develop similar overtones in the context of first person. In contrast, in a number of Tibeto-Burman languages, the combination of first person with direct evidential implies accidental, uncontrolled action of which the speaker was merely a passive participant.

Assumed and inferred evidentials have hardly any first-person-specific extensions. When used with second and third person, these evidentials may occasionally develop overtones of politeness. First person marking with a non-firsthand evidential may transmit the information about the speaker which is new to the addressee. It may then include two observers, 'you' and 'me' (as in Archi and in Meithei). There tend to be more restrictions on evidentiality choices with first person than with second or third. Some languages have evidentials used just to refer to information acquired by first person.

Verbs covering internal states may require an obligatory evidential choice depending on person. As a result of these correlations evidentials acquire the implicit value of person markers. They can then be considered person-marking strategies.

Evidentials interrelate with clause types and grammatical categories of mood, modality, negation, and tense and aspect in the following ways.

1. The maximum number of evidential specifications is distinguished in declarative main clauses.
2. The most frequent evidential in commands is reported ('do what someone else told you to'). The choice of an evidential in questions may contain reference to the source of information available to the speaker, to the addressee, or to both. As a result, the meaning of evidentials in interrogative clauses and in declarative clauses can be rather different; see Table 8.1.
3. Fewer evidentials may be used in negative clauses than in positive.
4. Non-indicative modalities (conditional, dubitative, and so on) tend to allow fewer evidential specifications than the indicative.
5. The maximum number of evidential specifications is expected in past tenses. There are often no evidentiality choices at all in future which is, by its nature, a kind of modality. These correlations can be accounted for by the nature of evidentiality, and its relations to the temporal setting of events. The evidence for an event is often based on its result, hence the link between firsthand or non-firsthand on the one hand, and past, perfect, perfective, and resultative on the other.

There are hardly any correlations between evidentials and any other categories.

(VI) Origins of evidentials

The development of an independent verb into an evidentiality marker is a frequently attested grammaticalization path. The historical origins of evidentials confirm their similarities with independent predicates. Evidentials often come from grammaticalized verbs. The verb of 'saying' is a frequent source for reported and quotative evidentials, and the verb 'feel, think, hear' can give rise to non-visual evidential in large systems. Closed word classes—deictics and locatives—may give rise to evidentials, in both small and large systems.

Evidentiality strategies involving past tenses and perfects, and nominalizations, can develop into small evidentiality systems (A1 and A2). The creation of a reported evidential may involve reanalysis of subordinate clauses (typically, complement clauses of verbs of speech) as main clauses. Non-indicative moods and modalities may give rise to a term in a large evidentiality system; however, there are no examples of a modal system developing into a system of evidentials. This confirms the separate status of evidentiality and modality. Large evidential systems tend to be heterogenous in origin.

Evidentiality is a property of a significant number of linguistic areas. It is highly diffusible: languages acquire evidentials through contact, and also lose them when under pressure from neighbouring languages with no evidentials. Evidentials make their way into contact languages. Their stability then depends on whether or not a particular variety of a contact language becomes the norm.

When a language becomes obsolescent, it may lose its evidentials, as part of general loss of its morphosyntactic complexity. An erstwhile evidential system may get readjusted to the system in a dominant language (for example, evidentials in Wintu were reinterpreted as epistemic markers under the influence of English).

(VII) Evidentials in discourse and their pragmatic implications

The use of evidentials depends on a variety of conventions. If several information sources are available, visual evidential is preferred over any other option, because of the value attributed to what one has actually seen (see Diagrams 10.1 and 10.2). The genre of a text may determine the choice of an evidential. Lexical conventions include preferential evidential choices for different classes of verbs. For instance, the non-visual evidential is preferred in a larger system when talking about what one feels or knows. To talk about what someone else feels or knows, another evidential will be employed. Evidentials can be manipulated in discourse as a stylistic device. Switching from a reported to a direct (or visual) evidential creates the effect of the speaker's participation and confidence. Switching to a non-firsthand evidential often implies a backgrounded 'aside'. The interplay of various evidentials within a text is what makes it polyphonic.

Choosing an evidential is quite unlike automatically applying specific rules. The pragmatics of evidential choice has to do with various competing factors, depending on which aspect of the situation the speaker intends to highlight. Diagram 12.1 (repeated from Diagram 10.3) shows the ways in which these choices can be and usually are restricted, and which one is preferred over the other, everything else being equal.

An evidential in a lexically fixed expression—such as a speech formula, or a fully lexicalized form—always remains the same. Discourse and narrative conventions override requirements dictated by the semantic class of the verb. If the genre of a story requires that it be cast in reported evidential, the reported evidential is used no matter what semantic class the verbs belong to or what other conventions there are which may prefer a particular evidential choice.

DIAGRAM 12.1 How to choose the correct evidential: restrictions and preferences

Lexically fixed expressions
↓
Textual genre
↓
Conventionalized evidential choice for description of types of experience
↓
Grammatical choice (e.g. depending on person)
↓
Preferred evidentials for competing information sources

The semantics of the verb overrides the first person effect: if the verb implies an uncontrollable state, the choice of non-visual evidential automatically goes with first person and does not have any further implications of lack of control. If there are competing information sources, and if everything else is equal, one applies the principle of the preferential status of visually acquired data.

The narrative genre as a macro-convention typically overrides all other preferences. Narrative conventions thus serve to narrow down the polysemy of evidentials depending on person and other factors.

(VIII) Evidentials and cultural conventions
Having obligatory evidentials implies being precise in stating one's information source. The diffusibility of evidentials further confirms their importance for human cognition and the ways in which people organize their thoughts when they speak. Failure to demonstrate one's competence in the use of evidentials, or a breach of evidential conventions, may inflict a blow to the speaker's reputation and stature in the community.

Speakers are aware of evidentials and their importance. This awareness is metalinguistically reflected in the ways people can discuss evidentials and explain why one evidential, and not another, was used in particular circumstances. Metalinguistic awareness of evidentials is realized through proverbs, and the ways in which people teach children to always be precise in saying how they know things. Evidentiality is interlinked with conventionalized attitudes to information and precision in stating the source of information.

Each evidential is associated with a certain information source. Different types of traditional knowledge and experience come to be associated with conventionalized sources. For instance, dreams can be treated on a par with directly observed reality (as in Jarawara, Quechua, Tuyuca, and Tatuyo). Or they can be represented as being outside conscious reality, and cast in reported or in non-firsthand evidential (as in Shipibo-Konibo, Yukaghir, Cree, and

Modern Eastern Armenian). The choice of evidential in a dream may depend on who the 'dreamer' is: dreams by ordinary humans in Tucano and Tariana are cast in non-visual evidential; such dreams are something not 'seen' in the same way as what one sees while awake. Shamanic dreams are cast in visual evidential; shamans 'see' what other people do not.

The distinction between 'self' and 'other' is typically reflected in the choice of evidentials: one talks about one's own feelings, states, and emotions differently from the ways in which one talks about someone else's. What social and other relationships underlie these conventions remains a topic for future studies.

An important issue in the semantics of evidentials and their correlations with cultural knowledge is how new cultural practices get incorporated and what evidentials they require. Introducing reading, television, and radio into the daily life of traditional communities has affected the ways in which evidentials are employed. Previously existing evidential conventions have often been simply extended to cover modern avenues of communication: what one sees on the television screen is marked as visual information. New conventions have been developed for other avenues: for instance, information acquired through reading is never reported in 'visual' evidential. It may be treated on a par with a verbal report, as in Shipibo-Konibo or Quechua. Evidentials can acquire new metaphorical extensions with the introduction of innovative means of communication: phone conversations in Tariana are now reported in visual evidential, just like any face-to-face communication.

Evidentials are a powerful and versatile avenue for human communication. They provide grammatical backing for the efficient realization of the various maxims of conversational implicature within Grice's 'cooperative principle' (Grice 1989: 26–8). Following the Maxim of Quantity, they allow speakers to make their contribution 'as informative as required'. In agreement with the Maxim of Manner, they help avoid both 'obscurity of expression' and 'ambiguity'. This is why lay people and even linguists often wish that familiar Indo-European languages could require as much precision of speech as is obligatory in languages with evidentials. The importance of evidentials for successful communication is what underlies their relevance for human cognition.

Speaking a language with obligatory evidentials implies adhering to strict cultural conventions. Beliefs, mental attitudes, and patterns of behaviour appear to correlate with these. Exactly how this happens remains to be investigated, and will have to be based on cross-cultural studies of traditional societies. So far, I have only been able to offer a few speculations, to be confirmed, or refuted, by future research.

The aim of this summary is to establish a unified set of properties and parameters as the basis for the further investigation of evidentials in previously undescribed or underdescribed systems. These parameters also lay a foundation for working out further parameters and insights into further kinds of evidential systems.

12.2 Evidentials: prospects and avenues for further investigation

As we saw in Chapter 1, linguistic scholars have been trying to come to grips with the notion of obligatory information source, unusual from the point of view of a European-biased approach, for a long time. The early grammarians of Quechua and Aymara did their best to background this salient feature: evidentials were discarded as mere 'ornate particles' with no real meaning attached to them. Modern linguistics bears witness to the opposite extreme. Once evidentials had been 'discovered' through the ground-breaking work of Boas, Jakobson, and Barnes, to name but a few, there has been an upsurge in attempts to show that familiar Indo-European languages are not deprived of this fascinating category. Studies of lexical expressions of information source in English, Dutch, or Modern Greek under the label of 'evidentiality' run the risk of submerging this grammatical category and obscuring its status in languages where it does exist. Yet other authors have been consistently trying to demote evidentiality into the domain of tense-aspect, modality, or mood, putting it under the umbrella terms of 'subjectivity', 'reliability of knowledge', or 'epistemic modality'. As a result, some grammars group evidentials together with 'modals', notwithstanding their distinct grammatical and semantic properties. This creates an additional challenge to a cross-linguistically informed typological study of the category.

All these pitfalls ought to be carefully avoided, in order to expand and amplify our knowledge of evidentials in the grammars of already known languages, and of those which are as yet uninvestigated.

A number of areas require further work in order to refine our understanding of grammatical evidentials. There is first and foremost an urgent need to provide good descriptive analytic studies of individual systems, especially in the areas of little-known, 'exotic' languages such as Amazonia and Papua New Guinea. Many languages with multiterm evidentials are spoken in Amazonia. As yet, very few systems have been analysed in full detail. Among East Tucanoan languages, in-depth studies are available for Tucano and for Tuyuca (with excellent work in progress on Wanano: Stenzel 2003). Other languages require much more study than has thus far been done. Among other language families which require in-depth studies of evidentials are Carib, Tupí (including the Tupí-Guaraní branch), Jê, and Bora-Witoto. For many of these, even the question of whether a language has one grammatical category of information source, or scattered evidentiality, remains open. Systematic study of Nambiquara languages, with their intricate evidentiality system hinted at by Lowe (1999), is an urgent priority, even more so in the light of their degree of endangerment.

Evidentials in New Guinea languages remain a puzzle. At least three languages have rather complex systems. One is Oksapmin, an isolate from Sandaun province (§2.2 and Lawrence 1987). The other two are from the Kutubuan family in the Southern Highlands—Foe (Rule 1977) and Fasu (May and Loeweke 1980: 71–4). No comprehensive grammar is available for any of these. Are there any more languages in Sandaun province or in the New Guinea highlands with large evidential systems? Given the linguistic diversity of the Sepik area (to which Sandaun (West Sepik) province belongs), one may expect the answer 'yes'. More studies are urgently needed.

Very few evidentiality systems have been described for African languages. Is this a mere coincidence? Again, urgent investigation of this issue is required. At least some languages of the Philippines have been reported to have evidentials. This 'reported' information needs to be substantiated with in-depth research.

Even for well-described languages there is often need for more detailed studies of evidentials, especially studies involving texts and conversations, as well as participant–observation results. Only further empirical work will further our knowledge of varied evidential systems, their semantics and pragmatics of use, and correlations between evidentials and other grammatical categories, especially in large systems. For languages of all types, all areas, and every genetic affiliation, we need further work on investigating dependencies between evidentials and narrative genres. Investigating evidentials and their use with different semantic groups of predicates requires in-depth analysis of the semantic structure of languages. How do speakers deal with competing information sources? What evidentials are used to talk about dreams, or paranormal phenomena? Only on the basis of full-fledged empirical study will we be able to further investigate the ways in which evidentials are employed in referring to cultural stereotypes and newly emerging cultural practices. Some suggestions for working with evidentials are given in the Fieldworker's guide below.

Child language acquisition of evidentials remains a notable gap. Yet quite a few languages with large evidentiality systems are being acquired by children. Quechua and Aymara have quite a high number of speakers. Tucano, with over ten-thousand speakers, has recently been accorded the status of one of the three official languages in the territory of Upper Rio Negro in the state of Amazonas in Brazil. Investigating how children acquire marking of information source will no doubt provide valuable insights into evidentials and their role in cognition. Nothing whatsoever is known about the dissolution of evidentials in aphasia.

Evidentials offer a fertile ground for collaborative research by descriptive linguists, typologists, sociolinguists, and psycholinguists, together with sociologists, philosophers, and psychologists. They offer numerous possibilities for projects in core areas of linguistics, as well as in a wide range of cross-disciplinary fields. The most important task, however, is first to pursue descriptive studies, in order to collect additional materials which may then assist us in building up on the existing analytical framework.

It is also important to note that, in spite of differences along many parameters, all evidentials reflect (in different ways) a single phenomenon—the categorization of information source, through human language. They reflect common cognitive mechanisms, and common semantic features, such as seeing, hearing, and reasoning.

This book includes facts from a mere fraction of the world's languages. Only further detailed studies of evidentials in languages of all sorts, including those previously undocumented or scarcely documented, will help deepen our understanding of the mechanisms of human cognition and communication.

Fieldworker's guide: How to gather materials on evidentiality systems

The aim of this guide is to provide field linguists working on a previously undescribed or insufficiently documented languages with orientation as to the questions which should be asked in order to establish a complete picture of how evidential systems and/or evidential strategies are organized in a language.[1]

PRELIMINARY INFORMATION is needed as a starting point. This includes:

(i) Morphological type: e.g. isolating, agglutinating, fusional; analytic, synthetic, polysynthetic; head-marking or dependent-marking.
(ii) Word classes: open classes (e.g. nouns, verbs, adjectives) and closed classes.
(iii) Grammatical categories for open classes (e.g. number for nouns, tense for verbs).
(iv) Transitivity classes of verbs.
(v) Marking of grammatical relations.
(vi) Clause types.
(vii) NATURE OF SOURCES: should be mostly based on participant–observation in speech community and on texts with corroborative grammatical and lexical elicitation.

One should concentrate on gathering and analysing texts in the language, starting near the beginning of any linguistic fieldwork. The evidential patterns found in texts of various genres should then be confirmed and systematically studied through participant–observation and, to a lesser extent, carefully directed elicitation in the language itself. Observing how evidentials are used in various circumstances in day-to-day life is crucial to the understanding of the system. Gossip, casual remarks, or overheard conversations often provide many more enlightening clues than narrated stories. We can recall that evidentials are often tokens of narrative genres; evidentials in traditional texts are hardly ever a matter for speaker's choice. Moreover, traditional stories (such as origin myths) are often told in reported evidential. As a result, there may be fewer evidentiality options in texts than there are in day-to-day communication, which involves a wide variety of situations and ways of acquiring information. That is, if a language has a complex system of evidentiality and its grammar is based only on the analysis of traditional texts, some of the complexities of marking information source may well be missed.

Trying to elicit an evidential system using a lingua franca (be it English, Spanish, Portuguese, Russian, or Mandarin Chinese) is not a sensible or profitable source of action. This is why grammars based on elicitation often miss evidentials altogether.

---

[1] This is based on the author's own field experience in different parts of the world, student supervision in Brazil and Australia, reading of grammars, and talking to other linguists about their field experience.

It is bad technique to ask a linguistically unsophisticated native speaker: 'Why did you use this morpheme?' But once the researcher has started speaking the language, they ought to try using different evidentials in varied circumstances, to test hypotheses about how evidentials are employed. The speakers' corrections are then likely to provide sufficient clues as to the evidentials' meaning and use. If at all possible, the researcher should take into account—but not entirely rely on—the intuitions of native speakers when trying to explain seemingly obscure and strange uses of evidentials. Extensive work with both texts and spontaneous conversations is indispensable for an understanding of how evidentials are used in discourse.

Ideally, the analysis of evidentials in a grammar ought to deal with as many of the topics listed below as possible. This may not be viable for an obsolescent language which is no longer actively used as means of communication. For such languages, we may never achieve a full understanding of evidentials (as of many other grammatical categories), their semantic nuances, and their uses. We saw, in Chapter 2, how little we know concerning the fascinating evidential systems in Euchee, Latundê, Diyari, Ngiyambaa, and a great many other languages which are or were at an advanced stage of language obsolescence at the time of their documentation. A linguist working with an obsolescent language does the best they can.

Evidentials in a language which has a speech community can only be studied within this community, and not outside it. A grammar based on work with one or two speakers of a 'healthy' language in an urban environment is likely to contain few insights into the use and meaning of evidentials. Since the participant–observation technique is crucial for working out how an information source is marked, elicited linguistic data with one or two native speakers in the context of a field methods class will not shed much light on the evidentiality system as it is used. Working with immigrant communities is also hardly advisable: we have seen that evidentials are extremely prone to diffusion and are likely to change under the impact of introducing new—and losing old—cultural practices. It is likely that patterns of evidential use of speakers of Serbian or Croatian in Melbourne or Los Angeles have changed under the subtle influence of the Anglophone environment. Studying these patterns is a fascinating issue from the point of view of how evidentials may get affected by language contact; but this can only be achieved if a preliminary analysis of evidentials in this language as it is spoken in the original community had already been accomplished.

Questions relevant for establishing and analysing evidentials are divided into nine broad areas. After each question, a brief explanation is given; relevant chapters of this book are indicated in parentheses.

I. Organization of evidential system (see Chapter 2)

1. Is evidentiality in the language an obligatory grammatical category? Or does the language have an evidentiality strategy? Or a combination of these?

2. If the language has obligatory evidentiality, how many terms are there in the system? What type of system (A, B, C, or D) is there? Give as full a description as possible, providing good examples from texts or conversations (not just from elicitation).

II. Expression of evidentials (see Chapter 3)

1. What are the grammatical means employed for expressing evidentiality?
2. Is there a functionally unmarked term in the system? Is one term formally unmarked, or less marked than others?
3. Can an evidential be omitted? Does the system have an evidentially neutral option?
4. Does the language have evidentials as one grammatical system? Or are evidentiality distinctions 'scattered' in various parts of the grammar? Is there more than one subsystem of evidentials?
5. Can an evidential occur more than once in a clause?
6. Can more than one information source be marked within a clause? If so, does it reflect different perceptions by multiple recipients, or do the two sources confirm and complement each other? (See the range of possibilities in Table 3.2.)
7. Can an evidential be within the scope of negation? Can an evidential be questioned? Can the time reference of an evidential be distinct from that of the clause's predicate? That is, can the reference to the time of the utterance be different from the reference to the time when the information was acquired from a particular source? Comment on the truth value of an evidential as compared to that of the predicate.

III. Evidential extensions of non-evidential categories, or evidentiality strategies (Chapter 4)

1. Are there any non-evidential categories which acquire an additional meaning to refer to the source of information? Do any of the following acquire any evidential overtones: non-indicative moods and modalities; past tenses, resultatives, and perfects; passives; nominalizations (including participles and infinitives) as heads of predicates and as part of complex predicates; complementation strategies; and person marking? Are any perceptual meanings expressed in demonstratives, and if yes, how do they correlate with perceptual meanings in evidentials? Does the language have any modal expressions (for instance, modal verbs) with evidential extensions?
2. Does the language have more than one evidential strategy? If so, what are the semantic differences between these?
3. How does the language mark reported speech? Is there a special indirect speech construction? If the language also has a reported evidential, how does this compare with reported speech strategies? Do direct quotations have any epistemic overtones?

IV. Semantics (Chapters 5 and 6)

1. What are the semantic parameters at work in the evidential system of the language? How do the parameters in §2.5 apply to the language (also see Tables 2.1, 5.2–4). If the language has an 'eyewitness' term, does this cover visual and non-visual sensory information? If there is a corresponding 'non-eyewitness' term, does this subsume reported and inferred information sources? What sorts of inference can be expressed (e.g. inference based on reasoning, inference based on observable results)? Is the 'reported' term used for secondhand and thirdhand? Is there a special quotative evidential?

2. Do any of the evidential terms have epistemic or hypothetical extensions? Does the 'reported' term have any connotation of 'unreliable' information?

3. Does any evidential term have a mirative extension? If so, is this extension independent of person and verb class, or not? If the language has evidentiality strategies, do these also have any mirative overtones?

V. Evidentiality and person (Chapter 7)

1. Does using an evidential presuppose a first person perceiver of information?

2. Do any of the evidential terms have a 'first person' effect (see Table 7.1)?

3. Are there any restrictions on using any evidential with first person?

4. Any comment on semantics of evidentials with non-first person?

5. If the language has a conjunct/disjunct distinction, how does it correlate with evidentiality?

6. How are evidentials used with verbs of internal state (feelings, emotions, physical conditions) depending on the person? Are evidentials in the language used as implicit person markers?

VI. Evidentiality and other grammatical categories (Chapter 8)

1. How are evidentials used in questions? Does the use of an evidential in a question presuppose the questioner's assumption about the answerer's source of information? Or does it presuppose the questioner's information source? Is there any evidential that implies information source of a third party? Are fewer evidentials used in questions than in indicative clauses?

2. How are evidentials used in commands (if used at all)?

3. Are evidentials used in dependent clauses of any type? What other clause types are evidentials used in, and how do these relate to the evidentials in statements?

4. How are evidentials used in negative clauses? Are there fewer evidential specifications in negative clauses than in positive clauses?

5. If there are non-indicative modalities (e.g. conditional, dubitative, frustrative), what evidentials are used there (if any at all)?

6. Are there any restrictions on the co-occurrence of evidentials with any tenses or aspects? Are there evidentiality distinctions in future tense?

7. Are there any dependencies between evidentials and other categories (such as politeness, grammatical relations, gender, and others)?

VII. Origin of evidentials (Chapter 9)

1. What can you say about the origin of evidentials in the language? Did they develop from grammaticalized verbs, or as the result of grammaticalization of an evidentiality strategy, or from some other source (e.g. copula construction, lexical verb or noun)?

2. Is evidentiality inherited from a proto-language, or is it diffused from neighbouring languages? Or a mixture of the two?

3. Is there any evidence of calquing evidentials into contact languages? Do you have any examples of miscommunication due to misuse of evidentials?

VIII. Evidentiality in discourse and lexicon (Chapter 10)

1. Are there any preferences for the use of evidentials in particular discourse genres (e.g. historical narratives or folklore)?

2. Can evidentials be manipulated as a stylistic device (e.g. to make the narrative more vivid)?

3. If there are competing information sources, which one is preferably marked with an evidential?

4. Are evidentials employed in any lexicalized speech formulae?

5. Are there different rules for evidentials depending on the semantic type of the verb used (e.g. verbs of feeling or of internal state)?

6. Does the tentative hierarchy of evidential choices formulated in Diagram 10.3 apply to the language?

IX. Evidentials, and cultural attitudes and conventions (Chapter 11)

1. Do you have any examples of the metalinguistic appraisal of evidentials by native speakers of the language? Are speakers of the language aware of the array of evidentials and, if this is the case, the lack of it in contact language(s)? Do the speakers rephrase evidentials with corresponding lexical items for the purposes of clarification?

2. How do evidentials correlate with conventionalized attitudes to information? For instance, does one have to use 'visual' evidential to talk about shamanic revelations? Are dreams told using 'visual' or another evidential? How are European innovations treated—can the visual evidential be used to describe what one had

seen on TV? How do speakers retell what they have read, or heard on the radio? Or over the telephone? And so on.

3. Can any speculations be made concerning the correlations between evidentials and cultural profiles?

I am aware that not all of the questions here are applicable to every language. And there may be additional issues not included here. It is hoped, however, that this preliminary set of points to cover will provide a basis for in-depth empirical studies of evidentials worldwide.

Glossary of terms

This short glossary explicates the ways in which some core linguistic terms are used throughout this book, within the context of problems linked to evidentiality, in order to avoid terminological confusion. The definitions here are based, among other sources, on Dixon's glossary (1980: 510–14) and Matthews (1997). Where appropriate, I give the number of a section where a particular point is discussed in detail. Complementary terms are referred to by Compl. Synonyms are referred to as Syn.

ADMIRATIVE: a mood-type paradigm with surprise as its main meaning (as in Albanian: Friedman 2003: 192).

ALLATIVE: case indicating movement to or towards something.

ANTERIOR: a verbal form focusing on the results of an action or process, thus relating a past event to the present. An event or a process is viewed as completed in the past but still relevant for the present. Syn: PERFECT, POST-TERMINAL ASPECT.

AORIST: a verbal form used to refer to events that occurred without regard to their extension over time, or states resulting from them.

ASSUMED EVIDENTIAL: information source based on conclusions drawn on the basis of logical conclusion and general knowledge and experience.

AUDITIVE: a term in Uralic linguistics used to refer to an evidential covering information acquired by hearing and sometimes also by hearsay.

COMPLEMENT CLAUSE: a special clause type whose exclusive function is to occupy the argument slot of a main verb.

COMPLEMENTATION STRATEGY: any construction type functionally similar to a complement clause (see Dixon 1995).

COMPLEMENTIZER: an overt marker of a complement clause.

CONFIRMATIVE: a term in Balkan linguistics referring to the eyewitness evidential. Compl: NON-CONFIRMATIVE. See Friedman (2003).

CONJUNCT/DISJUNCT: person-marking on the verb whereby first person subject in statements is expressed in the same way as second person in questions, and all other persons are marked in a different way. (Also used to describe cross-clausal co-reference.) Syn: LOCUTOR/NON-LOCUTOR and CONGRUENT/NON-CONGRUENT.

CONVERB: a non-finite verb form marking adverbial subordination (Haspelmath 1995).

CORE MEANING: main and default meaning of a category or a lexical item. Syn: MAIN MEANING. Compl: EXTENSION OF MEANING.

DATA SOURCE: same as INFORMATION SOURCE (term preferred by Hardman 1986 in her analysis of Aymara).

DEBITIVE: modality indicating obligation. Syn: DEONTIC.

DEICTIC: category related to DEIXIS.

DEIXIS: the ways in which the reference of an element is determined with respect to speaker, addressee, or temporal and spatial setting.

DEONTIC: form or category expressing obligation or recommendation.

DEPENDENT CLAUSE: a clause constituting a syntactic element within another clause.

DE-SUBORDINATION: a process whereby a subordinate clause acquires the status of a main clause (e.g. §9.1.4).

DIRECT EVIDENTIAL: an evidential which covers speakers' or participants' own sensory experience of any kind (e.g. §5.2.1). Often same as VISUAL EVIDENTIAL.

DIRECT SPEECH: verbatim quotation of what was said.

DIRECT SPEECH COMPLEMENT: verbatim quotation of what someone else had said as a COMPLEMENT CLAUSE of verb of speaking. See COMPLEMENT CLAUSE.

DISJUNCT: opposite of conjunct, SEE CONJUNCT/DISJUNCT.

EPISTEMIC: (*a*) as a philosophical term relating to knowledge or the degree of its validation; (*b*) as a linguistic term: indicating necessity, probability, or possibility. Also see EPISTEMIC MEANINGS.

EPISTEMIC MEANINGS: meanings of (*a*) possibility or probability of an event, or (*b*) of the reliability of information.

EPISTEMIC MODALITY: modality associated with epistemic meanings.

EPISTEMIC STANCE: speaker's attitude to the possibility or probability of an event or the reliability of information.

EPISTEMICS: the scientific study of knowledge, 'as opposed to the philosophical study of knowledge, which is known as EPISTEMOLOGY'. A more extended definition of epistemics is 'the construction of formal models of the processes—perceptual, intellectual, and linguistic—by which knowledge and understanding are achieved and communicated' (Bullock and Stallybrass 1988: 279); see §§1.2–3.

EPISTEMOLOGY: philosophical theory of knowledge which 'seeks to define and distinguish its principal varieties, identify its sources, and establish its limits' (Bullock and Stallybrass 1988: 279); see §§1.2–3.

EVIDENTIAL, EVIDENTIALITY: grammatical marking of information source. Syn: INFORMATION SOURCE, DATA SOURCE, VERIFICATIONAL, and VALIDATIONAL.

EVIDENTIAL EXTENSION: an extension for a non-evidential category (such as tense, aspect, or modality) to refer to an information source. Syn: EVIDENTIAL STRATEGY.

EVIDENTIALITY STRATEGY: use of a non-evidential category (such as tense, aspect, or modality) to refer to an information source. Syn: EVIDENTIAL EXTENSION.

EXPERIENTIAL: same as direct evidential.

EXTENSION OF MEANING: additional meaning of a category or a lexical item realized in particular circumstances. Compl: CORE MEANING.

EYEWITNESS EVIDENTIAL: an evidential—typically in a small system with two choices—referring to something the speaker has seen or witnessed. The term FIRSTHAND is used throughout this book. Further synonyms: FIRSTHAND and CONFIRMATIVE.

FIRSTHAND EVIDENTIAL: an evidential—typically in a small system with two choices—referring to something the speaker has seen, heard, or otherwise experienced. Opposite of NON-FIRSTHAND EVIDENTIAL. Syn: EYEWITNESS and CONFIRMATIVE.

FREE INDIRECT SPEECH: INDIRECT SPEECH form used as a main clause.

FRUSTRATIVE: verbal form (often classified as a type of modality) indicating that the action was done in vain.

GRAMMATICAL MEANING: a meaning which must be expressed in a given language (Boas 1938: 132; Jakobson 1959).

GRAMMATICALIZATION: typically the process whereby an item with lexical meaning changes into an item with grammatical meaning (see Heine and Kuteva 2001).

HEARSAY: information known through verbal report. Syn: REPORTED.

ILLATIVE: case indicating movement into something.

IMPERFECTIVE ASPECT: a verbal form used to refer to actions extending over a period of time, or continuously.

INDIRECT SPEECH: reporting of what someone else has said by adapting deictic categories (e.g. person) to the viewpoint of the reporter. Compl: DIRECT SPEECH.

INDIRECTIVE: a term predominantly used in Turkic linguistics for the non-firsthand or the non-eyewitness evidential. Syn: INDIRECTIVITY. See Johanson and Utas (2000) and Johanson (2003).

INFERENTIAL: (*a*) synonym for INFERRED EVIDENTIAL; (*b*) inference as part of the meaning of a non-firsthand evidential.

INFERRED EVIDENTIAL: information source based on conclusions drawn on the basis of what one can see, or the result of something happening.

INFORMATION SOURCE: the way in which a speaker or participant has learnt the information. See: EVIDENTIAL, EVIDENTIALITY.

INTRATERMINAL ASPECT: a verbal form used to refer to an action or an event within its limits or in its course, 'be doing' (Johanson 2000*a*: 62), similar to imperfective. Syn: INTRATERMINATIVE ASPECT.

IRREALIS: verbal form referring to hypothetical events and something that has not happened. Compl: REALIS. See Elliott (2000).

LANGUAGE OBSOLESCENCE: a process whereby language gradually falls into disuse.

LATENTIVE: a term in Uralic linguistics to refer to an evidential with a non-firsthand meaning (see Kuznetsova et al. 1980: 240–2).

LEXICAL REINFORCEMENT OF EVIDENTIALITY: situation when speakers add lexical justification for a particular evidential, e.g. visual, 'I saw it'.

LINGUISTIC AREA: a geographically delimited area including languages from two or more language families sharing significant traits (most of which are not found in languages from these families spoken outside the area). Syn: SPRACHBUND.

LOCUTOR/NON-LOCUTOR: person-marking on the verb whereby first person subject in statements is expressed in the same way as second person in questions, and all other choices are marked in a different way. Syn: CONJUNCT/DISJUNCT and CONGRUENT/NON-CONGRUENT.

LOGOPHORIC: pronouns employed in indirect speech to refer to the person whose speech is being reported. Logophoric pronouns indicate whether the speaker and the subject or another argument of the reported utterance are the same person or not.

MASDAR: deverbal noun (term used in Arabic and Caucasian traditions).

MEDIATIVE: a term in French linguistics referring to non-firsthand, non-eyewitness, and reported evidentiality, akin to INDIRECTIVITY.

MEDIATIVITY: a term in French linguistics used with a meaning similar to that of EVIDENTIALITY.

MIRATIVE: grammatical marking of 'unprepared mind', including unexpected and also surprising information; see Chapter 6 and Appendix to it.

MODAL VERB: a verb with epistemic or deontic meaning.

MODALITY: grammatical category covering the degree of certainty of the statement (see §1.3); sometimes understood as a kind of speech-act (see MOOD).

MODE: alternative to MOOD; or alternative to MODALITY (see discussion in §1.3).

MOOD: grammatical category expressing a speech-act (e.g. statement: indicative mood; question: interrogative mood; command: imperative mood), also sometimes defined as a category which 'characterizes the actuality of the event' (Chung and Timberlake 1985: 241).

NON-CONFIRMATIVE: a term in Balkan linguistics covering non-firsthand or the non-eyewitness evidential. Compl: CONFIRMATIVE. See Friedman (2003).

NON-EYEWITNESS EVIDENTIAL: an evidential—typically in a small system with two choices—referring to something the speaker has not seen or witnessed. Opposite of EYEWITNESS EVIDENTIAL. The term NON-FIRSTHAND is used throughout this book. Further synonyms: INDIRECTIVE, MEDIATIVE, and NON-CONFIRMATIVE.

NON-FIRSTHAND EVIDENTIAL: an evidential, typically in a small system with two choices, referring to something the speaker has not seen, heard, or otherwise experienced, and to something the speaker may have inferred, assumed, or (in some systems) learnt from someone else's verbal report. Opposite of FIRSTHAND EVIDENTIAL. Syn: NON-EYEWITNESS, INDIRECTIVE, MEDIATIVE, and NON-CONFIRMATIVE.

NON-VISUAL EVIDENTIAL: information source involving hearing, smelling, feeling, and sometimes also touching something.

PERFECT: a verbal form focusing on the results of an action or process, thus relating a past event to the present. An event or a process is viewed as completed in the past but still relevant for the present. Syn: ANTERIOR, POST-TERMINAL ASPECT, POST-TERMINATIVE ASPECT.

PERFECTIVE ASPECT: a verbal form which specifies that the event is regarded as a whole, without respect for its temporal constituency (even though it may be extended in time). Compl: IMPERFECTIVE ASPECT.

POST-TERMINAL ASPECT: a verbal form used to refer to an action or an event 'at point where its relevant limit is transgressed, "having done" ' (Johanson 2000a: 62). Syn: ANTERIOR, PERFECT, POST-TERMINATIVE ASPECT.

QUOTATIVE: (*a*) verbal form or a particle introducing a verbatim quotation of what someone else has said; (*b*) in some grammars of North and South American Indian languages, same as REPORTED (see §2.2 and §4.8).

REALIS: a verbal form generally referring to something that has happened or is happening. Compl: IRREALIS.

REPORTED: an evidential whose main meaning is marking what has been learnt from someone else's verbal report.

RESULTATIVE: a verbal form referring to the results of an action or a process.

SCOPE: the part of a sentence or clause with which an evidential (or negative, etc.) combines in meaning (cf. Matthews 1997: 331). See §2.4.

SECONDHAND: (*a*) based on verbal reported from someone who said it (as opposed to THIRDHAND); (*b*) same as REPORTED.

SENSORY: referring to perception by physical senses.

SUBORDINATE CLAUSE: Syn: DEPENDENT CLAUSE.

SUBORDINATOR: overt marker of a subordinate clause.

THIRDHAND: based on verbal report from someone else who in their turn acquired the information through another verbal report.

VALIDATIONAL: alternative term for DATA SOURCE and for VERIFICATIONAL used in studies of Andean languages (see Adelaar 1997). Syn: EVIDENTIAL.

VALIDATOR: alternative term to VALIDATIONAL, also used in studies of Andean languages.

VERBS OF INTERNAL STATE: verbs covering emotions, feelings, and internal physical and psychological states; these may have evidential preferences of their own.

VERIFICATIONAL: term used for grammatical marking of information source in some descriptions of North American Indian languages (see Jacobsen 1986). Syn: EVIDENTIAL.

VISUAL EVIDENTIAL: information source involving seeing something.

References

Adams, K. L., and Conklin, N. F. (1973). 'Towards a theory of natural classification', *Papers from the Annual Regional Meeting of the Chicago Linguistic Society* 9: 1–10.

Adelaar, W. F. H. (1977). *Tarma Quechua: Grammar, Texts, Dictionary*. Lisse: De Ridder.

—— (1987). *Morfologia del Quechua de Pacaraos*. Lima: Universidad Nacional Mayor de San Marcos.

—— (1997). 'Los marcadores de validación y evidencialidad en quechua: automatismo o elemento expresivo?' *Amérindia* 22: 4–13.

Aikhenvald, A. Y. (1998). 'Warekena', in D. C. Derbyshire and G. K. Pullum (eds.), *Handbook of Amazonian Languages*, vol. 4. Berlin: Mouton de Gruyter, 215–439.

—— (1999a). 'Multiple marking of syntactic function and polysynthetic nouns in Tariana', *Proceedings of the 35th Regional Meeting of the Chicago Linguistic Society* 2, 235–48.

—— (1999b). 'The Arawak language family', in Dixon and Aikhenvald (eds.) (1999: 65–101).

—— (2000). *Classifiers: A Typology of Noun Categorization Devices*. Oxford: Oxford University Press.

—— (2002). *Language Contact in Amazonia*. Oxford: Oxford University Press.

—— (2003a). 'Evidentiality in typological perspective', in Aikhenvald and Dixon (eds.) (2003: 1–31).

—— (2003b). 'Evidentiality in Tariana', in Aikhenvald and Dixon (eds.) (2003: 131–64).

—— (2003c). *A Grammar of Tariana, from Northwest Amazonia*. Cambridge: Cambridge University Press.

—— (2003d). 'A typology of clitics, with special reference to Tariana', in R. M. W. Dixon and A. Y. Aikhenvald (eds.), *Word: A Cross-linguistic Typology*. Cambridge: Cambridge University Press, 42–78.

—— (2003e). 'Mechanisms of change in areal diffusion: new morphology and language contact', *Journal of Linguistics* 39: 1–29.

—— (forthcoming). *Imperatives and commands*. Oxford: Oxford University Press.

—— and Dixon, R. M. W. (1998a). 'Dependencies between grammatical systems', *Language* 74: 56–80.

—— —— (1998b). 'Evidentials and areal typology: A case-study from Amazonia', *Language Sciences* 20: 241–57.

—— —— (1999). 'Other small families and isolates', in Dixon and Aikhenvald (eds.) (1999: 341–84).

—— ——, (eds.) (2003). *Studies in Evidentiality*. Amsterdam: John Benjamins.

——, and Green, D. (1998). 'Palikur and the typology of classifiers', *Anthropological Linguistics* 40: 429–80.

Akatsuka, N. (1978). 'Epistemology and Japanese syntax: complementizer choice', *Papers from the Fourteenth Regional Meeting. Chicago Linguistic Society*, 272–84.

—— (1985). 'Conditionals and the Epistemic Scale', *Language* 61: 625–39.

Aksu-Koç, A. A. (1988). *The Acquisition of Aspect and Modality: The Case of Past Reference in Turkish*. Cambridge: Cambridge University Press.

—— (2000). 'Some aspects of the acquisition of evidentials in Turkish', in Johanson and Utas (eds.) (2000: 15–28).

—— and Slobin, D. I. (1986). 'A psychological account of the development and use of evidentials in Turkish', in Chafe and Nichols (eds.) (1986: 159–67).

Alexander, R. M. (1988). 'A syntactic sketch of Ocotepec Mixtec', in Bradley and Hollenbach (eds.) (1988: 151–304).

Alhoniemi, A. (1993). *Grammatik des Tscheremissischen (Mari)*. Hamburg: Buske Verlag.

Alpher, B. (1987). 'Feminine as the unmarked grammatical gender: buffalo girls are no fools', *Australian Journal of Linguistics* 7: 169–87.

Ambrazas, V. (1990). *Sravnitelj'nyj sintaksis pričastij baltijskih jazykov* (Comparative syntax of participles in the Baltic languages). Vilnius: Mokslas.

Anderson, G. (1993). 'Obligatory double-marking of morphosyntactic categories', *Papers from the 29th Regional Meeting of the Chicago Linguistic Society*, vol. 1: 1–16.

—— (1998). *Xakas*. Munich: Lincom Europa.

Anderson, L. B. (1986). 'Evidentials, paths of change, and mental maps: typologically regular asymmetries', in Chafe and Nichols (eds.) (1986: 273–312).

Anderson, S. R. and Keenan, E. L. (1985). 'Deixis', in T. Shopen (ed.), *Language Typology and Syntactic Description*, vol. III. *Grammatical Categories and the Lexicon*. Cambridge: Cambridge University Press, 259–308.

Andrews, E. (1990). *Markedness Theory: The Union of Asymmetry and Semiosis in Language*. Durham: Duke University Press.

Anónimo (1586). *Arte, y vocabulario en la lengva general del Perv llamada Quichua, y en la lengua Española*. En los Reyes (Lima): Antonio Ricardo.

Anonymous (n.d.). *The Ponca Language*. MS.

Aoki, H. (1986). 'Evidentials in Japanese', in Chafe and Nichols (eds.) (1986: 223–38).

Aronson, H. I. (1967). 'The grammatical categories of the indicative in the contemporary Bulgarian literary language', in *To Honor Roman Jakobson*, vol. 1. The Hague: Mouton, 82–98.

Austin, P. (1978). 'A grammar of the Diyari language of north-east South Australia'. Ph.D. dissertation. ANU, Canberra.

—— (1981). *A Grammar of Diyari, South Australia*. Cambridge: Cambridge University Press.

Ballard, L. (1974). 'Telling it like it was said, part 1', *Notes on Translation* 51: 23–8.

Balode, L., and Holvoet, A. (2001). 'The Lithuanian language and its dialects', in Ö. Dahl and M. Koptjevskaja-Tamm (eds.), *Circum-Baltic Languages*, vol. 1. *Past and Present*. Amsterdam: John Benjamins, 41–80.

Bamgboṣe, A. (1986). 'Reported speech in Yoruba', in Coulmas (ed.) (1986: 77–97).

Bani, E. (1987). 'Masculine and feminine grammatical gender in Kala Lagaw Ya', *Australian Journal of Linguistics* 7: 189–201.

Barentsen, A. (1996). 'Shifting points of orientation in Modern Russian: Tense selection in "reported perception" ', in Janssen and van der Wurff (eds.) (1996: 15–55).

Barnes, J. (1979). 'Los imperativos en tuyuca', *Artículos, en lingüística y campos afines* 6: 87–94.

—— (1984). 'Evidentials in the Tuyuca Verb', *International Journal of American Linguistics* 50: 255–71.

—— (1999). 'Tucano', in Dixon and Aikhenvald (eds.) (1999: 207–26).

—— and Malone, T. (2000). 'El tuyuca', in M. S. González de Pérez and M. L. Rodríguez de Montes (eds.), *Lenguas indígenas de Colombia. Una visión descriptiva*, Santafé de Bogotá: Instituto Caro y Cuervo, 419–36.

Baron, D. E. (1982). *Grammar and Good Taste. Reforming the American Language.* New Haven: Yale University Press.

Bashir, E. (1988). 'Inferentiality in Kalasha and Khowar', *Papers from the 24th Regional Meeting of the Chicago Linguistic Society*, 47–59.

Basso, E. B. (1990). 'The Last Cannibal', in E. B. Basso (ed.), *Native Latin American Cultures through their Discourse.* Bloomington: Indiana University, 133–53.

Beier, C., Michael, L., and Sherzer, J. (2002). 'Discourse forms and processes in Indigenous Lowland South America: an areal–typological study', *Annual Review of Anthropology* 51: 121–45.

Bendix, E. H. (1992). 'The grammaticalization of responsibility and evidence: interactional potential of evidential categories in Newari', in Hill and Irvine (eds.) (1992: 226–47).

Bertonio Romano, L. (1603). *Arte de la Lengua Aymara.* Roma: Luis Zanetti.

Besnier, N. (1992). 'Reported speech and affect on Nukulaelae atoll', in Hill and Irvine (eds.) (1992: 161–81).

—— (2000). *Tuvaluan.* London: Routledge.

Bhat, D. N. S. (1999). *The Prominence of Tense, Aspect and Mood.* Amsterdam: John Benjamins.

Bickel, B. (2000). 'Introduction: person and evidence in Himalayan languages', *Linguistics of the Tibeto-Burman Area* 23: 1–11.

Blass, R. (1989). 'Grammaticalization of interpretive use: the case of *ré* in Sissala', *Lingua* 79: 299–326.

Bloomfield, L. (1933). *Language.* New York: Holt, Rinehart, and Winston.

—— (1962). *The Menomini Language.* New Haven and London: Yale University Press.

Boas, F. (1900). 'Sketch of the Kwakiutl language', *American Anthropologist* 2: 708–21. (Repr. in G. W. Stocking, Jr. (ed.) (1974). *The Shaping of American Anthropology 1883–1911: A Franz Boas Reader.* New York: Basic Books, Inc.)

—— (1910). *Kwakiutl. An Illustrative Sketch.* Washington: Government Printing Office.

—— (1911a). 'Introduction', in F. Boas (ed.), *Handbook of American Indian Languages.* Part 1. Smithsonian Institution. Bureau of American Ethnology Bulletin 40, 5–83.

—— (1911b). 'Kwakiutl', in F. Boas (ed.), *Handbook of American Indian Languages.* Part 1. Smithsonian Institution. Bureau of American Ethnology Bulletin 40, 423–557.

Boas, F. (1911c). 'Tsimshian', in F. Boas (ed.), *Handbook of American Indian Languages.* Part 1. Smithsonian Institution. Bureau of American Ethnology Bulletin 40, 223–422.

—— (1938). 'Language', in F. Boas (ed.), *General Anthropology.* Boston, New York: D. C. Heath and Company, 124–45.

—— (1942). 'Language and culture', in *Studies in the History of Culture: The Disciplines of the Humanities.* Menasha: The George Banta Publishing Co., 178–84.

—— (1947). 'Kwakiutl grammar, with a glossary of the suffixes', *Transactions of the American Philosophical Society* 37: 201–377.

—— and Deloria, E. (1939). *Dakota Grammar.* Washington: US Govt. Print. Office.

Boeder, W. (2000). 'Evidentiality in Georgian', in Johanson and Utas (eds.) (2000: 275–328).

Bokarev, E. A. (1967). 'Tsezskij jazyk' (Tsez language), in P. J. Skorik (ed.), *Jazyki Narodov SSSR*, vol. IV. Moscow-Leningrad: Nauka, 404–20.

Bolkentein, M. (1996). 'Reported speech in Latin', in Janseen and van der Wurff (eds.) (1996: 121–40).

Borgman, D. M. (1990). 'Sanuma', in D. C. Derbyshire and G. K. Pullum (eds.), *Handbook of Amazonian Languages*, vol. 2. Berlin: Mouton de Gruyter, 17–248.

Botne, R. (1995). 'The pronominal origin of an evidential', *Diachronica* XII: 201–21.

Bradley, C. H., and Hollenbach, B. E. (eds.) (1988). *Studies in the Syntax of Mixtecan Languages*, vol. 1. Dallas: Summer Institute of Linguistics and the University of Texas at Arlington.

Breen, G. (in preparation). 'The great Australian compass-point shift'.

Broadwell, G. A. (1991). 'Speaker and self in Choctaw', *International Journal of American Linguistics* 57: 411–25.

Bromley, H. M. (1981). *A Grammar of Lower Grand Valley Dani.* Canberra: Pacific Linguistics.

Brosnahan, P. (1961). *The Sounds of Language.* Cambridge: W. Heffer and Sons Ltd.

Bugenhagen, R. (1995). *A Grammar of Mangap-Mbula: An Austronesian Language of Papua New Guinea.* Canberra: Pacific Linguistics.

Bullock, A., and Stallybrass, O. (1988). *The Fontana Dictionary of Modern Thought.* London: Fontana/Collins.

Bulut, C. (2000). 'Indirectivity in Kurmanji', in Johanson and Utas (eds.) (2000: 147–84).

Bulygina, T. V., and Shmelev, A. D. (1997). *Jazykovaja konceptualizacija mira (na materiale russkoj grammatiki). (Linguistic conceptualization of the world (based on the Russian grammar).)* Moscow: Shkola Jazyki russkoj kuljtury.

Bunte, P. A., and Kendall, M. B. (1981). 'When is an error not an error? Notes on language contact and the question of interference', *Anthropological Linguistics* 23: 1–7.

Burgess, D. (1984). 'Western Tarahumara', in R. Langacker (ed.), *Southern Uto-Aztecan Grammatical Sketches.* Dallas: Summer Institute of Linguistics and University of Texas at Austin, 1–150.

Burridge, K. (2001). *Blooming English.* Sydney: ABC.

Bustamante, I. (1991). 'El presente perfecto o pretérito compuesto en el español quiteño'. *Lexis* 15/2: 195–231.

Bybee, J. (1985). *Morphology: A Study of the Relation between Meaning and Form*. Amsterdam: John Benjamins.

—— Perkins, R., and Pagliuca, W. (1994). *The Evolution of Grammar: Tense, Aspect, and Modality in the Languages of the World*. Chicago: University of Chicago Press.

Calvo Pérez, J. (1997). 'La gramática aimara de Bertonio (1603) y la escuela de Juli', in K. Zimmermann (ed.), *La descripción de las lenguas amerindias en la época colonial*. Frankfurt am Main: Vervuert; Madrid: Iberoamericana, 321–38.

Campbell, L. (1991). 'Some grammaticalization changes in Estonian and their implications', in E. C. Traugott and B. Heine (eds.), *Approaches to Grammaticalization*, vol. 1. Amsterdam: John Benjamins, 285–99.

Carlin, E. B. (2002). 'Patterns of language, patterns of thought. The Cariban languages', in E. B. Carlin and J. Arends (eds.), *Atlas of the Languages of Suriname*. Leiden: KITLV Press, 47–81.

Carpenter, K. (1991). 'Later rather sooner: Children's use of extralinguistic information in the acquisition of Thai classifiers', *Journal of Child Language* 18: 93–113.

Casad, E. (1984). 'Cora', in R. Langacker (ed.), *Southern Uto-Aztecan Grammatical Sketches*. Dallas: Summer Institute of Linguistics and University of Texas at Austin, 151–459.

—— (1992). 'Cognition, history and Cora *yee*', *Cognitive Linguistics* 3: 151–86.

Caughley, R. C. (1982). *The Syntax and Morphology of the Verb in Chepang*. Canberra: Pacific Linguistics.

Cerrón-Palomino, R. (1976). *Gramática quechua: Junín-Huanca*. Lima: Ministerio de Educación e Instituto de Estudios Peruanos.

Chafe, W. L. (1986). 'Evidentiality in English conversation and academic writing', in Chafe and Nichols (eds.) (1986: 261–72).

—— and Nichols, J. (eds.) (1986). *Evidentiality: The Linguistic Coding of Epistemology*. Norwood, NJ: Ablex.

Chamereau, C. (2000). *Grammaire du purépecha parlé sur des îles du lac de Patzcuaro*. München: Lincom Europa.

Chang, I. (1996). 'Representation médiate d'un suffixe verbal, *-teo-*, en coréen contemporain', in Guentchéva (ed.) (1996: 183–94).

Chappell, H. (2001). 'A typology of evidential markers in Sinitic languages', in H. Chappell (ed.), *Sinitic Grammar: Diachronic and Synchronic Perspectives*. Oxford: Oxford University Press, 56–84.

Charney, J. O. (1993). *A Grammar of Comanche*. Lincoln and London: The University of Nebraska Press.

Chelliah, S. L. (1997). *A Grammar of Meithei*. Berlin: Mouton de Gruyter.

Chelliah, S. L. (2003). 'Meithei', in Thurgood and LaPolla (eds.) (2003: 427–38).

Chirikba, V. (2003). 'Evidential category and evidential strategy in Abkhaz', in Aikhenvald and Dixon (eds.) (2003: 243–72).

Chun, S. A., and Zubin, D. A. (1990). 'Experiential vs. agentive constructions in Korean narrative', *Proceedings of the Sixteenth Annual Meeting of the Berkeley Linguistics Society. General Session and Parasession on the Legacy of Grice*, 81–93.

Chung, S., and Timberlake, A. (1985). 'Tense, aspect and mood', in T. Shopen (ed.), *Language Typology and Syntactic Description*, vol. III. *Grammatical Categories and the Lexicon.* Cambridge: Cambridge University Press, 202–58.

Cole, P. (1982). *Imbabura Quechua.* Amsterdam: North-Holland.

Comrie, B. (1976). *Aspect.* Cambridge: Cambridge University Press.

—— (2000). 'Evidentials: semantics and history', in Johanson and Utas (eds.) (2000: 1–12).

—— and Thompson, S. A. (1985).'Lexical nominalization', in T. Shopen (ed.), *Language Typology and Syntactic Description*, vol. III. *Grammatical categories and the lexicon.* Cambridge: Cambridge University Press, 349–98.

Conrad, R. J. (1987). 'Kinds of information in Bukiyip oral narrative discourse', *Language and Linguistics in Melanesia* 16: 23–40.

Cook, D. M., and Criswell, L. L. (1993). *El Idioma Koreguaje (Tucano Occidental).* Colombia: Asociación Instituto Lingüístico de Verano.

Coulmas, F. (1986). 'Reported speech: Some general issues', in Coulmas (ed.) (1986: 1–28).

—— (ed.) (1986). *Direct and Indirect Speech.* Berlin: Mouton de Gruyter.

Coupe, A. R. (2003). 'The Mongsen dialect of Ao, a language of Nagaland'. Ph.D. dissertation. La Trobe University.

Courtney, E. (1999). 'Child acquisition of Quechua affirmative suffix', *Santa Barbara Papers in Linguistics. Proceedings from the Second Workshop on American Indigenous Languages.* Department of Linguistics, University of California, Santa Barbara, 30–41.

Criswell, L. L., and Brandrup, B. (2000). 'Un bosquejo fonológico y gramatical del siriano', in M. S. González de Pérez and M. L. Rodríguez de Montes (eds.), *Lenguas indígenas de Colombia. Una visión descriptiva.* Santafé de Bogotá: Instituto Caro y Cuervo, 395–418.

Croft, W. (1990). *Typology and Universals.* Cambridge: Cambridge University Press.

—— (1996).' "Markedness" and "Universals": From the Prague School to Typology', in K. R. Jankowsky (ed.), *Multiple Perspectives on the Historical Dimensions of Language.* Münster: Nodus Publikationen, 15–21.

Crystal, D. (2000). *Language Death.* Cambridge: Cambridge University Press.

Csató, É. Á. (2000). 'Turkish MIş and IMIş items. Dimensions of a functional analysis', in Johanson and Utas (eds.) (2000: 29–43).

Culy, C. (1994). 'Aspects of logophoric marking', *Linguistics* 32: 1055–94.

Curnow, T. J. (1997). 'A grammar of Awa Pit'. Ph.D. dissertation. Canberra: ANU.

—— (2002*a*). 'Conjunct/disjunct marking in Awa Pit', *Linguistics* 40: 611–27.

—— (2002*b*). 'Conjunct/disjunct systems in Barbacoan languages', *Santa Barbara Papers in Linguistics* 11: 3–12.

—— (2002*c*). 'Three types of verbal logophoricity in African languages', *Studies in African Linguistics* 31: 1–25.

—— (2003*a*). 'Types of interaction between evidentials and first person subjects', *Anthropological Linguistics* 44: 178–96.

—— (2003*b*). 'Nonvolitionality expressed through evidentials', *Studies in Language* 27: 39–60.

Dahl, Ö. (1985). *Tense and Aspect Systems*. Oxford: Blackwell.

Dahlstrom, A. (forthcoming). *A Grammar of Fox (Algonquian)*. MS.

Dankoff, R. (ed. and trans. with J. Kelly). (1982). *Mahmud al-Kāšġarī. Compendium of the Turkic Dialects. (Dīwān luġāt at-Turk)*. Part 1. Cambridge: Tekin.

Davidson, M. (2002). 'Studies in Southern Wakashan (Nootkan) grammar'. Ph.D. dissertation, SUNY Buffalo.

Décsy, G. (1965). *Einführung in die finnish-ugrische Sprachwissenschaft*. Wiesbaden: Harrasowitz.

—— (1966). *Yurak Chrestomathy*. Bloomington, Indiana University, and The Hague: Mouton.

Dedenbach-Salazar Sáenz, S. (1997*a*). 'La descripción gramatical como reflejo e influencia de la realidad lingüística: la presentación de las relaciones hablante-enunciado e intra-textuales en tres gramáticas quechuas coloniales y ejemplos de su uso en el discurso quechua de la época', in K. Zimmermann (ed.), *La descripción de las lenguas amerindias en la época colonial*. Frankfurt am Main: Vervuert; Madrid: Iberoamericana, 291–320.

—— (1997*b*). 'Point of view and evidentiality in the Huarochirí texts (Peru, 17th Century)', in R. Howard-Malverde (ed.), *Creating Context in Andean Cultures*. New York: Oxford University Press, 149–67.

Deibler, E. W. (1971). 'Uses of the verb "to say" in Gahuku', *Kivung* 4: 101–10.

De Haan, F. (1997). *The Interaction of Modality and Negation: a Typological Study*. New York: Garland Publication.

—— (1998). 'The cognitive basis of visual evidentials', in A. Cienki, B. J. Luka, and M. B. Smith (eds.), *Conceptual and Discourse Factors in Linguistic Structure*. Stanford: CSLI Publications, 91–105.

—— (1999). 'Evidentiality and epistemic modality: Setting boundaries', *Southwest Journal of Linguistics* 18: 83–102.

—— (2001). 'The cognitive basis of visual evidentials', in A. Cienki, B. J. Luka, and M. B. Smith (eds.), *Conceptual and Discourse Factors in Linguistic structure*. Stanford: CSLI Publications, 91–105.

—— (n.d.) 'Evidentiality in Dutch'. MS.

DeLancey, S. (1985). 'Lhasa Tibetan evidentials and the semantics of causation', *Proceedings of the Eighth Annual Meeting of the Berkeley Linguistics Society*, 65–72.

—— (1986). 'Evidentiality and volitionality in Tibetan', in Chafe and Nichols (eds.) (1986: 203–13).

—— (1990*a*). 'A note on evidentiality in Hare', *International Journal of American Linguistics* 56: 152–8.

—— (1990*b*). 'Ergativity and the cognitive model of event structure in Lhasa Tibetan', *Cognitive Linguistics* 1: 289–321.

—— (1992). 'The historical status of the conjunct–disjunct pattern in Tibeto-Burman', *Acta Linguistica Hafniensia* 25: 39–62.

DeLancey, S. (1997). 'Mirativity: The grammatical marking of unexpected information', *Linguistic Typology* 1: 33–52.

—— (2001). 'The mirative and evidentiality', *Journal of Pragmatics* 33: 369–82.

—— (2003). 'Lhasa Tibetan', in Thurgood and LaPolla (eds.) (2003: 270–88).

Dench, A., and Evans, N. (1988). 'Multiple case-marking in Australian languages', *Australian Journal of Linguistics* 8: 1–47.

Dendale, P. (1993). 'Le conditionnel de l'information incertaine: marqueur modal ou marqueur évidentiel?', in G. Hilty (ed.), *XXe Congrès International de Linguistique et Philologie Romanes, Tome I, Section I. La phrase.* Tübingen: Francke, 165–76.

—— and Tasmowski, L. (2001). 'Introduction: Evidentiality and related notions', *Journal of Pragmatics* 33: 339–48.

Denny, J. P. (1976). 'What are noun classifiers good for?' *Papers from the Annual Regional Meeting of the Chicago Linguistic Society* 12: 122–32.

—— (1979). 'The "extendedness" variable in classifier semantics: Universal semantic features and cultural variation', in M. Mathiot (ed.), *Ethnology: Boas, Sapir and Whorf Revisited.* The Hague: Mouton, 97–119.

Derbyshire, D. C. (1985). *Hixkaryana.* Dallas: Summer Institute of Linguistics.

Dickinson, C. (1999). 'Semantic and pragmatic dimensions of Tsafiki evidential and mirative markers', *CLS 35. The Panels*: 29–44.

—— (2000). 'Mirativity in Tsafiki', *Studies in Language* 24: 379–421.

—— (2001). 'Mirativity, evidentiality and epistemics in Tsafiki (Colorado)'. Paper at the International Workshop on Evidentiality. RCLT, La Trobe University, August.

Dik, S. C., and Hengeveld, K. (1991). 'The hierarchical structure of the clause and the typology of perception-verb complements', *Linguistics* 29: 231–59.

Dimmendaal, G. (1996). 'Attitude markers and conversational implicatures in Turkana speech acts', *Studies in Language* 20: 249–74.

—— (2001). 'Logophoric marking and represented speech in African languages as evidential hedging strategies', *Australian Journal of Linguistics* 21: 131–57.

Dixon, R. M. W. (1972). *The Dyirbal Language of North Queensland.* Cambridge: Cambridge University Press.

—— (1980). *The Languages of Australia.* Cambridge: Cambridge University Press.

—— (1982). *Where Have All the Adjectives Gone? and Other Essays in Semantics and Syntax.* Berlin: Mouton.

—— (1988). *A Grammar of Boumaa Fijian.* Chicago: University of Chicago Press.

—— (1991a). *A New Approach to English Grammar, on Semantic Principles.* Oxford: Clarendon Press.

—— (1991b). 'A changing language situation: The decline of Dyirbal, 1963–1989', *Language in Society* 20: 183–200.

—— (1992). 'Naive linguistic explanation', *Language in Society* 21: 83–91.

—— (1994). *Ergativity.* Cambridge: Cambridge University Press.

—— (1995). 'Complement clauses and complementation strategies', in F. R. Palmer (ed.), *Grammar and Meaning. Essays in Honour of Sir John Lyons.* Cambridge: Cambridge University Press, 175–200.

—— (1997). *The Rise and Fall of Languages.* Cambridge: Cambridge University Press.

—— (1998). 'Review of Nicholas Evans, *A grammar of Kayardild, with historical-comparative notes on Tangkic*', *Studies in Language* 22: 507–15.

—— (2002). *Australian Languages: Their Nature and Development.* Cambridge: Cambridge University Press.

—— (2003). 'Evidentiality in Jarawara', in Aikhenvald and Dixon (eds.) (2003: 165–88).

—— (2004). *The Jarawara Language of Southern Amazonia.* Oxford: Oxford University Press.

—— (forthcoming). *Basic Linguistic Theory.*

—— and Aikhenvald, A. Y. (1999*a*). 'Introduction', in R. M. W. Dixon and A. Y. Aikhenvald (eds.), *Changing Valency: Case Studies in Transitivity.* Cambridge: Cambridge University Press, 1–29.

—— (1999*b*). 'Introduction', in Dixon and Aikhenvald (eds.) (1999: 1–21).

—— —— (eds.) (1999). *The Amazonian Languages.* Cambridge: Cambridge University Press.

Dobrushina, N., and Tatevosov, S. (1996). 'Usage of verbal forms', in Kibrik, Tatevosov and Eulenberg (eds.) (1996: 91–106).

Donabédian, A. (1996). 'Pour une interprétation des différentes valeurs du médiatif en arménien occidental', in Guentchéva (ed.) (1996: 87–108).

—— (2001). 'Towards a semasiological account of evidentials: An enunciative approach of *-er* in Modern Western Armenian', *Journal of Pragmatics* 33: 421–42.

Donaldson, T. (1980). *Ngiyambaa: The Language of the Wangaaybuwan.* Cambridge: Cambridge University Press.

Drapeau, L. (1984). 'Le traitement de l'information chez les Montagnais', *Recherches amérindiennes au Québec* 14: 24–35.

—— (1996). 'Conjurers: The use of evidentials in Montagnais second-hand narratives', in J. D. Nichols and A. C. Ogg (eds.), *nikotwâsik iskwâhtêm, pâskihtêpayih! Studies in Honour of H. C. Wolfart.* Manitoba: Algonquian and Iroquoian Linguistics, Memoir 13, 171–94.

Du Bois, J. W. (1986). 'Self-Evidence and Ritual Speech', in Chafe and Nichols (eds.) (1986: 313–36).

Dwyer, A. (2000). 'Direct and indirect experience in Salar', in Johanson and Utas (eds.) (2000: 45–59).

Ebbing, J. E. (1965). *Gramática y diccionario aymara.* La Paz: Don Bosco.

Echegoven, A., et al. (1979). *Luces contemporáneas del otomí. Gramática del otomí de la Sierra.* México: Instituto Lingüístico de Verano.

Egerod, S. (1985). 'Typological features in Akha', in G. Thurgood, J. A. Matisoff, and D. Bradley (eds.), *Linguistics of the Sino-Tibetan Area: The State of the Art (Papers Presented to Paul K. Benedict for his 71st Birthday).* Canberra: Pacific Linguistics, 96–104.

Elliott, J. (2000). 'Realis and irrealis: Forms and concepts of the grammaticalisation of reality', *Linguistic Typology* 4: 55–90.

Emeneau, M. B. (1956). 'India as a linguistic area', *Language* 32: 3–16.

Epps, P. (2005). 'Areal diffusion and the development of evidentiality: evidence from Hup', *Studies in Language* 29: 617–50.

Erelt, M. (2002*a*). 'Does Estonian have the jussive?' *Linguistica Uralica* 2: 110–17.

Erelt, M. (2002*b*). 'Evidentiality in Estonian and some other languages. Introductory remarks', *Linguistica Uralica* 2: 93–6.

Escobar, A. M. (1997). 'From time to modality in Spanish in contact with Quechua', *Hispanic Linguistics* 9: 64–99.

Faller, M. T. (2002). *Semantics and Pragmatics of Evidentials in Cuzco Quechua*. Ph.D. dissertation, Stanford University.

Farris, E. R. (1992). 'A syntactic sketch of Yosondúa Mixtec', in C. H. Bradley B. E. Hollenbach (eds.), *Studies in the Syntax of Mixtecan Languages*, vol. 4. Dallas: Summer Institute of Linguistics and the University of Texas at Arlington, 1–172.

Fennell, T. G., and Gelsen, H. (1980). *A Grammar of Modern Latvian*. The Hague: Mouton.

Fernandez-Vest, M. M. J. (1996). 'Du médiatif finno-ougrien: mode oblique en Estonien, particules en Finnois et en Same', in Guentchéva (ed.) (1996: 169–82).

Feuillet, J. (1996). 'Réflexions sur les valeurs du médiatif', in Guentchéva (ed.) (1996: 71–86).

Floyd, R. (1989). 'A cognitive study of evidentiality in Wanka', in *Fourth Meeting of the Pacific Linguistics Conference*. Eugene: University of Oregon, 134–53.

—— (1996*a*). 'The radial structure of the Wanka reportative', in E. Casad (ed.) *Cognitive Linguistics in the Redwoods: The Expansion of a New Paradigm in Linguistics*. Berlin: Mouton De Gruyter, 895–941.

—— (1996*b*). 'Experience, certainty and control, and the direct evidential in Wanka Quechua questions', *Functions of Language* 3: 69–93.

—— (1997). *La Estructura categorial de los evidenciales en el quechua wanka*. Lima: Instituto Lingüístico de Verano.

—— (1999). *The Structure of Evidential Categories in Wanka Quechua*. Dallas: Summer Institute of Linguistics and University of Texas at Arlington.

Foley, W. A. (1986). *The Papuan Languages of New Guinea*. Cambridge: Cambridge University Press.

Foris, D. (2000). *A Grammar of Sochiapan Chinantec*. Dallas: Summer Institute of Linguistics and the University of Texas at Arlington.

Fortescue, M. (1998). *Language Relations across Bering Strait: Reappraising the ArchaeoLogical and Linguistic Evidence*. London, New York: Cassell.

—— (2003). 'Evidentiality in West Greenlandic: A case of scattered coding', in Aikhenvald and Dixon (eds.) (2003: 291–306).

Foster, M. L. (1969). *The Tarascan Language*. Berkeley: University of California.

Fox, B. (2001). 'Evidentiality: Authority, responsibility, and entitlement in English conversation', *Journal of Linguistic Anthropology* 11: 167–92.

Frajzyngier, Z. (1985). 'Truth and the indicative sentence', *Studies in Language* 9: 243–54.

—— (1987). 'Truth and the compositionality principle: A reply to Palmer', *Studies in Language* 11: 211–16.

—— (1991). 'The de dicto domain in language', in E. C. Traugott and B. Heine (eds.), *Approaches to Grammaticalization*, vol. 1. Amsterdam: John Benjamins, 219–52.

—— (1995). 'Functional theory of complementizers', in J. Bybee and S. Fleischman (eds.), *Modality in Grammar and Discourse*. Amsterdam: John Benjamins, 473–502.

—— (1996). *Grammaticalization of the Complex Sentence: A Case Study in Chadic.* Amsterdam: John Benjamins.

—— and Jasperson, R. (1991). 'That clauses and other complements', *Lingua* 83: 133–53.

Franklin, K. (2001). 'Kutubuan (Foe and Fasu) and Proto Engan', in A. Pawley, M. Ross, and D. Tryon (eds.), *The Boy from Bundaberg: Studies in Melanesian Linguistics in Honour of Tom Dutton.* Canberra: Pacific Linguistics, 143–54.

Franklin, K. J. (1971). *A Grammar of Kewa, New Guinea.* Canberra: Pacific Linguistics.

—— and Franklin, J. (1978). *A Kewa Dictionary.* Canberra: Pacific Linguistics.

Freeland, L. S. (1951). *Language of the Sierra Miwok.* Supplement to *International Journal of American Linguistics* 17 (1), Memoir 6.

Friedman, V. A. (1978). 'On the semantic and morphological influence of Turkish on Balkan Slavic', in D. Farkas, W. Jacobsen, and K. Todrys (eds.), *Papers from the Fourteenth Regional Meeting: Chicago Linguistic Society.* Chicago: Chicago Linguistic Society, 108–18.

—— (1979). 'Toward a typology of status: Georgian and other non-Slavic languages of the Soviet Union', in *Papers from the Conference on non-Slavic Languages of the USSR.* University of Chicago: Chicago Linguistic Society, 338–49.

—— (1981). 'Admirativity and confirmativity', *Zeitschrift für Balkanologie* 17: 12–28.

—— (1982). 'Reportedness in Bulgarian: Category or stylistic variant?' *International Journal of Slavic Linguistics and Poetics* 25/26: 149–63.

—— (1986). 'Evidentiality in the Balkans: Bulgarian. Macedonian, and Albanian', in Chafe and Nichols (eds.) (1986: 168–87).

—— (1994). 'Surprise! Surprise! Arumanian has had an admirative!' *Indiana Slavic Studies* 7: 79–89.

—— (2000). 'Confirmative/nonconfirmative in Balkan Slavic, Balkan Romance, and Albanian with additional observations on Turkish, Romani, Georgian and Lak', in Johanson and Utas (eds.) (2000: 329–66).

—— (2003). 'Evidentiality in the Balkans with special attention to Macedonian and Albanian', in Aikhenvald and Dixon (eds.) (2003: 189–218).

Gabas Júnior, N. (1999). 'Grammar of Karo, Tupí (Brazil)'. Ph.D. dissertation. University of California, Santa Barbara.

—— (2002). 'Evidenciais em Karo', in Ana Suelly A. C. Cabral, and A. Dall'Igna Rodrigues (eds.), *Línguas indígenas brasileiras: Fonologia, gramática e história. Atas do I Encontro Internacional do Grupo de Trabalho sobre línguas indígenas da ANPOLL',* tomo 1. Belém: Editora Universitária UFPa, 254–68.

Garrett, E. J. (2001). 'Evidentiality and assertion in Tibetan'. Ph.D. dissertation. University of California, Los Angeles.

Genetti, C. (1986). 'The grammaticalization of the Newari verb ṭol', *Linguistics of the Tibeto-Burman Area* 9: 53–70.

Geniušienė, E., and Nedjalkov, V. P. (1988). 'Resultative, passive, and perfect in Lithuanian', in Nedjalkov (ed.) (1988: 369–86).

Givón, T. (1982). 'Evidentiality and epistemic space', *Studies in Language* 6: 23–49.

Givón, T., and Kimenyi, A. (1974). 'Truth, belief and doubt in Kinyarwanda', *Studies in African Linguistics. Supplement* 5: 95–113.

Goddard, C. (1983). 'A semantically-oriented grammar of the Yankunytjatjara dialect of the Western Desert language'. Ph.D. dissertation, ANU, Canberra.

Goddard, P. E. (1911). 'Athapascan (Hupa)', in F. Boas (ed.), *Handbook of American Indian Languages*, part 1. Smithsonian Institution. Bureau of American Ethnology Bulletin 40, 85–158.

Golla, V. (1996). 'Sketch of Hupa, an Athapaskan language', in I. Goddard (ed.), *Handbook of North American Indians*, vol. 17: *Languages*. Washington: Smithsonian Institution, 364–89.

Gomez, G. G. (1990). 'The Shiriana dialect of Yanam (Northern Brazil)'. Ph.D. dissertation. Columbia University.

Gomez-Imbert, E. (1986). 'Conocimiento y verdad en Tatuyo', *Revista de Antropologia* 2: 117–25.

—— (1996). 'When animals become "rounded" and "feminine": Conceptual categories and linguistic classification in a multilingual setting', in J. J. Gumpertz and S. C. Levinson (eds.), *Rethinking Linguistic Relativity*. Cambridge: Cambridge University Press, 131–64.

Gordon, D., and Lakoff, G. (1971). 'Conversational postulates', *Papers from the Seventh Regional Meeting. Chicago Linguistic Society*, 63–84.

Gordon, L. (1986a). 'The development of evidentials in Maricopa', in Chafe and Nichols (eds.) (1986: 75–88).

—— (1986b). *Maricopa Morphology and Syntax*. Berkeley: University of California Press.

Gralow, F. L. (1993). *Un bosquejo del idioma Koreguaje*. Bogotá: Asociación Instituto Lingüístico de Verano.

Greenberg, J. H. (1966). *Language Universals, with special reference to Feature Hierarchies*. The Hague: Mouton.

Grevisse, M. (1980). *Le bon usage*, 11e édition. Paris: Duclos.

Grice, P. (1989). *Studies in the Way of Words*. Cambridge, Mass.: Harvard University Press.

Grinevald, C. (1997). 'Language contact and language degeneration', in F. Coulmas (ed.), *The Handbook of Sociolinguistics*. London: Blackwell, 257–70.

Gronemeyer, C. (1997). 'Evidentiality in Lithuanian', *Working Papers* 46: 93–112. Lund University, Department of Linguistics.

Grunina, E. A. (1976). 'K istorii semanticheskogo razvitija perfekta -*miṣ*' (Towards the history of the semantic development of perfect -*miṣ*), *Sovetskaja tjurkologija* 7: 12–26.

Gruzdeva, E. J. (2001). 'Imperative sentences in Nivkh', in V. S. Xrakhovskij (ed.), *Typology of Imperative Constructions*. Munich: Lincom Europa, 59–77.

Guasch, A. (1956). *El idioma guaraní; gramática de prosa y verso*. 3a edición, refundida y acrecentada. Asunción: Casa América-Moreno Hnos.

Guentchéva, Z., Donabédian A., Meydan M., and Camus, R. (1994). 'Interactions entre le médiatif et la personne', *Faits de langues* 3: 139–48.

Guentchéva, Z. (ed.) (1996). *L'Énonciation médiatisée.* Louvain-Paris: Éditions Peeters.

Guillaume, A. (2004). 'A grammar of Cavineña'. Ph.D. dissertation, RCLT, La Trobe University.

Güldemann, T. (2001). *Quotative Constructions in African Languages: A Synchronic and Diachronic Survey.* Habilitationsschrift. Leipzig University.

——, and Roncador, M. von (eds.) (2002). *Reported Discourse. A Meeting Ground for Different Linguistic Domains.* Amsterdam: John Benjamins.

—— ——, and Wurff, W. van der. (2002). 'A comprehensive bibliography of reported discourse', in Güldemann and von Roncador (eds.) (2002: 363–415).

Gumperz, J. J. (1982). 'The linguistic bases of communicative competence', in D. Tannen (ed.), *Analyzing Discourse: Text and Talk.* Georgetown University Round Table on Languages and Linguistics 1981. Washington: Georgetown University Press, 323–34.

Gusev, V. J. (forthcoming). 'Evidencialjnostj v nganasanskom jazyke' (Evidentiality in Nganasan).

Gvozdanović, J. (1996). 'Reported speech in South Slavic', in Janssen and van der Wurff (eds.) (1996: 57–71).

Haarmann, H. (1970). *Die indirekte Erlebnisform als grammatische Kategorie. Eine Eurasische Isoglosse.* Wiesbaden: Harrassowitz.

Haas, M. R. (1941). *Tunica.* New York: J. J. Augustin Publisher.

Hadarcev, O. A. (2001). 'Evidencialjnye znachenija perfekta v persidskom jazyke' (Evidential meanings of perfect in Persian), in V. A. Plungian (ed.), *Issledovanija po teorii grammatiki* (*Investigations in the theory of grammar*). Moscow: Russkie slovari, 115–35.

Hagège, C. (1995). 'Le rôle des médiaphoriques dans la langue et dans le discours', *Bulletin de la Société de Linguistique de Paris* 90: 1–19.

Hagenaar, E. (1996). 'Free indirect speech in Chinese', in Janssen and van der Wurff (eds.) (1996: 289–98).

Haig, G. (2001). 'Linguistic diffusion in present-day Anatolia: From top to bottom', in A. Y. Aikhenvald and R. M. W. Dixon (eds.), *Areal Diffusion and Genetic Inheritance: Problems in Comparative Linguistics.* Oxford: Oxford University Press, 195–224.

Hale, A. (1980). 'Person markers: finite conjunct and disjunct verb forms in Newari', in R. L. Trail (ed.), *Papers in South-East Asian Linguistics,* No. 7. Canberra: Pacific Linguistics, 95–106.

Hansson, I.-L. (1994). 'The interplay between the verb particle "ɔ" and the sentence particles in Akha', Paper presented at the 27th International Conference on Sino-Tibetan Languages and Linguistics. Paris, 12–16 October.

—— (2003). 'Akha', in Thurgood and LaPolla (eds.) (2003: 236–52).

Hardman, M. J. (1981). 'Introductory essay', in Hardman (ed.) (1981: 3–17).

—— (ed.) (1981). *The Aymara Language in its Social and Cultural Context: A Collection of Essays on Aspects of Aymara Language and Culture.* Gainesville: University Presses of Florida.

—— (1986). 'Data-source marking in the Jaqi languages', in Chafe and Nichols (eds.) (1986: 113–36).

Hargreaves, D. (1991). 'The conceptual structure of intentional action: Data from Kathmandu Newari', *Proceedings of the Seventeenth Annual Meeting of the Berkeley Linguistics Society*, 379–89.

Harms, P. L. (1994). *Epena Pedee Syntax*. Dallas: Summer Institute of Linguistics and University of Texas at Arlington.

Harris, A. C. (1991). 'Mingrelian', in A. C. Harris (ed.), *The Indigenous Languages of the Caucasus*, vol. 1. *The Kartvelian Languages*. New York: Caravan Books, 313–94.

—— and Campbell, L. (1995). *Historical Syntax in Cross-linguistic Perspective*. Cambridge: Cambridge University Press.

Harris, A. (1985). *Diachronic Syntax: The Kartvelian Case. Syntax and Semantics*, vol. 18. New York: Seminar Press.

Haspelmath, M. (1993). *A Grammar of Lezgian*. Berlin: Mouton de Gruyter.

—— (1994). 'Passive participles across languages', in B. Fox and P. J. Hopper (eds.), *Voice: Form and Function*. Amsterdam: John Benjamins, 151–78.

—— (1995). 'The converb as a cross-linguistically valid category', in M. Haspelmath and E. König (eds.), *Converbs in Cross-linguistic Perspective*. Berlin: Mouton de Gruyter, 1–55.

Hassler, G. (2002). 'Evidentiality and reported speech in Romance languages', in Güldemann and von Roncador (eds.) (2002: 143–72).

Haugen, E. (1972). 'The inferential perfect in Scandinavian', *The Canadian Journal of Linguistics* 17: 132–9.

Haviland, J. (1987). 'Fighting words: evidential particles, affect and argument', *Berkeley Linguistics Society. Proceedings of the Thirteenth Annual Meeting. General Session and Parasession of Grammar and Cognition*, 343–54.

Hawkins, R. E. (1994). 'Evidentiality or emotionality in Wai Wai?' *Revista Lationamericana de estudios etnolingüísticos* 8: 49–64.

Hedinger, R. (1984). 'Reported speech in Akɔɔse', *The Journal of West African Languages* 14: 81–102.

Heine, B. (1982). 'African noun class systems', in H. Seiler and C. Lehmann (eds.), *Apprehension: Das sprachliche Erfassen von Gegenständen, Teil I: Bereich und Ordnung der Phänomene*. Tübingen: Narr Language Universals Series 1/1, 189–216.

—— (1995). 'Agent-oriented vs. epistemic modality', in J. Bybee and S. Fleischman (eds.), *Modality in Grammar and Discourse*. Amsterdam: John Benjamins, 17–53.

—— (1997). *Cognitive Foundations of Grammar*. Oxford: Oxford University Press.

—— and Kuteva, T. (2001). *World Lexicon of Grammaticalization*. Cambridge: Cambridge University Press.

Helimsky, E. A., and Nikolaeva, I. A. (1997). 'Yukaghirskij jazyk' (The Yukaghir language), in *Jazyki mira. Paleoaziatskie jazyki*. Moscow: Indrik, 155–68.

Hewitt, B. G. (1979). 'The expression of "inferentiality" in Abkhaz', *Journal of Linguistics* 15: 87–92.

—— (1995). *Georgian Grammar*. Amsterdam: John Benjamins.

Hickmann, M. (1993). 'The boundaries of reported speech in narrative discourse: Some developmental aspects', in Lucy (ed.) (1993a: 63–90).

Hill, H. (1995). 'Pronouns and reported speech in Adioukrou', *The Journal of West African Languages* 25: 87–106.

Hill, J. H. (2005). *A Grammar of Cupeño*. University of California Publications in Linguistics 136.

—— and Irvine, J. T. (1992). 'Introduction', in Hill and Irvine (eds.) (1992: 2–23).

——, and Irvine, J. T. (eds.) (1992). *Responsibility and Evidence in Oral Discourse*. Cambridge: Cambridge University Press.

Hill, K. E., and Black, M. (1998). 'A sketch of Hopi grammar', in *Hopi Dictionary*, compiled by the Hopi Dictionary Project, Bureau of Applied Research in Anthropology, University of Arizona. Tucson: University of Arizona Press, 861–900.

Hockett, C. (1948). 'Potawatomi', *International Journal of American Linguistics* 14: 139–49.

Hoff, B. (1986). 'Evidentiality in Carib', *Lingua* 69: 49–103.

Hoijer, H. (1933). 'Tonkawa', in F. Boas (ed.), *Handbook of American Indian Languages*. New York: Columbia University Press, pp. i–x, 1–148.

—— (1946). 'Tonkawa', in H. Hoijer et al., *Linguistic Structures of Native America*. New York: The Viking Fund, 289–311.

Holisky, D. A. (1991). 'Laz', in A. C. Harris (ed.), *The Indigenous Languages of the Caucasus*, vol. 1. *The Kartvelian Languages*. New York: Caravan Books, 395–472.

Hollenbach, B. E. (1992). 'A syntactic sketch of Copala Trique', in C. H. Bradley and B. E. Hollenbach (eds.), *Studies in the Syntax of Mixtecan Languages*, vol. 4. A publication of the Summer Institute of Linguistics and the University of Texas at Arlington, 173–341.

Holvoet, A. (2001). 'Impersonals and passives in Baltic and Finnic', in Ö. Dahl and M. Koptjevskaja-Tamm (eds.), *Circum-Baltic Languages, Vol. 2: Grammar and Typology*. Amsterdam: John Benjamins, 363–90.

Hopper, P. J. (1987). 'Emergent grammar', *Berkeley Linguistics Society. Proceedings of the Thirteenth Annual Meeting. General Session and Parasession on Grammar and Cognition*, 139–57.

Howard-Malverde, R. (1988). 'Talking about the past: Tense and testimonials in Quechua narrative discourse', *Amerindia* 13: 125–55.

Hyman, L. M., and Comrie, B. (1981). 'Logophoric reference in Gokana', *Journal of African Languages and Linguistics* 3: 19–37.

Ifantidou, E. (2001). *Evidentials and Relevance*. Amsterdam: John Benjamins.

Ikola, O. (1953). *Viron ja liivin obliquuksen historiaa*. Helsinki: SKS (Coll. Suomi 106).

Isaksson, B. (2000). 'Expressions of evidentiality in two Semitic languages—Hebrew and Arabic', in Johanson and Utas (eds.) (2000: 383–99).

Jackson, E. (1987). 'Direct and indirect speech in Tikar', *The Journal of West African Languages* 17: 98–109.

Jacobs, P. (1996). 'Le médiatif en Squamish: le caractère inhérent du degré du certain', in Guentchéva (ed.) (1996: 249–58).

Jacobson, S. (1990). *A Grammatical Sketch of Siberian Yupik Eskimo*. Fairbanks: Alaska Native Language Center.

Jacobsen, W. H. Jr. (1964). 'A grammar of the Washo language'. Ph.D. dissertation. University of California, Berkeley.

—— (1986). 'The heterogeneity of evidentials in Makah', in Chafe and Nichols (eds.) (1986: 3–28).

Jacquesson, F. (1996). 'Histoire du médiatif en Sibérie Orientale', in Guentchéva (ed.) (1996: 215–32).

Jake, J., and Chuquín, C. (1979). 'Validational suffixes in Imbabura Quechua', *Papers from the Fifteenth Regional Meeting Chicago Linguistic Society* 15: 172–84.

Jakobson, R. (1957). *Shifters, Verbal Categories, and the Russian Verb.* Cambridge: Harvard University.

—— (1959). 'Boas' view of grammatical meaning', in W. Goldschmidt (ed.), *The Anthropology of Franz Boas. Essays on the Centennial of his Birth. American Anthropologist* 61:5, part 2: Memoir 89: 139–45.

—— (1971). 'Shifters verbal categories and the Russian verb,' in R. Jakobson, Selected writings. Vol II. The Hague: Mouton, 130–147.

James, D. (1982). 'Past tense and the hypothetical: A cross-linguistic study', *Studies in Language* 6: 375–403.

—— Clarke, S., and Mackenzie, M. (2001). 'The encoding of information source in Algonquian: Evidentials in Cree/Montagnais/Naskapi', *International Journal of American Linguistics* 67: 229–63.

Janssen, T. A. J. M., and Wurff, W. van der (1996). 'Introductory remarks on reported speech and thought', in Janssen and van der Wurff (eds.) (1996: 1–14).

—— —— (eds.) (1996). *Reported Speech: Forms and Functions of the Verb.* Amsterdam: John Benjamins.

Jochelson, W. (1905). 'Essay on the grammar of the Yukaghir Language', *American Anthropologist Supplement* 7: 369–424.

Johanson, L. (1971). *Aspekt im Türkischen. Vorstudien zu einer Beschreibung des türkeitürkischen Aspektsystems.* Uppsala: Almquist and Wiksell.

—— (1996). 'On Bulgarian and Turkish indirectives', in N. Boretzky, W. Enninger, and T. Stolz (eds.), *Areale Kontakte, Dialekte, Sprache und ihre Dynamik in mehrsprachigen Situationen.* Bochum: Brockmeyer, 84–94.

—— (1998). 'Zum Kontakteinfluss türkischer Indirektive', in N. Demir and E. Taube (eds.), *Turkologie heute—Tradition und Perspektive.* Wiesbaden: Harrassowitz, 141–50.

—— (2000*a*). 'Turkic indirectives', in Johanson and Utas (eds.) (2000: 61–87).

—— (2000*b*). 'Viewpoint operators in European languages', in Ö. Dahl (ed.), *Tense and Aspect in the Languages of Europe.* Berlin and New York: Mouton de Gruyter, 27–187.

—— (2003). 'Evidentiality in Turkic', in Aikhenvald and Dixon (eds.) (2003: 273–91).

Johanson, L., and Utas, B. (eds.) (2000). *Evidentials. Turkic, Iranian and Neighbouring Languages.* Berlin: Mouton de Gruyter.

Johnson, A. F. (1988). 'A syntactic sketch of Jamiltepec Mixtec', in Bradley and Hollenbach (eds.) (1988: 11–150).

Jones, W., and Jones, P. (1991). *Barasano Syntax.* Dallas: Summer Institute of Linguistics and the University of Texas at Arlington.

Joseph, B. (2003). 'Evidentials. Summation, questions, prospects', in Aikhenvald and Dixon (eds.) (2003: 307–27).

Kakumasu, J. (1986). 'Urubu-Kaapor', in D. C. Derbyshire and G. K. Pullum (eds.), *Handbook of Amazonian Languages*, vol. 1. Mouton de Gruyter, Berlin, 326–403.

Kammerzell, F., and Peust, C. (2002). 'Reported speech in Egyptian: Forms, types and history', in Güldemann and von Roncador (eds.) (2002: 289–322).

Kany, C. (1944). 'Impersonal *dizque* and its variants in American Spanish', *Hispanic Review* 12: 168–77.

Kask, A. (1984). *Eesti murded ja kirjakeel*. Tallinn: Valgus.

Keenan, E. L., and Ochs, E. (1979). 'Becoming a competent speaker of Malagasy', in T. Shopen (ed.), *Languages and their Speakers*. Philadelphia: University of Pennsylvania Press, 113–58

Kendall, M. B. (1976). *Selected Problems in Yavapai Syntax. The Verde Valley Dialect*. New York: Garland.

Kerimova, A. A. (1966). 'Tajikskij jazyk' (The Tajik language), in P. J. Skorik (ed.), *Jazyki narodov SSSR*, vol. I. Moscow-Leningrad: Nauka, 212–36.

Kibrik, A. E. (1977). *Opyt strukturnogo opisanija archinskogo jazuka*. Tom II. *Taksonomicheskaja grammatika. (An essay in structural description of Archi*. Vol. II. *Taksonomic Grammar*.) Moscow: Izdateljstvo Moskovskogo Universiteta.

—— (ed.) (2001). *Bagvalal. Grammar. Texts. Dictionaries*. Moscow: Nasledie.

—— Tatevosov, S. G., and Eulenberg, A. (eds.) (1996). *Godoberi*. München: Lincom Europa.

—— and Testelec, J. G. (eds.) (1999). *Elementy tsakhurskogo jazyka v tipologicheskom osveschenii. (Elements of the Tsakhur language in Typological Perspective)*. Moscow: Nasledie.

Kiefer, F. (1986). 'Focus and modality', in J. L. Mey (ed.), *Language and Discourse: Test and Protest. A Festschrift for Petr Sgall*. Amsterdam: John Benjamins, 287–312.

Kimball, G. D. (1991). *Koasati Grammar*. Lincoln and London: University of Nebraska Press.

King, R., and Nadasdi, T. (1999). 'The expression of evidentiality in French-English bilingual discourse', *Language in Society* 28: 355–65.

Kirsner, R. S. (1969). 'The role of *zullen* in the grammar of modern Standard Dutch', *Lingua* 24: 101–54.

Kirsner, R. S., and Thompson, S. A. (1976). 'The role of pragmatic inference in semantics: A study of sensory verb complements in English', *Glossa* 10: 200–40.

Klaas, B. (2002). 'Reported commands in Lithuanian compared to Estonian', *Linguistica Uralica* 2: 118–25.

Klamer, M. (2000). 'How report verbs become quote markers and complementisers', *Lingua* 110: 69–98.

—— (2002). ' "Report" constructions in Kambera (Austronesian)', in Güldemann and von Roncador (eds.) (2002: 323–40).

König, C., and Heine, B. (forthcoming). *The !Xun Language*.

Koontz, J. E. (2000). 'Evidentials'. Paper presented at Siouan and Caddoan conference, Anadarko, Oklakhoma.

Kornfilt, J. (1997). *Turkish*. London: Routledge.

Koshal, S. (1979). *Ladakhi Grammar*. Delhi: Motilal Banarsidass.

Kovedjaeva, E. I. (1966). 'Marijskie jazuki' (Mari languages), in P. J. Skorik (ed.), *Jazyki narodov SSSR*, vol. III. Moscow-Leningrad: Nauka, 221–54.

Kozinceva, N. A. (1988). 'Resultative, passive and perfect in Armenian', in Nedjalkov (ed.) (1988: 449–68).

Kozintseva, N. (1994). 'Kategorija evidentsial'nosti (problemy tipologicheskogo analiza)'. (The category of evidentiality (problems of typological analysis).) *Voprosy Jazykoznanija* 3: 92–104.

—— (2000). 'Perfect forms as means of expressing evidentiality in Modern Eastern Armenian', in Johanson and Utas (eds.) (2000: 401–17).

Krejnovich, E. A. (1934). 'Nivkhskij (giljackij) jazyk' (The Nivkh (Gilyak) language), in *Jazyki i pis'mennost' narodov Severa: III. Jazyki i pis'mennost' paleoaziatskih narodov*. Moscow, Leningrad: Učpedgiz, 181–222.

—— (1979). 'Nivkhskij jazyk' (The Nivkh language), in *Jazyki Azii i Afriki. III. Jazyki drevnej perednej Azii (nesemitskie). Iberijsko-kavkazskie jazyki. Paleoaziatskije jazyki*. Moscow: Nauka, 295–329.

Krivoshein de Canese, N. (1983). *Gramática de la lengua guaraní*. Asunción: N. Krivoshein de Canese.

Kroeker, M. (2001). 'A descriptive grammar of Nambiquara', *International Journal of American Linguistics* 67: 1–87.

Kronning, H. (forthcoming). 'Modalité et médiation épistemiques', to appear in R. Delamotte-Legrand and L. Gosselin (eds.), *La médiation. Marquages en langue et en discours. Actes du colloque international de Rouen 2000*.

Kroskrity, P. V. (1993). *Language, History, and Identity. Ethnolinguistic Studies of the Arizona Tewa*. Tucson and London: University of Arizona Press.

Kroskrity, P. V. (1998). 'Discursive convergence with a Tewa evidential', in J. H. Hill, P. J. Mistry, and L. Campbell (eds.), *The Life of Language. Papers in Linguistics in Honor of William Bright*. Berlin: Mouton de Gruyter, 25–34.

Kruspe, N. (2004). *A Grammar of Semelai*. Cambridge: Cambridge University Press.

Kuiper, F. B. J. (1974). 'The genesis of a linguistic area', *International Journal of Dravidian Linguistics* 3: 135–53.

Kuipers, J. C. (1992). 'Obligations to the word: Ritual speech, performance, and responsibility among the Weyewa', in Hill and Irvine (eds.) (1992: 88–104).

Künnap, A. (1992). 'Elanud kord . . . .' (Once upon a time . . .) *Keel ja kirjandus* 4: 209–15.

—— (1999). *Enets*. Munich: Lincom Europa.

—— (2002). 'On the Enets evidential suffixes', *Linguistica Uralica* 2: 145–53.

Kuznetsova, A. I., Helimsky, E. A., and Grushkina, E. V. (1980). *Ocherki po seljkupskomu jazyku. Tazovskij dialekt. Tom 1. (Essays on the Selkup Language. The Taz Dialect. Vol. 1.)* Moscow: Izdateljstvo Moskovskogo Universiteta.

Laanest, A. (1975). *Sissejuhatus läänemeresoome keeltesse*. Tallinn: Eesti NSV Teaduste Akadeemia. Keele ja Kirjanduse Instituut.

—— (1982). *Einführung in die ostseefinnischen Sprachen*. Hamburg: Buske Verlag.

Lakoff, R. (1970). 'Tense and its relation to participants', *Language* 46: 838–49.

Landeweerd, R., and Vet, C. (1996). 'Tense in (free) indirect discourse in French', in Janssen and van der Wurff (eds.) (1996: 141–62).

Lang, A. (1973). *Enga Dictionary with English Index*. Canberra: Pacific Linguistics.

Langdon, M. (1970). *A Grammar of Diegueño. The Mesa Grande Dialect*. University of California Publications in Linguistics 66.

—— (1978). 'Auxiliary verb constructions in Yuman', *Journal of Californian Anthropology Papers in Linguistics* 1: 93–130.

LaPolla, R. J. (2003a). 'Evidentiality in Qiang', in Aikhenvald and Dixon (eds.) (2003: 63–78).

—— (2003b). 'Overview of Sino-Tibetan morphosyntax', in Thurgood and LaPolla (eds.) (2003: 22–42).

—— (2003c). 'Dulong', in Thurgood and LaPolla (eds.) (2003: 674–84).

Laprade, R. A. (1981). 'Some cases of Aymara influence on La Paz Spanish', in Hardman (ed.) (1981: 207–27).

Larson, M. L. (1978). *The Functions of Reported Speech in Discourse*. Dallas: Summer Institute of Linguistics and University of Texas at Arlington.

—— (1984). *Meaning-Based Translation. A Guide to Cross-language Equivalence*. Lanham: University Press of America.

Laughren, M. (1982). 'A preliminary description of propositional particles in Warlpiri', in S. Swartz (ed.), *Papers in Warlpiri Grammar: In Memory of Lothar Jagst. Work Papers of SIL-AAB*, Ser. A, vol. 6. Darwin: Summer Institute of Linguistics, 129–63.

Lawrence, M. (1987). 'Viewpoint in Oksapmin', *Language and Linguistics in Melanesia* 16: 54–70.

Lazard, G. (1957). 'Caractères distinctifs de la langue tadjik', *Bulletin de la Société de Linguistique de Paris* 52: 117–86.

—— (1985). 'L'inférenciel ou passé distancié en Persan', *Studia Iranica* 14: 27–42.

—— (1996). 'Le médiatif en Persan', in Guentchéva (ed.) (1996: 21–30).

—— (1999). 'Mirativity, evidentiality, mediativity, or other?', *Linguistic Typology* 3: 91–110.

—— (2001). 'On the grammaticalization of evidentiality', *Journal of Pragmatics* 33: 358–68.

Lee, D. D. (1938). 'Conceptual implications of an Indian language', *Philosophy of Science* 5: 89–102.

—— (1941). 'Some Indian texts dealing with the supernatural', *Review of Religion* 5: 403–11.

—— (1944). 'Linguistic reflection of Wintu thought', *International Journal of American Linguistics* 10: 181–7. (Reprinted in Lee 1959: 121–30.)

—— (1950). 'Notes on the conception of the self among the Wintu Indians', *Journal of Abnormal and Social Psychology* 45: 538–43. (Reprinted in Lee 1959: 131–40.)

—— (1959). *Freedom and Culture*. Englewood Cliffs: Prentice-Hall.

Lefebvre, C., and Muysken, P. (1988). *Mixed Categories. Nominalizations in Quechua*. Dordrecht: Kluwer Academic Publishers.

Leinonen, M. (2000). 'Evidentiality in Komi Zyryan', in Johanson and Utas (eds.) (2000: 419–40).

Levinsohn, S. (1975). 'Functional perspective in Inga', *Journal of Linguistics* 11: 13–37.

Li, C. (1986). 'Direct and indirect speech: a Functional study', in Coulmas (ed.) (1986: 29–45).

Liddicoat, A. J. (1997). 'The function of the conditional in French scientific writing', *Linguistics* 35: 767–80.

Lindström, E. (2002). 'Topics in the grammar of Kuot, a non-Austronesian language of New Ireland, Papua New Guinea'. Ph.D. dissertation, Stockholm University.

Linn, M. (2000). 'A grammar of Euchee (Yuchi)'. Ph.D. dissertation. University of Kansas.

Longacre, R. (1990). *Storyline Concerns and Word Order Typology in East and West Africa*. Los Angeles: The James S. Coleman African Studies Centre and the Department of Linguistics, UCLA.

Loos, E. (1999). 'Pano', in Dixon and Aikhenvald (eds.) (1999: 227–50).

Lowe, I. (1999). 'Nambiquara', in Dixon and Aikhenvald (eds.) (1999: 269–91).

Lucy, J. A. (1993). 'Metapragmatic representationals: reporting speech with quotatives in Yucatec Maya', in Lucy (ed.) (1993: 91–126).

Lucy, J. A. (ed.) (1993). *Reflexive Language. Reported Speech and Metapragmatics*. Cambridge: Cambridge University Press.

Lunn, P. V. (1995). 'The evaluative function of the Spanish Subjunctive', in J. Bybee and S. Fleischman (eds.), *Modality in Grammar and Discourse*. Amsterdam: John Benjamins, 429–50.

Lyons, J. (1977). *Semantics*. Cambridge: Cambridge University Press.

Lytkin, V. I. (1966a). 'Komi-permjackij jazyk' (The Komi-Permiak language), in P. J. Skorik (ed.), *Jazyki narodov SSSR*. vol. III. Moscow-Leningrad: Nauka, 281–99.

—— (1966b). 'Komi-zyrjanskij jazyk' (The Komi-Zyryan language), in P. J. Skorik (ed.), *Jazyki narodov SSSR*, vol. III. Moscow-Leningrad: Nauka, 281–99.

MacDonald, L. (1990a). 'Evidentiality in Tauya', *Language and Linguistics in Melanesia* 21: 31–46.

—— (1990b). *A Grammar of Tauya*. Berlin: Mouton de Gruyter.

Maisak, T. A., and Merdanova, S. P. (2002). 'Kategoria evidencialjnosti v aguljskom jazyke' (The category of evidentiality in Agul), *Kavkazovedenije* 1: 102–12.

—— and Tatevosov, S. G. (2001). 'Lichnaja zasvideteljstvovannostj', in Kibrik (ed.) (2001: 307–12).

Majtinskaja, K. E. (1979). *Istoriko-sopostaviteljnaja morfologia finno-ugorskih jazykov* (*Historic and Comparative Grammar of Finno-Ugric Languages*). Moscow: Nauka.

Malchukov, A. L. (1995). *Even*. Munich: Lincom Europa.

Malone, T. (1988). 'The Origin and Development of Tuyuca Evidentials', *International Journal of American Linguistics* 54: 119–40.

Martin, E. H. (1981). 'Data source in La Paz Spanish', in Hardman (ed.) (1981: 205–6).

Martins, S. A. (1994). 'Análise da morfosintaxe da língua Dâw (Maku-Kamã) e sua classificação tipológica'. MA thesis, Florianópolis, Brazil.

—— and Martins, V. (1999). 'Makú', in Dixon and Aikhenvald (eds.) (1999: 251–68).

Maslova, E. (2003). 'Evidentiality in Yukaghir', in Aikhenvald and Dixon (eds.) (2003: 219–36).

Mathiassen, T. (1996). *A Short Grammar of Lithuanian.* Columbus, Ohio: Slavica Publishers.

Matisoff, J. A. (1991). 'Areal and universal dimensions of grammatization in Lahu, in E. C. Traugott and B. Heine (eds.), *Approaches to Grammaticalization,* vol. 2. Amsterdam: John Benjamins, 383–453.

—— (2001). 'Genetic versus contact relationship: prosodic diffusibility in South-East Asian languages', in A. Y. Aikhenvald and R. M. W. Dixon (eds.), *Areal Diffusion and Genetic Inheritance: Problems in Comparative Linguistics.* Oxford: Oxford University Press, 291–327.

Matlock, T. (1989). 'Metaphor and the grammaticalization of evidentials', in *Proceedings of the Fifteenth Annual Meeting of the Berkeley Linguistics Society. General Session and Parasession on Theoretical Issues in Language Reconstruction,* 215–25.

Matras, Y. (1995). 'Verb evidentials and their discourse function in Vlach narratives', in Y. Matras (ed.), *Romani in Contact. The History, Structure and Sociology of a Language.* Amsterdam: John Benjamins, 95–123.

Matthews, P. H. (1997). *The Concise Oxford Dictionary of Linguistics.* Oxford: Oxford University Press.

May, J., and Loeweke, E. (1980). *General Grammar of Faso (Namo Me).* Repr. from Workpapers in Papua New Guinea Languages, vol. 27. Ukarumpa: Summer Institute of Linguistics.

McLendon, S. (1975). *Eastern Pomo.* Berkeley: University of California Publications in Linguistics.

—— (1982). 'Meaning, rhetorical structure, and discourse organization in myth', in D. Tannen (ed.), *Analyzing Discourse: Text and Talk.* Georgetown University Round Table on Languages and Linguistics 1981. Washington: Georgetown University Press.

—— (1996). 'Sketch of Eastern Pomo, a Pomoan language', in I. Goddard (ed.), *Handbook of North American Indians,* Vol. 17. *Languages.* Washington: Smithsonian Institution, 507–50.

—— (2003). 'Evidentials in Eastern Pomo with a comparative survey of the category in other Pomoan languages', in Aikhenvald and Dixon (eds.) (2003: 101–30).

Meillet, A. (1926). *Linguistique historique et linguistique générale.* Paris: Librairie Ancienne Honoré Champion.

Mennecier, P., and Robbe, B. (1996). 'La médiatisation dans le discours des inuit', in Guéntcheva (ed.) (1996: 215–32).

Merlan, F. (1981). 'Some functional relations among subordination, mood, aspect and focus in Australian languages', *Australian Journal of Linguistics* 1: 175–210.

—— and Rumsey, A. (2001). 'Aspects of ergativity and reported speech in Ku Waru', in A. Pawley, M. Ross, and D. Tryon (eds.), *The Boy from Bundaberg: Studies in Melanesian Linguistics in Honour of Tom Dutton.* Canberra: Pacific Linguistics, 215–31.

Metslang, H., and Pajusalu, K. (2002). 'Evidentiality in South Estonian', *Linguistica Uralica* 2: 98–109.

Michailovsky, B. (1996). 'L'inférentel du népali', in Guéntcheva (ed.) (1996: 109–24).

Middendorf, E. W. (1890). *Die einheimischen Sprachen Perus. Erster Band. Das Runa Simi oder die Keshua-Sprache wie sie gegenwärtig in der Provinz von Cuzco gesprochen wird.* Leipzig: F. A. Brockhaus.

Migliazza, E. (1972). 'Yanomama grammar and intelligibility'. Ph.D. dissertation, Indiana University.

Miller, A. (2001). *A Grammar of Jamul Tiipay.* Berlin: Mouton de Gruyter.

Miller, C. L., and Gilley, L. G. (forthcoming). 'Evidentiality and mirativity in Shilluk', in M. Reh and D. L. Payne (eds.), *Proceedings of the Eighth International Nilo-Saharan Linguistics Colloquium.* Cologne: Rüdiger Köppe.

Miller, M. (1999). *Desano Grammar.* Arlington: Summer Institute of Linguistics and University of Arlington Publication in Linguistics.

Miller, W. R. (1996). 'Sketch of Shoshone, a Uto-Aztecan language', in I. Goddard (ed.), *Handbook of North American Indians,* Vol. 17. *Languages.* Washington: Smithsonian Institution, 693–720.

Miracle, A. W. Jr., and Dioz Yapita Moya, J. de (1981). 'Time and space in Aymara', in Hardman (ed.) (1981: 33–56).

Mithun, M. (1986). 'Evidential diachrony in Northern Iroquoian', in Chafe and Nichols (eds.) (1986: 89–112).

—— (1999). *The Languages of Native North America.* Cambridge: Cambridge University Press.

Monserrat, R., and Dixon, R. M. W. (2003). 'Evidentiality in Mỹky', in Aikhenvald and Dixon (eds.) (2003: 237–42).

Mortensen, C. A. (1999). *A Reference Grammar of the Northern Embera Languages.* Texas: Summer Institute of Linguistics International and the University of Texas at Arlington.

Muižniece, L., Metslang, H., and Pajusalu, K. (1999). 'Past participle finitization in Estonian and Latvian', in M. Erelt (ed.), *Estonian: Typological Studies III.* Tartu: University of Tartu, 128–57.

Munro, P. (1978). 'Chemehuevi "say" and the Uto-Aztecan quotative pattern', in D. R. Tuohy (ed.), *Selected Papers from the Fourteenth Great Basin Anthropological Conference.* Socorro, New Mexico: Ballena Press, 149–71.

Mürk, H. W. (1991). 'The structure and development of estonian Morphology'. Ph.D. dissertation. Indiana University.

Mushin, I. (2001a). *Evidentiality and Epistemological Stance. Narrative Retelling.* Amsterdam: John Benjamins.

—— (2001b.) 'Japanese reportive evidentiality and the pragmatics of retelling', *Journal of Pragmatics* 33: 1361–90.

Muysken, P. (1977). *Syntactic Developments in the Verb Phrase of Ecuadorian Quechua.* Lisse: De Ridder.

—— (1995). 'Focus in Quechua', in K. É. Kiss (ed.), *Discourse Configurational Languages.* Oxford: Oxford University Press, 375–93.

Nazarova, Z. O. (1998). *Sistema ishkashimskogo glagola v sopostavlenii s badakhshansko-tajiikskoj.* (*The System of the Ishkashim Verb in Comparison with That in Badakhan-Tajik*). Moscow: The Academy of Sciences of the Republic of Tajikistan.

Nedjalkov, I. V. (1997). *Evenki.* London and New York: Routledge.

Nedjalkov, V. P. (ed.) (1988). *Typology of Resultative Constructions.* Amsterdam: John Benjamins.

——, and Jaxontov, S. J. (1988). 'The typology of resultative constructions', in Nedjalkov (ed.) (1988: 3–62).

Neukom, L. (2001). *Santali.* Munich: Lincom Europa.

Nichols, J. (1986). 'The bottom line: Chinese Pidgin Russian', in Chafe and Nichols (eds.) (1986: 239–57).

Nikolaeva, I. (1999). 'The semantics of Northern Khanty evidentials', *Journal de la Société Finno-Ougrienne* 88: 131–59.

—— and Tolskaya, M. (2001). *A Grammar of Udihe.* Berlin: Mouton de Gruyter.

Noonan, M. (1985). 'Complementation', in T. Shopen (ed.), *Language Typology and Syntactic Description*, Vol. II. *Complex Constructions.* Cambridge: Cambridge University Press, 42–140.

—— (2001). 'Direct speech as a rhetorical style in Chantyal', Paper presented at the Workshop on Tibeto-Burman Languages, University of California, Santa Barbara, July 2001.

Nordlinger, R., and Sandler, L. (2004). 'Nominal tense in cross-linguistic perspective', *Language* 80: 776–806.

Nuckolls, J. B. (1993). 'The semantics of certainty in Quechua and its implications for a cultural epistemology', *Language in Society* 22: 235–55.

Nuyts, J. (2001). 'Subjectivity as an evidential dimension in epistemic modal expressions', *Journal of Pragmatics* 33: 383–400.

Olbertz, H. (2003). 'Mirativity and evidentiality in Ecuadorian Highland Spanish'. Paper presented at CIL XVII, Prague.

Onishi, M. (2001). 'Non-canonically marked subjects and objects—Parameters and properties', in M. Onishi, A. Y. Aikhenvald, and R. M. W. Dixon (eds.), *Non-canonically Marked Subjects and Objects.* Amsterdam: John Benjamins, 1–51.

Ospina Bozzi, A. M. (2002). 'Les structures élémentaires du Yuhup Makú, langue de l'Amazonie colombienne: morfologie et syntaxe'. Ph.D. dissertation. Université Paris 7—Denis Diderot.

Oswalt, R. L. (1986). 'The evidential system of Kashaya', in Chafe and Nichols (eds.) (1986: 29–45).

Palmer, F. R. (1986). *Mood and Modality.* Cambridge: Cambridge University Press.

—— (1987). 'Truth indicative?' *Studies in Language* 11: 206–10.

Palmer, G. (1996). *Towards a Theory of Cultural Linguistics.* Austin: University of Texas Press.

Parks, D. (1972). *A Grammar of Pawnee.* New York: Garland Publishing.

Paul, L. (1998). *Zazaki. Grammatik und Versuch einer Dialektologie.* Wiesbaden: Dr. Ludwig Reichert Verlag.

Payne, J. R. (1985). 'Negation', in T. Shopen (ed.), *Language Typology and Syntactic Description*, Vol. I. *Clause Structure*. Cambridge: Cambridge University Press, 197–242.

Payne, T. W., and Payne, D. L. (1999). *Panare: A Cariban Language of Central Venezuela*. MS.

Perrison, H. (1996). 'Reported speech in Swedish', in Janssen and van der Wurff (eds.) (1996: 165–88).

Perrot, J. (1996). 'Un médiatif ouralien: l'auditif en Samoyède Nenets', in Guentchéva (ed.) (1996: 157–68).

Perry, J. R. (2000). 'Epistemic verb forms in Persian of Iran, Afghanistan and Tajikistan', in Johanson and Utas (eds.) (2000: 229–57).

Peterson. D. A. (2003). 'Hakha Lai', in Thurgood and LaPolla (eds.) (2003: 409–26).

Peterson, J. (2000). 'Evidentials, inferentials and mirativity in Nepali', *Linguistics of the Tibeto-Burman Area* 23: 13–37.

Peterson, M. N. (1955). *Ocherk litovskogo jazyka* (*A Sketch of Lithuanian*). Moscow: Academy of Sciences of the USSR.

Philips, S. U. (1992). 'Evidentiary standards for American trials: just the facts', in Hill and Irvine (eds.) (1992: 248–59).

Phosakritsana, P. (1978). *Laksana chapho' kho'ng phasa thai.* (*Distinguishing Features of the Thai Language.*) Bangkok: Ruamsan Press.

Pitkin, H. (1963). 'Wintu grammar'. Ph.D. dissertation. University of California.

—— (1984). *Wintu Grammar*. Berkeley: University of California Press.

Plungian, V. A. (1988). 'Resultative and apparent evidential in Dogon', in Nedjalkov (ed.) (1988: 481–93).

—— (1995). *Dogon*. München: Lincom Europa.

—— (2001). 'The place of evidentiality within the universal grammatical space', *Journal of Pragmatics* 33: 349–58.

Prokofjev, G. N. (1935). *Seljkupskaja (ostjako-samojedskaja) grammatika.* (*Selkup (Ostjako-samoyedic) grammar.*) Leningrad: Izdateljstv o Instituta Narodov Severa CIK SSSR.

—— (1996). 'Seljkupskij (ostjako-samoedskij) jazyk' (The Selkup (Ostjako-Samoyedic language)), in *Jazyki i pisjmennosti narodov severa*. Leningrad: Nauka, 91–124.

Pulte, W. (1985). 'The experienced and nonexperienced past in Cherokee', *International Journal of American Linguistics* 51: 543–4.

Ráez, J. F. M. (1917). *Gramáticas en el Quichua-Huanca y en el de Ayacucho*. Lima: Sanmarti y Ca.

Rakhilina, E. (1996). 'Jakoby comme procédé de médiatisation en russe', in Guentchéva (ed.) (1996: 299–304).

Ramat, P. (1996). ' "*Allegedly, John is ill again*": Stratégies pour le médiatif', in Guentchéva (ed.) (1996: 287–98).

Ramirez, H. (1992). *Bahwana: une nouvelle langue Arawak*. Paris: Chantiers Amerindiens.

—— (1994). *Le Parler Yanomami des Xamatauteri*. Paris.

—— (1997). *A Fala Tukano dos Yepâ-masa*. Tomo I. *Gramática*. Tomo II. *Dicionário*. Tomo III. *Método de aprendizagem*. Manaus: Inspetoria Salesiana.

Reed, I., Miyaoka, O., Jacobson, S., Afcan, P., and Krauss, M. (1987). *Yup'ik Eskimo Grammar.* Fairbanks: Alaska Native Language Center.

Reesink, G. P. (1986). *Structures and Their Functions in Usan, a Papuan Language of New Guinea.* Amsterdam: John Benjamins.

Reuse, W. J. de (1994). *Siberian Yupik Eskimo. The Language and its Contacts with Chukchi.* Salt Lake City: University of Utah Press.

—— (2003). 'Evidentiality in Western Apache', in Aikhenvald and Dixon (eds.) (2003: 79–100).

Reyburn, W. D. (1954). 'Cherokee verb morphology: III', *International Journal of American Linguistics* 20: 44–64.

Rodrigues, A. D. (1999). 'Tupí', in Dixon and Aikhenvald (eds.) (1999: 107–24).

Rombandeeva, E. I. (1966). 'Mansijskij jazyk' (The Mansi language), in P. J. Skorik (ed.), *Jazyki narodov SSSR*, vol. III. Moscow-Leningrad: Nauka, 343–62.

—— (1973). *Mansijskij jazyk. (The Mansi Language.)* Moscow: Nauka.

Rood, D. S. (1976). *Wichita Grammar.* New York: Garland Publications.

—— (1996). 'Sketch of Wichita, a Caddoan language', in I. Goddard (ed.), *Handbook of North American Indians*, Vol. 17. *Languages.* Washington: Smithsonian Institution, 580–608.

—— and Taylor, A. R. (1996). 'Sketch of Lakhota, a Siouan language', in I. Goddard (ed.), *Handbook of North American Indians*, Vol. 17. *Languages.* Washington: Smithsonian Institution, 440–82.

Ross, E. M. (1963). *Rudimento de gramática Aymara.* La Paz: Canadian Baptist Mission.

Rule, W. M. (1977). *A Comparative Study of the Foe, Huli and Pole Languages of Papua New Guinea.* Oceania Linguistic Monographs 20. Sydney: University of Sydney.

Sakel, J. (2003). 'A grammar of Mosetén'. Ph.D. dissertation. University of Nijmegen.

Sakita, T. I. (2002). 'Discourse perspectives on tense choice in spoken-English reporting discourse', in Güldemann and von Roncador (eds.) (2002: 173–98).

Salas, A. (1992). *El mapuche o araucano. Fonología, gramática y antlogía de cuentos.* Madrid: Editorial MAPFRE.

Santo Tomás, D. de (1560). *Grammatica o arte de la lengua general de los indios de los reynos del Peru.* Valladolid. Repr. in 1951. Lima: Instituto de Historia, Universidad Nacional Mayor de San Marcos.

Sapir, E. (1915). 'Abnormal types of speech in Nootka', *Canadian Department of Mines Geological Survey Memoir 62, Anthropological Series 5.* Repr. 1949, 1963 in D. Mandelbaum (ed.), *Selected Writings of Edward Sapir in Language, Culture, and Personality.* Berkeley: University of California, 179–96.

—— (1922). 'Takelma', in F. Boas (ed.), *Handbook of American Indian Languages*, part 2. Washington: Government Printing Office, 1–296.

—— (1924). 'The rival whalers, a Nitinat story (Nootka text with translation and grammatical analysis)', *International Journal of American Linguistics* 3: 76–102.

Saunders, R., and Davis, P. W. (1976). 'The expression of the cooperative principle in Bella Coola', *The Victoria Conference on Northwestern Languages. Heritage Record 4. British Columbia Provincial Museum*, 33–61.

Saxena, A. (1988). 'On syntactic convergence: The case of the verb "say" in Tibeto-Burman', *Berkeley Linguistics Society. Proceedings of the Fourteenth Annual Meeting. General Session and Parasession on Grammaticalization*, 375–88.

—— (1997). 'Aspect and Evidential Morphology in Standard Lhasa Tibetan: A Diachronic Study', *Cahiers de Linguistique—Asie Orientale* 26: 281–306.

Schauer, S., and Schauer, J. (1978). 'Una gramática del Yucuna', *Artigos en lingüística e campos afines* 5: 1–52.

Schlichter, A. (1986). 'The Origin and Deictic Nature of Wintu Evidentials', in Chafe and Nichols (eds.) (1986: 46–59).

Schmidt, A. (1985). *Young People's Dyirbal. An Example of Language Death from Australia.* Cambridge: Cambridge University Press.

Schöttelndryer, B. (1980). 'Person markers in Sherpa', in R. L. Trail (ed.), *Papers in South-East Asian Linguistics.* Canberra: Pacific Linguistics, 125–30.

Seki, L. (2000). *Gramática do Kamaiurá, língua Tupí-Guaraní do Alto Xingu.* Campinas: Editora da Unicamp.

Serebrjannikov, B. A. (1960). *Kategorii vremeni i vida v finno-ugorskih jazykah permskoj i volzhskoj grupp. (Categories of Tense and Aspect in Finno-Ugric Languages of Permic and Volga Groups.)* Moscow: Izdateljstvo Akademii nauk SSSR.

Sharp, J. (2004). *A Grammar of Nyangumarta.* Canberra: Pacific Linguistics.

Shell, O. A. (1978). 'Los modos del cashibo y el análisis del performativo', *Estudios Pano* I: 23–62.

Sherzer, J. (1973). 'Areal linguistics in North America', in T. Sebeok (ed.), *Current Trends in Linguistics* 10. The Hague: Mouton.

—— (1976). *An Areal-Typological Study of American Indian Languages North of Mexico* (North-Holland Linguistic Series, 20). North-Holland: Amsterdam.

Shields, J. K. (1988). 'A syntactic sketch of Silacayoapan Mixtec', in Bradley and Hollenbach (eds.) (1988: 305–449).

Shipley, W. F. (1964). *Maidu Grammar.* Berkeley and Los Angeles: University of California Press.

Silver, S., and Miller, M. (1997). *American Indian Languages. Cultural and Social Contexts.* Tucson: University of Arizona Press.

Silverstein, M. (1978). 'Deixis and deducibility in a Wasco-Wishram passive of evidence', in J. J. Jaeger and A. C. Woodbury (eds.), *Proceedings of the Fourth Annual Meeting of the Berkeley Linguistics Society.* Berkeley: University of California Press, 238–53.

Skribnik, E. K. (1998). 'K voprosu o neochevidnom naklonenii v mansijskom jazyke (struktura i semantika)' (On the unobvious mood in Mansi (structure and semantics)), in *Jazyki korennyh narodov Sibiri* 4. Novosibirsk, 197–215.

—— (2003). 'Non-finite verb forms and their categories'. Paper presented at CIL XVII, Prague.

—— and Ozonova, A. A. (forthcoming). 'Sredstva vyrazhenija zasvideteljstvovannosti i mirativnosti v altajskom jazyke'. (Means of expression of witness and mirativity in the Altaic language.)

Slobin, D. I., and Aksu-Koç, A. A. (1982). 'Tense, aspect, and modality in the use of the Turkish evidential', in P. J. Hopper (ed.), *Tense-Aspect: Between Semantics and Pragmatics*. Amsterdam: John Benjamins, 185–200.

Smeets, I. (1989). 'A Mapuche grammar'. Ph.D. dissertation, University of Leiden.

Smothermon, J. R., Smothermon, J. H., and Frank, P. S. (1995). *Bosquejo del Macuna*. Santafé de Bogotá: Instituto Lingüístico de Verano.

Sohn, H.-M. (1986). *Linguistic Expeditions*. Seoul: Hanshin.

—— (1994). *Korean*. London: Routledge.

Soper, J. (1996). *Loan Syntax in Turkic and Iranian*. Bloomington: Eurolingua.

Soto Ruiz, C. (1976). *Gramática quechua: Ayacucho-Chanca*. Lima: Ministerio de Educación e Instituto de Estudios Peruanos.

Sparing-Chávez, M. (2003). 'I want to but I can't: The frustrative in Amahuaca'. *Summer Institute of Linguistics Electronic Working Papers* SILEWP 2003-002, 13 pp.

Starke, G. (1985). 'Zum Modusgebrauch bei der Redewiederaufgabe in der Presse', *Sprachpflege* 34: 163–5.

Stebbins, T. (1999). 'Issues in Sm'algyax (Coast Tsimshian) lexicography'. Ph.D. dissertation, University of Melbourne.

Steever, S. (2002). 'Direct and indirect discourse in Tamil', in Güldemann and von Roncador (eds.) (2002: 91–108).

Stenzel, K. (2003). 'Assertion (presupposition) as an evidential category in Wanano and other Eastern Tukano languages'. Paper presented at CIL XVII, Prague, July.

Stolz, T. (1991). *Sprachbund im Baltikum? Estnisch und Lettisch im Zentrum einer sprachlichen Konvergenzlandschaft*. Bochum: Universitätsverlag Dr. N. Brockmeyer.

Storch, A. (1999). *Das Hone und seine Stellung im Zentral-Jukunoid*. Köln: Rüdiger Köppe Verlag.

Strom, C. (1992). *Retuarã Syntax*. Summer Institute of Linguistics and the University of Texas at Arlington.

Sumbatova, N. (1999). 'Evidentiality, transitivity and split ergativity', in W. Abraham and L. Kulikov (eds.), *Tense-Aspect, Transitivity and Causativity. Essays in Honour of Vladimir Nedjalkov*. Amsterdam: John Benjamins, 63–95.

Sun, J. T. S. (1993). 'Evidentials in Amdo-Tibetan', *Bulletin of the Institute of History and Philology, Academia Sinica* 63–4: 945–1001.

Swadesh, M. (1939). 'Nootka internal syntax', *International Journal of American Linguistics* 9: 77–102.

Swanton, J. (1911). 'Haida', in F. Boas (ed.), *Handbook of American Indian Languages*, part 1. Smithsonian Institution. Bureau of American Ethnology Bulletin 40, 205–82.

Tarpent, M.-L. MS. 'Evidential particles in Nisq'ah'.

Tasmowski, L., and Dendale, P. (1994). 'Pouvoir: un marqueur d'évidentialité', *Langue Française* 102: 41–55.

Tatevosov, S. G. (2001a). 'From resultatives to evidentials: Multiple uses of the perfect in Nakh-Daghestanian languages', *Journal of Pragmatics* 33: 443–64.

—— (2001b). 'Kosvennaja zasvideteljstvovannostj' (Oblique evidentiality), in Kibrik (ed.) (2001: 294–307).

Tatevosov, S. G., and Maisak, T. A. (1999*a*). 'Formy realjnogo naklonenija' (Forms of realis mood), in Kibrik and Testelec (eds.) (1999: 206–47).

—— —— (1999*b*). 'Formy admirativnoj semantiki' (Forms with admirative semantics), in Kibrik and Testelec (eds.) (1999: 289–92).

Tauli, V. (1973–83) *Standard Estonian Grammar*, 2 vols. Uppsala: Studia Uralica et Altaica Upsaliensia.

Telles, S. (2002). 'Fonologia e gramátiaa Latundê/Lakondê'. Ph.D. dissertation. Vrije Universiteit Amsterdam.

Ten Cate, A. P. (1996). 'Modality of verb forms in German reported speech', in Janssen and van der Wurff (eds.) (1996: 189–211).

Tepljashina, T. I. (1967). 'Udmurtskij jazyk' (The Udmurt language), in P. J. Skorik (ed.), *Jazyki narodov SSSR*, vol. III. Moscow-Leningrad: Nauka, 261–80.

—— and Lytkin, V. I. (1976). 'Permskije jazyki' (The Permic languages), in *Osnovy Finno-ugorskogo Jazykoznanija. Marijskij. Permskije i Ugorskije Jazyki. (Foundations of Finno-Ugric Linguistics; Mari, Permic and Ugric Languages.)* Moscow: Nauka, 97–228.

Tereschenko, N. M. (1966). 'Enetskij jazyk' (The Enets language), in P. J. Skorik (ed.), *Jazyki narodov SSSR*, vol. III. Moscow-Leningrad: Nauka, 438–57.

—— (1973). *Sintaksis samodijskih jazykov. (Syntax of Samoyedic Languages.)* Leningrad: Nauka.

—— (1979). *Nganasanskij jazyk. (The Nganasan language.)* Leningrad: Nauka.

Thiesen, W. (1996). *Gramática del idioma Bora*. Peru: Instituto Lingüístico de Verano.

Thomason, S. G., and Kaufman, T. (1988). *Language Contact, Creolization and Genetic Linguistics*. Berkeley and Los Angeles: University of California Press.

Thompson, L. (1979). 'Salishan and the Northwest', in L. Campbell and M. Mithun (eds.), *The Languages of Native America*. Austin and London: University of Texas Press, 692–765.

—— and Thompson, M. T. (1992). *The Thompson Language*. University of Montana occasional papers in linguistics 8. Missoula: The University of Montana Press.

Thompson, S. (2002). ' "Object complements" and conversation: Towards a realistic account', *Studies in Language* 26: 125–64.

Thurgood, G. (1981). 'The historical development of the Akha evidentials system', *Proceedings of the Seventh Annual Meeting of the Berkeley Linguistics Society*, 295–302.

—— (1986). 'The nature and origins of the Akha evidentials system', in Chafe and Nichols (eds.) (1986: 214–22).

Thurgood, G., and LaPolla, R. J. (eds.) (2003). *The Sino-Tibetan Languages*. London: Routledge.

Timberlake, A. (1982). 'The impersonal passive in Lithuanian', *Proceedings of the Eighth Annual Meeting of the Berkeley Linguistics Society*, 508–23.

Torres Rubio, D. de (1616). *Arte de la lengua aymara*. Lima: Francisco del Canto.

Tosco, M. (2000). 'Is there an "Ethiopian linguistic area"?' *Anthropological Linguistics* 42: 329–65.

Tournadre, N. (1994). 'Personne et médiatifs en tibétain', *Faits de langues* 3: 149–58.

—— (1996). 'Comparaison des systèmes médiatifs de quatre dialectes tibétains (tibétain central, ladakhi, dzongha et amdo)', in Guentchéva (ed.) (1996: 195–213).

Trask, L. (1999). *Key Concepts in Language and Linguistics*. London and New York: Routledge.

Traugott, E. C. (1989). 'On the rise of epistemic meanings in English: An example of subjectification in semantic change', *Language* 65: 31–55.

Travis, C. (forthcoming). 'Dizque: A Colombian evidentiality strategy', *Linquistics*.

Trivedi, G. M. (1991). *Descriptive Grammar of Byansi, a Bhotiya Language*. Calcutta: Anthropological Survey of India, Government of India, Ministry of Human Resource Development, Department of Culture.

Tschenkéli, K. (1958). *Einführung in die Georgische Sprache*. Band 1. Theoretischer Teil. Zürich: Amirani Verlag.

Tuldava, J. (1994). *Estonian Textbook*. Bloomington: Indiana University.

Urmston, J. O. (1952). 'Parenthetical verbs', *Mind* 61: 480–96.

Usenkova, E. V. (forthcoming). 'Renarrativ v nganasanskom jazyke'. (Renarrative in Nganasan.)

Vakhtin, N. B. (1995). *Syntaksis jazyka asiatskih eskimosov*. (*Syntax of the language of the Asian Eskimo*.) Sankt-Peterburg: Izdateljstvo Evropejskogo Doma.

Valenzuela, P. (2003). 'Evidentiality in Shipibo-Konibo, with a comparative overview of the category in Panoan', in Aikhenvald and Dixon (eds.) (2003: 33–62).

van der Auwera, J., and Plungian, V. A. (1998). 'On modality's semantic map', *Linguistic Typology* 2: 79–124.

van der Auwera, J. (1999). 'On the semantic and pragmatic polyfunctionality of modal verbs', in K. Turner (ed.), *The Semantics/Pragmatics Interface from Different Points of View*. Oxford: Elsevier, 49–64.

van den Berg, H. (1995). *A Grammar of Hunzib*. Munich: Lincom Europa.

van den Berg, R. (1997). 'Spatial deixis in Muna (Sulawesi)', in G. Senft (ed.), *Referring to Space: Studies in Austronesian and Papuan Languages*. Oxford: Oxford University Press, 197–220.

van Eijk, J. (1997). *The Lillooet Language. Phonology. Morphology. Syntax*. Vancouver: UBC Press.

Veksler, B. H., and Jurik, V. A. (1975). *Latyshskij jazyk*. (*The Latvian Language*.) 2nd ed. Riga: Zvajgzne.

Viitso, T.-R. (1998). 'Estonian', in D. Abondolo (ed.), *The Uralic languages*. London: Routledge, 115–48.

Vinogradov, V. V. (1947). *Russkij jazyk*. (*The Russian Language*.) Moscow and Leningrad: Uchpedgiz.

Voort, H. van der (2000). 'A grammar of Kwaza'. Ph.D. dissertation, University of Leiden.

Vries, de. L. J. (1990). 'Some remarks of direct quotation in Kombai', in H. Pinkster and I. Genee (eds.), *Unity in Diversity: Papers Presented to Siom C. Dik on his 50th Birthday*. Dordrecht: Foris, 291–309.

Wagner, G. (1934). *Yuchi*. New York: Columbia University Press.

Wälchli, B. (2000). 'Infinite predication as marker of evidentiality and modality in the languages of the Baltic region', *Sprachtypologie und Universalienforschung* 53: 186–210.

Waltz, N., and Waltz. C. (1997). *El agua, la roca y el humo. Estudios sobre la cultura wanana del Vaupés.* Santafé de Bogotá: Instituto Lingüístico del Verano.

Watanabe, Y. (1984). 'Transitivity and evidentiality in Japanese', *Studies in Language* 8: 235–51.

Watkins, L. (1984). *A Grammar of Kiowa.* Lincoln and London: University of Nebraska Press.

Watters, D. E. (2002). *A Grammar of Kham.* Cambridge: Cambridge University Press.

Weber, D. J. (1986). 'Information perspective, profile, and patterns in Quechua', in Chafe and Nichols (eds.) (1986: 137–55).

—— (1989). *A Grammar of Huallaga (Huánuco) Quechua.* Berkeley: University of California Press.

—— (1996). *Una gramática del quechua del Huallaga (Huánuco).* Lima: Instituto Lingüístico de Verano.

—— and Thiesen, W. (forthcoming). *A Grammar of Bora.*

Weinreich, U. (1963). 'On the semantic structure of language', in J. H. Greenberg (ed.), *Universals of Language.* Cambridge, Mass.: MIT Press, 114-71.

West, B. (1980). *Gramática Popular del Tucano.* Santafé de Bogotá: Instituto Lingüístico de Verano.

Wheeler, A. (1987). *Gantëya Bain. El Pueblo Siona del río Putumayo, Colombia.* Tomo 1. *Etnología, Gramática, Textos.* Santafé de Bogotá: Instituto Lingüístico de Verano.

Whistler, K. W. (1986). 'Evidentials in Patwin', in Chafe and Nichols (eds.) (1986: 60–74).

Whorf, B. L. (1941). 'The relation of habitual thought and behavior to language', in L. Spier, A. I. Hallowell, and S. S. Newmann (eds.), *Language, Culture and Personality. Essays in Memory of Edward Sapir.* Menasha, Wisconsin: Sapir Memorial Publication Fund, 75–93.

Wiemer, B. (1998). 'Pragmatical inferences at the threshold to grammaticalization. The case of Lithuanian predicative participles and their functions', *Linguistica Baltica* 7: 229–43.

Wierzbicka, A. (1996). *Semantics. Primes and Universals.* Oxford: Oxford University Press.

—— (1994). 'Semantics and epistemology: The meaning of "evidentials" in a cross-linguistic perspective', *Language Sciences* 16: 81–137.

Wilkins, D. P. (1989). 'Mparntwe Arrernte (Aranda): Studies in the structure and semantics of grammar'. Ph.D. dissertation, ANU, Canberra.

Willett, T. (1988). 'A cross-linguistic survey of the grammaticization of evidentiality', *Studies in Language* 12: 51–97.

—— (1991). *A Reference Grammar of Southeastern Tepehuan.* Dallas: Summer Institute of Linguistics and University of Texas at Arlington.

Wilson, P. (1992). *Gramática del Achagua (Arawak).* Bogotá: Instituto Lingüístico de Verano.

Windfuhr, G. (1982). 'The verbal category of inference in Persian', in *Acta Iranica 22. Monumentum Georg Morgenstierne II.* Leiden: Brill, 264–87.

Winkler, E. (2001). *Udmurt.* Munich: Lincom Europa.

Wise, M. R. (1999). 'Small language families and isolates in Peru', in Dixon and Aikhenvald (eds.) (1999: 307–40).

Woodbury, A. C. (1981). 'Study of the Chevak dialect of Central Yupi'k Eskimo'. Ph.D. dissertation, University of California, Berkeley.

—— (1986). 'Interactions of tense and evidentiality: A study of Sherpa and English', in Chafe and Nichols (eds.) (1986: 188–202).

Yu, D. (2003). 'Evidentiality in Shibacha Lisu'. Paper presented at 36th International Conference on Sino-Tibetan Languages and Linguistics. Melbourne.

Zeisler, B. (2000). 'Narrative conventions in Tibetan languages: The issue of mirativity', *Linguistics of the Tibeto-Burman Area* 23: 39–77.

Zúñiga, F. (2000). *Mapudungun.* Munich: Lincom Europa.

—— (n.d.) 'Some notes on the Mapudungun evidential'. MS.

Zylstra, C. F. (1991). 'A syntactic sketch of Alazatlatzala Mixtec', in C. H. Bradley and B. E. Hollenbach (eds.), *Studies in the Syntax of Mixtecan Languages,* vol. 3. Dallas: Summer Institute of Linguistics and the University of Texas at Arlington, 1–178.

Index of languages

Abkhaz (Northwest Caucasian) 29–30, 38, 67, 70,
  82, 142, 241–2, 250, 253, 256, 261, 293
  evidentials and modalites 258
  evidentials and person 222–3, 238
  evidentials in discourse 108, 137, 313, 316–18,
    323–4, 346, 350
  mirative extensions of evidentials 196, 199,
    207–8
  origin of evidentials 109, 272–3, 277
  semantics of evidentials 158, 186
Achagua (Arawak) 32, 292, 301
Adioukrou (Kwa, Niger-Congo) 135
Afghan Persian (Iranian, Indo-European) 109
African languages 116, 133, 291, 383
Aguaruna (Jívaro) 137, 141
Agul (Northeast Caucasian) 115, 143, 228
Akha (Tibeto-Burman, Sino-Tibetan) 69, 96–7,
    103, 204, 256, 261, 272, 277, 284–5, 291, 369
Albanian (Indo-European) 40, 108, 130, 158, 197,
    279, 280, 288, 296
Algonquian 41, 187, 279, 291
Amahuaca (Panoan) 357
Amazonian languages 61, 76, 292, 357, 359, 382
Amdo Tibetan (Tibeto-Burman, Sino-Tibetan)
    45, 100, 160, 229–30, 232, 238, 260, 269,
    326, 345, 350
Andean Spanish 21, 109, 277, 297–9, 335–6,
    see also Spanish, Andean
Anglophone environment 386
Apache (Athabaskan) 291, see also Western
    Apache
Arabela (Zaparoan) 32, 292
Arabic (Semitic) 10
Aranda (Australian), see Arrernte, Mparntwe
    Arrernte
Arapaho (Algonquian) 291
Arawá languages 292, see also Madí dialect
    complex
Arawak languages 32, 278–9, 285, 292, 296, 310
Archi (Northeast Caucasian) 29, 72, 83, 96, 156,
    199, 207, 210, 222, 233–4, 238, 241, 256,
    279, 377
Arizona Tewa (Kiowa-Tanoan) 42, 69–70, 96,
    136, 139–40, 145, 185, 294–5, 313, see also
    Tewa

Armenian (Indo-European) 113, 289, 323, 346,
    360, 381, see also Modern Eastern
    Armenian, Western Armenian
Aromanian (Romance, Indo-European) 288
Arrernte (Australian) 33, 69, 180–1, 183, 193, 251,
    284, 293, 299, 310, 312–14, 322, see also
    Mparntwe Arrernte
Aslian (Mon-Khmer) 234
Athabaskan languages 31, 53, 291, 358
Australian languages 33–5, 76, 87, 110, 132, 193,
    293, 314
Avar (Northeast Caucasian) 38
Aymara (Jaqi) 12, 14–15, 18, 43, 114, 142, 250,
    296–7, 391, see also Jaqi
  semantics of evidentials 162
  usage of evidentials 335–6, 338–9, 357–8

Bagvalal (Northeast Caucasian) 155, 280, 316, 325,
    341
Bahwana (Arawak) 46
Balinese (Western Austronesian) 356
Balkan Slavic (Slavic, Indo-European) 40, 158,
    197, 279, 288–9
Balkan languages 15, 77, 150, 264, 288–9, 293, 297
Balto-Finnic (Finno-Ugric, Uralic) 77, 123, 140,
    282, 290
Baltic languages (Indo-European) 77, 140,
    278, 290
Banawá (Arawá) 292
Baniwa (Arawak) 32, 34, 95, 242, 253, 258, 285, 292,
    294, 310, see also Baniwa of Içana
Baniwa of Içana (Arawak) 32, 34, 95, 242, 253, 258,
    285, 292, 294, 310, see also Baniwa
Bantu languages 275
Barasano (East Tucanoan, Tucanoan) 51, 312
Barbacoan 54, 124, 293, 325
Basque (isolate) 284
Bedauye (Cushitic, Afroasiatic) 137
Bella Coola (Salish) 59
Benue-Congo (Niger-Congo) 132
Biansi (Tibeto-Burman, Sino-Tibetan) 274
Bora (Bora-Witoto) 44, 72, 83, 91, 93, 103, 162–4,
    187, 243–4, 258, 265, 292, 310, 341, 369, 373
Bora-Witoto languages 104, 382
Boumaa Fijian (Oceanic, Austronesian) 122

Bukiyip Arapesh (Arapesh, Papuan area) 109
Bulgar (Turkic) 289
Bulgarian (Slavic, Indo-European) 14–15, 111, 136, 138, 140, 264, 277, 288–9, 294, 298

Caddoan languages 56, 59, 291
Capanawa (Panoan) 46
Carib languages 382
Cashibo (Panoan) 32
Caucasian languages 17, 28, 112, 277, 316
Cavineña (Tacanan) 250
Central Pomo (Pomoan) 61, 232
Central Siberian Eskimo 148, 182, *see also* Eskimo language
Central Tucanoan (Tucanoan) 49–50
Chadic languages 120
Chantyal (Tibeto-Burman, Sino-Tibetan) 137
Chemehuevi (Uto-Aztecan) 51
Chepang (Tibeto-Burman, Sino-Tibetan) 127, 204
Cheyenne (Algonquian) 291
Cherokee (Iroquoian) 26–8, 41, 77, 154–5, 352
Chinese Pidgin Russian (Creole) 8, 31, 253, 263–4, 283, 325, 328, 368
Chimakuan languages 291
Chinantecan (Oto-Manguean) 291
Chinese, Mandarin (Sino-Tibetan) 385
Chipewyan (Athabaskan) 31
Choco languages 58, 293
Choctaw (Muskogean) 96, 256, 350
Chukchi (Chukotko-Kamchatkan) 148
Chukotko-Kamchatkan languages 290
Circassian (Northwest Caucasian) 277, 293
Colombian Spanish (Romance, Indo-European) 111, 141–2, 151, 179, 205–6, 228, 324, *see also* Spanish, Colombian
Comanche (Uto-Aztecan) 50, 92–3, 177, 218
Copala Trique (Oto-Manguean) 178
Cora (Uto-Aztecan) 57–8, 64, 177, 182, 250, 272
Cree (Algonquian) 42, 157–8, 278–9, 314, 316–17, 345–6, 360, 380, *see also* Cree/Montagnais/Naskapi
Cree/Montagnais/Naskapi (Algonquian) 42, 157–8, 278–9, 314, 316–17, 345–6, 360, 380
Creole languages 8, 368
Crimean Tatar (Turkic) 289
Croatian (Slavic, Indo-European) 110, 386
Cupeño (Uto-Aztecan) 32, 87, 182, 213, 314

Daco-Romanian (Romance, Indo-European) 111, 277, 288
Dakota (Siouan) 50, *see also* Lakota, Lakhota

Dani (Papuan area) 132
Dardic languages (Indo-European) 24, 254, 289
Dargwa (Northeast Caucasian) 228, 279, 281, 284
Dâw (Makú) 32, 286, 292
Desano (East Tucanoan, Tucanoan) 60, 120, 175, 265, 267, 294–6, 311–12
Diegueño (Yuman) 83, 182, 193, 257, 273, 284, *see also* Jamul Tiipay
Diyari (Australian) 35–6, 154, 193, 200, 386
Dogon (Niger-Congo) 114
Donno Sɔ (Dogon, Niger-Congo) 133
Dulong (Tibeto-Burman, Sino-Tibetan) 47, 274
Dutch (Germanic, Indo-European) 17, 382
Dyirbal (Australian) 76, 130–2, 149, 300, 356

East Tucanoan (Tucanoan) 51–2, 60, 69–70, 82, 242–3, 247, 253–4, 263, 266–7, 274, 285, 292–6, 298, 325, 349
Eastern Armenian, Modern (Indo-European) 113, 289, 323, 346, 360, 381, *see also* Armenian, Western Armenian
Eastern Quebec Cree (Algonquian) 106, *see also* Cree
Eastern Pomo (Pomoan) 52–3, 67, 242, 250, 253, 256, 263, 267
    evidentials and other catergories 72, 243–4
    evidentials and person 226, 235, 238
    evidentials, more than once in a clause 91–3, 103, 218, 332
    semantics of evidentials 167, 170–1, 174–5, 185, 219
    usage of evidentials 314, 321–2, 358
Enets (Samoyedic, Uralic) 47–8, 241, 284–5
Enga (Engan, Papuan area) 32, 293
Engan family (Papuan area) 32, 83, 293
English (Germanic, Indo-European) 4, 7–8, 10, 17, 76, 120–2, 133, 137, 142, 148, 150, 154, 235, 297–9, 302, 314, 335, 337–8, 355, 357, 360, 382, 385
Eskimo language (Eskimo-Aleut) 130, *see also* Central Siberian Eskimo
Eskimo languages (Eskimo-Aleut) 63, 287
Eskimo-Aleut 290
Estonian, Standard (Balto-Finnic, Finno-Ugric) 10, 33, 68–9, 77, 110–1, 122, 256, 258, 264, 270, 277, 281–3
    mirative extensions of evidentials 200, 225, 238
    origin of evidentials 111, 119, 123, 140, 281–3, 290
    semantics of evidentials 7, 180, 193
    usage of evidentials 76, 310

Estonian South dialects (Balto-Finnic,
  Finno-Ugric) 77, 111, 277–8, 283, *see also*
  South Estonian dialects
Ethiopian Plateau, languages of 132
Euchee (isolate) 37–8, 73, 249, 251, 275, 328, 340–1,
  386, *see also* Yuchi
European languages 5–7, 76, 148, 333, 355, 360
Even (Tungusic) 106
Evenki (Tungusic) 106

Fasu (Kutubuan, Papuan area) 62–3, 253, 383
Finnic languages (Finno-Ugric, Uralic) 99
Finno-Ugric languages (Uralic) 28, 68, 263, 267,
  279, 289
Foe (Kutubuan, Papuan area) 61–2, 176, 383
Fox (Algonquian) 109, 143
French (Romance, Indo-European) 10–11, 17,
  106–8, 134, 177

Gahuku (Gorokan, Papuan area) 139–40
Galician (Romance, Indo-European) 141
Gavião (Tupí) 32
Georgian (South Caucasian) 11, 38, 77, 113, 204,
  232, 264, 272, 279, 324
German (Germanic, Indo-European) 15, 76,
  107–8, 110–11, 134–5, 150
Germanic languages (Indo-European) 5
Godoberi (Northeast Caucasian) 28, 311
Greek (Indo-European) 150–1, 272, 293, 296,
  see also Greek, Modern; Modern Greek
Greek, Modern (Indo-European) 142,
  150–1, 382
Guahibo languages 32
Guaraní, Paraguayan (Tupí-Guarani, Tupí)
  32, 292
Gur languages (Niger-Congo) 32
Gypsy languages, *see* Romani

Hakha Lai (Tibeto-Burman, Sino-Tibetan) 275
Hare (Athabaskan) 31, 204, 222
Hatti (isolate) 290
Hebrew (Semitic, Afroasiatic) 10
Hill Patwin (Wintun) 176, 277, 284, *see also*
  Patwin
Hittite (Anatolian, Indo-European) 290
Hixkaryana (Carib) 63, 73, 292, 324
Hokan languages 291
Hone (Central Jukunoid) 214
Hopi (Uto-Aztecan) 15, 45, 69, 294–5, 313
Hungarian (Ugric, Finno-Ugric) 108, 148
Hunzib (Northeast Caucasian) 29, 232
Hupa (Athabaskan) 31, 53, 275, 291

Hup (Makú) 60, 68, 72, 242, 259, 261, 273–4,
  286–7, 292, *see also* Hupda
Hupda (Makú) 60, 68, 72, 242, 259, 261, 273–4,
  286–7, 292, *see also* Hup

Ignaciano (Arawak) 32, 292
India as a linguistic area 291
Indo-Aryan languages (Indo-European) 291
Indo-European languages 11, 18, 133, 148
Iranian languages 11, 16, 68, 77, 112, 279, 289
Irantxe (isolate) 24, 71, 82–3, 156, 232, 242, 256,
  see also Mỹky
Iroquoian 26
Ishkashim (Iranian, Indo-European) 38, 113–14
Istanbul Judezmo (Jewish Spanish language;
  Romance, Indo-European) 114
Itelmen (Chukotko-Kamchatkan) 116

Jamamadí (Arawá) 292
Jamiltepec Mixtec (Oto-Manguean) 182
Jamul Tiipay (Yuman) 83, 182, 193, 257, 273, 284,
  see also Diegueño
Japanese (isolate) 10, 14, 81, 100, 122–3, 128, 268,
  324–5, 356
Jaqi 12, 14–15, 18, 43, 114, 142, 250, 296–7, 391,
  see also Aymara
Jarawara (Arawá) 23–4, 26–7, 29, 68, 70, 77, 130,
  242, 250, 253, 258, 264, 267
  evidentials and person 218, 220–1, 223–4, 234,
    238
  evidentials, more than once in a clause 88,
    93–5, 103
  markedness in evidentials 71–2
  mirative extensions of evidentials 197–8, 207
  origin of evidentials 275, 292
  semantics of evidentials 23–4, 154, 156, 158
  subsystems of evidentials 84–5
  usage of evidentials in discourse 308–9, 311,
    326–7, 334, 341, 345, 360, 380
Jê languages 382
Jívaro languages 137
Jinghpaw (Tibeto-Burman, Sino-Tibetan) 178

Kalapalo (Carib) 321, 330, 337
Kalasha (Dardic, Indo-European) 24, 28, 79, 120,
  154–5, 157, 197, 210, 222, 263, 289
Kamaiurá (Tupí-Guaraní, Tupí) 18, 69, 78, 94,
  280–1, 292
Kambera (Western Austronesian) 140–1
Karachay-Balkar (Turkic) 289
Karaim (Turkic) 296
Karatjarri (Australian) 110

Karitiana (Tupí) 32
Karo (Tupí) 63
Kashaya (Pomoan) 60–1, 204, 233, 266, 307–8, 310
Kato (Athabaskan) 31, 291
Kazakh (Turkic) 40
Ket (isolate) 290
Kewa (Engan, Papuan area) 83
Kham (Tibeto-Burman, Sino-Tibetan)
    mirativity 211–12
    reported evidential in 32–4, 137–8, 177, 179, 193,
        232, 248, 273, 301
Khanty (Ob-Ugric, Finno-Ugric) 31, 155–6, 290,
    see also Northern Khanty
Khazar (Turkic) 289
Khowar (Dardic, Indo-European) 24, 28, 79, 157,
    222, 261, 289
Kinyarwanda (Bantu) 11, 120
Kiowa (Kiowa-Tanoan) 42, 178, 227, 266, 291,
    330–1
Kiowa-Tanoan 42, 69, 291
Koasati (Muskogean) 232
Kombai (Awyu-Dumut, Papuan area) 137, 256
Komi (Finno-Permic, Finno-Ugric) 28, 68–9,
    156, 232, 264, 279, 281, 316
Komi Zyryan (Finno-Permic, Finno-Ugric) 28,
    68–9, 156, 232, 264, 279, 281, 316, *see also*
    Komi
Korean (isolate) 128–9, 214, 325, 356
Koreguaje (West Tucanoan, Tucanoan) 44, 72,
    162, 187, 373
Kunama (Nilo-Saharan) 137
Kuot (New Ireland, Papuan area) 343
Kurdish (Iranian, Indo-European) 289
Kurmanjî Kurdish (Iranian, Indo-European),
    see Kurdish
Kutubuan languages (Papuan area) 61–2
Kwakiutl (Wakashan) 12–13, 59, 130, 285, 345
Kwakwala, *see* Kwakuitl
Kwaza (isolate) 132
Kypchak (Turkic) 289

Ladakhi (Tibeto-Burman, Sino-Tibetan) 53, 82,
    211, 232
Lak (Northeast Caucasian) 250
Lakhota (Siouan) 50, 75, *see also* Dakota, Lakota
Lakota (Siouan) 50, 75, *see also* Dakota, Lakhota
Latundê/Lakondê (Nambiquara) 36–7, 72, 178,
    341, 386
Latvian (Baltic, Indo-European) 33, 123, 140, 258,
    281–2, 290
Laz (South Caucasian)
Lega (Bantu) 275, 291

Lezgian (Northeast Caucasian) 31–3, 272–3
Lhasa Tibetan (Tibeto-Burman, Sino-Tibetan)
    69, 125–8, 133–4, 204, 284
Lillooet (Salish) 59
Lisu (Tibeto-Burman, Sino-Tibetan) 69
Lithuanian (Baltic, Indo-European) 33, 117, 119,
    123, 140, 238, 281–2, 290
    mirative extensions of evidentials 200, 205,
        207–8, 218, 225, 228
Livonian (Balto-Finnic, Finno-Ugric) 33, 68, 123,
    282, 290
Luvian (Anatolian, Indo-European) 290

Macedonian (Slavic, Indo-European) 40, 257,
    288–9, 298, 311, 317, 346, 354
Macuna (East Tucanoan, Tucanoan) 52
Madí dialect complex (Arawá) 284, 292
Mah Meri (Aslian, Mon-Khmer) 234
Maidu (Maidun) 46, 252, 291
Makah (Wakashan) 63, 80, 176, 212, 258,
    285, 345
Makú languages 32, 60, 274, 286, 292
Malagasy (Western Austronesian) 130
Mamainde (Nambiquara) 56–7, 61, 123, 234
Manambu (Ndu, Papuan area) 343
Mandarin Chinese (Sino-Tibetan) 385
Mangap-Mbula (Oceanic, Austronesian) 28, 293
Mangarayi (Australian) 108–9
Mansi (Ob-Ugric, Finno-Ugric) 31, 118, 155, 196,
    198, 281–2, 290
Mao Naga (Tibeto-Burman, Sino-Tibetan) 241
Mapuche (isolate) 42, 200, *see also* Mapudungun
Mapudungun (isolate) 42, 200, *see also* Mapuche
Mari (Finno-Permic, Finno-Ugric) 28, 68, 278
Maricopa (Yuman) 47, 69, 96, 162, 182, 187–8, 193,
    228, 235, 256, 272–3, 308, 373
Mayan 291
Meglено-Romanian (Romance,
    Indo-European) 288
Megrelian (South Caucasian) 31, 113, 289
Meithei (Tibeto-Burman, Sino-Tibetan) 31, 144,
    233–4, 238, 251, 263, 275, 311, 377
Menomini (Algonquian) 33, 77, 132, 138, 140
Mingrelian (South Caucasian) 31, 113, 289, *see
    also* Megrelian
Miwok (Miwok-Costanoan) 291
Mixtecan (Oto-Manguean) 291
Modern Eastern Armenian (Indo-European) 113,
    289, 323, 346, 360, 381, *see also* Armenian
    (Indo-European), Western Armenian
Modern Greek (Indo-European) 142, 150–1, 382,
    see also Modern Greek

Modern Persian (Iranian, Indo-European)
114–15
Mon-Khmer 234
Mosetén (isolate) 44, 160–1, 171, 330
Mparntwe Arrernte (Australian) 33, 69, 180–1,
183, 193, 251, 284, 293, 299, 310, 312–14, 322,
see also Arrernte
Muna (Western Austronesian) 131
Munda languages (Austroasiatic) 131
Mỹky (isolate) 24, 71, 82–3, 156, 232, 242, 256,
see also Irantxe

Nadëb (Makú) 286, 292
Nambiquara languages 36, 56, 61, 215, 234, 292,
341, 383
Nax (Nax-Daghestanian, Northeast Caucasian) 28
Nenets (Samoyedic, Uralic) 31, 241, 281, 284–5
Nepali (Indo-Aryan, Indo-European) 156,
197, 291
Newari (Tibeto-Burman, Sino-Tibetan) 115, 124,
204, 274, 291
Nganasan (Samoyedic, Uralic) 47–50, 59, 82,
241–2, 245, 290
evidentials and other categories 250, 264–5,
266–7
evidentials and person 218–19, 226, 238
forms unmarked for evidentiality 74–5
mirative extensions of evidentials 200–1, 207
origin of evidentials 284–5
semantics of evidentials 163–4, 166, 178, 180,
183, 193
usage of evidentials 142, 314, 325, 328, 349–50
Ngiyambaa (Australian) 34–5, 68, 82, 227, 254,
257, 386
semantics of evidentials 64, 154, 159, 184, 193
usage of evidentials 330, 341
Niger-Congo languages 133
Nivkh (isolate) 252, 255, 290, 300, 356
Nootka (Wakashan) 13, 51, 80
North American Indian languages 13–15, 17, 28,
31, 33, 45, 50–1, 82, 290–1, 395
Northeast Caucasian languages 79, 263, 267,
280, 289
Northern Embera (Choco) 58
Northern Iroquoian (Iroquoian) 108
Northern Khanty (Ob-Ugric, Finno-Ugric) 279,
341
mirative extensions of evidentials 196–7, 199,
207–8, 217, 221
semantics of evidentials 155–6
Northern Paiute (Uto-Aztecan) 291, 298–9, 333,
see also Paiute

Northern Samoyedic (Uralic) 284
Nyangumarta (Australian) 110–11, 133

Ob-Ugric languages (Finno-Ugric, Uralic) 68,
118
Oceanic languages (Austronesian) 28, 99
Ocotepec Mixtec (Oto-Manguean) 182
Oksapmin (Papuan area) 46–7, 69, 72, 163, 268,
293, 383
Omaha (Siouan) 33–4, 70
Oto-Manguean languages 178, 182

Paiute (Uto-Aztecan) 291, 298–9, 333, *see also*
Southern Paiute and Northern Paiute
Palaic (Anatolian, Indo-European) 290
Palikur (Arawak) 130
Panare (Carib) 118–19, 253
Panoan languages 45–6, 292
Papuan area 32, 46, 61–2, 83, 109, 132, 137, 140, 176,
182, 293, 382–3
Paraguayan Guaraní (Tupí-Guaraní, Tupí)
32, 292
Pareci (Arawak) 32, 292
Patwin (Wintun) 176, 277, 284, *see also*
Hill Patwin
Paumarí (Arawá) 284
Pawnee (Caddoan) 56, 72, 310
Penutian languages 291
Permic languages (Finno-Ugric, Uralic) 15
Persian (Iranian, Indo-European) 38–9, 112, 204
Persian, Modern (Iranian, Indo-European)
114–15
Philippine languages (Austronesian) 14, 32,
293, 383
Piapoco (Arawak) 32, 34, 284, 292, 310
Pidgins 8, 368
Piro (Arawak) 32, 292
Pomoan languages 32, 61, 279–80
Ponca (Siouan) 33–4, 45, 70
Portuguese (Romance, Indo-European) 10, 76,
337, 360, 385
Portuguese, South American 142, 179
Portuguese, of northwest Amazonia 206, 297–9,
339, 343
Potawatomi (Algonquian) 32, 310
Proto-Abkhaz (Northwest Caucasian) 289
Proto-Algonquian 279
Proto-Arawak 87
Proto-Baniwa-Tariana (Arawak) 287
Proto-Circassian (Northwest Caucasian) 289
Proto-Eskimo 285
Proto-Eskimo-Aleut 287

Proto-Indo-European 355
Proto-Nax 28
Proto-Tucanoan 355
Purépecha (isolate) 41–2, 118, 185, *see also*
    Tarascan

Qiang (Tibeto-Burman, Sino-Tibetan) 43–5,
    72–3, 84, 97, 242, 250, 256, 263, 267, 269, 291
    evidentiality strategies 120, 148
    evidentials and person 218, 229–30, 232,
        235, 238
    evidentials, more than once in a clause 89,
        92–3, 103, 369
    mirative extensions of evidentials 198, 201,
        207–9, 328, 376
    semantics of evidentials 160, 162–4, 187,
        190, 373
    usage of evidentials 310, 353
Quechua (Quechua) 12, 14–15, 43, 68–70, 213,
        245, 247, 250, 252–3, 256, 258, 260, 266–8,
        277, 297
    acquisition of evidentials 362
    evidentials and cultural stereotypes 349–50,
        353, 358–61, 380–1
    evidentials and other categories 72, 242
    mirative extensions of evidentials 202–3,
        207, 249
    omission of evidentials 79
    semantics of evidentials 7, 159–60, 165–6,
        169–71, 175, 178, 183, 187, 189–90, 193, 373–4
    usage of evidentials 313, 318–21, 325, 337
    see also Quechua Wanka, Quechua Cuzco,
        Quechua Cuzco-Collao variety, Quechua
        Huallaga, Quechua of Huarochirí texts,
        Quechua Junín, Quechua Pastaza,
        Quechua Tarma
Quechua Wanka 43, 252–3, 268–9, *see also*
    Quechua
    evidentials and other categories 230–1, 239,
        245, 247, 261–2
    mirative extensions of evidentials 202–3
    scope of evidentials 97–8, 103, 242, 369
    semantics of evidentials 159–62, 165, 219
    usage of evidentials 318–19, 344–5
Quechua Cuzco 12, 79, 162, 245, 248, *see also*
    Quechua
Quechua, Cuzco-Collao variety 362, *see also*
    Quechua
Quechua Huallaga 79, 162, 166, 230, 322, 330, 337,
    see also Quechua
Quechua of Huarochirí texts 320–1, *see also*
    Quechua

Quechua Junín 213, *see also* Quechua
Quechua Pastaza 162, 316, 319–21, *see also*
    Quechua
Quechua Tarma 162, 213, 245, *see also* Quechua

Resígaro (Arawak) 32, 292
Retuarā (Central Tucanoan, Tucanoan) 49–50,
    242, 296
Rio Grande Tewa (Kiowa-Tanoan) 295
Romance languages (Indo-European) 5, 12, 288
Romani, also Gypsy (Indo-Aryan,
    Indo-European), 112, 288, 293–4,
        see also Vlach Romani
Romanian (Romance, Indo-European) 118, 288
Russian (Slavic, Indo-European) 10, 76, 121–2,
    149, 316, 385

Salar (Turkic) 223, 234, 270, 281, 312, 315–16, 354
Salish languages 59, 291
Samoyedic (Uralic) 47, 82, 241, 290
Santali (Munda, Austroasiatic) 131
Sanuma (Yanomami) 18, 46
Scandinavian languages (Germanic,
    Indo-European) 112
Secoya (West Tucanoan, Tucanoan) 28
Selkup (Samoyedic, Uralic) 232, 241, 266–7, 300
Semelai (Aslian, Mon-Khmer) 109, 210–11
Serbian (Slavic, Indo-European) 110, 288, 386
Shasta (Shastan) 43, 160, 187, 373
Sherpa (Tibeto-Burman, Sino-Tibetan) 124, 233
Shibacha Lisu (Tibeto-Burman, Sino-Tibetan)
    54, 274, 286
Shilluk (Nilotic) 43–4, 214, 226, 234, 256, 291
Shipibo-Konibo (Panoan) 55–6, 68, 261, 267–8
    and other categories 243, 245, 253, 256
    evidentials, more than once in a clause 89–90,
        93, 103, 369
    mirative extensions of evidentials 201, 207, 226
    origin of evidentials 278
    semantics of evidentials 7, 24, 64, 70, 72, 78,
        171–2, 175–6, 179–80, 184–5, 192–3, 308, 375
    usage of evidentials 6, 310, 322, 335–6, 346, 348,
        351–3, 360–1, 380–1
Shoshone (Uto-Aztecan) 33–4, 70, 130
Sierra Miwok (Miwok-Costanoan) 116
Sign Languages 8, 368
Silacayoapan Mixtec (Oto-Manguean) 182
Sinitic languages (Sino-Tibetan) 115
Siona (West Tucanoan, Tucanoan) 46
Siouan languages 291
Siriano (East Tucanoan, Tucanoan) 52
Sissala (Gur, Niger-Congo) 32, 185, 275, 291

Skidegate Haida (Haida) 46
Slovene (Slavic, Indo-European) 110
Sm'algyax (Tsimshianic) 13, 300, *see also* Tsimshian
Sochiapan Chinantec (Oto-Manguean) 182, 249–50, 313
South American languages 14, 17, 28, 32, 45, 70, 82
South Caucasian languages 289
South Estonian dialects 77, 111, 277–8, 283, *see also* Estonian South dialects
Southeastern Tepehuan (Uto-Aztecan) 58–9
Southern Nambiquara (Nambiquara) 61, 234, 268–9
Southern Paiute (Uto-Aztecan) 291, 298–9, 333, *see also* Paiute
Spanish (Romance, Indo-European) 10, 106, 135, 337–8, 385, *see also* Spanish, Andean; Spanish, Bolivian; Spanish, Colombian; Spanish, European; Spanish, Ecuadorian Highlands; Spanish of La Paz; Spanish, South American
Spanish, Andean 21, 109, 277, 297–9, 335–6, *see also* Andean Spanish, Spanish
Spanish, Bolivian 338, *see also* Spanish
Spanish, Colombian 111, 141–2, 151, 179, 205–6, 228, 324, *see also* Colombian Spanish, Spanish
Spanish, Ecuadorian Highlands 205, 297–9, *see also* Spanish
Spanish, European 141–2, 360, *see also* Spanish
Spanish of La Paz 114, 136, 142–3, 204–5, 227–8, *see also* Spanish
Spanish, South American 141–2, 297–9, *see also* Spanish
Squamish (Salish) 151
Sunwar (Tibeto-Burman, Sino-Tibetan) 204
Suruí (Tupí) 32
Svan (South Caucasian) 31, 76–7, 113, 158, 198, 264, 267, 269–70, 346

Tajik (Iranian, Indo-European) 25, 39, 112, 197, 279, 289, 294
Takelma (isolate) 41, 72, 241
Tamil (Dravidian) 138, 140
Tarascan (isolate) 41–2, 118, 185, *see also* Purépecha
Tariana (Arawak) 1–3, 60, 68, 73, 77, 87, 95, 120, 130, 146, 257
    evidentials and cultural stereotypes 333, 336–7, 341–2, 346–9, 350–4, 360–1
    evidentials and modalities 259–60
    evidentials and person 218–19, 223–5, 230, 236–8

    evidentials and tense 8, 78, 263, 265–7
    evidentials in dependent clauses 253–5
    evidentials in questions and commands 242–3, 245–7, 250
    mirative construction 213
    omission of evidentials 78–9
    origin of evidentials 69, 273–4, 278–9, 284–6, 294–6
    semantics of evidentials 7, 64, 98–9, 136, 138–40, 153, 167–9, 171, 175–9, 184, 191–3
    subsystems of evidentials 85–7
    time reference of evidentials 100–2
    usage of evidentials 305–7, 309, 311–12, 315, 322–3, 325, 327–9, 332, 339–40
Tariana, traditional 52, 86
Tatuyo (East Tucanoan, Tucanoan) 51, 345, 347, 360, 380
Tauya (Papuan area) 32, 140, 182, 193, 272, 293
Terêna (Arawak) 32, 292
Tewa (Kiowa-Tanoan) 42, 69–70, 96, 136, 139–40, 145, 185, 294–5, 313, *see also* Arizona Tewa
Thai (Tai-Kadai) 343, 363
Thompson (Salish) 59
Tibetan (Tibeto-Burman, Sino-Tibetan) 14, 28, 69, 205, 211, 264, 272, 291
Tibeto-Burman languages (Sino-Tibetan) 17, 32, 53–4, 69–70, 96, 124, 204, 213, 220, 228, 232–3, 237, 272, 275, 291, 311, 377
Tikar (Benue-Congo, Niger-Congo) 132
Tonkawa (isolate) 51, 273, 291
Trio (Carib) 292
Tsafiki (Barbacoan) 54, 69, 72–3, 83–4, 136, 242, 245, 350
    evidentials and other categories 231, 258, 339
    evidentials, more than once in a clause 90–1, 93, 103, 369
    mirative extensions of evidentials 201–2, 204, 207, 209, 211–12
    origin of evidentials 293
    person marking 124–6
    semantics of evidentials 172–5, 178–9, 189, 192, 374
Tsakhur (Northeast Caucasian) 316
Tsez (Northeast Caucasian) 28, 245, 314
Tsimshian (Tsimshianic) 13, 300, *see also* Sm'algyax
Tucano (East Tucanoan, Tucanoan) 51–2, 68, 78, 101, 382–3
    evidentiality strategies 119–20
    evidentials and cultural stereotypes 342, 346–7, 350, 352, 354, 359–60
    evidentials and modalities 258–9

evidentials and person 218–19, 223–6, 230, 235–8
evidentials and tense 265–7
evidentials in dependent clauses 253–4
evidentials in questions and commands 242–3, 245–7, 250
origin of evidentials 295–6
semantics of evidentials 167–9, 171, 176–7, 193
subsystems of 85–7
usage of evidentials 309, 311–12, 325, 329–30, 332, 336–7, 339
Tucanoan languages 72, 250, 265, 292, 355
Tungusic languages 99
Tunica (isolate) 77
Tupí languages 32, 63, 382
Tupí-Guaraní languages (Tupí) 18, 69, 94, 280, 292, 382
Turkana (Nilo-Saharan) 148
Turkic languages 11–12, 15–16, 30–1, 40, 77, 112, 248, 250, 253, 289, 296–7, 342–3, 345
evidentials and tense 158
evidentials and tense 68
mirative extensions of evidentials 196
origin of evidentials 279, 281
semantics of evidentials 153
Turkish (Turkic) 15–16, 30, 38, 40–1, 112, 114, 288–9
acquisition of evidentials 362–3
mirative extensions of evidentials 207–8, 210, 212, 217, 221
semantics of evidentials 155, 317–18, 323
usage of evidentials 311, 342
Turkmen (Turkic) 40
Tuvaluan (Oceanic, Austronesian) 359
Tuvan (Turkic) 281
Tuyuca 14, 16, 60, 68, 78, 86–7, 100, 120, 146, 260, 294, 382
evidentials and other categories 243, 265, 267
origin of evidentials 274, 280
semantics of evidentials 170, 175–6, 192
usage of evidentials 305–7, 311, 325, 345, 360, 380

Ubykh (Northwest Caucasian) 293
Udihe (Tungusic) 178, 272
Udmurt (Finno-Permic, Finno-Ugric) 28, 68, 156, 264
Ugric languages 290
Uralic family 310
Usan (Numugenan, Papuan area) 139–40
Uto-Aztecan languages 50–1, 57–8, 69, 182, 193, 272, 291

Uyghur (Turkic) 40, 281
Uzbek (Turkic) 40, 294

Vaupés linguistic area 1–3, 51, 86, 153–4, 170, 274, 285–6, 292, 295–7, 311–12, 323, 342
Verde Valley Yavapai (Yuman) 117, 298–9, 333, see also Yavapai
Vlach Romani (Indo-Aryan, Indo-European) 38, 158, 232, 324, see also Gypsy, Romani

Wai Wai (Carib) 292
Wakashan languages 80, 82, 130, 176, 241, 250, 285, 291
Wanano (East Tucanoan, Tucanoan) 72, 120, 382
Warluwarra (Australian) 293
Warlpiri (Australian) 14, 33, 69, 96, 250–1, 293
acquisition of evidentials 363
semantics of evidentials 181–3, 193, 314, 316, 322, 330–1
Wasco-Wishram (Chinookan) 39, 69, 117, 275–6
Washo (isolate) 46, 201, 207, 210, 291
Waurá (Arawak) 32
Wayana (Carib) 292
West Caucasian 289
West Greenlandic (Eskimo-Aleut) 80–1, 250
origin of evidentials 272, 284–5
semantics of evidentials 176, 182, 185
usage of evidentials 310, 313, 353
West Tibetan (Tibeto-Burman, Sino-Tibetan) 205
West Tucanoan (Tucanoan) 46
Western Apache (Athabaskan) 31, 63, 74, 81–2, 93–4, 102, 148, 358
mirative extensions of evidentials 203–4, 209, 212
semantics of evidentials 185–6, 342
Western Armenian (Indo-European) 113, 289, 323, 346, 360, 381, see also Armenian, Modern Eastern Armenian
Western Austronesian languages (Austronesian) 32, 140, 293
Western Desert language (Australian) 33, 69, 182, 193, 250, 293, 310, 314, see also Yankunytjatjara
Western Torres Straits language 356
Western Türk (Turkic) 289
Weyewa (Western Austronesian) 359
Wichita (Caddoan) 59–60, 75, 226
Wintu (Wintun) 13, 36, 67, 70, 82, 167, 226, 238, 245, 284–5, 291, 300–2, 310, 314, 337, 348, 351, 366
origin of evidentials 273–4, 275

Wintu, traditional (Wintun) 36, 60, 300–2

Xakas (Turkic) 30
Xamatauteri (Yanomami) 18, 56, 85, 90, 93, 103,
    177, 284, 311
!Xun (Khoisan) 149

Yana (isolate) 291
Yanam (Yanomami) 18, 28, 241
Yankunytjatjara (Australian) 33, 69, 182, 193, 250,
    293, 310, 314, *see also* Western Desert
    language
Yanomami languages 18, 28, 46, 56, 292
Yavapai (Yuman) 117, 298–9, 333, *see also* Verde
    Valley Yavapai
Yokuts (Youkutsan) 291
Yoruba (Benue-Congo, Niger-Congo) 136–7
Yosondúa Mixtec (Oto-Manguean) 182
Yucatec Maya (Mayan) 137

Yuchi (isolate) 37–8, 73, 249, 251, 275, 328, 340–1,
    386, *see also* Euchee
Yucuna (Arawak) 296
Yuhup (Makú) 274, 286, 292
Yukaghir (isolate) 27–8, 67–8, 70, 72–3, 77, 82,
    149, 241, 250, 267, 290, 308, 311
    evidentials and other categories 68, 221–2,
        237–8, 244, 262–3, 266
    mirative extensions of evidentials 198–9, 202,
        207–9, 212
    semantics of evidentials 24, 102–3, 154–5, 157–8
    usage of evidentials 317, 326, 328, 346,
        360, 380
Yuman languages 83, 298
Yupik (Eskimo Aleut) 182, *see also* Eskimo
    language, Central Siberian Eskimo

Zaparoan languages 32, 292
Zazaki (Iranian, Indo-European) 38–9, 112

Index of authors

Adams, K. L. 338
Adelaar, W. F. H. 162, 164 n.1, 165, 202, 205 n.3, 208, 213, 245 n.5, 258, 268, 395
Aikhenvald, A. Y. 8, 16, 32, 68–71, 73, 76, 86–8, 95, 100 n.16, 101 n.17, 112 n.6, 116, 130, 146, 218 n.1, 243, 245–6, 250, 252–3, 257, 264 n.8, 273–4, 278, 285, 288, 292, 294–6, 298, 300–1, 337–8, 340, 355–7, 365
Akatsuka, N. 123 n.17
Aksu-Koç, A. A. 40–1, 196–7, 210, 212, 319, 323, 342, 362–3
Alexander, R. M. 182
Alhoniemi, A. 28
Alpher, B. 357 n.8
Ambrazas, V. 117
Anderson, G. 30, 87
Anderson, L. B. 8 n.7, 16 n.12, 69 n.1, 257
Anderson, S. R. 130
Andrews, E. 71 n.3
Anónimo 12
Anonymous 45
Aoki, H. 10, 14, 81, 100, 128, 264 n.8, 268
Aronson, H. I. 15
Austin, P. 34–5, 200

Ballard, L. 14, 32, 293
Balode, L. 290
Bamgboṣe, A. 136–7
Bani, E. 356
Barentsen, A. 121
Barnes, J. 14, 16 n.12, 44, 60, 68, 100 n.14, 146, 170, 175, 232, 260, 265, 296, 305–7, 345, 382
Baron, D. E. 357
Bashir, E. 24, 28, 120, 154, 157, 197, 210, 222, 261, 289
Basso, E. B. 321, 330, 337
Bavin, E. 182, 263
Beier, C. 315
Bendix, E. H. 337
Bertonio Romano, L. 12
Besnier, N. 359
Bhat, D. N. S. 53, 82, 211
Bickel, B. 291
Black, M. 45 n.12
Blass, R. 32, 150, 249, 275
Bloomfield, L. 19, 33, 138, 310

Boas, F. 1, 3, 12–13, 16 n.12, 51, 59, 130, 300, 343, 345 n.5, 351, 354, 382, 393
Boeder, W. 113, 289, 324
Bokarev, E. A. 28
Borgman, D. M. 18, 46, 275 n.2
Botne, R. 275
Brandrup, B. 52
Breen, G. 284, 293, 299 n.18
Broadwell, G. A. 96, 214, 256, 350
Bromley, H. M. 132
Brosnahan, P. 356
Bugenhagen, R. 28, 293
Bullock, A. 5 n.1, 6 n.2, 392
Bulut, C. 149, 289, 311
Bulygina, T. V. 149 n.29
Bunte, P. A. 298–9
Burridge, K. 135–6
Bustamante, I. 205, 297, 299
Bybee, J. 7 n.3, 112 n.6, 279

Calvo Pérez, J. 12
Campbell, L. 33, 69, 123, 272, 281
Carlin, E. B. 292 n.15
Carpenter, K. 363
Casad, E. 57–9, 64, 182, 272
Caughley, R. C. 127
Cerrón-Palomino, R. 165, 245, 268
Chafe, W. L. 5 n.1, 7 n.4, 14, 16 n.12, 344
Chamereau, C. 42 n.9, 118
Chang, I. 129 n.20
Chappell, H. 115 n.10
Charney, J. O. 50
Chelliah, S. L. 31, 144, 233, 251, 263, 311
Chirikba, V. 29, 38, 67, 108–9, 113 n.9, 142, 186, 196, 199, 222, 256, 258, 260, 290 n.12, 272, 277, 289, 293, 316–18, 323–4, 346, 350
Chun, S. A. 129 n.20
Chung, S. 5 n.1, 394
Chuquín, C. 14
Clarke, S. 42, 157, 278–9, 314, 346
Comrie, B. 28, 112, 118 n.13, 133, 222, 245, 264, 279, 289 n.10, 314
Conklin, N. F. 338
Conrad, R. J. 109
Cook, D. M. 44

Courtney, E. 362
Criswell, L. L. 44, 52
Croft, W. 71
Crystal, D. xiii
Csató, É. Á. 30 n.6
Culy, C. 133, 135 n.22
Curnow, T. J. 124, 133, 218

Dahl, Ö. 7 n.3, 8 n.6, 279
Dahlstrom, A. 109, 143
Dankoff, R. 12 n.9
Daguman, J. 32
Davidson, M. 214
Davis, P. W. 59
de Dioz Yapita Moya, J. 336
De Haan, F. 7, 16 n.12, 17 n.13, 96, 256–7, 273, 275, 279–80, 285
Décsy, G. 15, 31 n.7, 241, 281
Dedenbach-Salazar Sáenz, S. 12, 258, 320–1
Deibler, E. W. 139
DeLancey, S. 7, 8, 14, 20, 28, 31, 69, 72, 94, 127, 134, 195–7, 199, 204, 210–11, 213–4, 222, 264, 284
Deloria, E. 51
Dench, A. 87
Dendale, P. 5–6 n.1, 10, 106
Denny, J. P. 130, 355, 365, 368 n.1
Derbyshire, D. C. 63 n.19, 73, 292 n.15, 324
Dickinson, C. 54, 73, 83, 91, 93, 124–6, 172, 176, 178–9, 202, 231, 245, 258, 339, 350
Dik, S. C. 122
Diller, A. 343
Dimmendaal, G. 133, 135 n.22, 148
Dixon, R. M. W. xiii, 8, 10, 19 n.14, 23–4, 32, 70–1, 72 n.5, 75–6, 82–5, 87–8, 94, 112 n.6, 116, 121–2, 130, 149, 198, 218 n.1, 220–1, 232, 234, 242 n.2, 256–7, 264 n.8, 269, 275, 284, 292, 299, 308, 311, 326–7, 341, 345, 355–7, 391
Dobrushina, N. 28
Donabédian, A. 4, 39, 155, 222, 248, 289, 311, 323
Donaldson, T. 34–5, 159, 184, 227, 254, 330
Drapeau, L. 158, 278, 317
Du Bois, J. W. 344
Dwyer, A. 223, 234, 269, 312, 315–16, 354

Ebbing, J. E. 12
Egerod, S. 96
Elliott, J. 393
Emeneau, M. B. 288
Epps, P. 60, 68, 72, 168, 242 n.3, 246 n.6, 259, 261, 274, 286, 292
Erelt, M. 110, 119
Escobar, A. M. 277

Eulenberg, A. 311
Evans, N. 87

Faller, M. T. 79, 165, 245, 248
Farris, E. R. 182, 291
Fennell, T. G. 258
Fernandez-Vest, M. M. J. 77, 119 n.14, 123 n.16, 180, 261
Feuillet, J. 107–8
Floyd, R. 12, 43, 97, 159–61, 164–6, 178, 202–3, 231, 239, 245, 247–8, 252, 261–2, 269, 313, 318–19, 344–5
Foley, W. A. 293
Foris, D. 182, 249, 291, 313
Fortescue, M. 80, 82, 148, 176, 182, 185, 250, 272, 284–5, 287, 290, 310, 313, 353, 359
Foster, M. L. 41, 185
Fox, B. 10, 148
Frajzyngier, Z. 6, 7 n.3, 120, 149, 257
Frank, P. S. 52
Franklin, K. 62, 83
Freeland, L. S. 116
Friedman, V. A. 12 n.9, 15, 38, 40, 77, 108, 111, 114, 130 n.21, 142, 150–1, 158, 210, 257, 264, 272, 277, 279–80, 289, 293–4, 297, 311, 317, 338, 346, 354, 391, 394

Gabas Júnior, N. 63
Gelsen, H. 258
Genetti, C. 115, 274
Geniušienė, E. 112 n.6
Gilley, L. G. 43, 214, 226, 234, 256
Givón, T. 8 n.7, 11, 120
Goddard, C. 33, 181–2, 250
Goddard, P. E. 53
Golla, V. 53, 275
Gomez, G. G. 18, 28, 241
Gomez-Imbert, E. 51, 296, 347
Gordon, D. 149
Gordon, L. 47, 69, 96, 162, 182, 187, 228 n.5, 235, 272–3, 308, 373
Gralow, F. L. 44
Green, D. 130
Greenberg, J. H. 71
Grevisse, M. 106
Grice, P. 149, 334, 361, 381
Grinevald, C. 299
Gronemeyer, C. 117, 200, 205, 225, 228, 281
Grunina, E. A. 40–1
Grushkina, E. V. 31 n.7, 300, 393
Gruzdeva, E. Ju. 252, 300
Guasch, A. 32, 292

Guentchéva, Z.   15, 30 n.6, 157, 231, 311
Guillaume, A.   250
Güldemann, T.   132–3, 137, 310
Gumperz, J. J.   323
Gusev, V. Ju.   47, 49–50, 59, 74, 82, 163, 180, 183, 201,
    245, 264, 284, 314, 328, 349
Gvozdanović, J.   110, 138

Haarmann, H.   15, 33, 106 n.1, 290
Haas, M. R.   77
Hadarcev, O. A.   38, 77, 114
Hagège, C.   15
Haig, G.   295
Hale, A.   124
Hansson, I.-L.   96
Hardman, M. J.   4, 12, 14–15, 17, 43, 162, 203, 296,
    335–6, 338–9, 360, 391
Hargreaves, D.   149
Harris, A. C.   113 n.9, 123, 272, 281
Haspelmath, M.   31, 116, 118 n.13, 272, 391
Hassler, G.   5, 135
Haugen, E.   112
Haviland, J.   291
Hawkins, R. E.   292 n.15
Heine, B.   87, 149, 272, 361, 393
Helimsky, E. A.   31 n.7, 300, 393
Hengeveld, K.   122
Hewitt, B. G.   28–9, 31, 38, 77, 113, 204, 232, 277
Hickmann, M.   133
Hill, H.   135
Hill, J. H.   32, 51, 87, 182, 213, 314, 338, 344
Hill, K. E.   45 n.12
Hockett, C.   32, 310
Hoff, B.   5
Hoijer, H.   51, 273
Hollenbach, B. E.   178, 291
Holvoet, A.   117 n.12, 290
Hopper, P. J.   287 n.8
Howard-Malverde, R.   320
Hyman, L. M.   133

Ifantidou, E.   6 n.1, 150
Ikola, O.   123, 281
Irvine, J. T.   338, 344

Jacobsen, W. H. Jr.   3–4, 46, 80, 176, 201, 210, 214,
    284–5, 290–1, 345 n.5, 395
Jacquesson, F.   116, 290 n.13
Jake, J.   14
Jakobson, R.   13–14, 345 n.5, 350, 382, 393
James, D.   42, 106 n.1, 149, 157, 278–9,
    314, 346

Janssen, T. A. J. M.   132–3
Jasperson, R.   120
Jaxontov, S. Je.   112 n.6
Jochelson, W.   158, 346
Johanson, L.   15–16, 25 n.2, 30, 40, 67, 78, 112, 248,
    258, 264, 279, 281, 289 n.11, 296, 311, 317,
    393–4
Johnson, A. F.   182
Jones, P.   51, 312
Jones, W.   51, 312
Joseph, B.   150, 290 n.12, 287, 293, 362

Kammerzell, F.   132
Kany, C.   140, 142 n.28
Kask, A.   283
Kaufman, T.   288 n.9
Keenan, E. L.   130, 357
Kendall, M. B.   117, 298–9
Kerimova, A. A.   112
Kibrik, A. E.   29, 72, 83, 96, 199, 210, 222,
    233, 256, 311
Kiefer, F.   108 n.4
Kimball, G. D.   232
Kimenyi, A.   11, 120
King, R.   10, 148
Kirsner, R. S.   121
Klamer, M.   140, 272, 293
König, C.   149
Koontz, J. E.   34, 46 n.13, 70
Kornfilt, J.   40
Koshal, S.   53, 232
Kovedjaeva, E. I.   28 n.4
Kozintseva, N. A.   112 n.6, 289, 346
Krejnovich, E. A.   300
Krivoshein de Canese, N.   32, 292
Kroeker, M.   56, 61, 234
Kroskrity, P. V.   42, 70, 96, 139, 185, 295, 313
Kruspe, N.   109, 211, 234
Kuiper, F. B. J.   291
Kuipers, J. C.   359
Künnap, A.   48 n.16, 119, 290, 284–5, 310 n.2
Kuteva, T.   272, 393
Kuznetsova, A. I.   31 n.7, 241, 300, 393

Laanest, A.   123, 282
Lakoff, G.   149
Landeweerd, R.   134
Lang, A.   32
Langdon, M.   83, 284
LaPolla, R. J.   44, 47, 67, 70 n.2, 74, 84, 89, 97, 120,
    148, 160, 164, 201, 229, 256, 274, 291,
    310, 353

Laprade, R. A.   114, 136, 142–3, 205, 228, 297, 335
Larson, M. L.   132, 137, 141 n.26
Laughren, M.   14, 33, 97, 137, 181, 183, 248, 250–1, 314, 330
Lawrence, M.   46, 268, 383
Lazard, G.   7, 8, 11, 15, 25 n.2, 38–9, 112, 157–8, 195–6, 204, 207, 210, 214, 279, 311, 316, 376
Lee, D. D.   13, 36, 60, 245, 300, 348, 351
Lees, A.   225
Lees, B.   123 n.6
Lefebvre, C.   68
Lehiste, I.   180
Leinonen, M.   28, 69 n.1, 281, 316, 328
Levinsohn, S.   14
Li, C.   132
Liddicoat, A. J.   106–7
Lindström, E.   343
Linn, M.   37, 249, 251, 275, 328, 340
Loeweke, E.   62, 383
Longacre, R.   116, 132
Loos, E.   45
Lowe, I.   61, 215, 234, 269, 383
Lucy, J. A.   133, 137, 291
Lunn, P. V.   106 n.1
Lytkin, V. I.   28 n.4, 232, 264 n.8

MacDonald, L.   32, 140, 182, 272
Mackenzie, M.   42, 157, 278–9, 314, 346
Maisak, T. A.   115, 143, 155, 199, 214, 228, 316, 325
Majtinskaja, K. E.   31
Malchukov, A. L.   106 n.1
Malone, T.   14, 28, 52, 69, 86, 120, 243, 274, 280, 325, 350
Martin, E. H.   114
Martins, S. A.   32, 286
Martins, V.   32
Maslova, E.   27, 67, 102, 149, 157, 199, 209, 221, 244, 258, 262–3, 311, 317
Mathiassen, T.   77, 117
Matisoff, J. A.   275
Matlock, T.   273
Matras, Y.   38, 112 n.7, 158, 232, 288, 324
Matthews, P. H.   5 n.1, 6 n.2, 7, 14 n.10, 391, 395
May, J.   62, 383
McLendon, S.   52–3, 61, 67, 91–2, 169–70, 174, 185, 226, 235, 243–4, 279–80, 314, 321–2, 358
Meillet, A.   153
Merdanova, S. P.   115, 143, 155, 228
Merlan, F.   108, 137 n.24

Metslang, H.   33, 76–7, 111, 119, 123 n.16, 277–8, 281, 283 n.7
Michael, L.   315
Michailovsky, B.   156, 291
Middendorf, E. W.   12 n.8
Migliazza, E.   18
Miller, A.   83, 182, 257, 273, 284
Miller, C. L.   43, 214, 226, 234, 256
Miller, M.   31, 33, 44, 60, 70, 120 n.15, 160, 177 n.3, 265, 274, 296–9, 311, 335–6, 341, 344
Miller, W. R.   130
Miracle, A. W. Jr.   336
Mithun, M.   37, 61, 108, 232, 245, 310
Monserrat, R.   24, 71, 75, 82, 232, 256
Mortensen, C. A.   58, 293
Muižniece, L.   119, 281
Munro, P.   51, 58, 69, 182, 272, 310
Mürk, H. W.   283
Mushin, I.   6 n.1, 8 n.5, 324 n.5
Muysken, P.   68, 70, 253, 268

Nadasdi, T.   10, 148
Nazarova, Z. O.   38, 77, 113–4
Nedjalkov, I. V.   106 n.1
Nedjalkov, V. P.   112 n.6
Neucom, L.   131
Nichols, J.   5 n.1, 7 n.4, 8, 14, 16 n.12, 31, 197, 253, 263–4, 283, 325, 328, 344, 368
Nikolaeva, I.   31, 155, 178, 196–7, 272, 279, 290
Noonan, M.   123 n.17, 137 n.24
Nordlinger, R.   88
Nuckolls, J. B.   162, 319–20
Nuyts, J.   5 n.1

Ochs, E.   357
Olbertz, H.   205, 297, 299
Ospina Bozzi, A. M.   274, 292 n.16
Oswalt, R. L.   60, 204, 233, 266 n.8, 307, 310
Ozonova, A. A.   290

Pagliuca, W.   112 n.6, 279
Pajusalu, K.   33, 76–7, 111, 119, 123 n.16, 277–8, 281, 283 n.7
Palmer, F. R.   7 n.3
Palmer, G.   337, 343
Parks, D.   56, 310
Paul, L.   38–9, 112 n.8
Payne, D. L.   118
Payne, T. W.   99, 118
Payne, J. R.   99
Perkins, R.   112 n.6, 279

Perrot, J. 28, 118, 119 n.14, 123 n.16, 232, 241, 281, 283
Perry, J. R. 109
Peterson. D. A. 275
Peterson, J. 291
Peterson, M. N. 77
Peust, C. 132
Phosakritsana, P. 343
Pitkin, H. 36, 56, 60, 67, 245, 273, 275, 300–1
Plungian, V. A. 7 n.3, 68, 114, 193 n.5
Prokofjev, G. N. 232
Pulte, W. 26, 41, 352

Ráez, J. F. M. 12
Rakhilina, E. 10, 142, 149 n.29
Ramat, P. 148, 150
Ramirez, H. 18, 46, 51, 56, 85, 86 n.12, 90, 119, 168–71, 177, 223, 230, 243 n.4, 245–6, 250, 253, 259, 284, 295, 311 n.3, 342, 347
de Reuse, W. J. 63, 74, 93, 102, 148, 182, 186, 203–4, 342, 358
Reesink, G. P. 140
Reyburn, W. D. 41
Rodrigues, A. D. 32
Rombandeeva, E. I. 31
Roncador, M. von 132–3
Rood, D. S. 60, 75, 214, 226
Ross, E. M. 12
Rule, W. M. 61–2, 176, 383
Rumsey, A. 137 n.24

Sakel, J. 44, 160, 330
Sakita, T. I. 133, 137
Salas, A. 200
Sandler, L. 88
Santo Tomás, D. de 11
Sapir, E. 13, 41, 51, 75, 80, 116
Saunders, R. 59
Saxena, A. 178, 284, 291
Schauer, J. 296
Schauer, S. 296
Schlichter, A. 56, 171, 226, 273–4, 284–5, 310, 314, 348
Schmidt, A. 300
Schöttelndryer, B. 124
Seki, L. 18, 78, 94, 281
Serebrjannikov, B. A. 232, 279
Sharp, J. 110
Shell, O. A. 32
Sherzer, J. 14, 288, 290–1, 315
Shields, J. K. 182, 291
Shipley, W. F. 46, 252

Shmelev, A. D. 149 n.29
Silver, S. 31, 33, 44, 70, 160, 177 n.3, 297–9, 335–6, 341, 344
Silverstein, M. 39, 69, 117, 275–6
Skribnik, E. K. 7, 31, 118, 155, 196, 198 n.1, 281, 282 n.6, 290
Slobin, D. I. 40–1, 196–7, 210, 212, 323
Smeets, I. 42 n.9
Smothermon, J. H. 52
Smothermon, J. R. 52
Sohn, Ho-Min. 128, 129 n.20, 214
Soper, J. 294
Soto Ruiz, C. 165
Sparing-Chávez, M. 357 n.9
Stallybrass, O. 5 n.1, 6 n.2, 392
Starke, G. 108
Stebbins, T. 300
Steever, S. 136, 138
Stenzel, K. 72 n.6, 382
Stolz, T. 33, 290
Storch, A. 214
Strom, C. 49–50, 296
Subin, D. A. 129 n.20
Sumbatova, N. 31, 76–7, 113 n.9, 158, 198, 269, 289, 346
Sun, J. T. S. 45, 100 n.15, 160, 229–30, 232, 260 n.7, 269, 326, 345, 350
Swadesh, M. 13
Swanton, J. 46

Tasmovski, L. 5–6 n.1, 10
Tatevosov, S. G. 28, 199, 214, 228 n.4, 279–81, 311, 316, 325
Tauli, V. 123 n.16
Taylor, A. R. 75
Telles, S. 36, 75, 341
ten Cate, A. P. 107 n.3, 108
Tepljashina, T. I. 28 n.4, 232, 264 n.8
Tereschenko, N. M. 31 n.7, 118, 241
Thiesen, W. 44, 83, 91, 98, 163, 243, 341
Thomason, S. G. 288 n.9
Thompson, L. 59
Thompson, M. T. 59
Thompson, S. A. 118 n.13, 121, 123 n.17
Thurgood, G. 272, 277, 284–5
Timberlake, A. 5 n.1, 117, 394
Tolskaya, M. 178, 272
Torres Rubio, D. de. 12
Tosco, M. 288
Tournadre, N. 127, 272
Trask, L. 7 n.3
Travis, C. 141, 206, 324 n.5

Trivedi, G. M.   274
Tschenkéli, K.   38, 113 n.9
Tuldava, J.   119

Urmston, J. O.   10
Usenkova, E. V.   50, 226, 245
Utas, B.   16, 30 n.6, 393

Valenzuela, P.   6, 24, 55–6, 68, 70, 72, 78, 89, 172,
    179–80, 184–5, 201, 205 n.3, 207, 226, 250,
    256, 261, 278, 292, 308, 310, 335–6, 346,
    348–9, 351–2, 375–6
van den Berg, H.   29, 232
van den Berg, R.   131
van der Auwera, J.   7 n.3, 68
van der Voort, H.   132
van der Wurff, W.   132–3
van Eijk, J.   59
Vet, C.   134
Viitso, T.-R.   119 n.14
Vinogradov, V. V.   14 n.10
Vries, de L. J.   137 n.25, 256

Wagner, G.   37
Wälchli, B.   77, 119, 123, 140, 281–2
Waltz, C.   120 n.15

Waltz, N.   120 n.15
Watkins, L.   42 n.10, 178, 227, 266, 330
Watters, D. E.   32, 137, 179, 210–12, 232, 248,
    273, 310
Weber, D. J.   14, 44, 79, 83, 98, 162–3, 166, 243, 261,
    319, 322, 330, 337, 358
Weinreich, U.   15 n.11
West, B.   119
Wheeler, A.   46
Whistler, K. W.   176, 277, 284
Whorf, B. L.   355
Wiemer, B.   140
Wierzbicka, A.   7 n.4, 16 n.12
Wilkins, D. P.   33, 180, 183, 251
Willett, Th.   7 n.3, 14, 57–9, 66, 96, 153, 368
Windfuhr, G.   38, 112 n.8
Winkler, E.   156
Wise, M. R.   32, 83, 91
Woodbury, A. C.   124, 130

Yu, Defen.   54, 274

Zeisler, B.   205, 207
Zeshan, U.   368
Zubin, D. A.   129 n.20
Zúñiga, F.   42 n.9, 200

Subject index

acquisition of evidentials 362–83
active verbs 269
adjective 81
admirative 108, 213–24, 259–60, 391
adverb 10, 284
affirmative clauses 242, *see also* declarative clause
agglutinating 8, 385
analytic 8, 385
anaphora 131, 145–6, 371
anterior 381, *see also* perfect
apprehensive 242, 252, 254–5, 300
aspect 7, 28–9, 198, 241, 261–7, 270, 284, 328, 365, 369–72, 376–7, 389, *see also* tense-aspect
assumed evidential 265–7, 307–10, 367–72, 377, 391
  and cultural innovations 351–4
  in C2 systems 54–7, 207, 224, 243
  in D1 systems 1–3, 60, 100, 168, 224, 260
  in narratives 311, 322–3
  in questions 246–7
  origin of 274, 284–7, 302
  with first person 230–1, 236, 239
  with verbs of internal states 325–9
assumption 2–3, 27–8, 63–5, 90, 110, 113, 116–17, 145–7, 149–51, 158, 163–4, 174–6, 279, *see also* assumed evidential
attrition, of language, *see* language obsolescence, language death
auditive 31, 232, 391
audibility, in demonstratives 105, 130–2, *see also* demonstrative pronouns
auditory information 24, 121, 159–60, *see also* hearing
  in A4 systems 34–5, 366–71
  in A5 systems 37–8, 73, 249, 251, 366–71
  in B1 systems 43–4, 159–60
  in demonstrative systems 105, 130–2
  in multiterm systems 60
augmentative 8
auxiliary verb 38, 44, 69, 84–5, 119, 211, 214, 277, 283–5
awareness, of evidentials 9–10, 153, 325, 360, 380–1, 389, *see also* metalinguistic valuation

backgrounding 9, 315–24
Balkan linguistic tradition 15
borrowing 4, 21, 294–5, 355, *see also* calque, diffusion, language contact

calque 294–9, *see also* borrowing, diffusion, language contact
case, *see* grammatical relations
certainty 3, 5, 13, 153, 161, 166, 171–2, 191, 358, 373, *see also* uncertainty
classifier 87, 338, 343, 356, 363, 365
clitic 8, 67–9, 95
cognition 21, 333–9, 343–62, 381, 383–4
cognitive states, verbs of 193, 324–5
command 9, 20, 110–11, 113, 162, 241–2, 249–53, 270, 294, 378, 388, *see also* imperative
commentative function of an evidential 313, 315–24
commitment to truth of statement 162, 176–7
common sense, inference based on 3, 155–6
communication 21, 333–62
complement clause 20, 51, 105, 111, 120–3, 133–4, 253–6, 271–3, 281–3, 302, 387, 391, *see also* complementiser
complementation strategy, *see* complement clause
complementiser, *see* complement clause
conditional 11, 80, 82, 105–11, 116, 147, 255, 257–60, 270, 369, 378, 388
confirmative 15, 391, *see also* non-confirmative
  as alternative to firsthand 25
congruent/noncongruent person marking, *see* conjunct/disjunct, locutor/non-locutor
conjecture 3, 85, 90, 164, 174, 176, 258, 373–4
conjunct person marking, *see* conjunct/disjunct person marking
conjunct/disjunct person marking 123–8, 133, 145–7, 204–5, 207, 231, 271–2, 286, 391
contact language 10, 288, 296–302, 389, *see also* diffusion, language contact
content question, *see* question
control 114, 127, 136, 161–3, 171, 173, 188, 197, 204–5, 237–8, 326–7, 372
  lack of control 114, 127, 186, 188, 207–9, 217, 221, 223–4, 227
conversation sustainer 86–7, 243, 294, 309, 324–5

copula 69, 81, 127–8, 133–4, 211, 271, 283–4, 389
cultural innovations 339–43, 351–4, 359–61,
    381, 389
cultural practices 9, 21, 315, 339–43, 363, 366,
    379–1

data source 4, 15, 18, 391
declarative clause 30, 33, 242, 251–3, 255, 268–9,
    270, 278–9, 378
default evidential 72, 308
deferred realisation 156–8, 203–4, 209, 222, 376
definiteness 1
deictic 130–2, 271, 275–6, 287, 302, 378, 391,
    see also demonstrative pronouns
demonstrative pronouns 20, 105, 130–2, 145,
    356, 371
dependent clause 69, 71, 242, 253–6, 370–1, 388,
    392, *see also* subordinate clause
dependent-marking language 8, 385
de-subordination 69, 107, 110–11, 145–7, 271,
    281–3, 370–1, 392
diffusion 21, 101, 271, 288–99, 302, 335, 355, 360,
    389, *see also* language contact, linguistic
    area
diminutive 8
direct evidential 24, 159–62, 366–77, 392
    acquisition of 362
    and cultural innovations 351–4
    and internal states 349–50
    and supernatural phenomena 348–9, 360
    in B1 systems 43–6, 159–62, 337
    in C2 systems 54–7, 167–73
    in C3 systems 57–9, 167–73
    in commands 213–14
    in dreams 345–8, 360–1
    in narratives 318–24
    in questions 245–8
    origin of 284–5
    with first person 228–30, 235
    with future 261–2
direct speech complement 137–40, 392, *see also*
    direct speech, complement clause
direct speech 137–40, 392, *see also* direct speech
    complement
disclaimer 42, 158, 182
discourse effects of evidentials 158, 205, 310–24,
    354, 366, 379–80
discourse genre 9, 153, 294–6, 310–24, 337, *see also*
    genre, discourse effects of evidentials
disjunct, *see* conjunct/disjunct
distancing effect 108, 111, 135, 157, 181, 186, 188,
    209, 222, 316–17, 323, 352

dizque as an evidentiality strategy in Colombian
    Spanish 111, 141–2, 151, 179, 182, 205–6, 228,
    298–9, 324
double marking of gender 87–8
    of grammatical function, or double case 87
    of information source 4, 19, 83, 87–95, 103, 322,
        369, 387
    of person 89, 218, 229, 235
    of tense 87, 100–2
doubt 20, 59, 116–17, 146, 158, 165, 176, 184–5, 260,
    342, 373–4
dreams 14, 59, 158, 173, 222, 232, 285, 309, 326, 332,
    344–8, 380–1, 383, *see also* revelative
    evidence
dubitative 110, 116, 143, 257–60, 270, 278, 284–5,
    369, 378, 388, *see also* modality

endangered language 299–301, *see also* language
    obsolescence, language death
epistemic meaning 107, 111, 120, 262, 284–5, 287,
    302, 365, 392
epistemic extensions of evidentials 6, 33, 41–2,
    66, 143, 145, 147, 153, 186–93, 228, 354, 367,
    370, 372–7
    in two-term systems 157–9
    in three-term systems 161–6
    in multiterm systems 167–76
    of evidentiality strategies 105, 132, 135–6, 205,
        387–8
    of evidentials in questions 247–8
    of reported evidentials 176–86, 312–13
epistemic modality 6, 7, 257–60, 270, 302, 344,
    365, 372, 382, 392, *see also* epistemic
    meaning, probability, possibility
epistemology 5, 6, 186, 392
ergative 356–7
evidence, definition of 4
evidential extensions 11, 21, 38–40, 45, 69, 77,
    105–51, 237, 260, 264, 270, 297–8, 324,
    365–6, 369–73, 386–7, 392, *see also*
    evidentiality strategy
evidentiality strategy 45, 77, 105–51, 237, 260, 264,
    270, 297–8, 324, 365–6, 369–73, 386–7, 392
    as origin for evidentials 271, 276–84, 288–9
    mirative extension of 204–6, 297
    with first person 227–8
evidentiality systems 387
    A1 15, 23–9, 75, 77–8, 82, 105–6, 112, 186–7, 205,
        207, 219–23, 237–8, 255, 288–9, 297–8,
        308–9, 311, 316, 366, 372, 375, 378–9
    distinguishing between A1 and A2 systems
        39–41, 77–8

distinguishing between A1, A2 and A3
41–2, 185
mirative meanings in 195–200, 207–9
semantics 154–9
A2 23, 25, 29–31, 83, 105–6, 112, 186–8, 205,
207–9, 219–30, 237–8, 248, 288–9, 293, 311,
316, 366, 368, 372–3, 378–9
distinguishing from evidentiality strategies
38–9, 77
mirative meanings in 195–200
semantics of 154–9
A3 23, 25, 31–4, 70, 77, 81, 83, 85–7, 95, 105,
186–8, 207–9, 237–8, 242–3, 248, 255, 366,
368, 372–3
semantics of, *see* reported evidential
A4 25, 34–7, 75, 82, 86–7, 366, 372, 375
semantics of 154–9
A5 25, 37–8, 75, 366, 368, 373
semantics of 154–9
B1 42–6, 49, 88–9, 186–7, 190, 366, 368, 373, 375
mirative meanings in 201–3, 207–9, 238
semantics of 159–66
B2 42–3, 46, 49, 75, 82, 85–7, 186–7, 190, 207–9,
242–3, 255, 366, 373, 375
semantics of 159–66
B3 42–3, 46–7, 49, 186–8, 190, 207–9, 243, 366,
368, 373, 375
semantics of 159–66
B4 43, 50–1, 75, 186–8, 190, 207–9
mirative meanings in 200–1
semantics of 159–66
verb unmarked for evidential in 49–50
B5 43, 50–1, 75, 77, 92, 159–66, 190, 367, 374
C1 51–4, 75, 82, 85–6, 189–93, 166–76, 223, 238,
242–3, 367, 374, 375
C2 51, 54–7, 75, 83–4, 89–91, 189–93, 166–76,
367, 374–5
mirative meanings in 201–2, 207–9
C3 51, 57–60, 75, 166–76, 189–93, 367, 374–5
D1 60, 82, 86–7, 95, 166–76, 189–93, 223, 238,
242–3, 255, 367, 374
semantic parameters in 63–6, 153–93, 388
time reference of 4, 99–103, 261, 294
two-term systems 15, 23–42, 154–9, *see also* A1,
A2, A3, A4, A5, firsthand evidential, non-
firsthand evidential, reported evidential,
sensory evidential
three-term systems 25, 43–51, 159–66, *see also*
B1, B2, B3, B4, B5, direct evidential,
inferred evidential, non-visual evidential,
quotative evidential, reported evidential,
visual evidential

four-term systems 25, 51–60, 166–76, *see also*
C1, C2, C3, assumed evidential, direct
evidential, inferred evidential, non-visual
evidential, quotative evidential, reported
evidential, visual evidential
multiterm systems 24–5, 60–3, 166–76, *see also*
D1, assumed evidential, direct evidential,
inferred evidential, non-visual evidential,
quotative evidential, reported evidential,
visual evidential
evidentials as person markers 225, 235–7, 239, 325
evidentials, frequency of 239, 301, 315
evidentiality neutral forms 23, 39–41, 49–50, 66,
71–8, 187, 317, 366–8, 373, 387, *see also*
unmarked for evidentiality
experienced, as alternative term to 'firsthand' 25
experiential 392, *see* direct evidential
eyewitness evidential 388, 392, *see* firsthand
evidential

fieldwork methodology 18–19, 385–6
first person 8–9, 89, 114, 123–8, 136, 157, 169–71,
183, 192, 325–9, 377–8,
see also person
and mirative meanings 195, 197, 200, 205–6,
208, 218, 225
restrictions on evidentials with 231–3
with direct and visual evidentials 228–30, 235
with evidentiality strategies 227–8
with firsthand and visual evidentials 228,
237–8
with inferred and assumed evidentials 230–1,
236, 239
with nonfirsthand evidentials 217, 219–35, 237–8
with nonvisual evidentials in C1 and D1
systems 223–5, 231, 235–8
with reported evidentials 225–7
firsthand evidential 1, 18–19, 23–4, 42, 88, 264,
289, 297–9, 308–9, 366, 369–70, 392
alternative terms 25
and cultural innovations 352–3
and dreams 345–9, 360–1
in A1 systems 26–9, 40, 77–8, 105, 154–9
in narratives 311–18, 334
in small systems 186–93, 372–3
with first person 228, 237–8, 377–8
with verbs of internal states 326–8
focus 95, 268, 317–18
foregrounding 9, 315–24
formal markedness 44, 54, 56, 59, 63, 72–5, 172,
286, 368–9, 387, *see also* markedness
free indirect speech 134–5, 392

frequency of evidentials 239, 301, 315
frustrative 258–60, 342, 357, 388, 392
functional markedness 71–2, 308, 368–9, 387,
    see also markedness
fusional 8, 385
future 8, 29, 67, 74, 88, 105, 109, 113, 146, 162, 241,
    261–7, 270, 276–7, 369–72, 389

gender 1, 4, 8, 52, 71, 87–8, 148, 221, 270, 343,
    356–7, 389
general knowledge, inference based on 3, 54, 56,
    61, 63–5, 367–8
generalization, inductive 19
genre 21, 33, 35, 106–8, 116, 153, 181, 293–6, 301, 304,
    310–16, 331–2, 359, 369, 379–80, 383, 389, *see
    also* discourse
    effects of evidentials, discourse genre
grammatical category 1, 5, 11–15, 17, 73, 80, 195,
    209–10, 214–15, 382–3, 385–6
grammatical relations 218, 236, 269–70, 356,
    385, 389
grammaticalisation 20–1, 31, 40, 69, 77, 87, 103,
    105, 140–2, 145, 205–6, 271–88, 294, 302,
    378–9, 389, 393
Grice's maxim 21, 149, 334–6, 361, 381,
    see also maxim

habitual 31, 263, 266, 272
head-marking language 12, 385
hearing 1, 2, 19, 23–4, 159–60, 367–8, *see also*
    direct evidential, firsthand evidential,
    non-firsthand evidential, non-visual
    evidential
    in A1 systems 26
    in B3 systems 47
    in C2 systems 54–5
    in multiterm systems 62, 167, 173
hearsay 1, 3, 4, 7–10, 19–20, 42, 64–6, 79, 81–7,
    90–6, 98–9, 103, 112, 116, 118, 121, 123, 143,
    148, 151–6, 186–7, 207, 393, *see also* reported
    evidential
    alternative terms for 25
hypothetical 7, 210–11, 262

imperative 9, 20, 110–11, 113, 162, 241–2, 249–53,
    270, 294, 378, 388, *see also* command
imperfect 28, 116
imperfective 114–15, 149, 366, 393
impersonal 236–7
inclusive vs exclusive 'we' 236–7
indirect speech 132–4, 138–40, 393
indirective 25, 393

inference 1–3, 19, 23, 80–1, 84–5, 110, 112, 115–17,
    120, 143, 145–7, 149–50, 186–93, 266–7, 279,
    370–2, 388, *see also* inferred evidential
    in two-term systems 154–9
    in three-term systems 160–1, 183, 188, 229
    in multiterm systems 170, 173–6, 189–93, 224
inferential 18, 61, 258–9, 285, 393
inferred evidential 1–3, 9, 19, 23, 63–6, 82–4, 86–7,
    89–91, 93–4, 100, 105, 207, 210, 229, 254–5,
    259–60, 265–9, 306–10, 341, 366–7, 388, 393,
    see also inference
    and conjunct-disjunct person marking
    126–7
    as a meaning of reported evidential 31
    in A1 systems 27–8
    in A2 systems 29–31
    in B1 systems 43–6, 163–6
    in B2 systems 46, 163–6
    in B4 systems 47–50, 163–6
    in C1 systems 51–4
    in C2 systems 54–7
    in C3 systems 57–9
    in commands 252–3
    in D1 systems 1–2, 60
    in narratives 311–12, 318–24, 331–2
    in questions 244–7, 249
    origin of 274–5, 285–7, 302
    with first person 230–1, 236, 239
    with future 262–3
    with verbs of internal states 325–9, 331–2, 350,
    360–1
inflection and derivation 82
intentional action 114, 127, 157, 217, 223–5, 227–30,
    237–8, 326–7, 331, *see also* intentionality,
    unintentional action
intentionality 114, 127, 157, 217, 223–5, 227–30,
    237–8, 326–7, 331, *see also* intentional
    action
interjection 199
intonation 199, 251
internal state, verbs of 11, 219, 223–5, 235–7, 246,
    268–9, 324–9, 341, 349–51, 360–1, 388–9,
    395
interrogative verb form 82, 109–10, 143
intraterminal aspect 393
irrealis 7, 35, 68, 105, 108–10, 165, 210–11, 257–8,
    365, 369–70, 393
irony and evidentials 166, 183–4, 188, 226, 231,
    323–4
isolating 8, 385

kinship relationships 172, 350

language contact 21, 95, 288–302, 355, 379, *see also*
    diffusion, linguistic area
language death 21, 36–8, 73, 299–302, 366, 379,
    393, *see also* language obsolescence
language obsolescence 21, 36–8, 73, 299–302, 366,
    379, 393, *see also* language death
language type 8, 12, 385
lexical evidentiality 10, 147–51, 324, 338, 355
lexical reinforcement of evidentials 3, 10, 34, 36,
    103, 153, 338–40, 347–8, 393
lexicon, also lexical categories 1, 21, 305, 324–32
linguistic area 23, 288–99, 302, 311, 379, 393, *see
    also* diffusion, language contact,
    Sprachbund
locational 287, 302, *see also* locative markers
locative marker 271, 275–6, 287, 302, 378, *see also*
    locational
locutor/non-locutor person marking 393, *see*
    conjunct/disjunct person marking,
    congruent/noncongruent person marking
logophoricity 133–4, 393
lying with evidentials 98–9, 136, 358–9

markedness 6, 19, 41, 44, 69, 70–9, 286, 308, *see
    also* formal markedness, functional
    markedness
maxim 21, 149, 334–6, 361, 381, *see also* Grice's
    maxim
mediative 15, 25, 125, 393
médiaphorique 15
mediativity, *see* mediative
metalinguistic valuation of evidentials 9, 339–43,
    360, 380, 389, *see also* awareness of
    evidentials
mirative meaning 8, 20, 66, 71, 125–6, 145, 148–51,
    153, 157, 166, 185–6, 193–215, 237–8, 269–70,
    376–7, 388
    and first person 195, 197, 200, 205–6, 208, 218,
        225, 325
    in A1 and A2 systems 28, 195–200, 207–9, 221,
        309, 328
    in multiterm systems 201–2, 207–9
    in three-term systems 200–4, 207–9, 238
    of evidentials in questions 242, 249
    of evidentiality strategy 204–9, 228, 297
    of inferred evidentials 200–1, 207–9
    of reported evidentials 202–4
    with pronouns 214
modal verb 6, 10, 150, 394
modality 6, 9, 20, 68, 82, 105–11, 145–7, 192, 241,
    257–60, 270–1, 276–9, 302, 365, 369–72,
    378–9, 387–8, 394

mode 13, 33, 241, 394
mood 6, 9, 11, 13, 20, 31, 44–5, 53, 67–8, 82, 105–11,
    116, 144–7, 211, 241, 270, 365, 369–72, 378–9,
    387, 394
multiple sources of information 4, 19, 83, 87–95,
    103, 322, 369, 387, *see also* double marking
    of information source

narrative 33, 34, 78–9, 91–6, 153, 181, 294–6, 305,
    310–15, 331–2, 343–4, 379–80, 388, *see also*
    genre
negation 4, 19, 82, 96–7, 99, 241, 255–7, 270, 365,
    369, 378, 387–8
    negation, scope of 96–7, 103, 261, 369
nominalisation 20, 69, 81, 105, 117–20, 144–7, 149,
    253, 271, 281, 302, 365, 369–73, 378–9
non-confirmative 15, 394, *see also* confirmative
    as alternative to non-firsthand evidential 25
non-experienced, as alternative to non-firsthand
    evidential 25
non-eyewitness evidential, as alternative to
    non-firsthand evidential 25, 388, 394
non-firsthand evidential 1, 3, 6, 15, 19, 23–4, 83,
    96, 153–4, 207, 256–8, 262–4, 266–7, 308–9,
    341, 366, 368–70, 394
    acquisition of 362–3
    alternative terms 25
    and cultural innovations 354–5
    and dreams 345–9, 360–1, 380–1
    as functionally unmarked term 71–2, 95
    as meaning of evidentiality strategy 109,
        112–17, 142–4, 373
    in A1 systems 26–9, 71–2, 77–8, 95, 105–6,
        154–9, 186–93, 210, 372–3
    in A2 systems 29–31, 39, 105–6, 154–9, 186–93,
        372–3
    in narratives 311–18, 324
    in questions 248–9, 251
    origin of 69, 275–7, 279–81, 283–4, 289, 291,
        296–9
    restrictions on person value 232, 377–8
    with verbs of internal states 325–9, 350, 360–1
non-visual evidential 20, 23, 63–5, 82–3, 85–7,
    91–2, 99, 153–4, 254–7, 259–60, 265–7,
    300–1, 306–10, 358, 366–77, 380, 394
    and cultural conventions 353–4
    in B2 systems 46, 162–3, 187, 189–93
    in B3 systems 46–7, 162–3, 187, 189–93
    in B4 systems 47–50, 162–3, 187, 189–93
    in C1 systems 51–4, 167–73, 189–93
    in D1 systems 1–2, 60, 100, 167–73, 189–93
    in dreams 345–8, 381

non-visual evidential (*cont.*)
  in multiterm systems 62–3, 167–73, 175, 189–93
  in narratives 312, 331–2
  in questions 244–7
  origin of 273–4, 284–7, 294, 302
  with first person 123, 223–5, 231, 235–8
  with supernatural experience 341–2,
    348–9, 360
  with verbs of internal states 325–9, 331–2,
    349–50, 360–1
number 1, 52, 75–6, 217–18, 270

obligatory marking of evidentiality 1–3, 16, 333–4
omission of evidential 2, 6, 70, 78–9, 387

parenthetic expression 10
participation 63, 124, 154, 156, 172–3, 186, 191, 199,
    208, 224, 315–24, 372
particle 5, 12, 33, 50, 57–8, 67, 69, 81–2, 148–51, 155,
    199, 293, 313, 371, 382
participle 33, 39, 69, 105, 116–18, 123, 271–3, 278,
    281–3, 302, 324
passive 11, 20, 39, 105, 116–17, 144–7, 228, 270, 276,
    369–72, 387
past tense 8, 20, 39, 85, 105, 112–16, 143–4, 261–7,
    270–1, 279–81, 302, 318, 324, 337, 362–3, 365,
    369–72, 378–9, 387
perfect 11, 20, 38, 77, 117–19, 261–7, 270, 297, 324,
    369–73, 378–9, 387, 394, *see also* anterior
  and A1 systems 28
  as evidentiality strategy 77, 105, 112–16, 144,
    271, 279–81, 302
  experiential 112
  non-firsthand meaning of 38–9
perfective 119, 263–4, 269–70, 365, 369–72, 378–9,
    387, 394
performative evidential 60, 232–3, 307–8
person 8, 20, 44, 52, 89, 105, 123–30, 261–2, 267,
    270, 325–9, 331–2, 356, 377, 388, *see also*
    conjunct/disjunct person marking, first
    person, second person, third person,
    person marking
person marking 73, 123–31, 144–7, 312, 325,
    369–72, *see also* conjunct/disjunct person
    marking, first person, person, second
    person, third person
pivot 269
pluperfect 114, 204–5, 227–8, 297
polar question, *see also* question
politeness 234, 243, 268, 343, 389
polysynthetic 8, 78, 385

possibility 6, 117, 186–93, 365, *see also* epistemic
    modality
potential 110–1, 241, 278, 369
preferred evidentials 21, 99, 257, 305–9, 327–9,
    331–2, 338, 379–80, 383, 389
presumptive mood 108, 111, 288
probability 6, 7, 116, 153, 158, 165, 186–93, 365, 372,
    see also epistemic modality
proverb 339, 360
purposive 242, 253

question 143, 255, 294, 342, 387
  content question 72, 248–9
  evidentials in 4, 9, 19–20, 86–7, 162, 241–9, 270,
    388
  person marking in 124–31
  polar question 248–9
  rhetorical question 230–1, 242, 249
  scope of, with evidentials 97–8, 103, 369
quotation 50–1, 132–45, 342, 387
quotative 13, 64–5, 80, 84, 105, 177–8, 193–4, 367,
    374–7, 388, 394
  as alternative term to reported 31, 177,
    193–4
  as different from reported 25, 178, 193–4
  in B5 systems 50–1, 75, 92, 227
  in C3 systems 57–9
  in general 64–5
  in multiterm systems 61
  origin of 69, 271–4, 281–3, 302
  reported as quotative 101

realis 394
reanalysis 69, 123, 140–2, 146–7, 271–4, 281–7, 302,
    372, 378–9, 389
reasoning, inference based on 3, 27–8, 48, 54–5,
    63–5, 89–90, 155–6, 163–4
relative clauses 253–6
reliability of information 5, 6, 33, 135, 180, 183–4,
    186, 352, 358, 365, 382
reported evidential 1, 3, 4, 7–10, 19–20, 42, 61–6,
    79, 81–7, 90–6, 98–9, 103, 112, 116, 118, 121,
    123, 143, 148, 151–6, 186–7, 207, 257–60,
    265–7, 300–1, 306–10, 366–71, 387–8, 394,
    see also hearsay, secondhand
  acquisition of 363
  alternative terms for 25
  and cultural innovations 351–3, 361
  and reported speech 105, 132–42
  as meaning of non-firsthand evidential in A1
    systems 26–9

as meaning of non-firsthand evidential in A2
    systems 29–30
in A3 systems 31–4, 75–8, 97
in A4 systems 34–7
in B3 systems 43–6
in B4 systems 46–7
in B5 systems 50–1, 75
in C1 systems 51–4
in C2 systems 54–7
in C3 systems 57–9
in commands 250–3, 270, 378
in D1 systems 1–3, 60, 100–2, 337
in dependent clauses 253–5, 270
in dreams 345–9
in narratives 310–24, 331–2, 334, 340–4,
    379–80, 385
in questions 243–5, 247–9, 270, 378
in speech formulae 330
origin of 271–5, 277–8, 284–8, 302, 290–4
restrictions on person in 232
semantic parameters in 159, 176–86, 193–4,
    374–7
with first person 123, 225–7
reported speech 105, 119, 132–42, 369–71, 387
and reported evidential 105, 132–42
reported speech complement 107, 145–7
responsibility 105–6, 128, 135, 153, 157, 162, 165,
    170–1, 173, 182, 196, 221, 374–6
resultative 112–16, 118, 143–7, 271, 279–81, 302,
    369–72, 378–9, 387, 394
revelative evidence 14, 59, 158, 173, 222, 232, 285,
    309, 326, 332, 344–8, 380–1, 383,
    see also dreams
rhetorical question, *see* question

scattered coding of evidentiality 9, 63, 67, 80–2,
    185–6, 290, 382–3, 387
second person 123–8, 233–5, 239, *see also* person
secondhand 15, 19, 24, 395, *see also* reported
    evidential
sensory evidential 366–71, 395, *see also*
    non-visual evidential
in A4 systems 34–6, 154–9, 186, 188
in multiterm systems 61–3
in speech formula 330
sex 270, 315, 354
shamanic knowledge 74–5, 99, 347–9, 360, 389
smelling 1, 19, 159, 173, 309, 367–8, *see also* direct
    evidential, firsthand evidential, non-
    firsthand evidential, non-visual
    evidential
in A4 systems 34

in B3 systems 47
in C2 systems 54–5
in multiterm systems 62, 168
speech formulae, evidentials in 329–30
Sprachbund 23, 288–99, 302, 311, 379, 393, *see also*
    linguistic area
Standard Average European 7, 334
stative verbs 269, 363
stylistic overtones of evidentials 9, 21, 137–8, 222,
    315–24, 379–80, 389
subjunctive 111, 258
subordinate clause 30, 69, 71, 143, 242, 253–6,
    271–3, 281–3, 302, 370–1, 388, 392, 395, *see
    also* dependent clause
subordinator 395, *see* subordinate clause
substratum 142
surprise, *see* mirative meaning
synthetic 8, 385

tense 1–3, 7, 10, 20, 44, 52, 67–8, 70, 78–9, 87, 95,
    100–3, 105, 133, 148, 241, 261–7, 270, 365,
    369–72, 389
tense-aspect 7, 28–9, 198, 241, 261–7, 270, 284, 328,
    365, 369–72, 376–7, 389
third person 89, 229, 233–5, 239,
    see also person
thirdhand 19, 59, 63, 178–9, 193, 375, 388, 395
time reference of evidential 4, 99–103,
    261, 294

uncertainty 33, 106, 146, 158, 165, 171–2, 174, 176,
    260, 372, *see also* certainty
unintentional action 114, 127, 157, 217, 223–5,
    227–30, 237–8, 326–7, 331, *see also*
    intentional action, intentionality
unmarked for evidentiality 23, 39–41, 49–50, 66,
    71–8, 187, 317, 366–8, 373, 387, *see also*
    evidentiality neutral forms
unmarked evidential, *see* markedness

validational 3, 15, 395
validator 395, *see* validational
verbal report, *see* reported evidential
verbs of cognitive states 193, 324–5
verbs of internal state 11, 219, 223–5, 235–7,
    246, 268, 324–9, 341, 349–51, 360–1,
    388–9, 395
verbs of perception and cognition 120–2, 269,
    273–4, 324–32, 370–1, 388–9
verbs of speech 271–3, 302, 328–9
verificational 3, 15, 73, 395
viewpoint as a grammatical category 268

visual, as a semantic parameter 63–6, *see also*
    direct evidential, firsthand evidential,
    visual evidential, visually acquired
    information
visual evidential 1–4, 13, 19, 82–7, 90, 98–9, 153–4,
    254–5, 259–60, 265–7, 300–1, 338, 361,
    366–9, 395
    and cultural innovations 352–4, 381
    as preferred evidential 305–10
    formally unmarked 44, 103
    functionally unmarked 71
    in B1 systems 43–4, 72–3, 159–62, 187–93
    in B2 systems 46, 159–62, 187–93
    in B3 systems 46–7, 159–62, 187–93
    in C1 systems 51–4, 167–73, 189–93, 223
    in C2 systems 54–7, 167–73, 189–93
    in D1 systems 1–2, 60–3, 100, 167–73, 175,
        189–93, 223–4
    in dreams 345–8, 360–1
    in narratives 312, 318–24, 332, 340, 389

in questions 245–7
in speech formulae 330–2
origin of 273–5, 278–9, 284–7, 302
semantics of 24, 63–6, 373–7
with first person 228–30, 235, 237–8, 377–8
with verbs of internal states 325–9, 331–2, 350,
    360–1
visually acquired information 80, 89, 120, 162,
    167, 229, 305–10, 338
    in A1 systems 26, 155
    in A2 systems 30
    in A4 systems 34–5
    in B4 systems 49–50, 74–5
    expressed with demonstratives 105, 131
visibility in demonstratives 130–2
vocative 70
vowel systems 186

zero-marking of evidentiality, *see* markedness,
    evidentiality neutral forms

Made in the USA
Middletown, DE
19 September 2018